PRISON SCHOOL

Akira Hiramoto

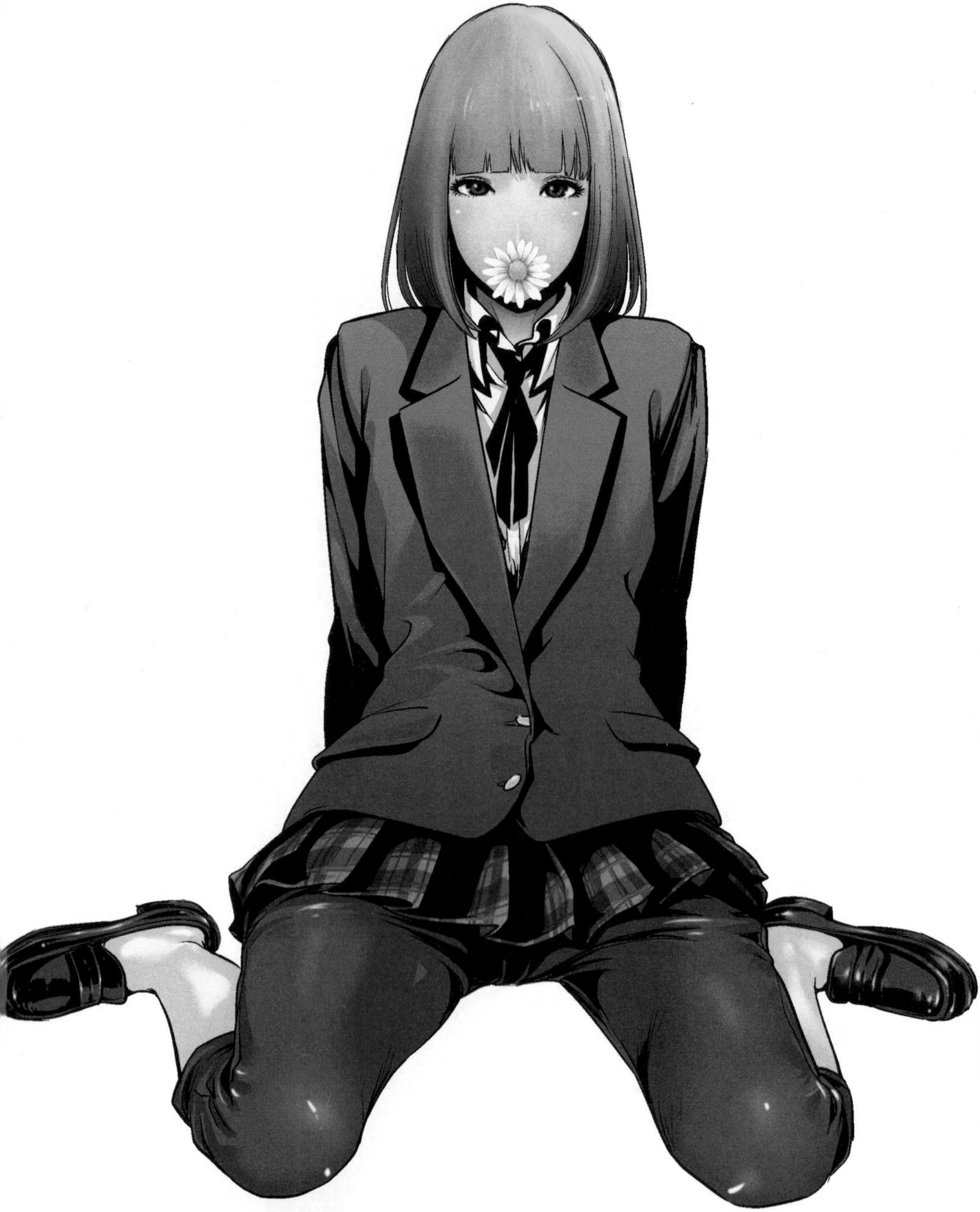

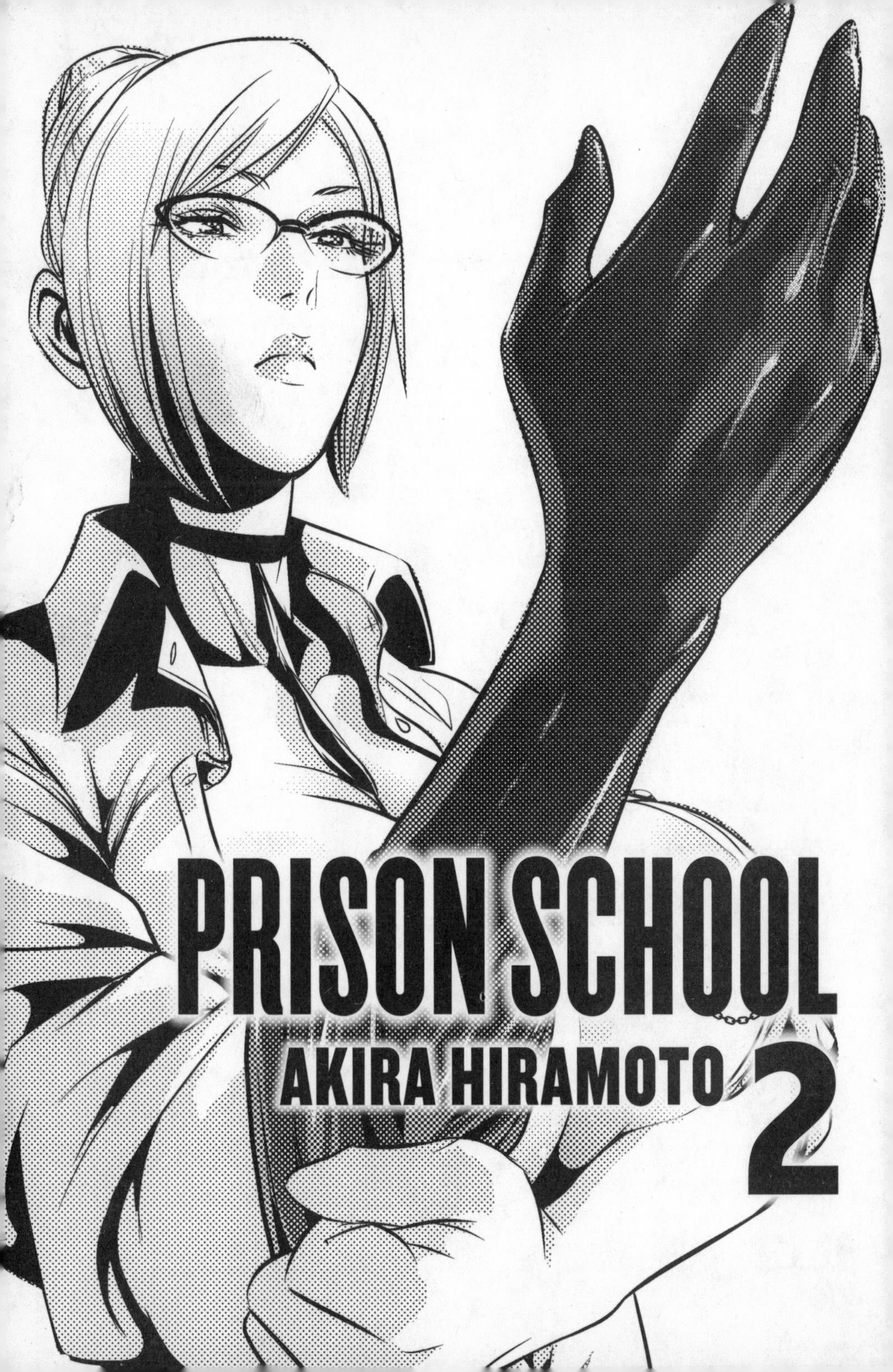

PRISON SCHOOL

AKIRA HIRAMOTO

2

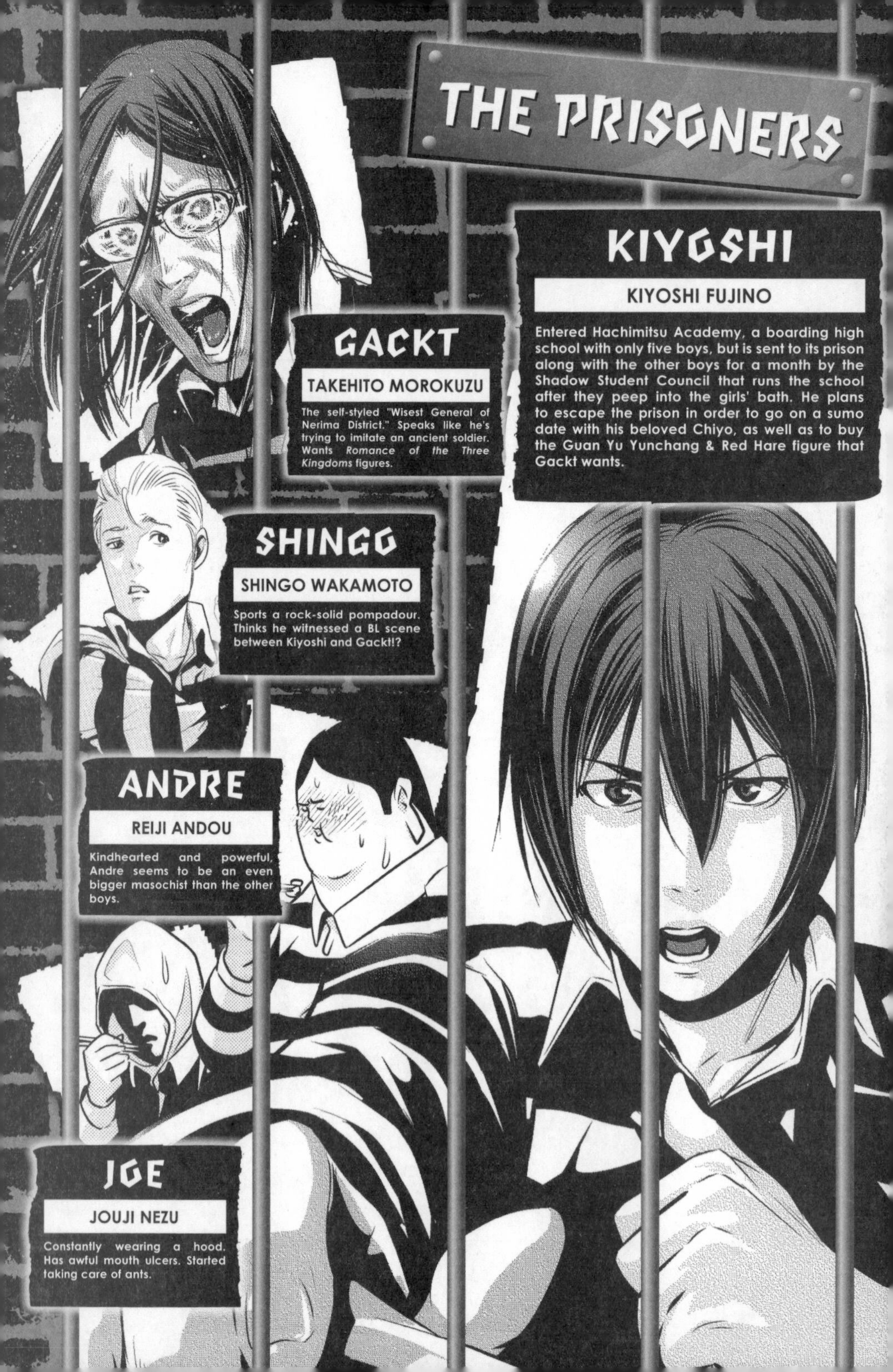
THE PRISONERS
KIYOSHI
KIYOSHI FUJINO
Entered Hachimitsu Academy, a boarding high school with only five boys, but is sent to its prison along with the other boys for a month by the Shadow Student Council that runs the school after they peep into the girls' bath. He plans to escape the prison in order to go on a sumo date with his beloved Chiyo, as well as to buy the Guan Yu Yunchang & Red Hare figure that Gackt wants.
GACKT
TAKEHITO MOROKUZU
The self-styled "Wisest General of Nerima District." Speaks like he's trying to imitate an ancient soldier. Wants *Romance of the Three Kingdoms* figures.
SHINGO
SHINGO WAKAMOTO
Sports a rock-solid pompadour. Thinks he witnessed a BL scene between Kiyoshi and Gackt!?
ANDRE
REIJI ANDOU
Kindhearted and powerful, Andre seems to be an even bigger masochist than the other boys.
JOE
JOUJI NEZU
Constantly wearing a hood. Has awful mouth ulcers. Started taking care of ants.

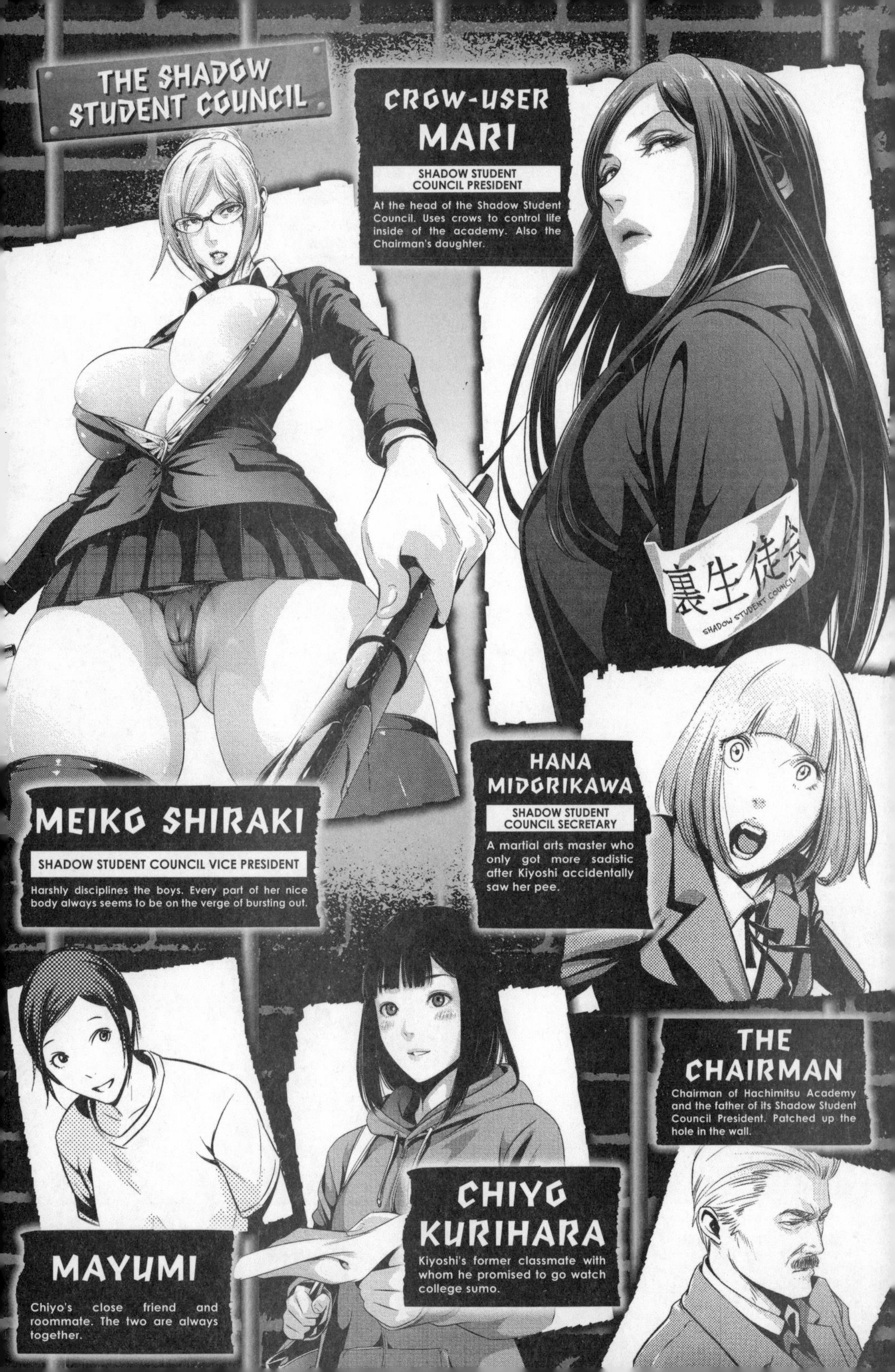
THE SHADOW STUDENT COUNCIL
CROW-USER MARI
SHADOW STUDENT COUNCIL PRESIDENT
At the head of the Shadow Student Council. Uses crows to control life inside of the academy. Also the Chairman's daughter.
裏生徒会
SHADOW STUDENT COUNCIL
MEIKO SHIRAKI
SHADOW STUDENT COUNCIL VICE PRESIDENT
Harshly disciplines the boys. Every part of her nice body always seems to be on the verge of bursting out.
HANA MIDORIKAWA
SHADOW STUDENT COUNCIL SECRETARY
A martial arts master who only got more sadistic after Kiyoshi accidentally saw her pee.
THE CHAIRMAN
Chairman of Hachimitsu Academy and the father of its Shadow Student Council President. Patched up the hole in the wall.
CHIYO KURIHARA
Kiyoshi's former classmate with whom he promised to go watch college sumo.
MAYUMI
Chiyo's close friend and roommate. The two are always together.

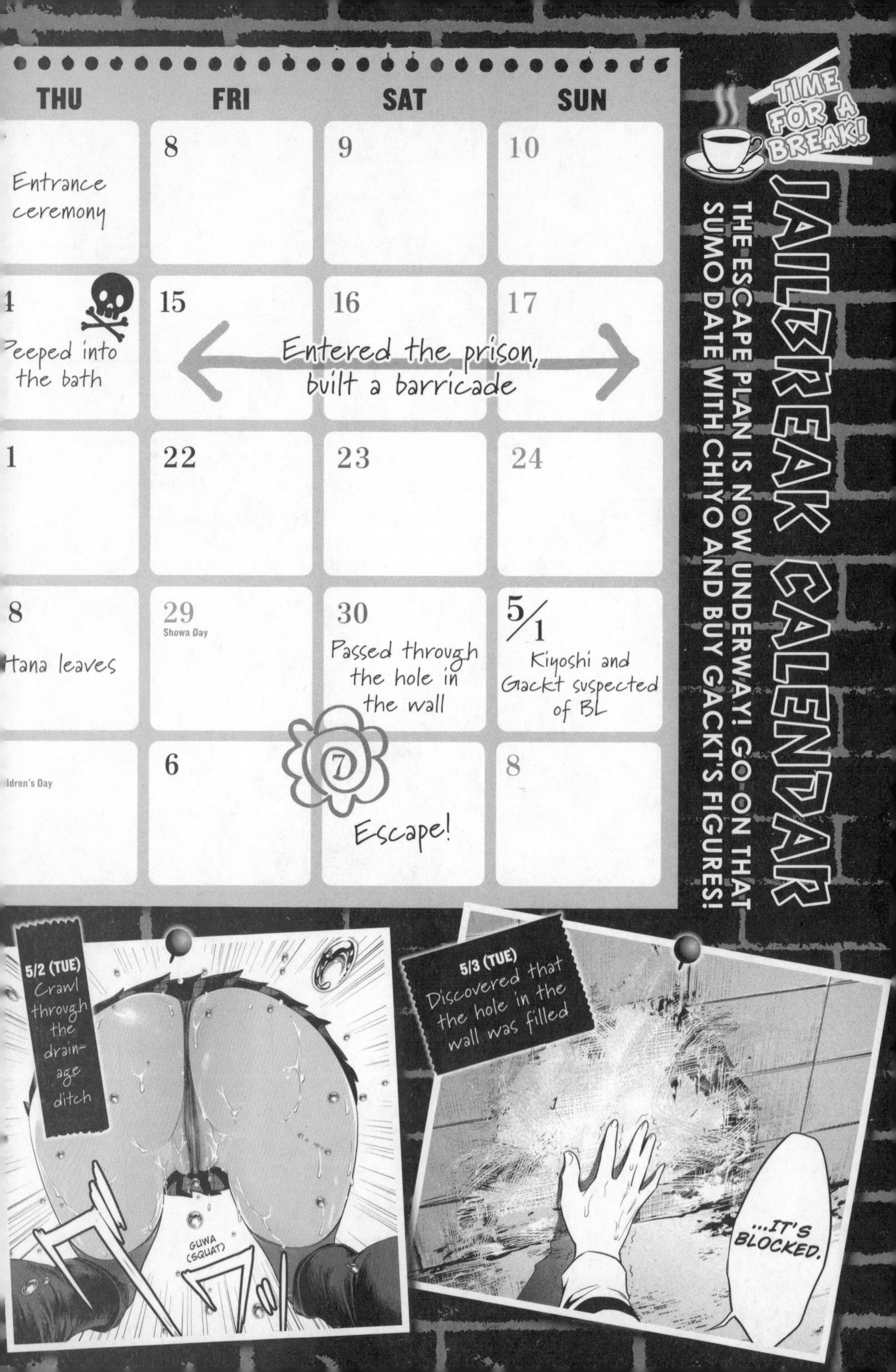
TIME FOR A BREAK!
JAILBREAK CALENDAR
THE ESCAPE PLAN IS NOW UNDERWAY! GO ON THAT SUMO DATE WITH CHIYO AND BUY GACKT'S FIGURES!
THU
FRI
SAT
SUN
8
9
10
Entrance ceremony
15
16
17
Peeped into the bath
Entered the prison, built a barricade
22
23
24
29
Showa Day
30
5/1
Hana leaves
Passed through the hole in the wall
Kiyoshi and Gackt suspected of BL
6
7
8
Escape!
5/2 (TUE)
Crawl through the drain-age ditch
GUWA (SQUAT)
5/3 (TUE)
Discovered that the hole in the wall was filled
...IT'S BLOCKED.

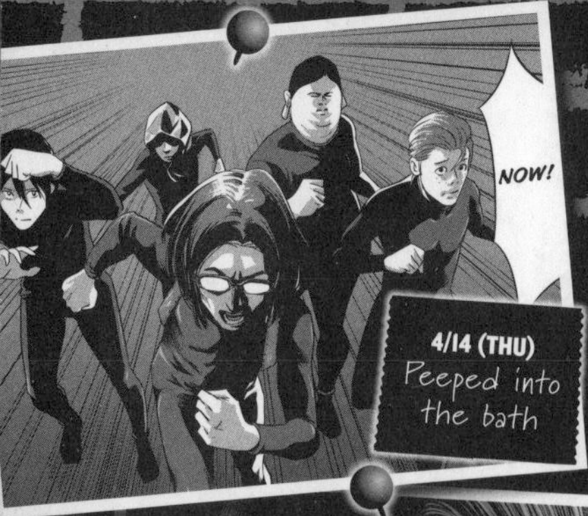
NOW!
4/14 (THU)
Peeped into the bath

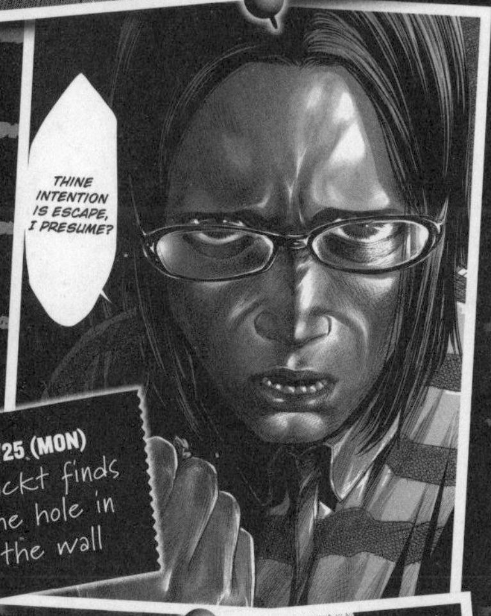
THINE INTENTION IS ESCAPE, I PRESUME?
4/25 (MON)
Gackt finds the hole in the wall

MON	TUE	WED
4/4	5	6
11	12	13
18 Clover gathering	19 Begin cultivating the wasteland	20
25 Gackt finds the hole in the wall	26 Join forces with Gackt	27 Destroy the building in the dump
2 Crawl through the drainage ditch	3 Constitution Memorial Day Discovered that the hole in the wall was filled	4 Greenery Day

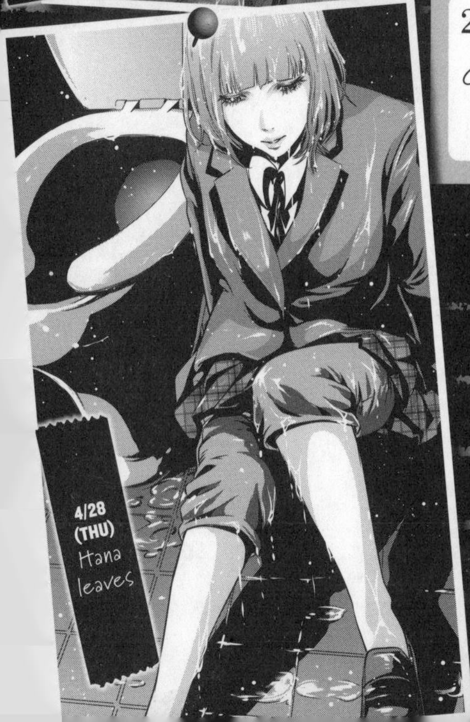
4/28 (THU)
Hana leaves

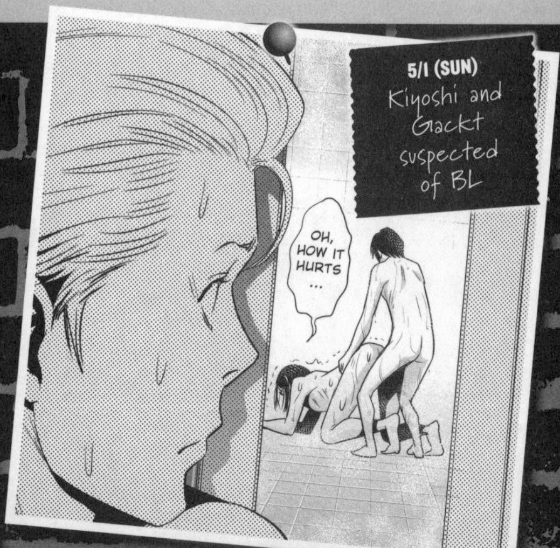
5/1 (SUN)
Kiyoshi and Gackt suspected of BL
OH, HOW IT HURTS ...

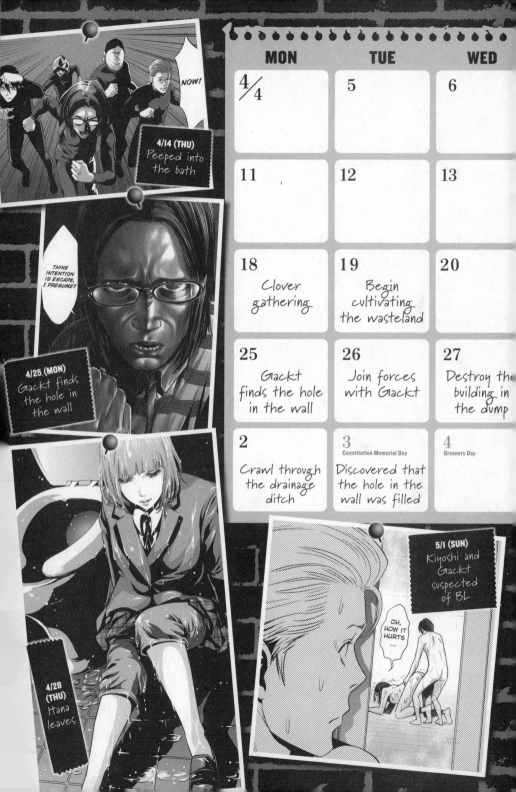

CONTENTS

PRISON SCHOOL

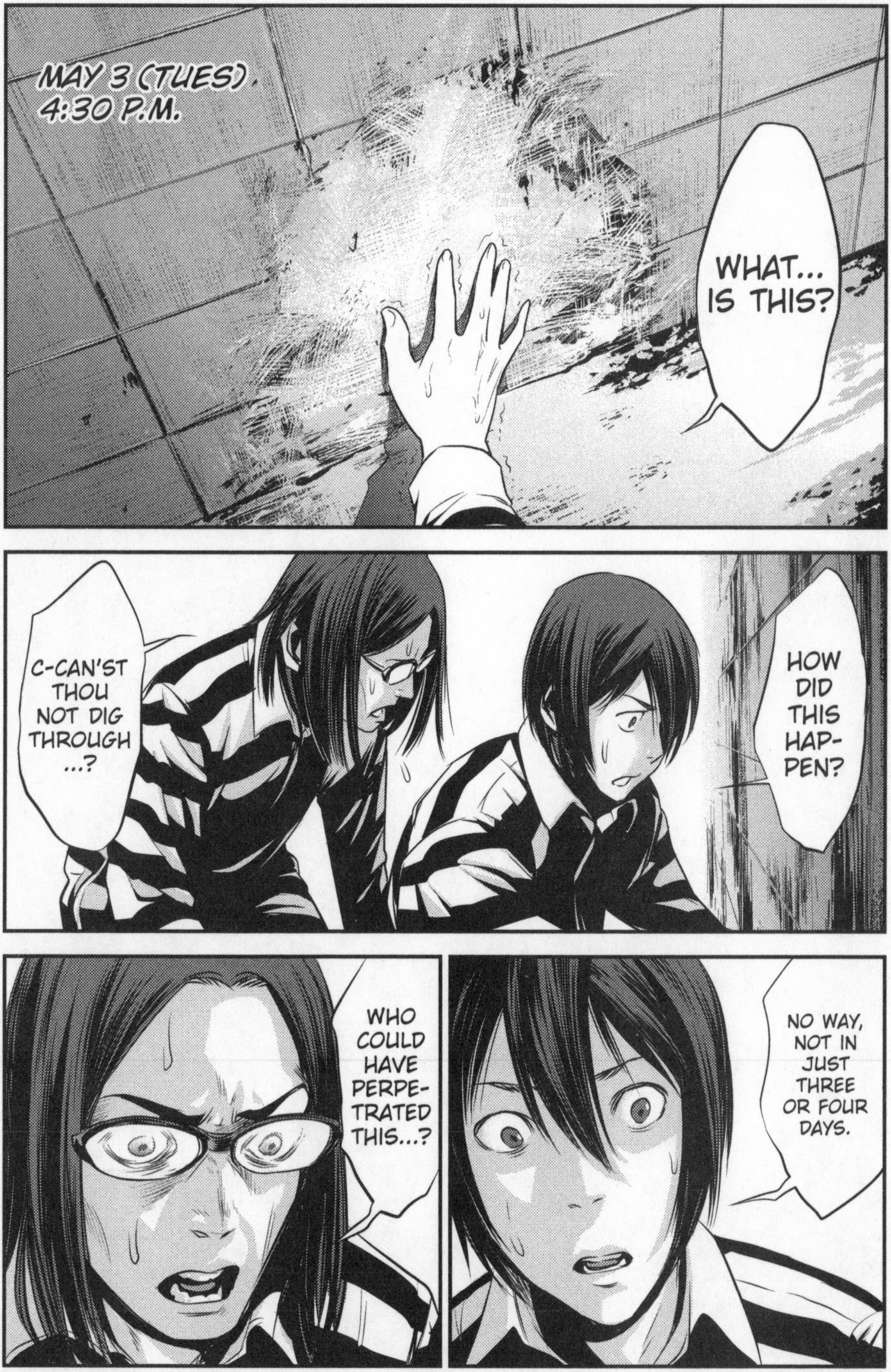
MAY 3 (TUES) 4:30 P.M.
WHAT... IS THIS?
HOW DID THIS HAP-PEN?
C-CAN'ST THOU NOT DIG THROUGH ...?
NO WAY, NOT IN JUST THREE OR FOUR DAYS.
WHO COULD HAVE PERPE-TRATED THIS...?

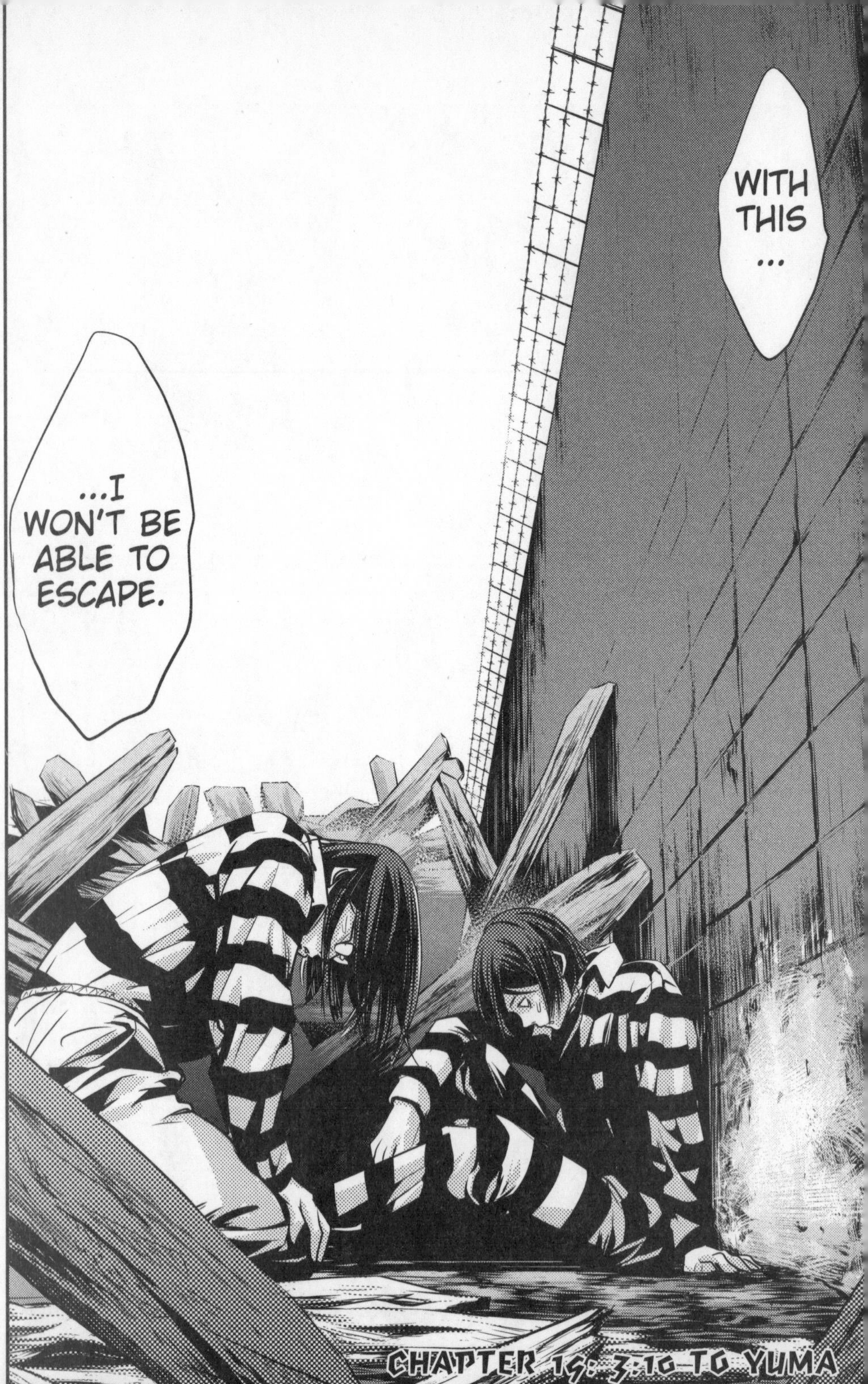
WITH THIS ...
...I WON'T BE ABLE TO ESCAPE.
CHAPTER 15: 3:10 TO YUMA

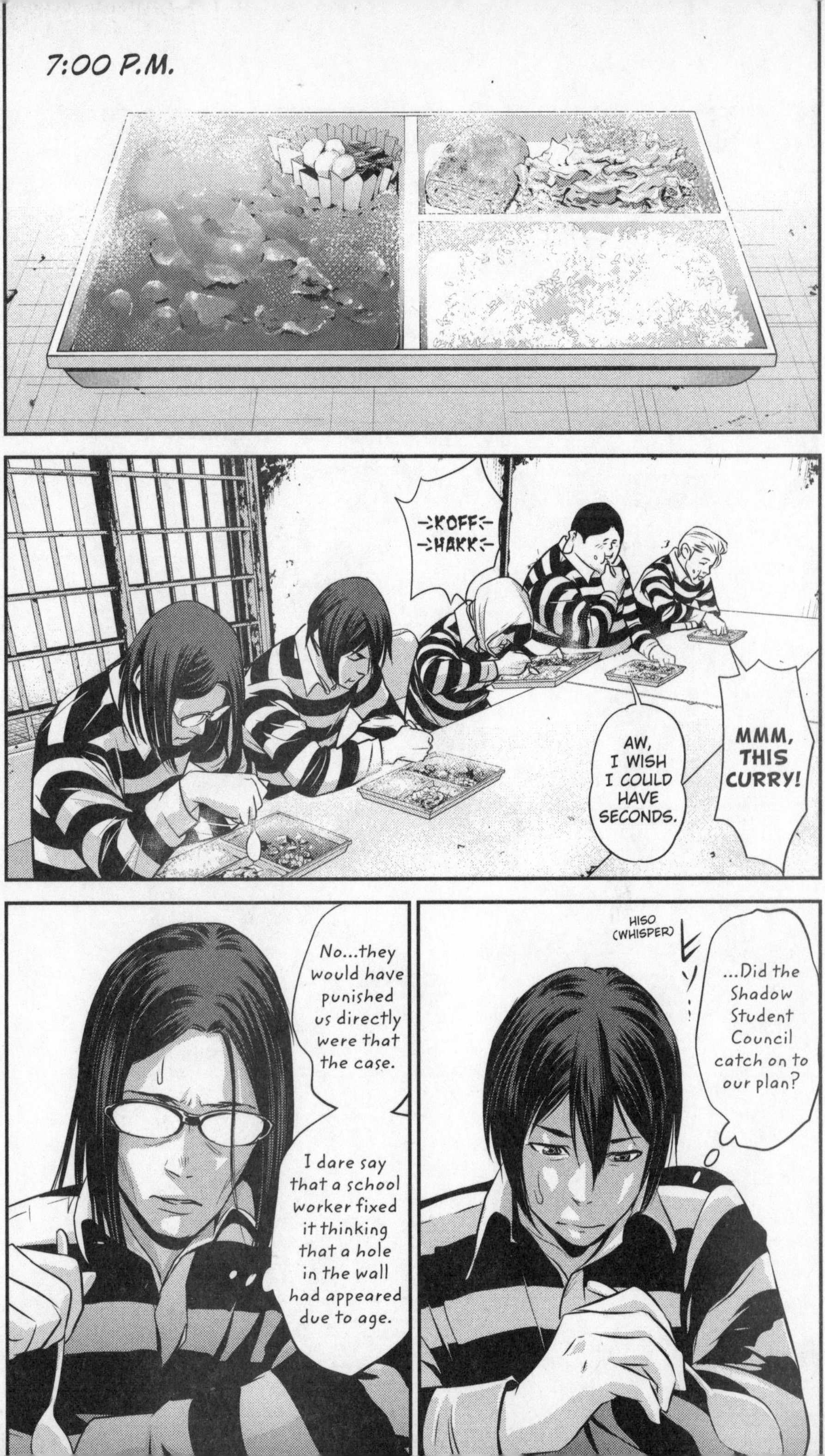
7:00 P.M.
MMM, THIS CURRY!
AW, I WISH I COULD HAVE SECONDS.
KOFF HAKK
HISO (WHISPER)
...Did the Shadow Student Council catch on to our plan?
No...they would have punished us directly were that the case.
I dare say that a school worker fixed it thinking that a hole in the wall had appeared due to age.

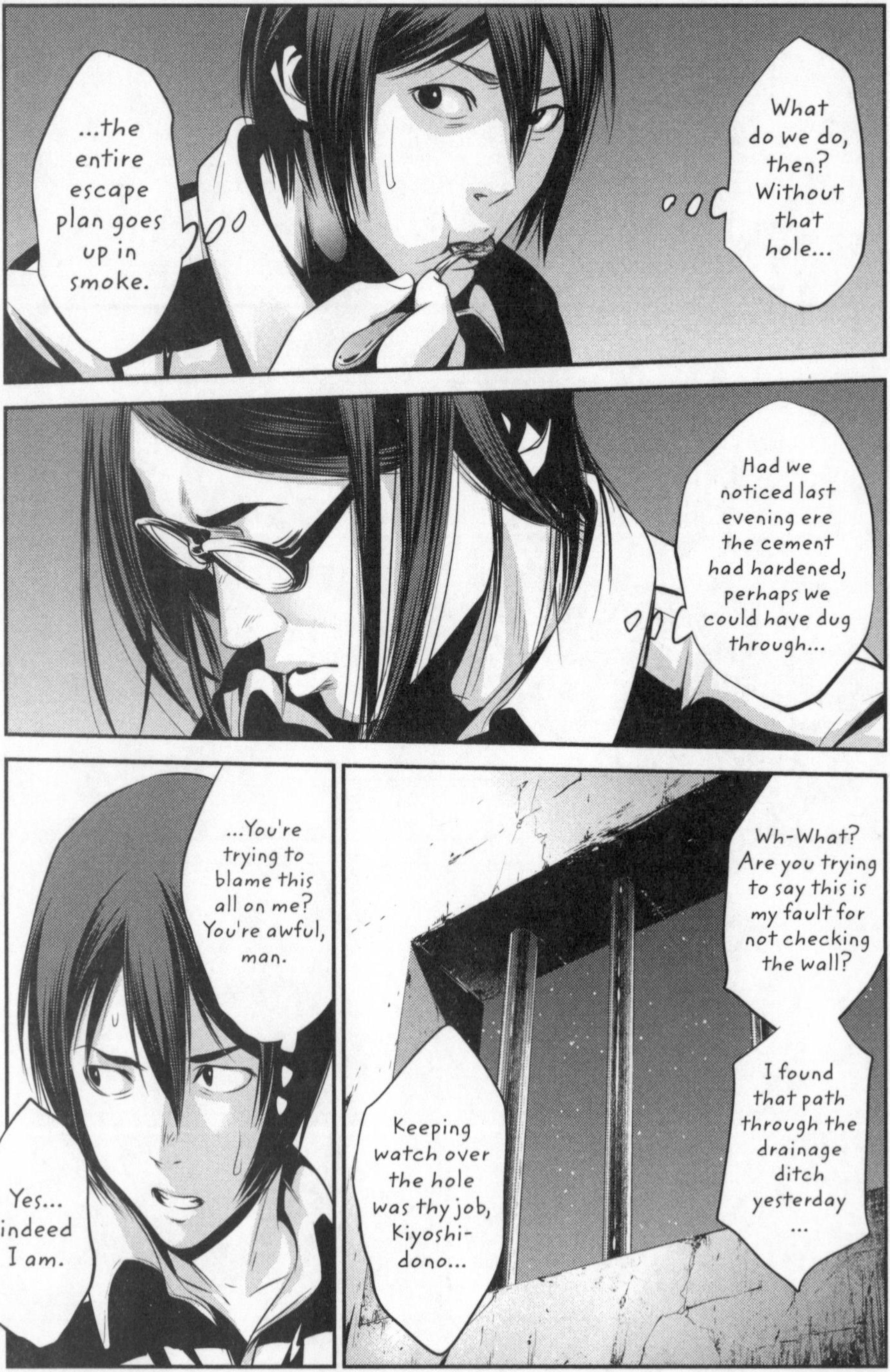
What do we do, then? Without that hole...
...the entire escape plan goes up in smoke.
Had we noticed last evening ere the cement had hardened, perhaps we could have dug through...
Wh-What? Are you trying to say this is my fault for not checking the wall?
I found that path through the drainage ditch yesterday ...
Keeping watch over the hole was thy job, Kiyoshi-dono...
...You're trying to blame this all on me? You're awful, man.
Yes... indeed I am.

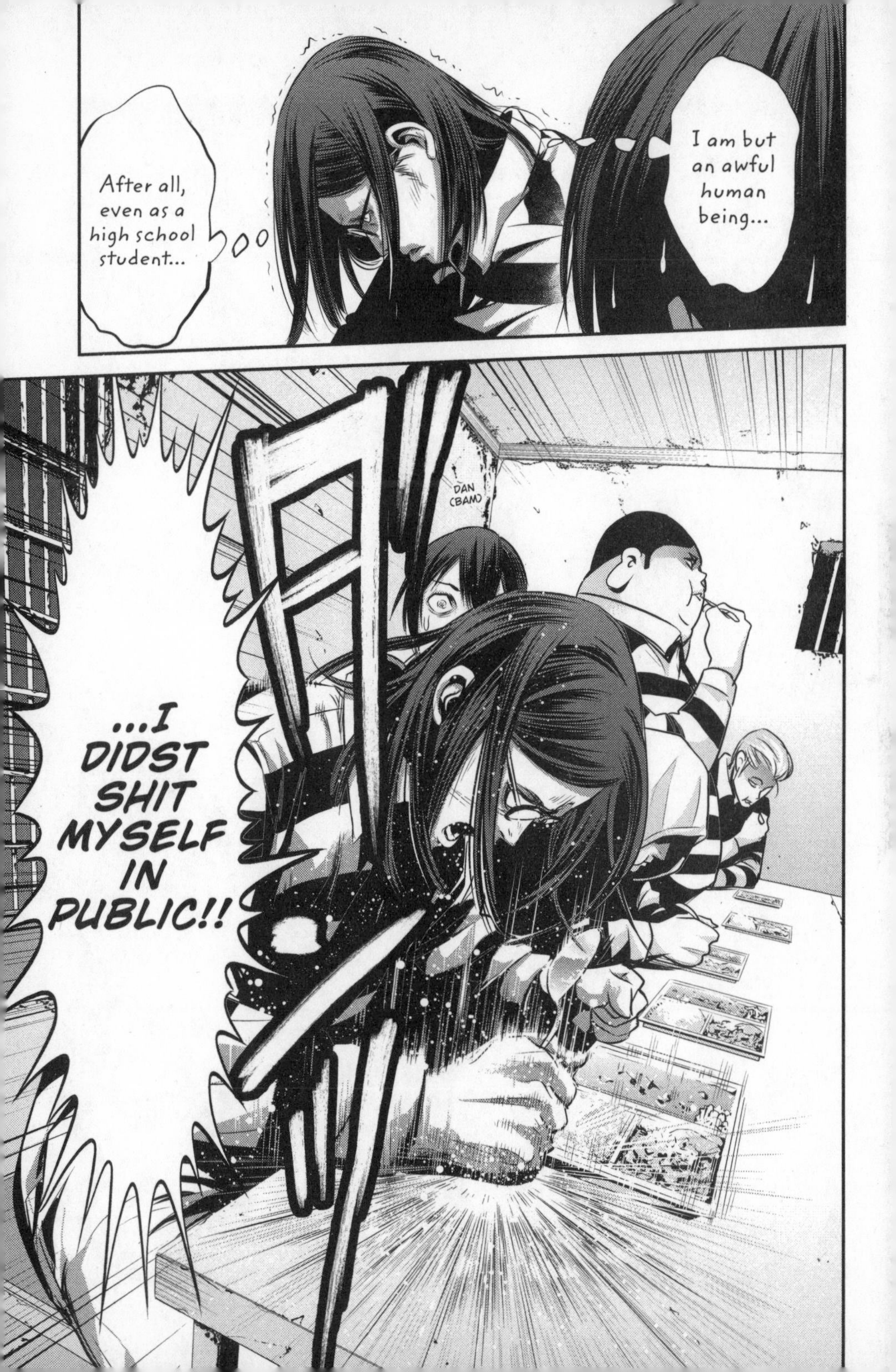

I am but an awful human being...
After all, even as a high school student...
DAN (BAM)
...I DIDST SHIT MYSELF IN PUBLIC!!

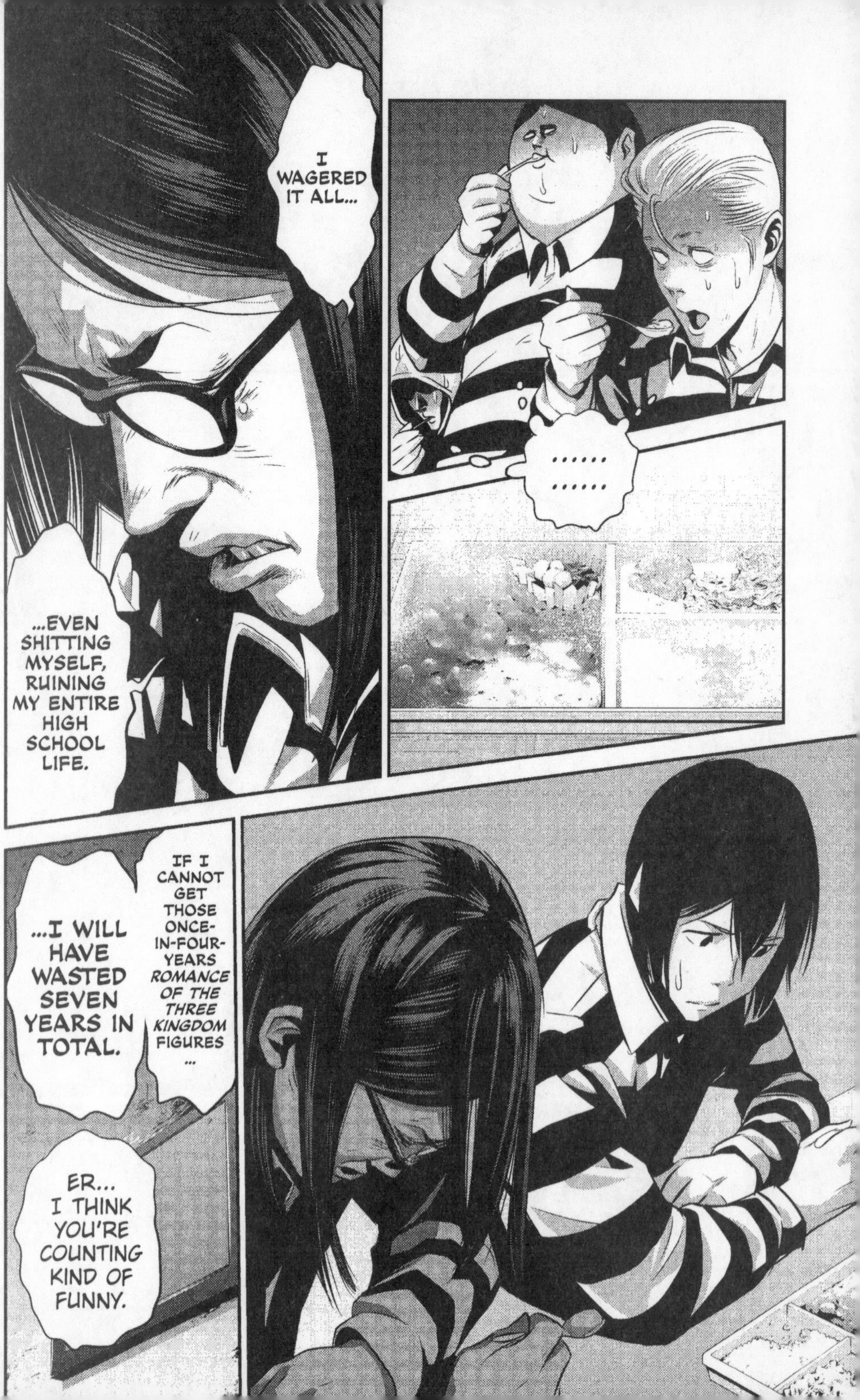
......
......
I WAGERED IT ALL...
...EVEN SHITTING MYSELF, RUINING MY ENTIRE HIGH SCHOOL LIFE.
IF I CANNOT GET THOSE ONCE-IN-FOUR-YEARS *ROMANCE OF THE THREE KINGDOM* FIGURES...
...I WILL HAVE WASTED SEVEN YEARS IN TOTAL.
ER... I THINK YOU'RE COUNTING KIND OF FUNNY.

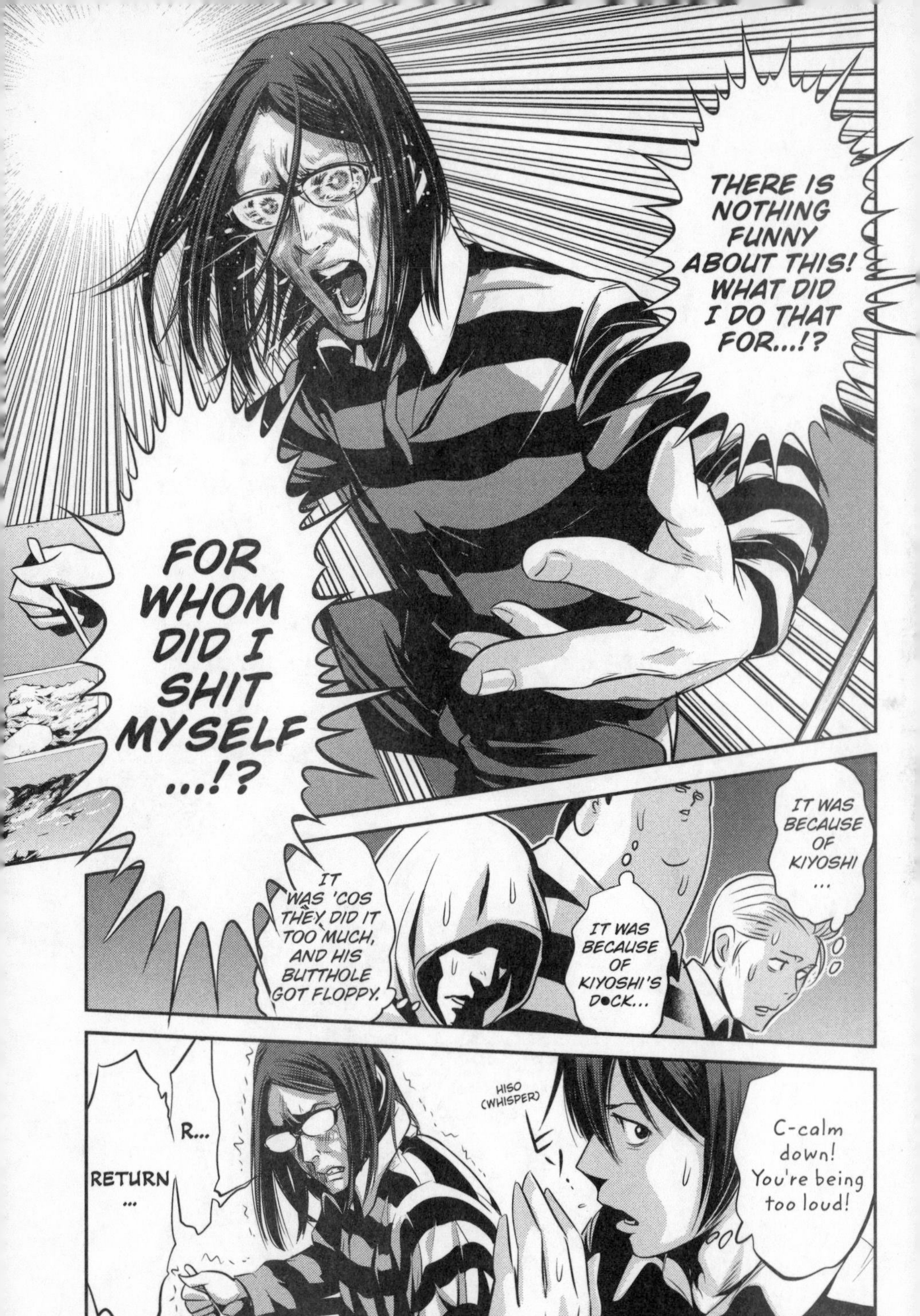
THERE IS NOTHING FUNNY ABOUT THIS! WHAT DID I DO THAT FOR...!?
FOR WHOM DID I SHIT MYSELF ...!?
IT WAS BECAUSE OF KIYOSHI ...
IT WAS BECAUSE OF KIYOSHI'S D●CK...
IT WAS 'COS THEY DID IT TOO MUCH, AND HIS BUTTHOLE GOT FLOPPY.
C-calm down! You're being too loud!
HISO (WHISPER)
R...
RETURN ...

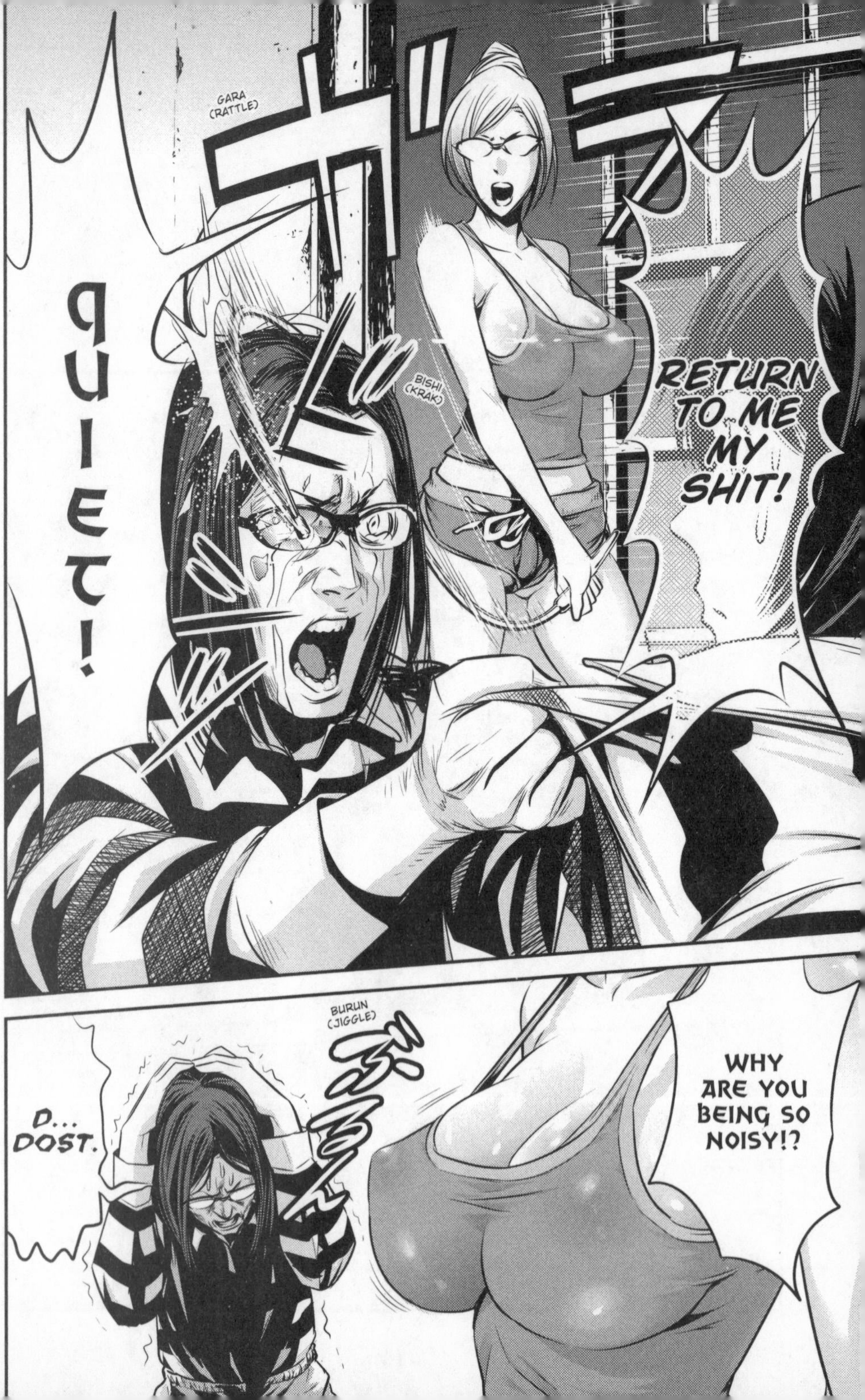
GARA
(RATTLE)
RETURN TO ME MY SHIT!
BISHI
(KRAK)
QUIET!
WHY ARE YOU BEING SO NOISY!?
BURUN
(JIGGLE)
D... DOST.

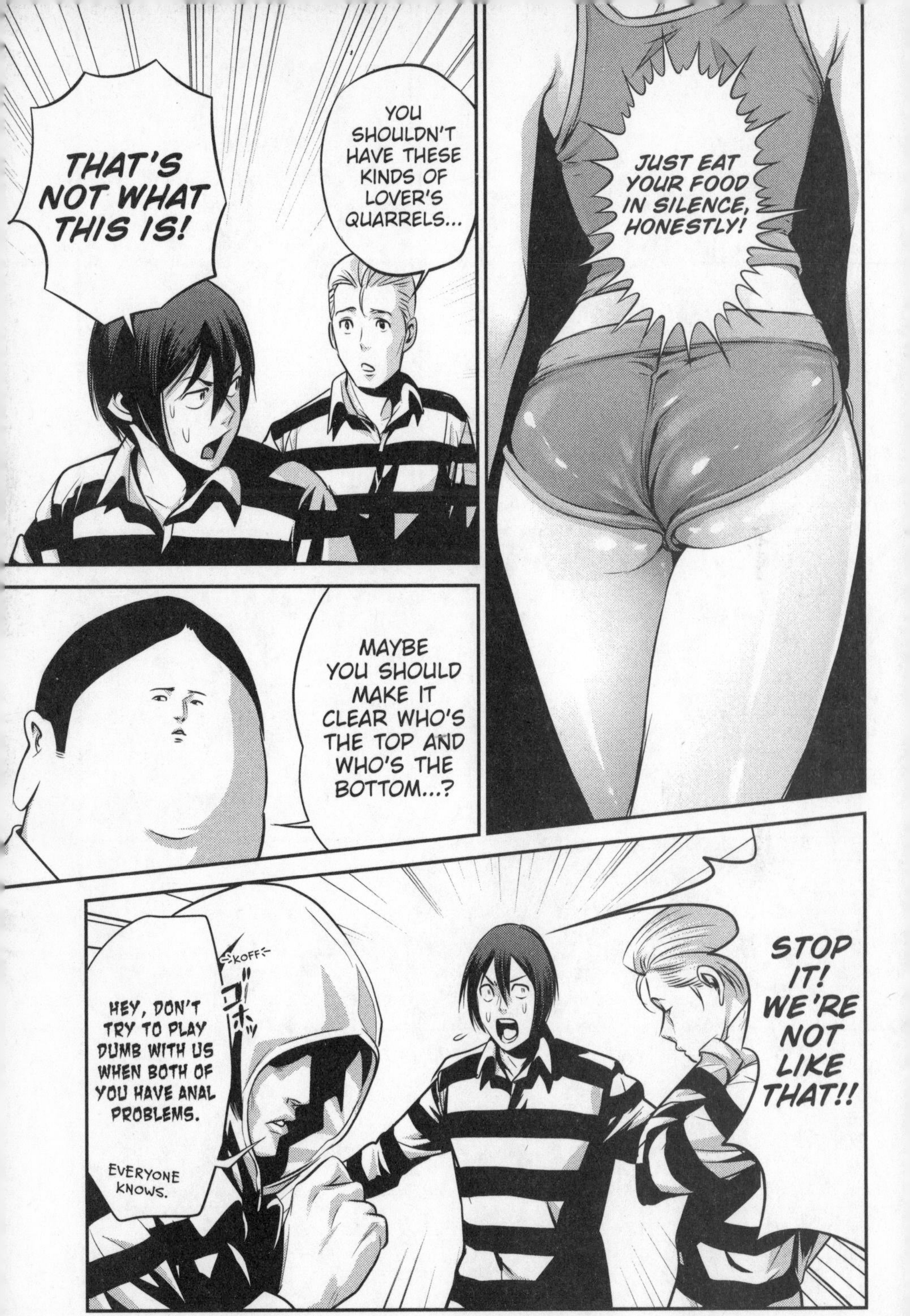
JUST EAT YOUR FOOD IN SILENCE, HONESTLY!
YOU SHOULDN'T HAVE THESE KINDS OF LOVER'S QUARRELS...
THAT'S NOT WHAT THIS IS!
MAYBE YOU SHOULD MAKE IT CLEAR WHO'S THE TOP AND WHO'S THE BOTTOM...?
STOP IT! WE'RE NOT LIKE THAT!!
KOFF
ゴホッ
HEY, DON'T TRY TO PLAY DUMB WITH US WHEN BOTH OF YOU HAVE ANAL PROBLEMS.
EVERYONE KNOWS.

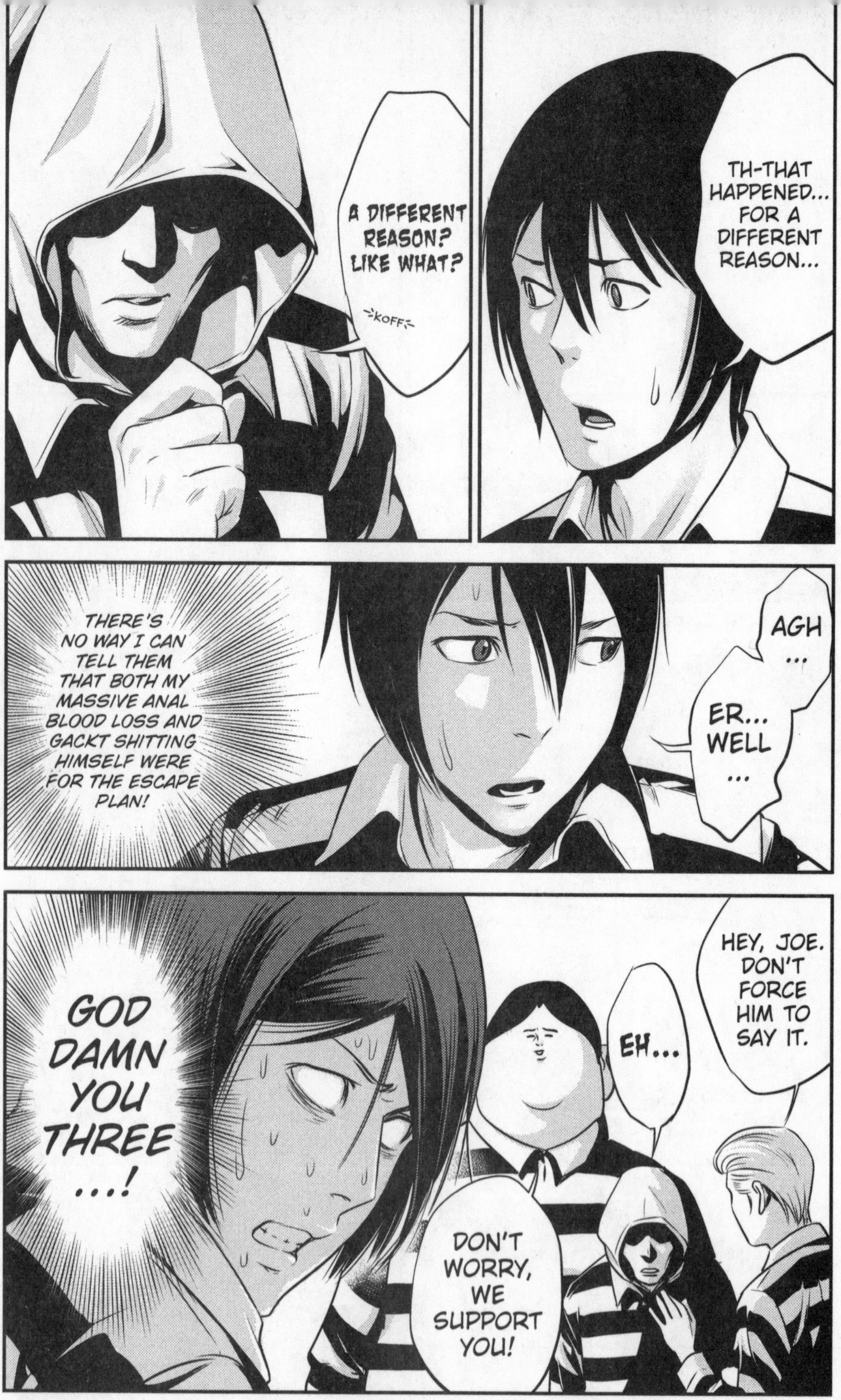
TH-THAT HAPPENED... FOR A DIFFERENT REASON...
A DIFFERENT REASON? LIKE WHAT?
KOFF
AGH ...
ER... WELL ...
THERE'S NO WAY I CAN TELL THEM THAT BOTH MY MASSIVE ANAL BLOOD LOSS AND GACKT SHITTING HIMSELF WERE FOR THE ESCAPE PLAN!
HEY, JOE. DON'T FORCE HIM TO SAY IT.
EH...
DON'T WORRY, WE SUPPORT YOU!
GOD DAMN YOU THREE ...!

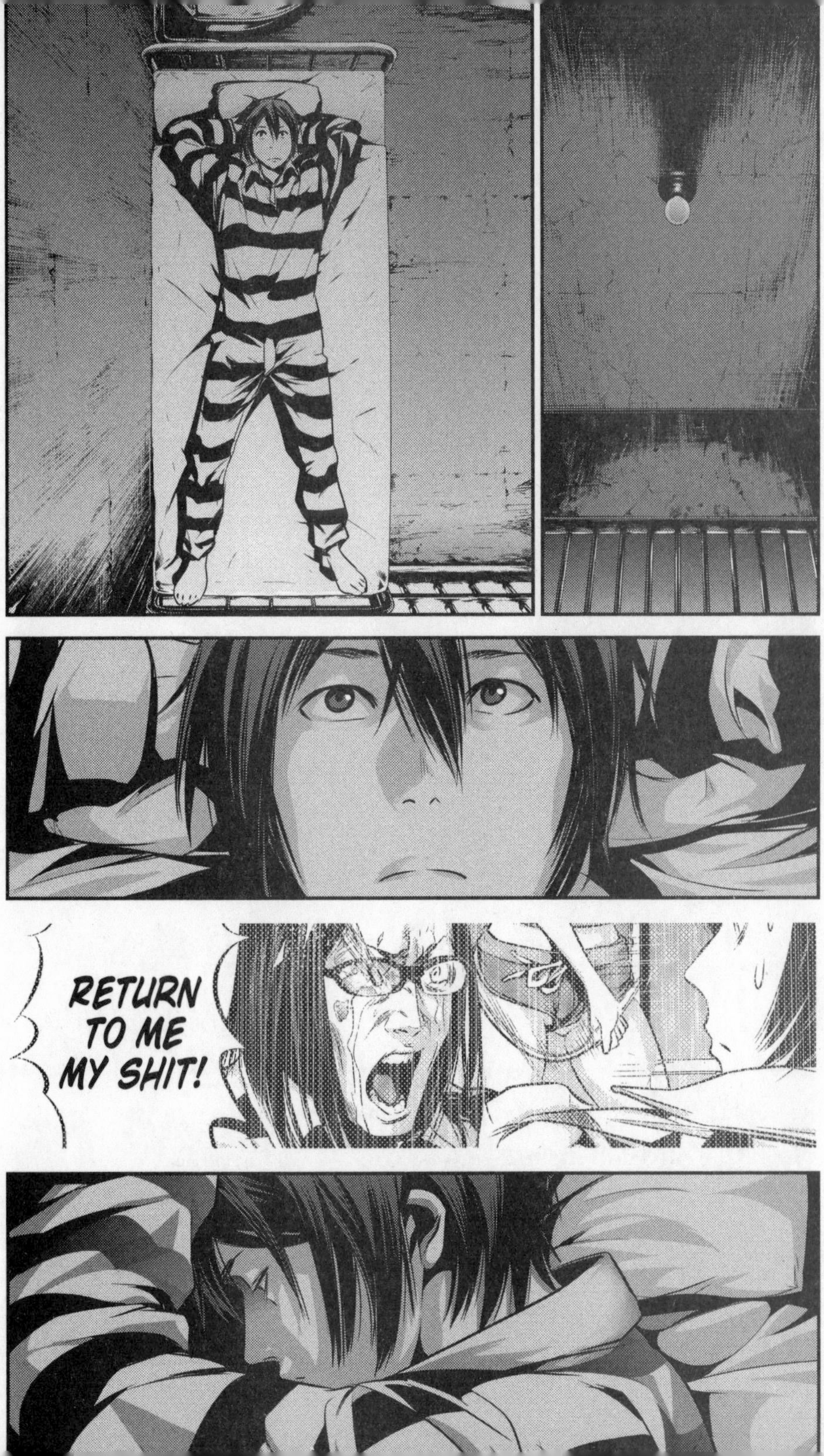
RETURN TO ME MY SHIT!

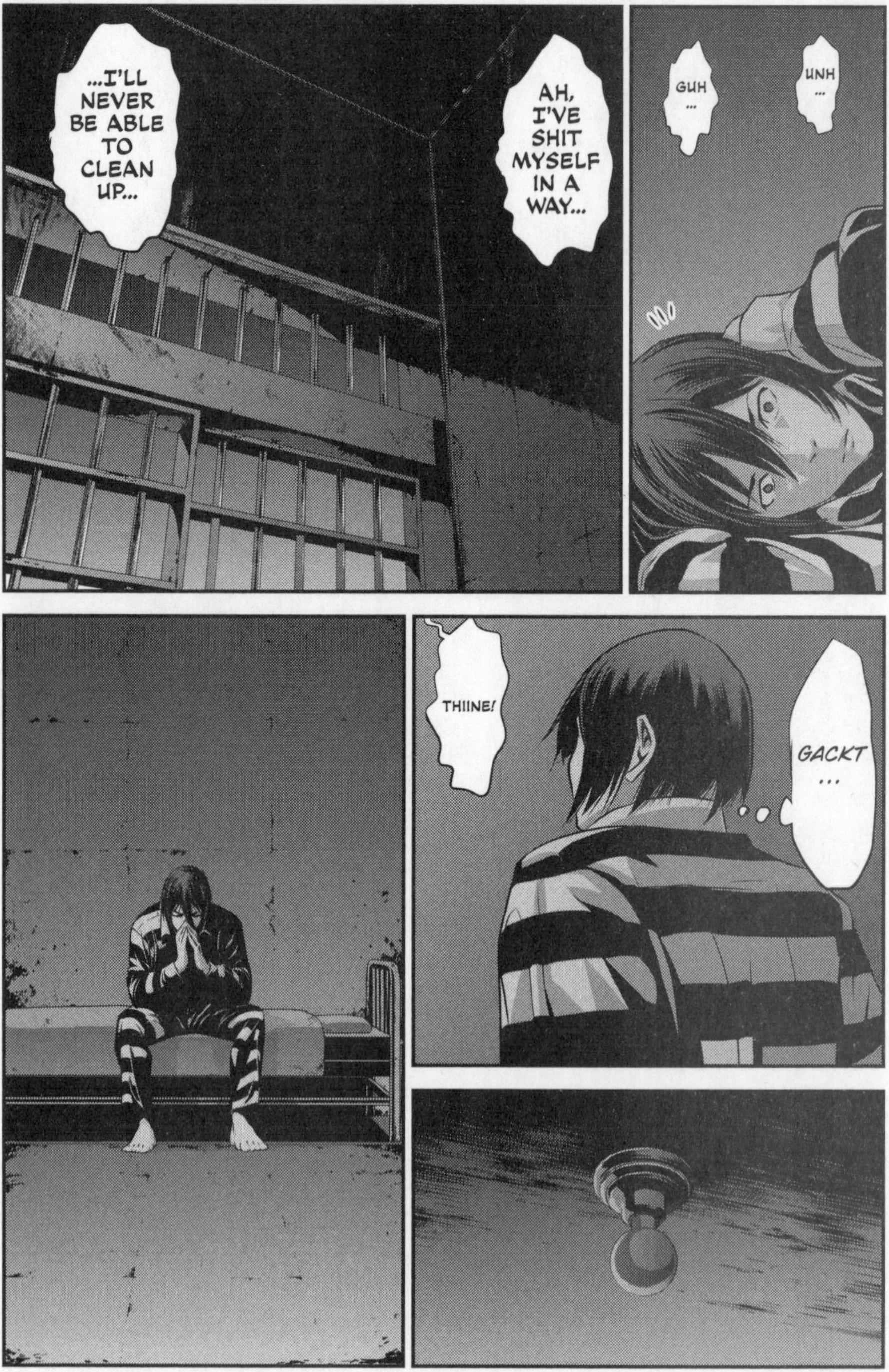
UNH ...
GUH ...
AH, I'VE SHIT MYSELF IN A WAY...
...I'LL NEVER BE ABLE TO CLEAN UP...
GACKT ...
THIINE!

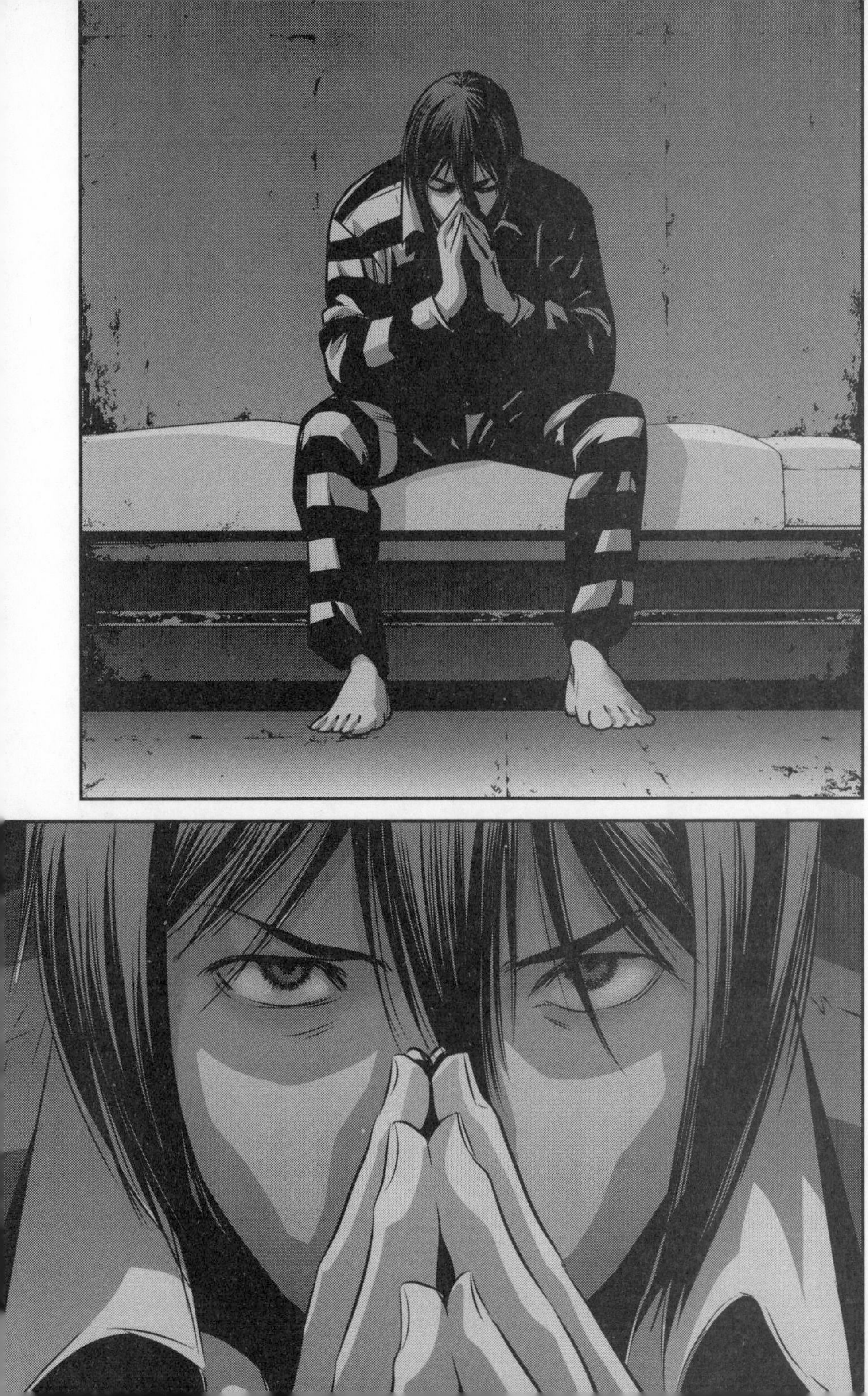

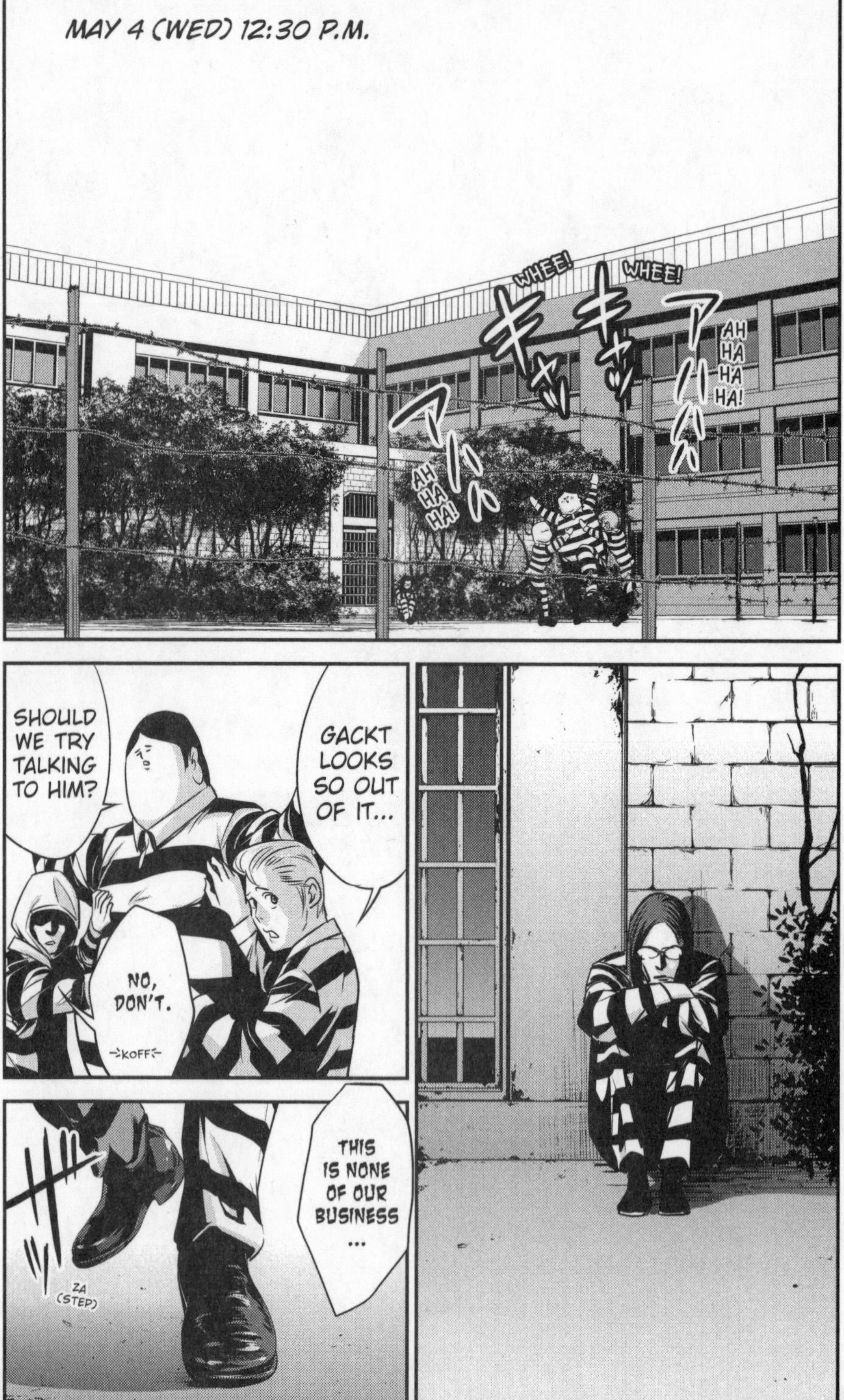
MAY 4 (WED) 12:30 P.M.
WHEE!
WHEE!
AH HA HA HA!
AH HA HA!
GACKT LOOKS SO OUT OF IT...
SHOULD WE TRY TALKING TO HIM?
NO, DON'T.
KOFF
THIS IS NONE OF OUR BUSINESS ...
ZA (STEP)

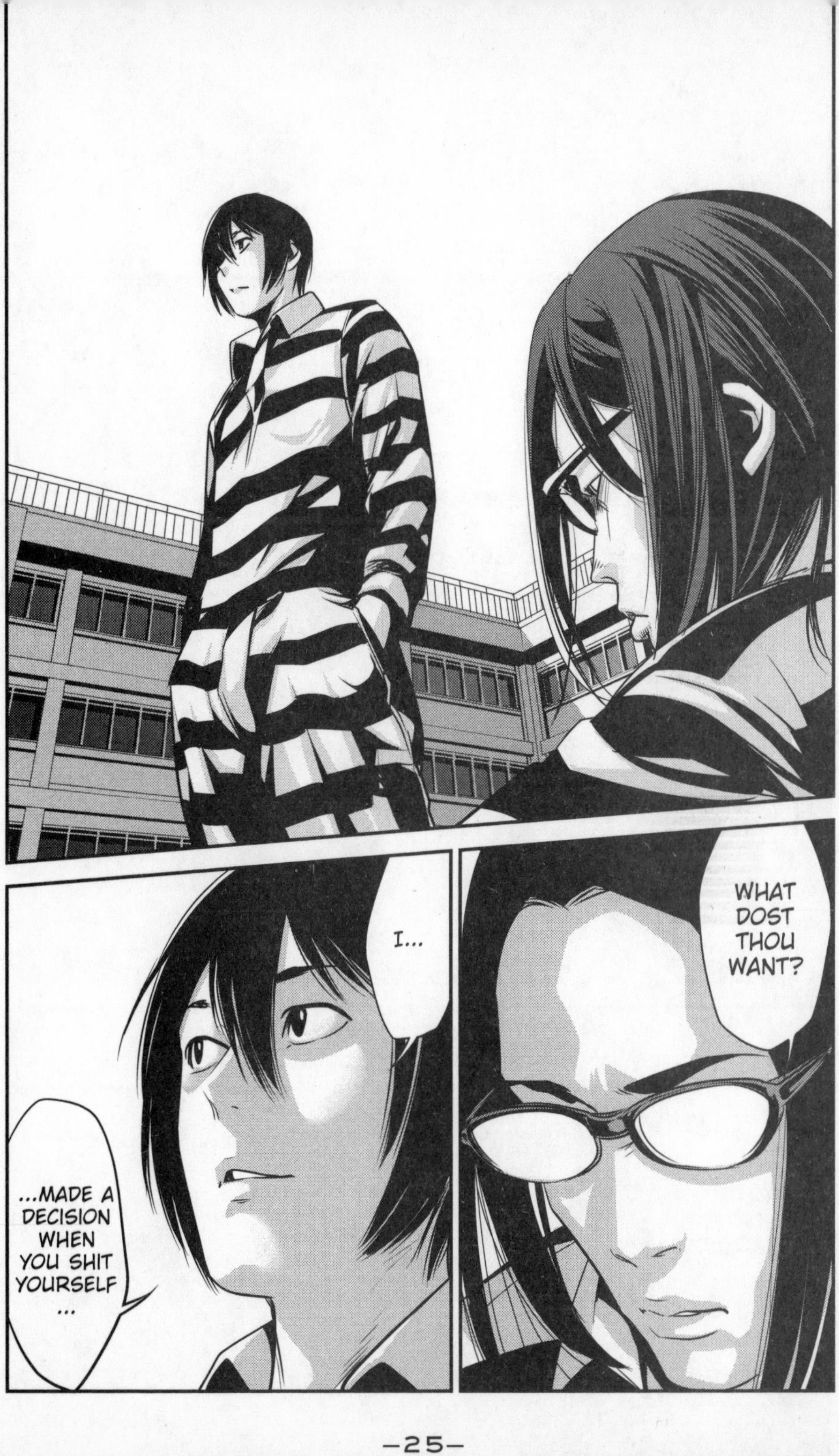
WHAT DOST THOU WANT?
I...
...MADE A DECISION WHEN YOU SHIT YOURSELF ...

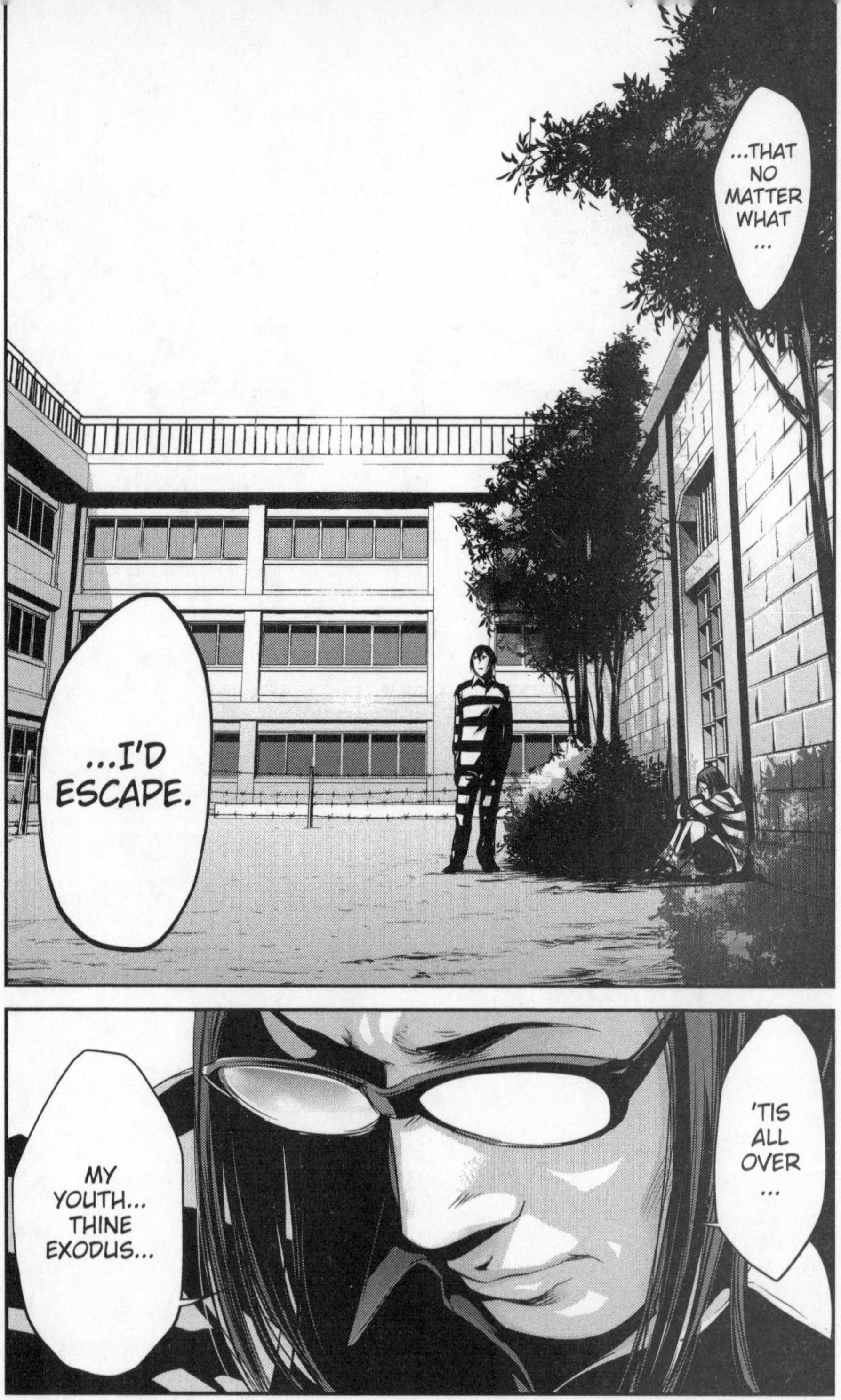
...THAT NO MATTER WHAT ...
...I'D ESCAPE.
'TIS ALL OVER ...
MY YOUTH... THINE EXODUS...

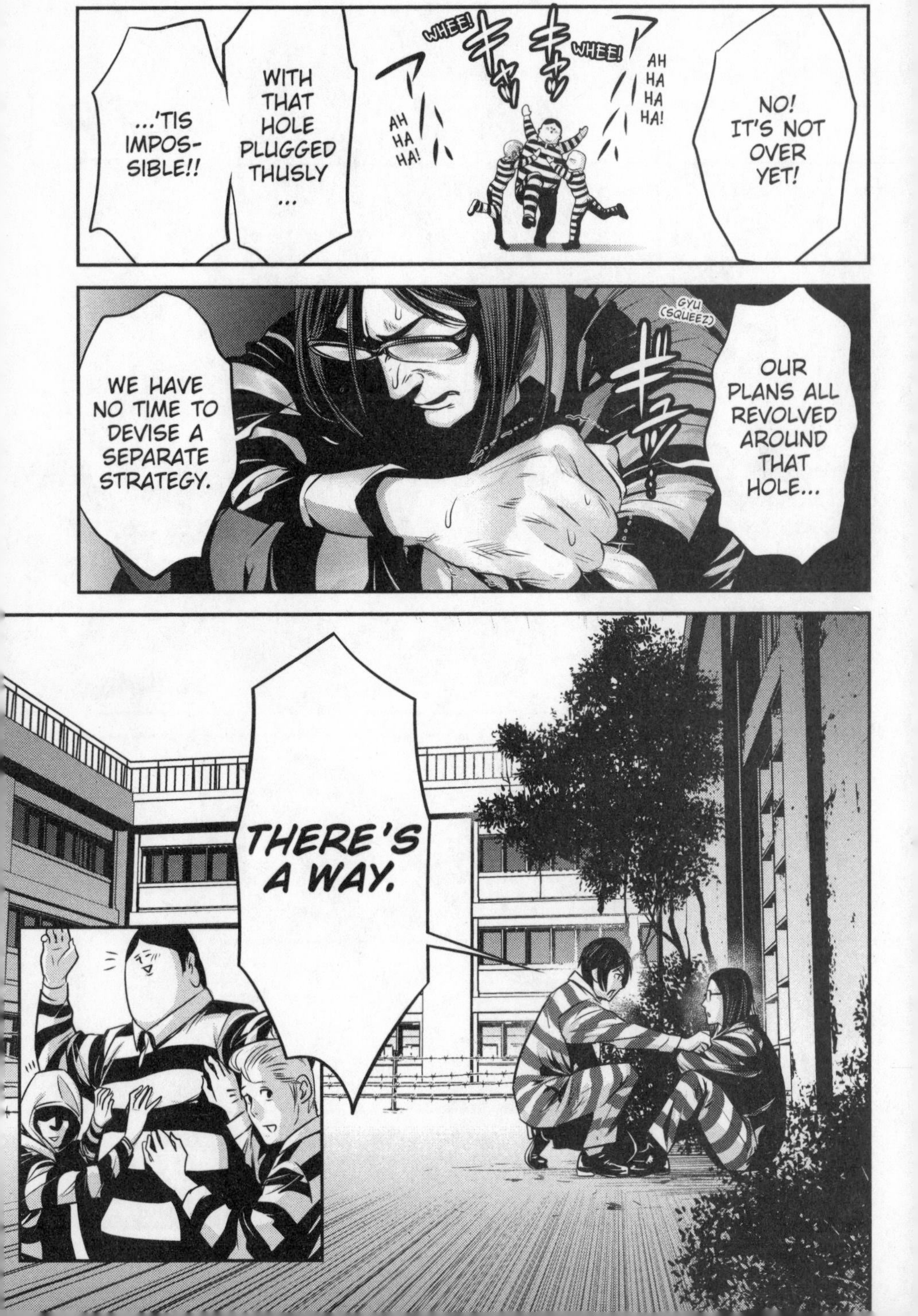
NO! IT'S NOT OVER YET!
AH HA HA HA!
WHEE!
WHEE!
AH HA HA!
WITH THAT HOLE PLUGGED THUSLY ...
...'TIS IMPOSSIBLE!!
OUR PLANS ALL REVOLVED AROUND THAT HOLE...
GYU (SQUEEZ)
WE HAVE NO TIME TO DEVISE A SEPARATE STRATEGY.
THERE'S A WAY.

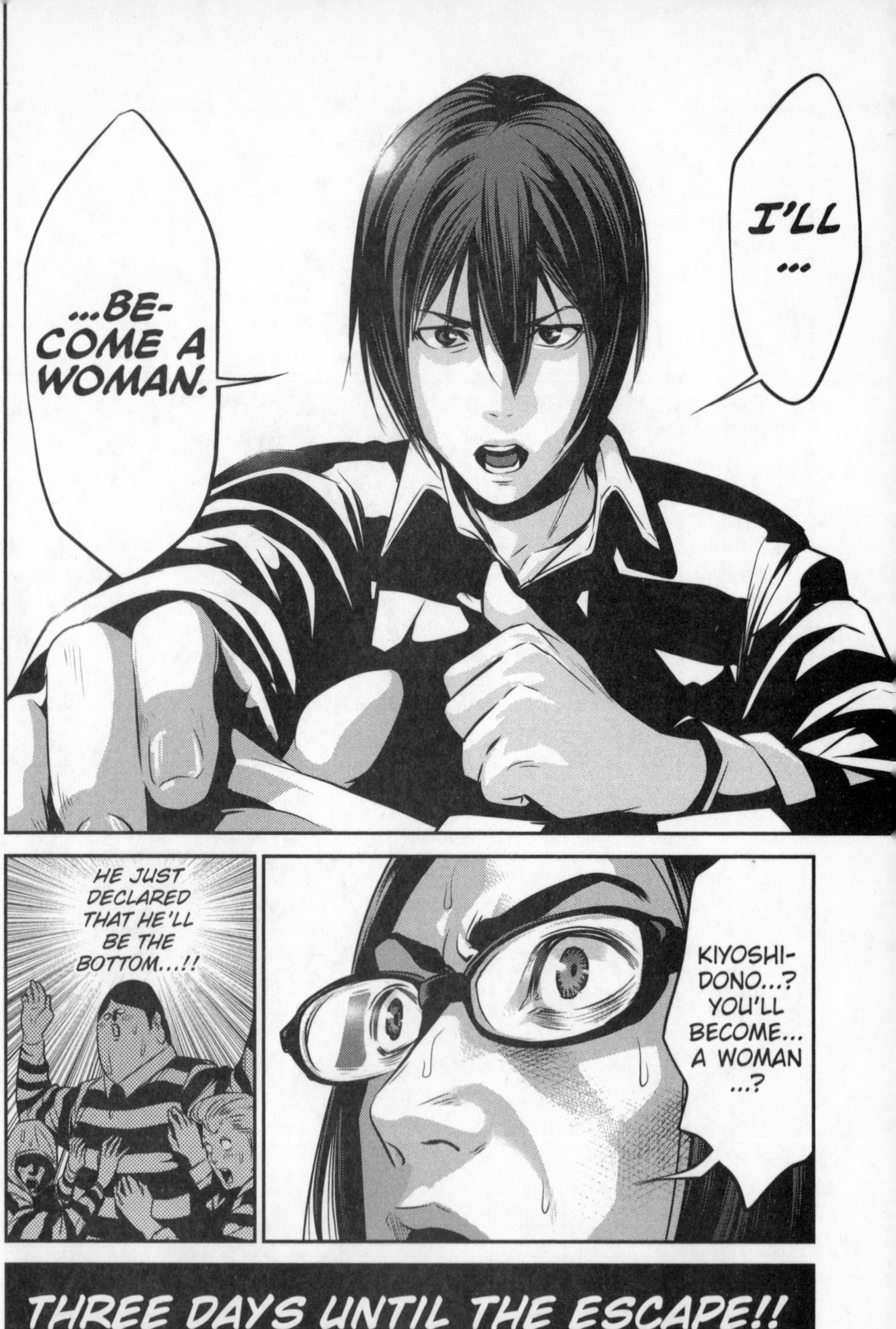
I'LL ...
...BE-COME A WOMAN.
KIYOSHI-DONO...? YOU'LL BECOME... A WOMAN ...?
HE JUST DECLARED THAT HE'LL BE THE BOTTOM...!!
THREE DAYS UNTIL THE ESCAPE!!

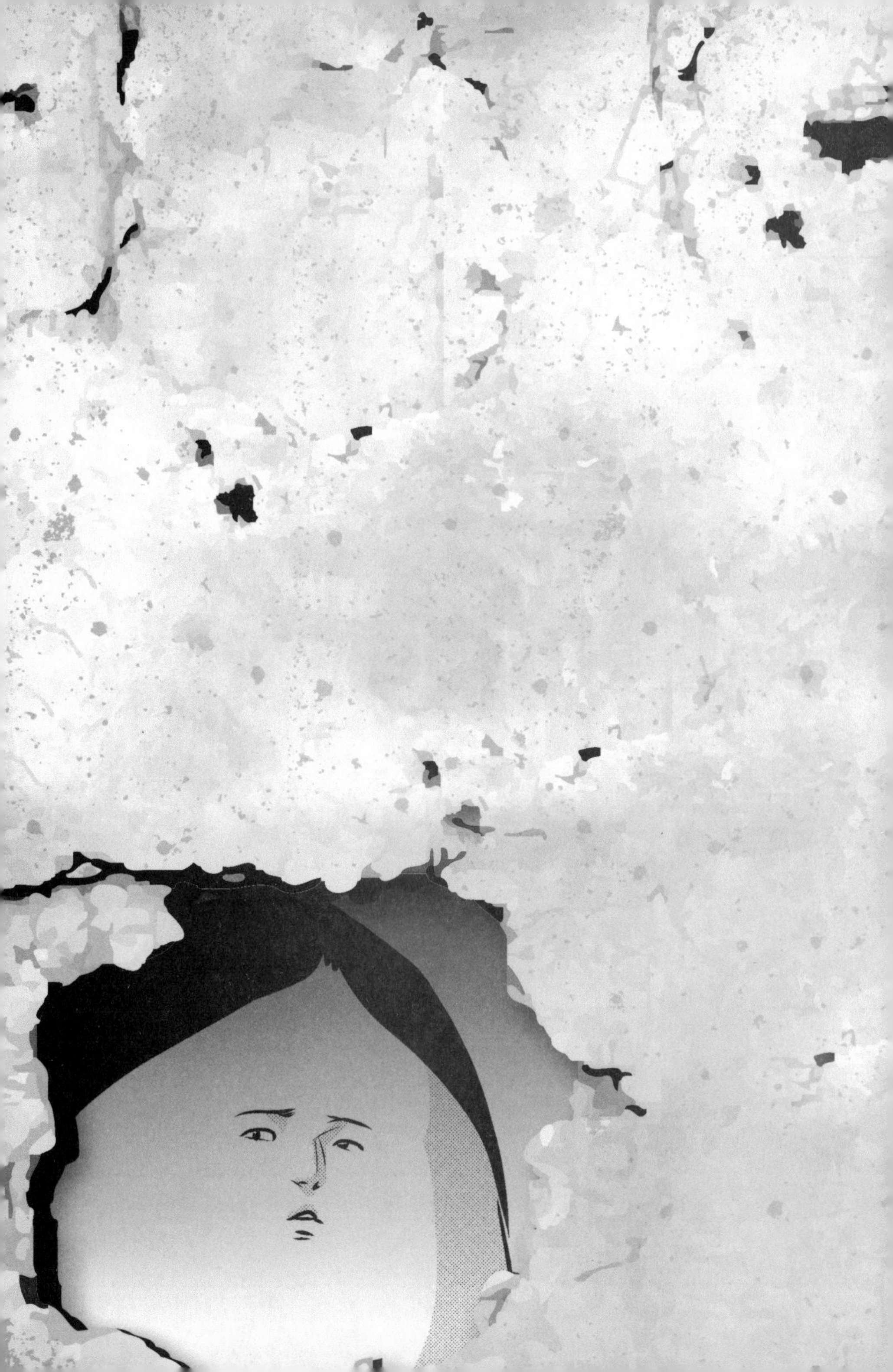

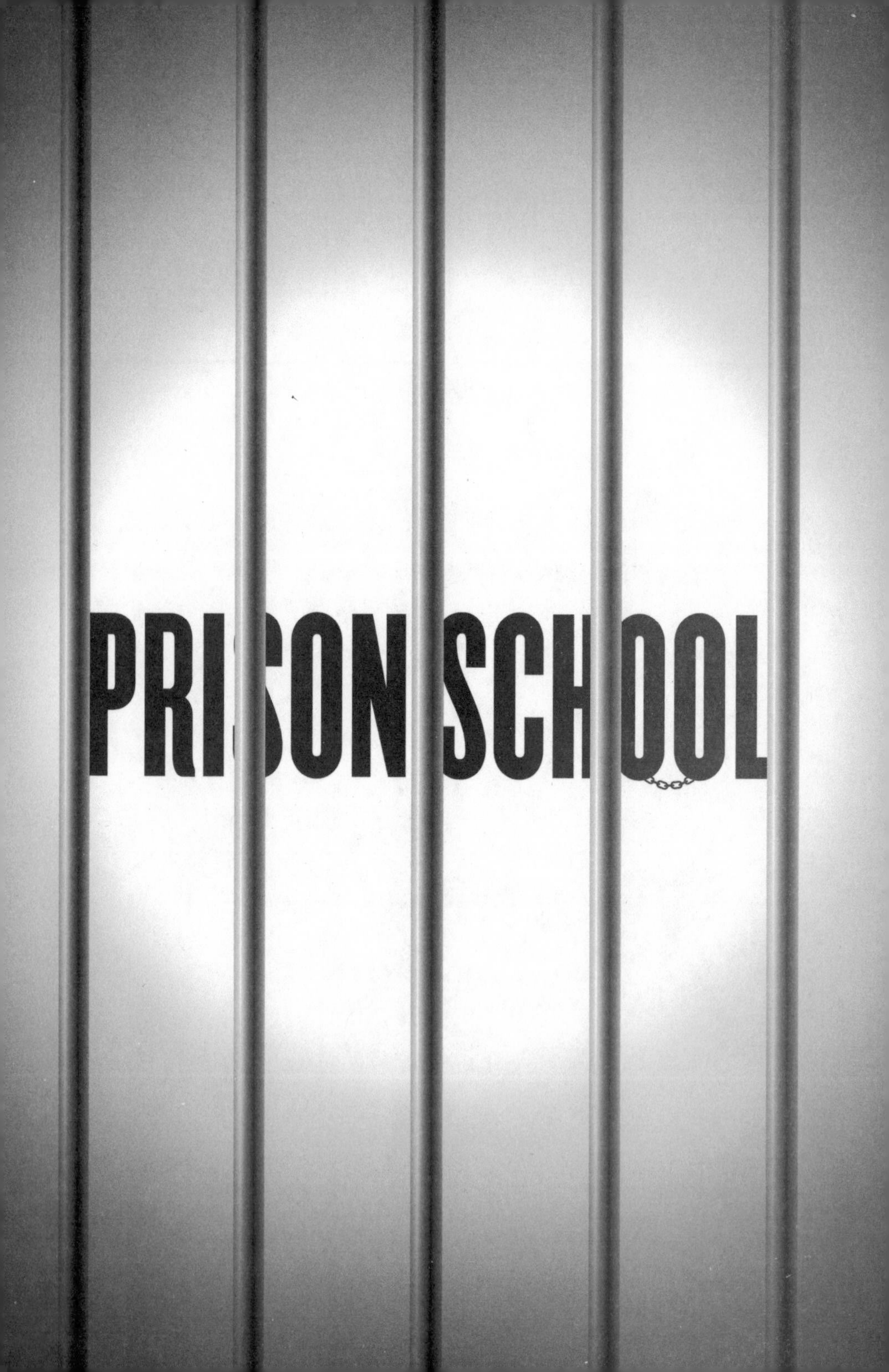
PRISON SCHOOL

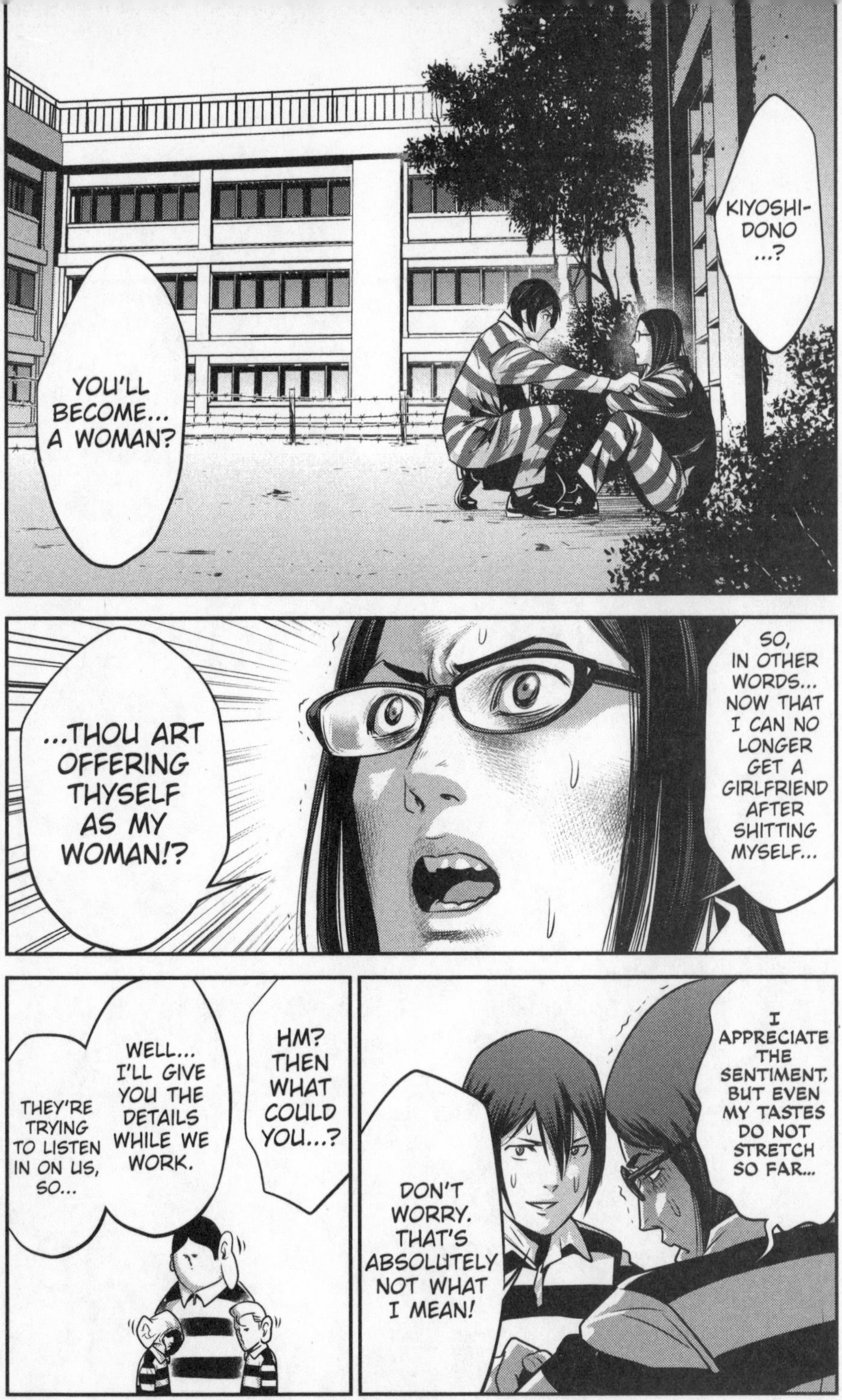
KIYOSHI-DONO ...?
YOU'LL BECOME... A WOMAN?
SO, IN OTHER WORDS... NOW THAT I CAN NO LONGER GET A GIRLFRIEND AFTER SHITTING MYSELF...
...THOU ART OFFERING THYSELF AS MY WOMAN!?
I APPRECIATE THE SENTIMENT, BUT EVEN MY TASTES DO NOT STRETCH SO FAR...
DON'T WORRY. THAT'S ABSOLUTELY NOT WHAT I MEAN!
HM? THEN WHAT COULD YOU...?
WELL... I'LL GIVE YOU THE DETAILS WHILE WE WORK.
THEY'RE TRYING TO LISTEN IN ON US, SO...

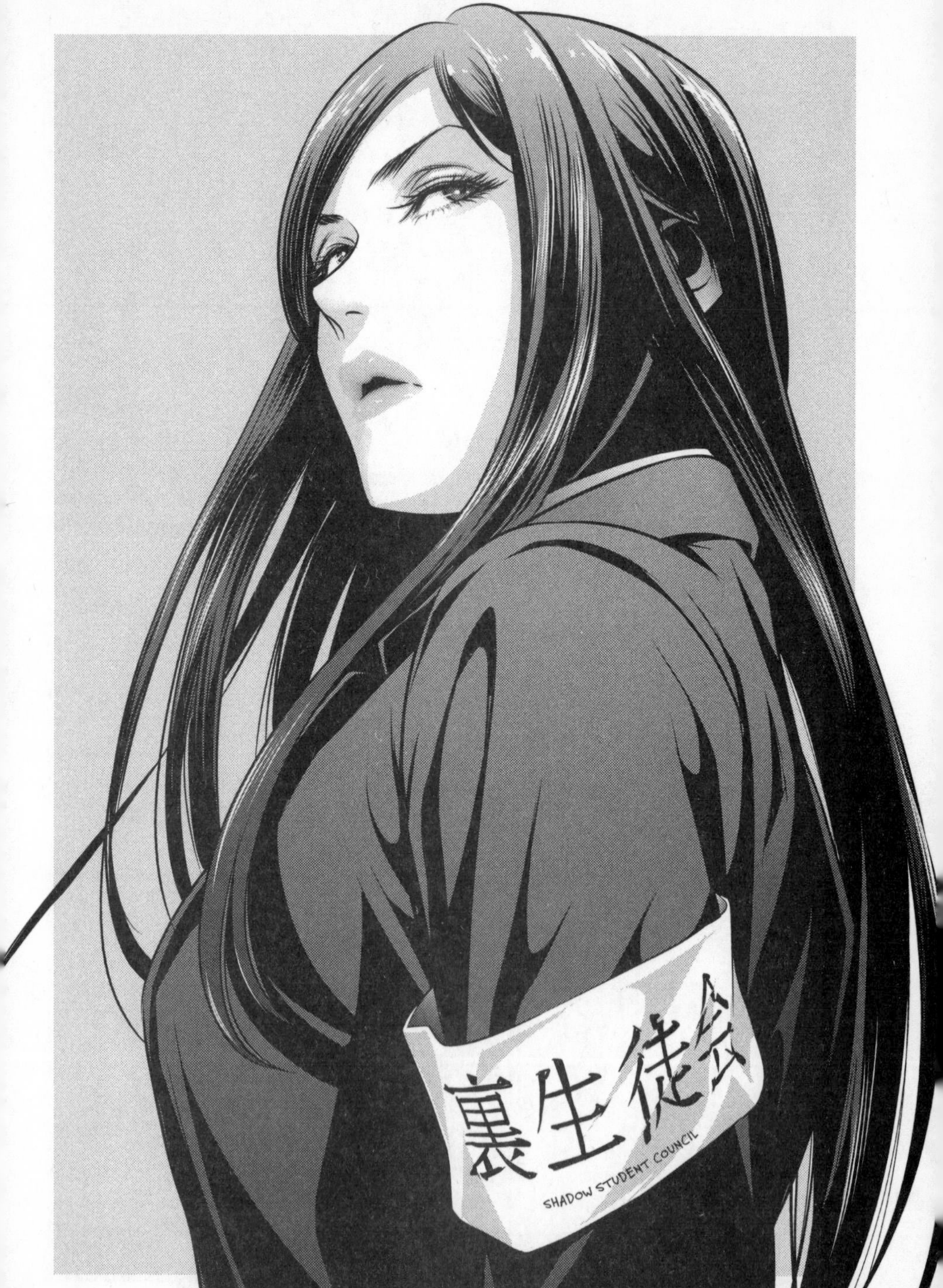
裏生徒会
SHADOW STUDENT COUNCIL

CHAPTER 20: PRETTY WOMAN

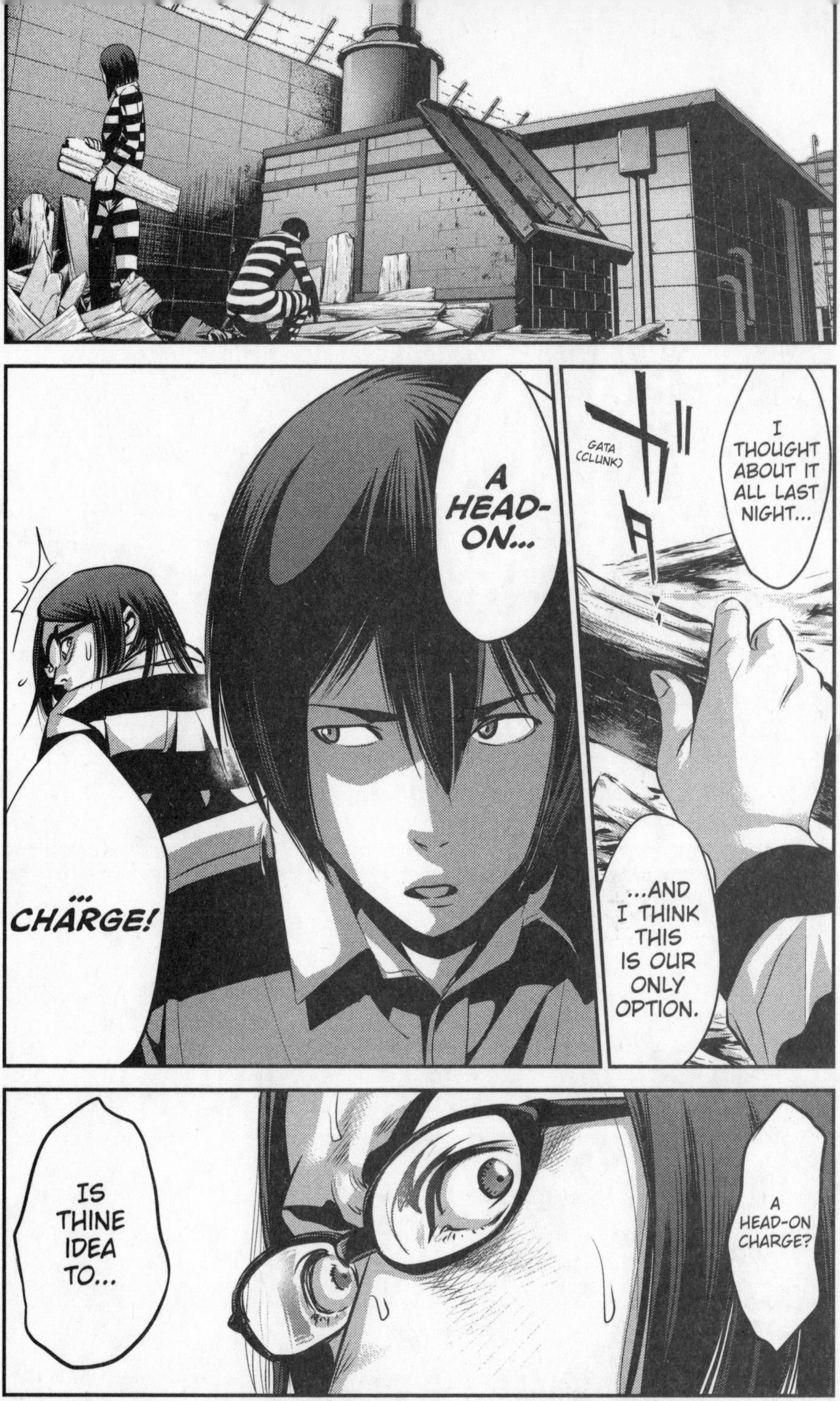
I THOUGHT ABOUT IT ALL LAST NIGHT...
GATA (CLUNK)
...AND I THINK THIS IS OUR ONLY OPTION.
A HEAD-ON...
... CHÄRGE!
A HEAD-ON CHARGE?
IS THINE IDEA TO...

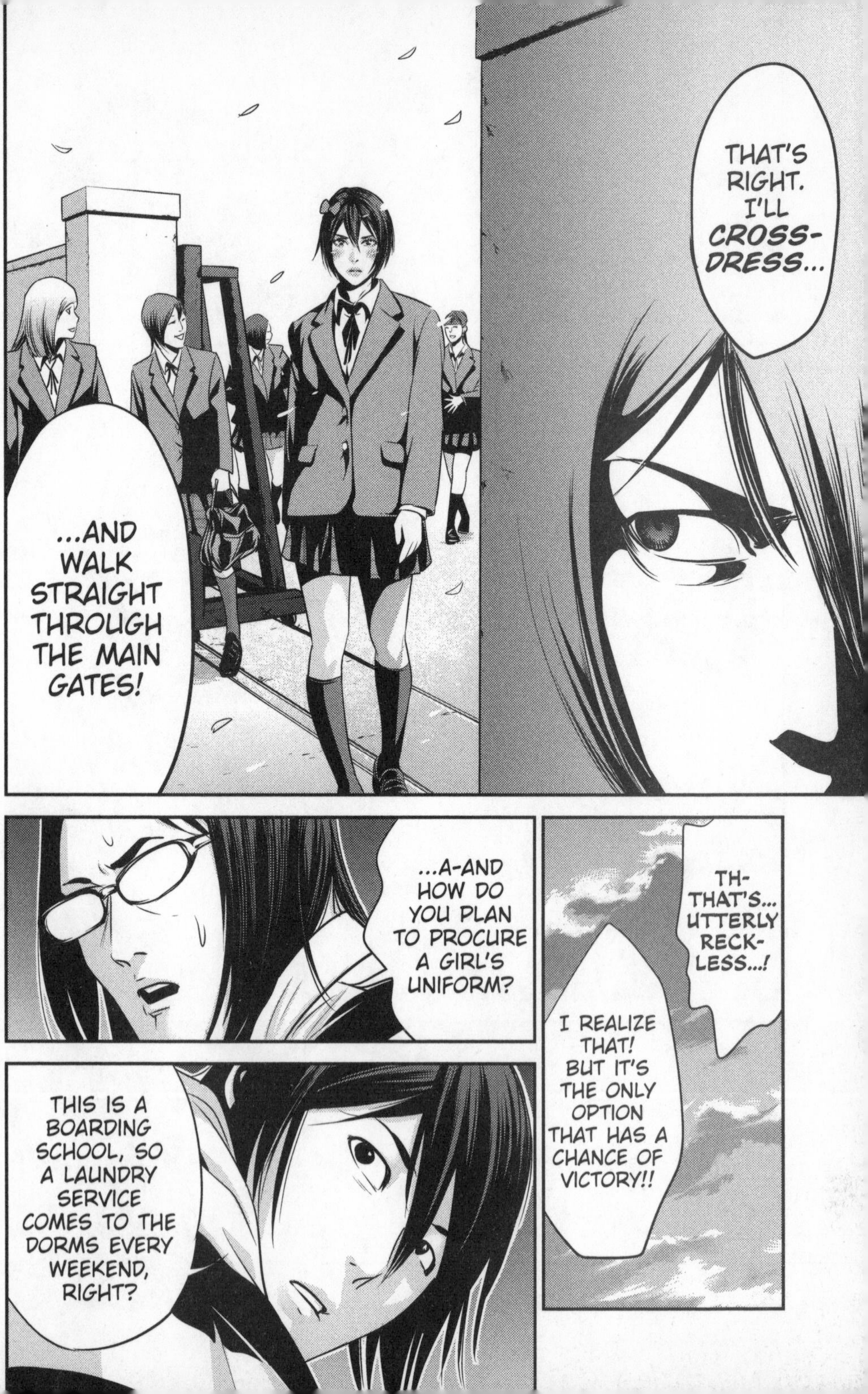
THAT'S RIGHT. I'LL CROSS-DRESS...
...AND WALK STRAIGHT THROUGH THE MAIN GATES!
TH-THAT'S... UTTERLY RECKLESS...!
I REALIZE THAT! BUT IT'S THE ONLY OPTION THAT HAS A CHANCE OF VICTORY!!
...A-AND HOW DO YOU PLAN TO PROCURE A GIRL'S UNIFORM?
THIS IS A BOARDING SCHOOL, SO A LAUNDRY SERVICE COMES TO THE DORMS EVERY WEEKEND, RIGHT?

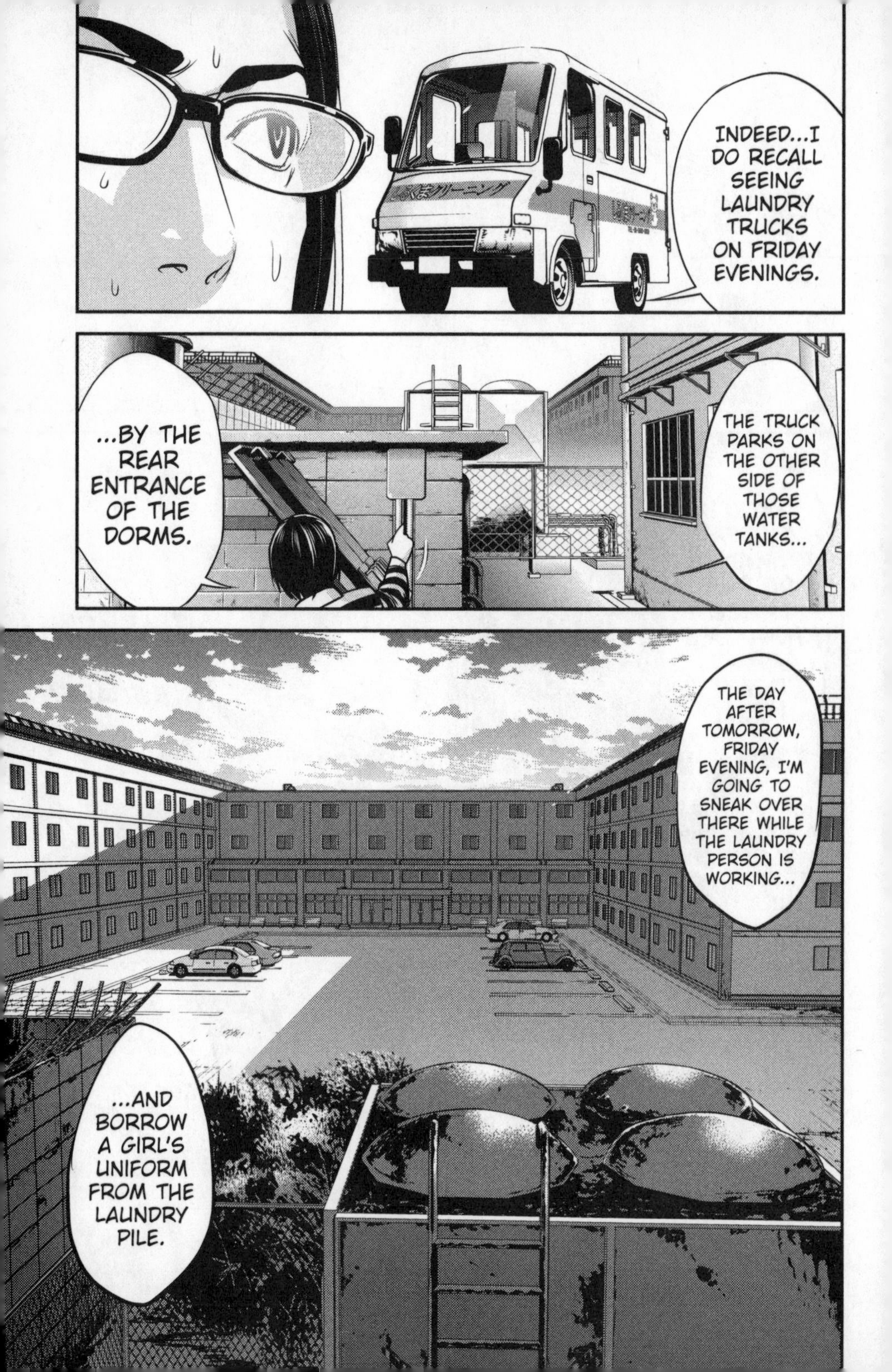
INDEED...I DO RECALL SEEING LAUNDRY TRUCKS ON FRIDAY EVENINGS.
THE TRUCK PARKS ON THE OTHER SIDE OF THOSE WATER TANKS...
...BY THE REAR ENTRANCE OF THE DORMS.
THE DAY AFTER TOMORROW, FRIDAY EVENING, I'M GOING TO SNEAK OVER THERE WHILE THE LAUNDRY PERSON IS WORKING...
...AND BORROW A GIRL'S UNIFORM FROM THE LAUNDRY PILE.

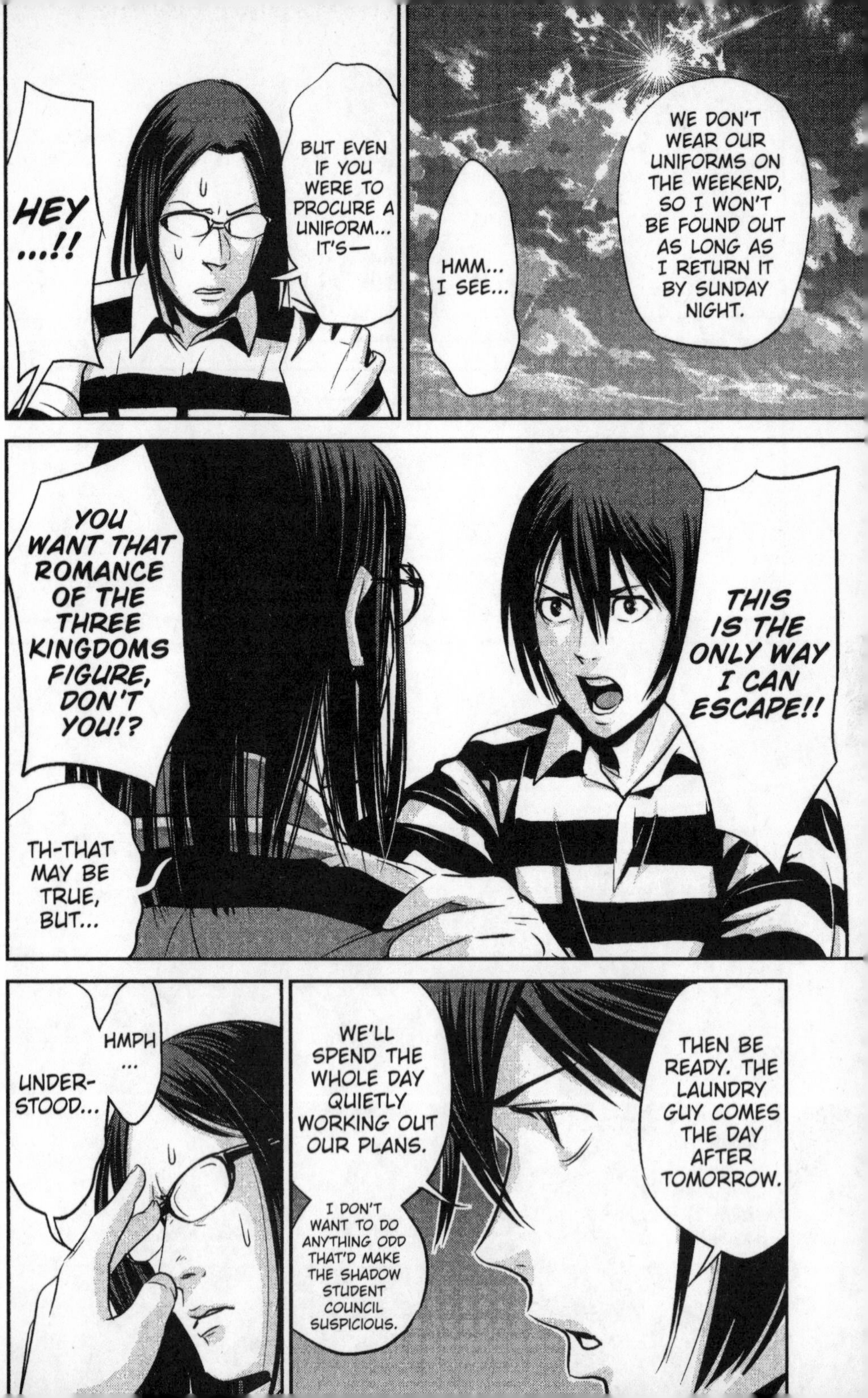
WE DON'T WEAR OUR UNIFORMS ON THE WEEKEND, SO I WON'T BE FOUND OUT AS LONG AS I RETURN IT BY SUNDAY NIGHT.
HMM... I SEE...
BUT EVEN IF YOU WERE TO PROCURE A UNIFORM... IT'S—
HEY ...!!
THIS IS THE ONLY WAY I CAN ESCAPE!!
YOU WANT THAT ROMANCE OF THE THREE KINGDOMS FIGURE, DON'T YOU!?
TH-THAT MAY BE TRUE, BUT...
THEN BE READY. THE LAUNDRY GUY COMES THE DAY AFTER TOMORROW.
WE'LL SPEND THE WHOLE DAY QUIETLY WORKING OUT OUR PLANS.
I DON'T WANT TO DO ANYTHING ODD THAT'D MAKE THE SHADOW STUDENT COUNCIL SUSPICIOUS.
HMPH ...
UNDER-STOOD...

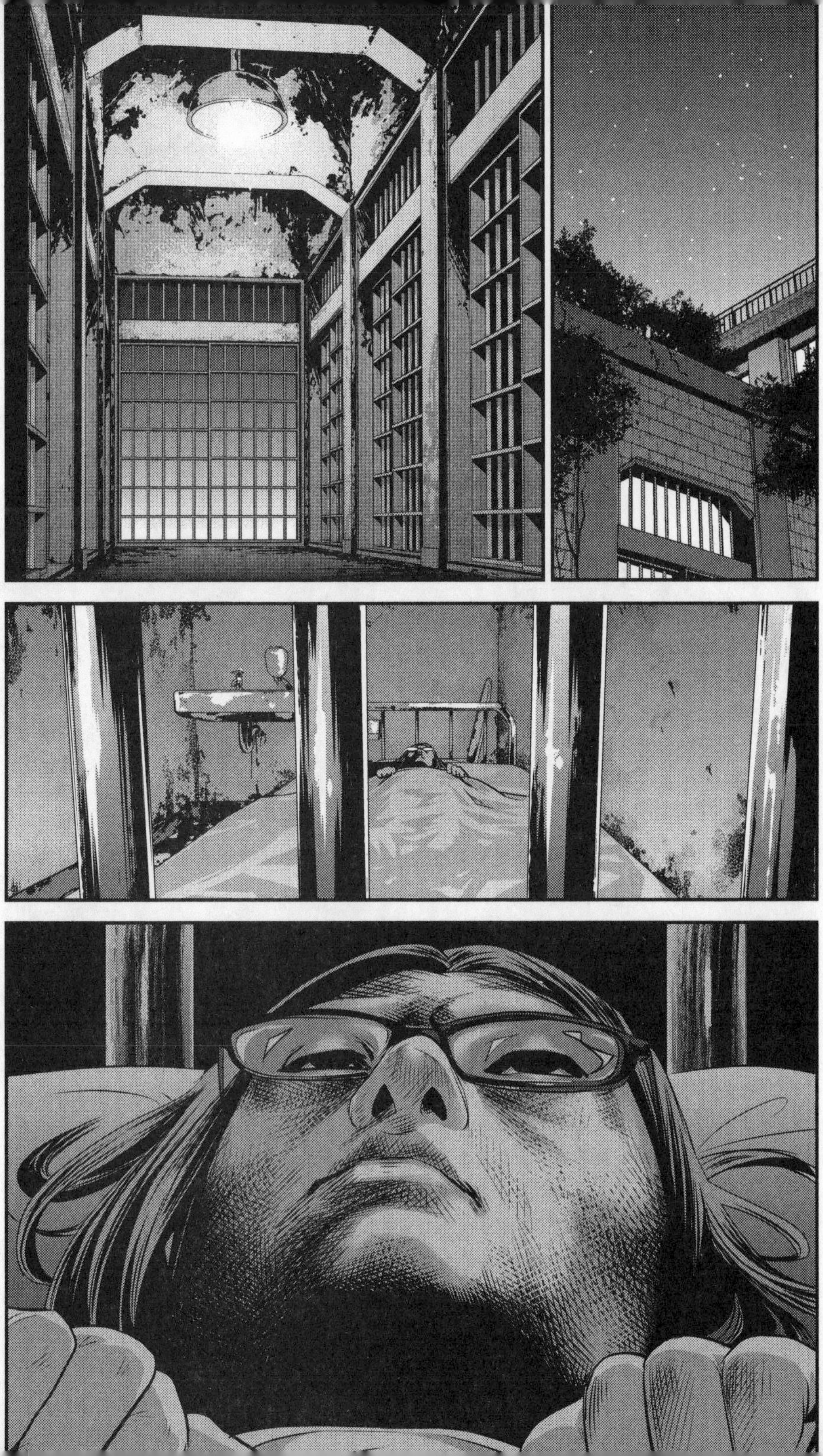

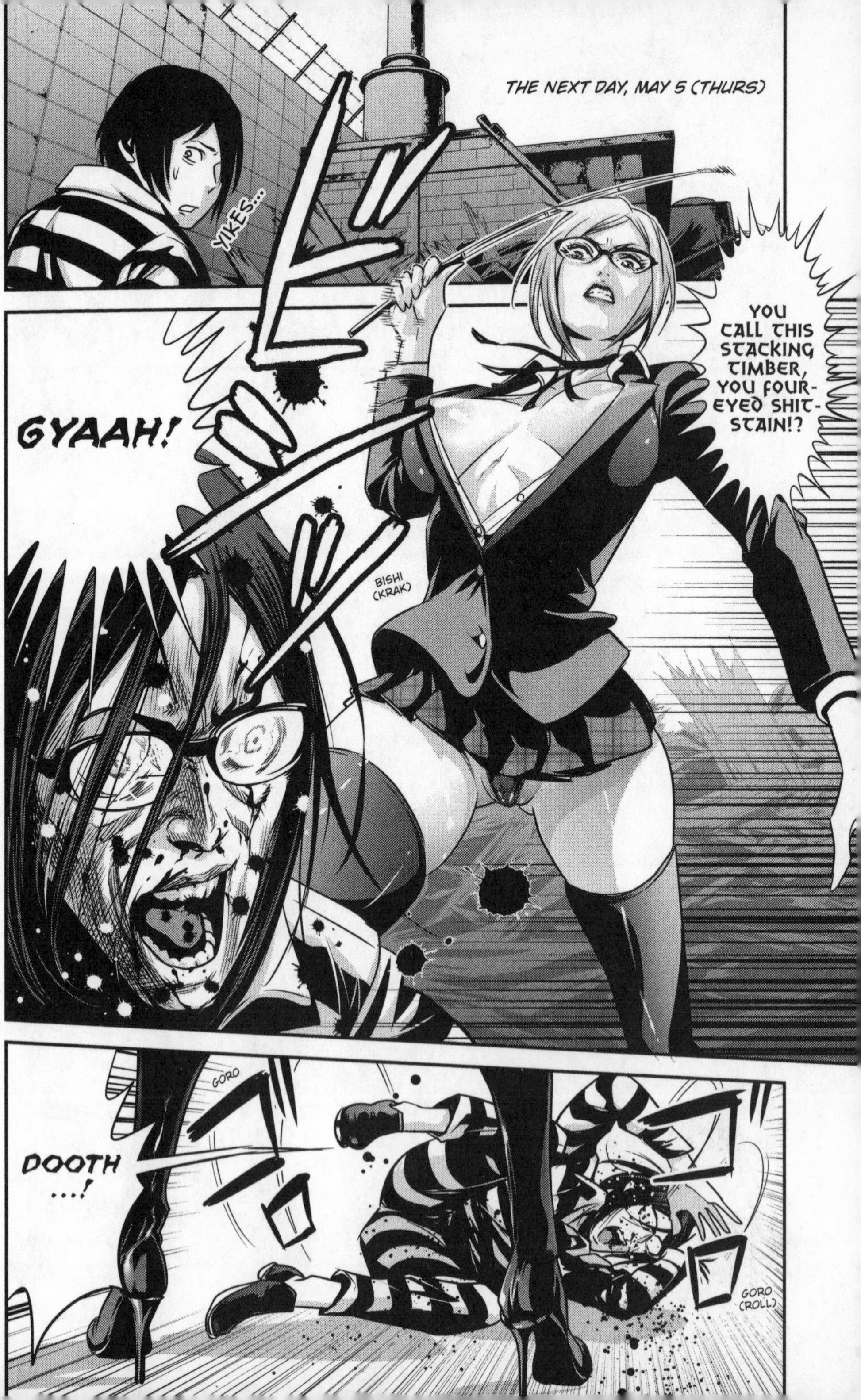
THE NEXT DAY, MAY 5 (THURS)
YIKES...
YOU CALL THIS STACKING TIMBER, YOU FOUR-EYED SHIT-STAIN!?
GYAAH!
BISHI (KRAK)
GORO
DOOTH ...!
GORO (ROLL)

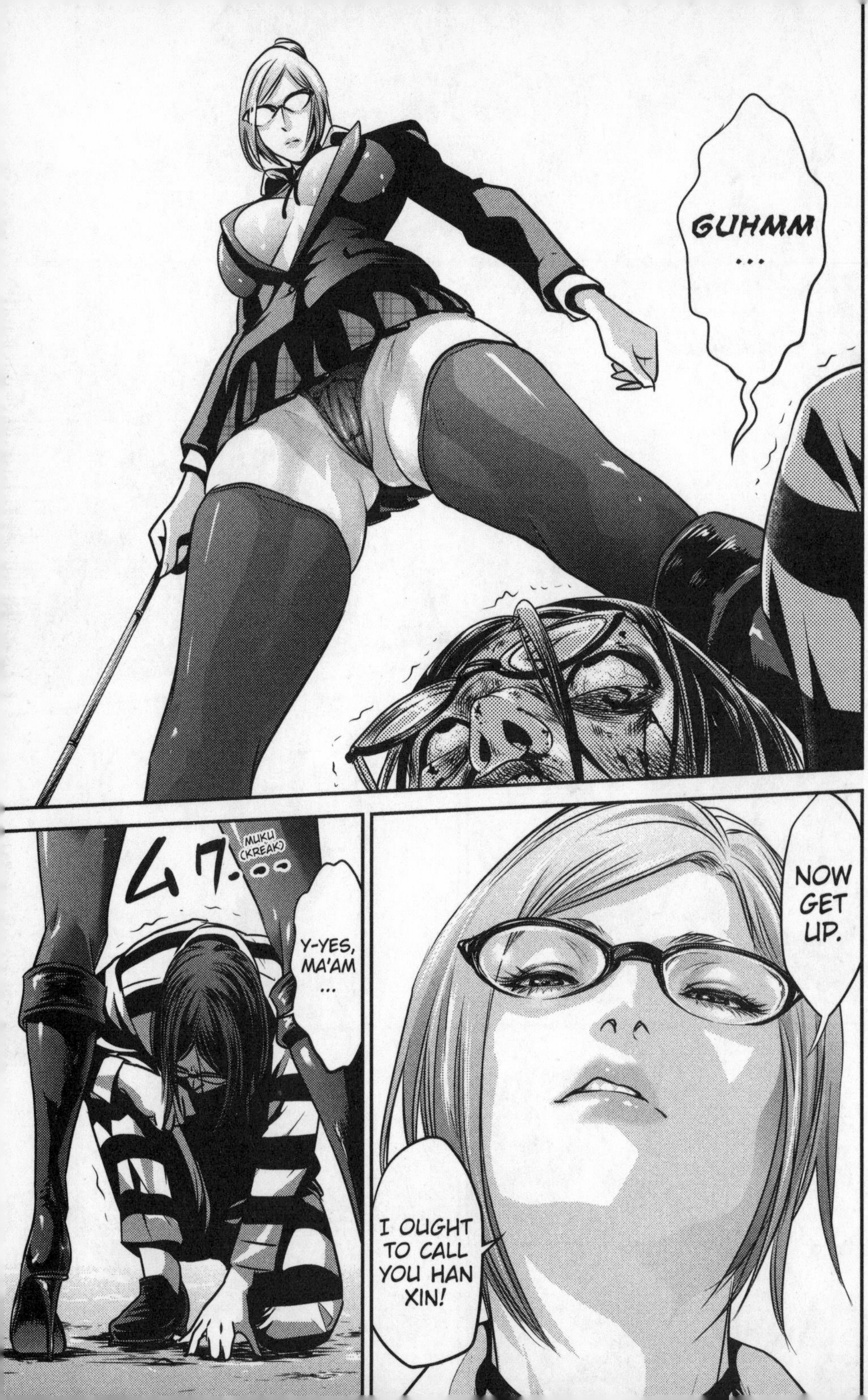
GUHMM ...
NOW GET UP.
I OUGHT TO CALL YOU HAN XIN!
ムク
MUKU (KREAK)
Y-YES, MA'AM ...

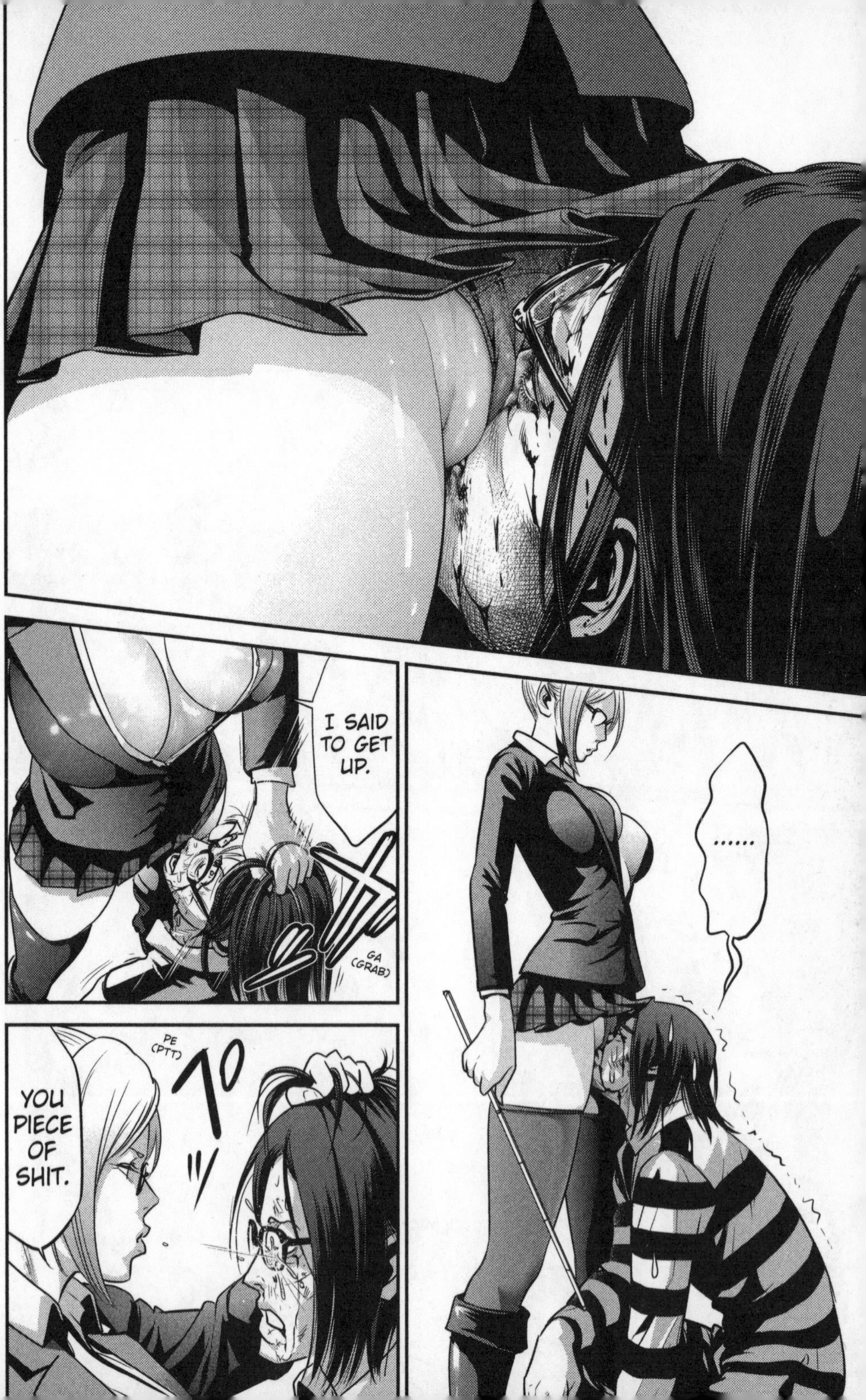
......
I SAID TO GET UP.
GA (GRAB)
PE (PTT)
YOU PIECE OF SHIT.

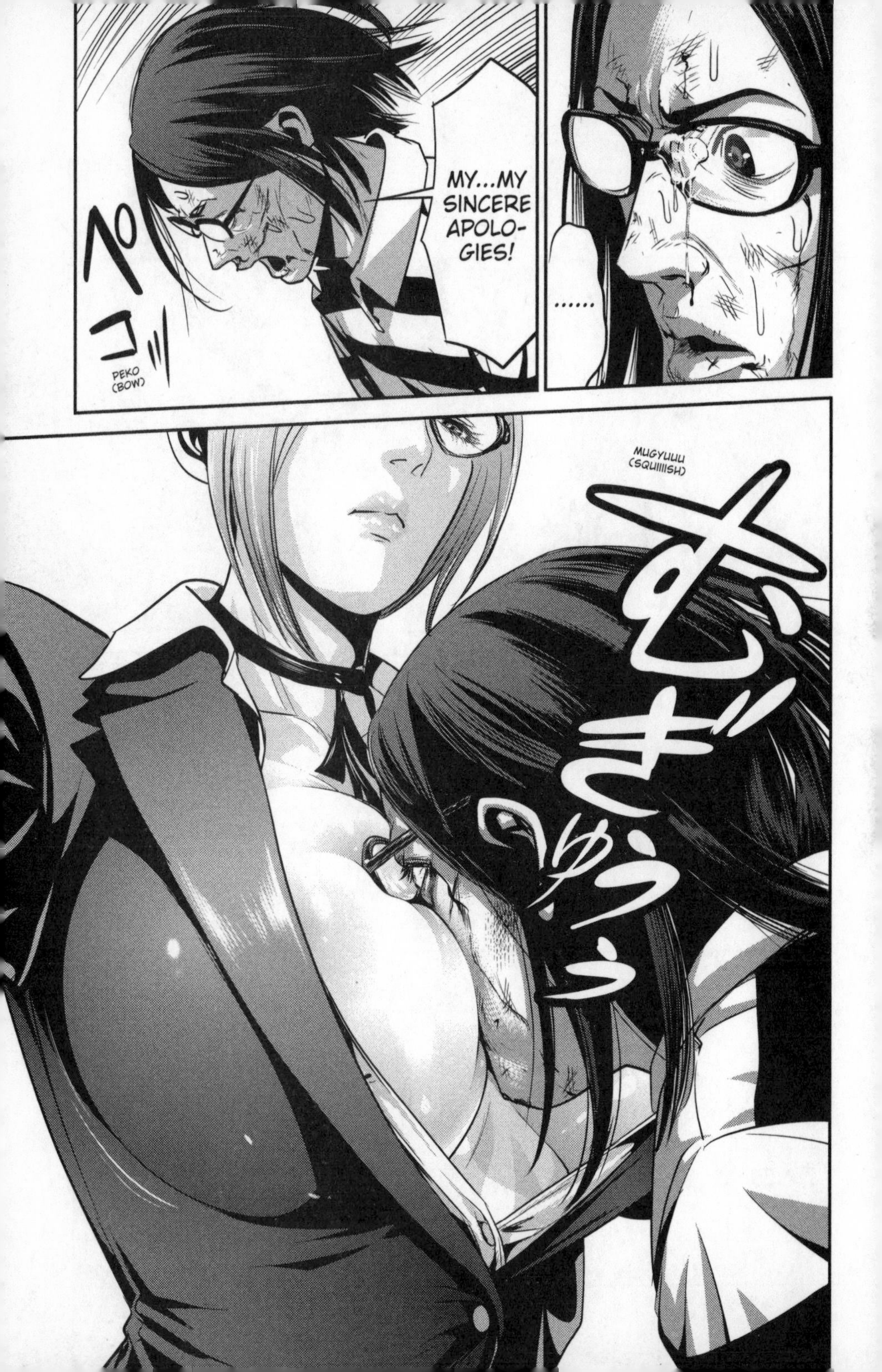
......
MY...MY SINCERE APOLO-GIES!
PEKO (BOW)
MUGYUUU (SQUIIIISH)

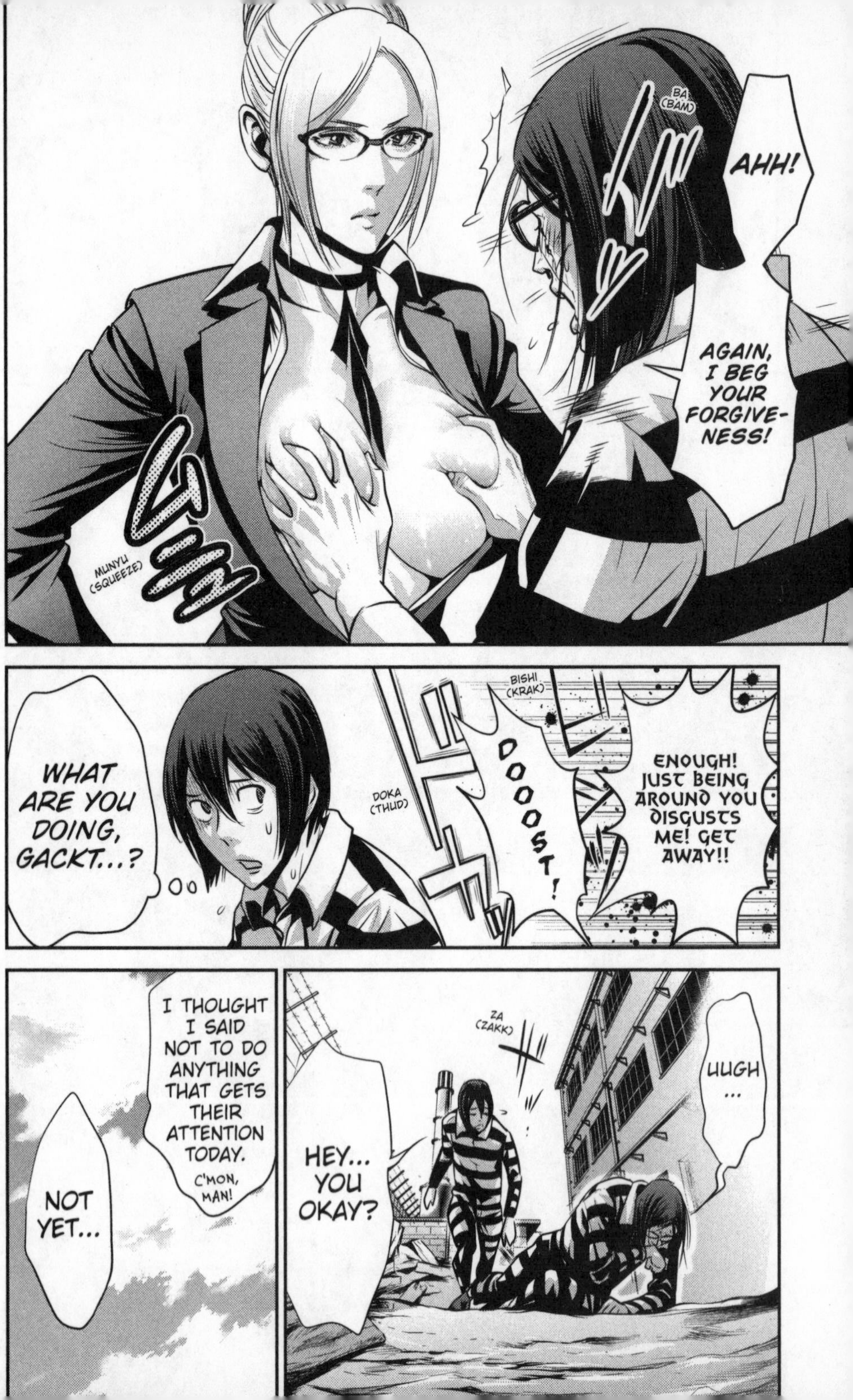
BA (BAM)
AHH!
AGAIN, I BEG YOUR FORGIVE-NESS!
MUNYU (SQUEEZE)
BISHI (KRAK)
ENOUGH! JUST BEING AROUND YOU DISGUSTS ME! GET AWAY!!
DOOOST!
DOKA (THUD)
WHAT ARE YOU DOING, GACKT...?
ZA (ZAKK)
UUGH ...
HEY... YOU OKAY?
I THOUGHT I SAID NOT TO DO ANYTHING THAT GETS THEIR ATTENTION TODAY.
C'MON, MAN!
NOT YET...

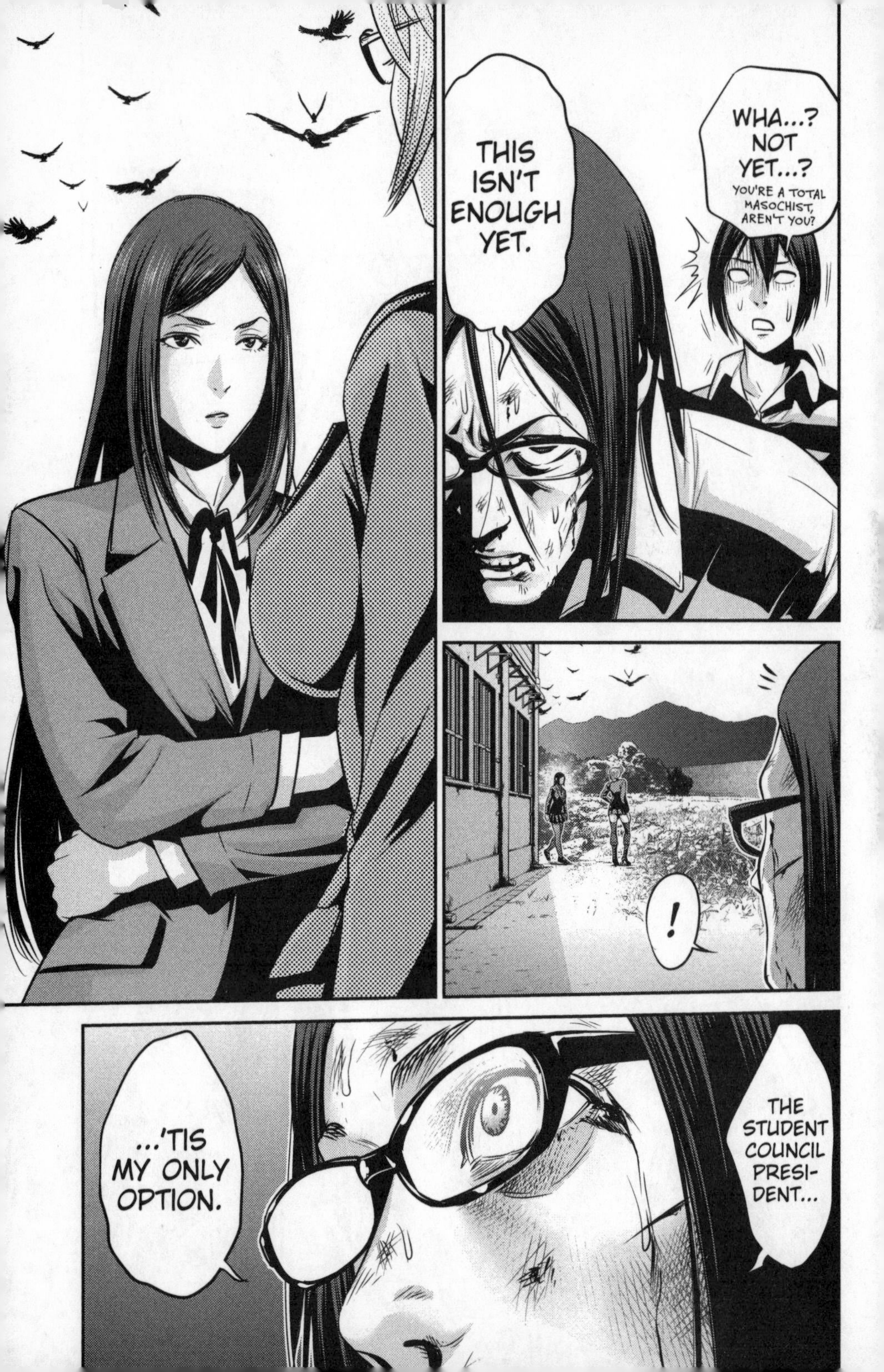
WHA...? NOT YET...? YOU'RE A TOTAL MASOCHIST, AREN'T YOU?
THIS ISN'T ENOUGH YET.
!
THE STUDENT COUNCIL PRESI-DENT...
...'TIS MY ONLY OPTION.

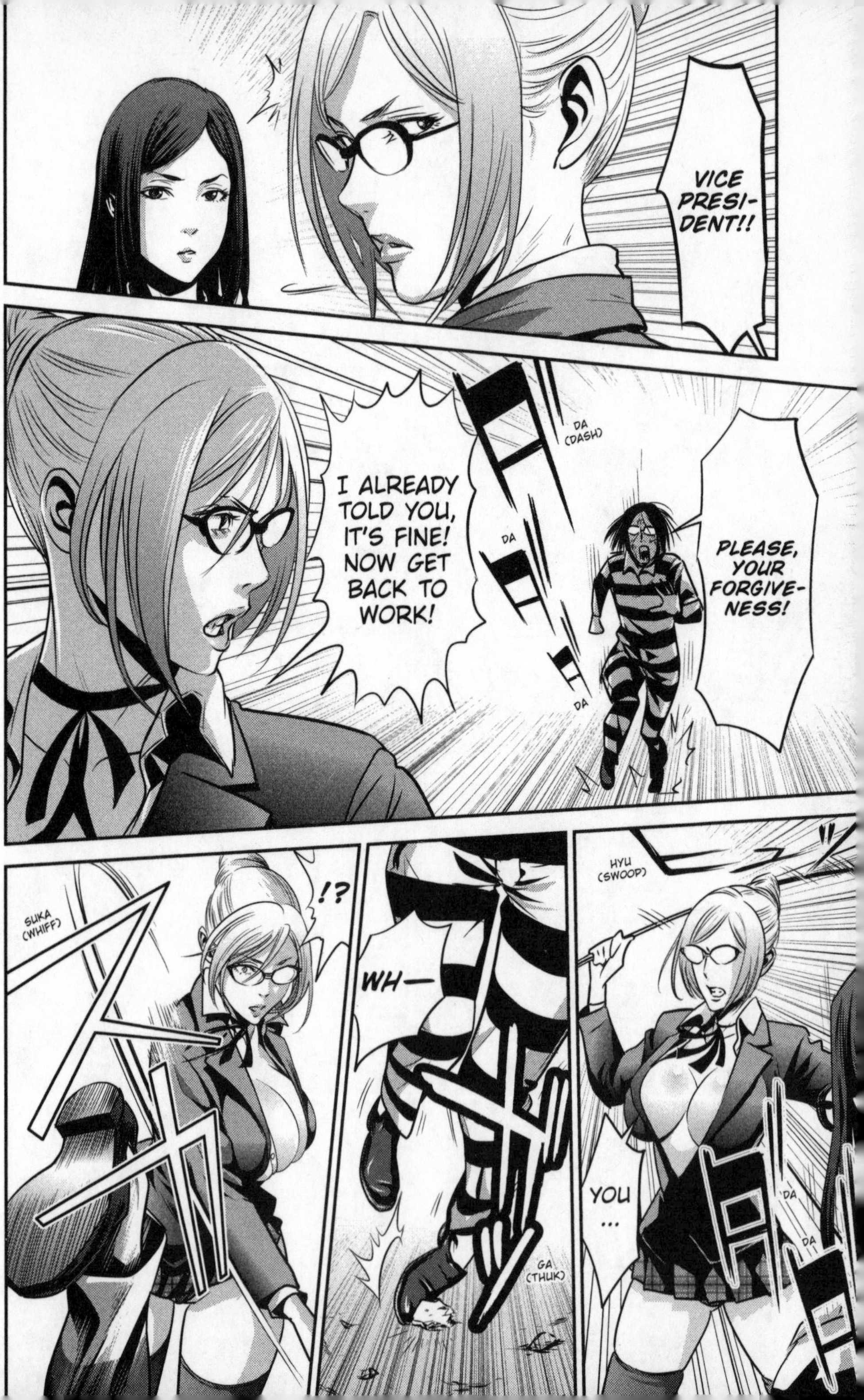
VICE PRESIDENT!!
PLEASE, YOUR FORGIVENESS!
DA (DASH)
DA
DA
I ALREADY TOLD YOU, IT'S FINE! NOW GET BACK TO WORK!
HYU (SWOOP)
YOU...
DA
DA
WH—
GA (THUK)
!?
SUKA (WHIFF)

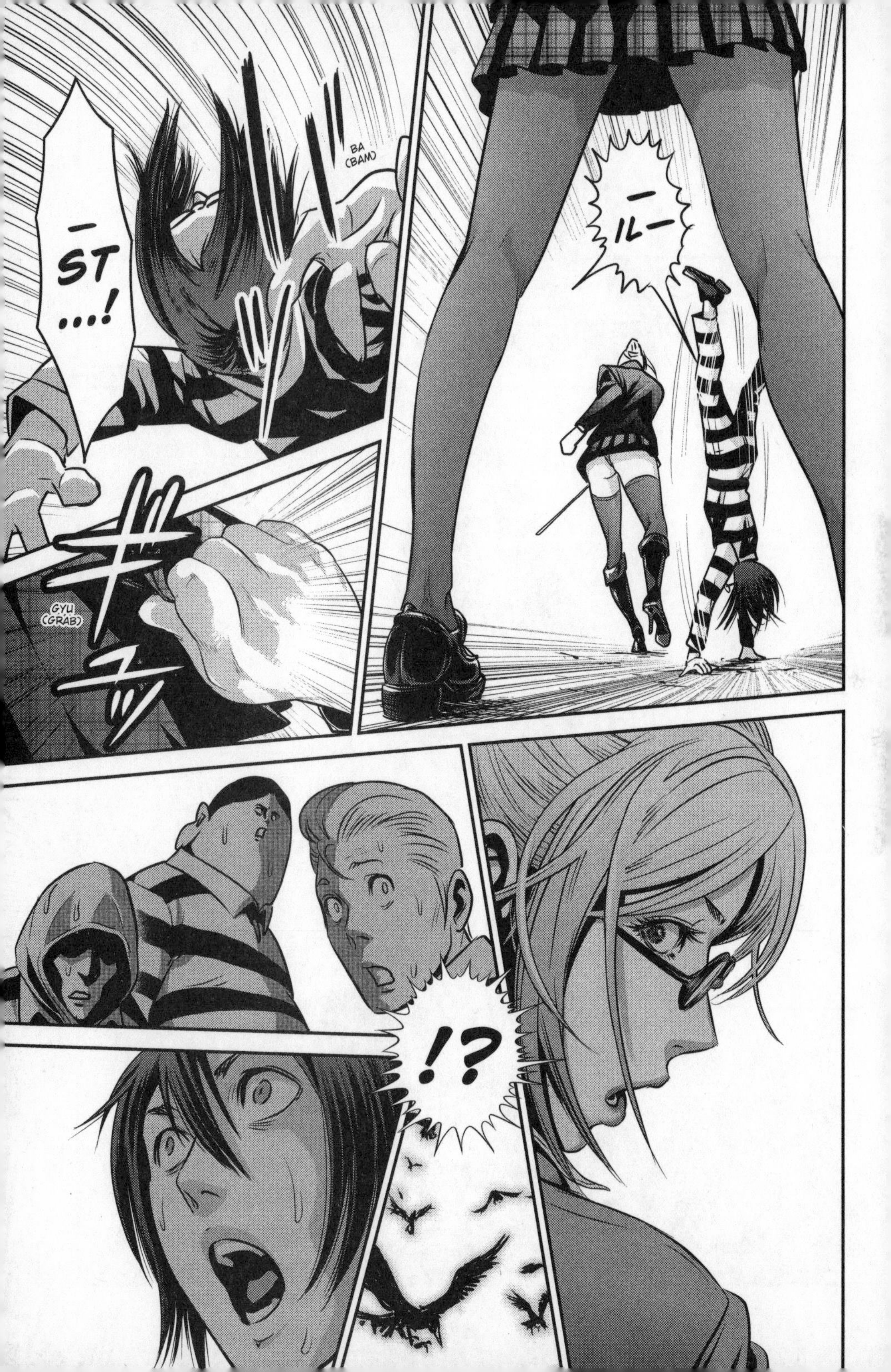
BA
(BAM)
—ST...!
GYU
(GRAB)
—ル—
!?

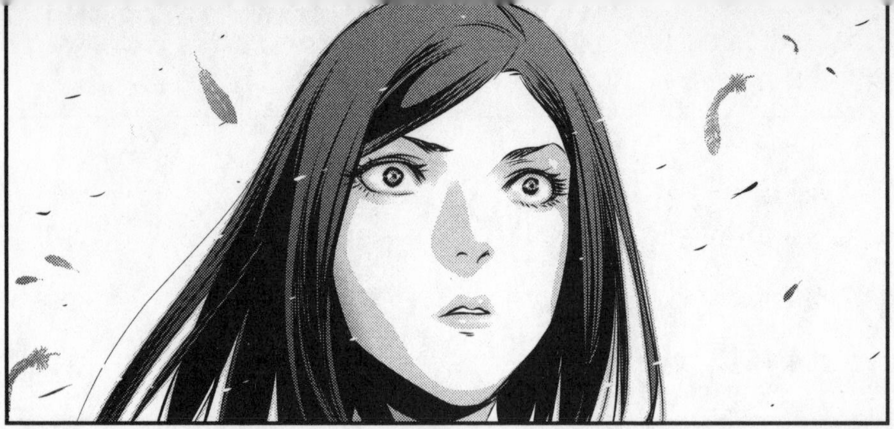

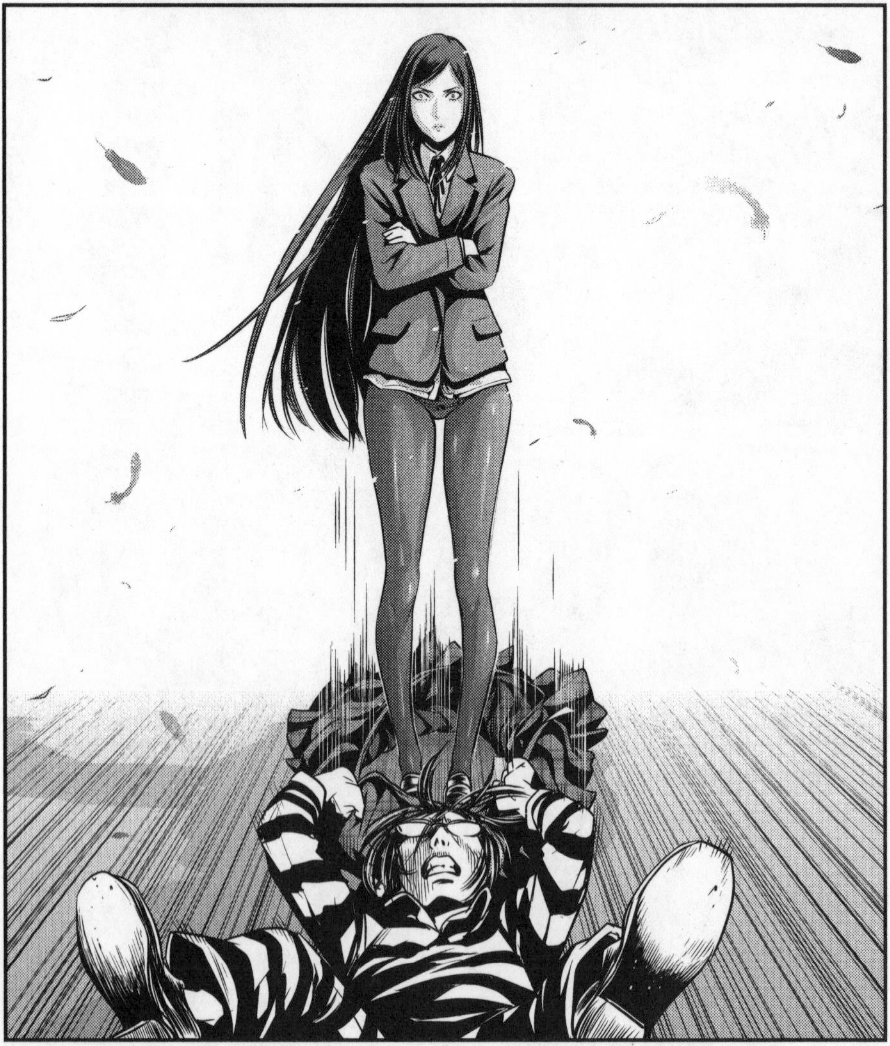

CHAPTER 21: THE SACRIFICE

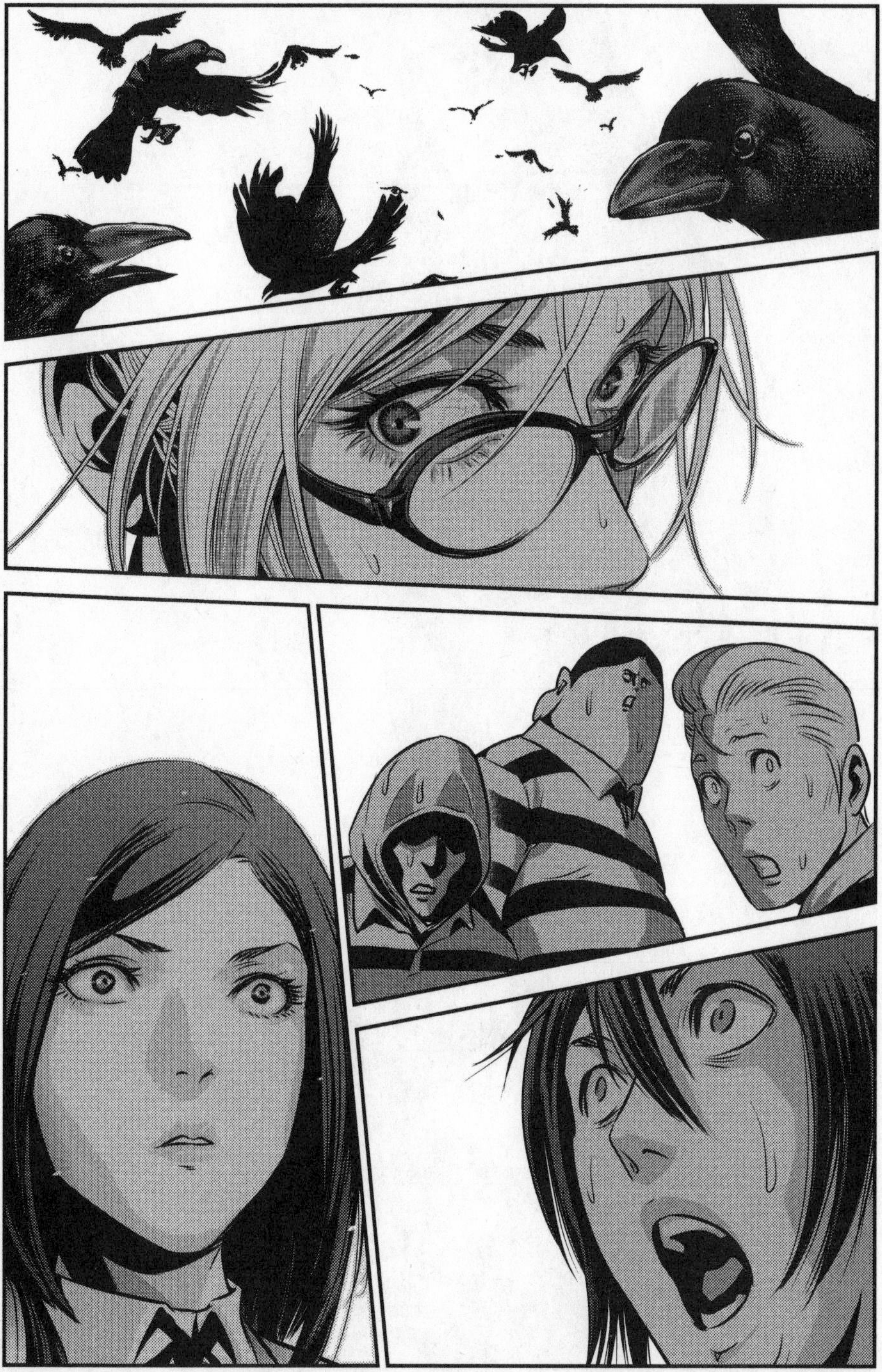

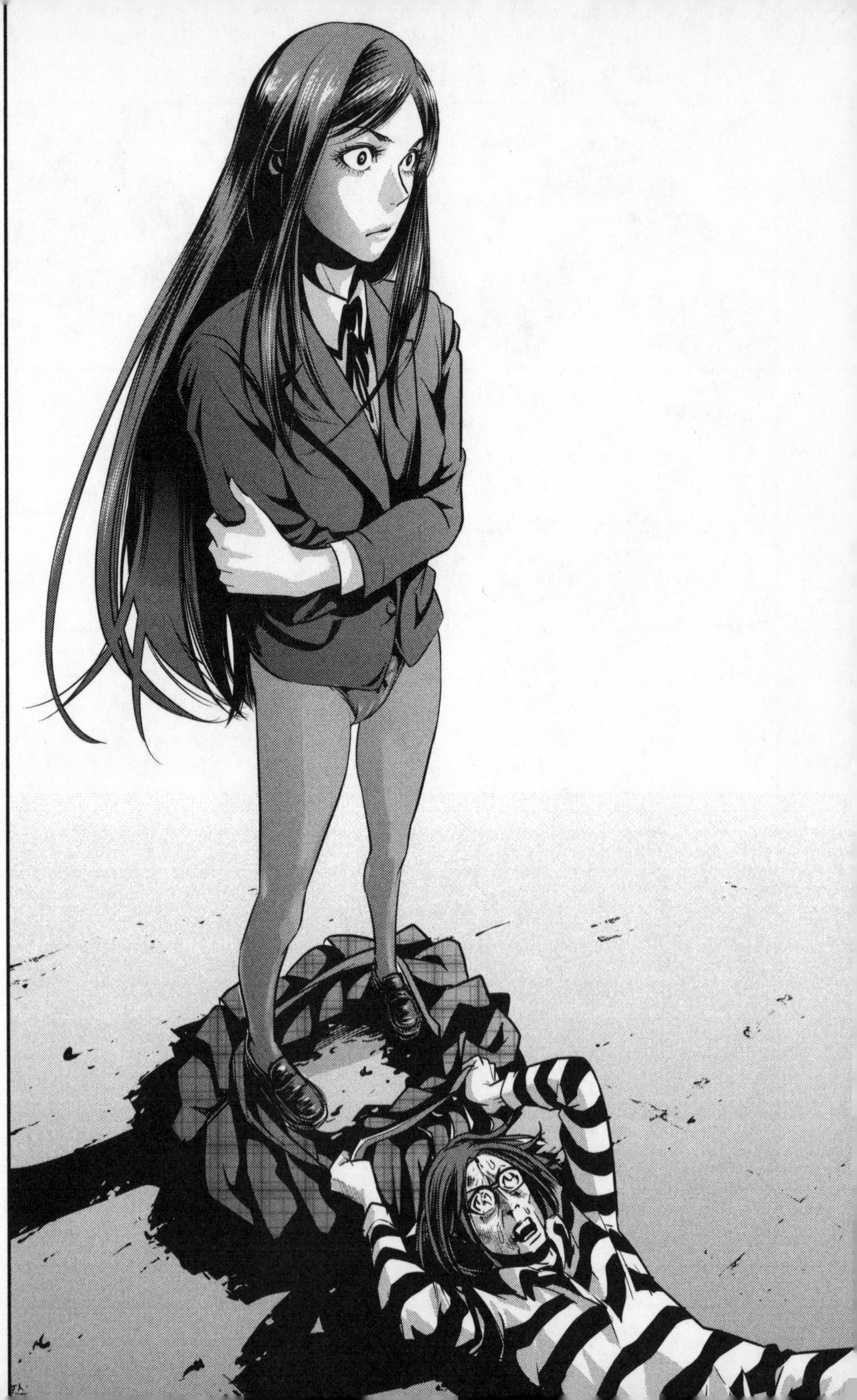

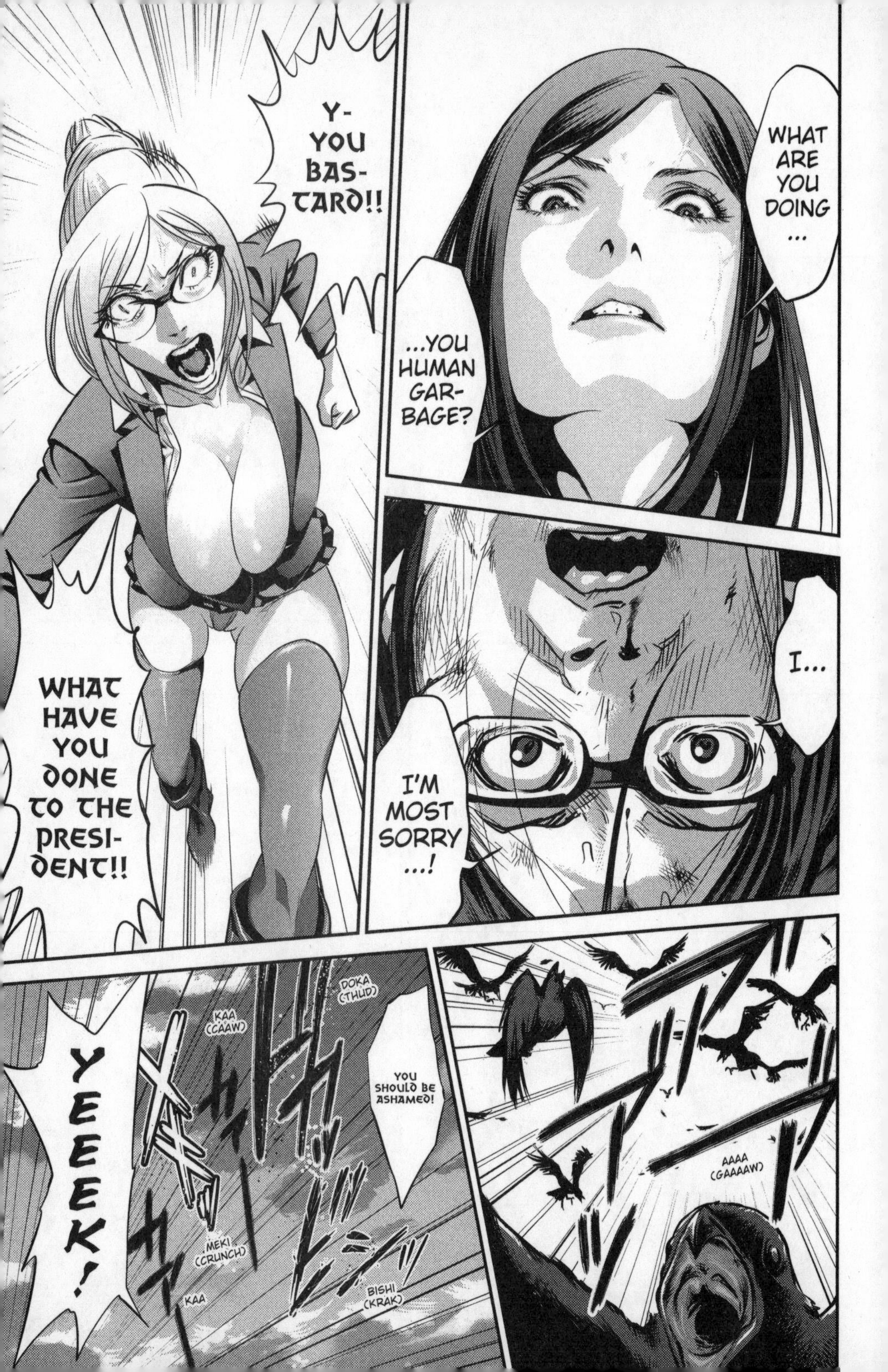
WHAT ARE YOU DOING ...
...YOU HUMAN GAR-BAGE?
I...
I'M MOST SORRY ...!
Y-YOU BAS-TARD!!
WHAT HAVE YOU DONE TO THE PRESI-DENT!!
AAAA (GAAAAW)
DOKA (THUD)
KAA (CAAW)
YOU SHOULD BE ASHAMED!
YEEEK!
MEKI (CRUNCH)
BISHI (KRAK)
KAA

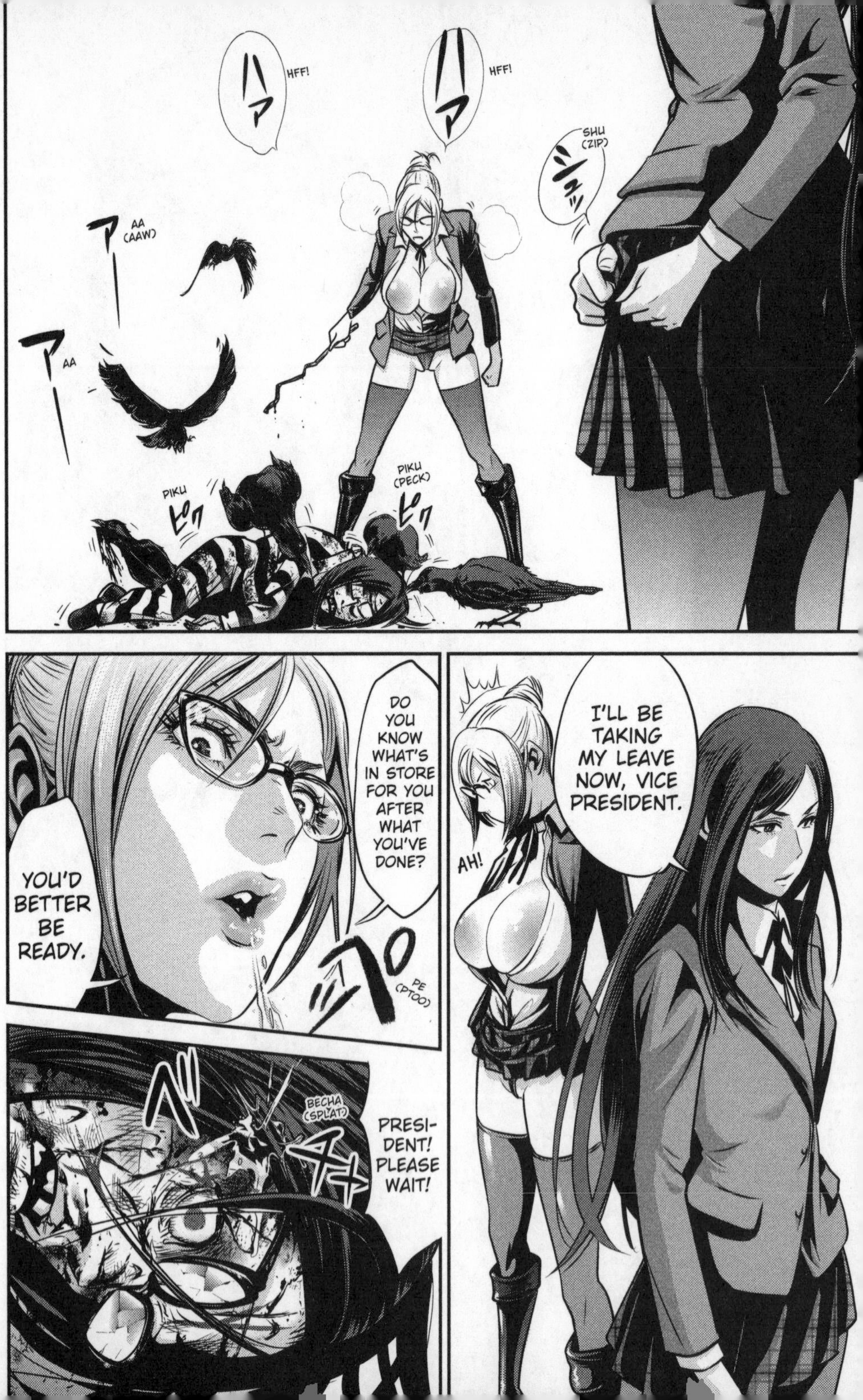

SHU (ZIP)
HFF!
HFF!
AA (AAW)
AA
PIKU (PECK)
PIKU
I'LL BE TAKING MY LEAVE NOW, VICE PRESIDENT.
AH!
DO YOU KNOW WHAT'S IN STORE FOR YOU AFTER WHAT YOU'VE DONE?
PE (PTOO)
YOU'D BETTER BE READY.
PRESI-DENT! PLEASE WAIT!
BECHA (SPLAT)

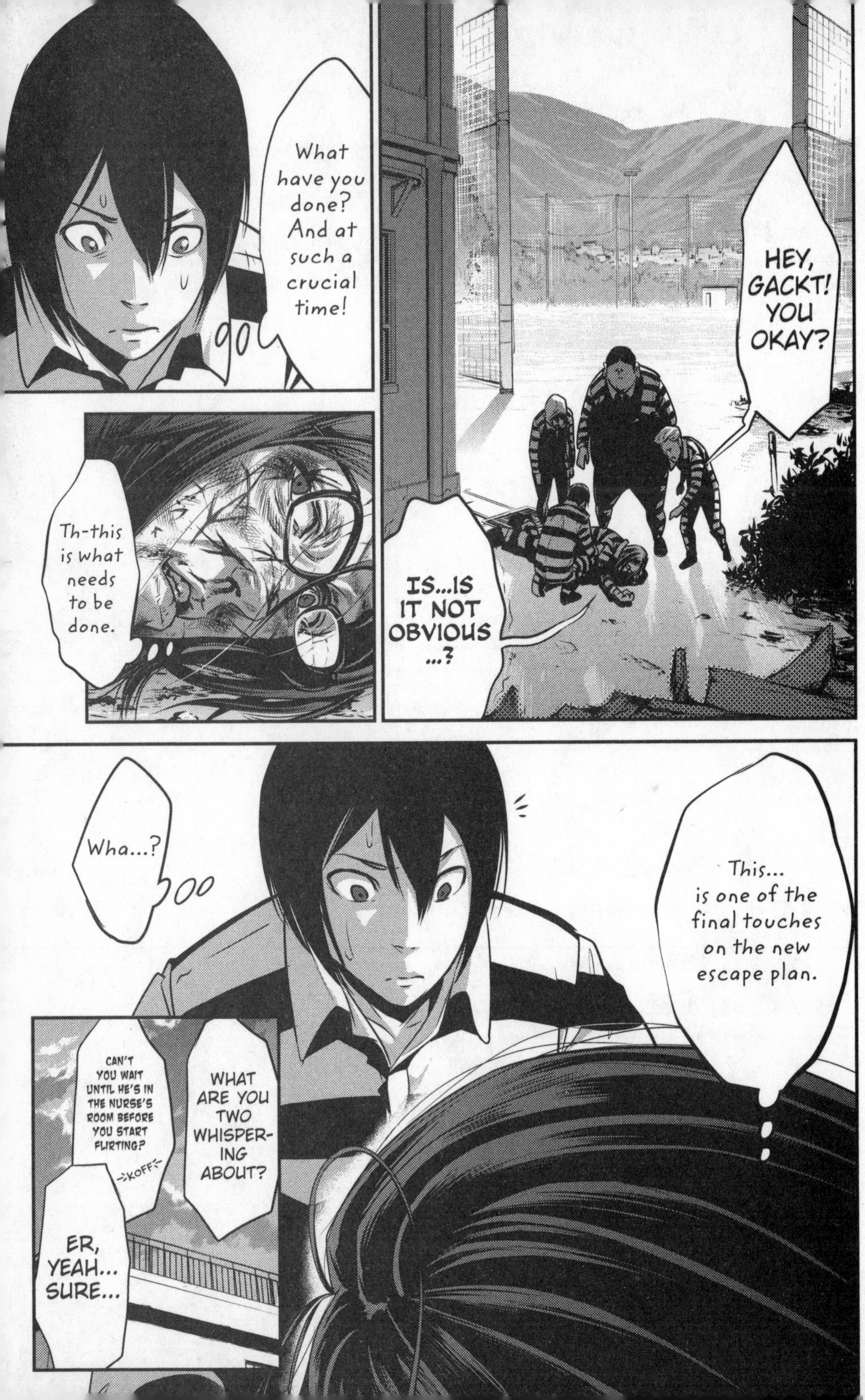
HEY, GACKT! YOU OKAY?
IS...IS IT NOT OBVIOUS ...?
What have you done? And at such a crucial time!
Th-this is what needs to be done.
This... is one of the final touches on the new escape plan.
Wha...?
WHAT ARE YOU TWO WHISPERING ABOUT?
CAN'T YOU WAIT UNTIL HE'S IN THE NURSE'S ROOM BEFORE YOU START FLIRTING?
~KOFF
ER, YEAH... SURE...

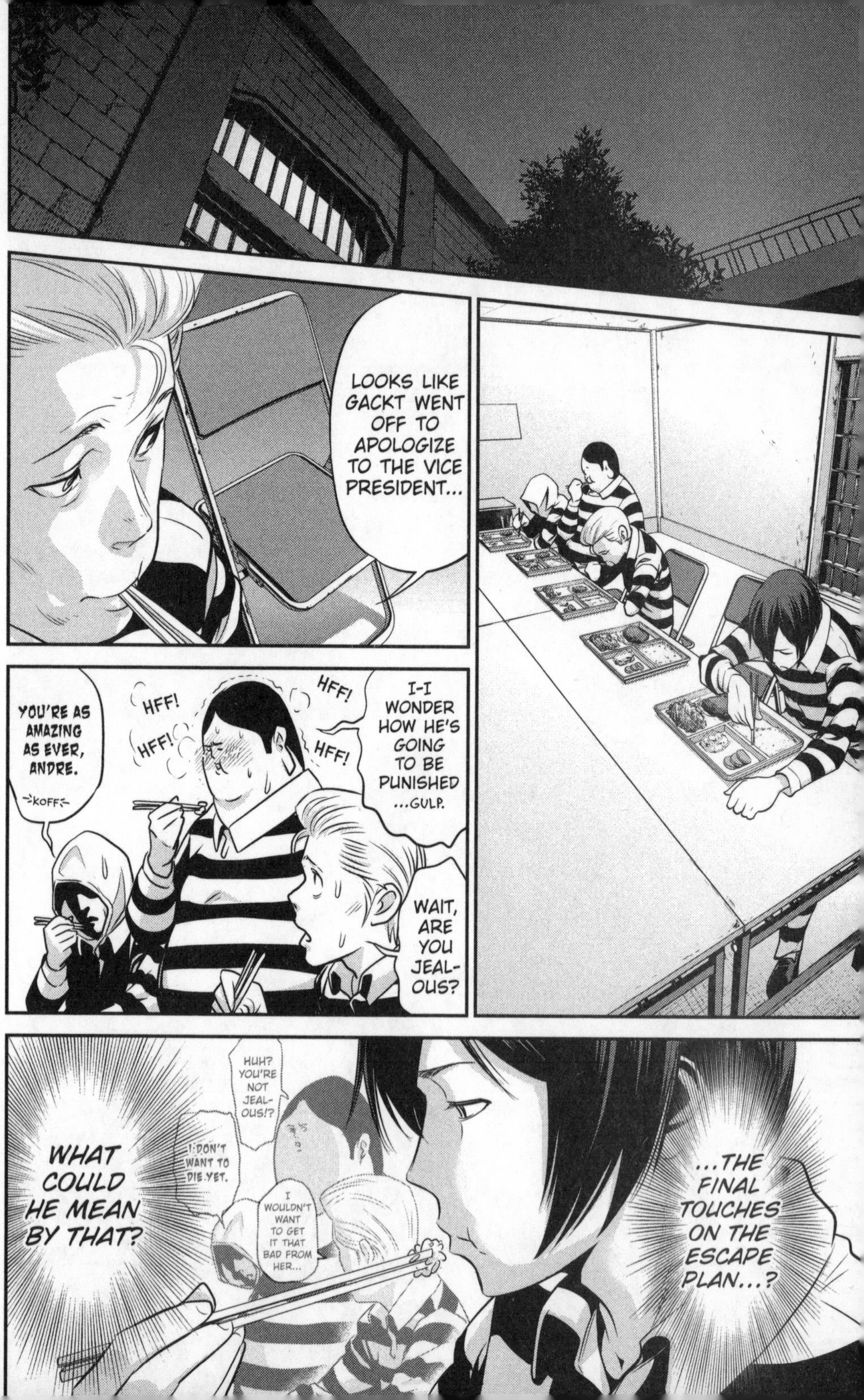

LOOKS LIKE GACKT WENT OFF TO APOLOGIZE TO THE VICE PRESIDENT...
I-I WONDER HOW HE'S GOING TO BE PUNISHED ...GULP.
HFF!
HFF!
HFF!
HFF!
YOU'RE AS AMAZING AS EVER, ANDRE.
KOFF
WAIT, ARE YOU JEAL-OUS?
...THE FINAL TOUCHES ON THE ESCAPE PLAN...?
HUH? YOU'RE NOT JEAL-OUS!?
I DON'T WANT TO DIE YET.
I WOULDN'T WANT TO GET IT THAT BAD FROM HER...
WHAT COULD HE MEAN BY THAT?

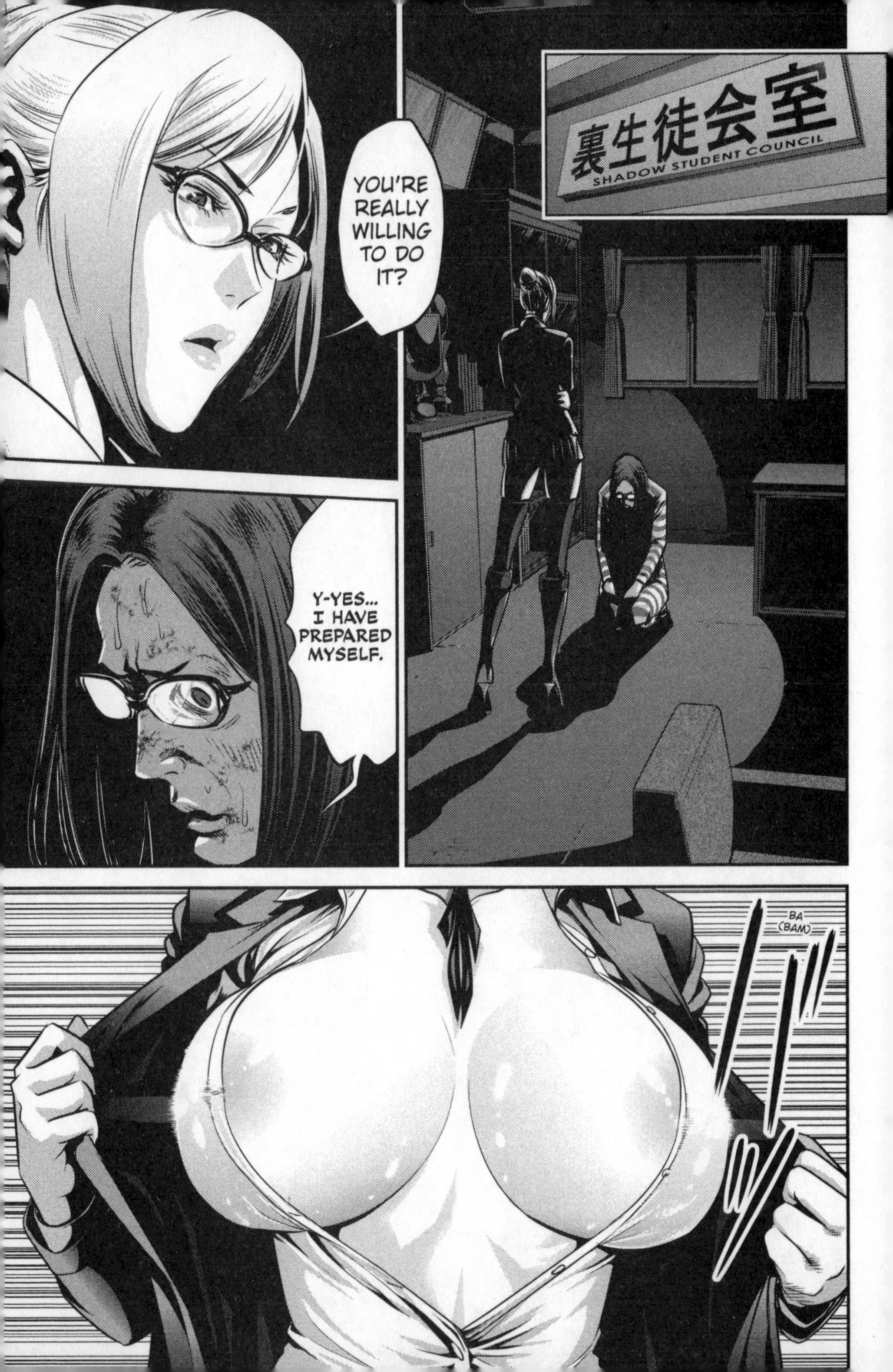
裏生徒会室
SHADOW STUDENT COUNCIL
YOU'RE REALLY WILLING TO DO IT?
Y-YES... I HAVE PREPARED MYSELF.
BA (BAM)

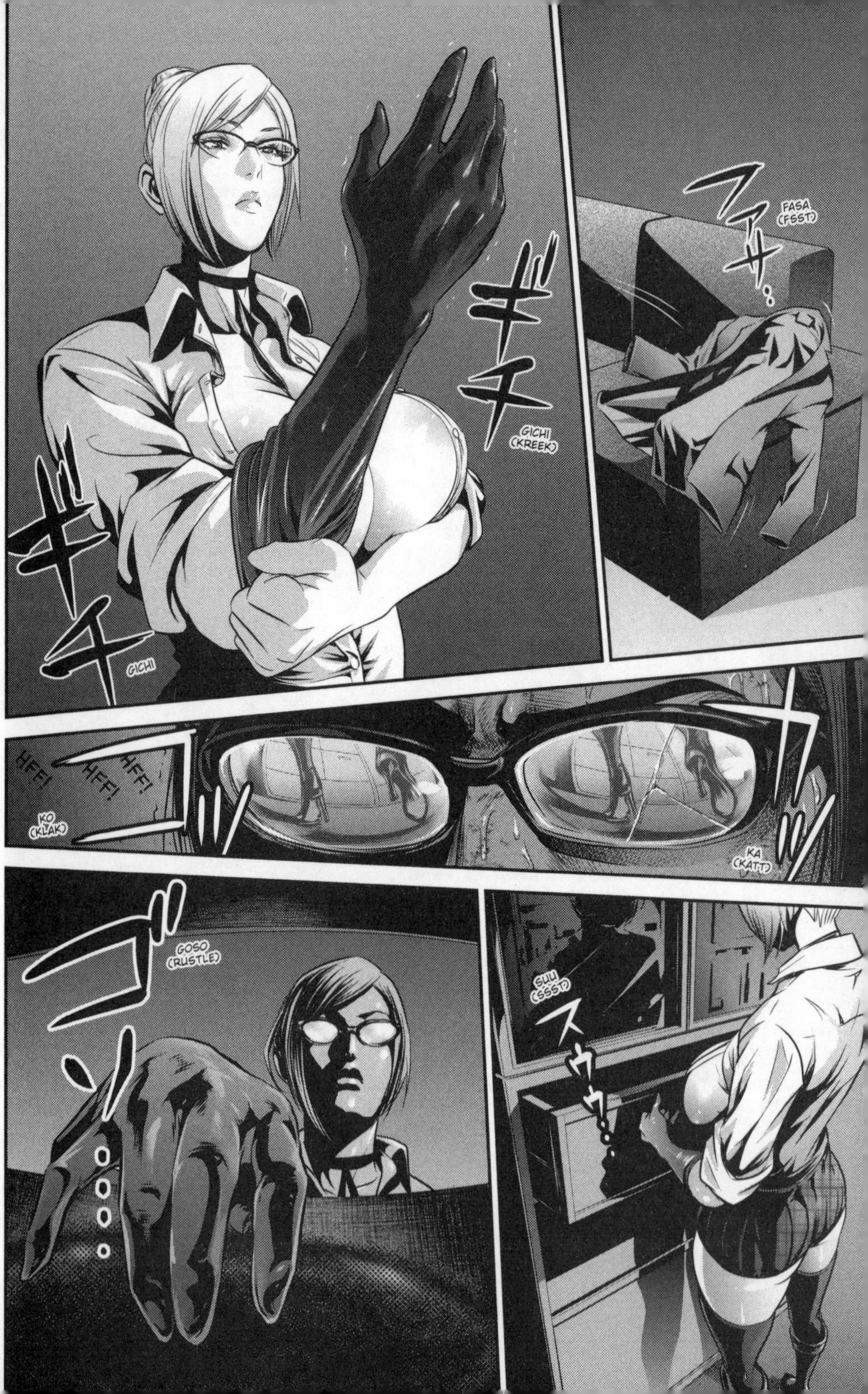
FASA (FSST)
GICHI (KREEK)
GICHI
KA (KATT)
HFF! HFF!
KO (KLAK)
SUU (SSST)
GOSO (RUSTLE)

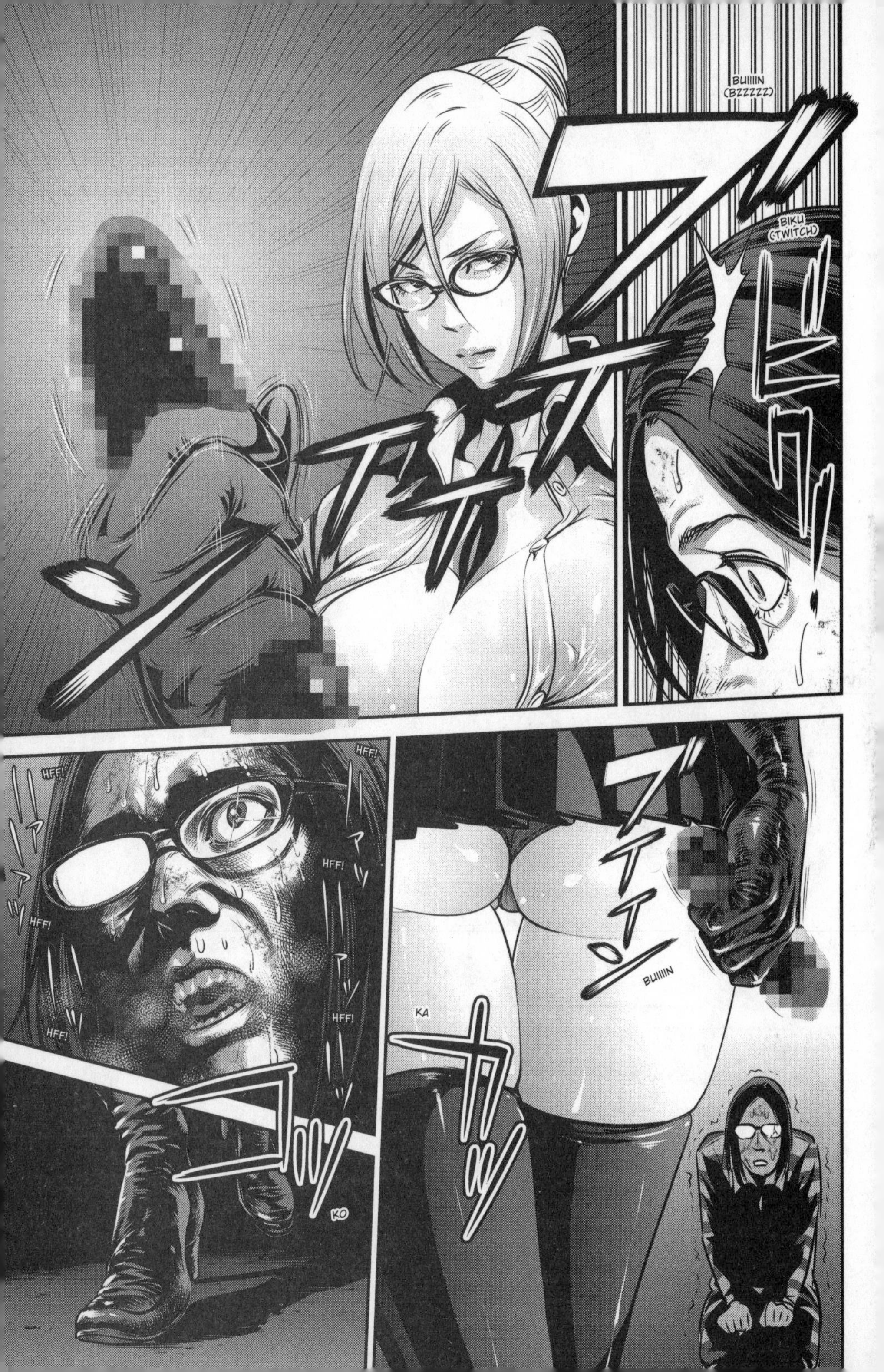
BUIIIIN
(BZZZZZ)
BIKU
(TWITCH)
BUIIIIN
KA
HFF!
HFF!
HFF!
HFF!
HFF!
HFF!
KO

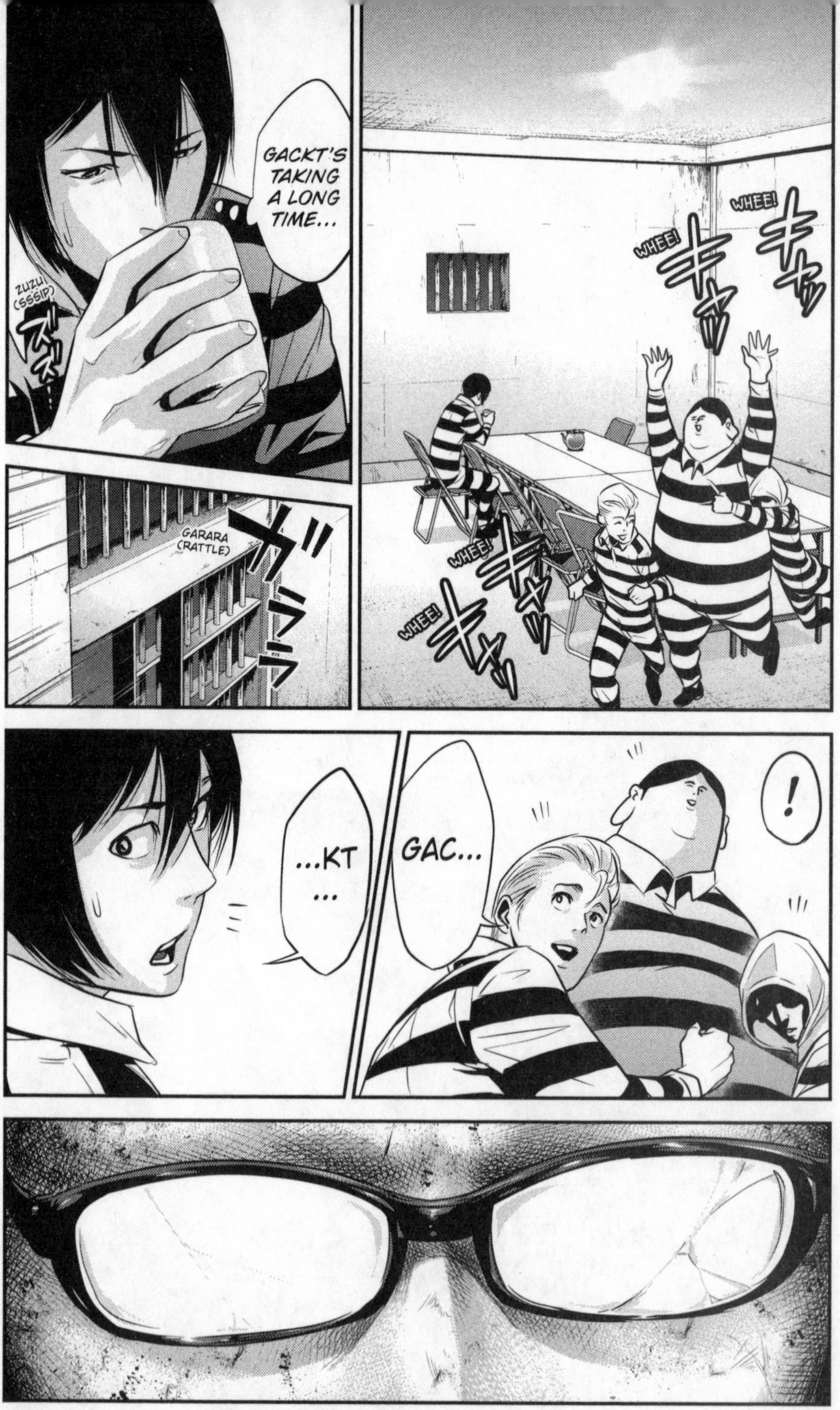
WHEE!
WHEE!
WHEE!
WHEE!
GACKT'S TAKING A LONG TIME...
ZUZU (SSSIP)
GARARA (RATTLE)
!
GAC...
...KT ...

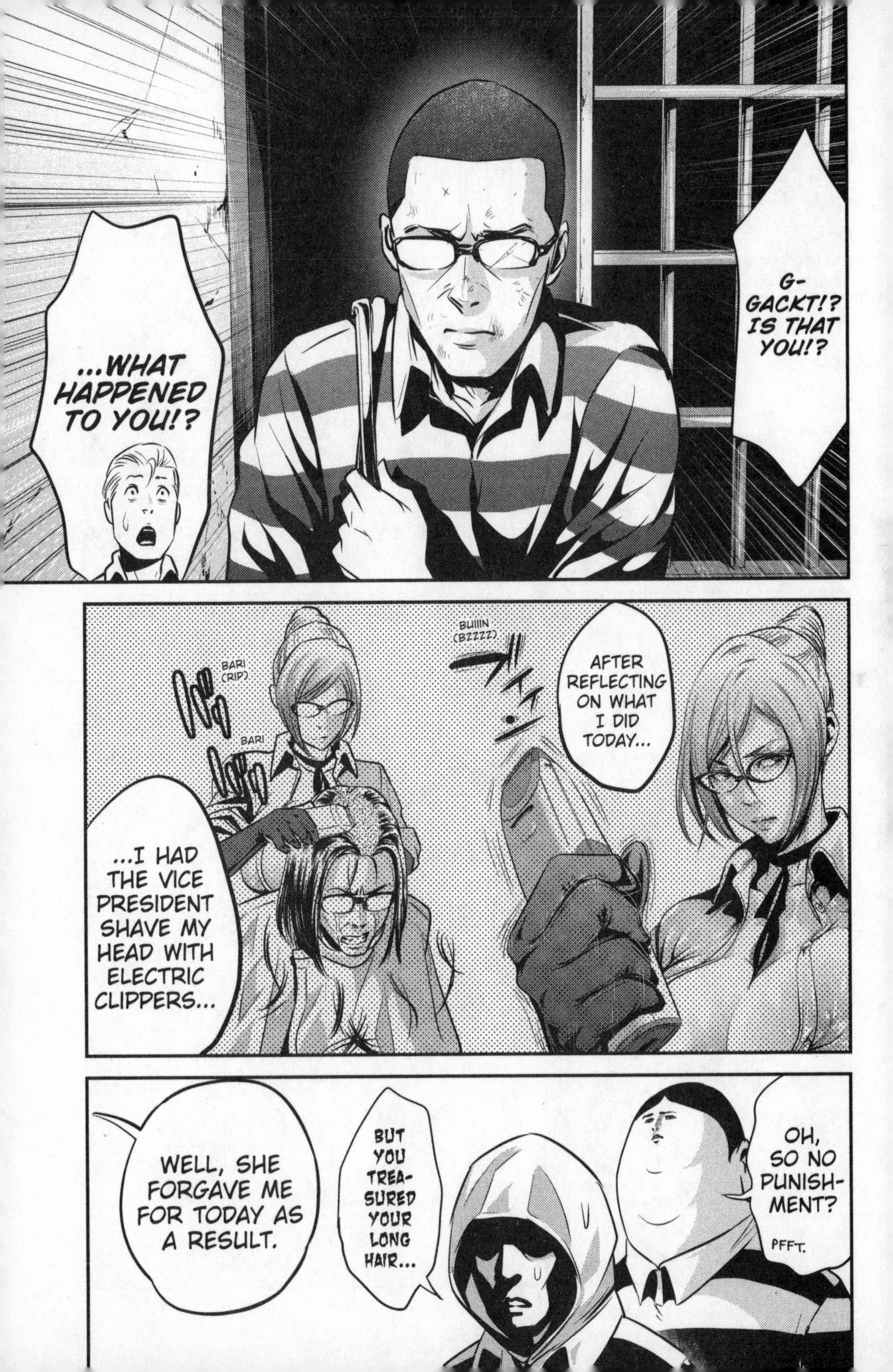
G-GACKT!? IS THAT YOU!?
...WHAT HAPPENED TO YOU!?
BUIIIN (BZZZZ)
AFTER REFLECTING ON WHAT I DID TODAY...
BARI (RIP)
BARI
...I HAD THE VICE PRESIDENT SHAVE MY HEAD WITH ELECTRIC CLIPPERS...
OH, SO NO PUNISH-MENT?
PFFT.
BUT YOU TREA-SURED YOUR LONG HAIR...
WELL, SHE FORGAVE ME FOR TODAY AS A RESULT.

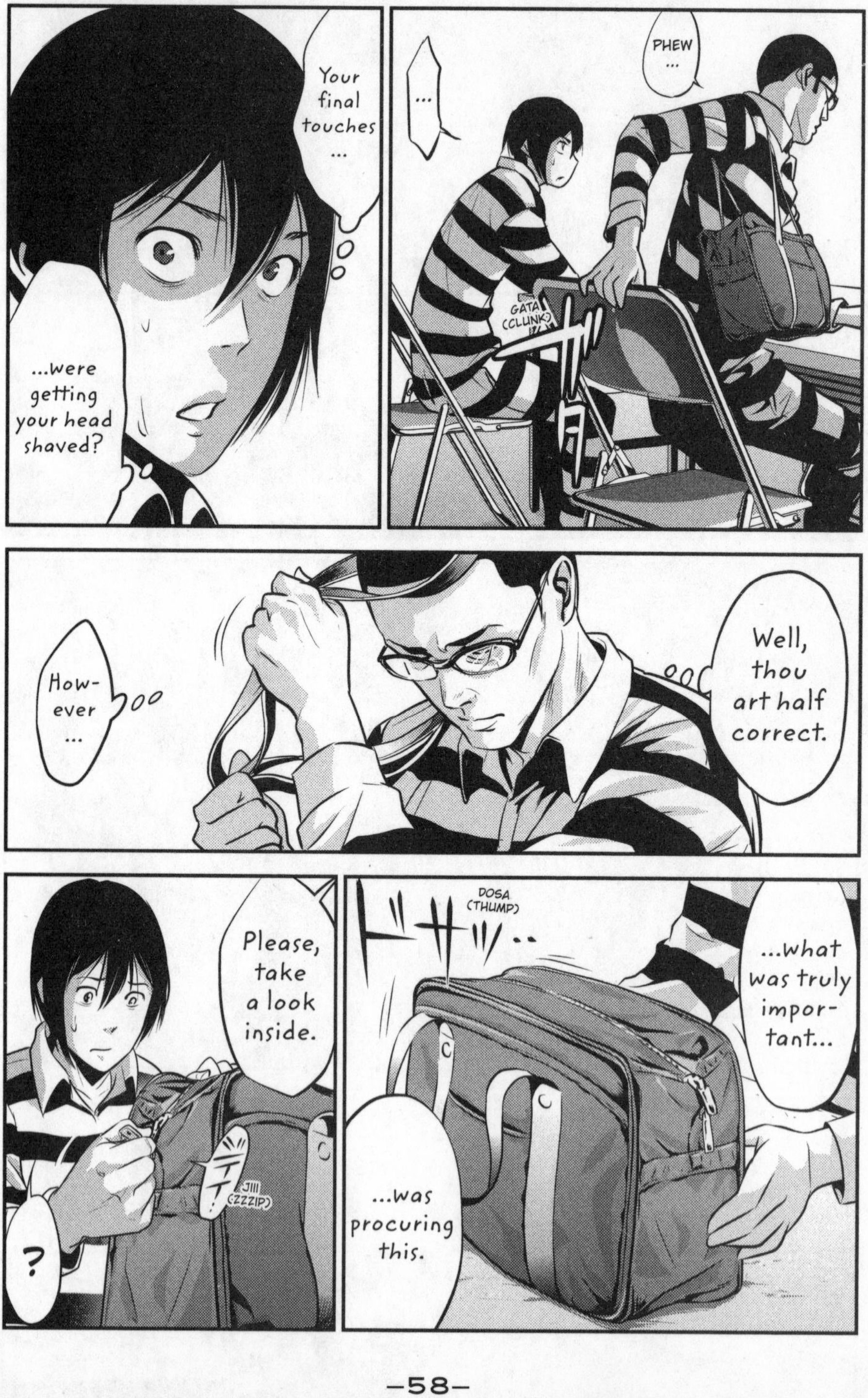
PHEW ...
...
GATA (CLUNK)
Your final touches ...
...were getting your head shaved?
Well, thou art half correct.
How-ever ...
DOSA (THUMP)
...what was truly impor-tant...
...was procuring this.
Please, take a look inside.
JIII (ZZZIP)
?

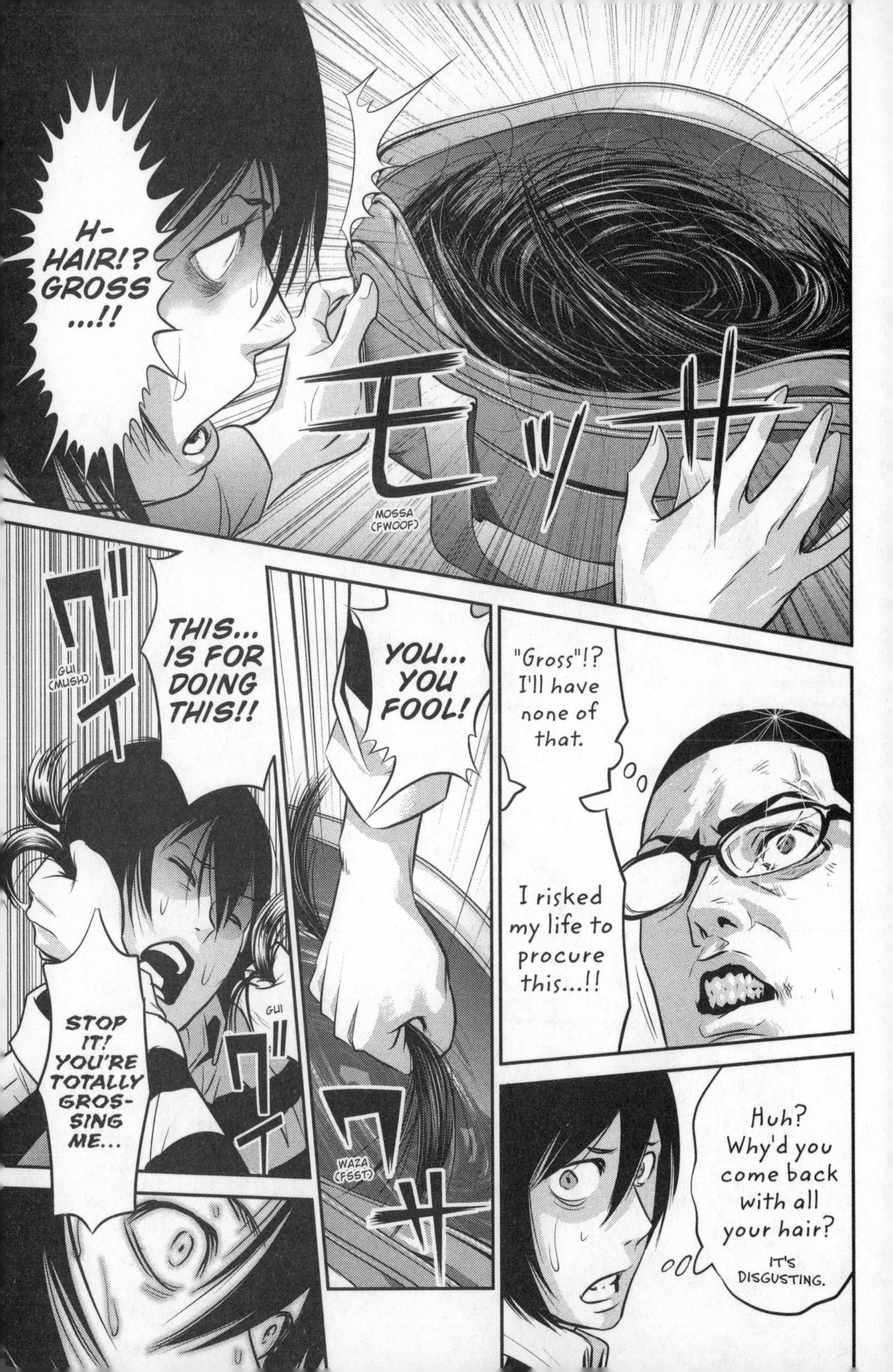
H-HAIR!? GROSS...!!
MOSSA (FWOOF)
"Gross"!? I'll have none of that.
I risked my life to procure this...!!
Huh? Why'd you come back with all your hair?
IT'S DISGUSTING.
YOU... YOU FOOL!
WAZA (FSST)
THIS... IS FOR DOING THIS!!
GUI (MUSH)
GUI
STOP IT! YOU'RE TOTALLY GROS-SING ME...

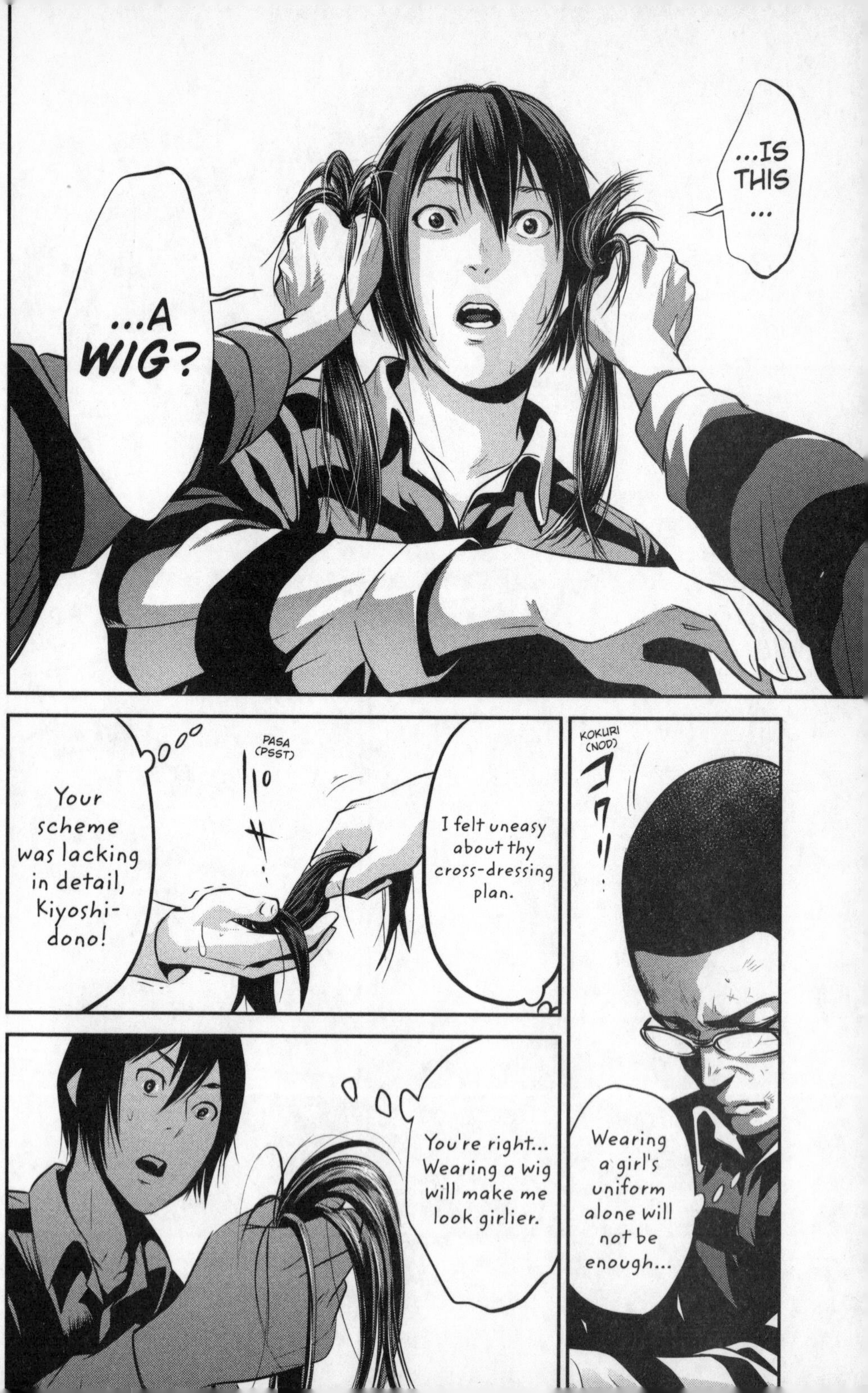
...IS THIS ...
...A WIG?
KOKURI (NOD)
Wearing a girl's uniform alone will not be enough...
I felt uneasy about thy cross-dressing plan.
PASA (PSST)
Your scheme was lacking in detail, Kiyoshi-dono!
You're right... Wearing a wig will make me look girlier.

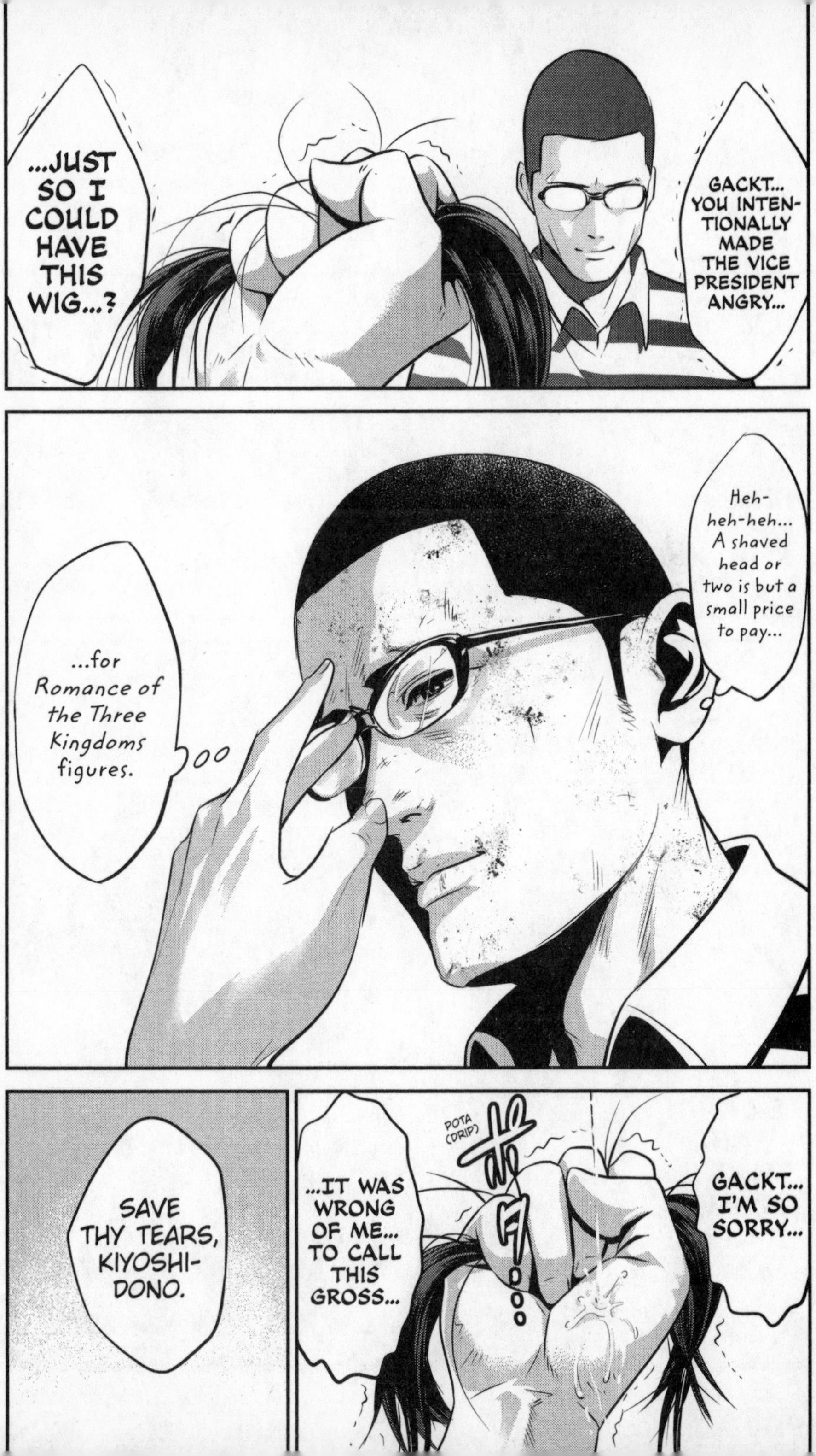

GACKT... YOU INTENTIONALLY MADE THE VICE PRESIDENT ANGRY...
...JUST SO I COULD HAVE THIS WIG...?
Heh-heh-heh... A shaved head or two is but a small price to pay...
...for Romance of the Three Kingdoms figures.
GACKT... I'M SO SORRY...
POTA (DRIP)
...IT WAS WRONG OF ME... TO CALL THIS GROSS...
SAVE THY TEARS, KIYOSHI-DONO.

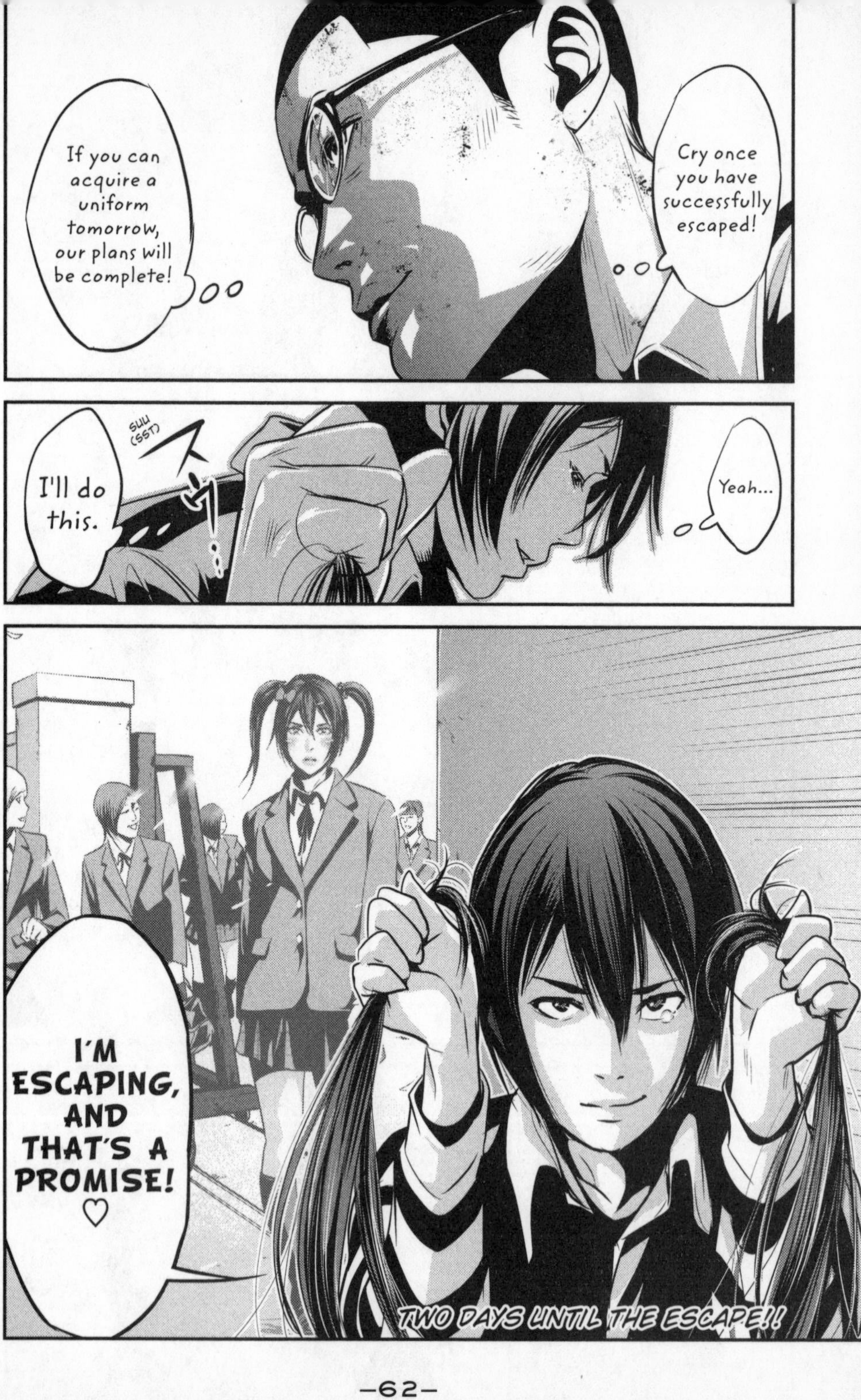
Cry once you have successfully escaped!
If you can acquire a uniform tomorrow, our plans will be complete!
Yeah...
SUU (SST)
I'll do this.
I'M ESCAPING, AND THAT'S A PROMISE! ♡
TWO DAYS UNTIL THE ESCAPE!!

CHAPTER 22: SUNSHINE CLEANING

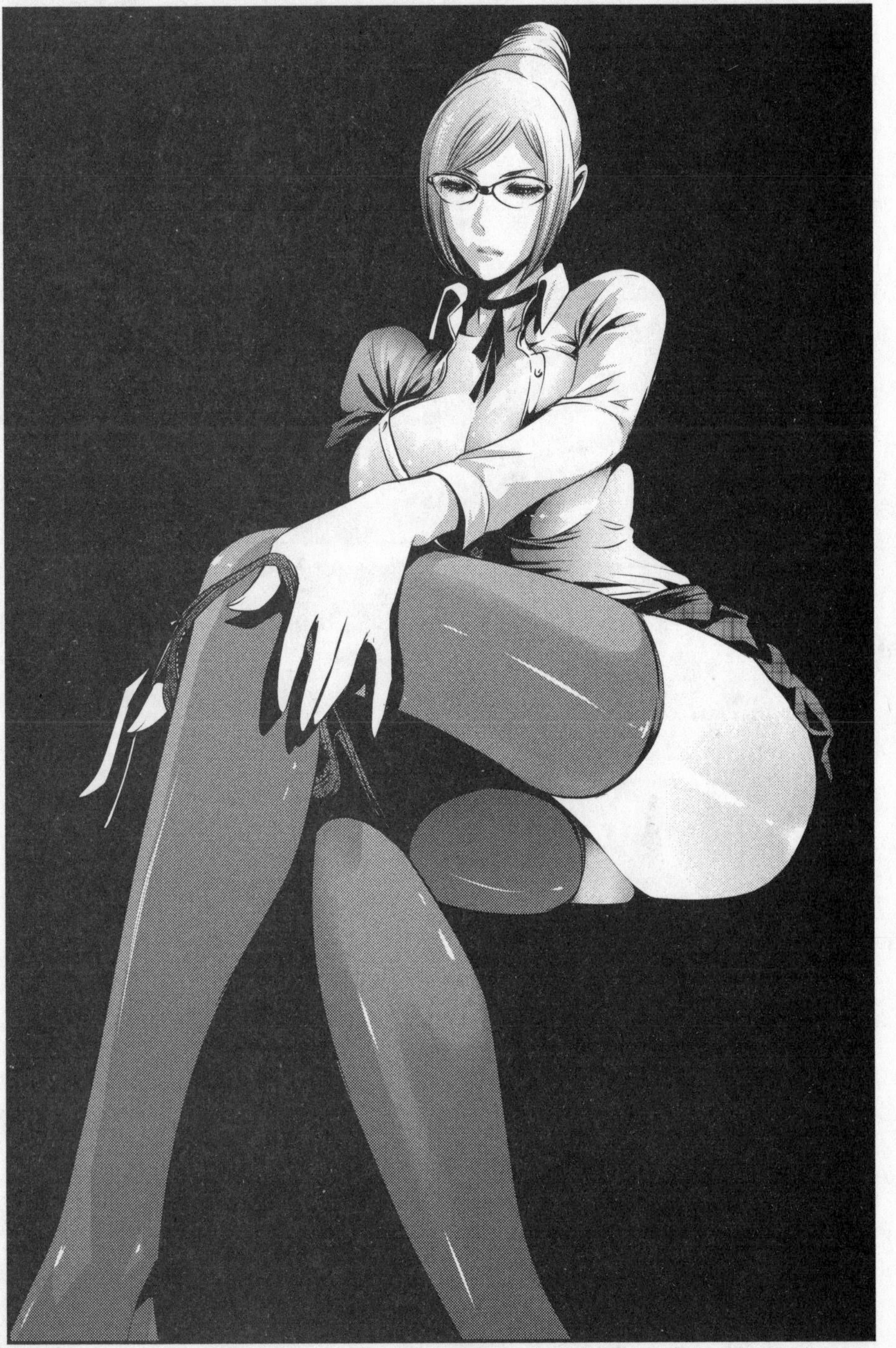

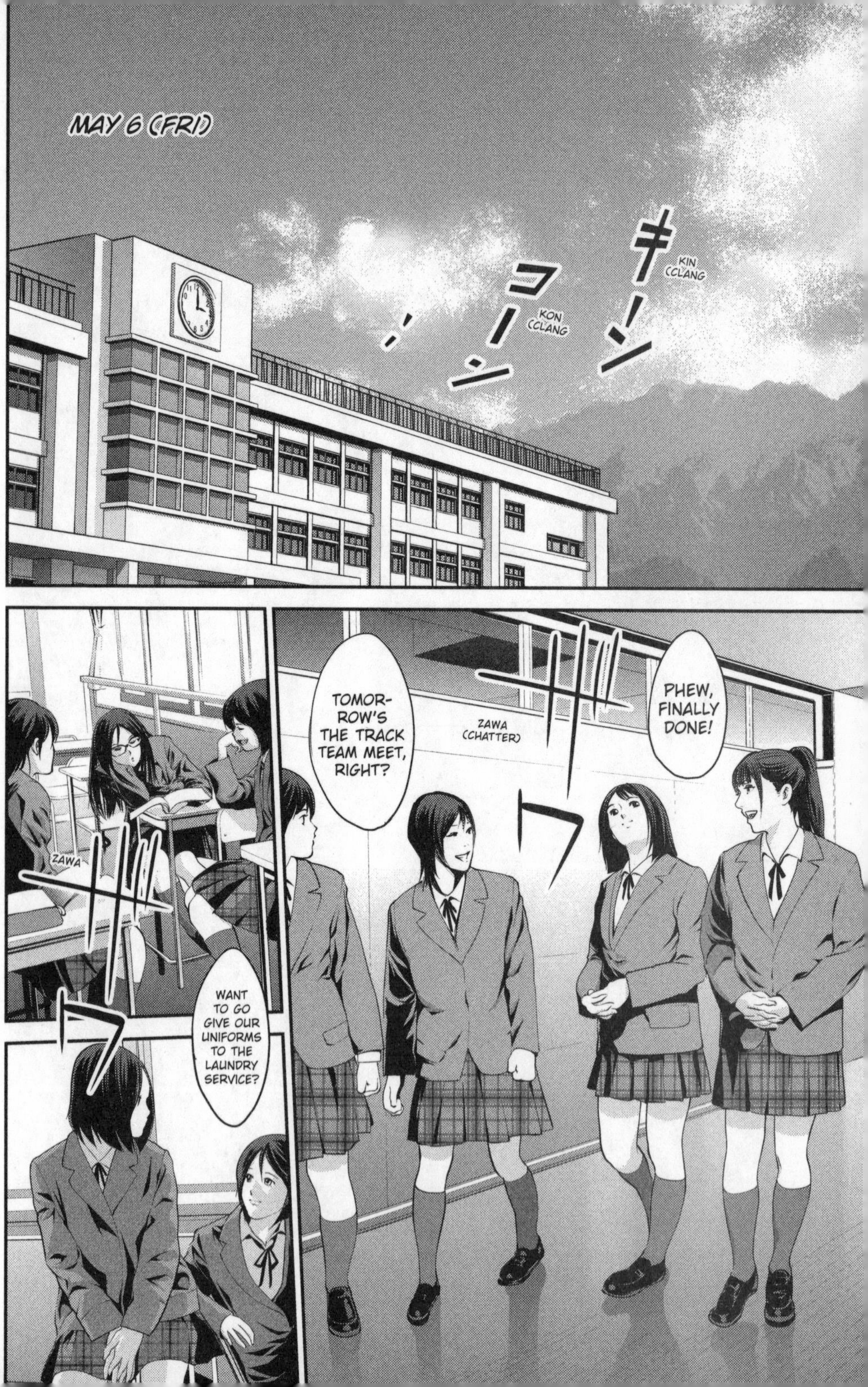
MAY 6 (FRI)
KIN (CLANG)
KON (CLANG)
PHEW, FINALLY DONE!
ZAWA (CHATTER)
TOMOR-ROW'S THE TRACK TEAM MEET, RIGHT?
ZAWA
WANT TO GO GIVE OUR UNIFORMS TO THE LAUNDRY SERVICE?

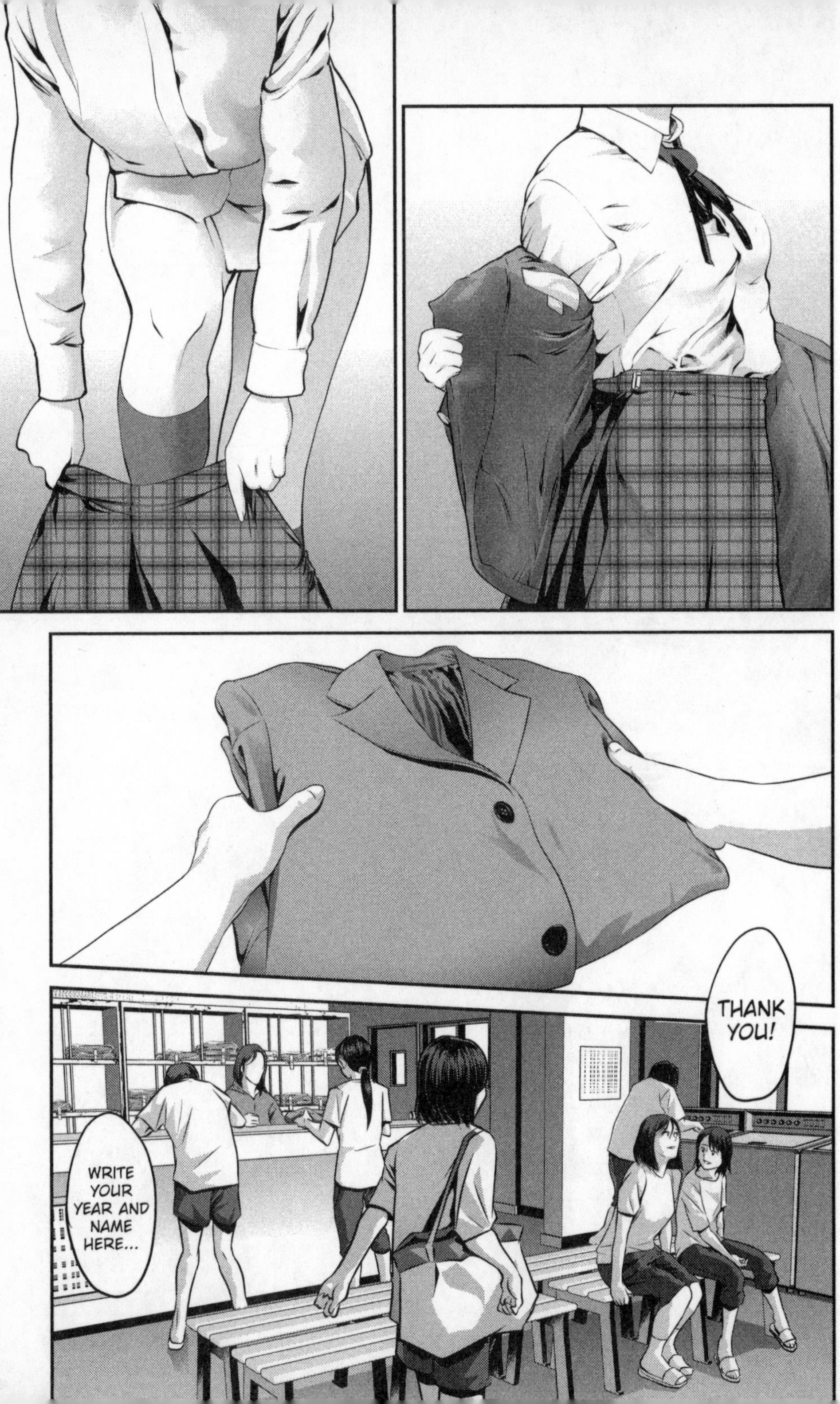
THANK YOU!
WRITE YOUR YEAR AND NAME HERE...

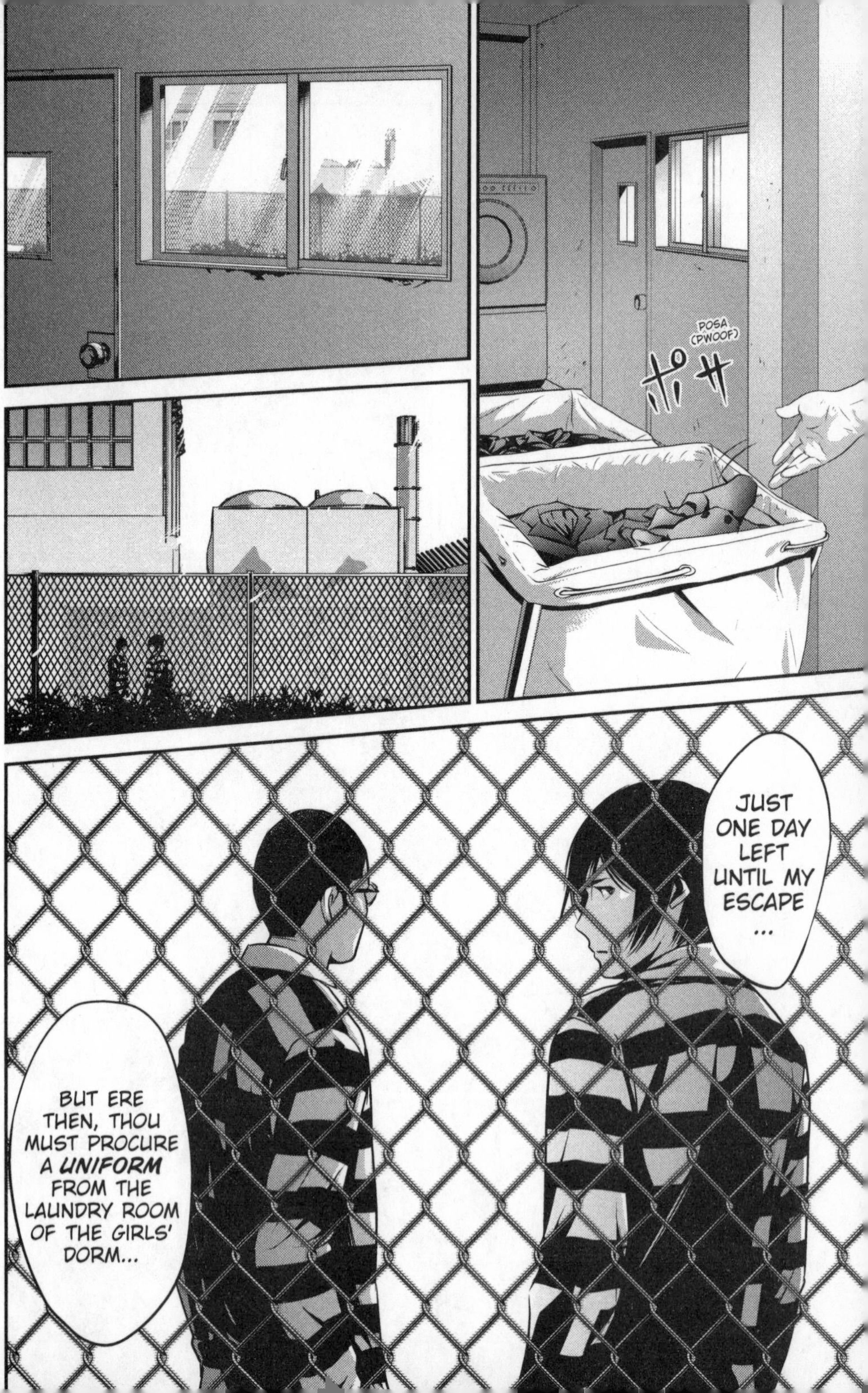
POSA (PWOOF)
ポサ
JUST ONE DAY LEFT UNTIL MY ESCAPE ...
BUT ERE THEN, THOU MUST PROCURE A UNIFORM FROM THE LAUNDRY ROOM OF THE GIRLS' DORM...

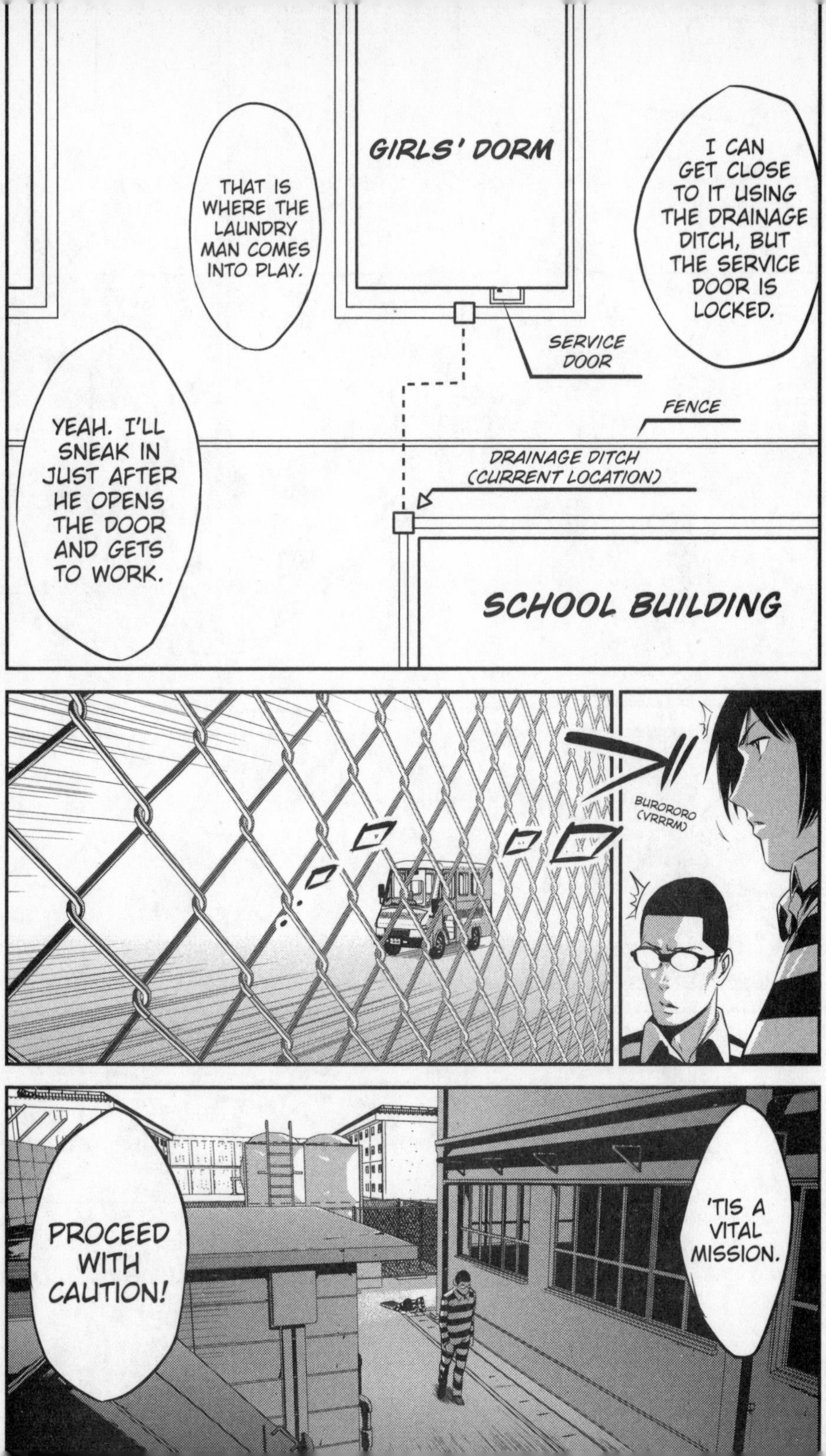
GIRLS' DORM
I CAN GET CLOSE TO IT USING THE DRAINAGE DITCH, BUT THE SERVICE DOOR IS LOCKED.
THAT IS WHERE THE LAUNDRY MAN COMES INTO PLAY.
SERVICE DOOR
FENCE
DRAINAGE DITCH (CURRENT LOCATION)
YEAH. I'LL SNEAK IN JUST AFTER HE OPENS THE DOOR AND GETS TO WORK.
SCHOOL BUILDING
BURORORO (VRRRM)
'TIS A VITAL MISSION.
PROCEED WITH CAUTION!

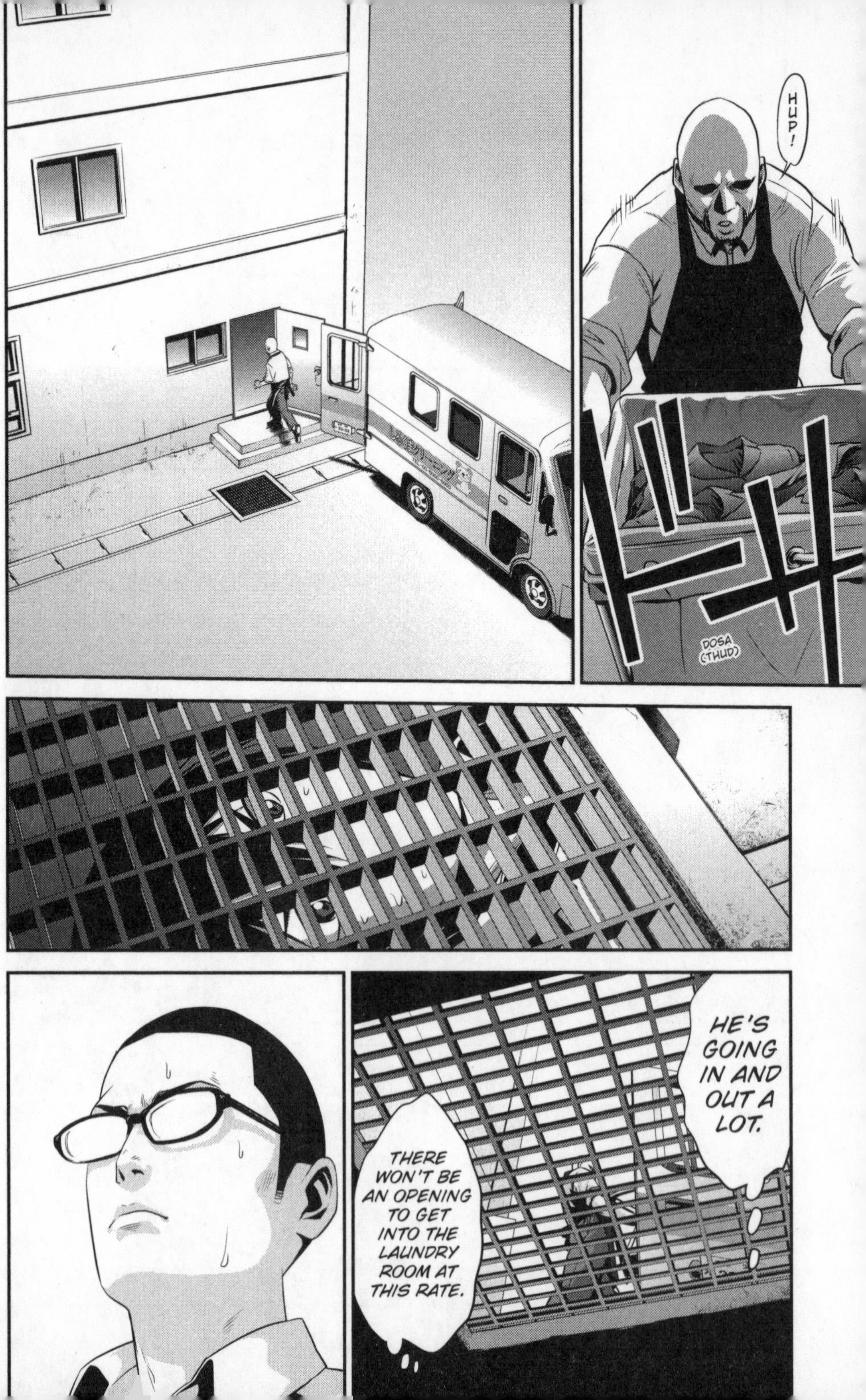
HUP!
DOSA (THUD)
HE'S GOING IN AND OUT A LOT.
THERE WON'T BE AN OPENING TO GET INTO THE LAUNDRY ROOM AT THIS RATE.

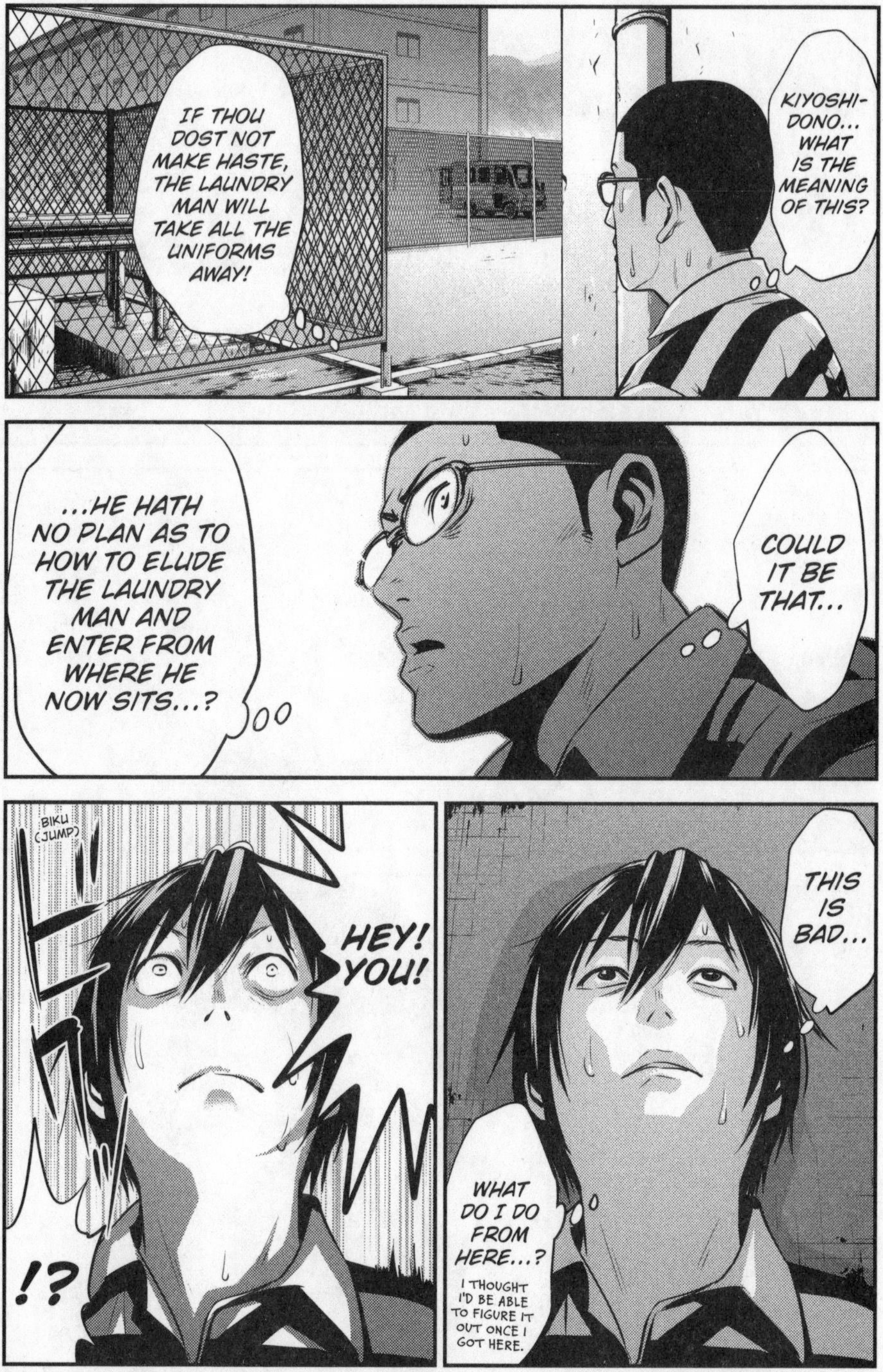
KIYOSHI-DONO... WHAT IS THE MEANING OF THIS?
IF THOU DOST NOT MAKE HASTE, THE LAUNDRY MAN WILL TAKE ALL THE UNIFORMS AWAY!
COULD IT BE THAT...
...HE HATH NO PLAN AS TO HOW TO ELUDE THE LAUNDRY MAN AND ENTER FROM WHERE HE NOW SITS...?
THIS IS BAD...
WHAT DO I DO FROM HERE...?
I THOUGHT I'D BE ABLE TO FIGURE IT OUT ONCE I GOT HERE.
BIKU (JUMP)
HEY! YOU!
!?

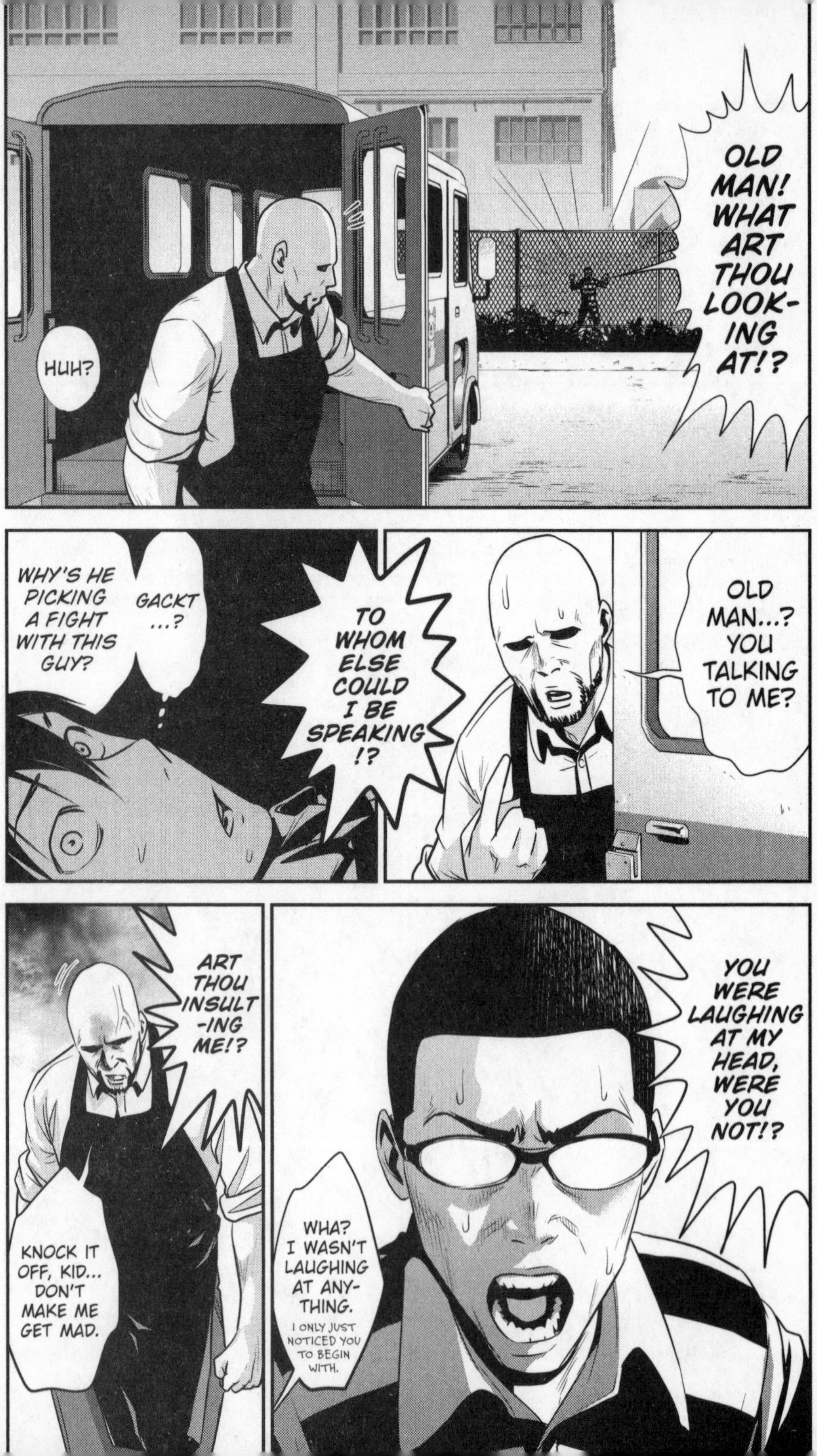
OLD MAN! WHAT ART THOU LOOKING AT!?
HUH?
OLD MAN...? YOU TALKING TO ME?
TO WHOM ELSE COULD I BE SPEAKING!?
GACKT...?
WHY'S HE PICKING A FIGHT WITH THIS GUY?
YOU WERE LAUGHING AT MY HEAD, WERE YOU NOT!?
ART THOU INSULT-ING ME!?
WHA? I WASN'T LAUGHING AT ANY-THING. I ONLY JUST NOTICED YOU TO BEGIN WITH.
KNOCK IT OFF, KID... DON'T MAKE ME GET MAD.

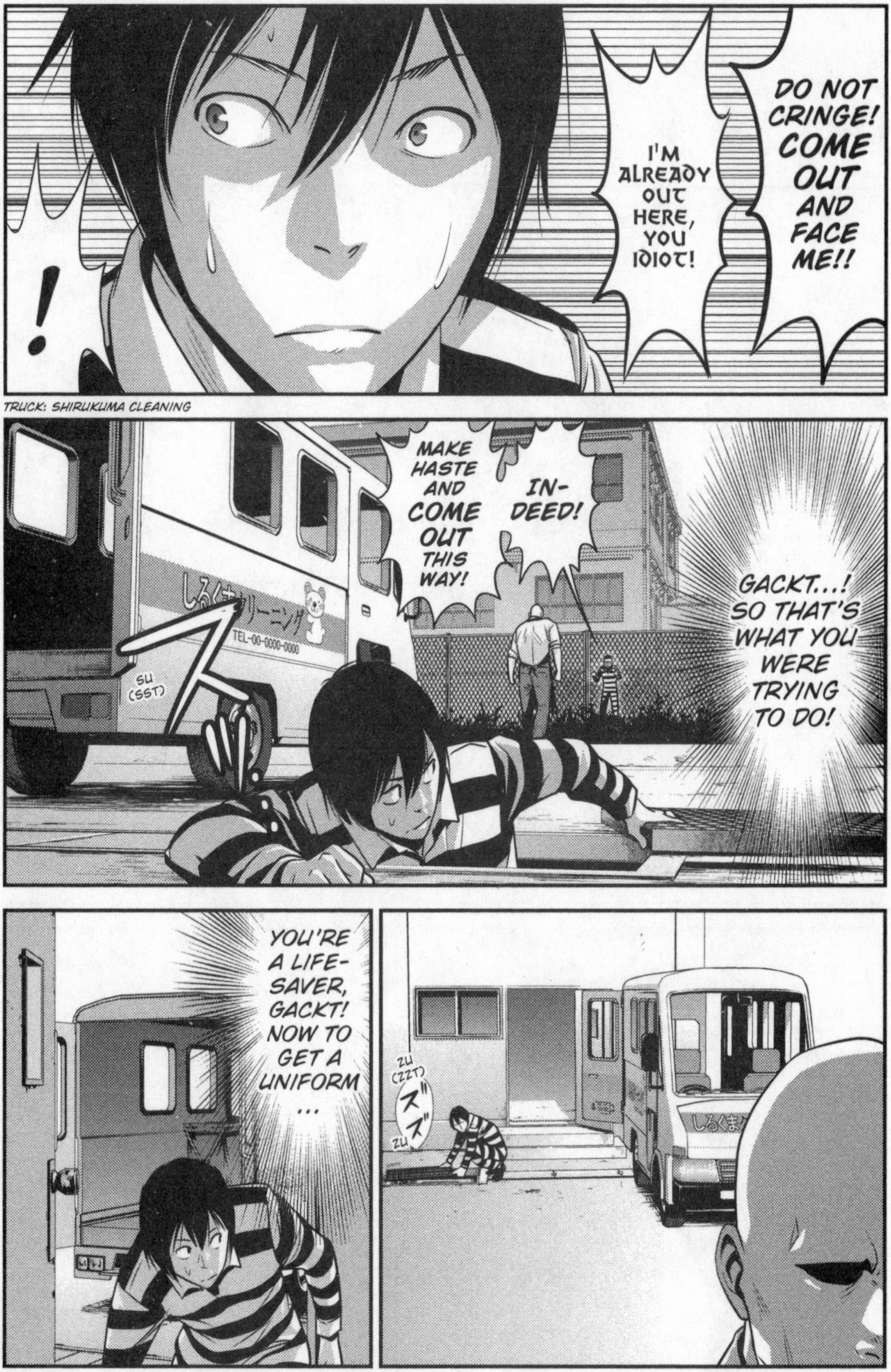
DO NOT CRINGE! COME OUT AND FACE ME!!
I'M ALREADY OUT HERE, YOU IDIOT!
!
TRUCK: SHIRUKUMA CLEANING
IN-DEED!
MAKE HASTE AND COME OUT THIS WAY!
GACKT...! SO THAT'S WHAT YOU WERE TRYING TO DO!
SU (SST)
ZU (ZZT) ズズ ZU
YOU'RE A LIFE-SAVER, GACKT! NOW TO GET A UNIFORM ...

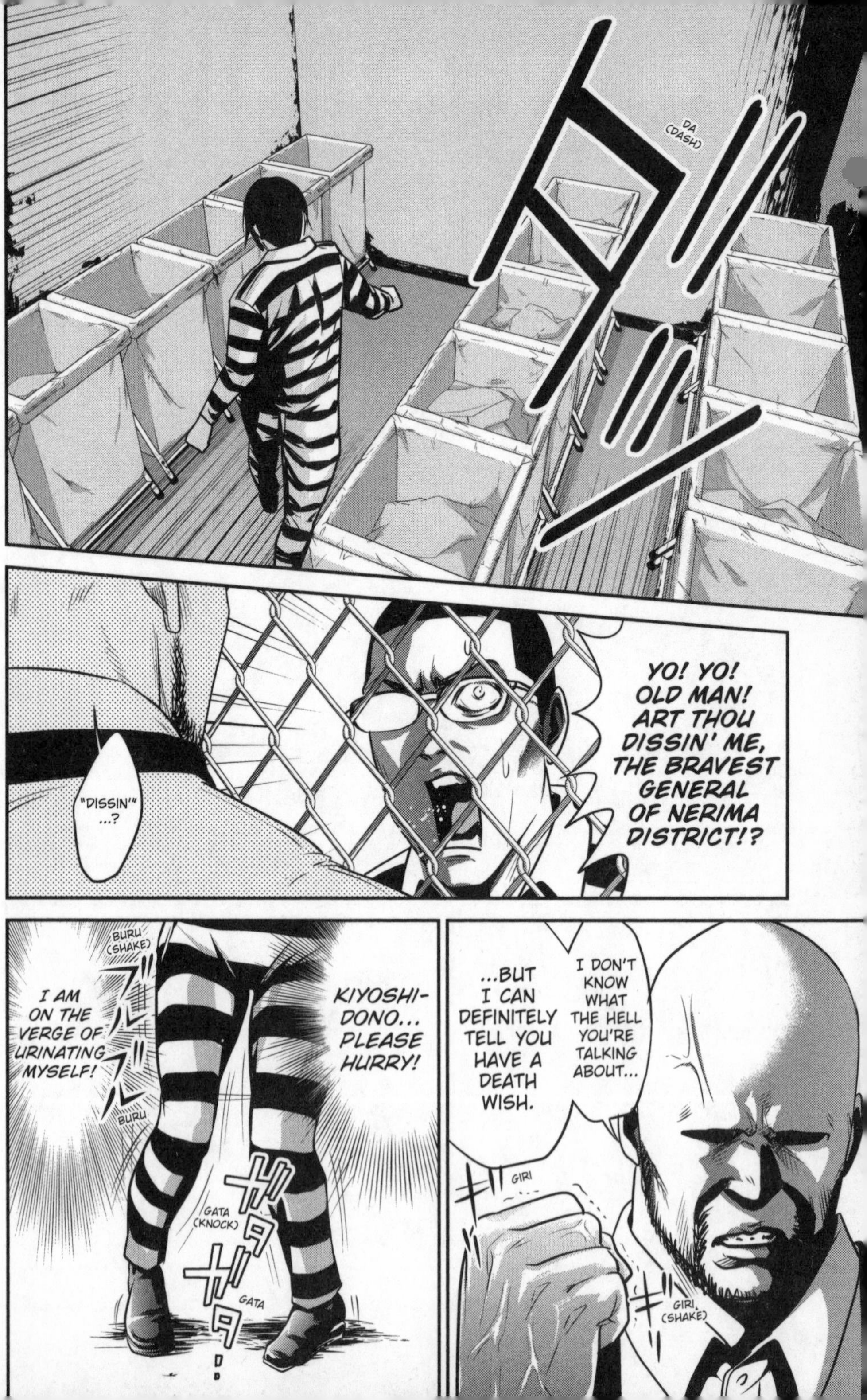
DA (DASH)
YO! YO! OLD MAN! ART THOU DISSIN' ME, THE BRAVEST GENERAL OF NERIMA DISTRICT!?
"DISSIN'" ...?
I DON'T KNOW WHAT THE HELL YOU'RE TALKING ABOUT...
...BUT I CAN DEFINITELY TELL YOU HAVE A DEATH WISH.
GIRI
GIRI (SHAKE)
KIYOSHI-DONO... PLEASE HURRY!
I AM ON THE VERGE OF URINATING MYSELF!
BURU (SHAKE)
BURU
GATA (KNOCK)
GATA

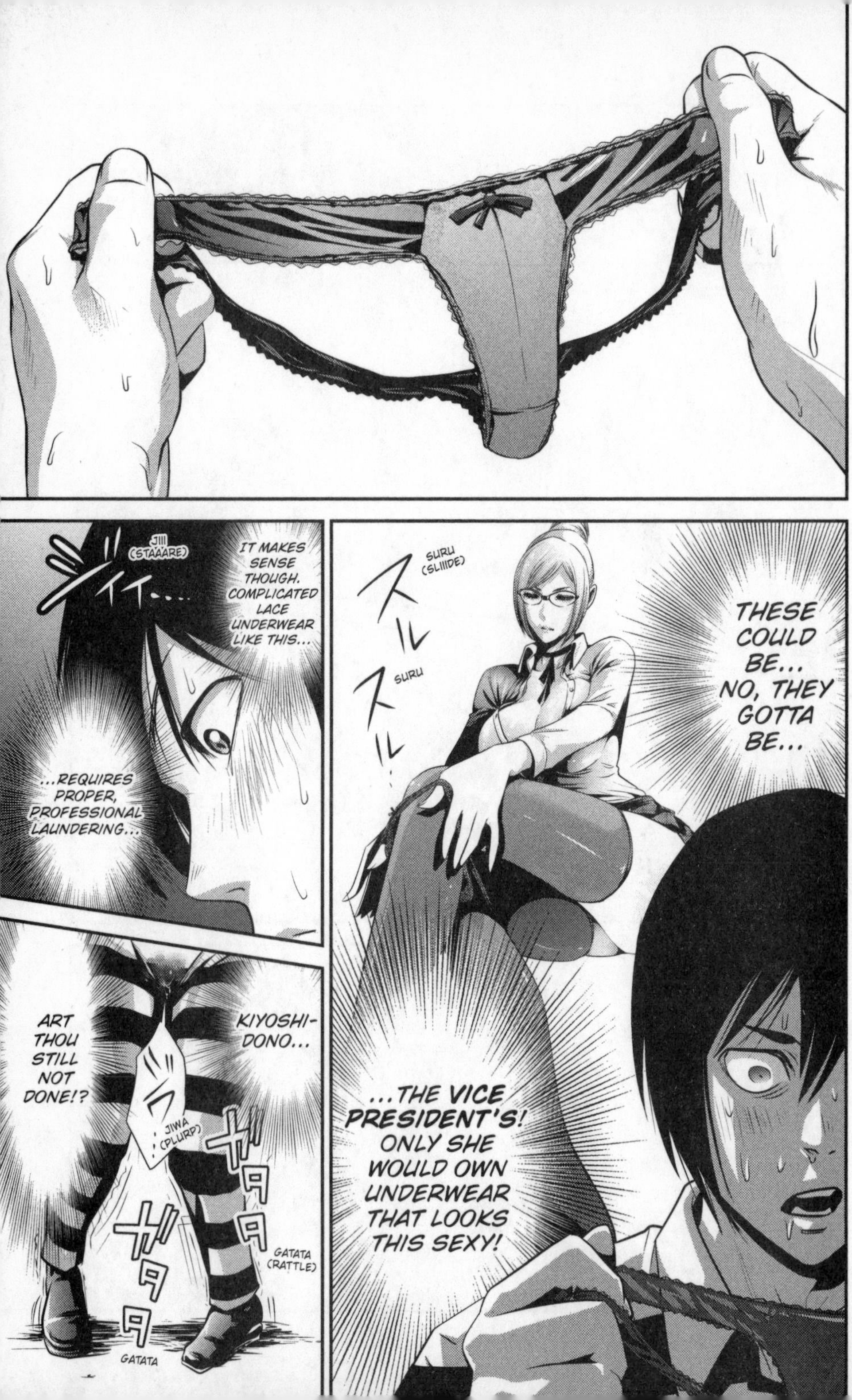

JIII (STAAARE)
IT MAKES SENSE THOUGH. COMPLICATED LACE UNDERWEAR LIKE THIS...
...REQUIRES PROPER, PROFESSIONAL LAUNDERING...
THESE COULD BE... NO, THEY GOTTA BE...
SURU (SLIIIDE)
SURU
KIYOSHI-DONO...
ART THOU STILL NOT DONE!?
JIWA (PLURP)
GATATA (RATTLE)
GATATA
...THE VICE PRESIDENT'S! ONLY SHE WOULD OWN UNDERWEAR THAT LOOKS THIS SEXY!

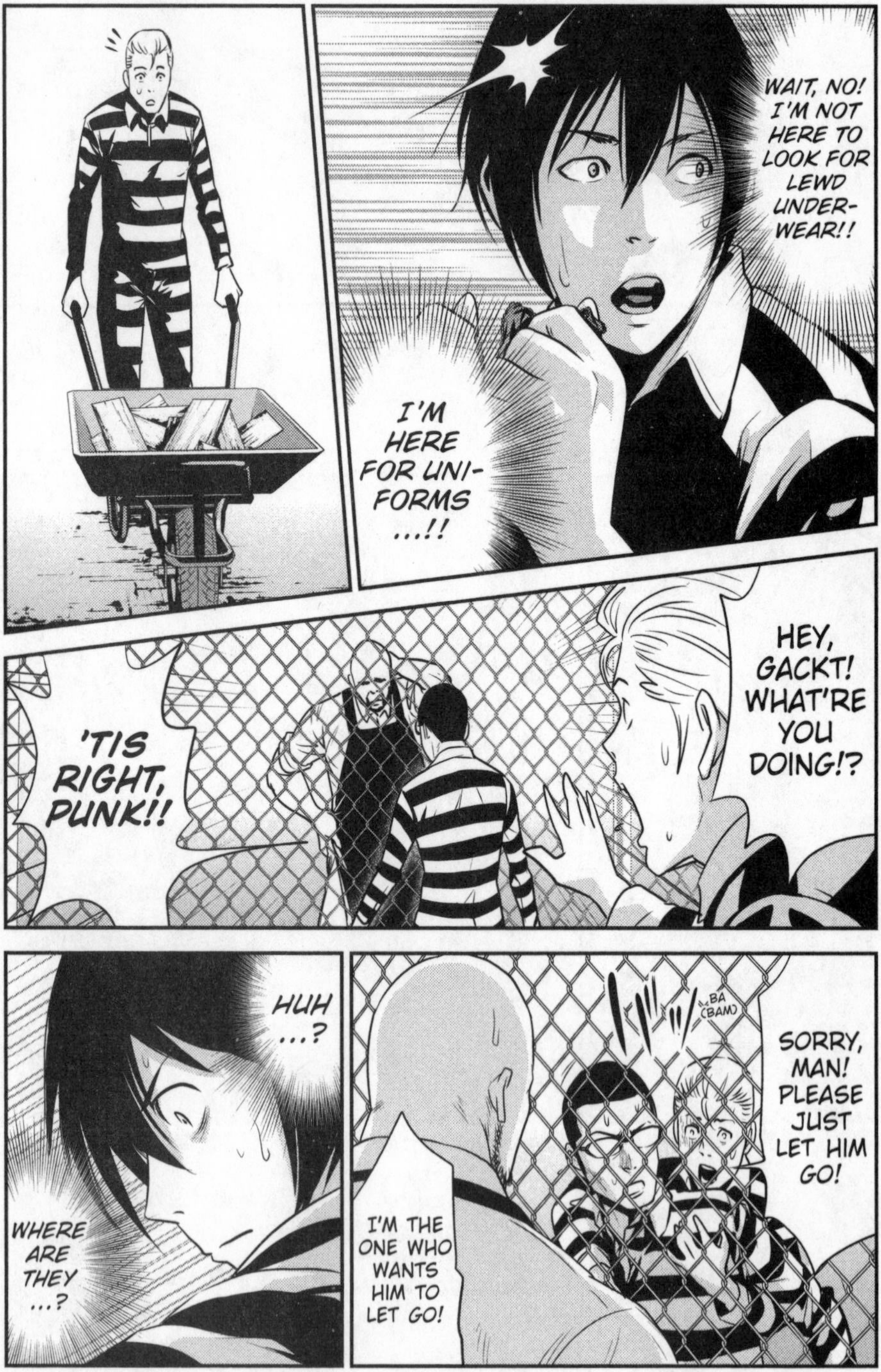
WAIT, NO! I'M NOT HERE TO LOOK FOR LEWD UNDER-WEAR!!
I'M HERE FOR UNI-FORMS ...!!
HEY, GACKT! WHAT'RE YOU DOING!?
'TIS RIGHT, PUNK!!
BA (BAM)
SORRY, MAN! PLEASE JUST LET HIM GO!
I'M THE ONE WHO WANTS HIM TO LET GO!
HUH ...?
WHERE ARE THEY ...?

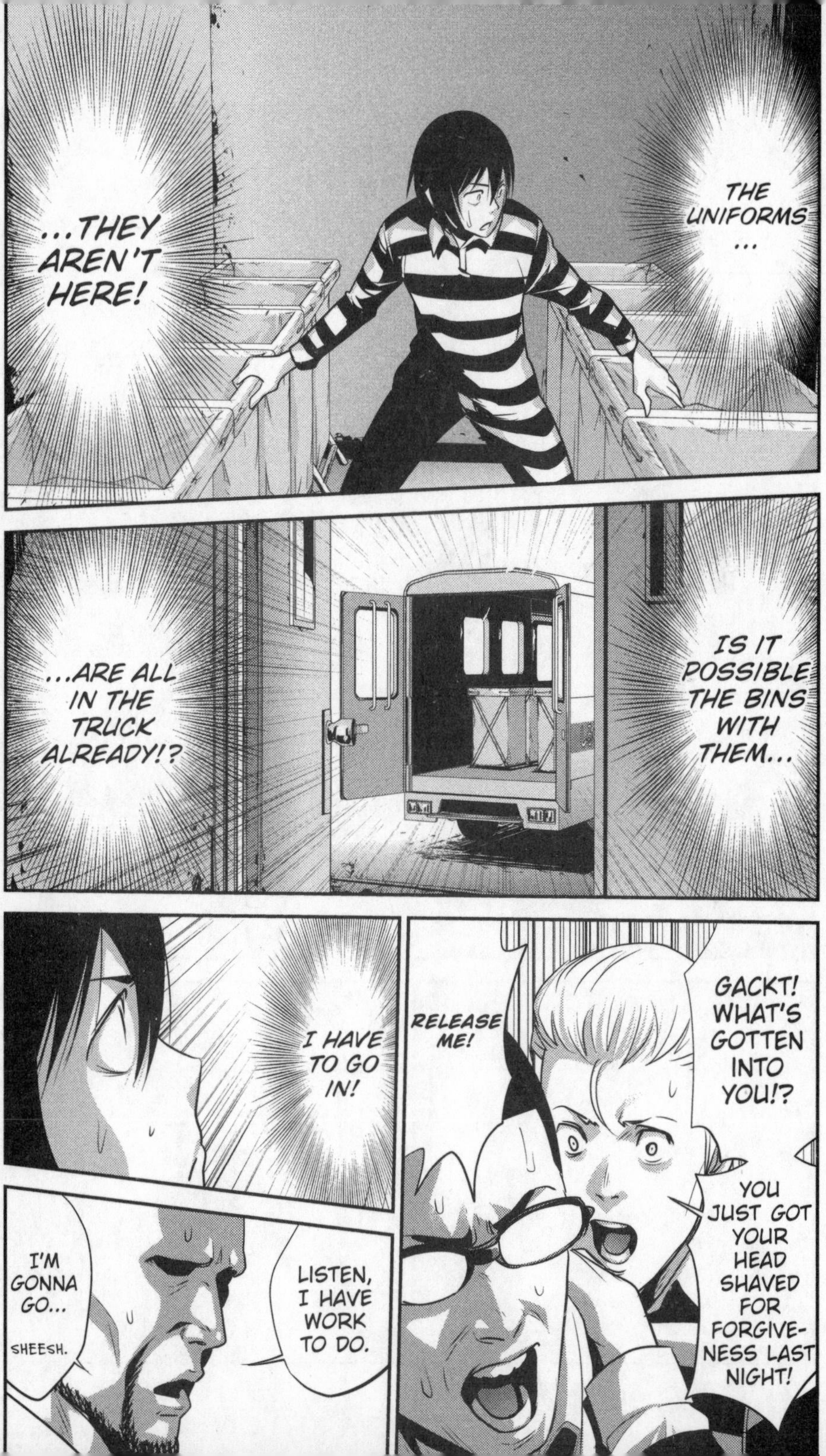
THE UNIFORMS...
...THEY AREN'T HERE!
IS IT POSSIBLE THE BINS WITH THEM...
...ARE ALL IN THE TRUCK ALREADY!?
GACKT! WHAT'S GOTTEN INTO YOU!?
RELEASE ME!
YOU JUST GOT YOUR HEAD SHAVED FOR FORGIVE-NESS LAST NIGHT!
I HAVE TO GO IN!
LISTEN, I HAVE WORK TO DO.
I'M GONNA GO...
SHEESH.

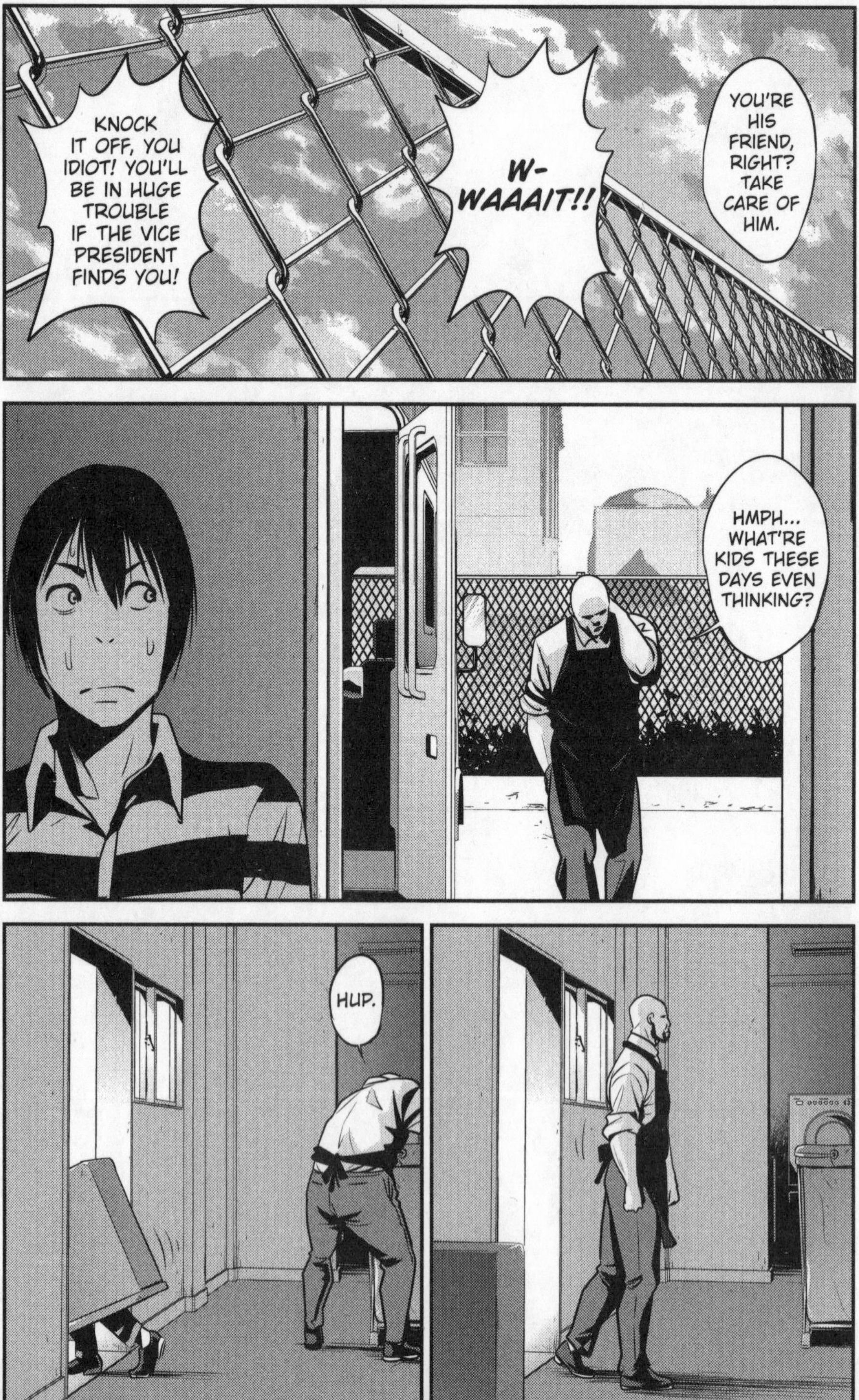
YOU'RE HIS FRIEND, RIGHT? TAKE CARE OF HIM.
W-WAAAIT!!
KNOCK IT OFF, YOU IDIOT! YOU'LL BE IN HUGE TROUBLE IF THE VICE PRESIDENT FINDS YOU!
HMPH... WHAT'RE KIDS THESE DAYS EVEN THINKING?
HUP.

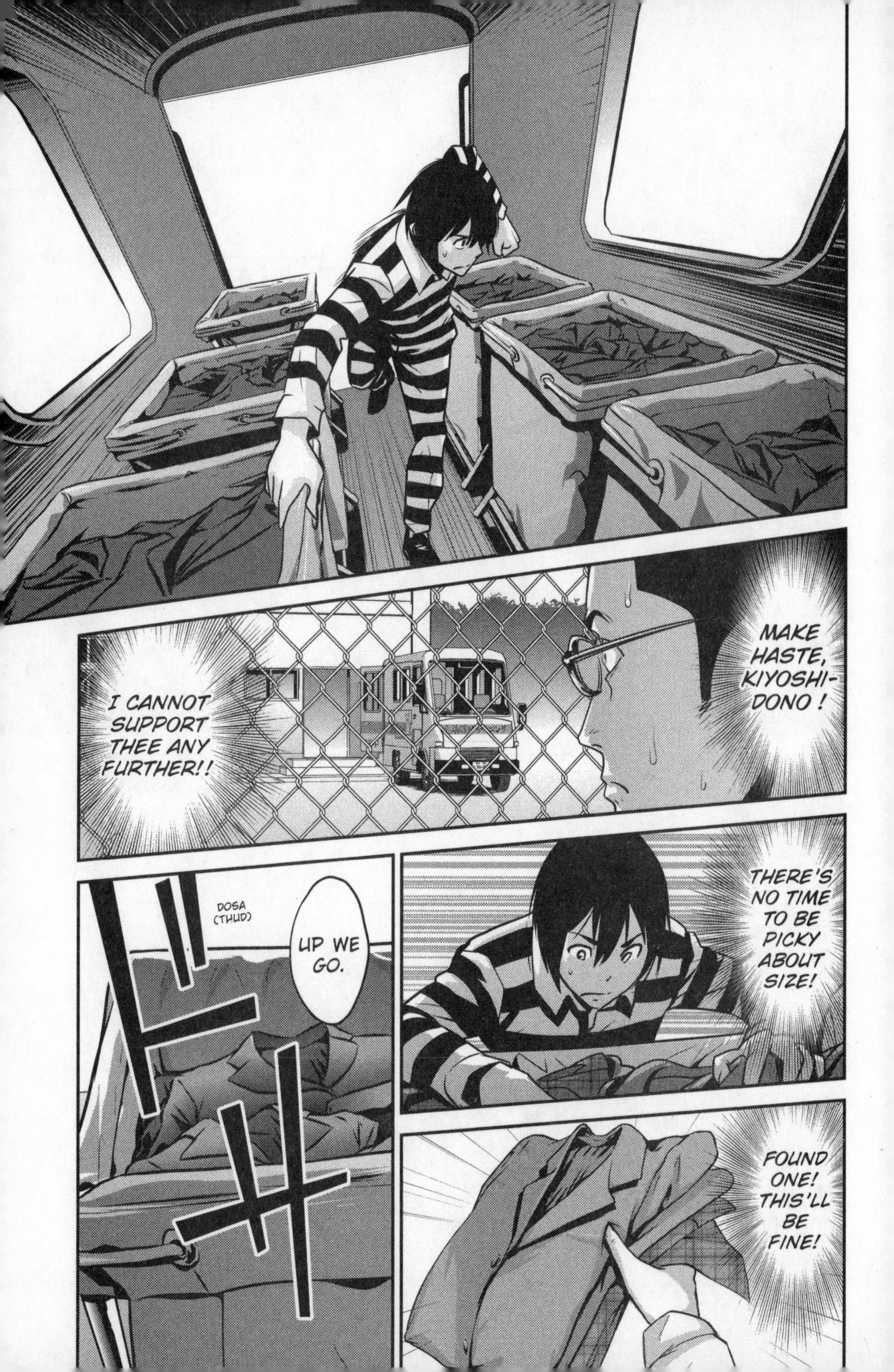
MAKE HASTE, KIYOSHI-DONO !
I CANNOT SUPPORT THEE ANY FURTHER!!
THERE'S NO TIME TO BE PICKY ABOUT SIZE!
UP WE GO.
DOSA (THUD)
FOUND ONE! THIS'LL BE FINE!

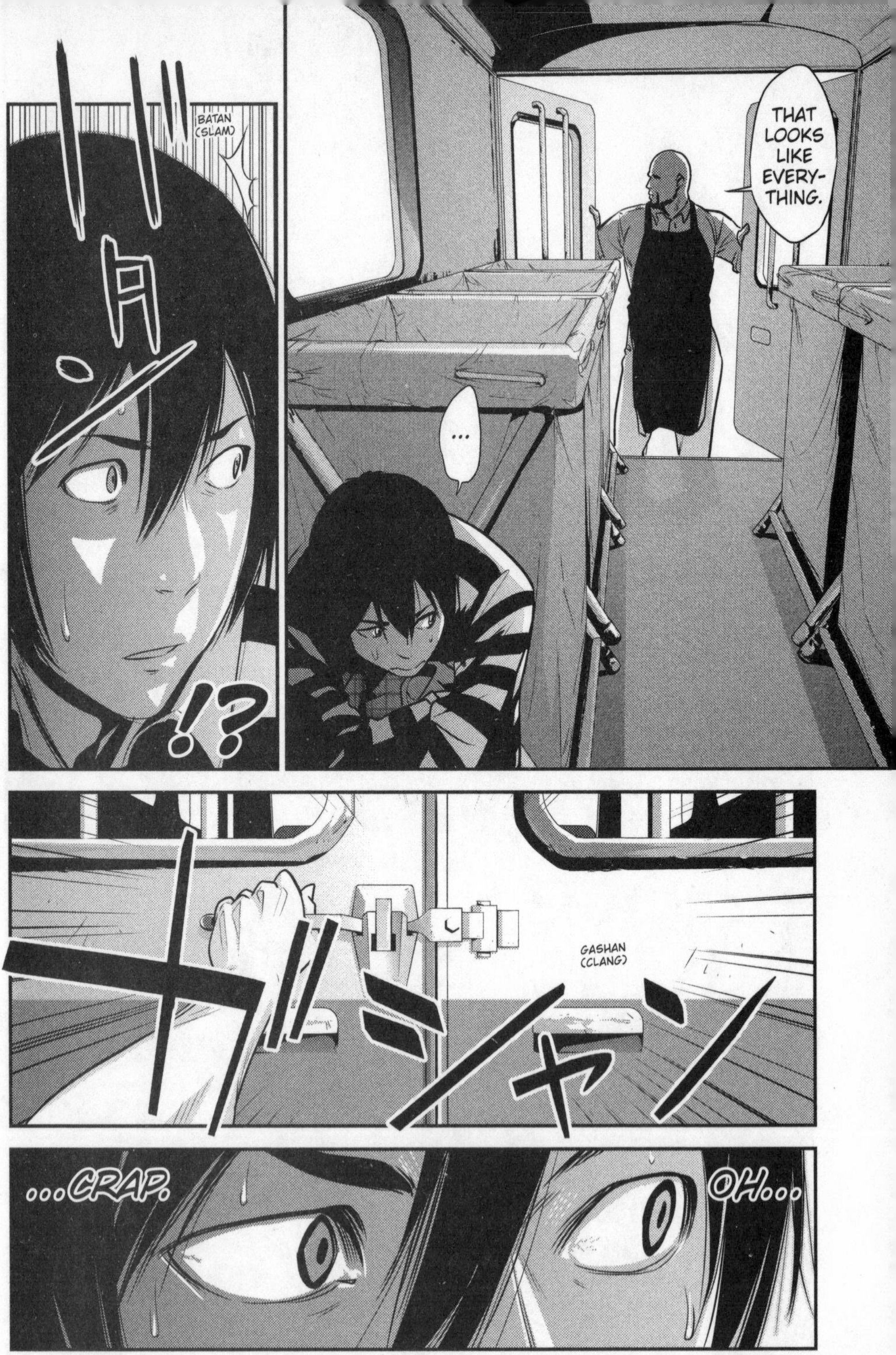
THAT LOOKS LIKE EVERY-THING.
...
BATAN (SLAM)
!?
GASHAN (CLANG)
OH...
...CRAP.

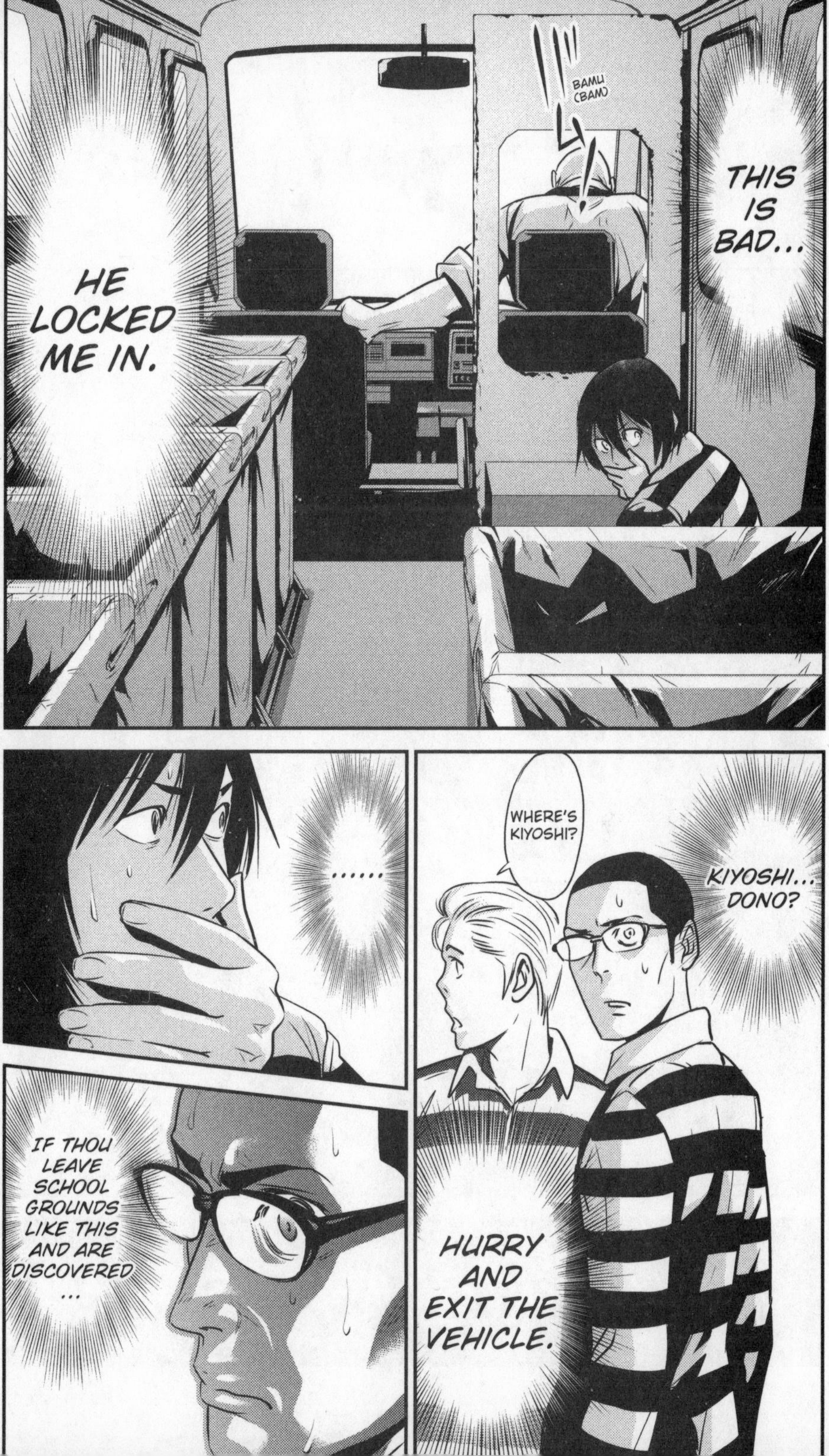
BAMU (BAM)
THIS IS BAD...
HE LOCKED ME IN.
KIYOSHI... DONO?
WHERE'S KIYOSHI?
......
HURRY AND EXIT THE VEHICLE.
IF THOU LEAVE SCHOOL GROUNDS LIKE THIS AND ARE DISCOVERED ...

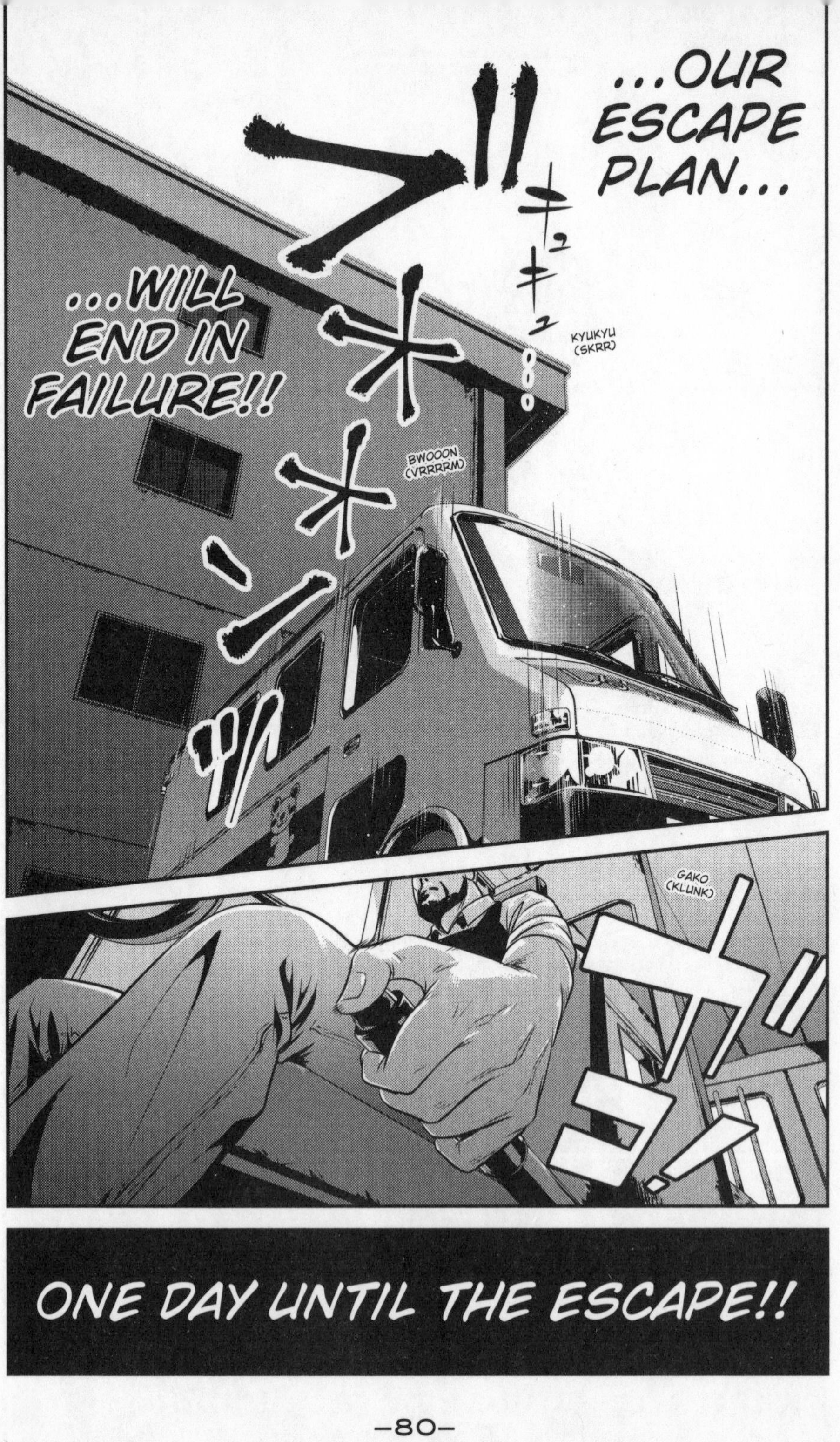
...OUR ESCAPE PLAN...
KYUKYU (SKRR)
...WILL END IN FAILURE!!
BWOOON (VRRRRM)
GAKO (KLUNK)

ONE DAY UNTIL THE ESCAPE!!

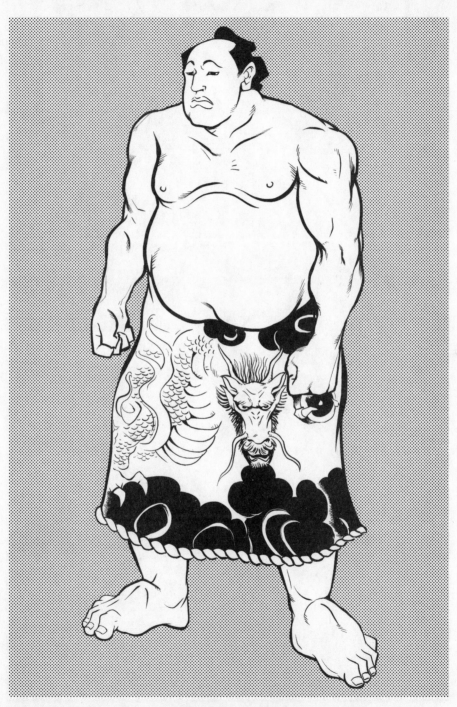

CHAPTER 23: TOMORROW NEVER DIES

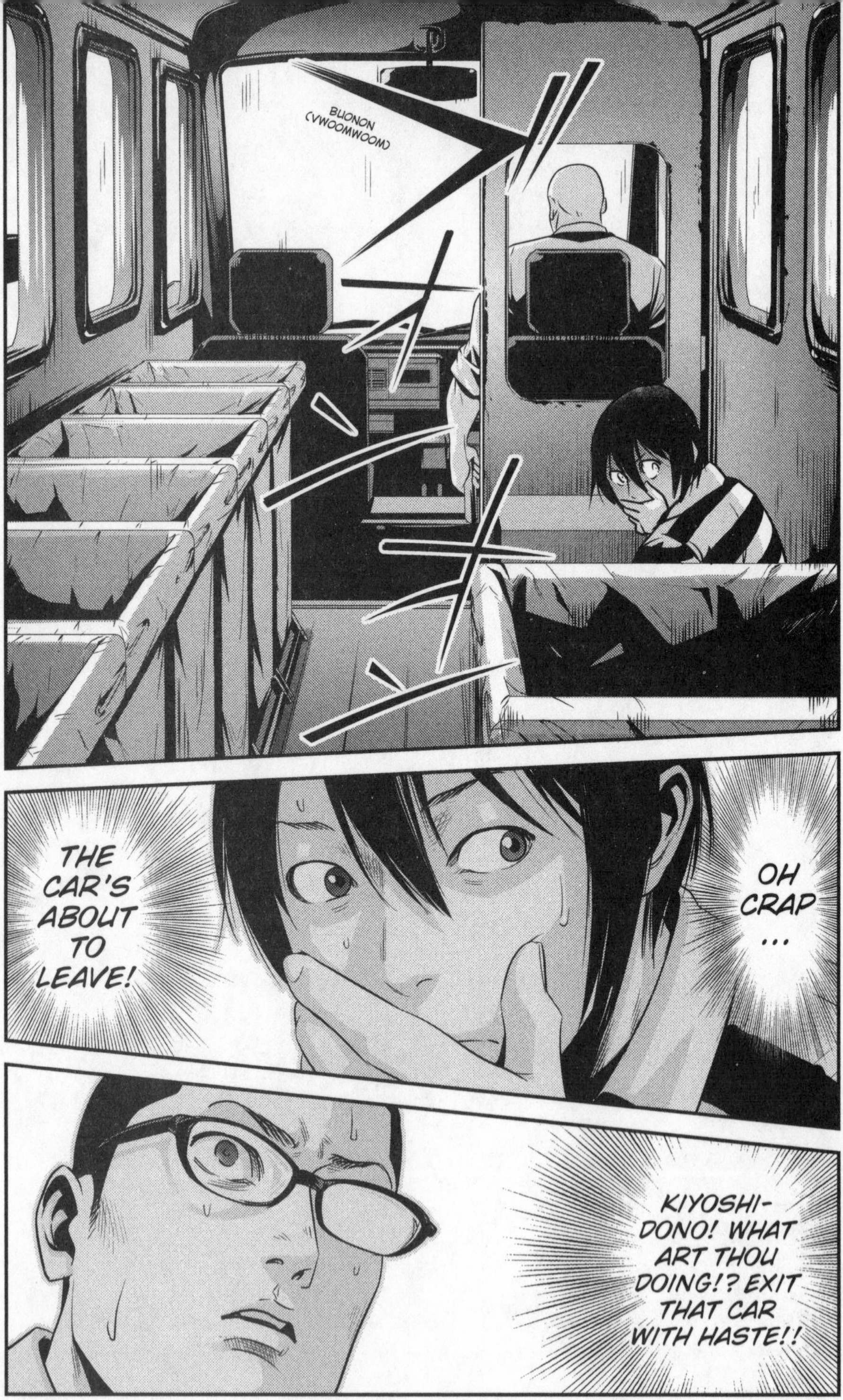
BUONON (VWOOMWOOM)
OH CRAP...
THE CAR'S ABOUT TO LEAVE!
KIYOSHI-DONO! WHAT ART THOU DOING!? EXIT THAT CAR WITH HASTE!!

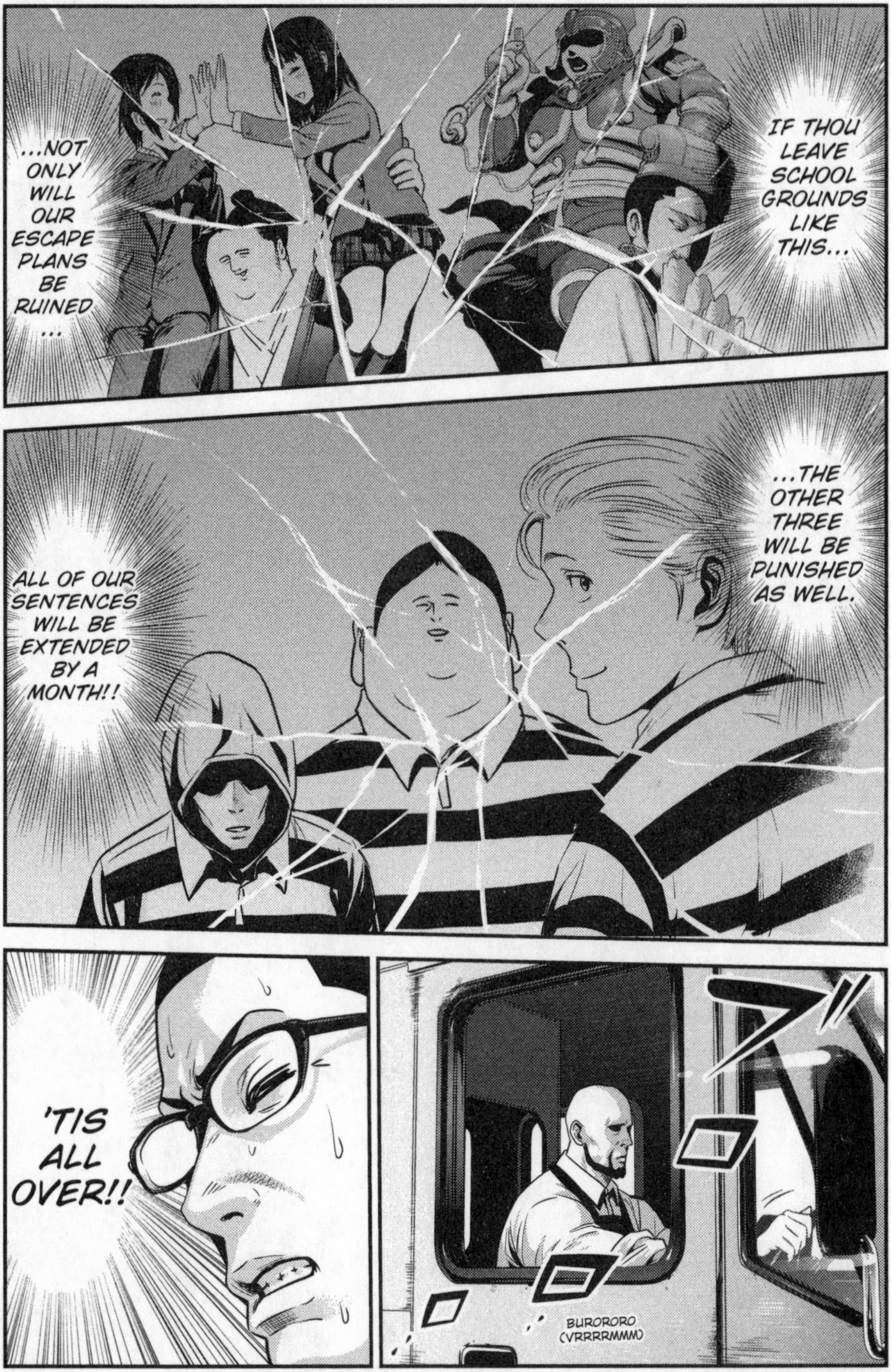
IF THOU LEAVE SCHOOL GROUNDS LIKE THIS...
...NOT ONLY WILL OUR ESCAPE PLANS BE RUINED ...
...THE OTHER THREE WILL BE PUNISHED AS WELL.
ALL OF OUR SENTENCES WILL BE EXTENDED BY A MONTH!!
BUROROROR (VRRRRMMM)
'TIS ALL OVER!!

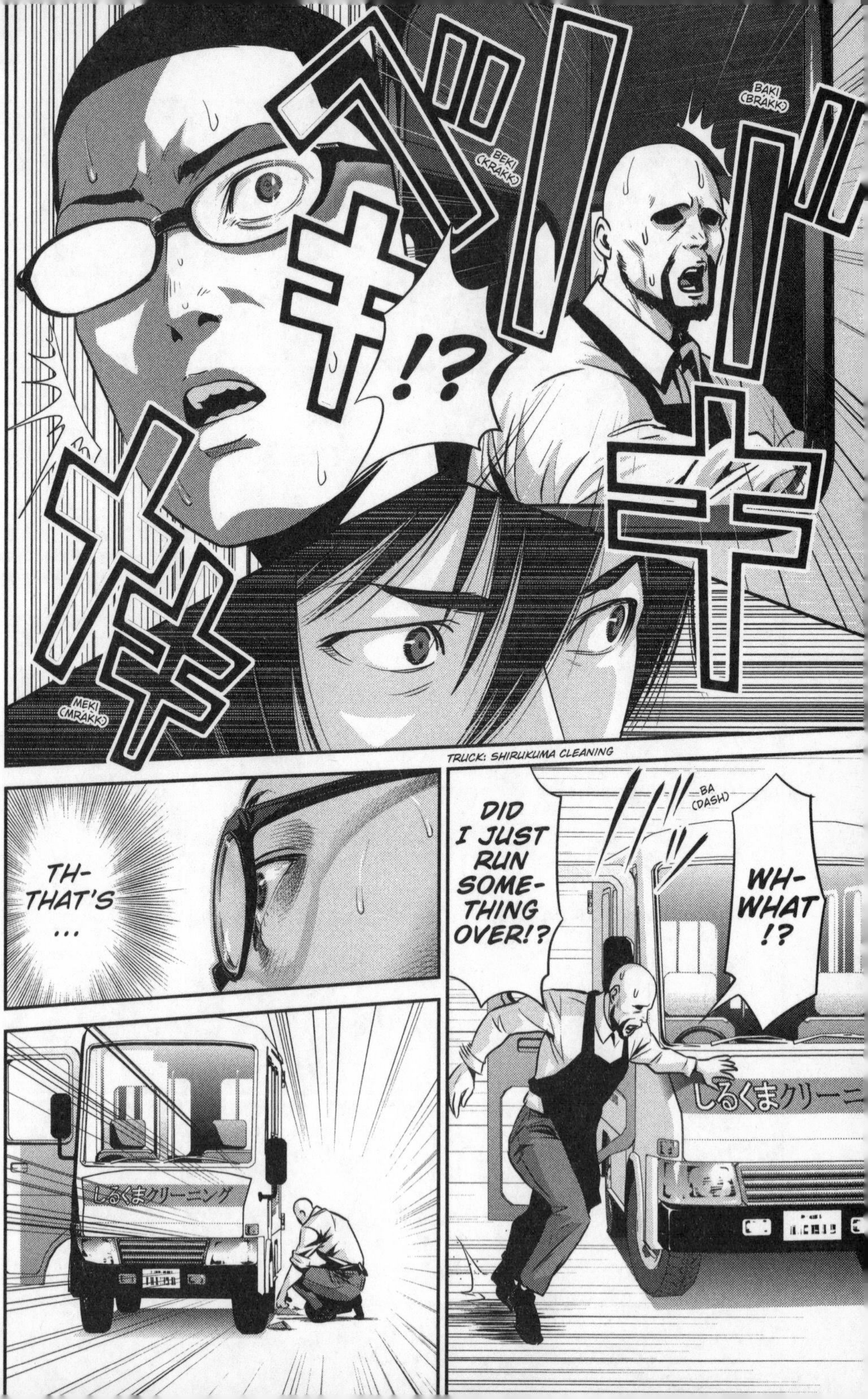
BAKI (BRAKK)
BEKI (KRAKK)
!?
MEKI (MRAKK)
TRUCK: SHIRUKUMA CLEANING
WH-WHAT!?
BA (DASH)
DID I JUST RUN SOMETHING OVER!?
TH-THAT'S ...
しるくまクリーニング

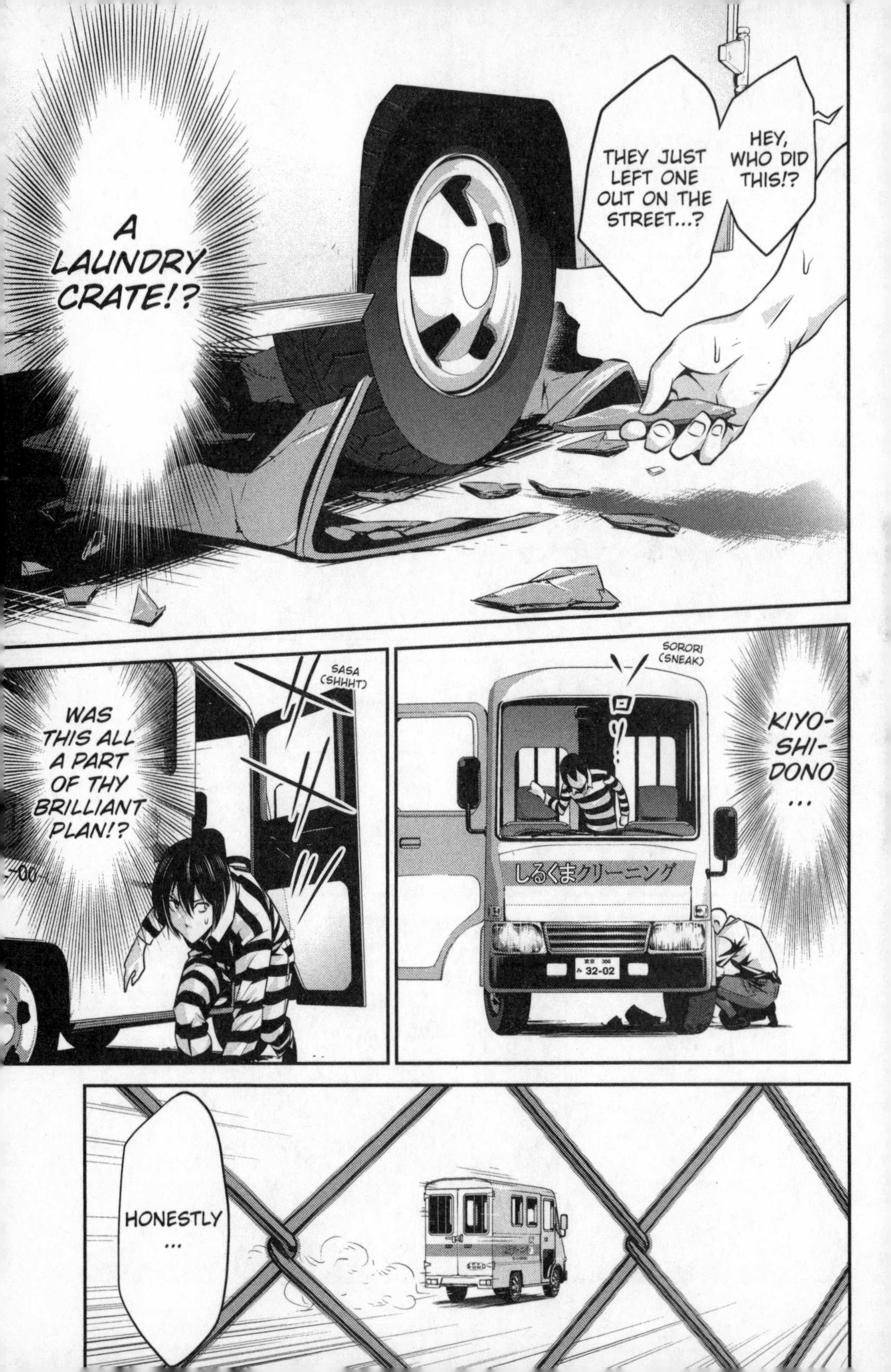
HEY, WHO DID THIS!?
THEY JUST LEFT ONE OUT ON THE STREET...?
A LAUNDRY CRATE!?
KIYO-SHI-DONO ...
SORORI (SNEAK)
しるくまクリーニング
32-02
SASA (SHHHT)
WAS THIS ALL A PART OF THY BRILLIANT PLAN!?
HONESTLY ...

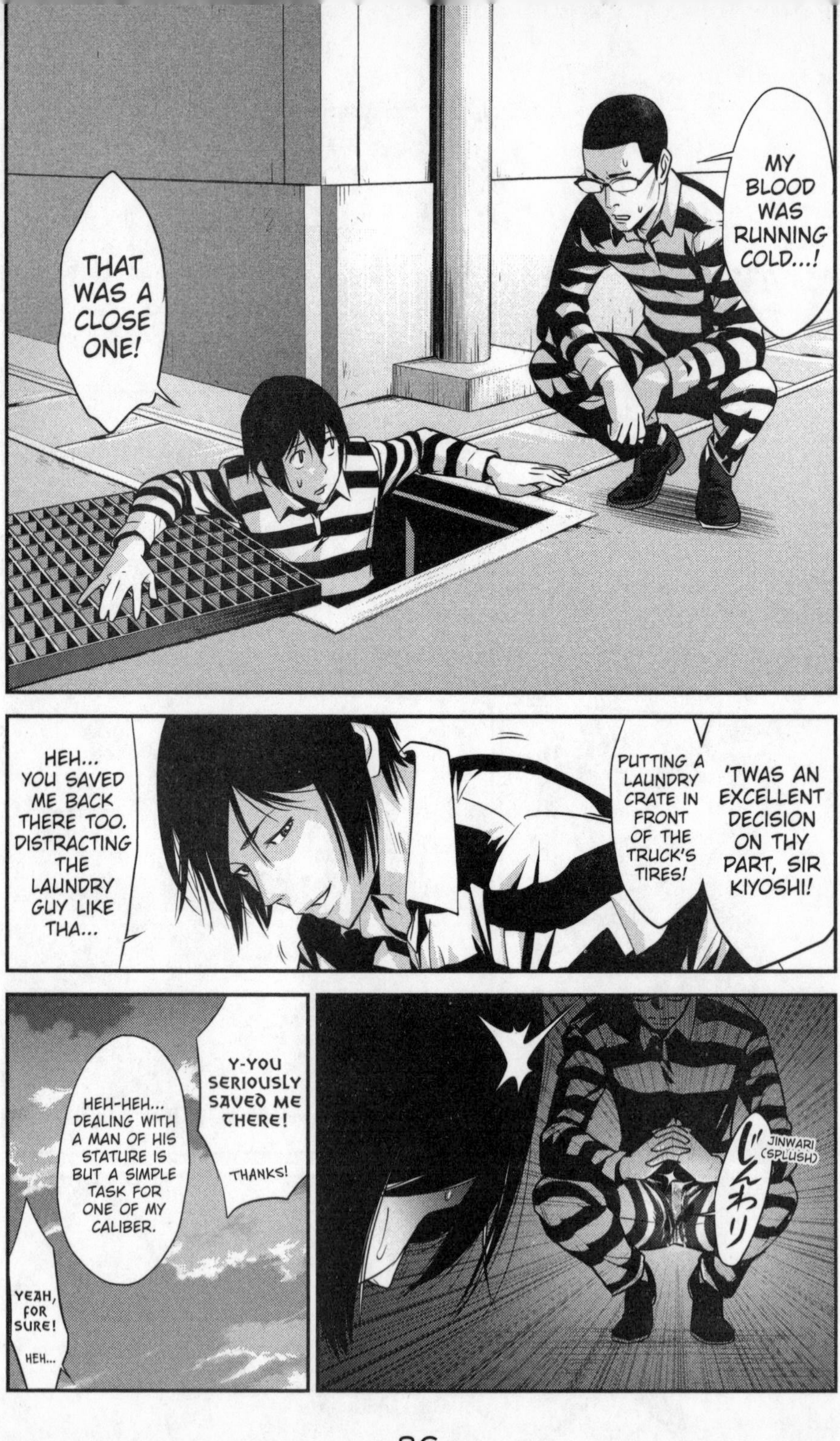
MY BLOOD WAS RUNNING COLD...!
THAT WAS A CLOSE ONE!
'TWAS AN EXCELLENT DECISION ON THY PART, SIR KIYOSHI!
PUTTING A LAUNDRY CRATE IN FRONT OF THE TRUCK'S TIRES!
HEH... YOU SAVED ME BACK THERE TOO. DISTRACTING THE LAUNDRY GUY LIKE THA...
じんわり
JINWARI (SPLUSH)
Y-YOU SERIOUSLY SAVED ME THERE!
THANKS!
HEH-HEH... DEALING WITH A MAN OF HIS STATURE IS BUT A SIMPLE TASK FOR ONE OF MY CALIBER.
YEAH, FOR SURE!
HEH...

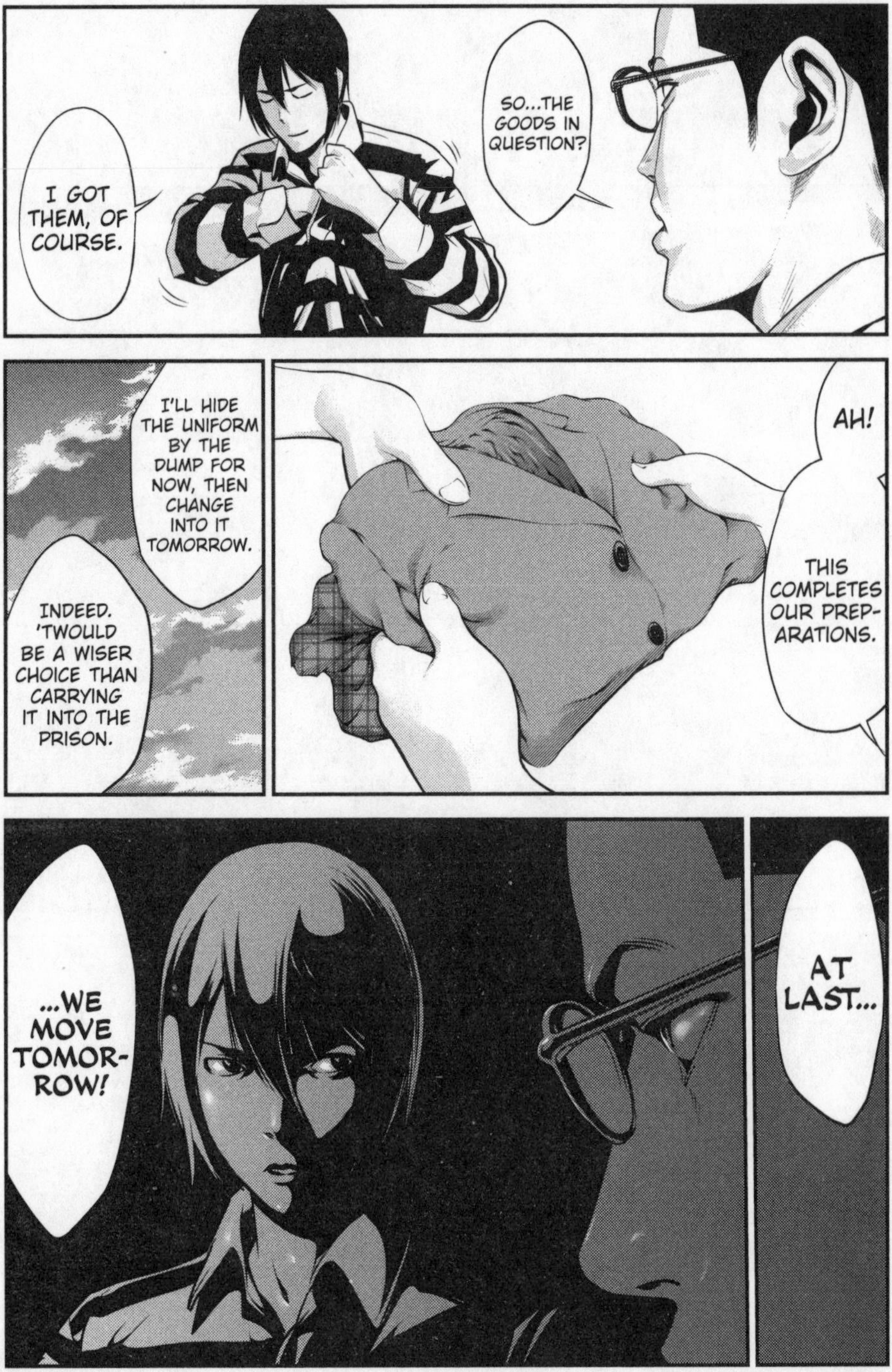
SO...THE GOODS IN QUESTION?
I GOT THEM, OF COURSE.
AH!
THIS COMPLETES OUR PREP-ARATIONS.
I'LL HIDE THE UNIFORM BY THE DUMP FOR NOW, THEN CHANGE INTO IT TOMORROW.
INDEED. 'TWOULD BE A WISER CHOICE THAN CARRYING IT INTO THE PRISON.
AT LAST...
...WE MOVE TOMOR-ROW!

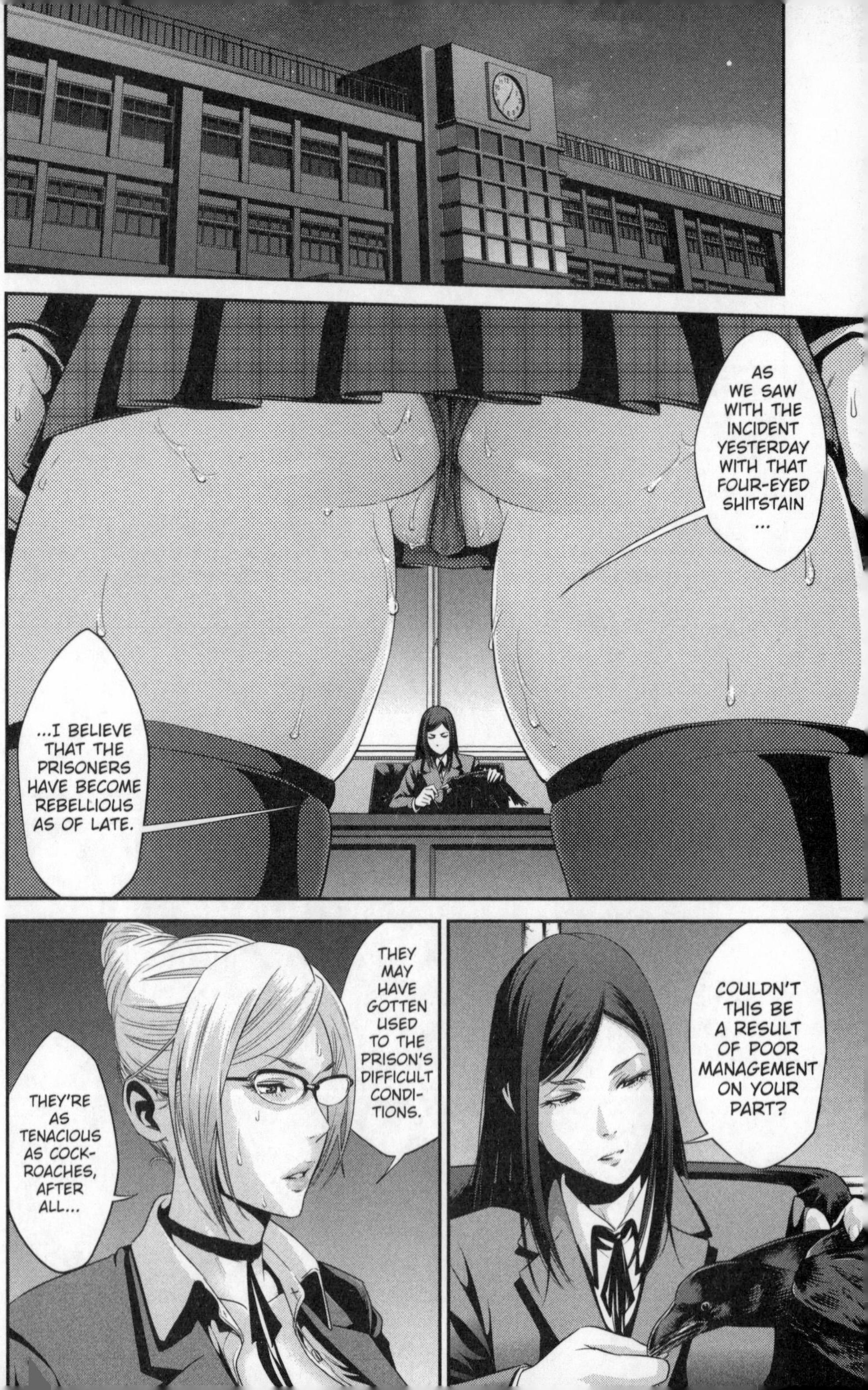
AS WE SAW WITH THE INCIDENT YESTERDAY WITH THAT FOUR-EYED SHITSTAIN ...
...I BELIEVE THAT THE PRISONERS HAVE BECOME REBELLIOUS AS OF LATE.
COULDN'T THIS BE A RESULT OF POOR MANAGEMENT ON YOUR PART?
THEY MAY HAVE GOTTEN USED TO THE PRISON'S DIFFICULT CONDI-TIONS.
THEY'RE AS TENACIOUS AS COCK-ROACHES, AFTER ALL...

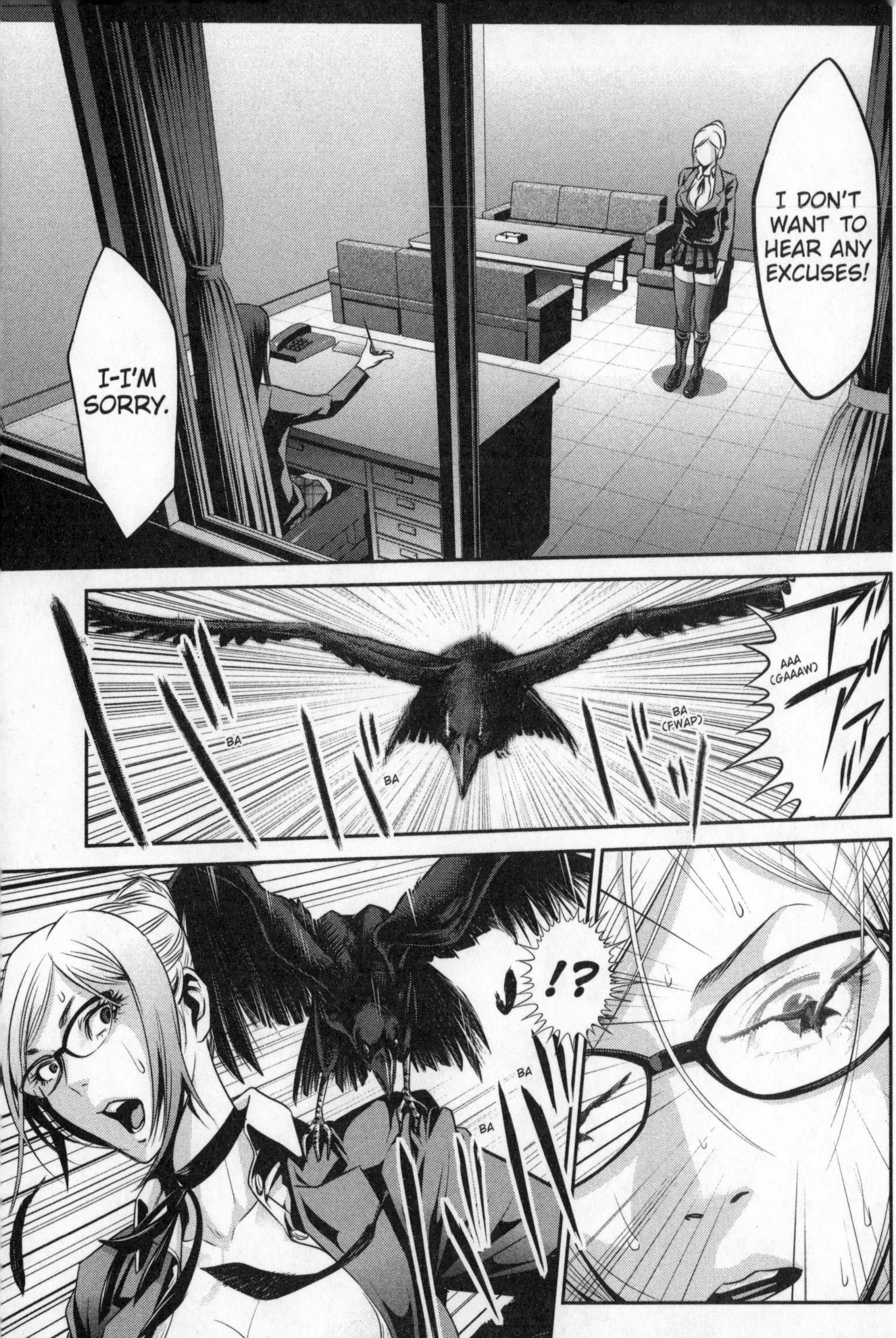
I DON'T WANT TO HEAR ANY EXCUSES!
I-I'M SORRY.
AAA (GAAAW)
BA (FWAP)
BA
BA
!?
BA
BA

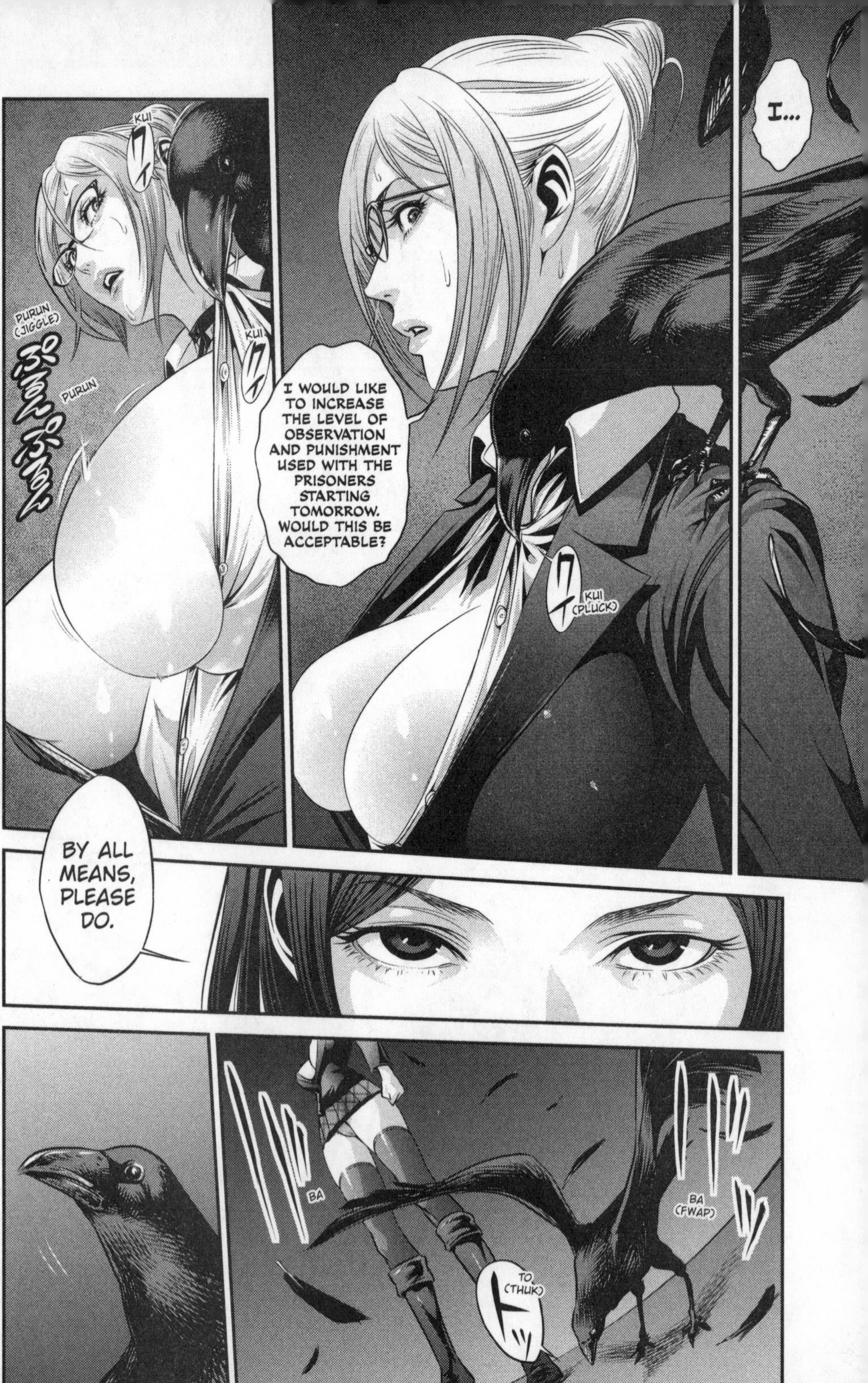

I...
I WOULD LIKE TO INCREASE THE LEVEL OF OBSERVATION AND PUNISHMENT USED WITH THE PRISONERS STARTING TOMORROW. WOULD THIS BE ACCEPTABLE?
KUI (PLUCK)
KUI
KUI
PURUN (JIGGLE)
PURUN
BY ALL MEANS, PLEASE DO.
BA (FWAP)
TO (THUK)
BA

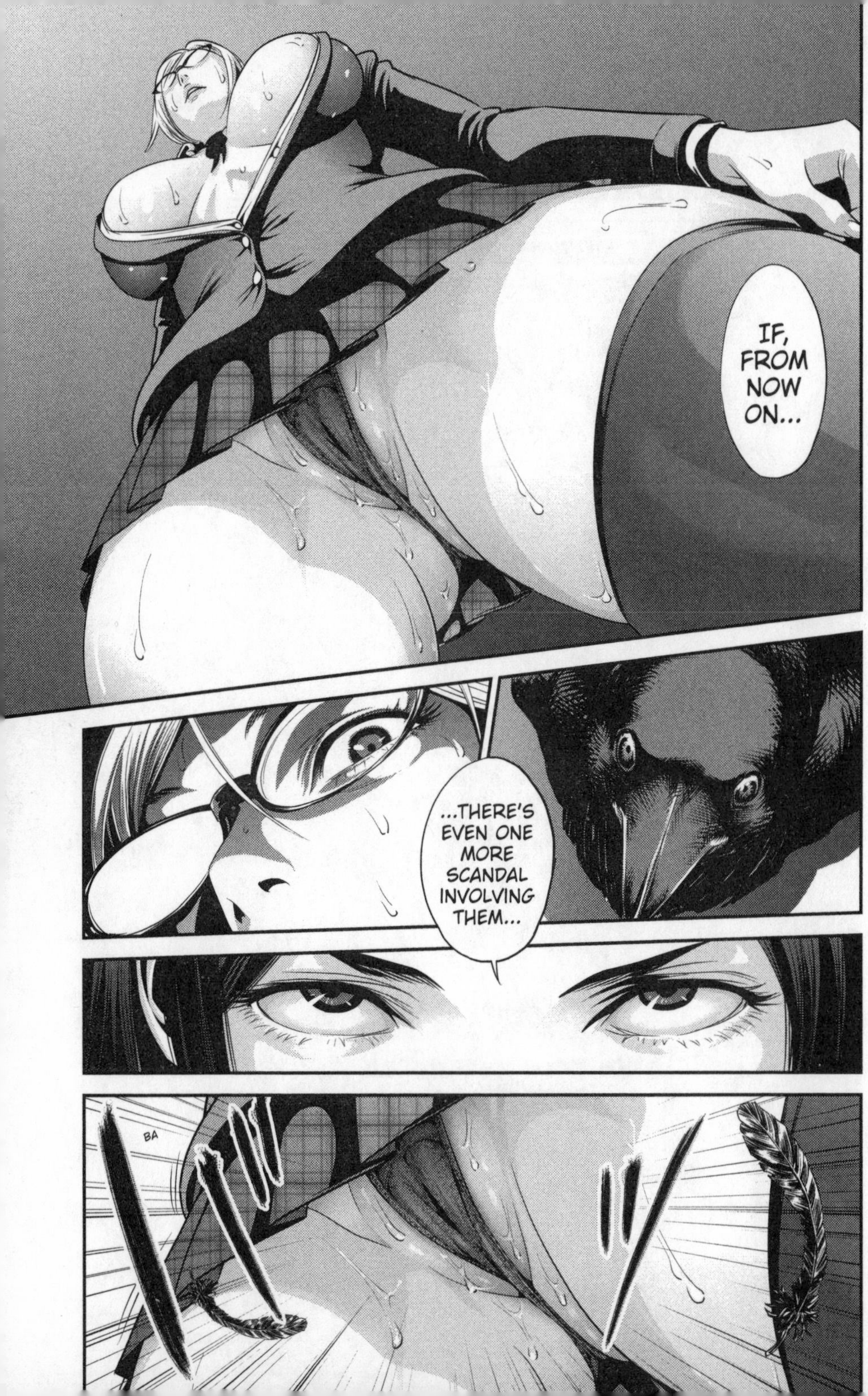
IF, FROM NOW ON...
...THERE'S EVEN ONE MORE SCANDAL INVOLVING THEM...
BA

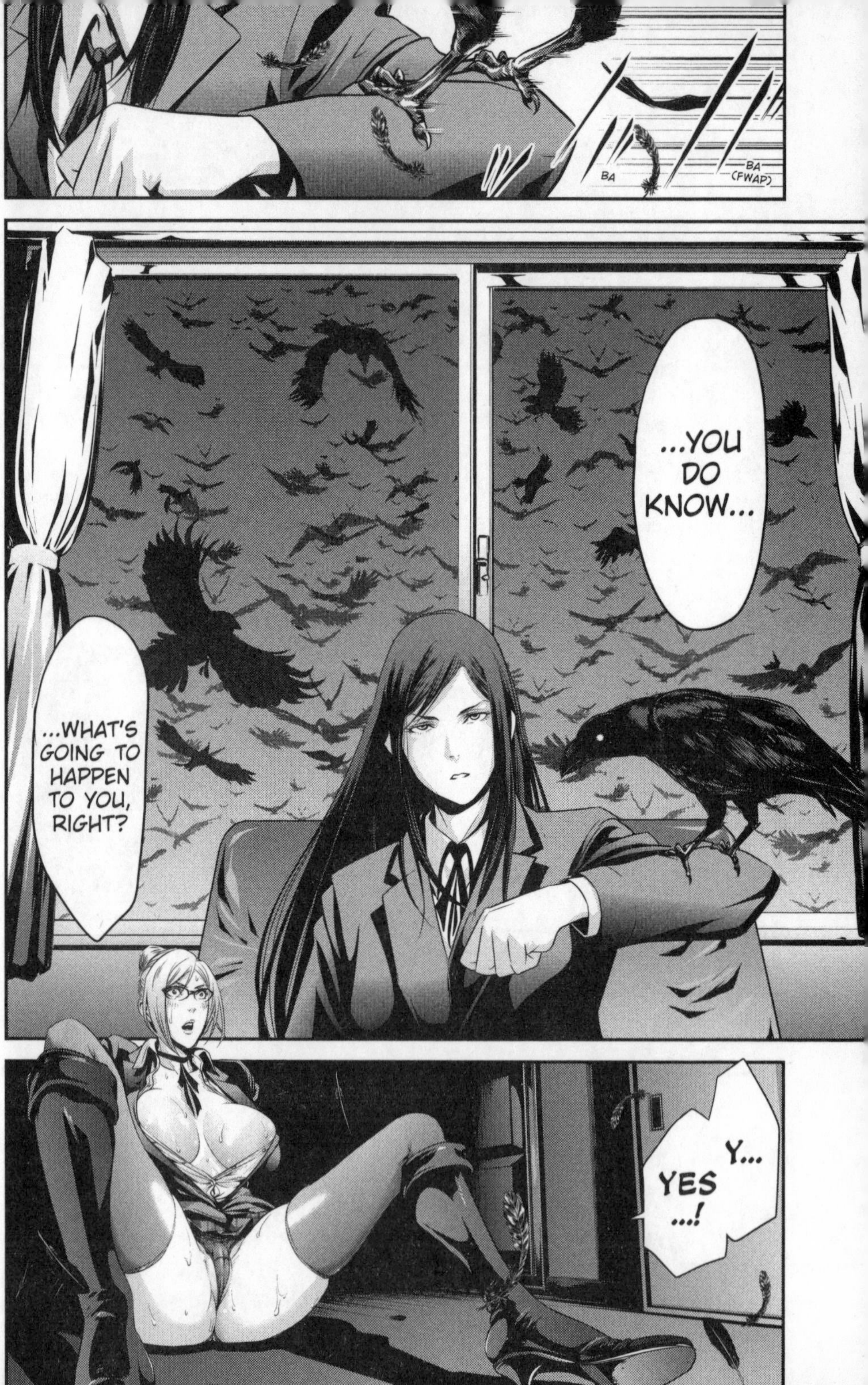
BA
(FWAP)
BA
...YOU DO KNOW...
...WHAT'S GOING TO HAPPEN TO YOU, RIGHT?
Y... YES ...!

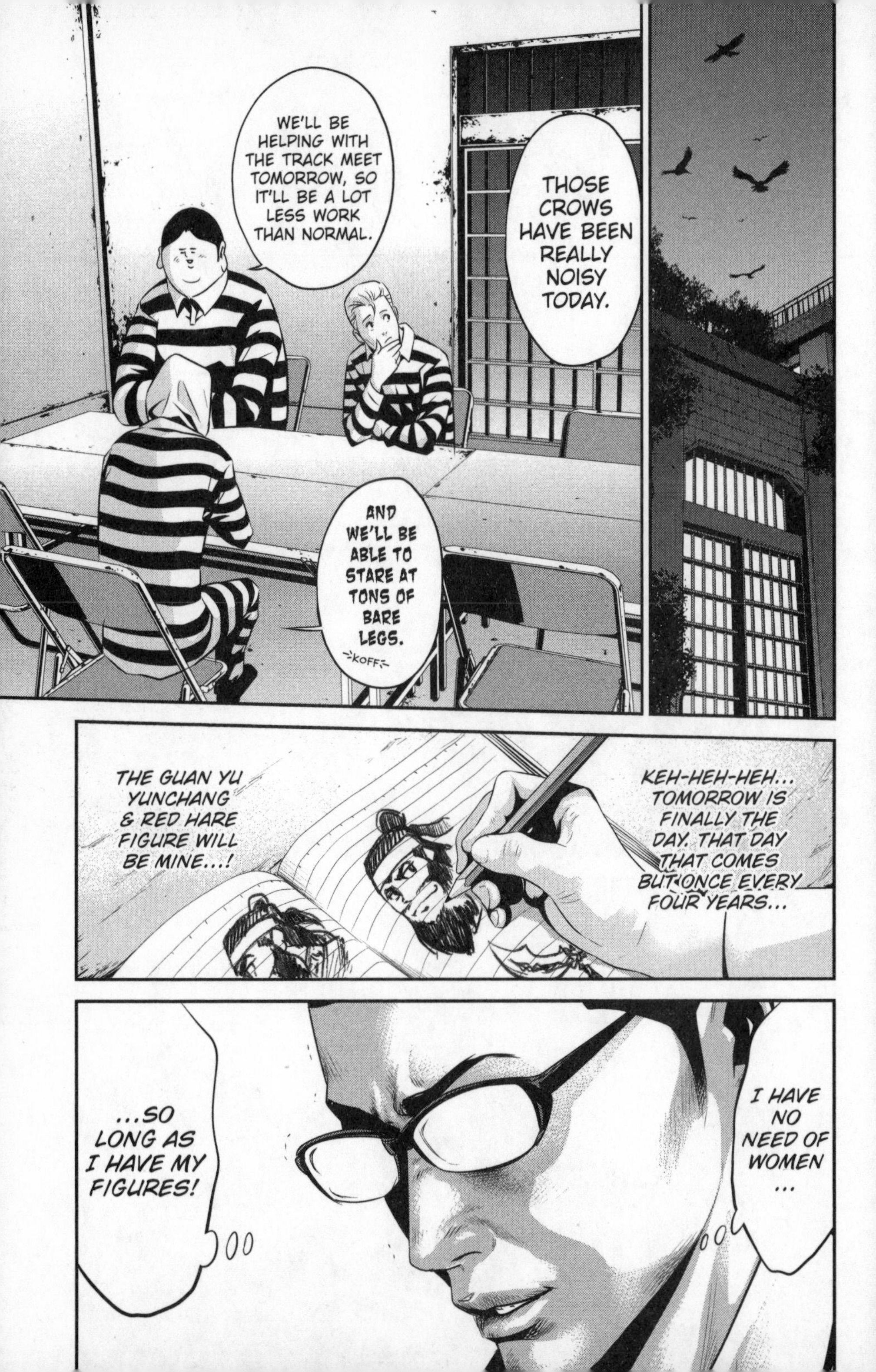
THOSE CROWS HAVE BEEN REALLY NOISY TODAY.
WE'LL BE HELPING WITH THE TRACK MEET TOMORROW, SO IT'LL BE A LOT LESS WORK THAN NORMAL.
AND WE'LL BE ABLE TO STARE AT TONS OF BARE LEGS.
KOFF
KEH-HEH-HEH... TOMORROW IS FINALLY THE DAY. THAT DAY THAT COMES BUT ONCE EVERY FOUR YEARS...
THE GUAN YU YUNCHANG & RED HARE FIGURE WILL BE MINE...!
I HAVE NO NEED OF WOMEN...
...SO LONG AS I HAVE MY FIGURES!

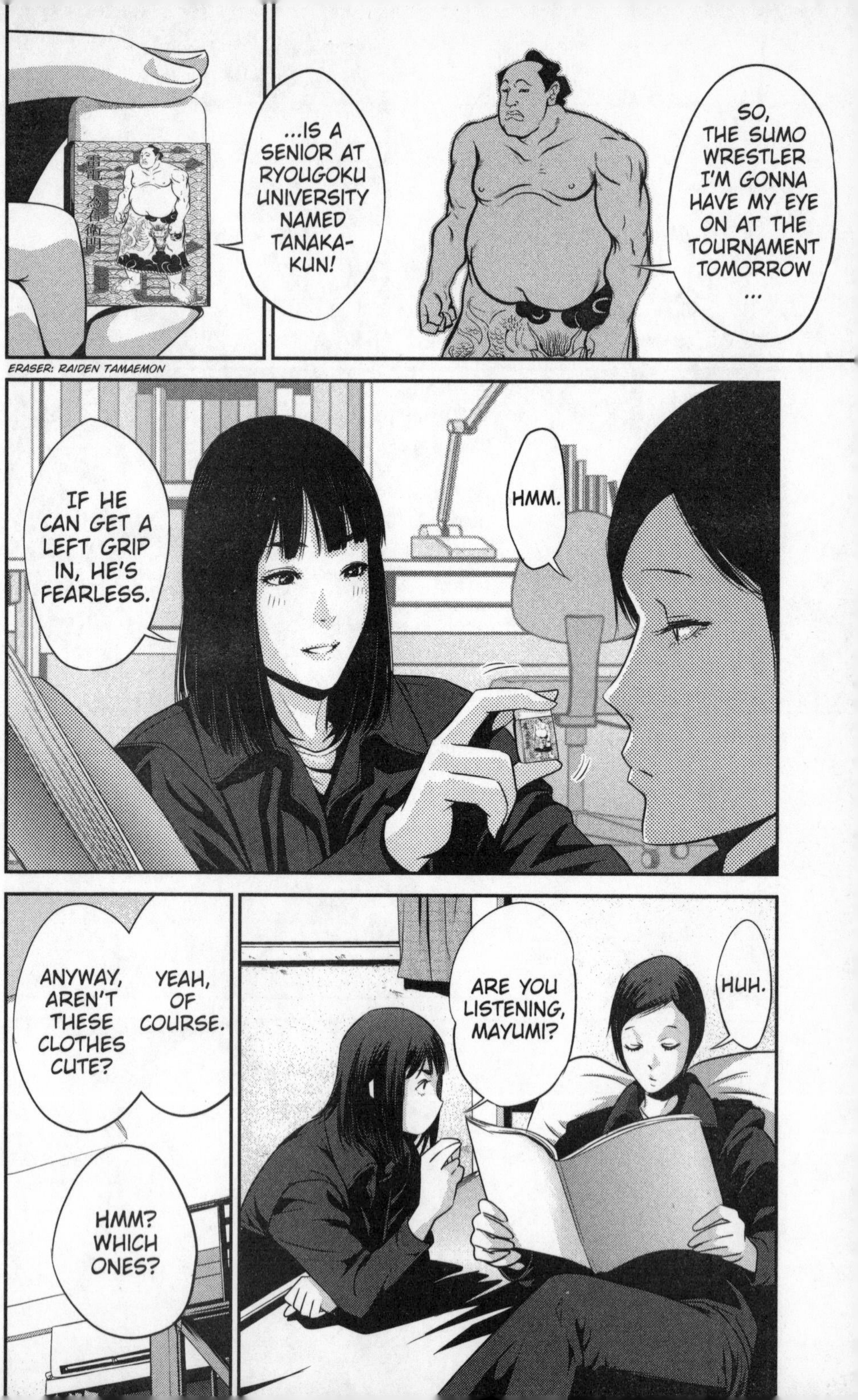
SO, THE SUMO WRESTLER I'M GONNA HAVE MY EYE ON AT THE TOURNAMENT TOMORROW ...
...IS A SENIOR AT RYOUGOKU UNIVERSITY NAMED TANAKA-KUN!
雷電 為右衛門
ERASER: RAIDEN TAMAEMON
IF HE CAN GET A LEFT GRIP IN, HE'S FEARLESS.
HMM.
HUH.
ARE YOU LISTENING, MAYUMI?
YEAH, OF COURSE.
ANYWAY, AREN'T THESE CLOTHES CUTE?
HMM? WHICH ONES?

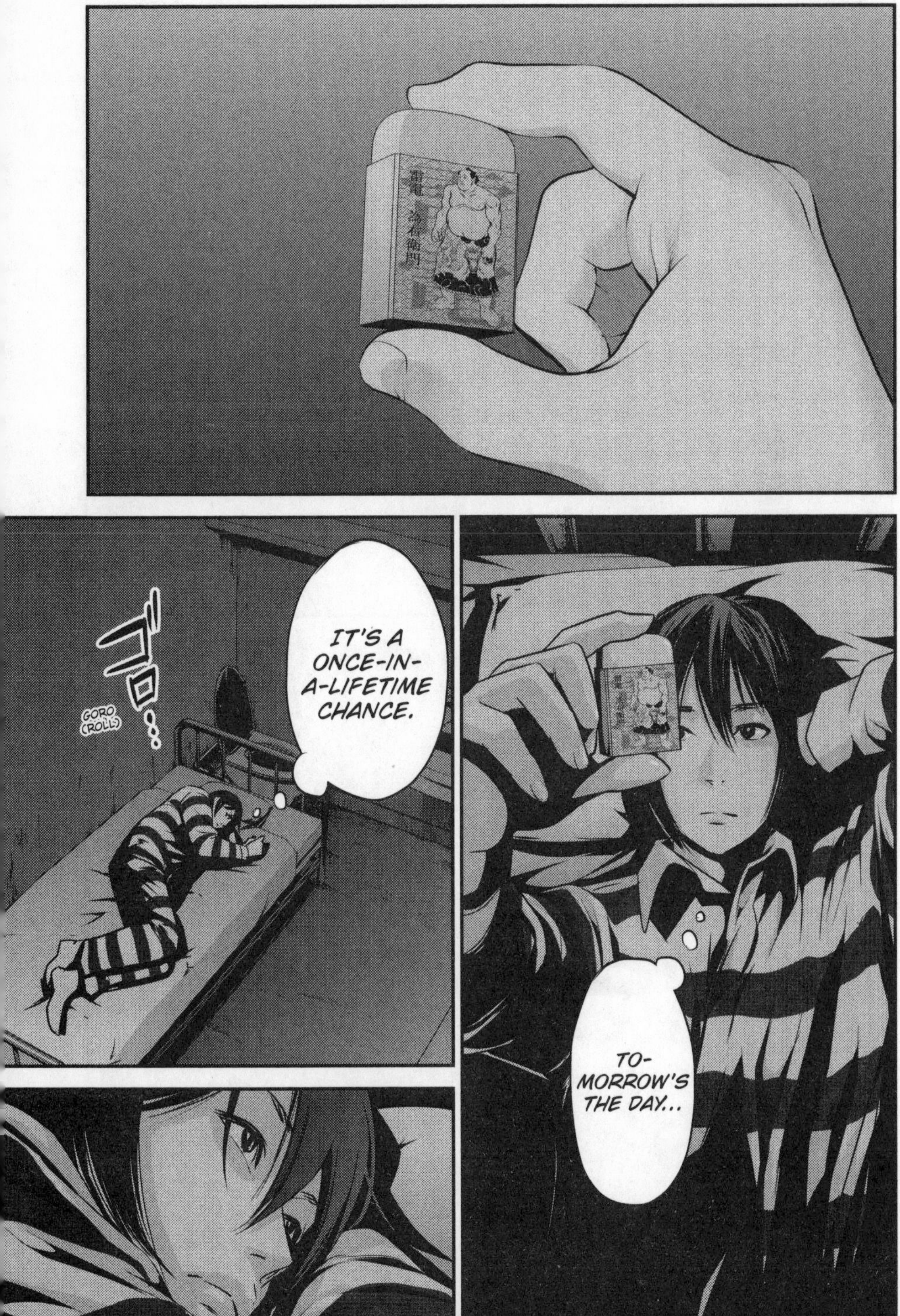
ゴロ…
GORO (ROLL)
IT'S A ONCE-IN-A-LIFETIME CHANCE.
TO-MORROW'S THE DAY...

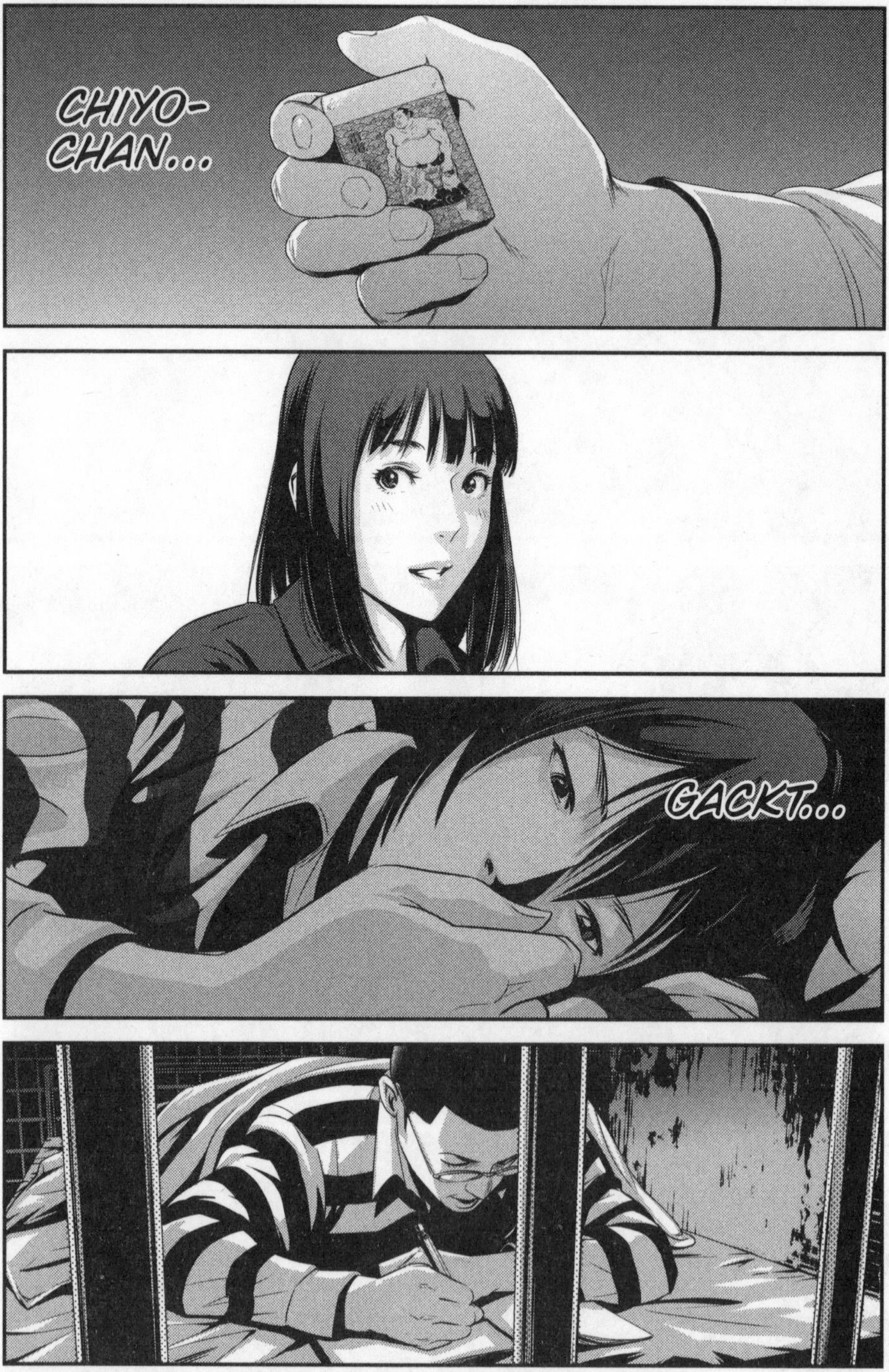
CHIYO-
CHAN...
GACKT...

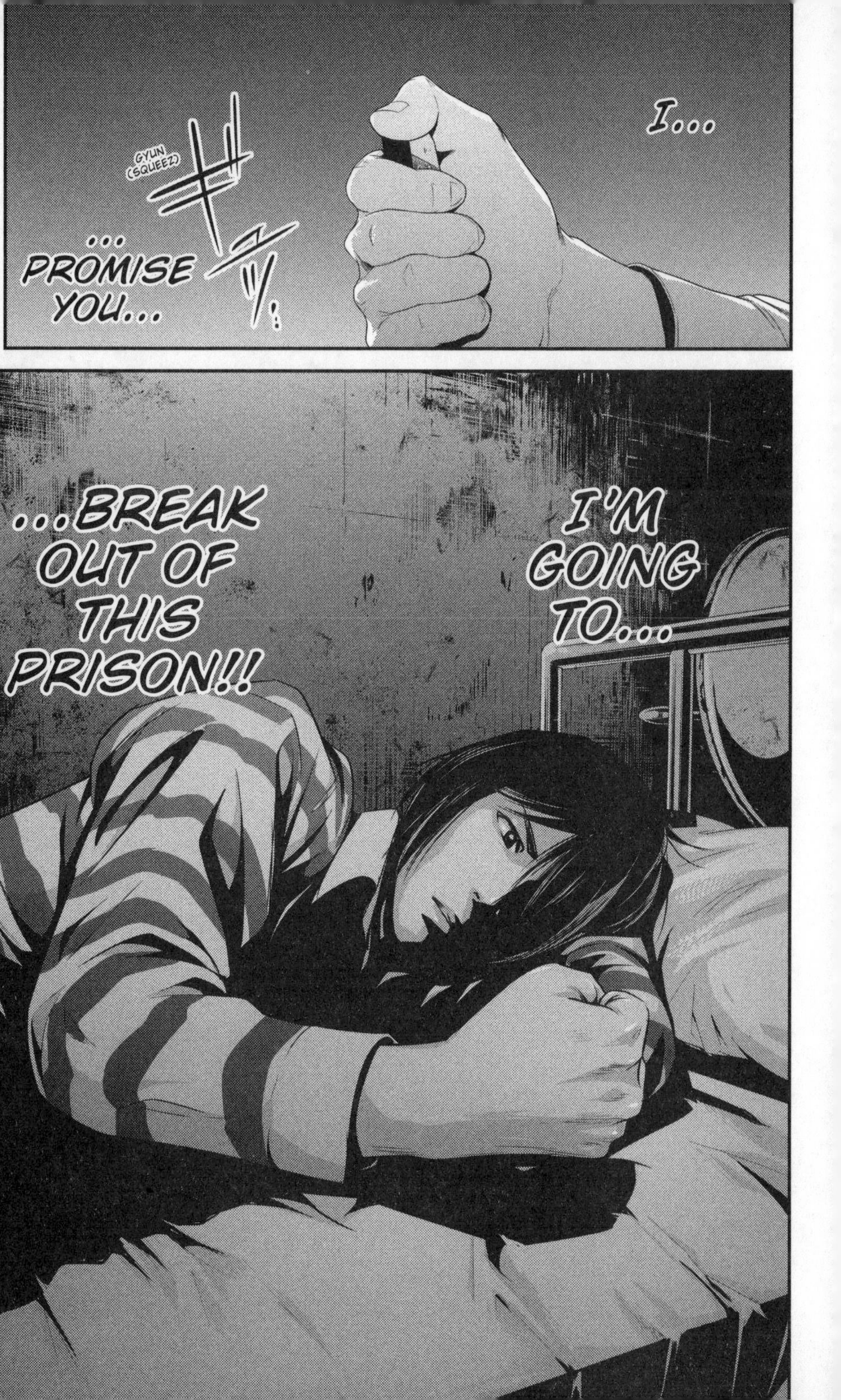
I...
GYUN (SQUEEZ)
...PROMISE YOU...
I'M GOING TO...
...BREAK OUT OF THIS PRISON!!

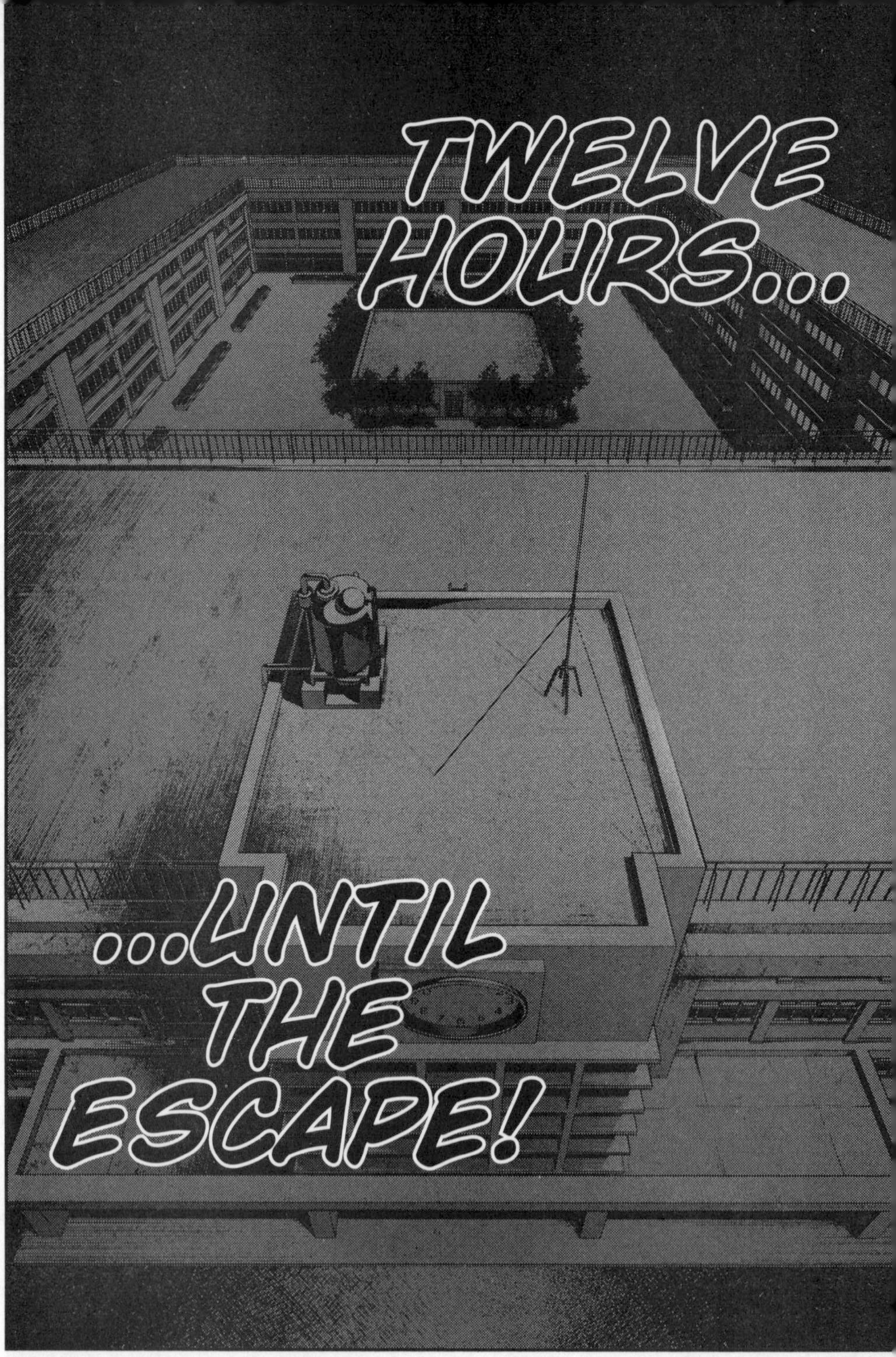
TWELVE HOURS...
...UNTIL THE ESCAPE!

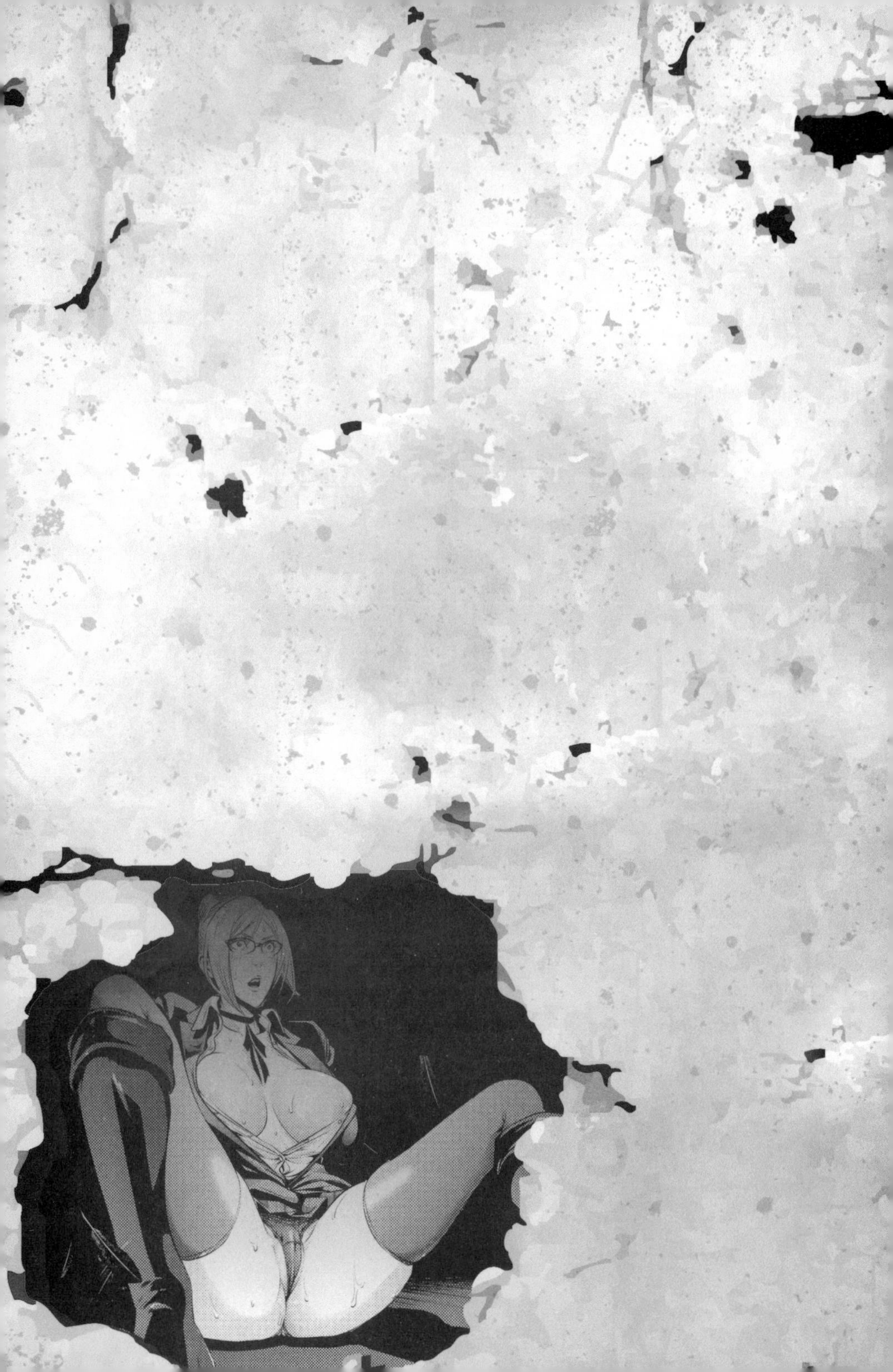

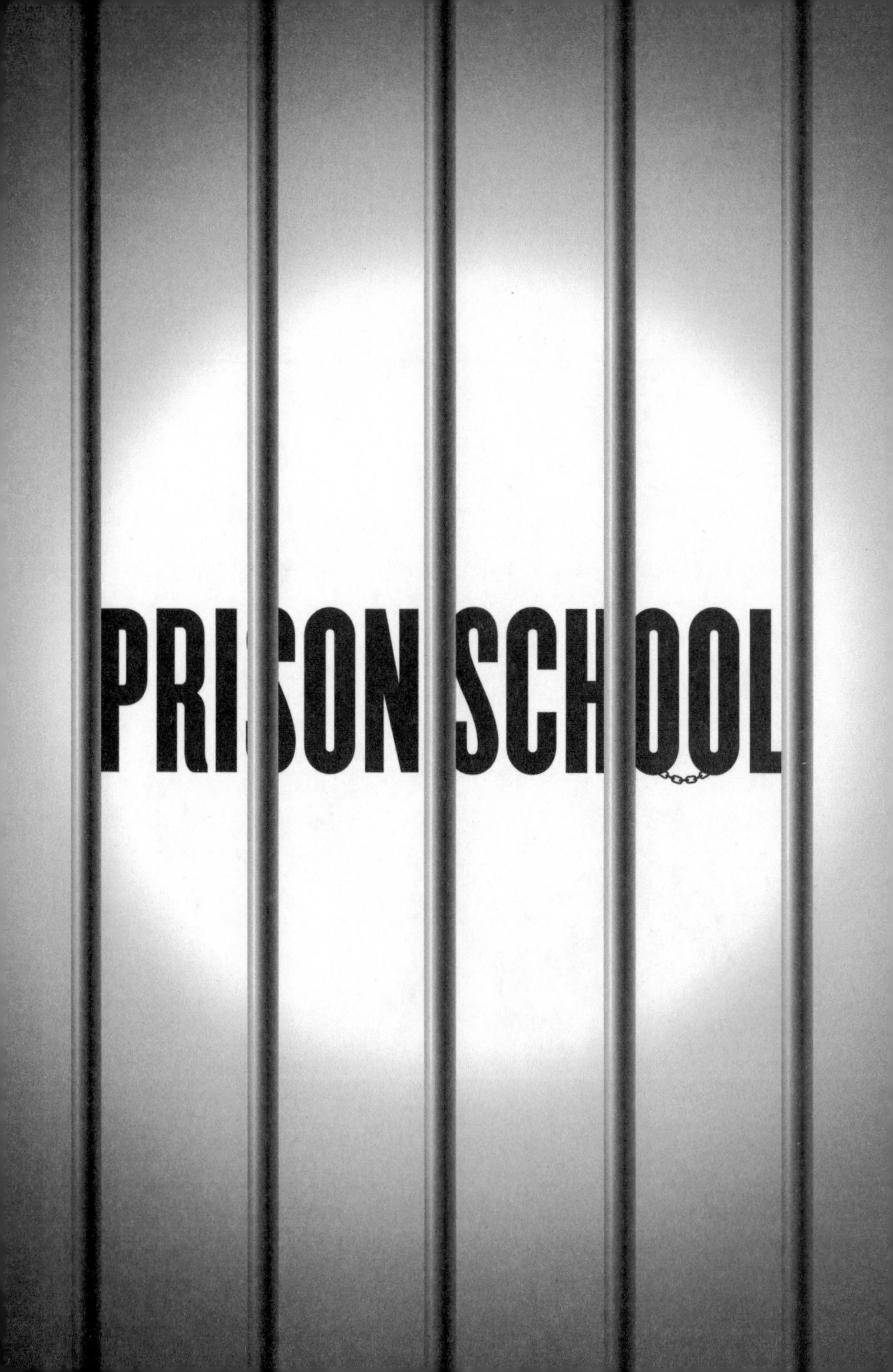
PRISON SCHOOL

よリ
YORI (TWIST)
よリ
YORI
GOSO (RUSTLE)
ゴソ
KYU (SQUEEZ)
キュッ

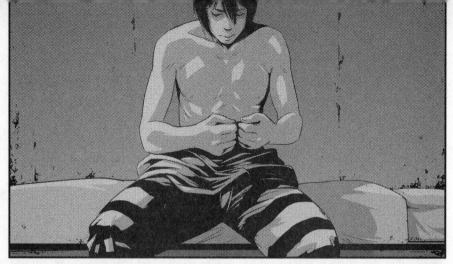

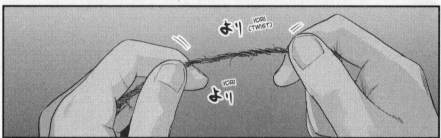

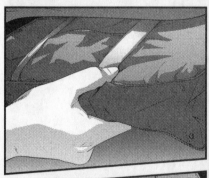

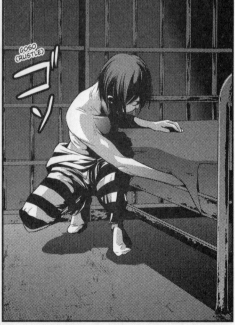

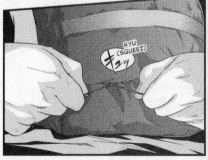

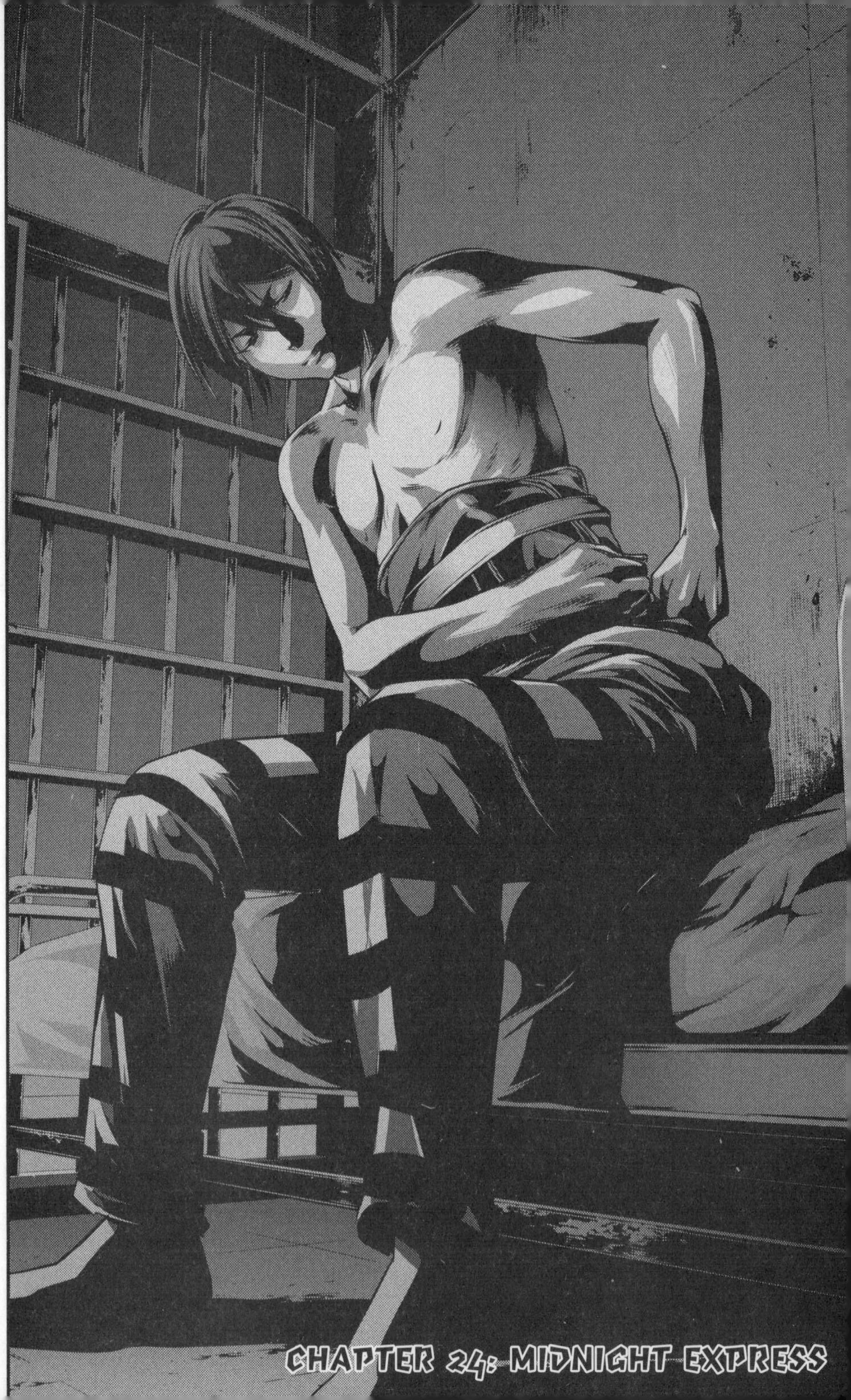
CHAPTER 24: MIDNIGHT EXPRESS

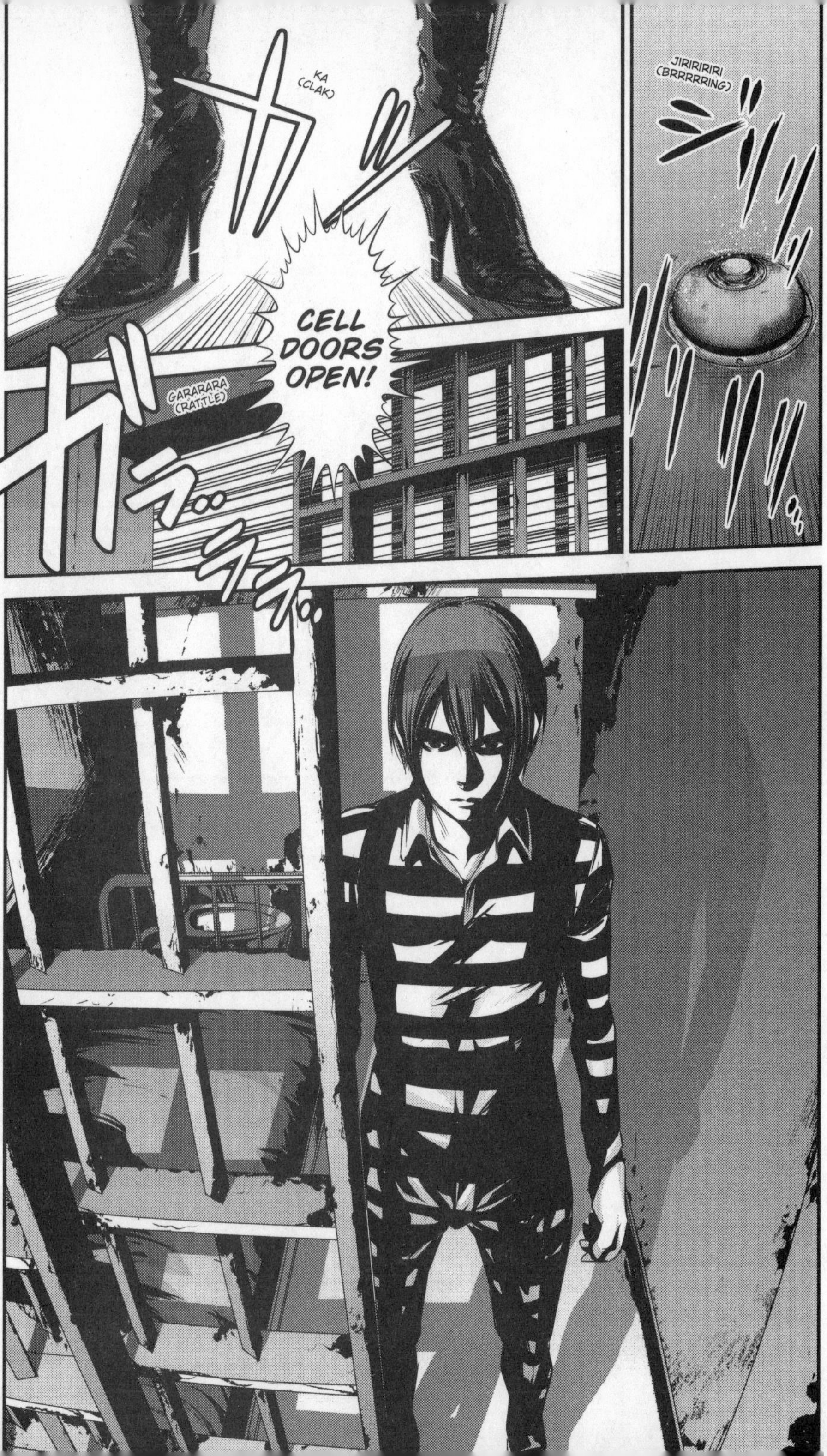
JIRIRIRIRI
(BRRRRRING)
KA
(CLAK)
CELL DOORS OPEN!
GARARARA
(RATTLE)

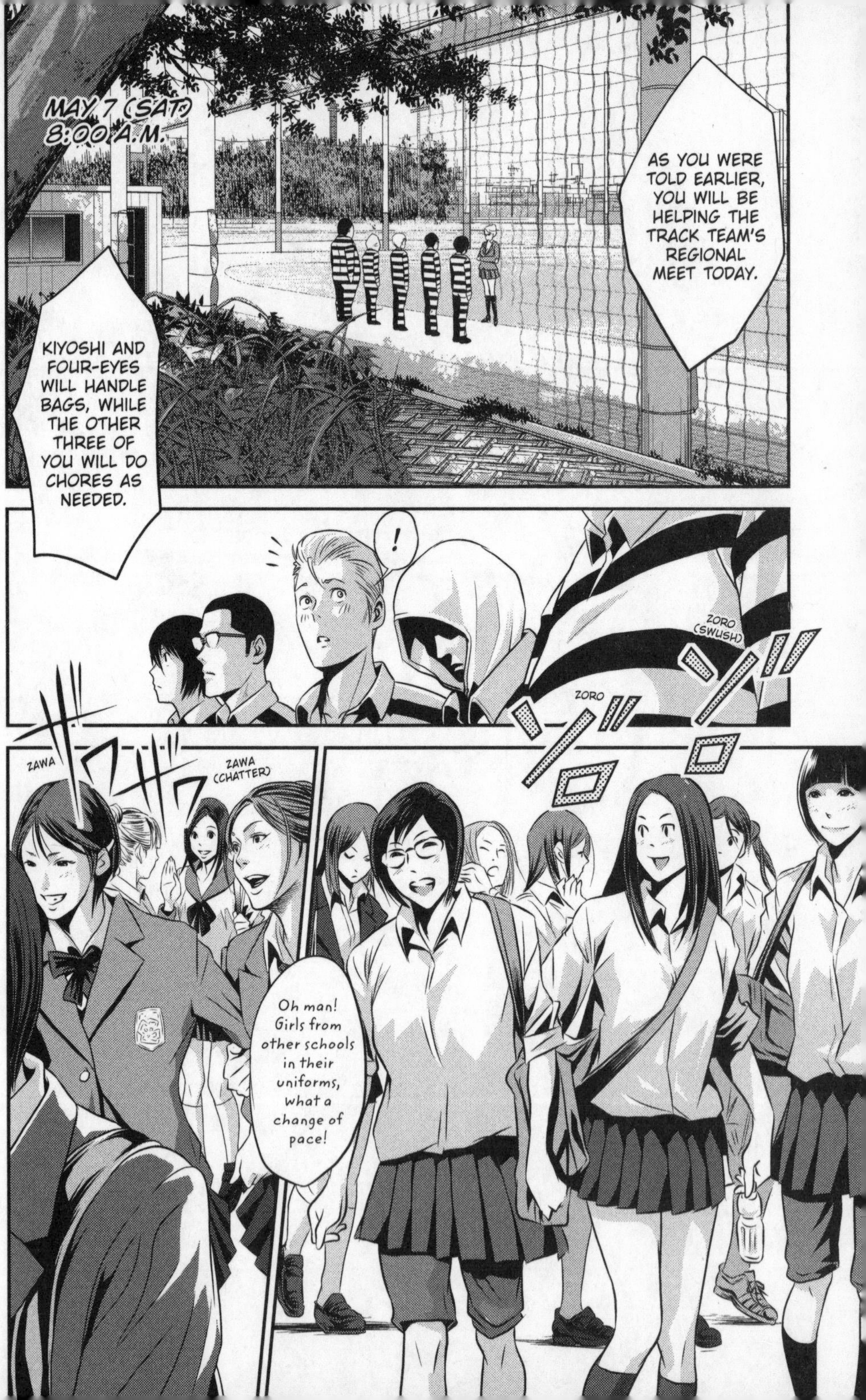
MAY 7 (SAT) 8:00 A.M.
AS YOU WERE TOLD EARLIER, YOU WILL BE HELPING THE TRACK TEAM'S REGIONAL MEET TODAY.
KIYOSHI AND FOUR-EYES WILL HANDLE BAGS, WHILE THE OTHER THREE OF YOU WILL DO CHORES AS NEEDED.
!
ZORO (SWUSH)
ZORO
ZAWA
ZAWA (CHATTER)
Oh man! Girls from other schools in their uniforms, what a change of pace!

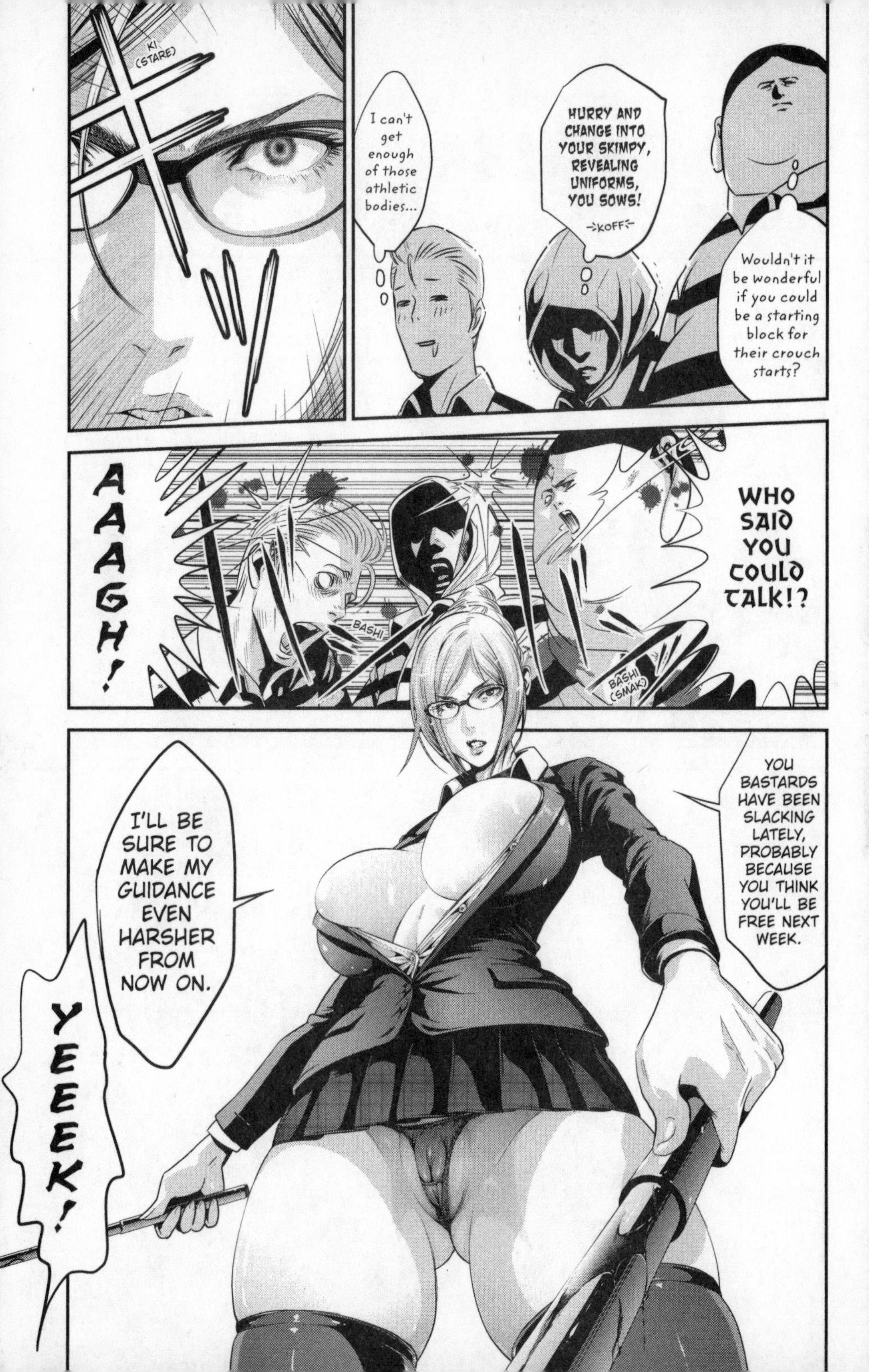
Wouldn't it be wonderful if you could be a starting block for their crouch starts?
HURRY AND CHANGE INTO YOUR SKIMPY, REVEALING UNIFORMS, YOU SOWS!
KOFF
I can't get enough of those athletic bodies...
KI (STARE)
WHO SAID YOU COULD TALK!?
BASHI (SMAK)
BASHI
AAAGH!
YOU BASTARDS HAVE BEEN SLACKING LATELY, PROBABLY BECAUSE YOU THINK YOU'LL BE FREE NEXT WEEK.
I'LL BE SURE TO MAKE MY GUIDANCE EVEN HARSHER FROM NOW ON.
YEEEK!

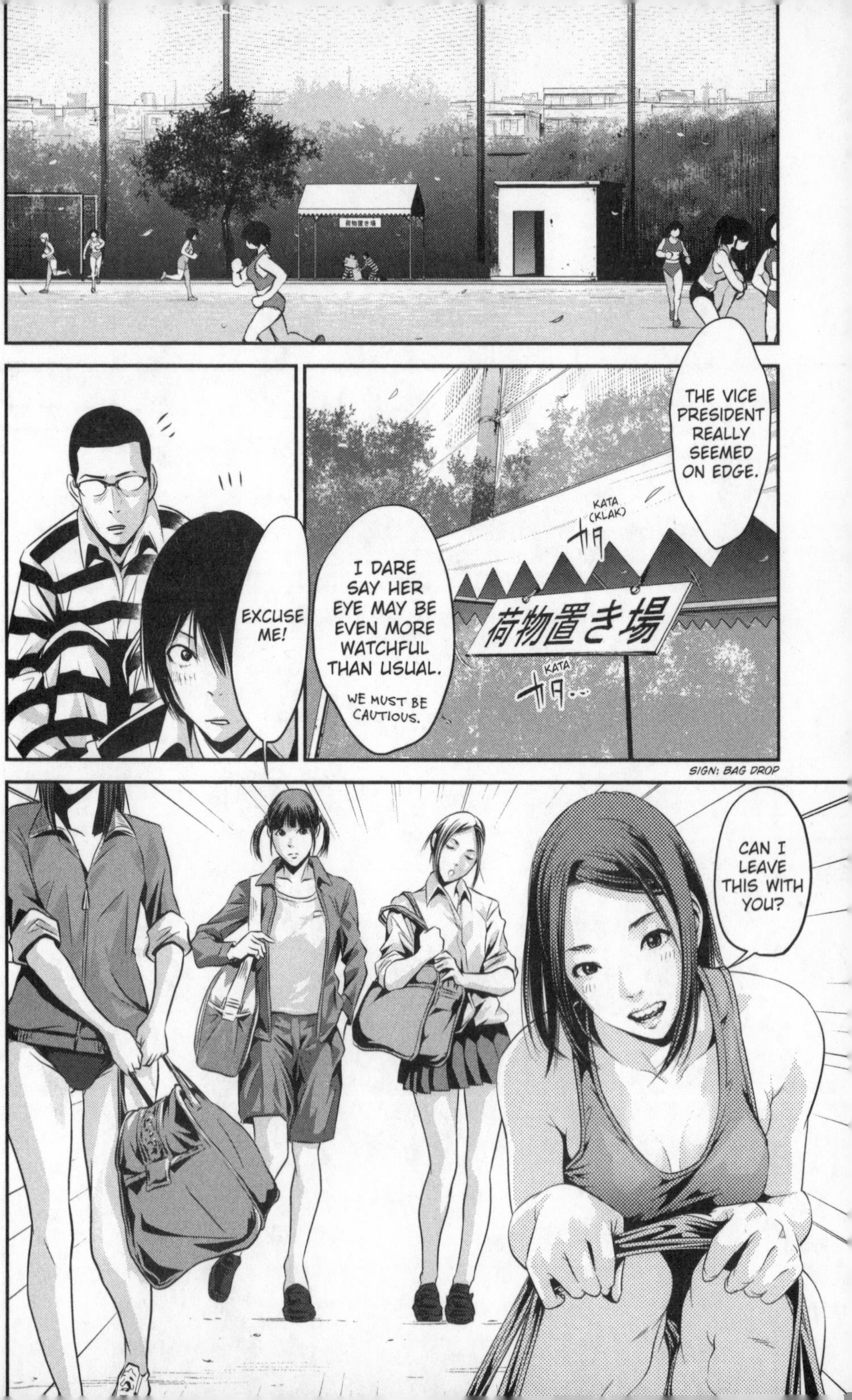
荷物置き場
THE VICE PRESIDENT REALLY SEEMED ON EDGE.
KATA (KLAK)
カタ
荷物置き場
I DARE SAY HER EYE MAY BE EVEN MORE WATCHFUL THAN USUAL.
WE MUST BE CAUTIOUS.
KATA
カタ…
EXCUSE ME!
SIGN: BAG DROP
CAN I LEAVE THIS WITH YOU?

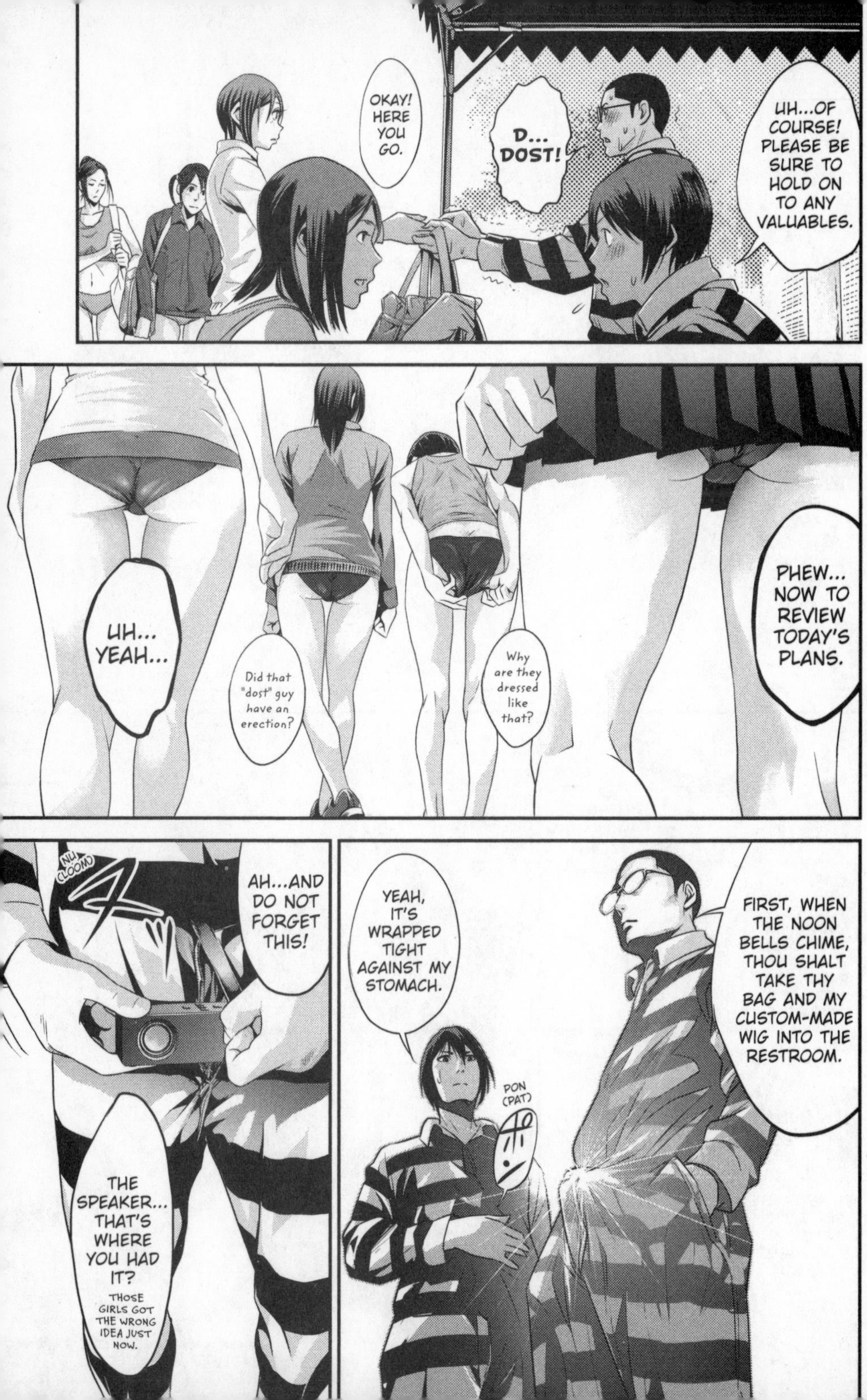
UH...OF COURSE! PLEASE BE SURE TO HOLD ON TO ANY VALUABLES.
D... DOST!
OKAY! HERE YOU GO.
PHEW... NOW TO REVIEW TODAY'S PLANS.
Why are they dressed like that?
Did that "dost" guy have an erection?
UH... YEAH...
FIRST, WHEN THE NOON BELLS CHIME, THOU SHALT TAKE THY BAG AND MY CUSTOM-MADE WIG INTO THE RESTROOM.
PON (PAT)
YEAH, IT'S WRAPPED TIGHT AGAINST MY STOMACH.
AH...AND DO NOT FORGET THIS!
NU (LOOM)
THE SPEAKER... THAT'S WHERE YOU HAD IT?
THOSE GIRLS GOT THE WRONG IDEA JUST NOW.

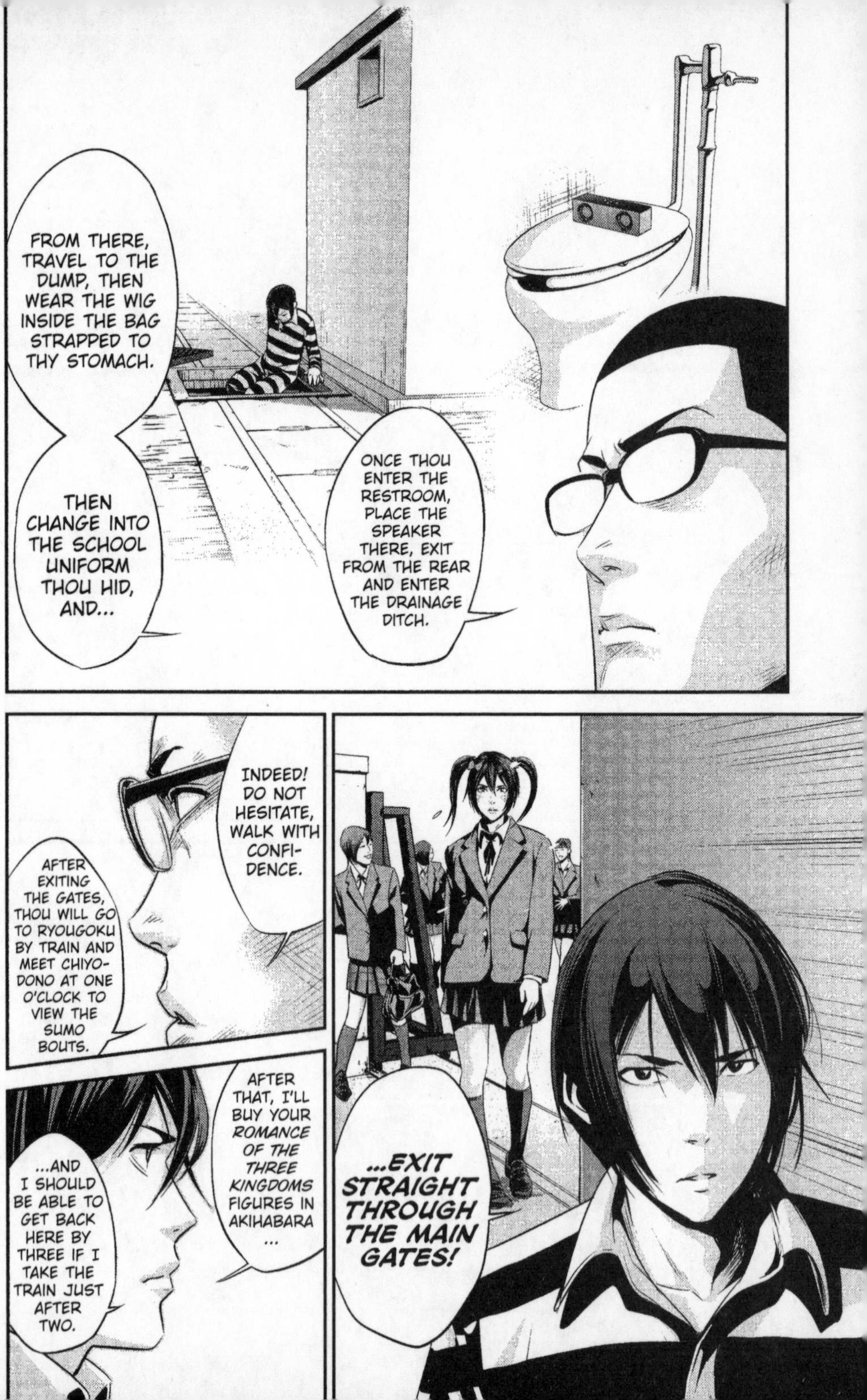
ONCE THOU ENTER THE RESTROOM, PLACE THE SPEAKER THERE, EXIT FROM THE REAR AND ENTER THE DRAINAGE DITCH.
FROM THERE, TRAVEL TO THE DUMP, THEN WEAR THE WIG INSIDE THE BAG STRAPPED TO THY STOMACH.
THEN CHANGE INTO THE SCHOOL UNIFORM THOU HID, AND...
...EXIT STRAIGHT THROUGH THE MAIN GATES!
INDEED! DO NOT HESITATE, WALK WITH CONFI-DENCE.
AFTER EXITING THE GATES, THOU WILL GO TO RYOUGOKU BY TRAIN AND MEET CHIYO-DONO AT ONE O'CLOCK TO VIEW THE SUMO BOUTS.
AFTER THAT, I'LL BUY YOUR *ROMANCE OF THE THREE KINGDOMS* FIGURES IN AKIHABARA ...
...AND I SHOULD BE ABLE TO GET BACK HERE BY THREE IF I TAKE THE TRAIN JUST AFTER TWO.

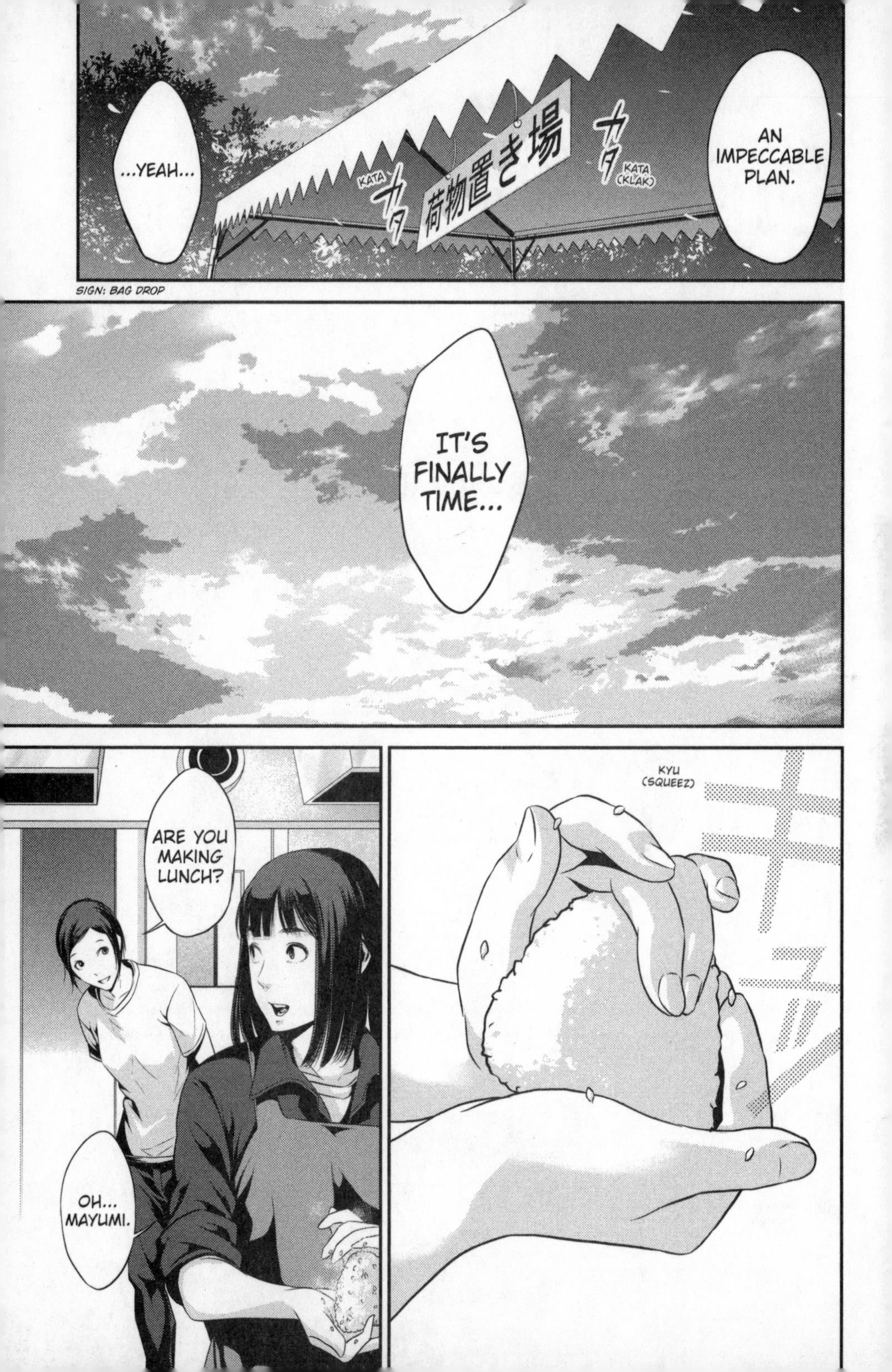
AN IMPECCABLE PLAN.
KATA (KLAK)
KATA
荷物置き場
...YEAH...
SIGN: BAG DROP
IT'S FINALLY TIME...
KYU (SQUEEZ)
ARE YOU MAKING LUNCH?
OH... MAYUMI.

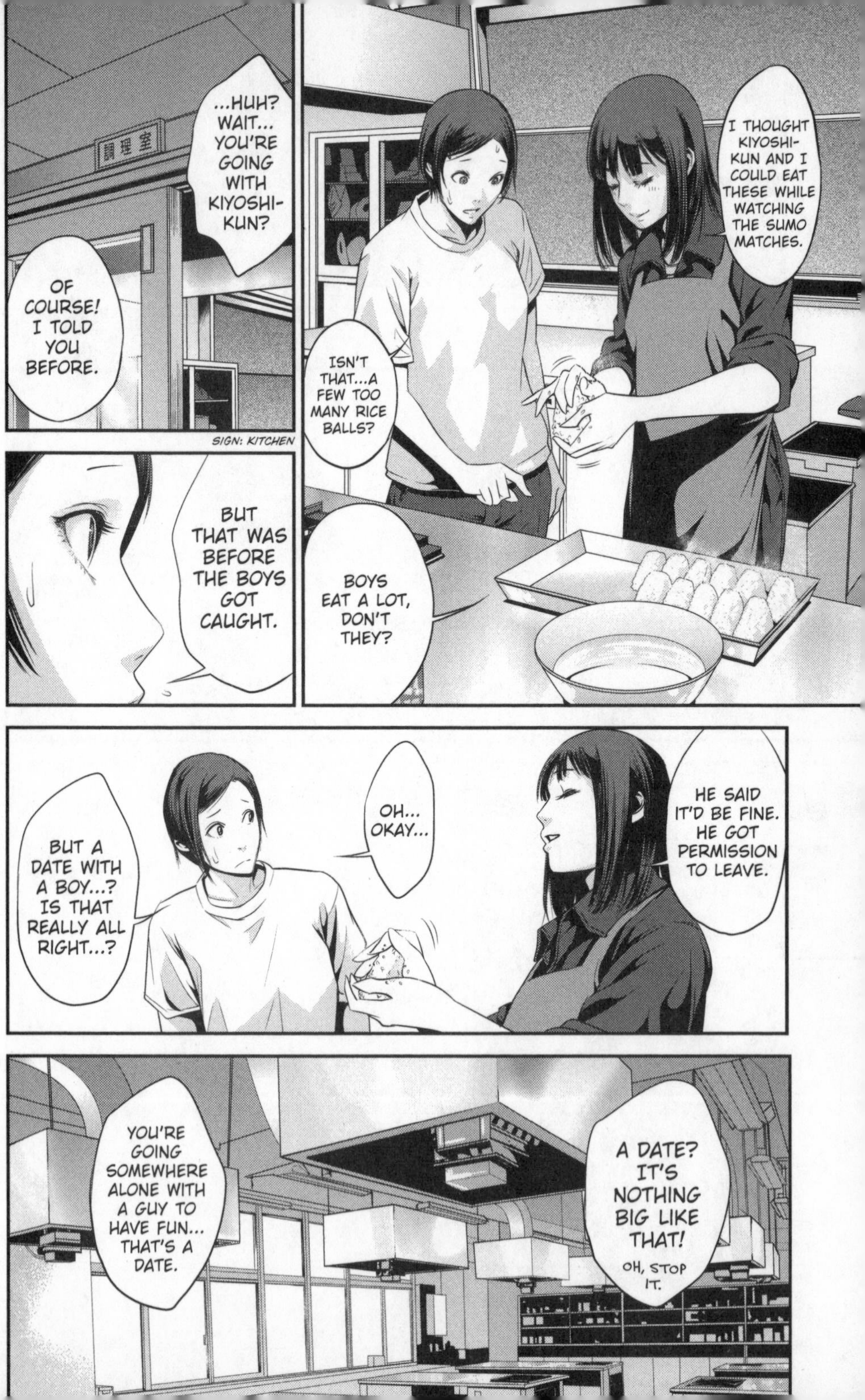
I THOUGHT KIYOSHI-KUN AND I COULD EAT THESE WHILE WATCHING THE SUMO MATCHES.
ISN'T THAT...A FEW TOO MANY RICE BALLS?
BOYS EAT A LOT, DON'T THEY?
調理室
...HUH? WAIT... YOU'RE GOING WITH KIYOSHI-KUN?
OF COURSE! I TOLD YOU BEFORE.
SIGN: KITCHEN
BUT THAT WAS BEFORE THE BOYS GOT CAUGHT.
HE SAID IT'D BE FINE. HE GOT PERMISSION TO LEAVE.
OH... OKAY...
BUT A DATE WITH A BOY...? IS THAT REALLY ALL RIGHT...?
A DATE? IT'S NOTHING BIG LIKE THAT!
OH, STOP IT.
YOU'RE GOING SOMEWHERE ALONE WITH A GUY TO HAVE FUN... THAT'S A DATE.

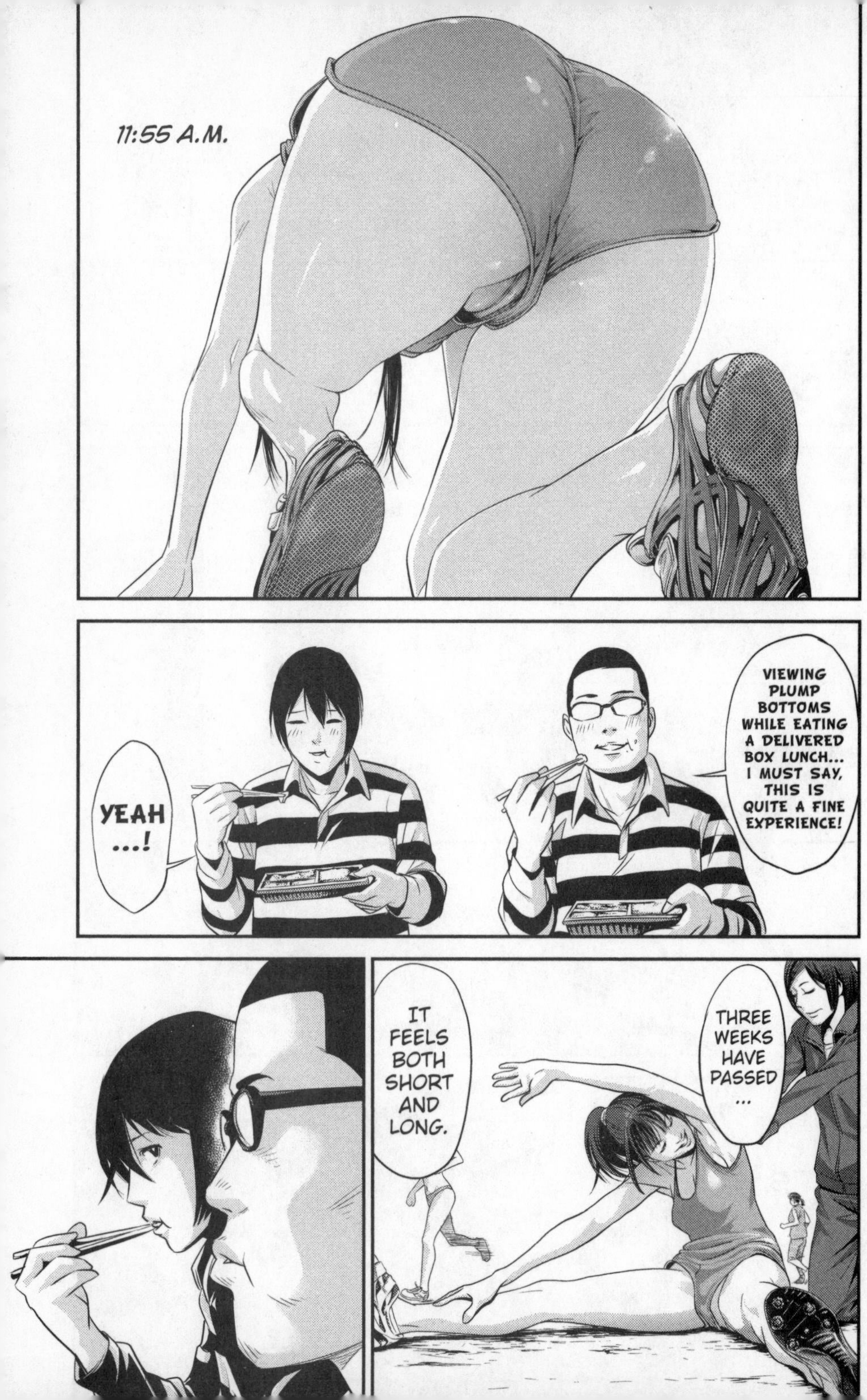
11:55 A.M.
VIEWING PLUMP BOTTOMS WHILE EATING A DELIVERED BOX LUNCH... I MUST SAY, THIS IS QUITE A FINE EXPERIENCE!
YEAH ...!
THREE WEEKS HAVE PASSED ...
IT FEELS BOTH SHORT AND LONG.

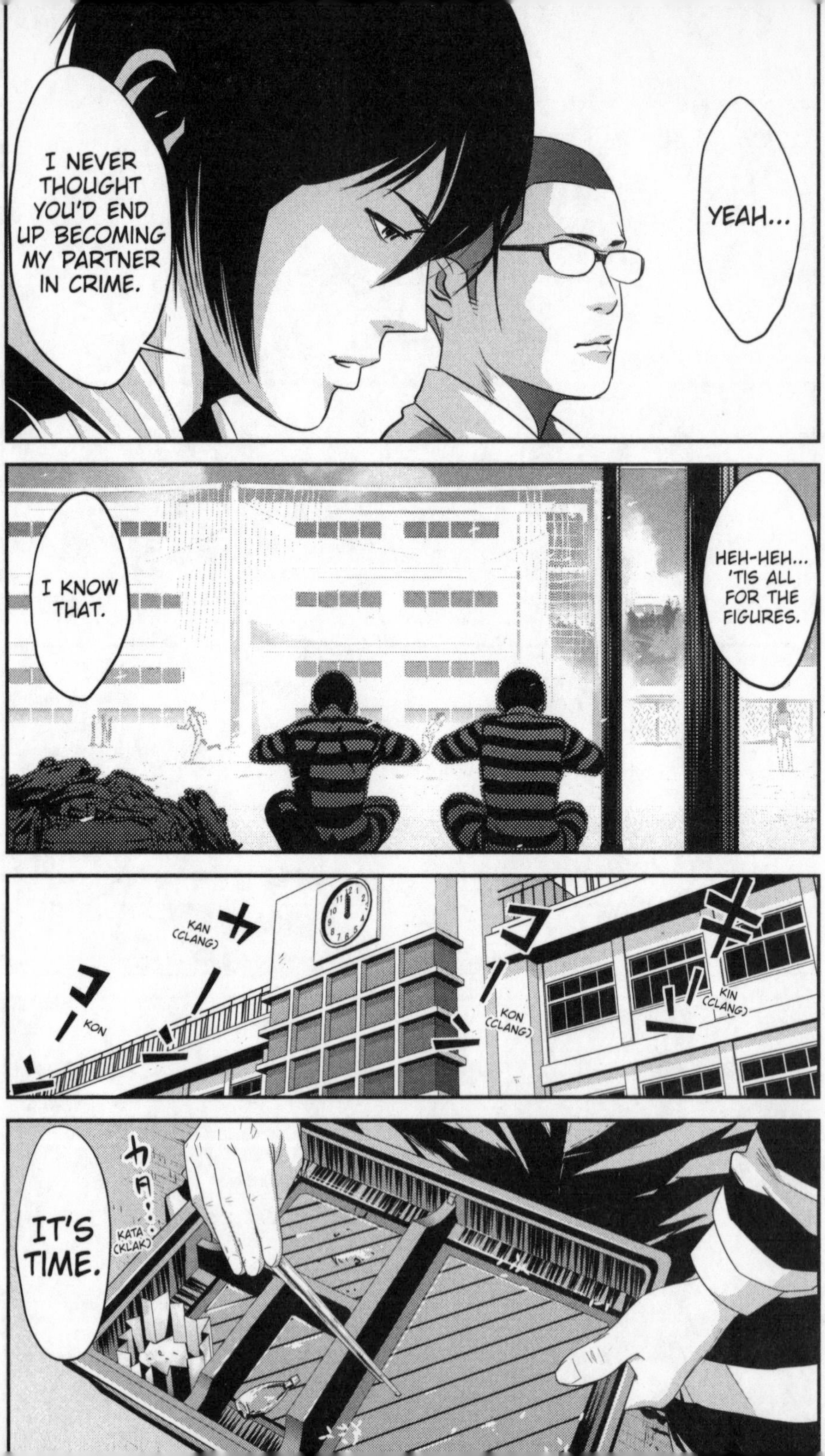
YEAH...
I NEVER THOUGHT YOU'D END UP BECOMING MY PARTNER IN CRIME.
HEH-HEH... 'TIS ALL FOR THE FIGURES.
I KNOW THAT.
KIN (CLANG)
KON (CLANG)
KAN (CLANG)
KON
KATA (KLAK)
IT'S TIME.

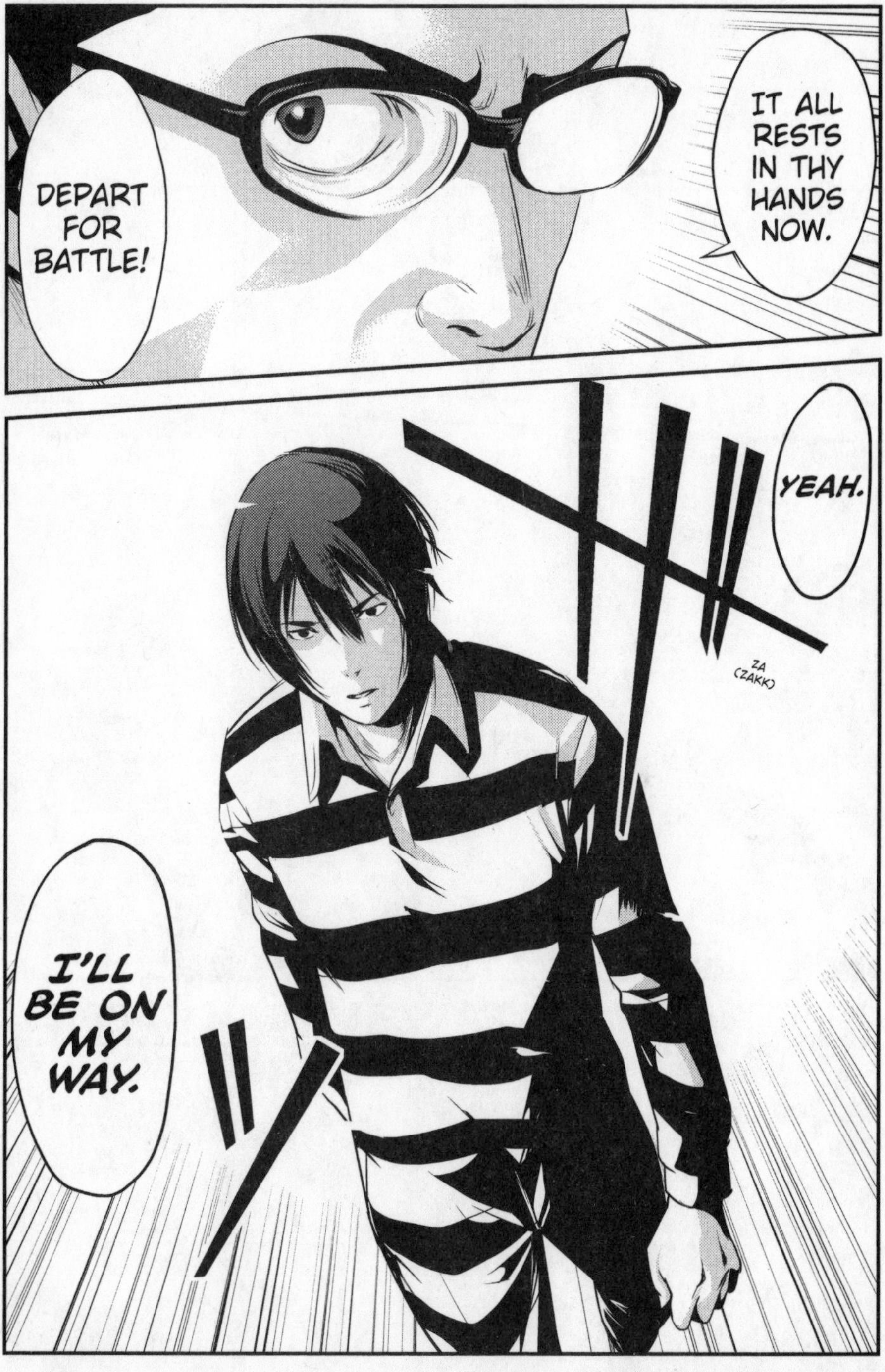
IT ALL RESTS IN THY HANDS NOW.
DEPART FOR BATTLE!
YEAH.
ZA (ZAKK)
I'LL BE ON MY WAY.

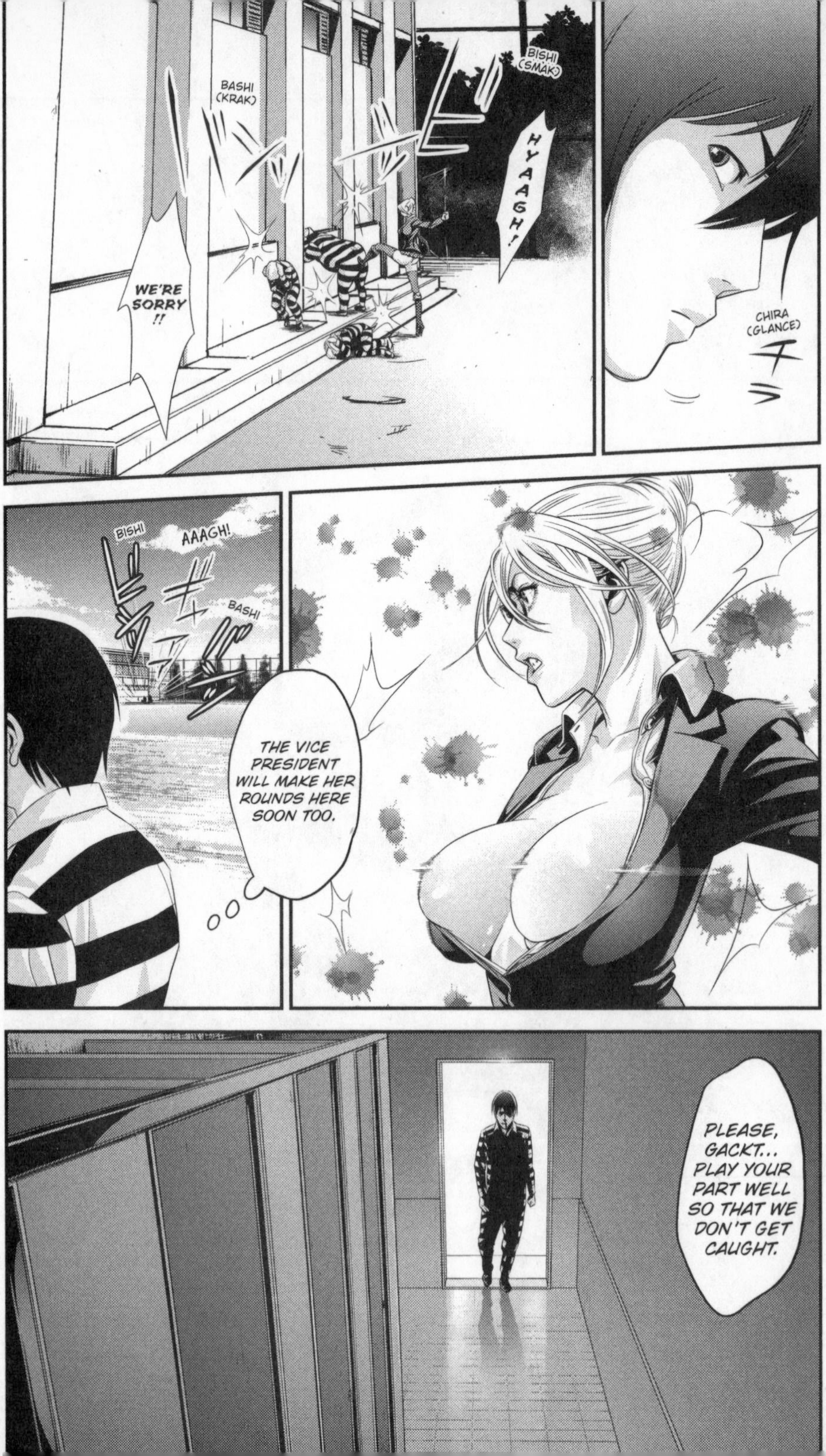
CHIRA (GLANCE)
BISHI (SMAK)
HYAAGH!
BASHI (KRAK)
WE'RE SORRY !!
THE VICE PRESIDENT WILL MAKE HER ROUNDS HERE SOON TOO.
BISHI
AAAGH!
BASHI
PLEASE, GACKT... PLAY YOUR PART WELL SO THAT WE DON'T GET CAUGHT.

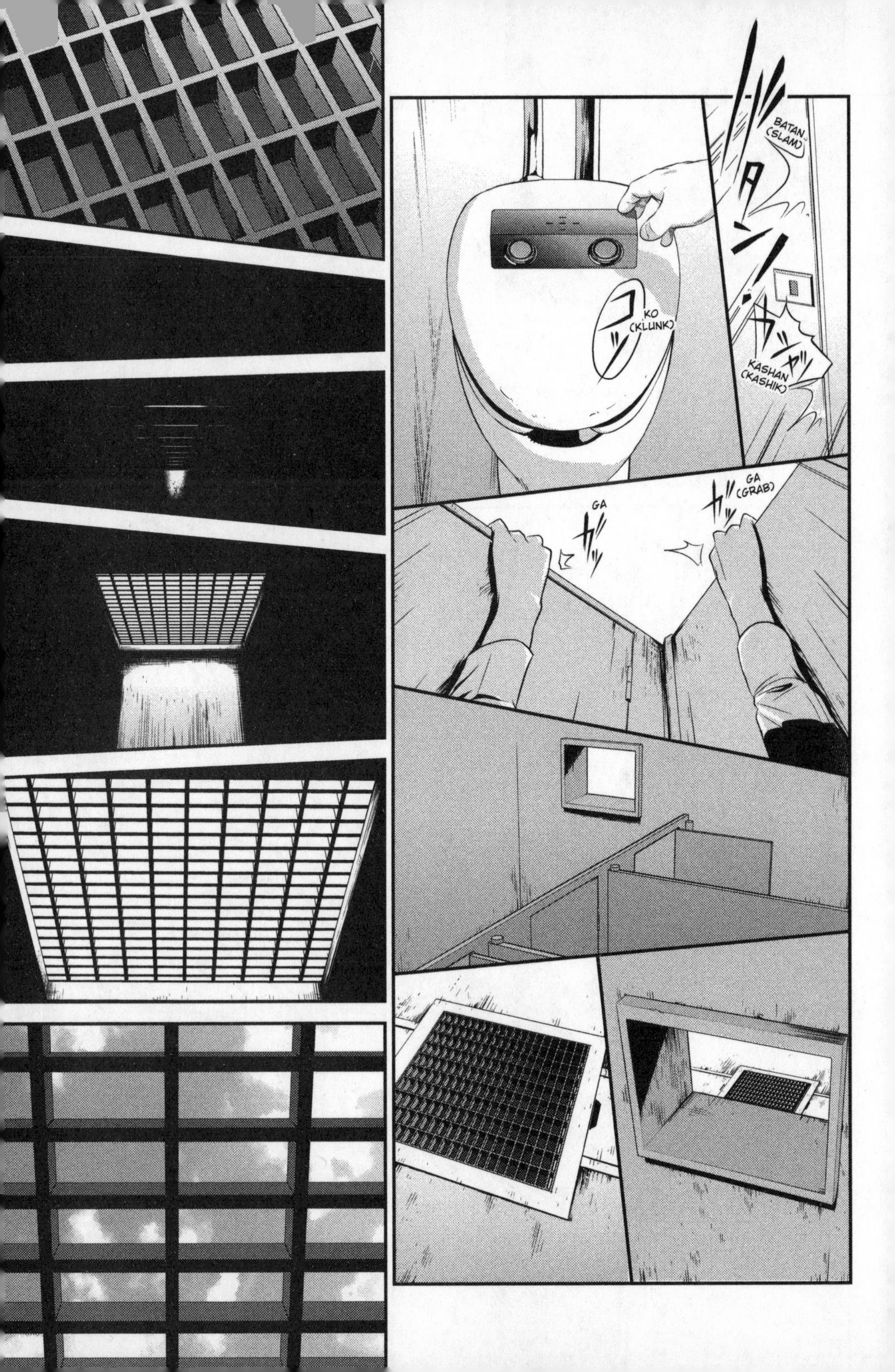
BATAN (SLAM)
KO (KLUNK)
KASHAN (KASHIK)
GA (GRAB)
GA

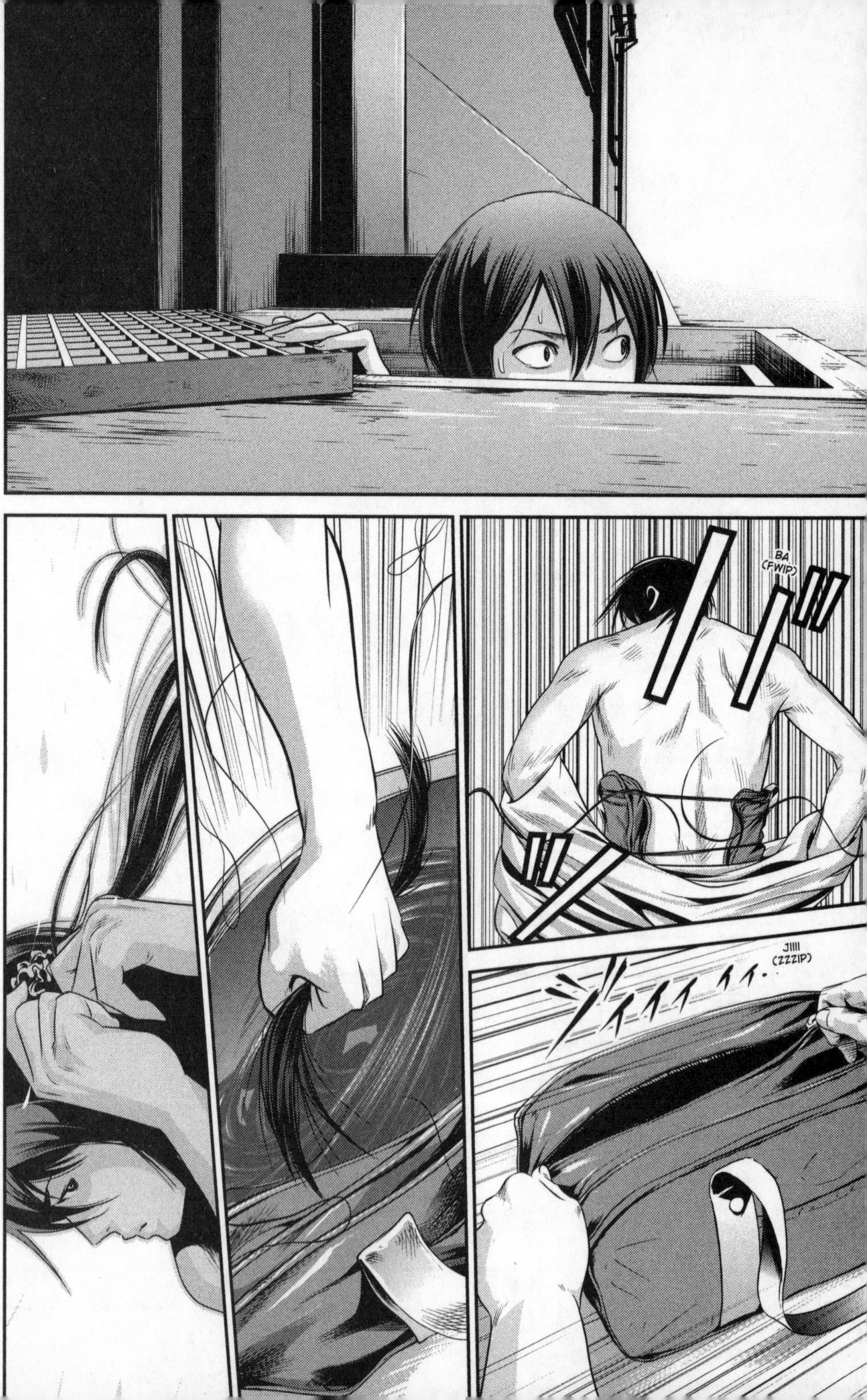
BA
(FWIP)
JIIII
(ZZZIP)

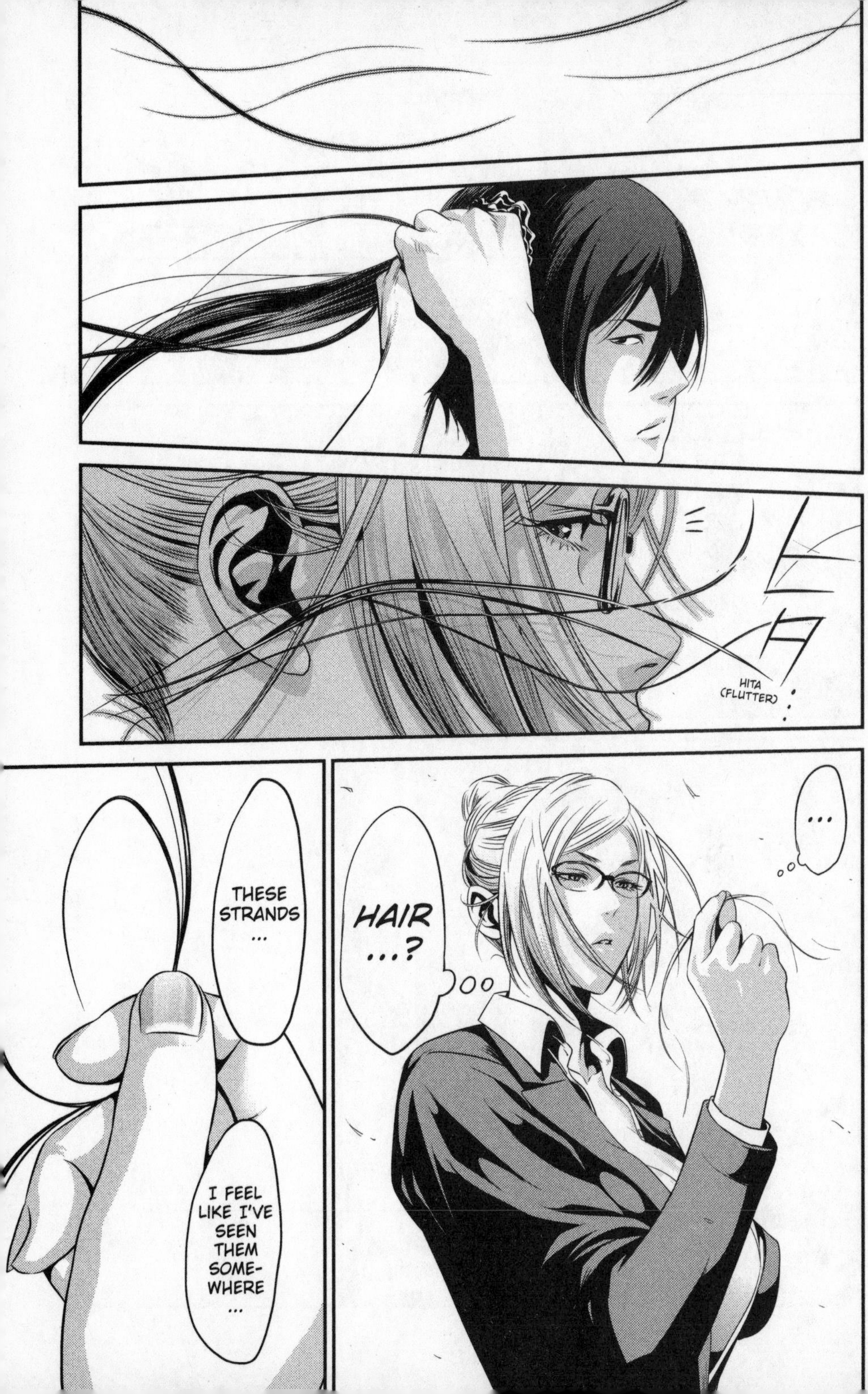
HITA (FLUTTER)
...
HAIR ...?
THESE STRANDS ...
I FEEL LIKE I'VE SEEN THEM SOME-WHERE ...

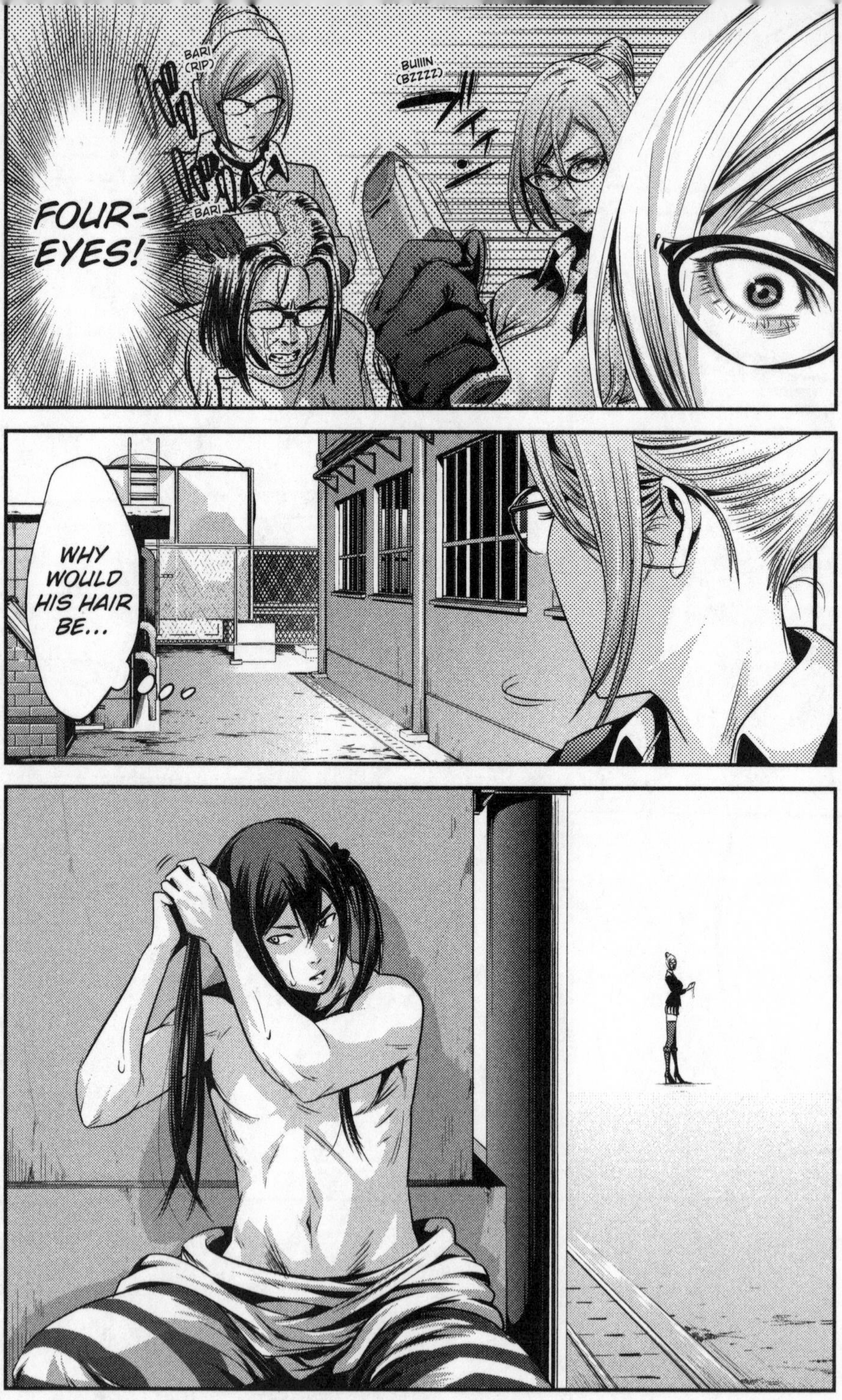
BUIIIN (BZZZZ)
BARI (RIP)
BARI
FOUR-EYES!
WHY WOULD HIS HAIR BE...

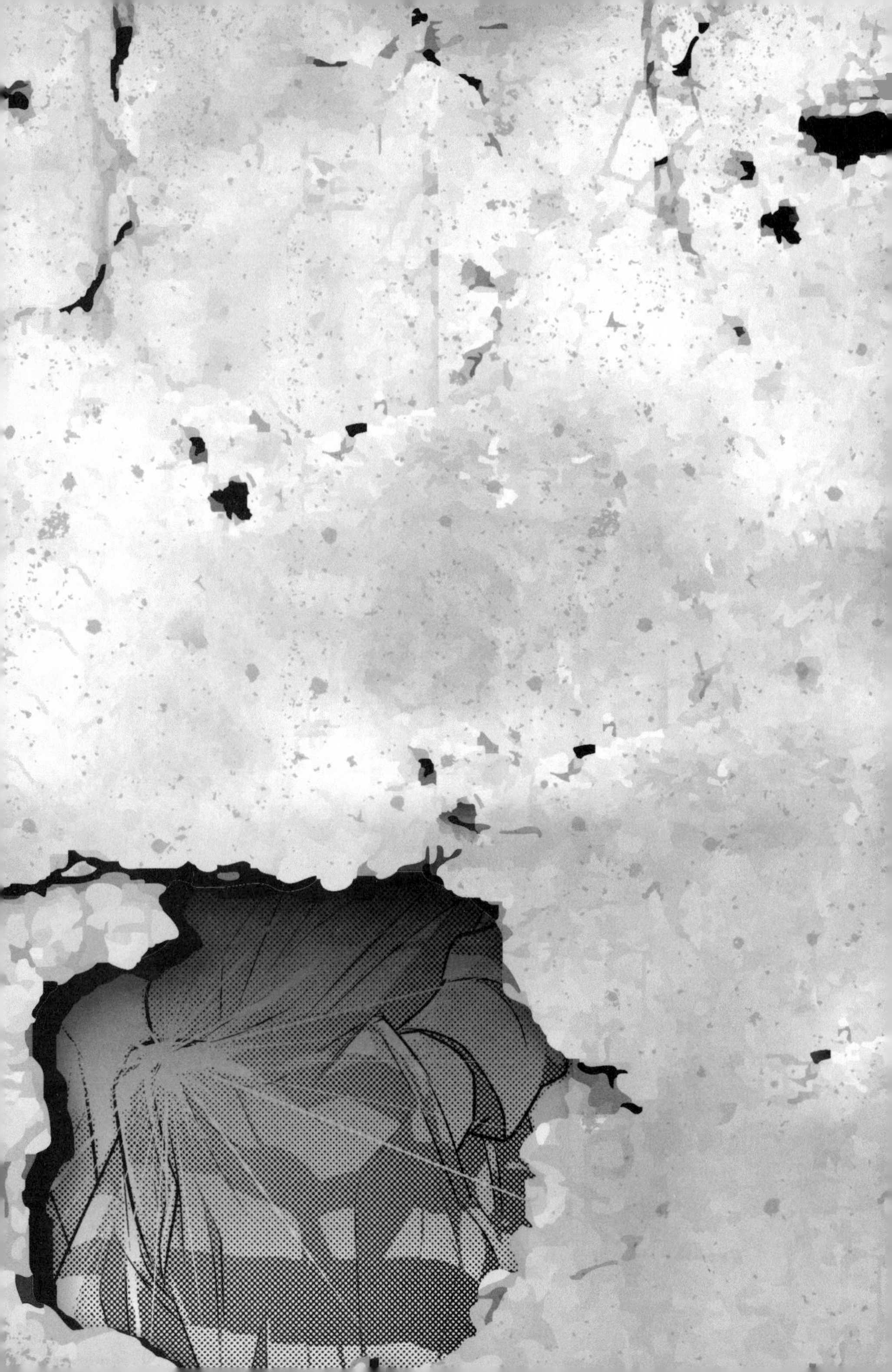

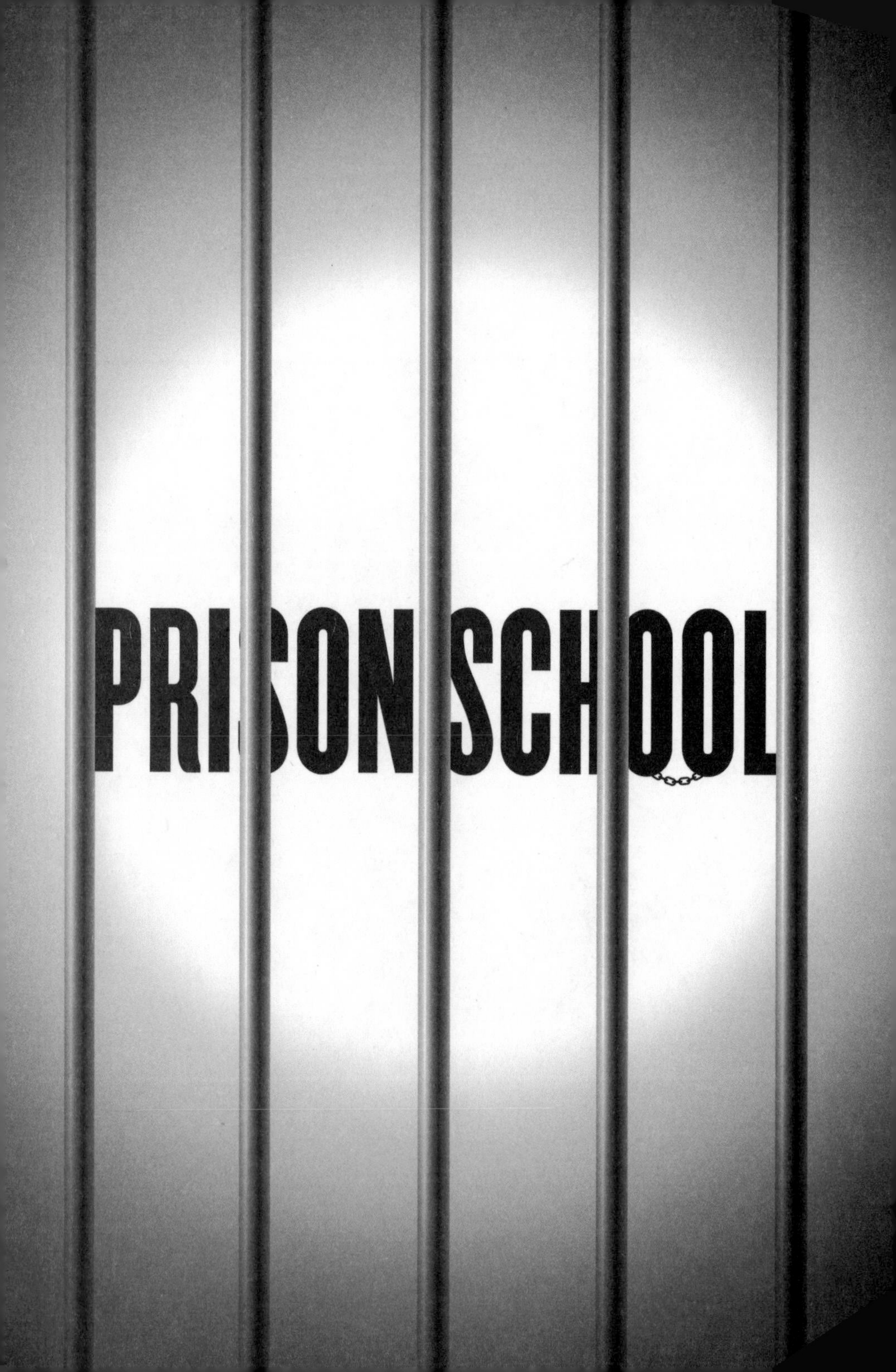
PRISON SCHOOL

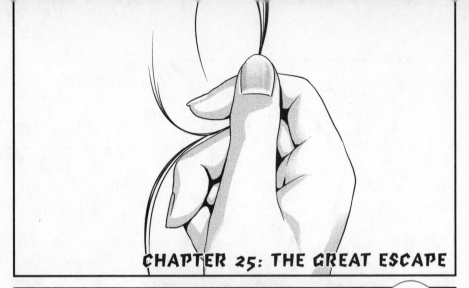

CHAPTER 25: THE GREAT ESCAPE

I THOUGHT I SHAVED FOUR-EYES BALD. WHY WOULD HIS HAIR BE HERE?

IT FLEW THIS WAY FROM OVER THERE...

I SHOULD GO CHECK JUST IN CASE.

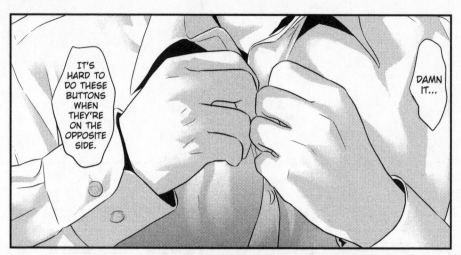

IT'S HARD TO DO THESE BUTTONS WHEN THEY'RE ON THE OPPOSITE SIDE.

DAMN IT...

......

SOOO (PEER)

そおぉ...

JARI (KRUNCH)

HUH?

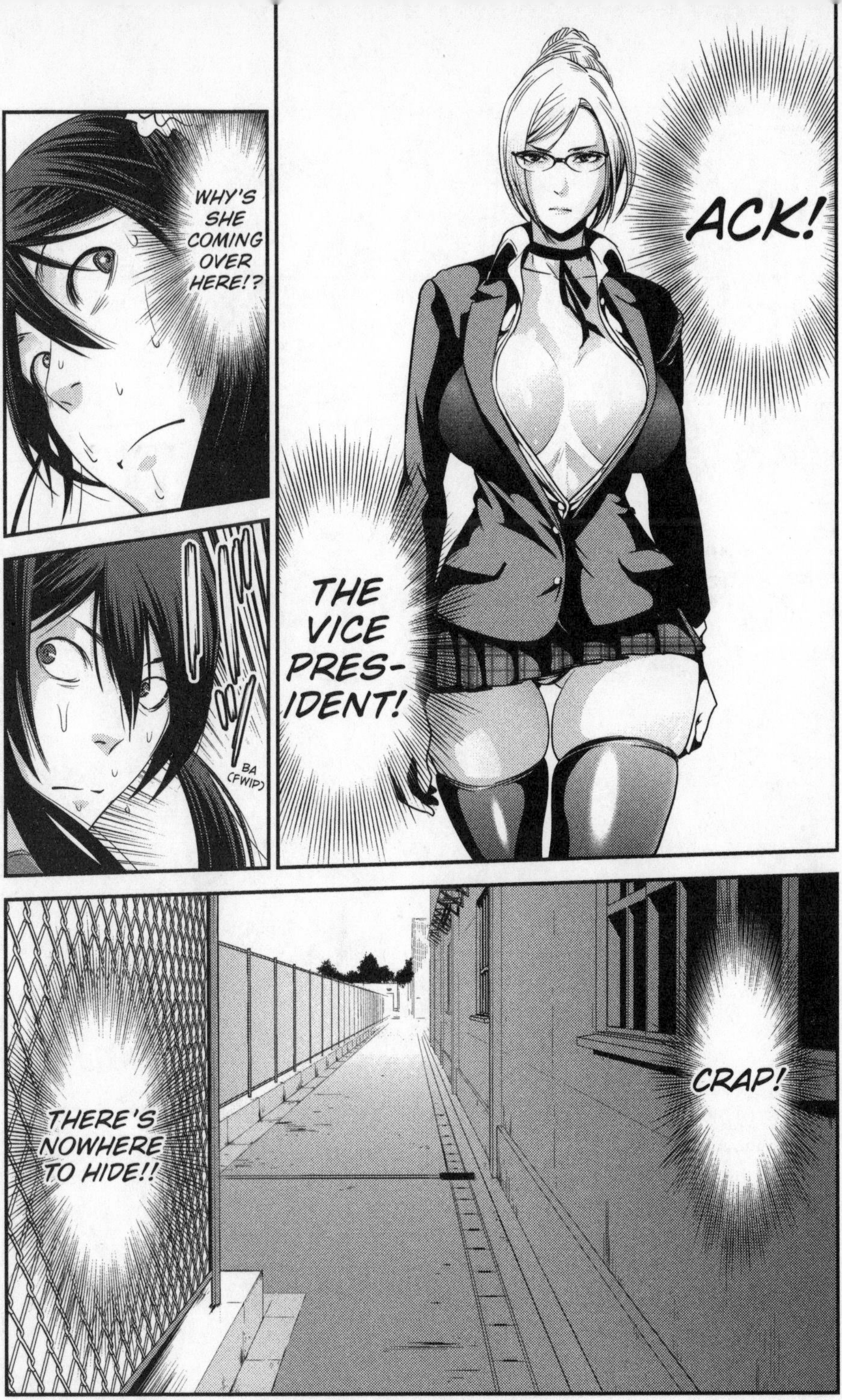
ACK!
THE VICE PRESIDENT!
WHY'S SHE COMING OVER HERE!?
BA (FWIP)
CRAP!
THERE'S NOWHERE TO HIDE!!

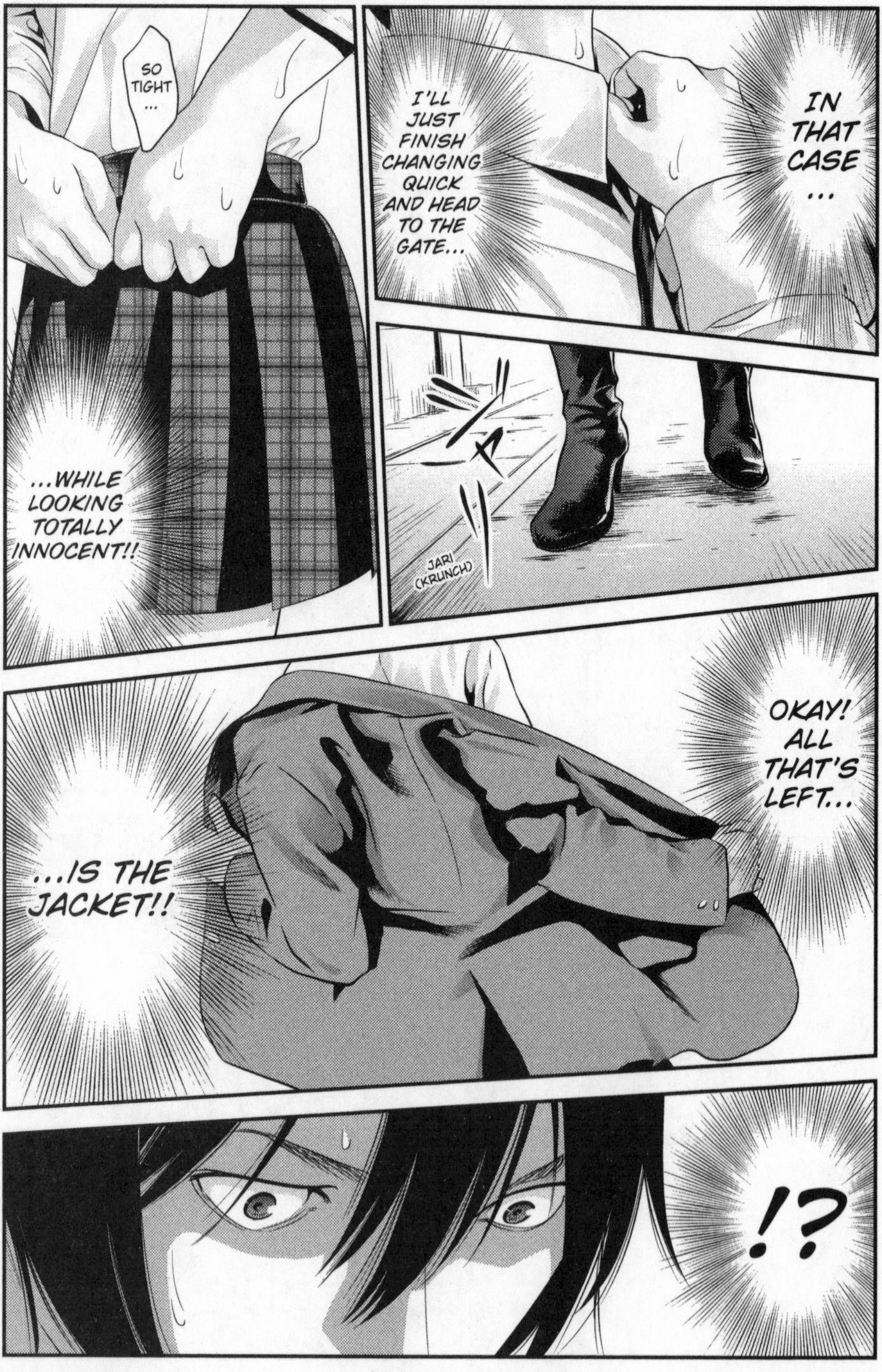
IN THAT CASE...
I'LL JUST FINISH CHANGING QUICK AND HEAD TO THE GATE...
SO TIGHT...
...WHILE LOOKING TOTALLY INNOCENT!!
JARI (KRUNCH)
OKAY! ALL THAT'S LEFT...
...IS THE JACKET!!
!?

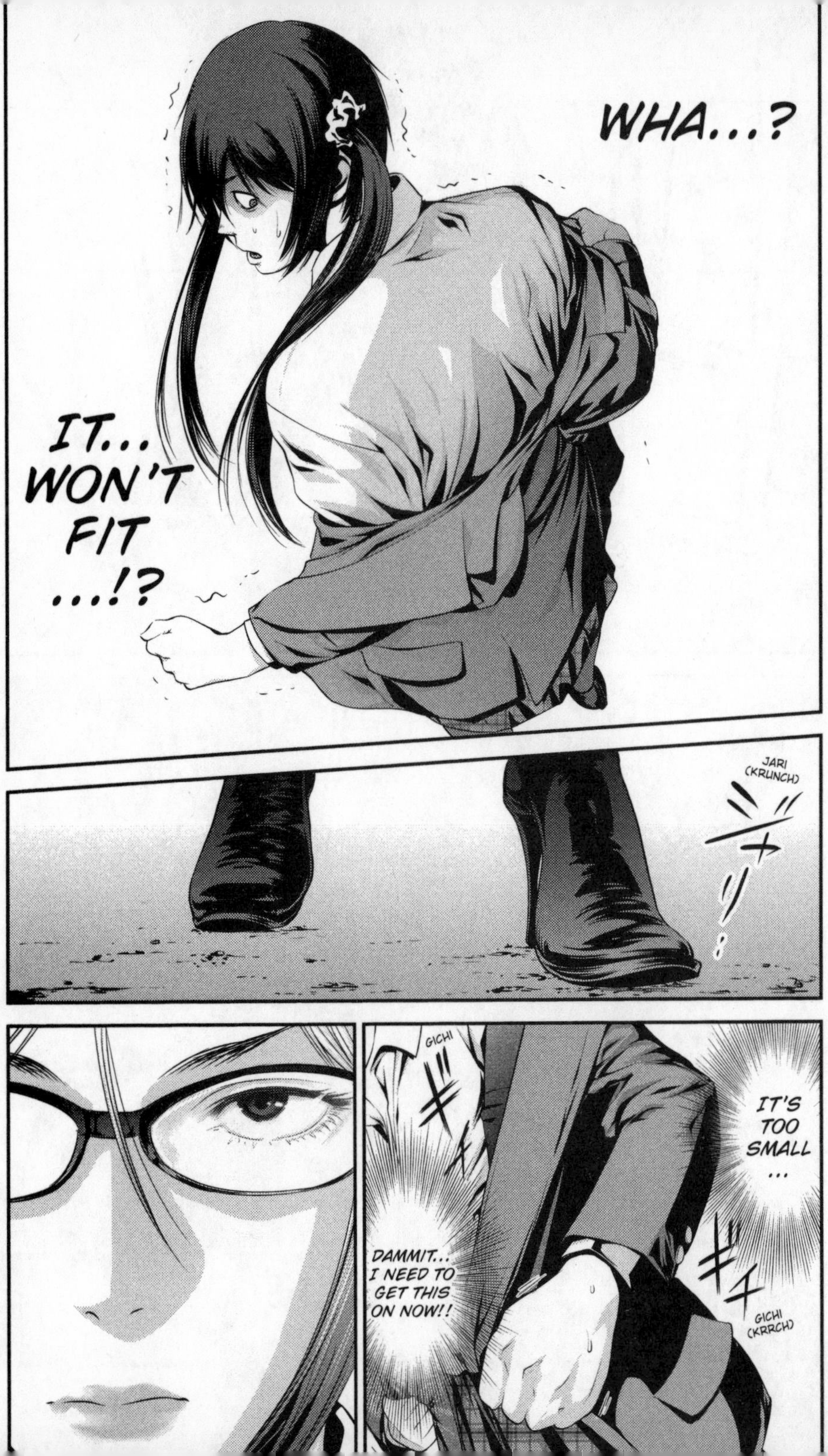
WHA...?
IT... WON'T FIT ...!?
JARI (KRUNCH)
IT'S TOO SMALL ...
GICHI
DAMMIT... I NEED TO GET THIS ON NOW!!
GICHI (KRRCH)

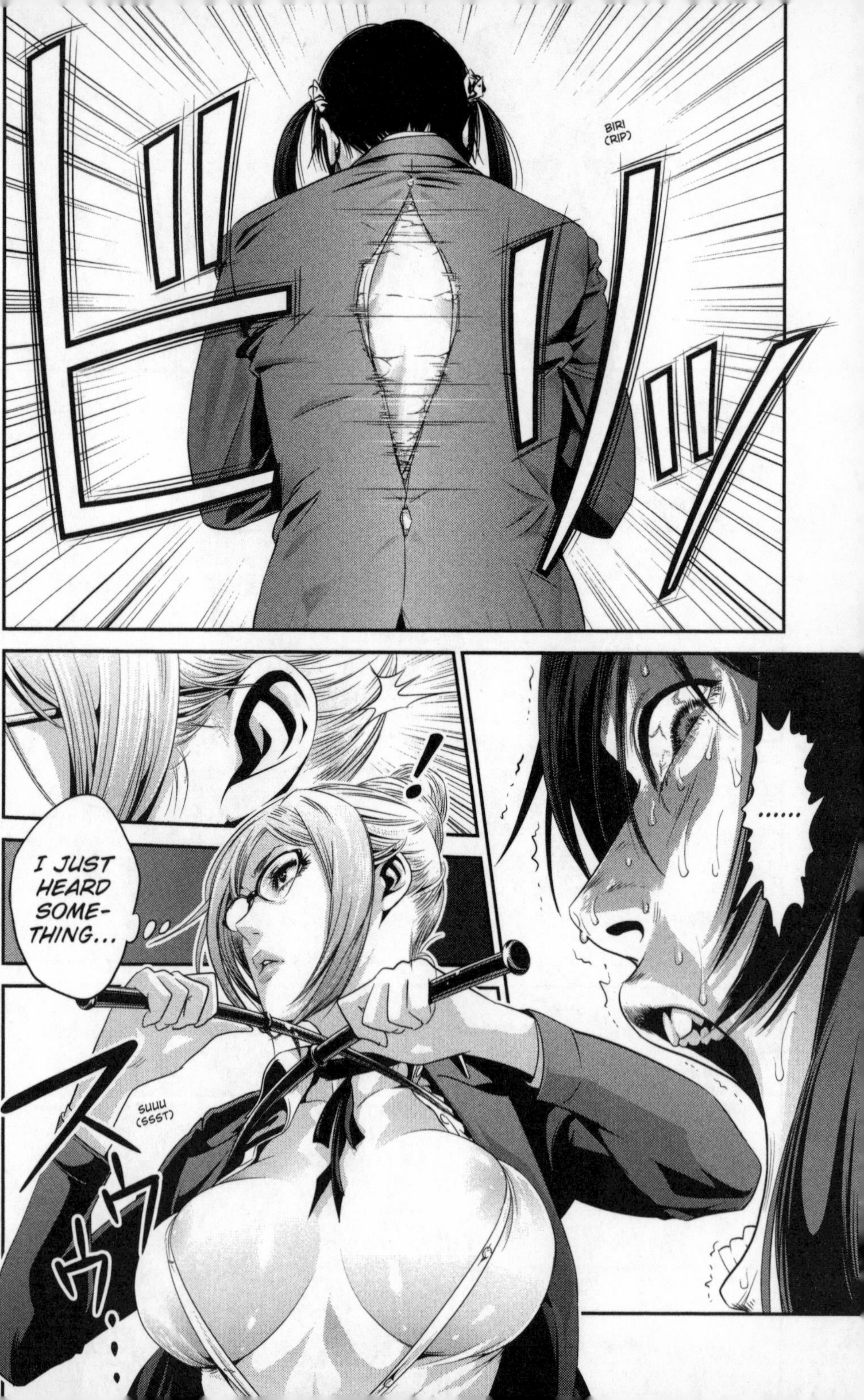
BIRI (RIP)
I JUST HEARD SOME-THING...
......
SUUU (SSST)

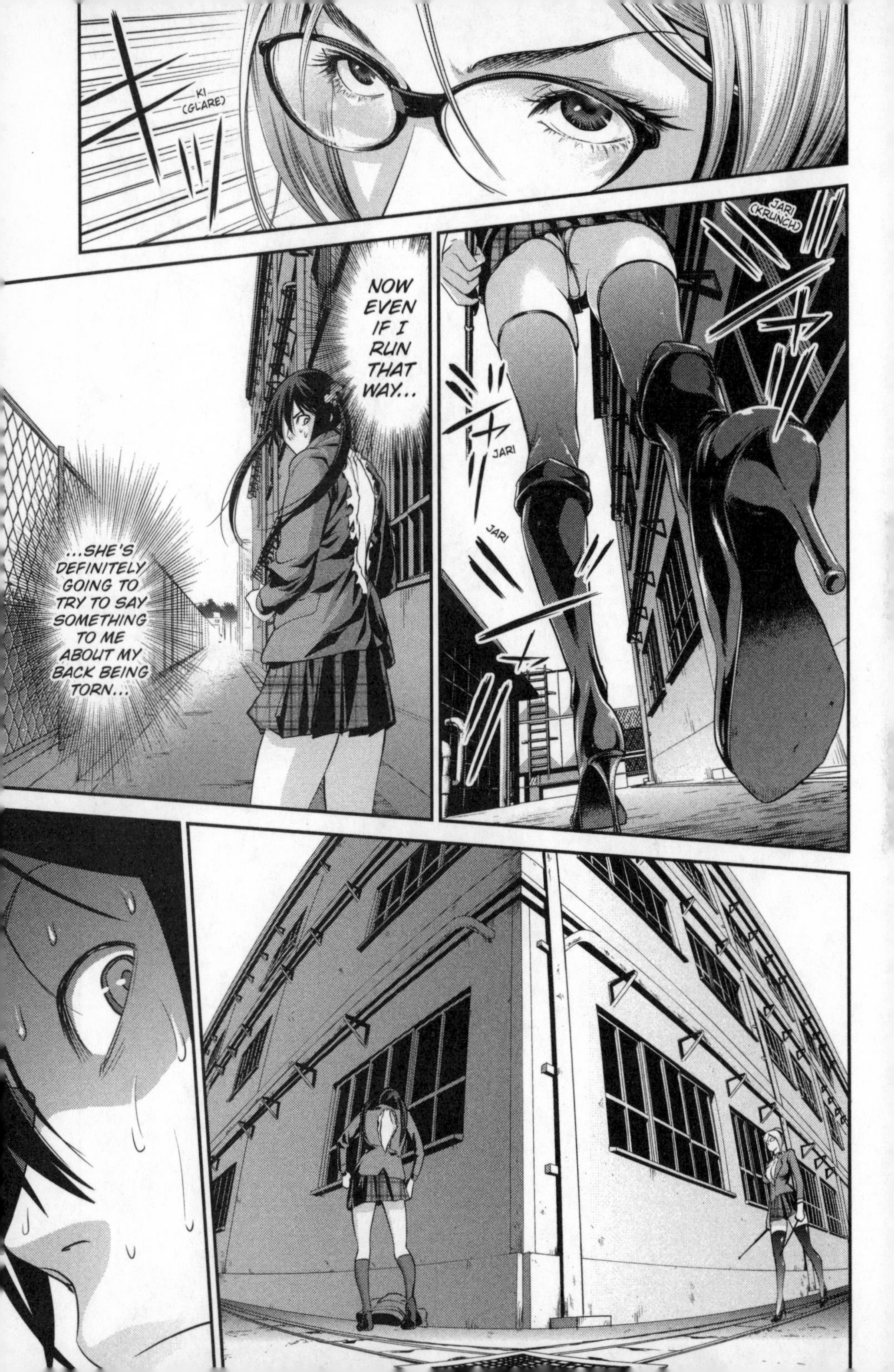
KI
(GLARE)
JARI
(KRUNCH)
JARI
JARI
NOW EVEN IF I RUN THAT WAY...
...SHE'S DEFINITELY GOING TO TRY TO SAY SOMETHING TO ME ABOUT MY BACK BEING TORN...

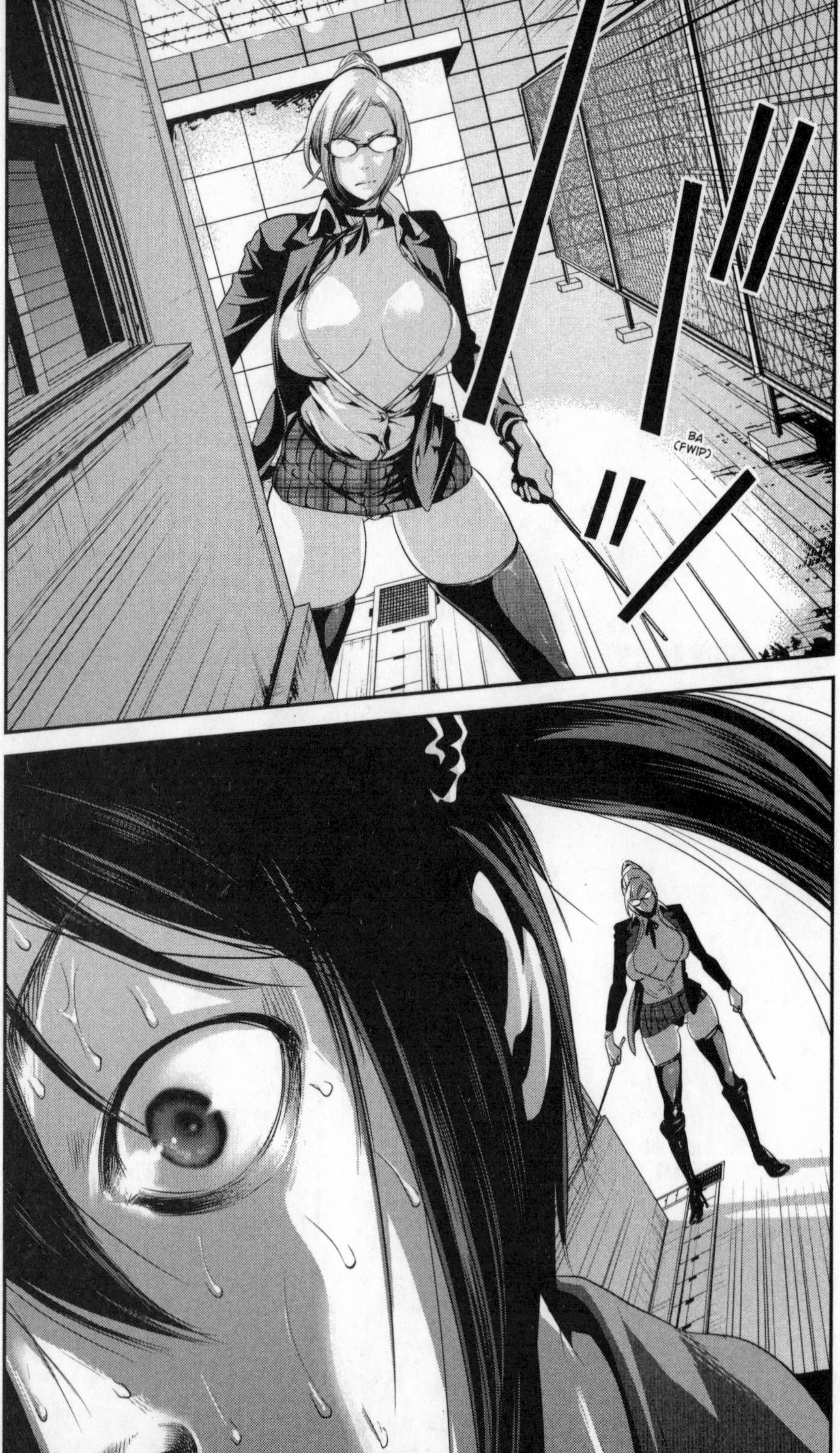
BA
(FWIP)

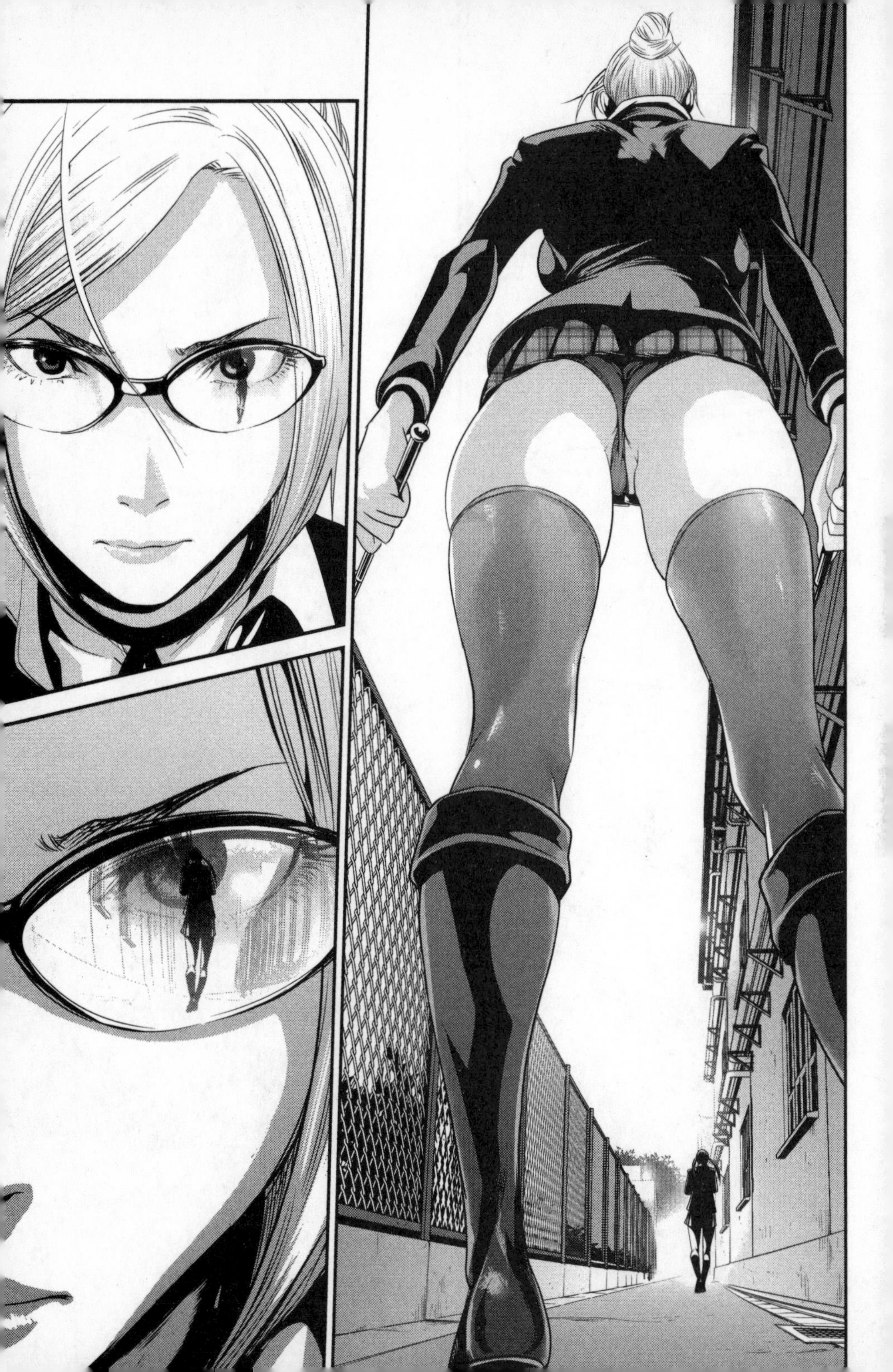

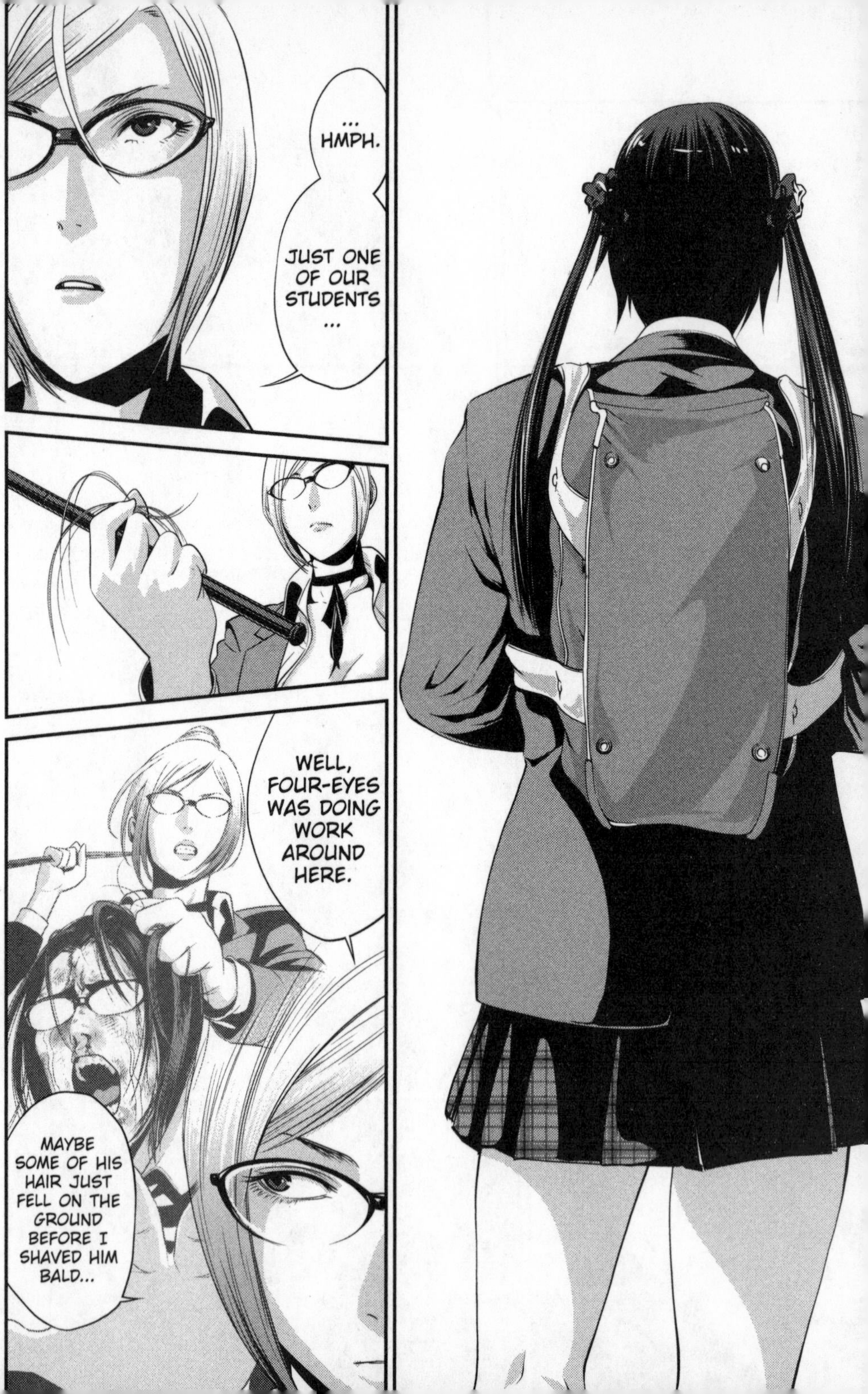
... HMPH.
JUST ONE OF OUR STUDENTS ...
WELL, FOUR-EYES WAS DOING WORK AROUND HERE.
MAYBE SOME OF HIS HAIR JUST FELL ON THE GROUND BEFORE I SHAVED HIM BALD...

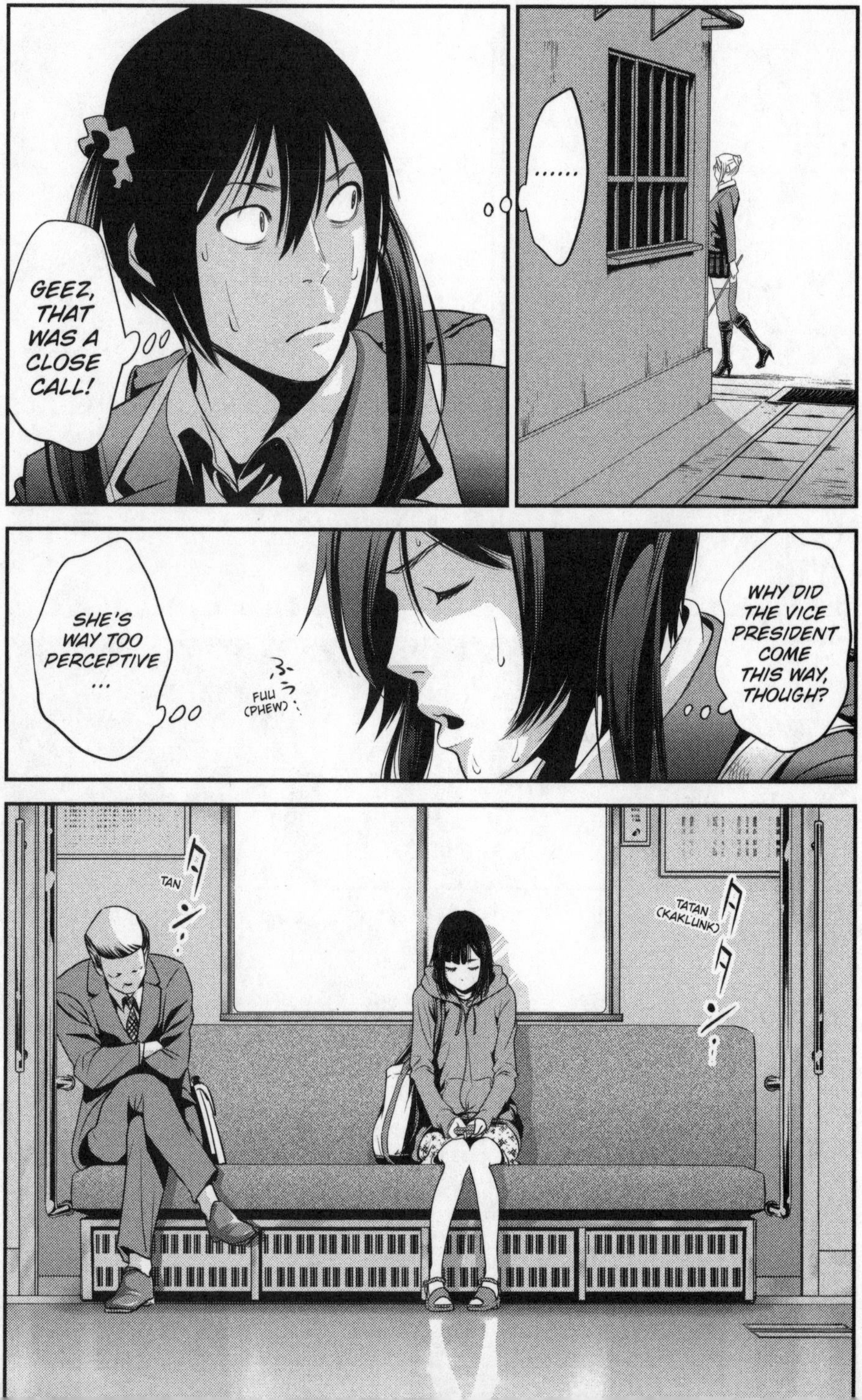
......
GEEZ, THAT WAS A CLOSE CALL!
WHY DID THE VICE PRESIDENT COME THIS WAY, THOUGH?
ふう
FUU (PHEW)
SHE'S WAY TOO PERCEPTIVE ...
TATAN (KAKLUNK)
TAN

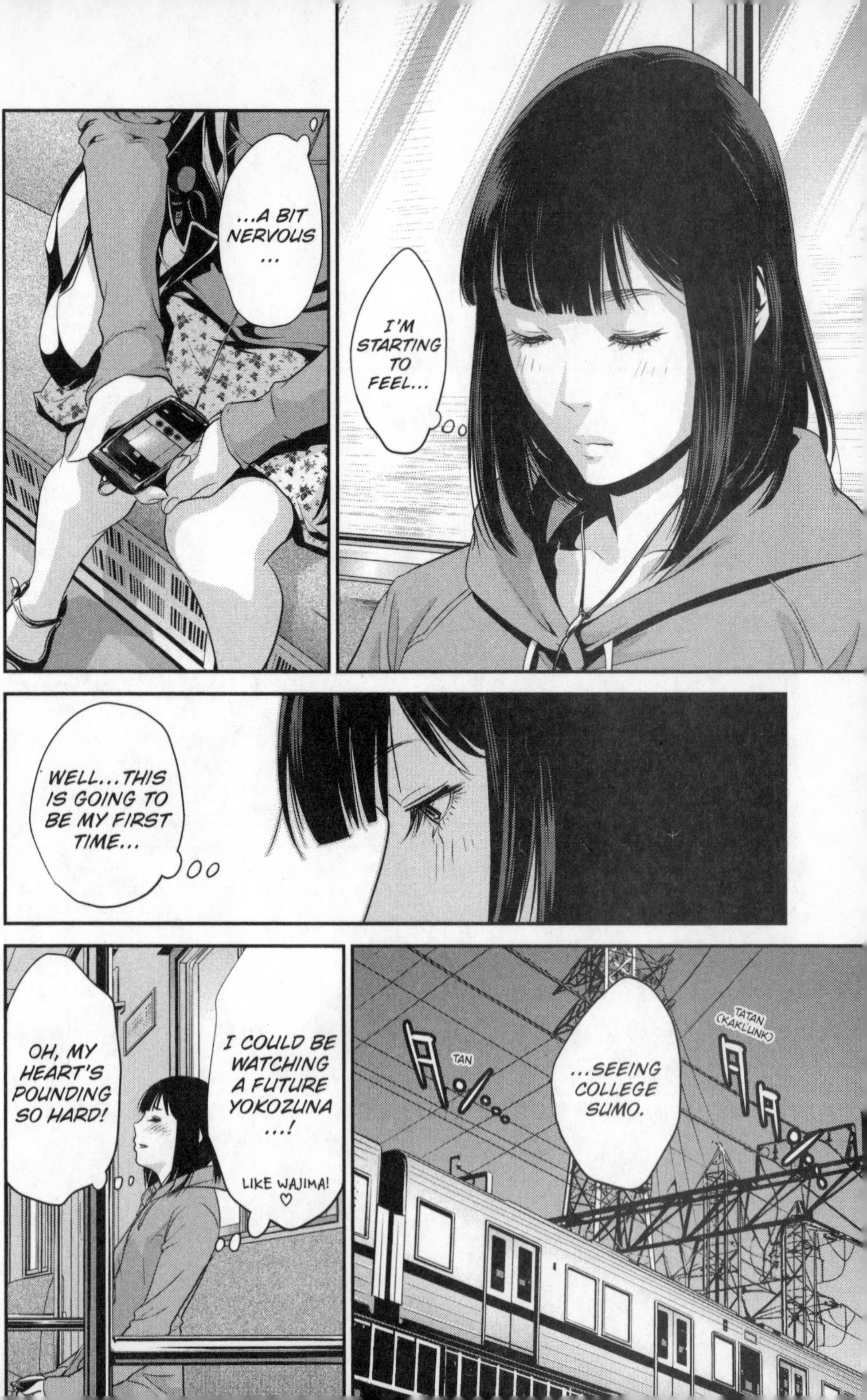
I'M STARTING TO FEEL...
...A BIT NERVOUS ...
WELL...THIS IS GOING TO BE MY FIRST TIME...
TATAN (KAKLUNK)
TAN
...SEEING COLLEGE SUMO.
I COULD BE WATCHING A FUTURE YOKOZUNA ...!
LIKE WAJIMA! ♥
OH, MY HEART'S POUNDING SO HARD!

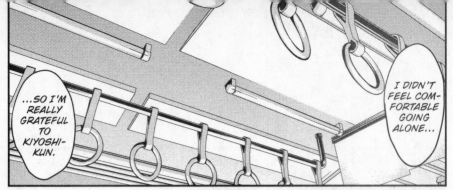

I DIDN'T FEEL COM-FORTABLE GOING ALONE...
...SO I'M REALLY GRATEFUL TO KIYOSHI-KUN.
I GUESS IT'S ALSO...
...MY FIRST TIME WATCHING SUMO WITH A BOY.
THAT'S A DATE!
NO, IT'S NOT A DATE! WE'RE JUST GOING TO WATCH SUMO!

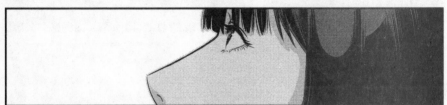

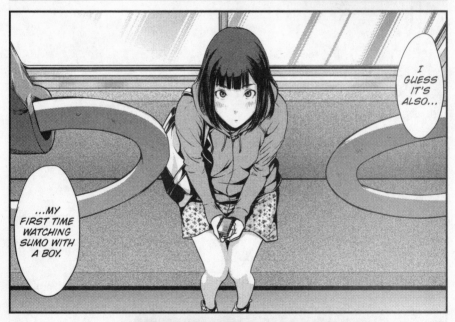

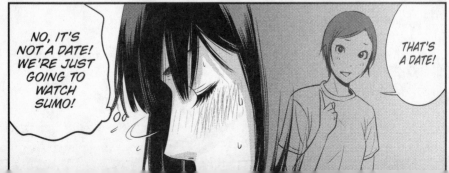

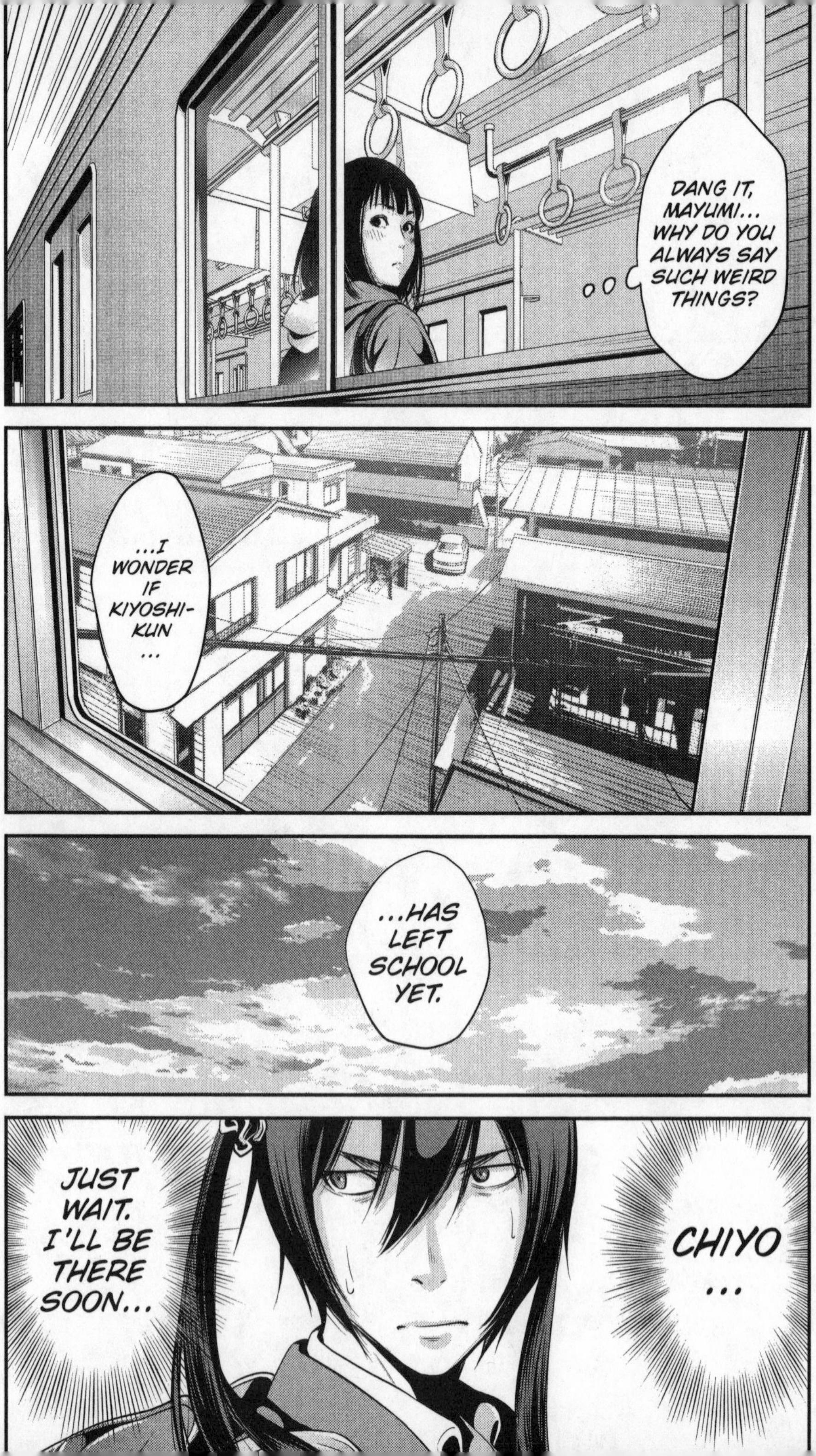

DANG IT, MAYUMI... WHY DO YOU ALWAYS SAY SUCH WEIRD THINGS?
...I WONDER IF KIYOSHI-KUN...
...HAS LEFT SCHOOL YET.
CHIYO...
JUST WAIT. I'LL BE THERE SOON...

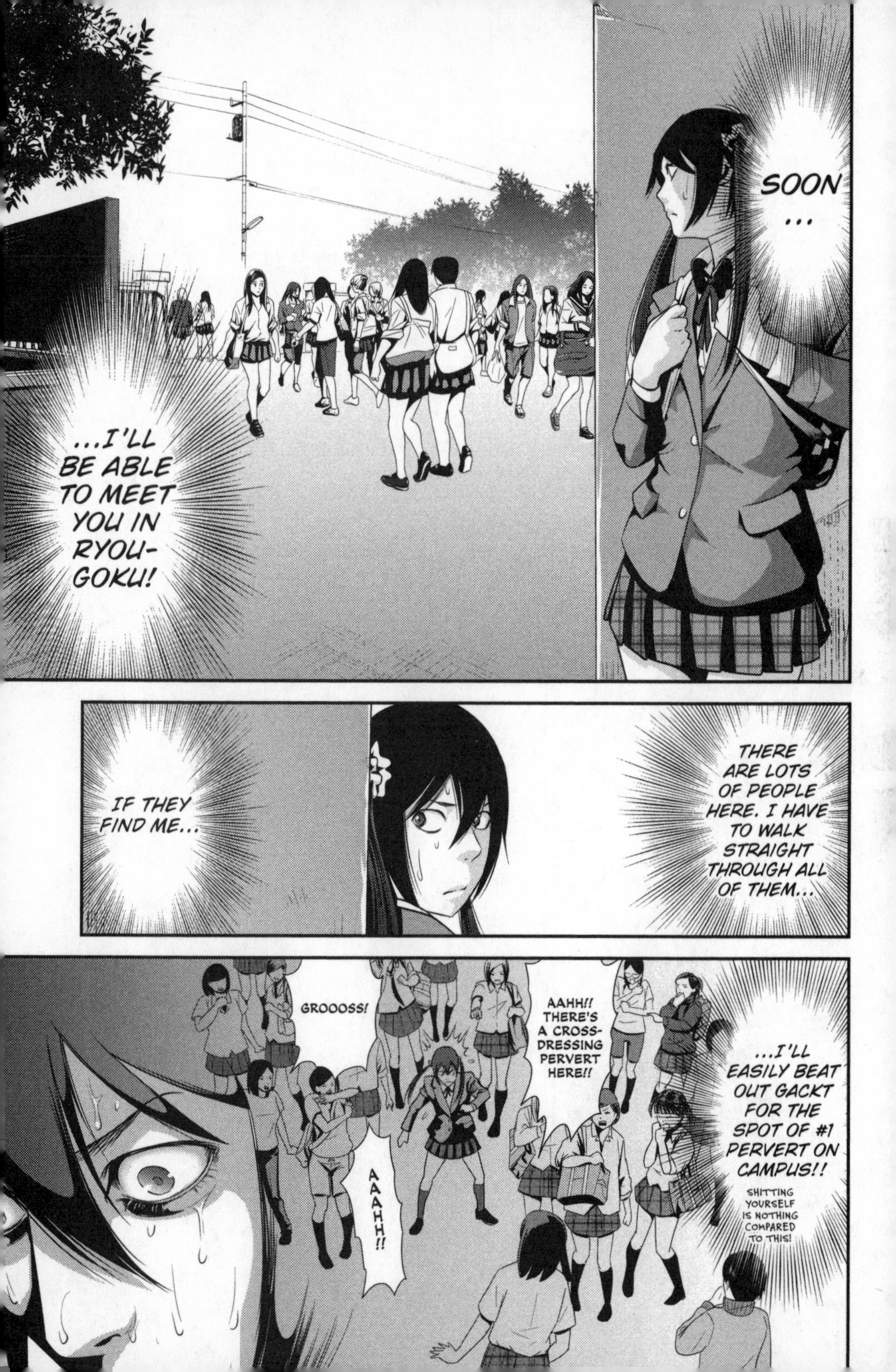
SOON ...
...I'LL BE ABLE TO MEET YOU IN RYOU-GOKU!
THERE ARE LOTS OF PEOPLE HERE. I HAVE TO WALK STRAIGHT THROUGH ALL OF THEM...
IF THEY FIND ME...
...I'LL EASILY BEAT OUT GACKT FOR THE SPOT OF #1 PERVERT ON CAMPUS!!
SHITTING YOURSELF IS NOTHING COMPARED TO THIS!
AAHH!! THERE'S A CROSS-DRESSING PERVERT HERE!!
GROOOSS!
AAAHH!!

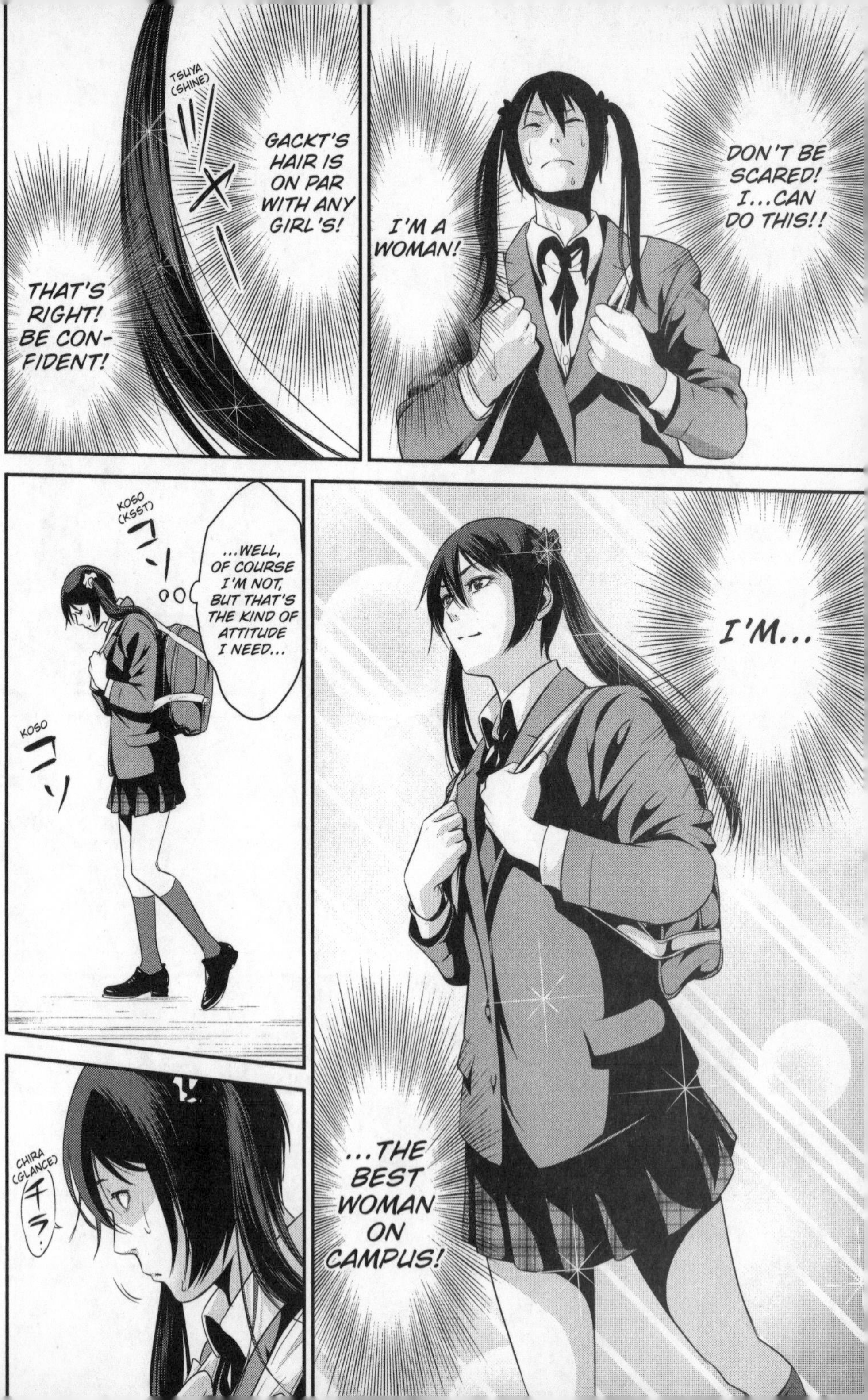
DON'T BE SCARED! I...CAN DO THIS!!
I'M A WOMAN!
TSUYA (SHINE)
GACKT'S HAIR IS ON PAR WITH ANY GIRL'S!
THAT'S RIGHT! BE CON-FIDENT!
I'M...
...THE BEST WOMAN ON CAMPUS!
KOSO (KSST)
...WELL, OF COURSE I'M NOT, BUT THAT'S THE KIND OF ATTITUDE I NEED...
KOSO
CHIRA (GLANCE)

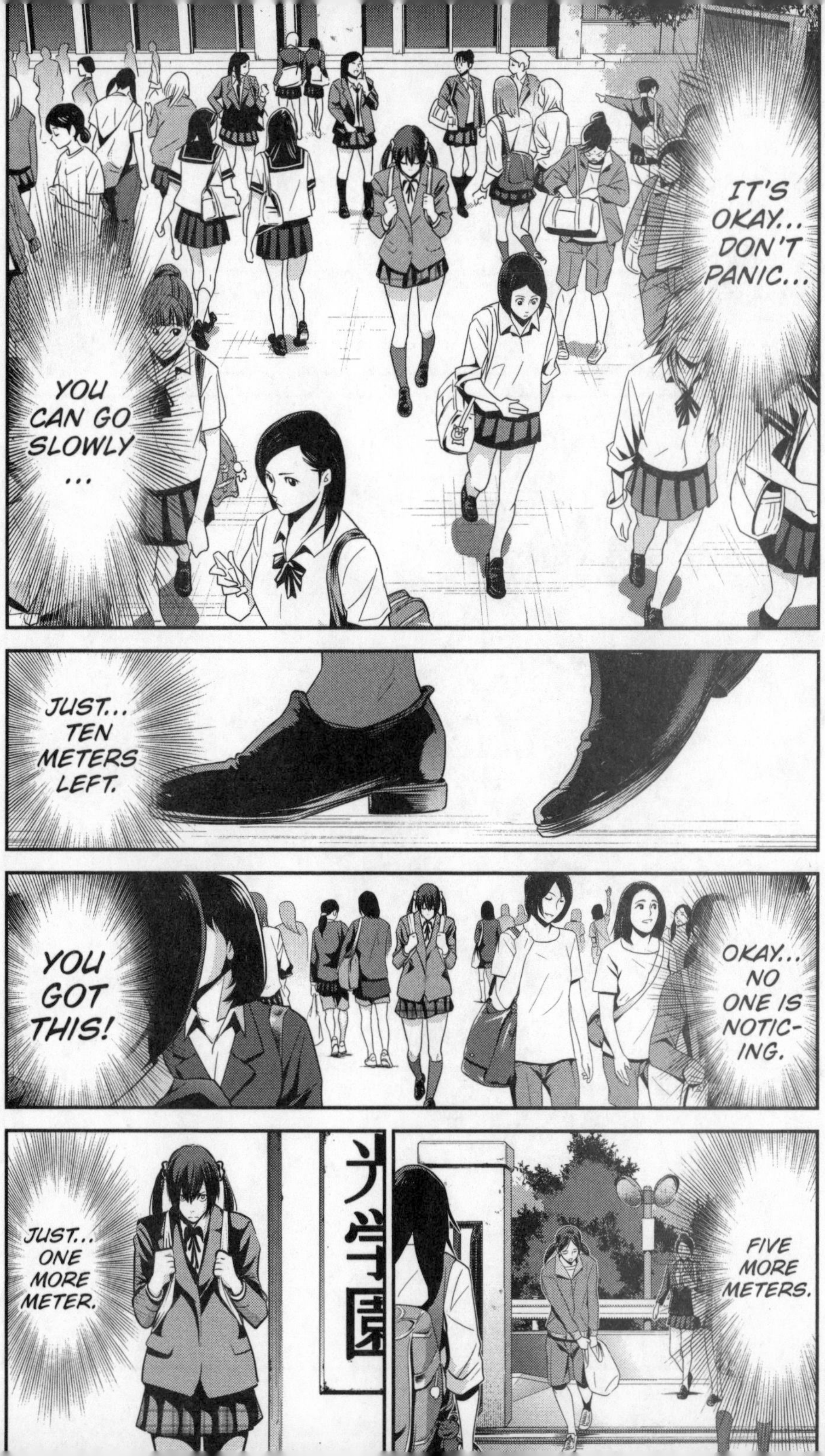
IT'S OKAY... DON'T PANIC...
YOU CAN GO SLOWLY ...
JUST... TEN METERS LEFT.
OKAY... NO ONE IS NOTIC-ING.
YOU GOT THIS!
FIVE MORE METERS.
JUST... ONE MORE METER.

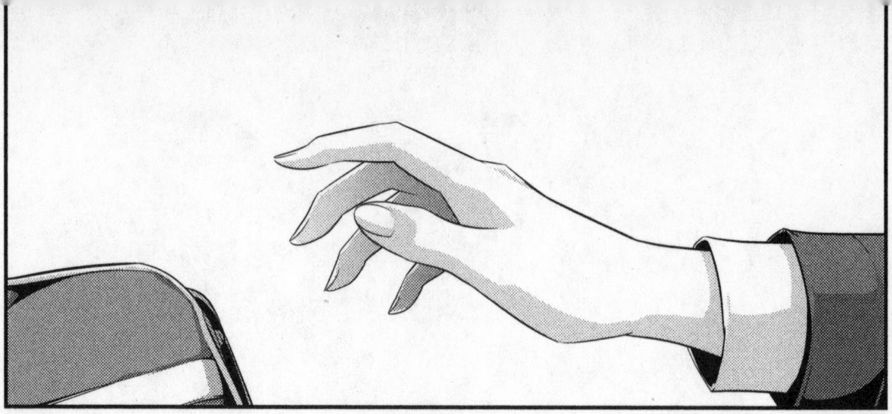

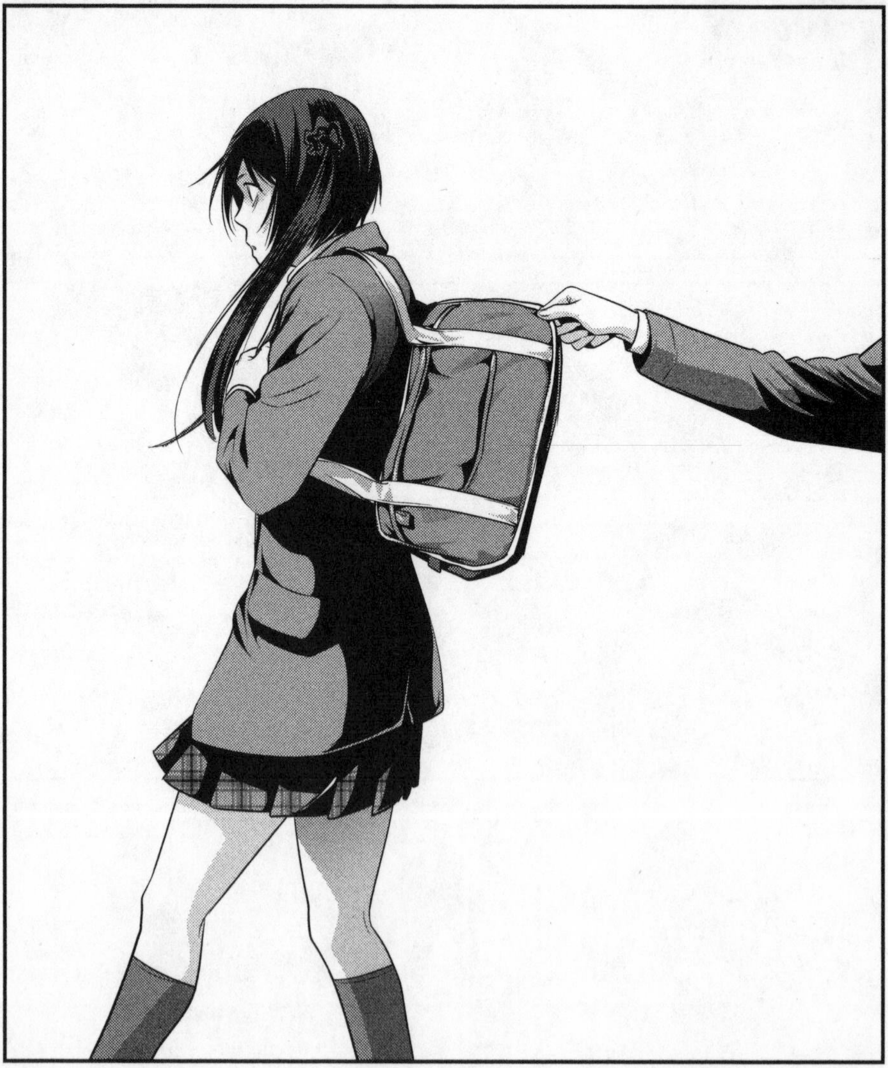

CHAPTER 26: THE GETAWAY

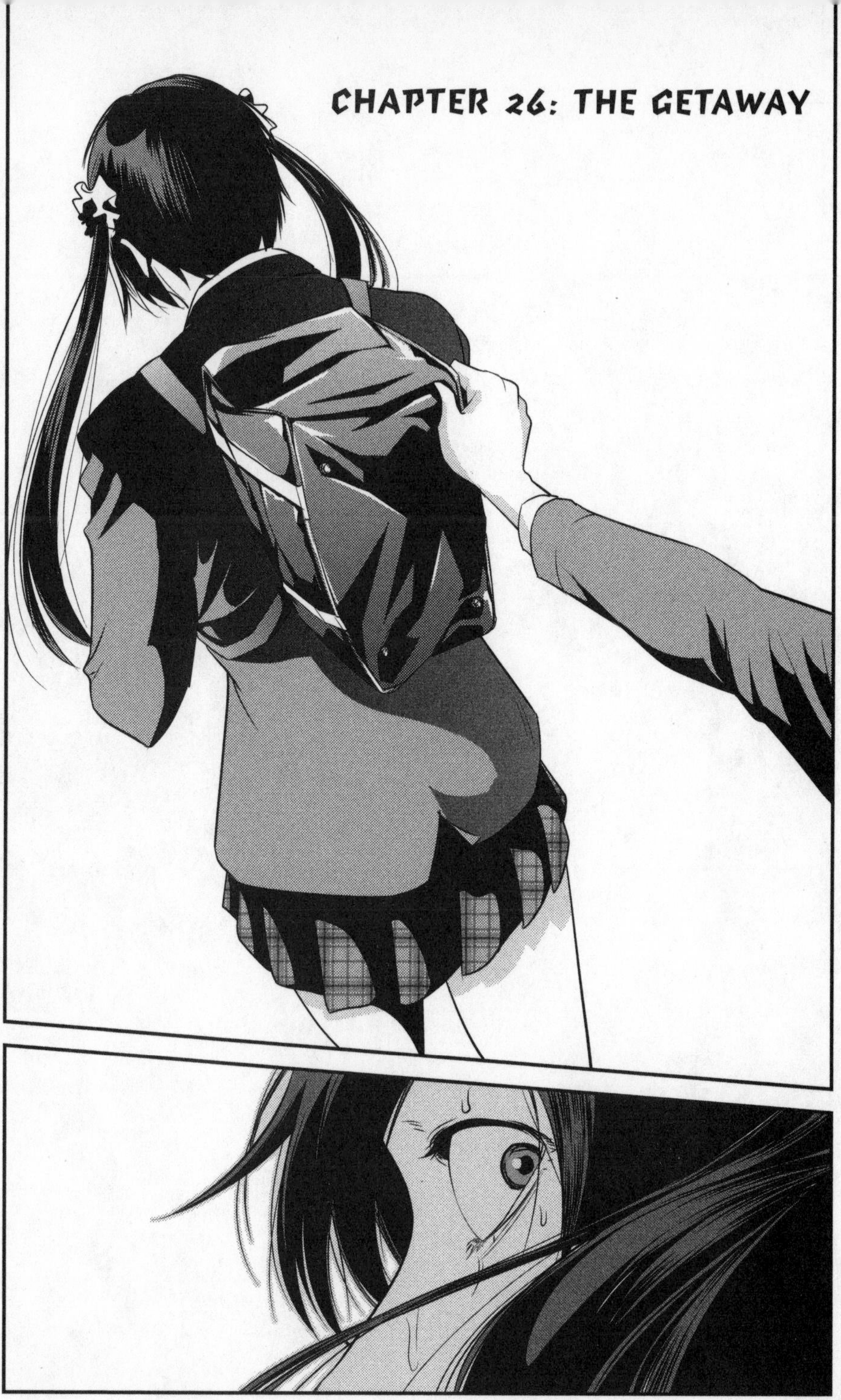

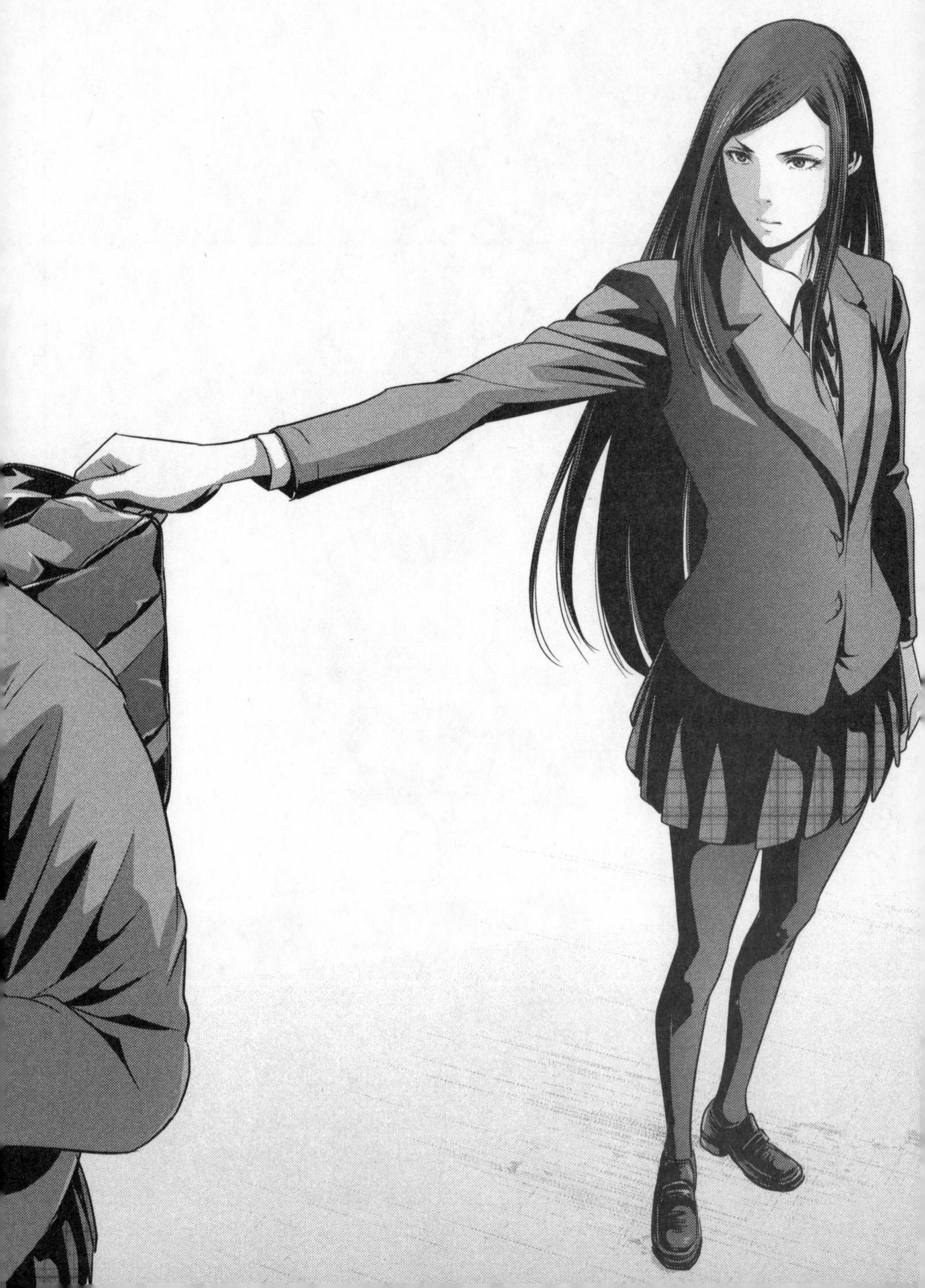

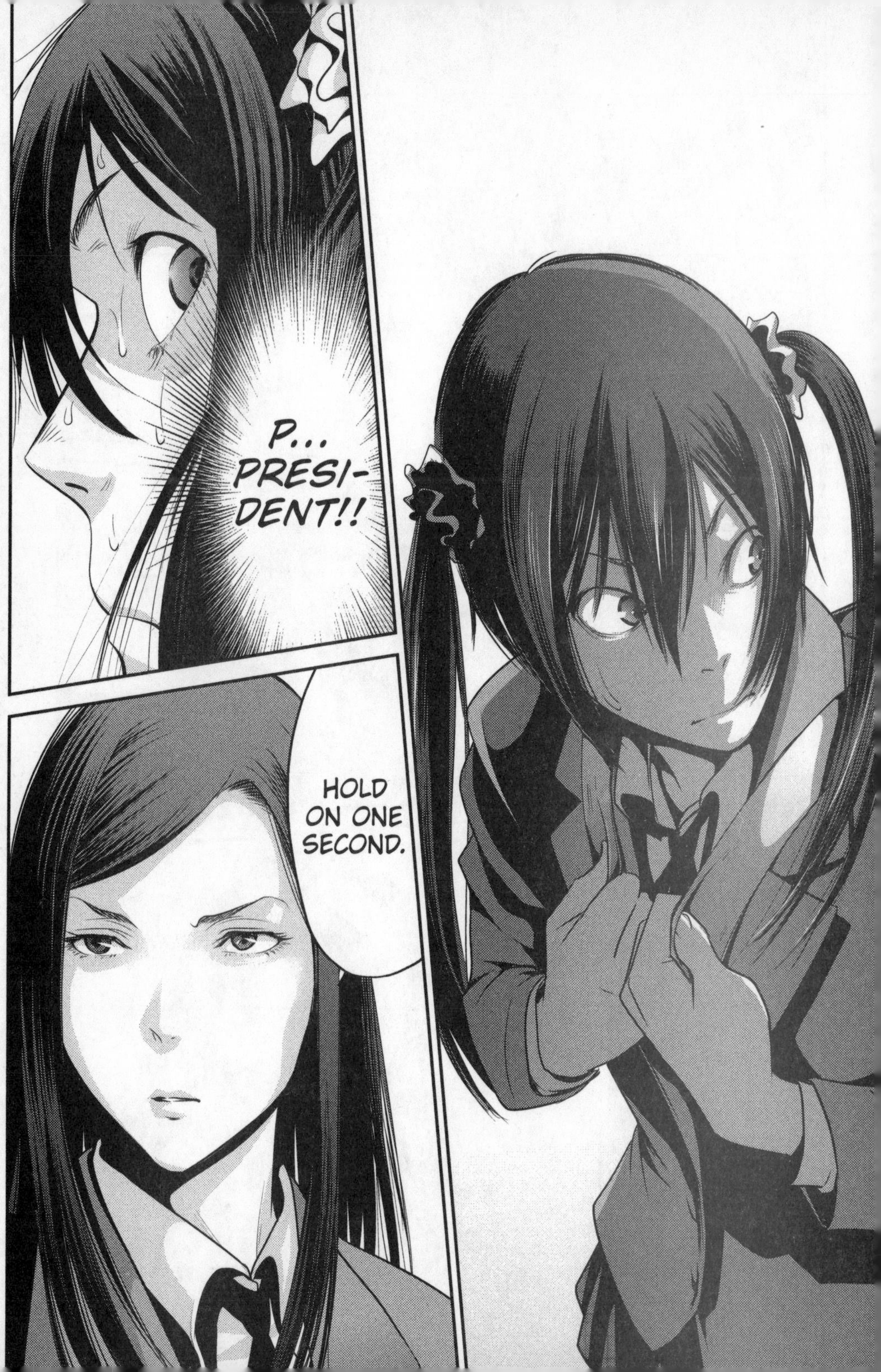
P... PRESI-DENT!!
HOLD ON ONE SECOND.

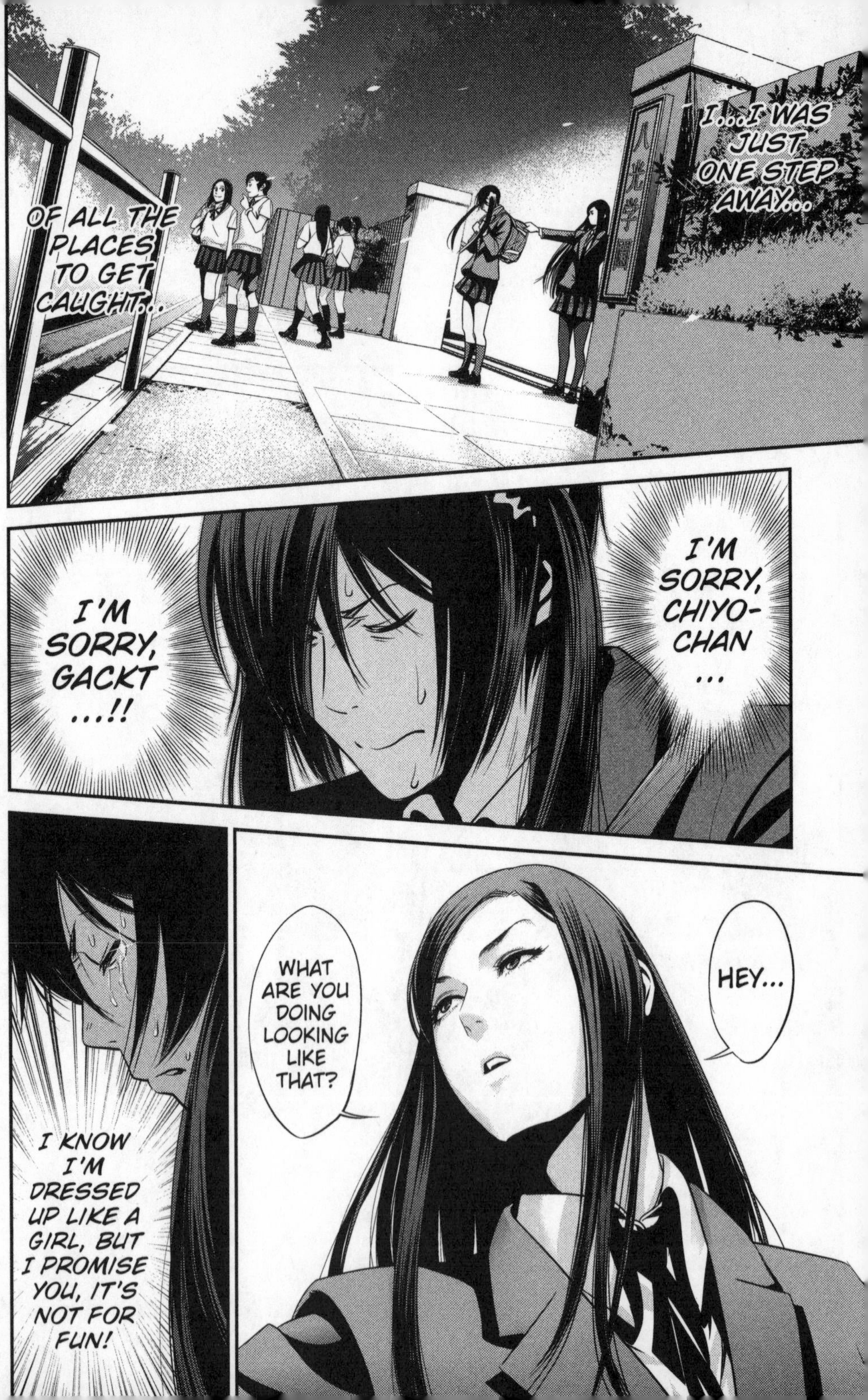

I...I WAS JUST ONE STEP AWAY...
OF ALL THE PLACES TO GET CAUGHT...
I'M SORRY, CHIYO-CHAN...
I'M SORRY, GACKT...!!
HEY...
WHAT ARE YOU DOING LOOKING LIKE THAT?
I KNOW I'M DRESSED UP LIKE A GIRL, BUT I PROMISE YOU, IT'S NOT FOR FUN!

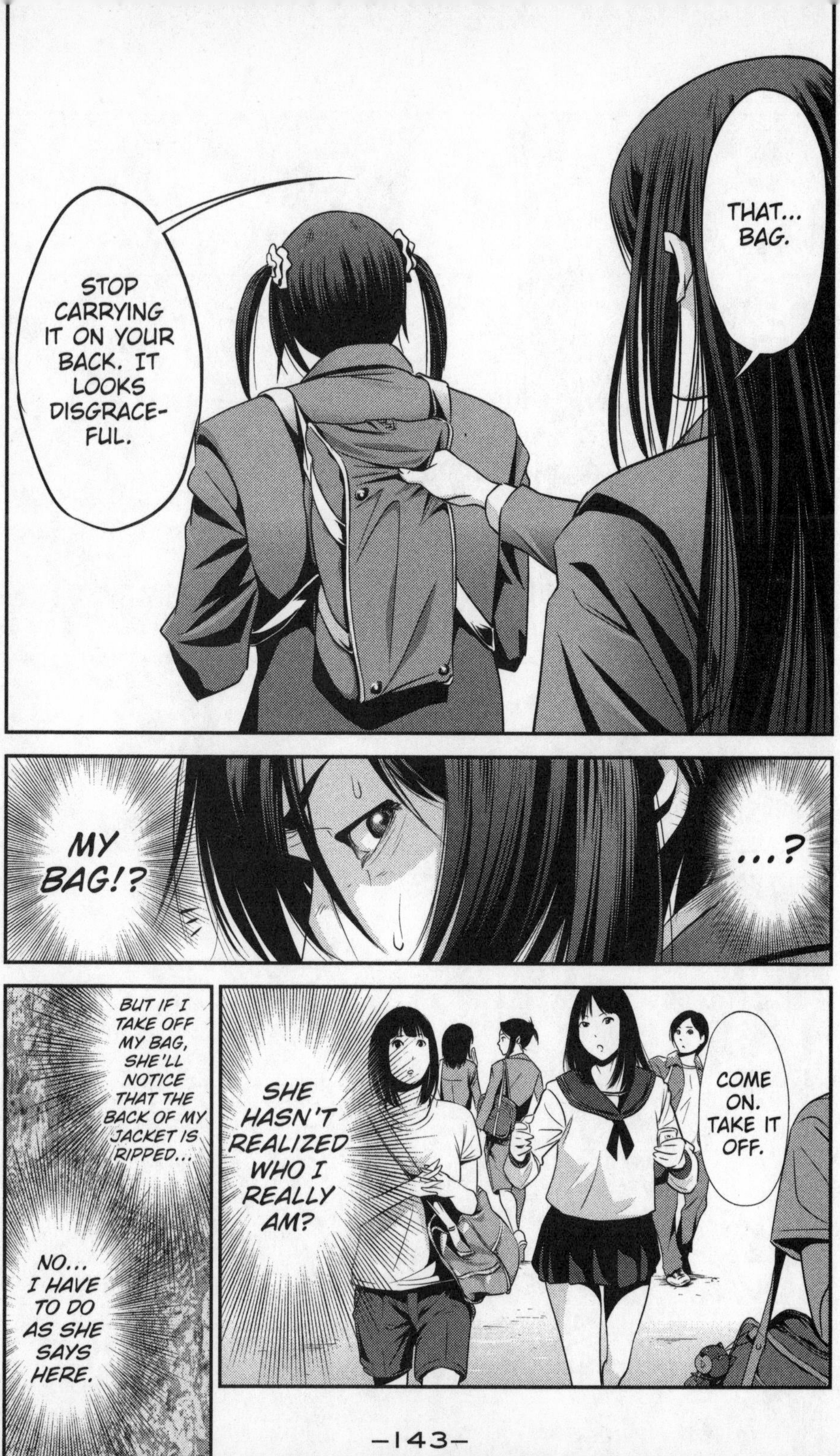
THAT... BAG.
STOP CARRYING IT ON YOUR BACK. IT LOOKS DISGRACE-FUL.
...?
MY BAG!?
COME ON. TAKE IT OFF.
SHE HASN'T REALIZED WHO I REALLY AM?
BUT IF I TAKE OFF MY BAG, SHE'LL NOTICE THAT THE BACK OF MY JACKET IS RIPPED...
NO... I HAVE TO DO AS SHE SAYS HERE.

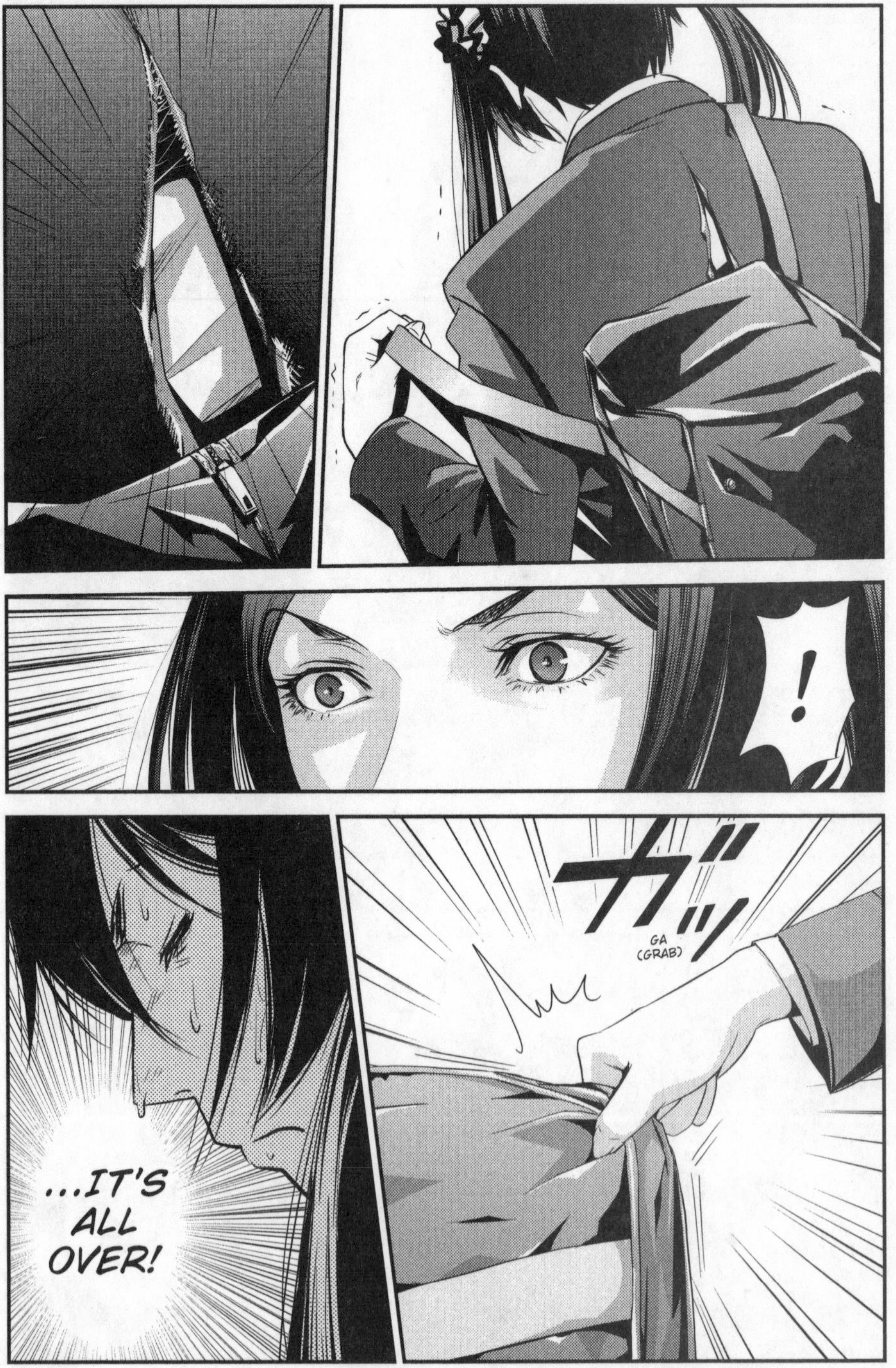
!
ガッ
GA
(GRAB)
...IT'S ALL OVER!

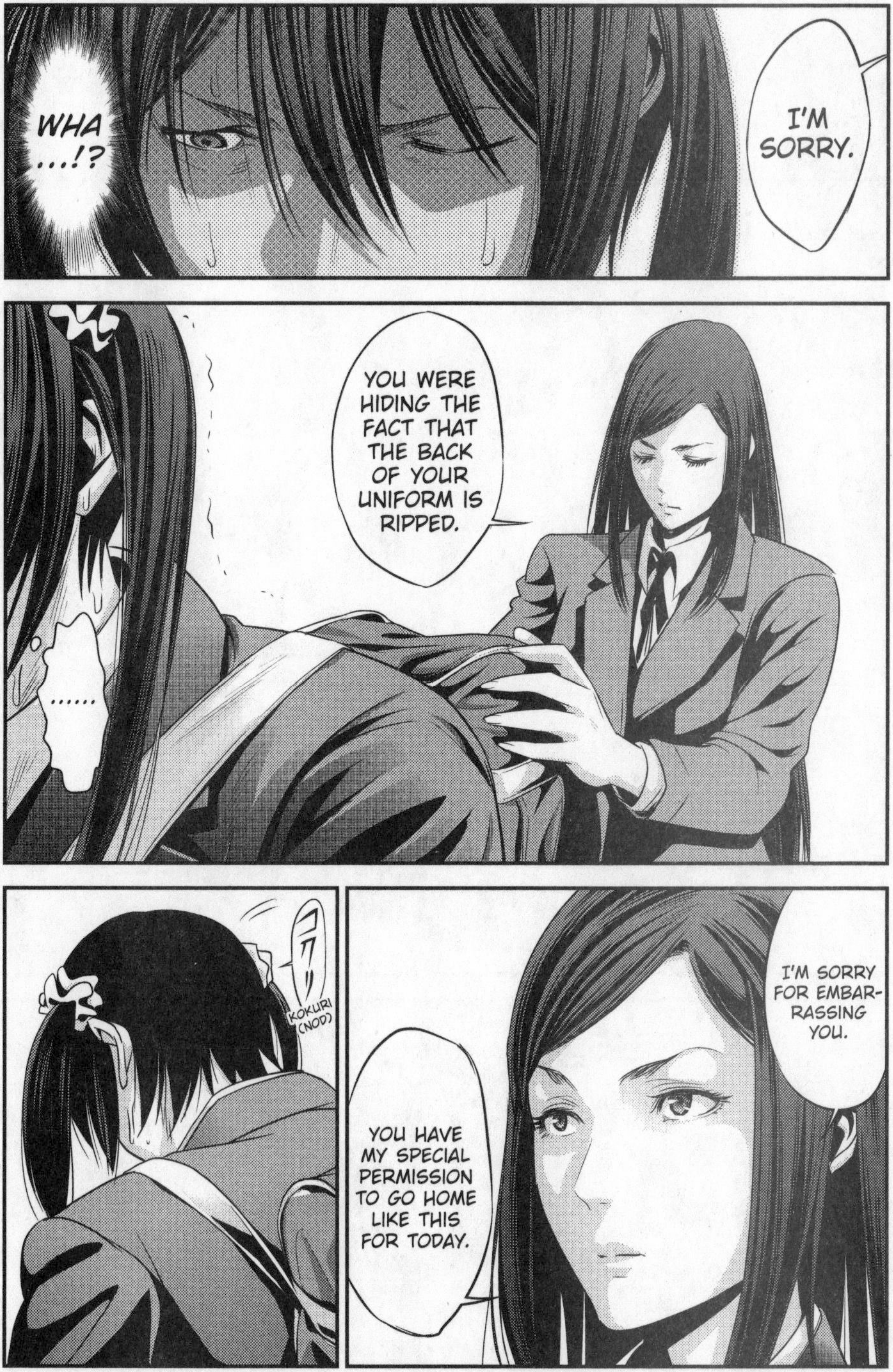
I'M SORRY.
WHA ...!?
YOU WERE HIDING THE FACT THAT THE BACK OF YOUR UNIFORM IS RIPPED.
......
I'M SORRY FOR EMBAR-RASSING YOU.
YOU HAVE MY SPECIAL PERMISSION TO GO HOME LIKE THIS FOR TODAY.
コクリ
KOKURI (NOD)

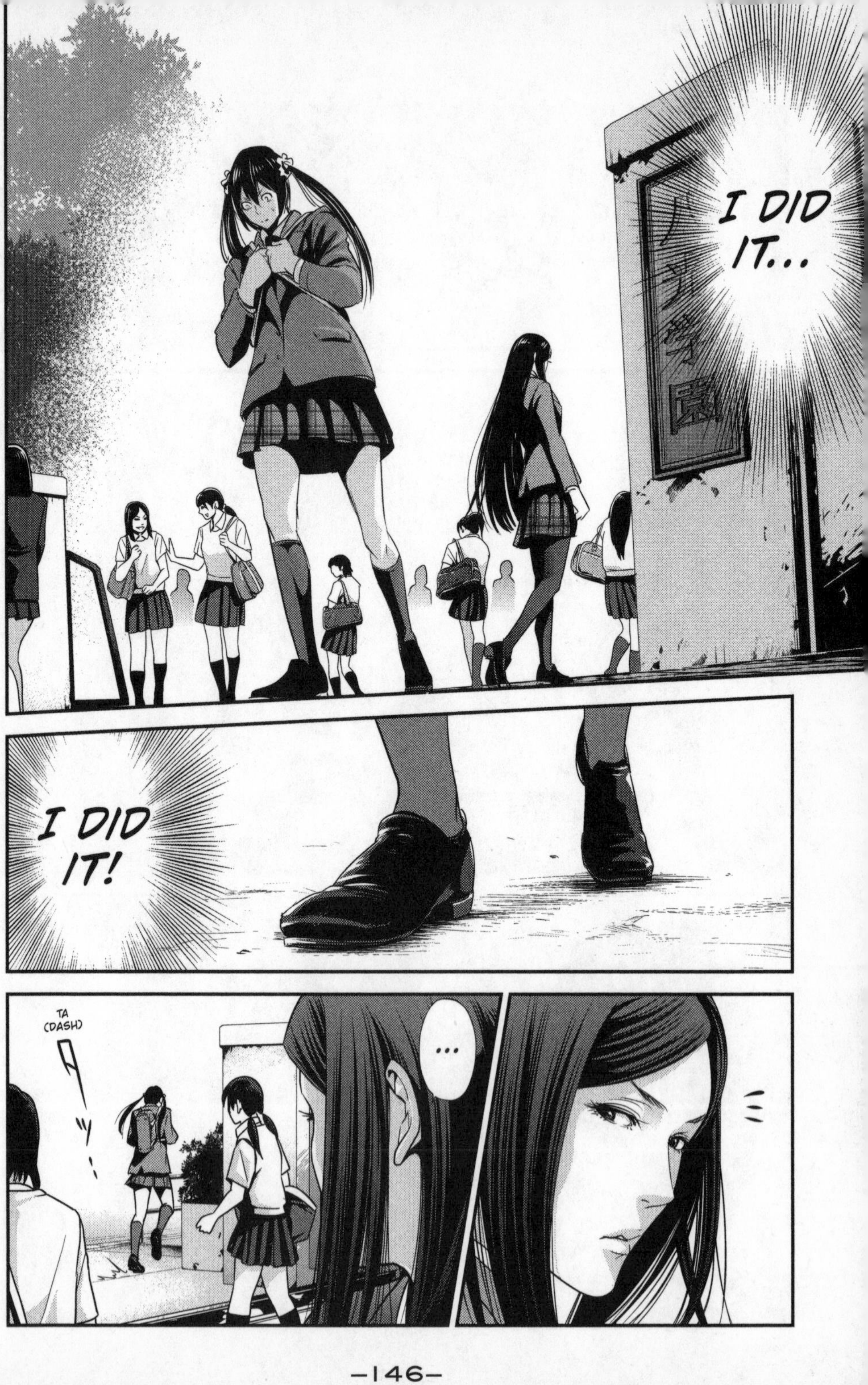
I DID IT...
I DID IT!
...
TA (DASH)

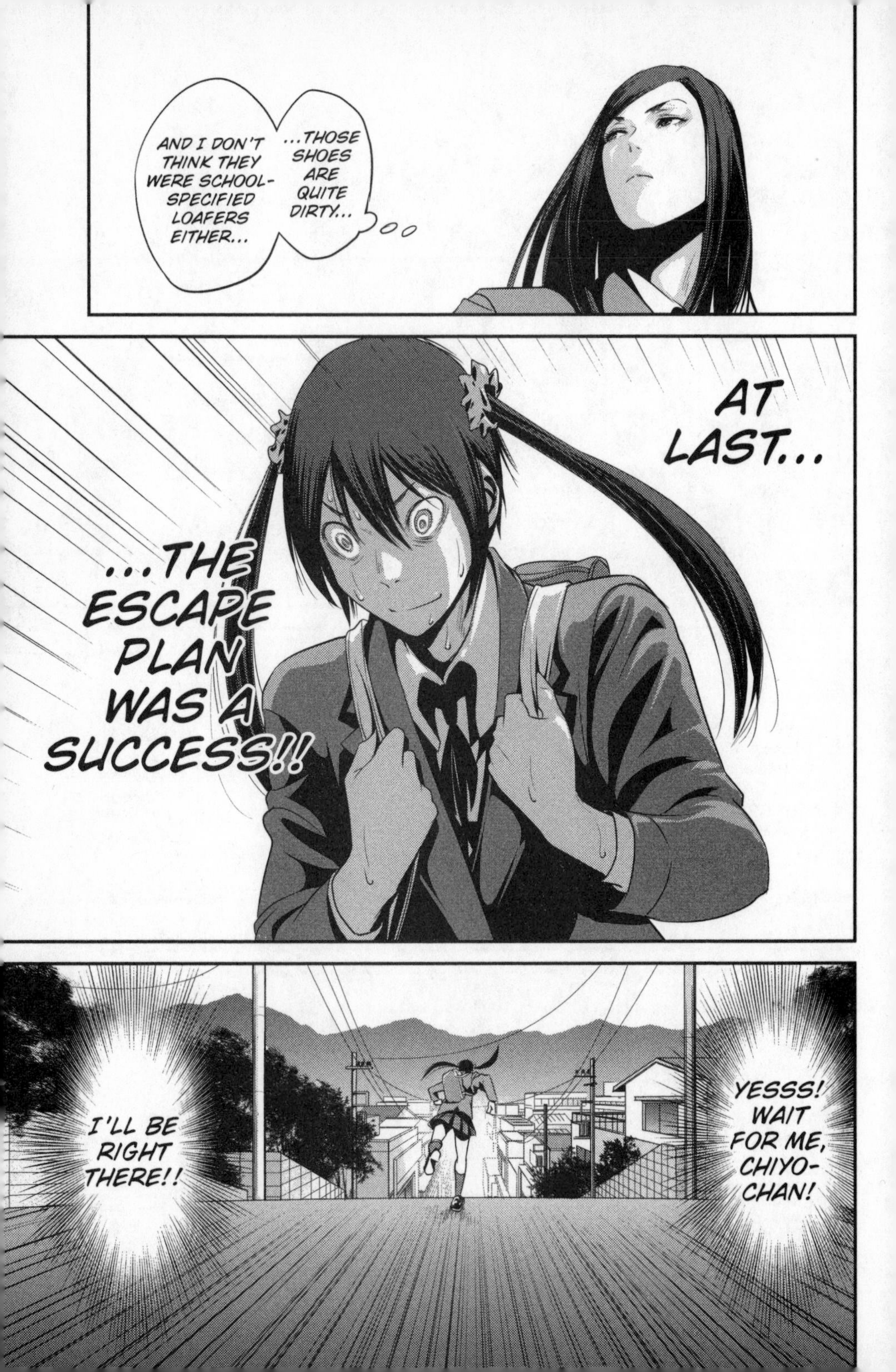
...THOSE SHOES ARE QUITE DIRTY...
AND I DON'T THINK THEY WERE SCHOOL-SPECIFIED LOAFERS EITHER...
AT LAST...
...THE ESCAPE PLAN WAS A SUCCESS!!
YESSS! WAIT FOR ME, CHIYO-CHAN!
I'LL BE RIGHT THERE!!

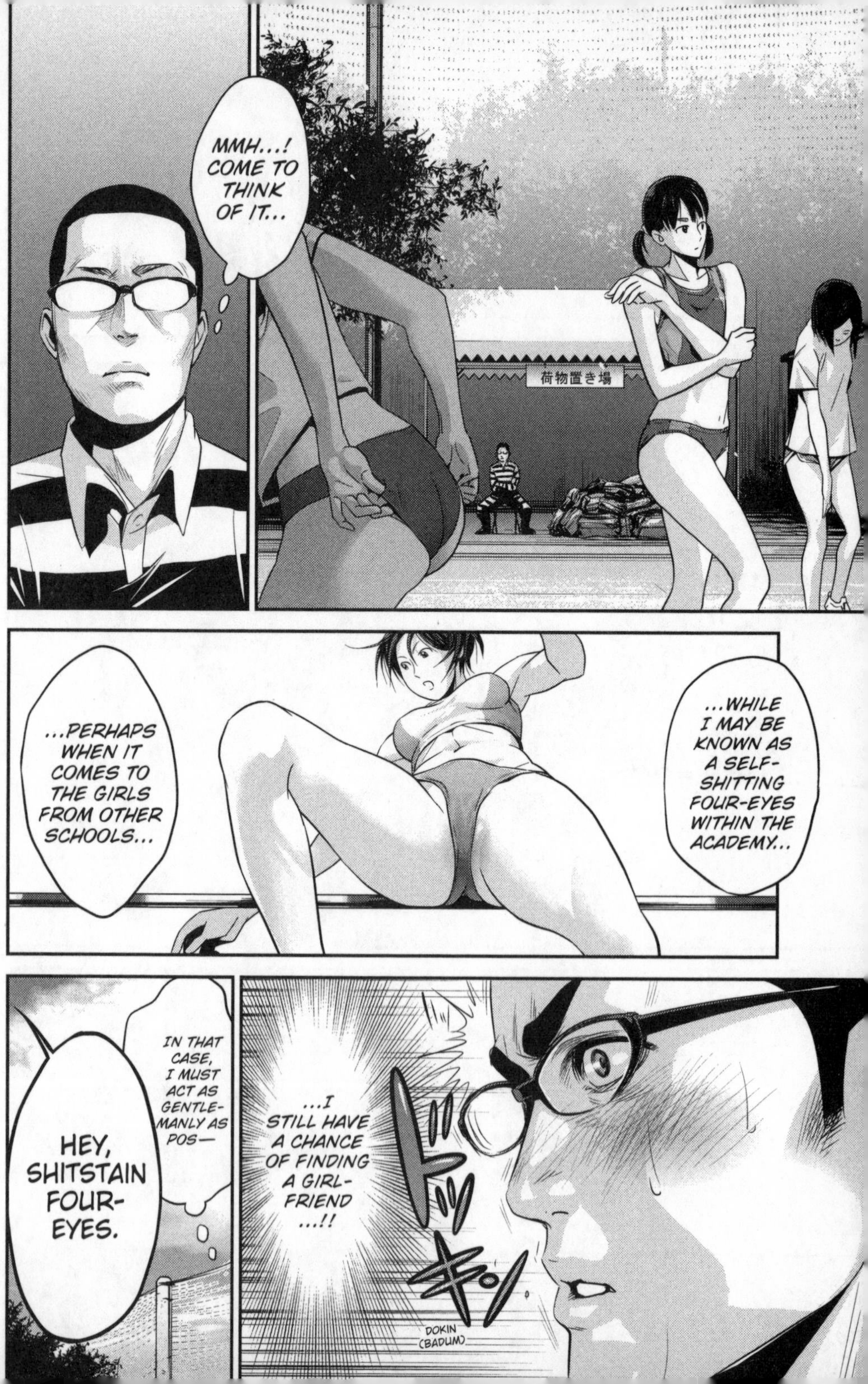
荷物置き場
MMH...! COME TO THINK OF IT...
...WHILE I MAY BE KNOWN AS A SELF-SHITTING FOUR-EYES WITHIN THE ACADEMY...
...PERHAPS WHEN IT COMES TO THE GIRLS FROM OTHER SCHOOLS...
...I STILL HAVE A CHANCE OF FINDING A GIRL-FRIEND ...!!
DOKIN (BADUM)
IN THAT CASE, I MUST ACT AS GENTLE-MANLY AS POS—
HEY, SHITSTAIN FOUR-EYES.

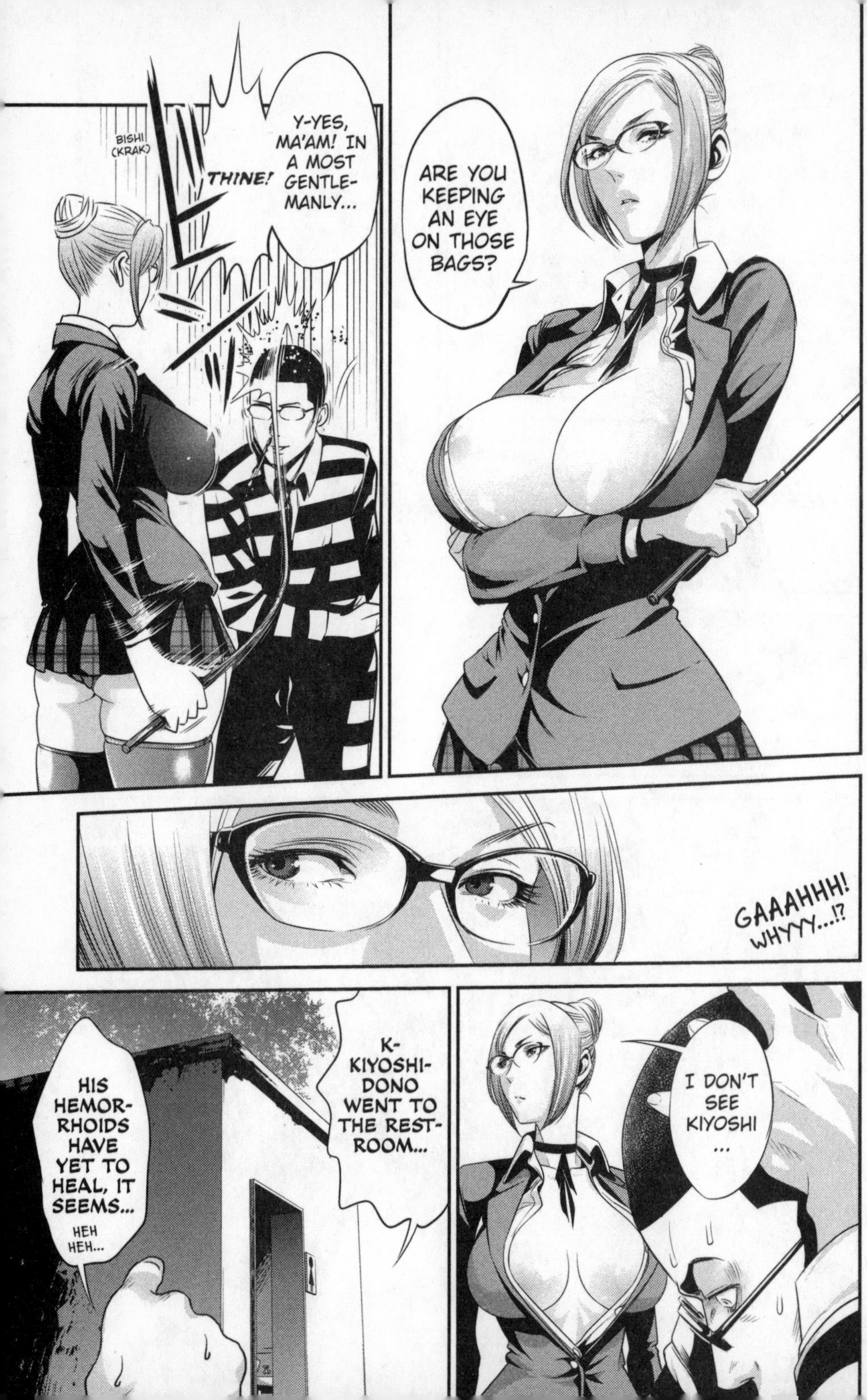
ARE YOU KEEPING AN EYE ON THOSE BAGS?
Y-YES, MA'AM! IN A MOST GENTLE-MANLY...
THINE!
BISHI (KRAK)
GAAAHHH! WHYYY...!?
I DON'T SEE KIYOSHI ...
K-KIYOSHI-DONO WENT TO THE REST-ROOM...
HIS HEMOR-RHOIDS HAVE YET TO HEAL, IT SEEMS...
HEH HEH...

HEY, YOU...

WHAT A HOPELESS CASE, INDEED.

Y-YES?

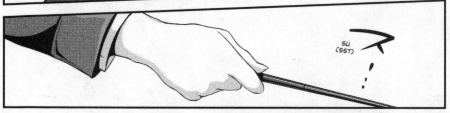

SU (SST)

!

AH!!

PAKKURI (PLOP)

WHAT'S THE MEANING OF THIS?

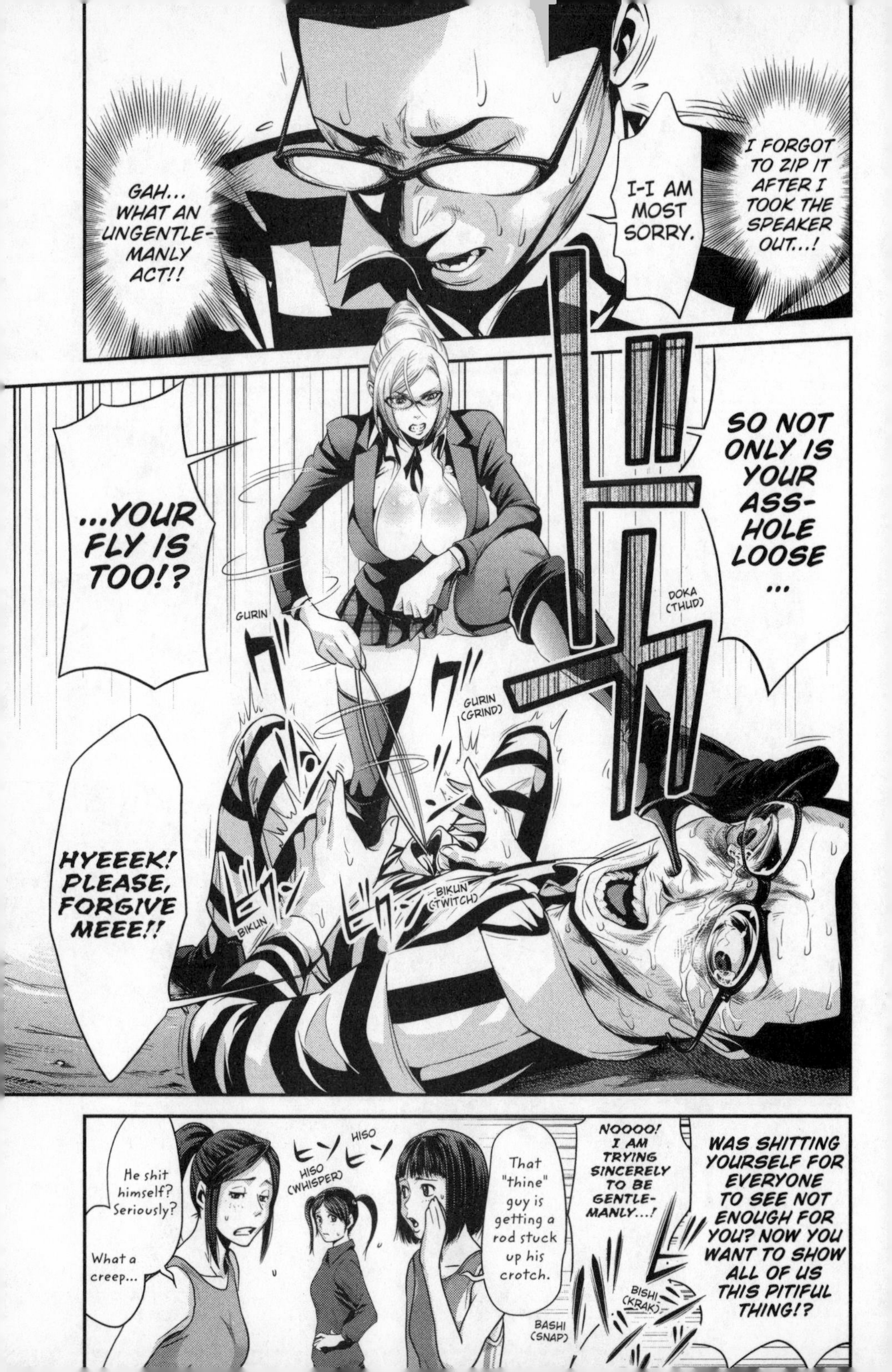
I FORGOT TO ZIP IT AFTER I TOOK THE SPEAKER OUT...!
I-I AM MOST SORRY.
GAH... WHAT AN UNGENTLE-MANLY ACT!!
SO NOT ONLY IS YOUR ASS-HOLE LOOSE ...
DOKA (THUD)
...YOUR FLY IS TOO!?
GURIN
GURIN (GRIND)
BIKUN (TWITCH)
BIKUN
HYEEEK! PLEASE, FORGIVE MEEE!!
WAS SHITTING YOURSELF FOR EVERYONE TO SEE NOT ENOUGH FOR YOU? NOW YOU WANT TO SHOW ALL OF US THIS PITIFUL THING!?
NOOOO! I AM TRYING SINCERELY TO BE GENTLE-MANLY...!
BISHI (KRAK)
BASHI (SNAP)
That "thine" guy is getting a rod stuck up his crotch.
HISO
HISO (WHISPER)
He shit himself? Seriously?
What a creep...

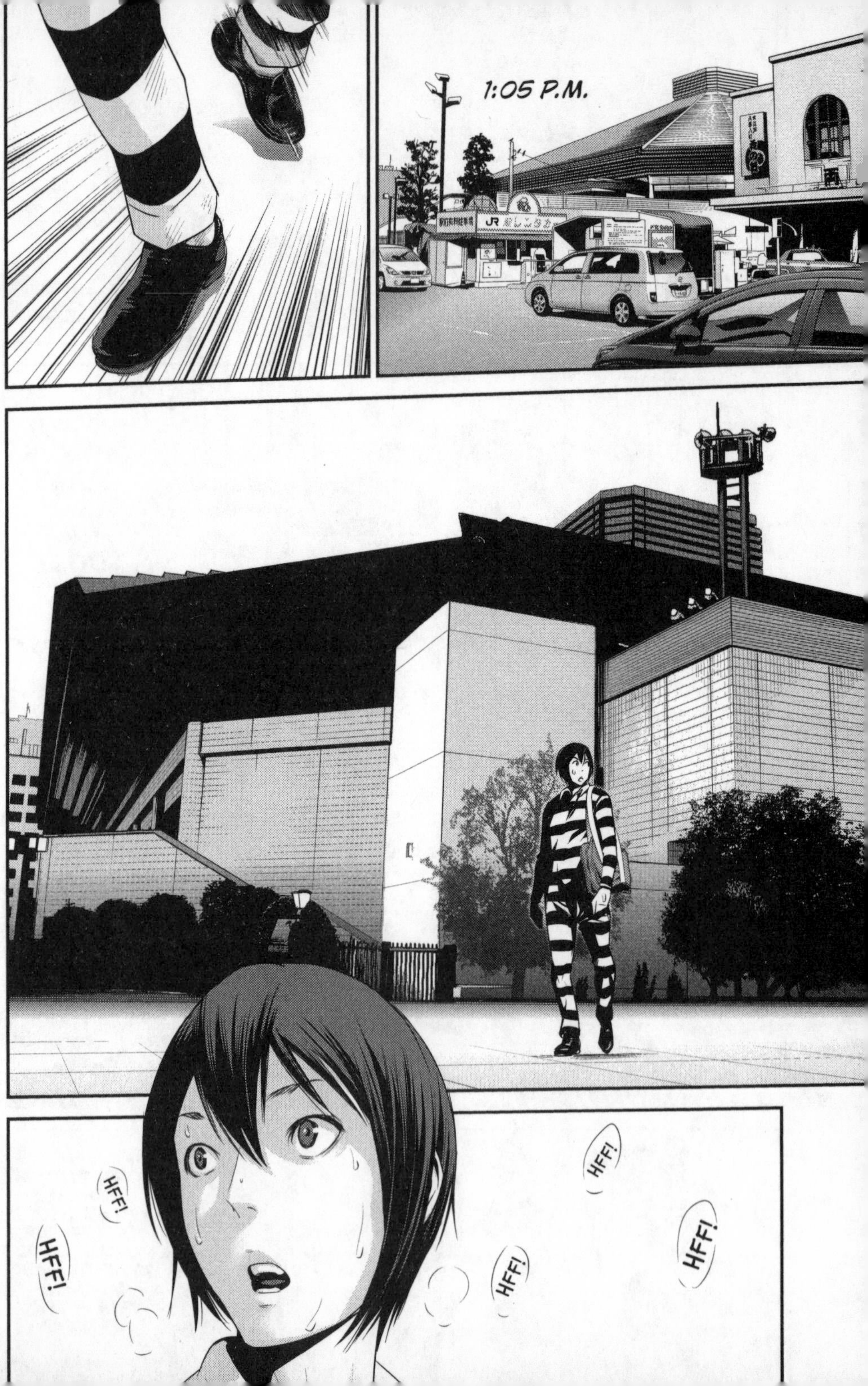
1:05 P.M.
HFF!
HFF!
HFF!
HFF!
HFF!

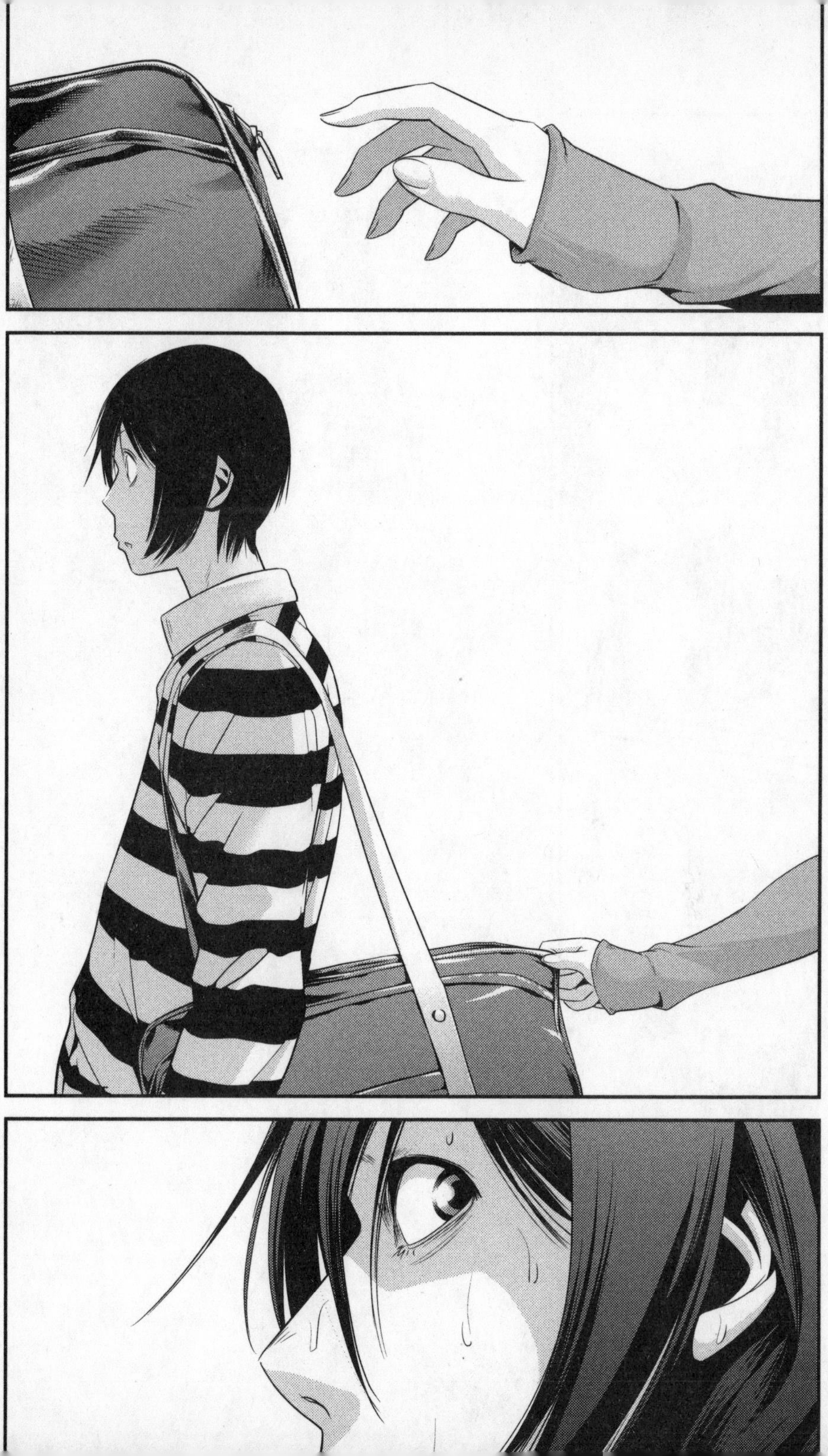

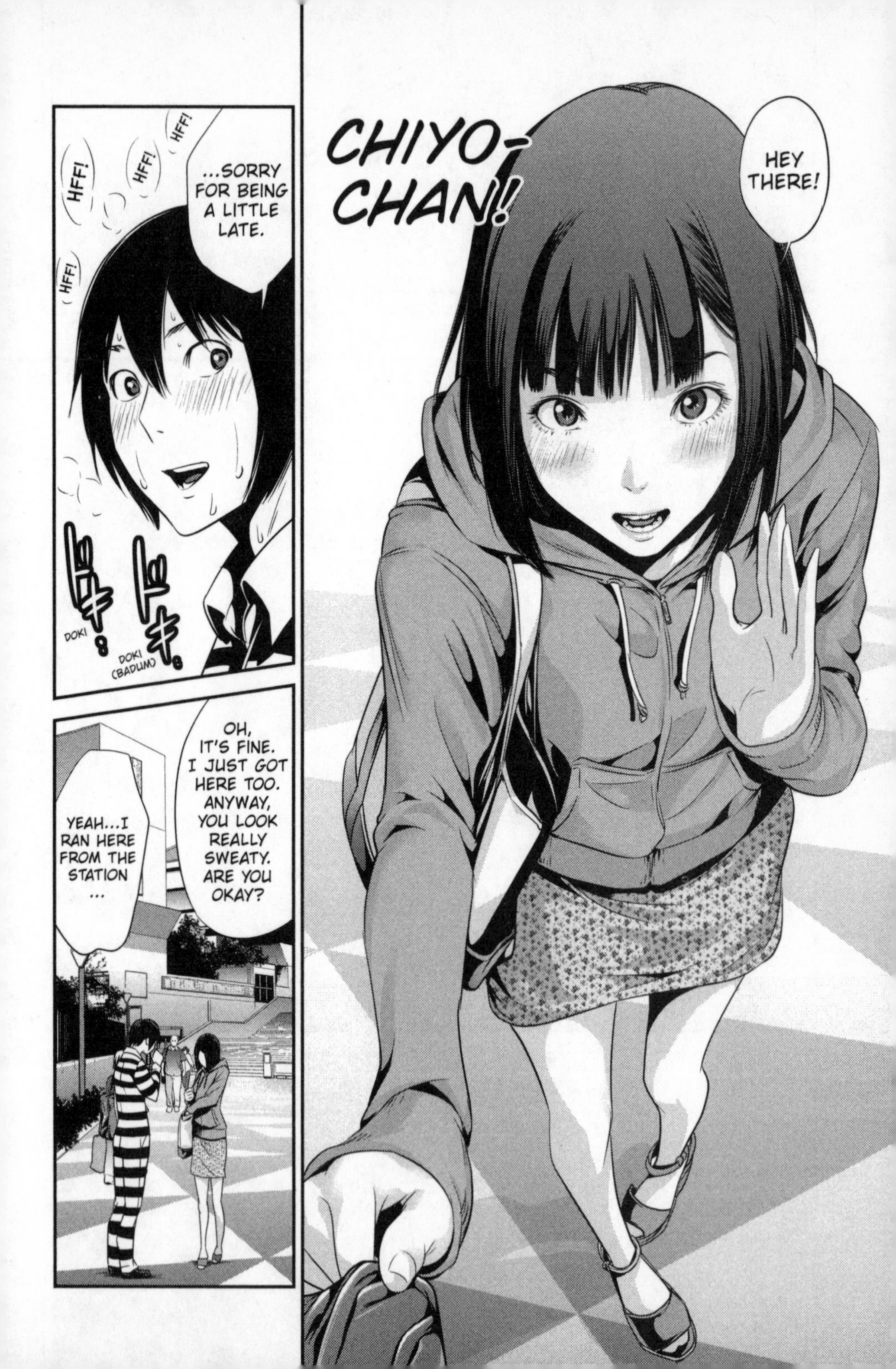
HEY THERE!
CHIYO-CHAN!!
...SORRY FOR BEING A LITTLE LATE.
HFF!
HFF!
HFF!
HFF!
DOKI
DOKI (BADUM)
OH, IT'S FINE. I JUST GOT HERE TOO. ANYWAY, YOU LOOK REALLY SWEATY. ARE YOU OKAY?
YEAH...I RAN HERE FROM THE STATION ...

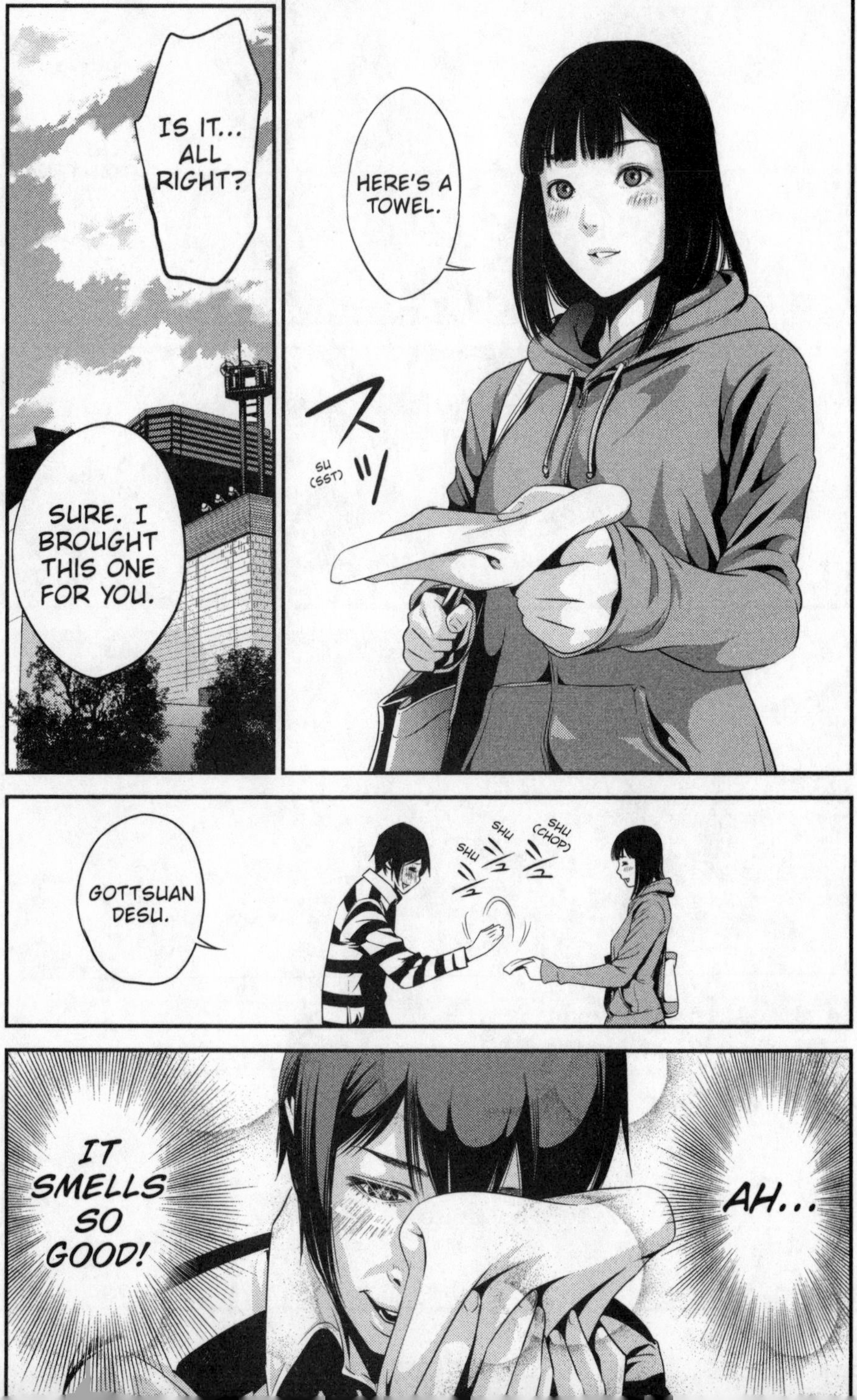
HERE'S A TOWEL.
スッ
SU (SST)
IS IT... ALL RIGHT?
SURE. I BROUGHT THIS ONE FOR YOU.
SHU (CHOP)
SHU
SHU
GOTTSUAN DESU.
AH...
IT SMELLS SO GOOD!

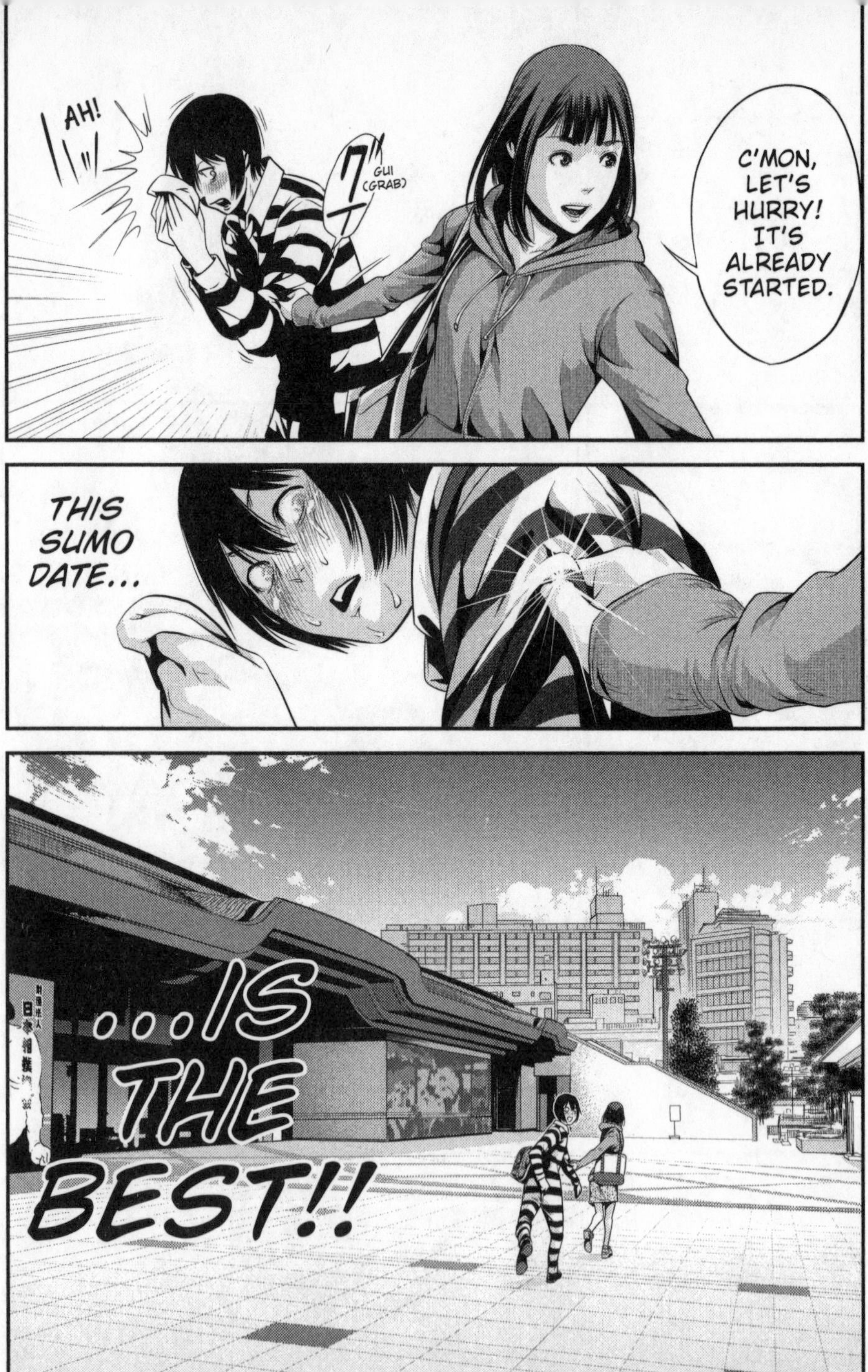
C'MON, LET'S HURRY! IT'S ALREADY STARTED.
GUI (GRAB)
AH!
THIS SUMO DATE...
...IS THE BEST!!

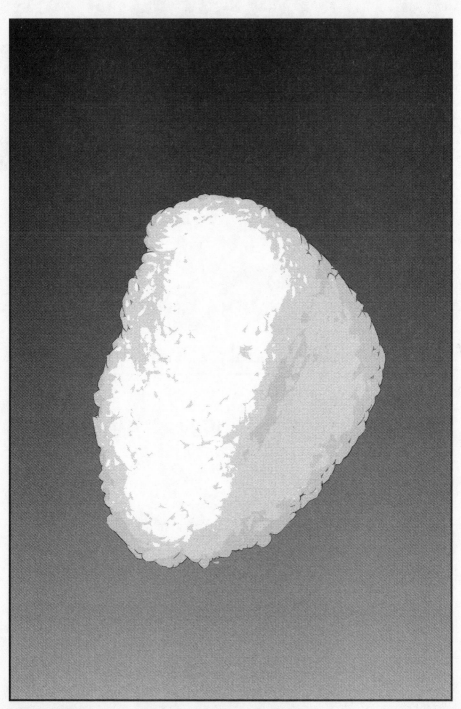

CHAPTER 27: TAKE ME TO SUMO

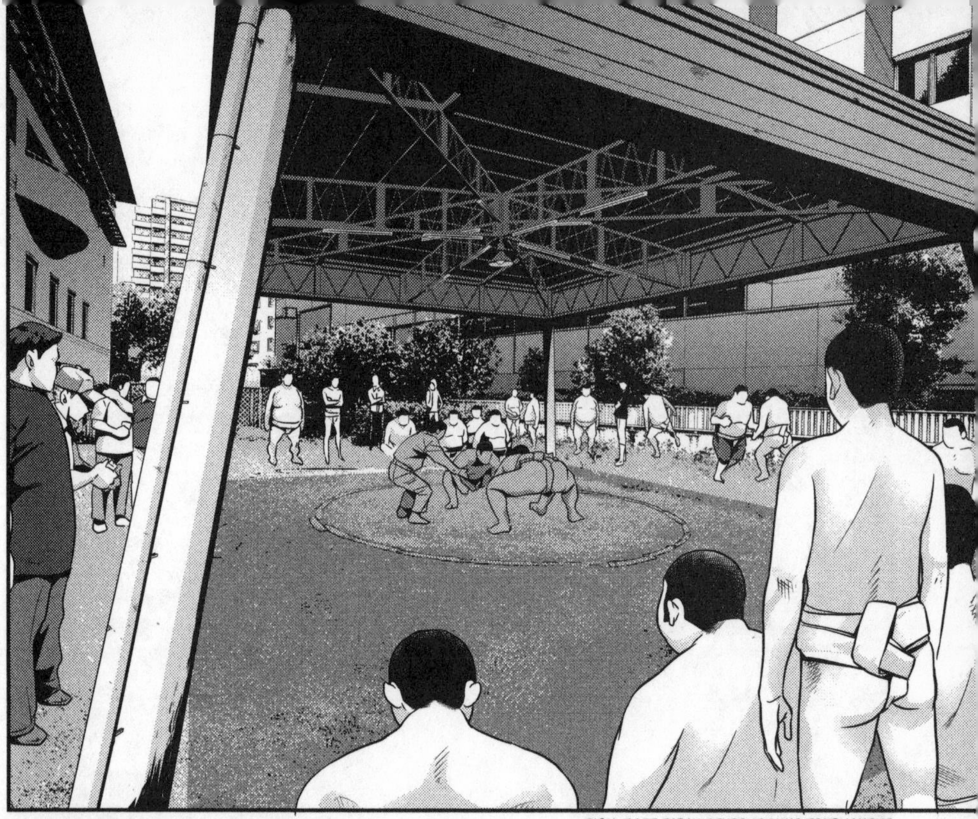

SIGN: EAST JAPAN STUDENT SUMO TOURNAMENT

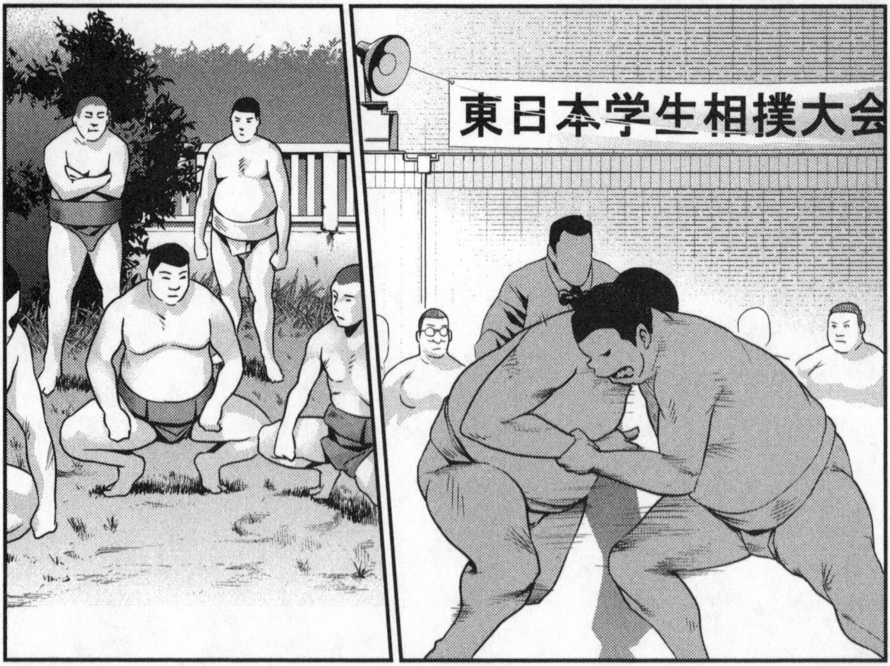
東日本学生相撲大会

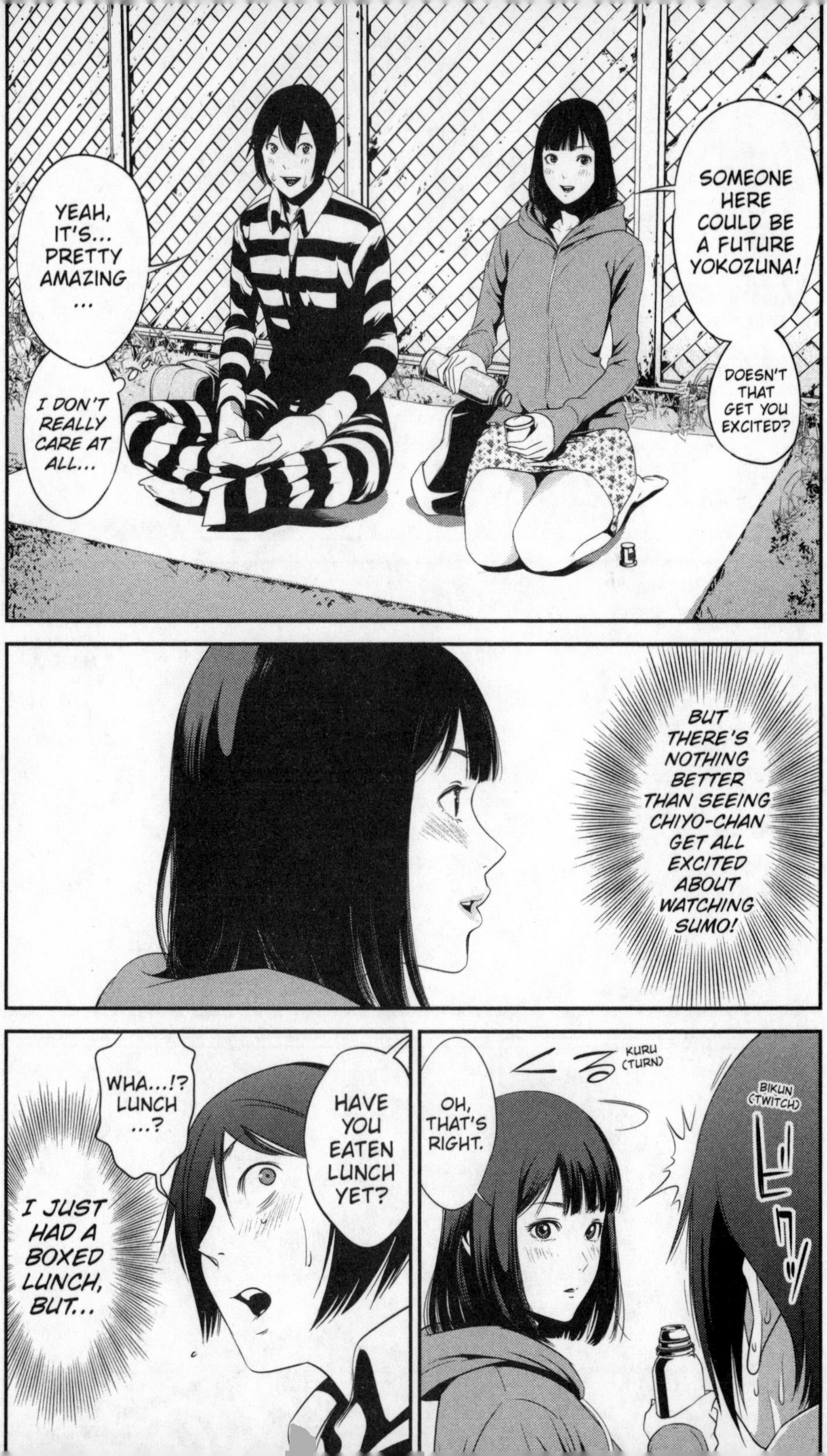
SOMEONE HERE COULD BE A FUTURE YOKOZUNA!
DOESN'T THAT GET YOU EXCITED?
YEAH, IT'S... PRETTY AMAZING ...
I DON'T REALLY CARE AT ALL...
BUT THERE'S NOTHING BETTER THAN SEEING CHIYO-CHAN GET ALL EXCITED ABOUT WATCHING SUMO!
BIKUN (TWITCH)
KURU (TURN)
OH, THAT'S RIGHT.
HAVE YOU EATEN LUNCH YET?
WHA...!? LUNCH ...?
I JUST HAD A BOXED LUNCH, BUT...

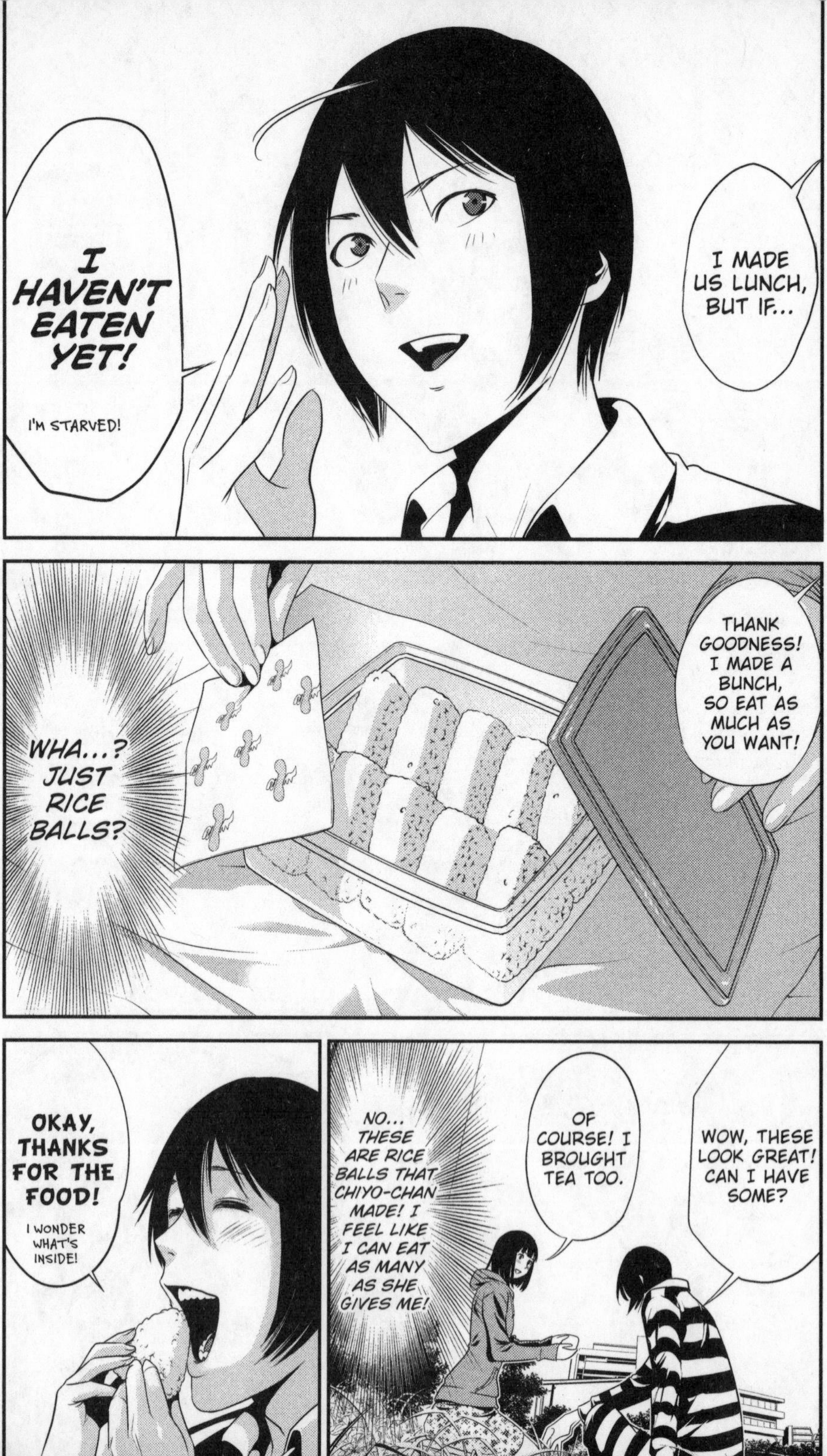
I MADE US LUNCH, BUT IF...
I HAVEN'T EATEN YET!
I'M STARVED!
THANK GOODNESS! I MADE A BUNCH, SO EAT AS MUCH AS YOU WANT!
WHA...? JUST RICE BALLS?
WOW, THESE LOOK GREAT! CAN I HAVE SOME?
OF COURSE! I BROUGHT TEA TOO.
NO... THESE ARE RICE BALLS THAT CHIYO-CHAN MADE! I FEEL LIKE I CAN EAT AS MANY AS SHE GIVES ME!
OKAY, THANKS FOR THE FOOD!
I WONDER WHAT'S INSIDE!

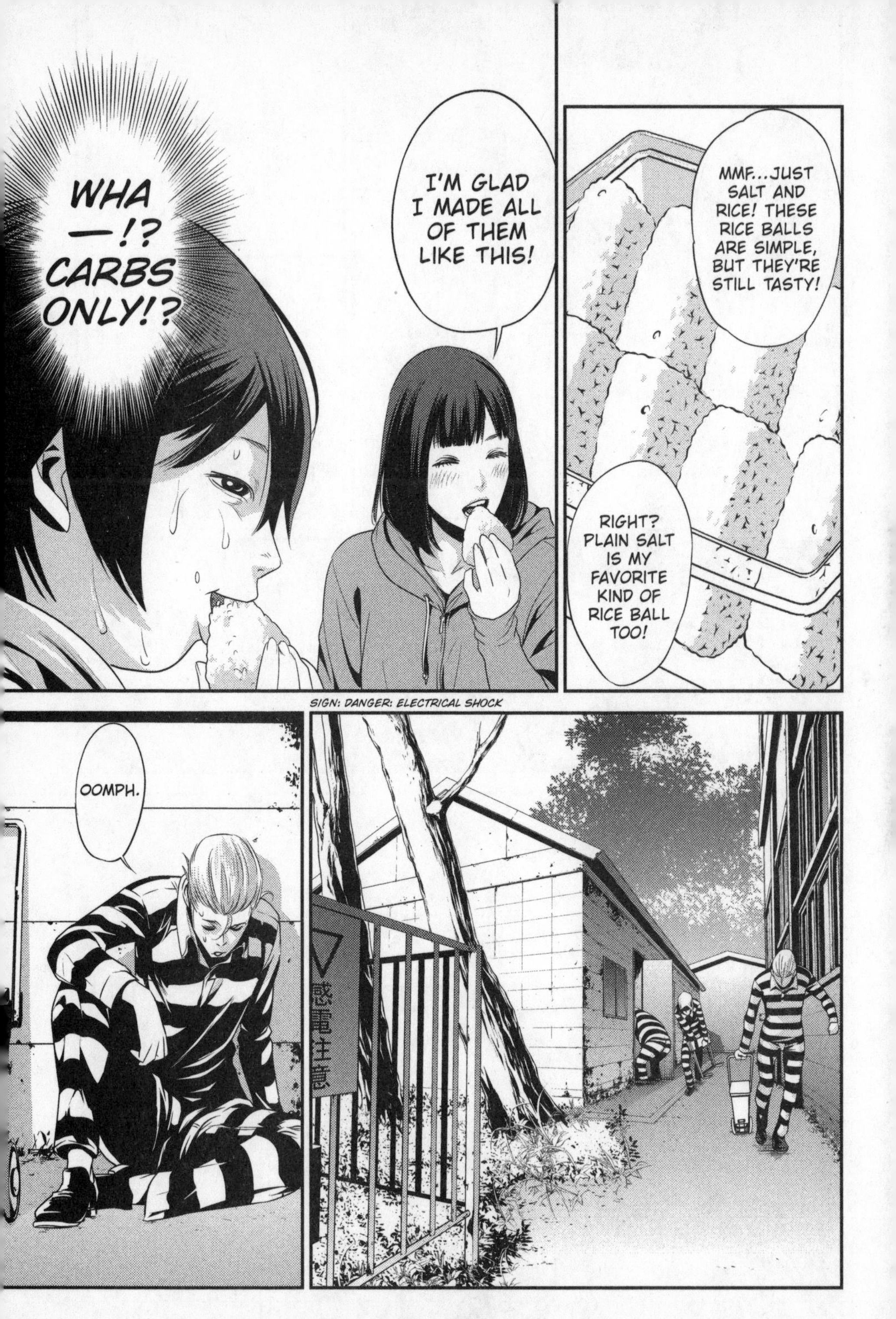
MMF...JUST SALT AND RICE! THESE RICE BALLS ARE SIMPLE, BUT THEY'RE STILL TASTY!
RIGHT? PLAIN SALT IS MY FAVORITE KIND OF RICE BALL TOO!
I'M GLAD I MADE ALL OF THEM LIKE THIS!
WHA—!? CARBS ONLY!?
SIGN: DANGER: ELECTRICAL SHOCK
感電注意
OOMPH.

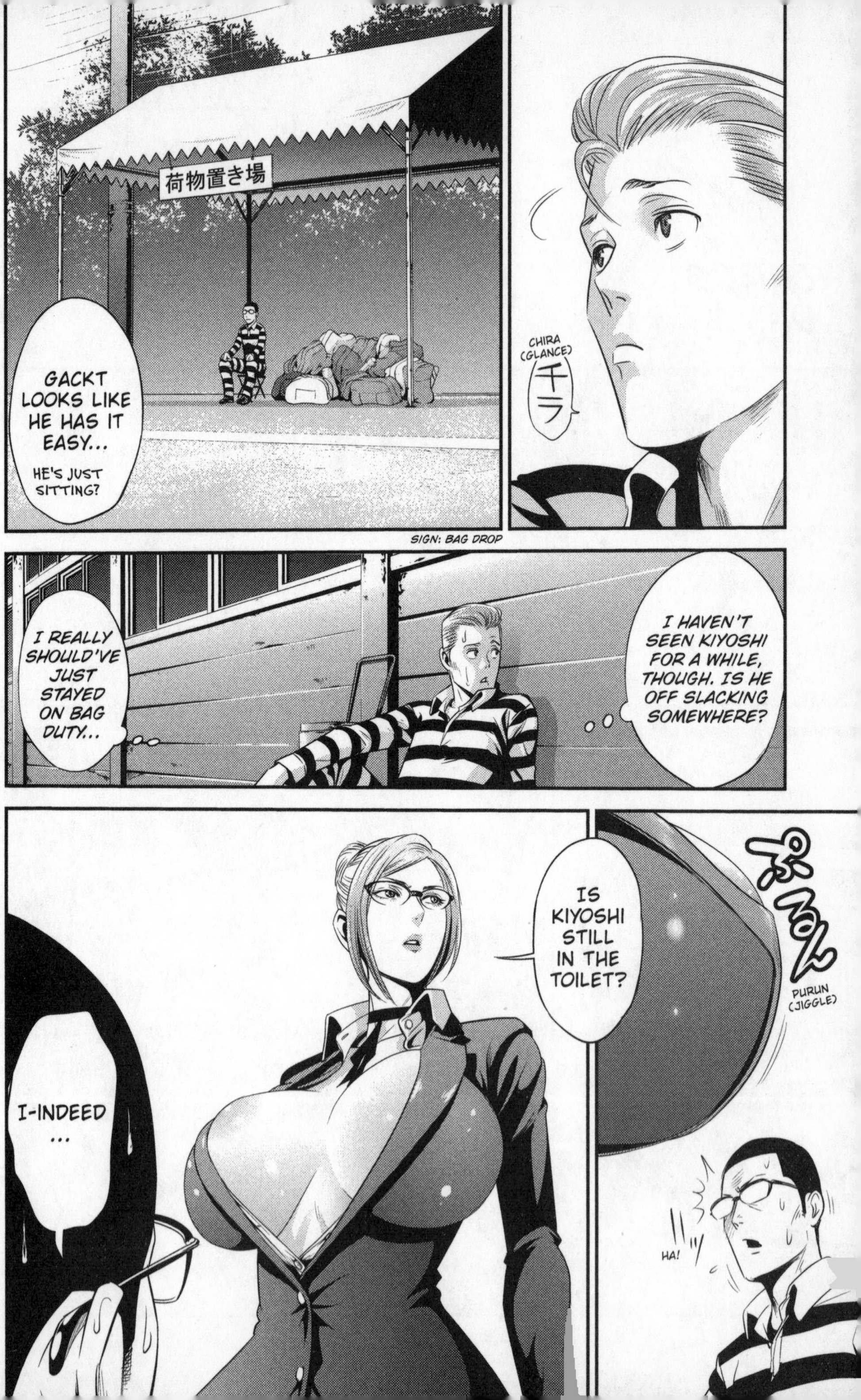
CHIRA (GLANCE)
チラ
荷物置き場
GACKT LOOKS LIKE HE HAS IT EASY...
HE'S JUST SITTING?
SIGN: BAG DROP
I HAVEN'T SEEN KIYOSHI FOR A WHILE, THOUGH. IS HE OFF SLACKING SOMEWHERE?
I REALLY SHOULD'VE JUST STAYED ON BAG DUTY...
ぷるん
PURUN (JIGGLE)
HA!
IS KIYOSHI STILL IN THE TOILET?
I-INDEED...

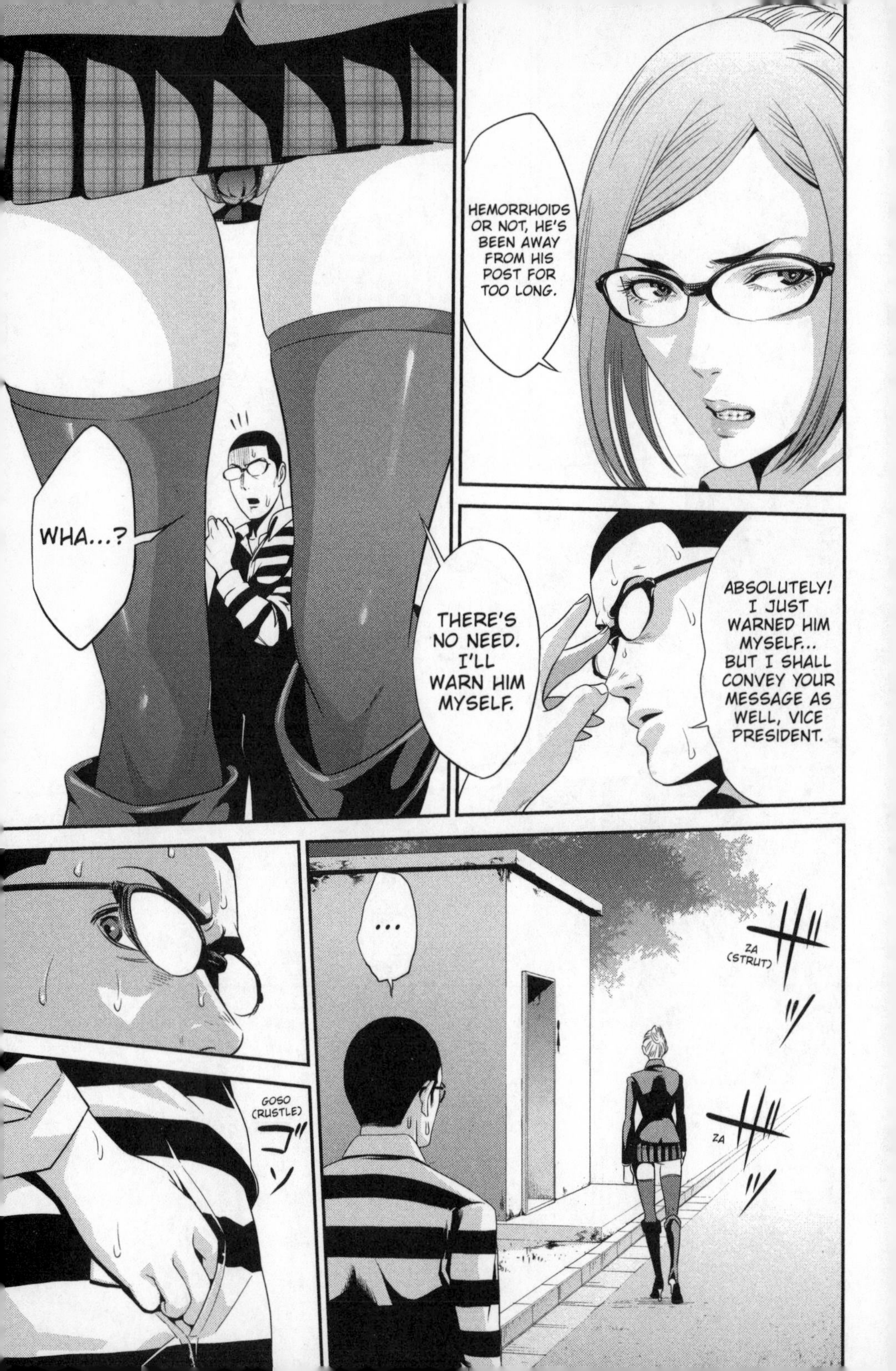
HEMORRHOIDS OR NOT, HE'S BEEN AWAY FROM HIS POST FOR TOO LONG.
ABSOLUTELY! I JUST WARNED HIM MYSELF... BUT I SHALL CONVEY YOUR MESSAGE AS WELL, VICE PRESIDENT.
THERE'S NO NEED. I'LL WARN HIM MYSELF.
WHA...?
ZA (STRUT)
ZA
...
GOSO (RUSTLE)

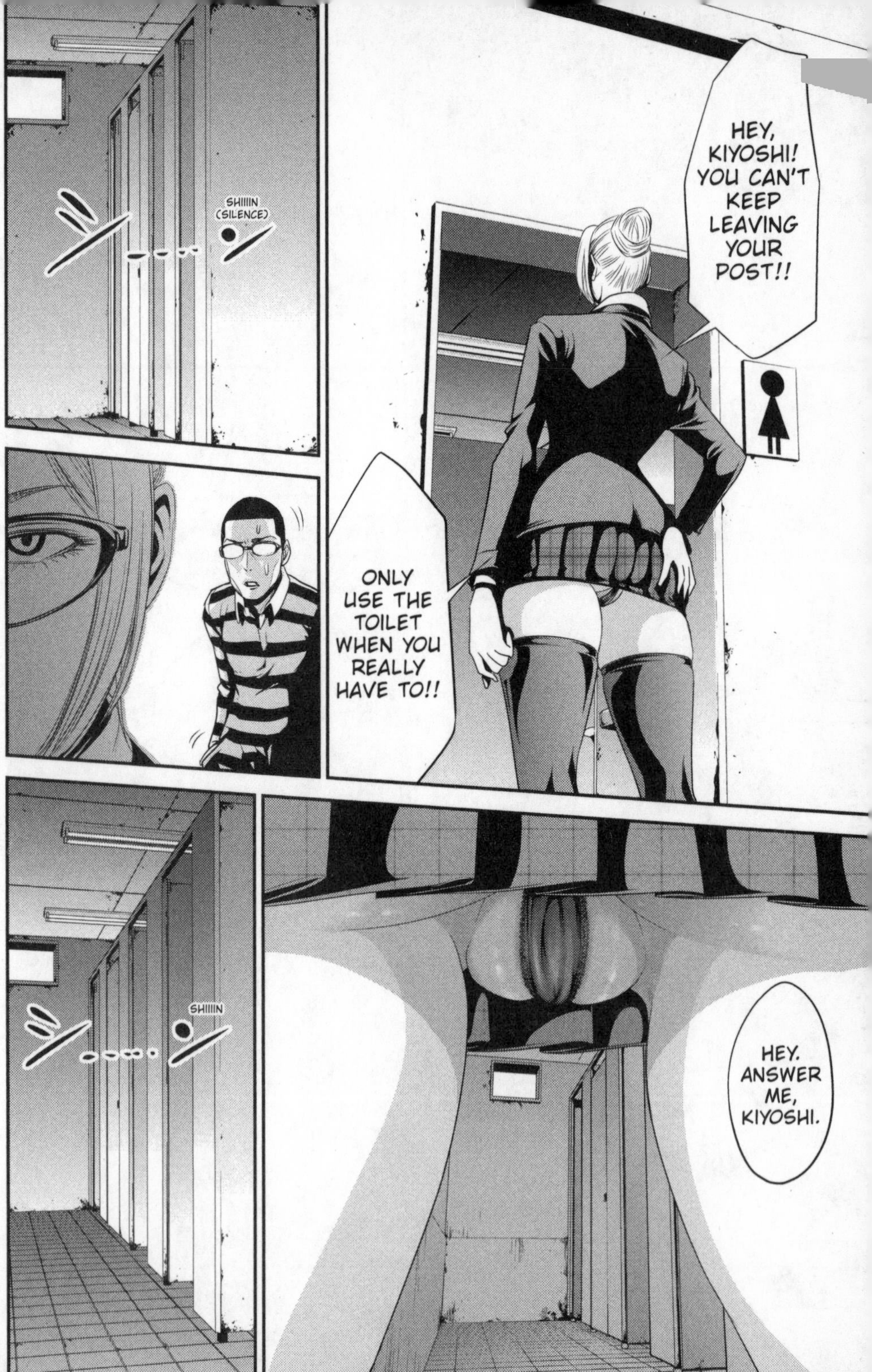
HEY, KIYOSHI! YOU CAN'T KEEP LEAVING YOUR POST!!
ONLY USE THE TOILET WHEN YOU REALLY HAVE TO!!
SHIIIN (SILENCE)
HEY. ANSWER ME, KIYOSHI.
SHIIIN

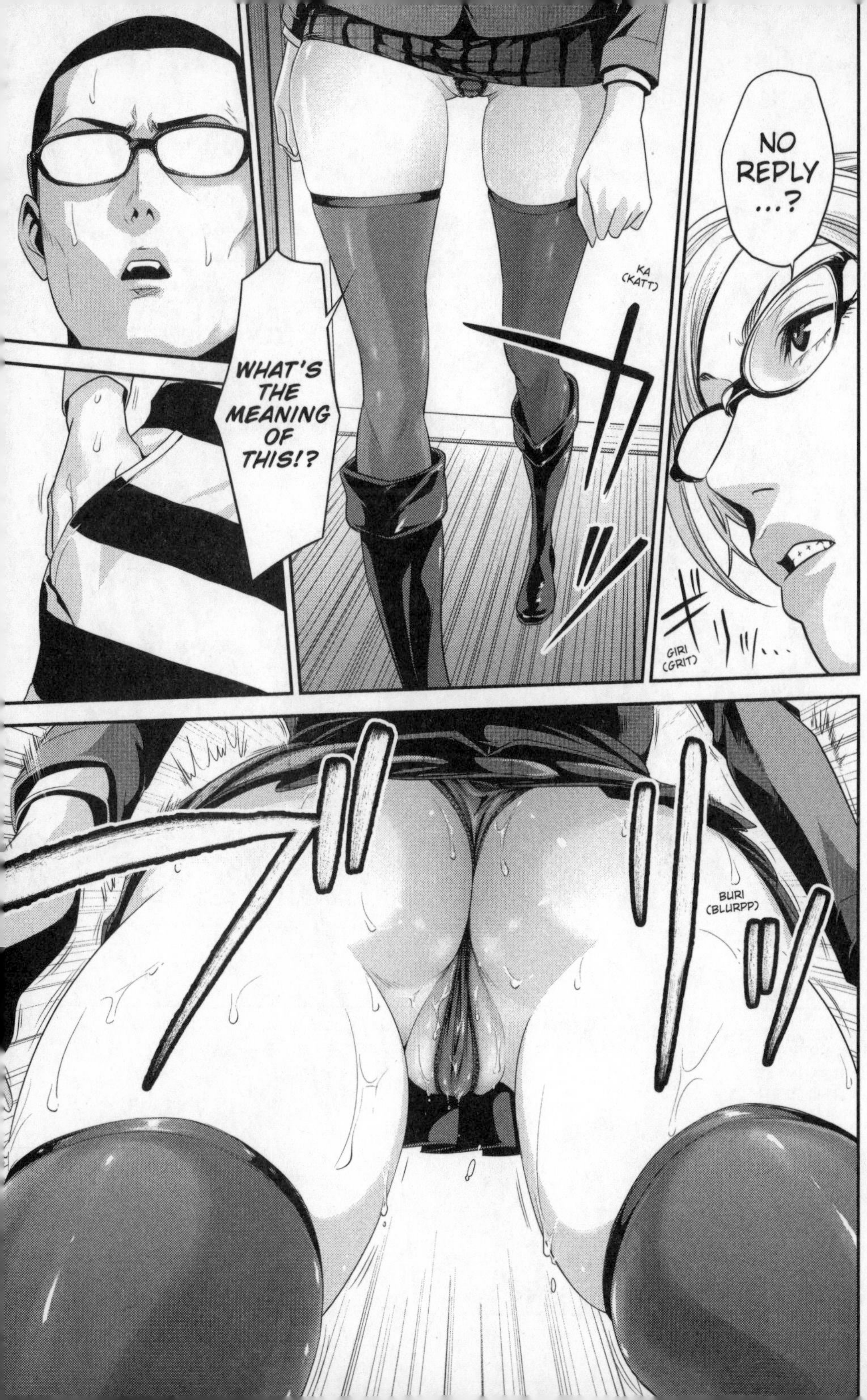
NO REPLY ...?
GIRI (GRIT)
KA (KATT)
WHAT'S THE MEANING OF THIS!?
BURI (BLURPP)

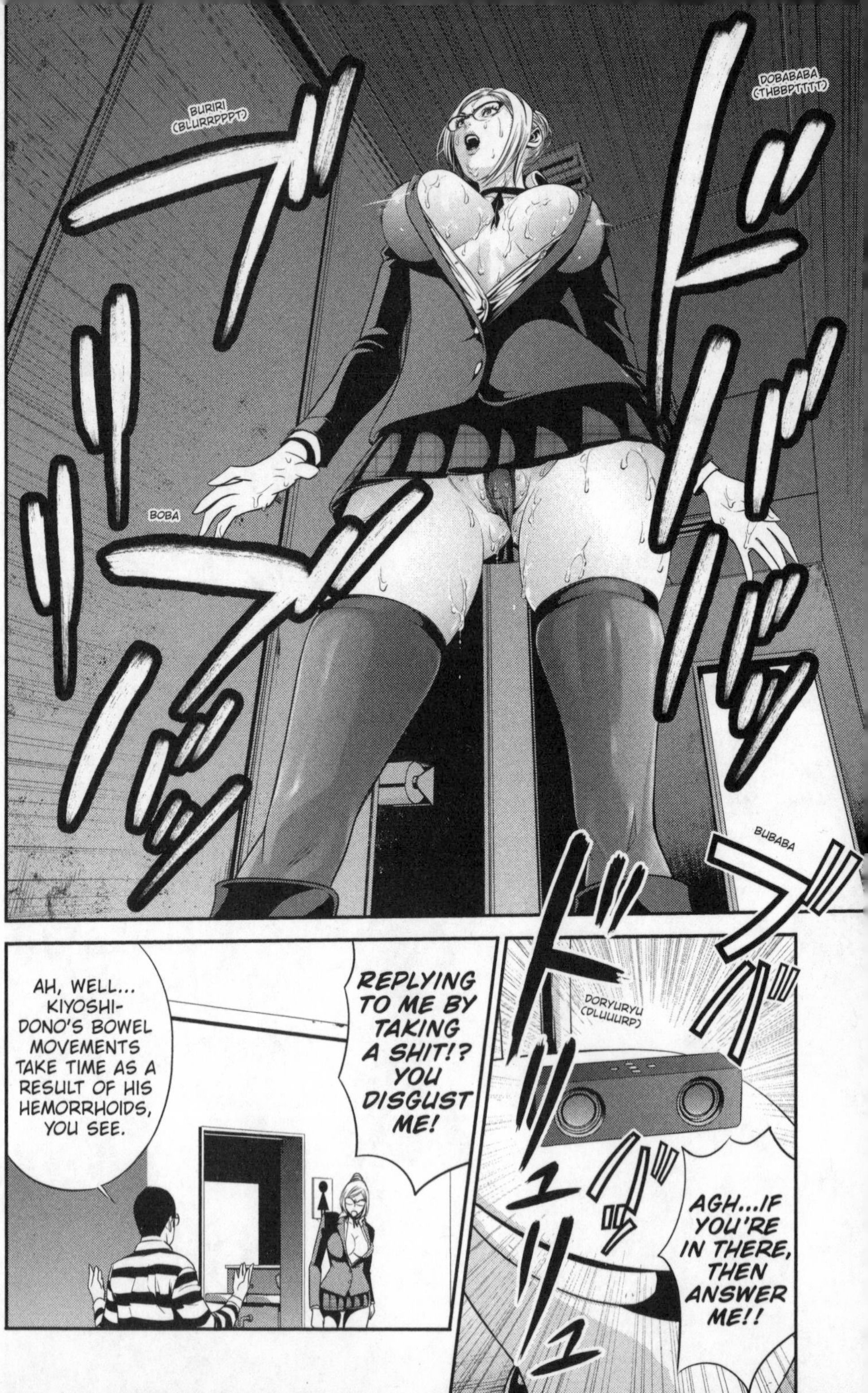
DOBABABA (THBBPTTTTT)
BURIRI (BLURRPPPT)
BOBA
BUBABA
DORYURYU (DLUUURP)
AGH...IF YOU'RE IN THERE, THEN ANSWER ME!!
REPLYING TO ME BY TAKING A SHIT!? YOU DISGUST ME!
AH, WELL... KIYOSHI-DONO'S BOWEL MOVEMENTS TAKE TIME AS A RESULT OF HIS HEMORRHOIDS, YOU SEE.

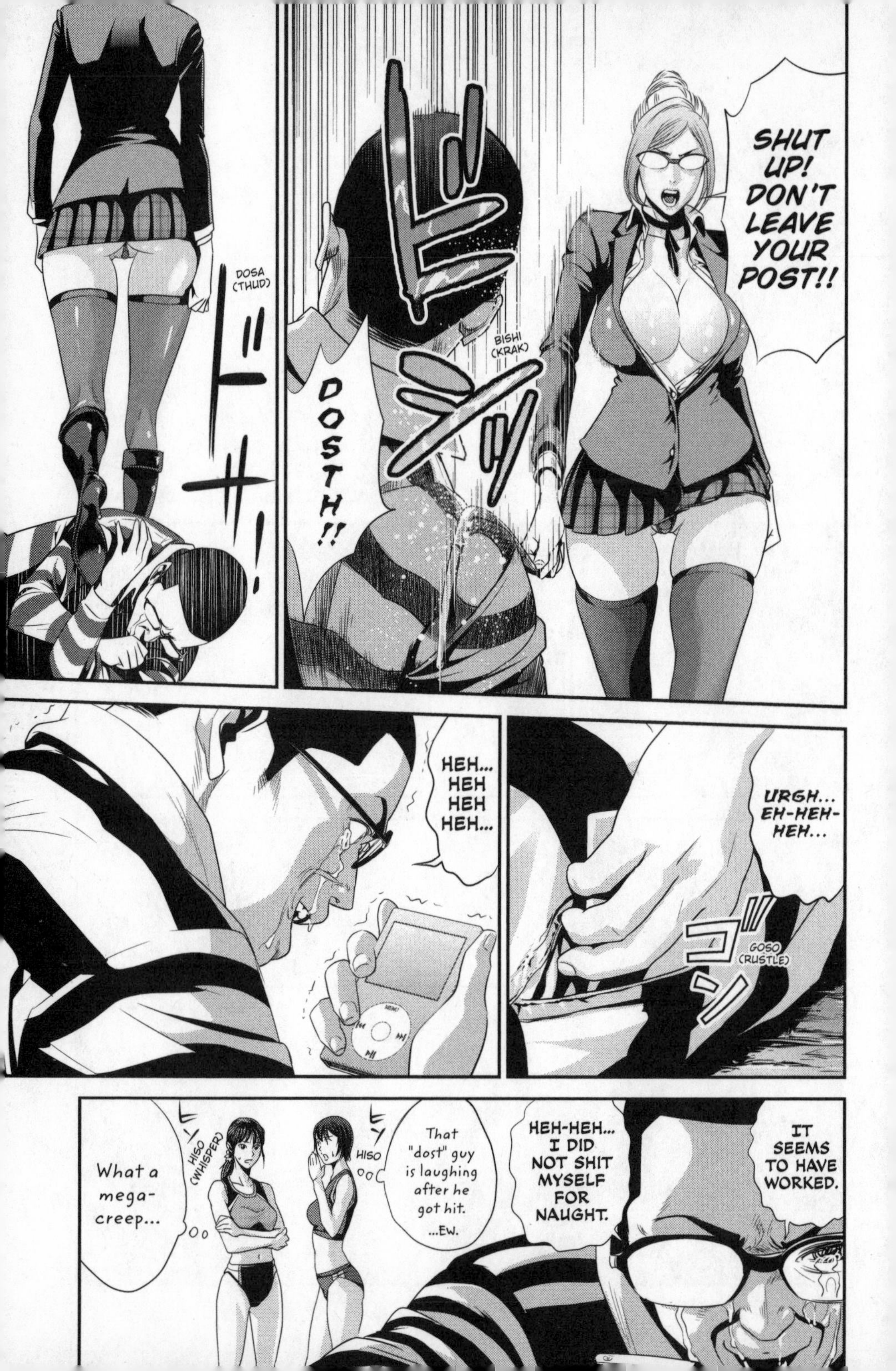
SHUT UP! DON'T LEAVE YOUR POST!!
BISHI (KRAK)
DOSTH!!
DOSA (THUD)
URGH... EH-HEH-HEH...
GOSO (RUSTLE)
HEH... HEH HEH HEH...
IT SEEMS TO HAVE WORKED.
HEH-HEH... I DID NOT SHIT MYSELF FOR NAUGHT.
That "dost" guy is laughing after he got hit. ...Ew.
HISO
HISO (WHISPER)
What a mega-creep...

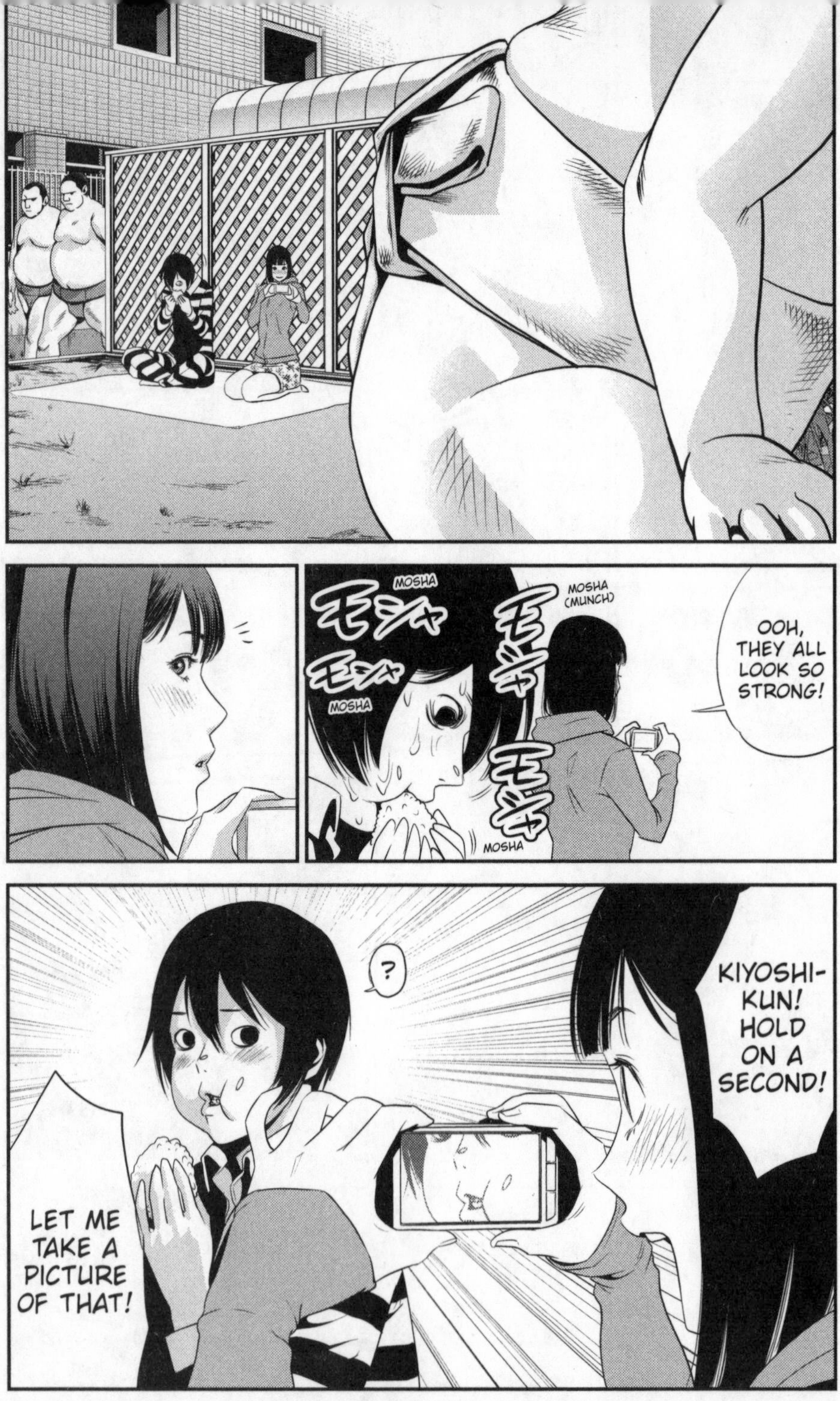

OOH, THEY ALL LOOK SO STRONG!
MOSHA (MUNCH)
MOSHA
MOSHA
MOSHA
KIYOSHI-KUN! HOLD ON A SECOND!
?
LET ME TAKE A PICTURE OF THAT!

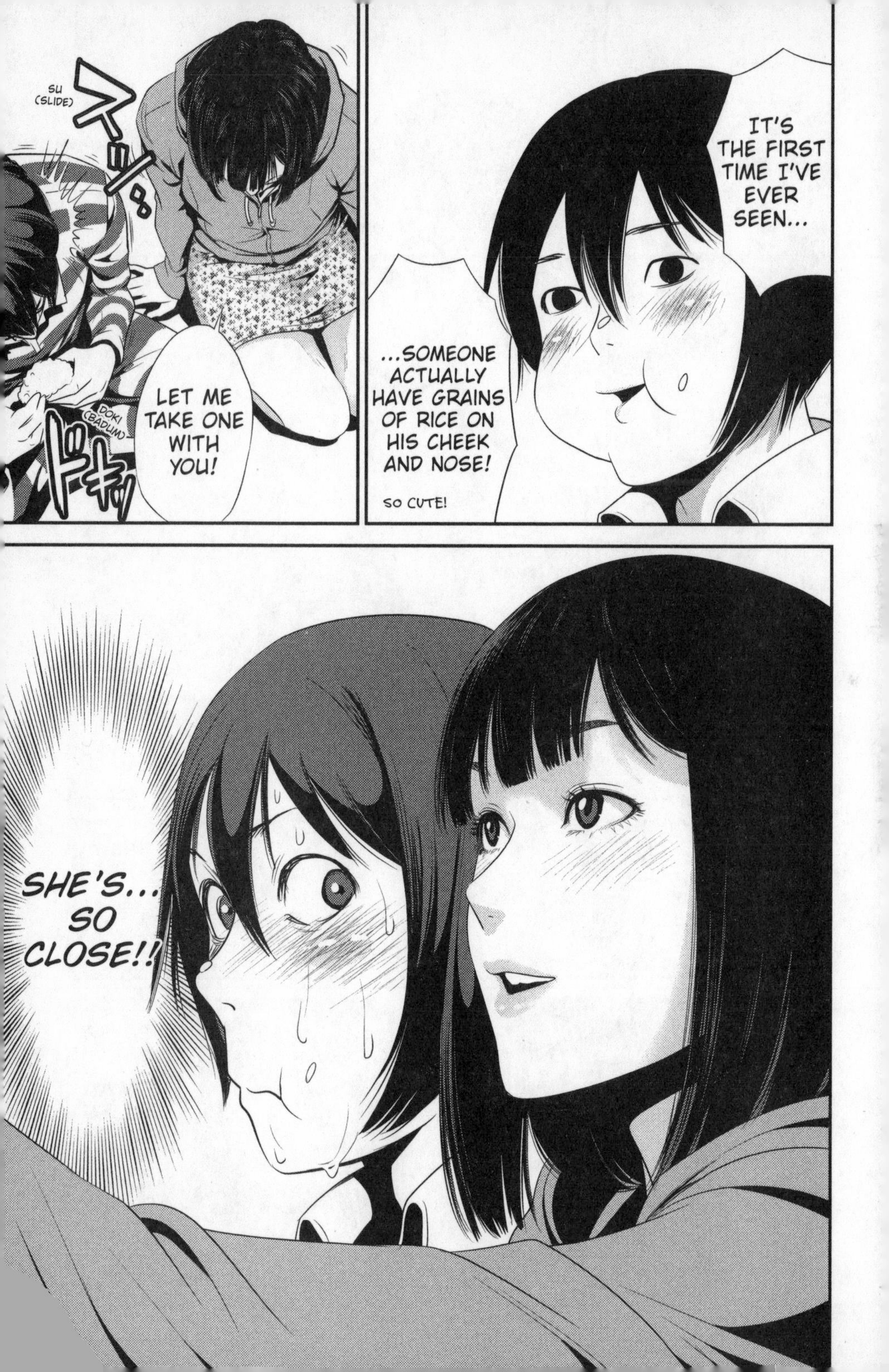
IT'S THE FIRST TIME I'VE EVER SEEN...
...SOMEONE ACTUALLY HAVE GRAINS OF RICE ON HIS CHEEK AND NOSE!
SO CUTE!
SU (SLIDE)
LET ME TAKE ONE WITH YOU!
DOKI (BADUM)
SHE'S... SO CLOSE!!

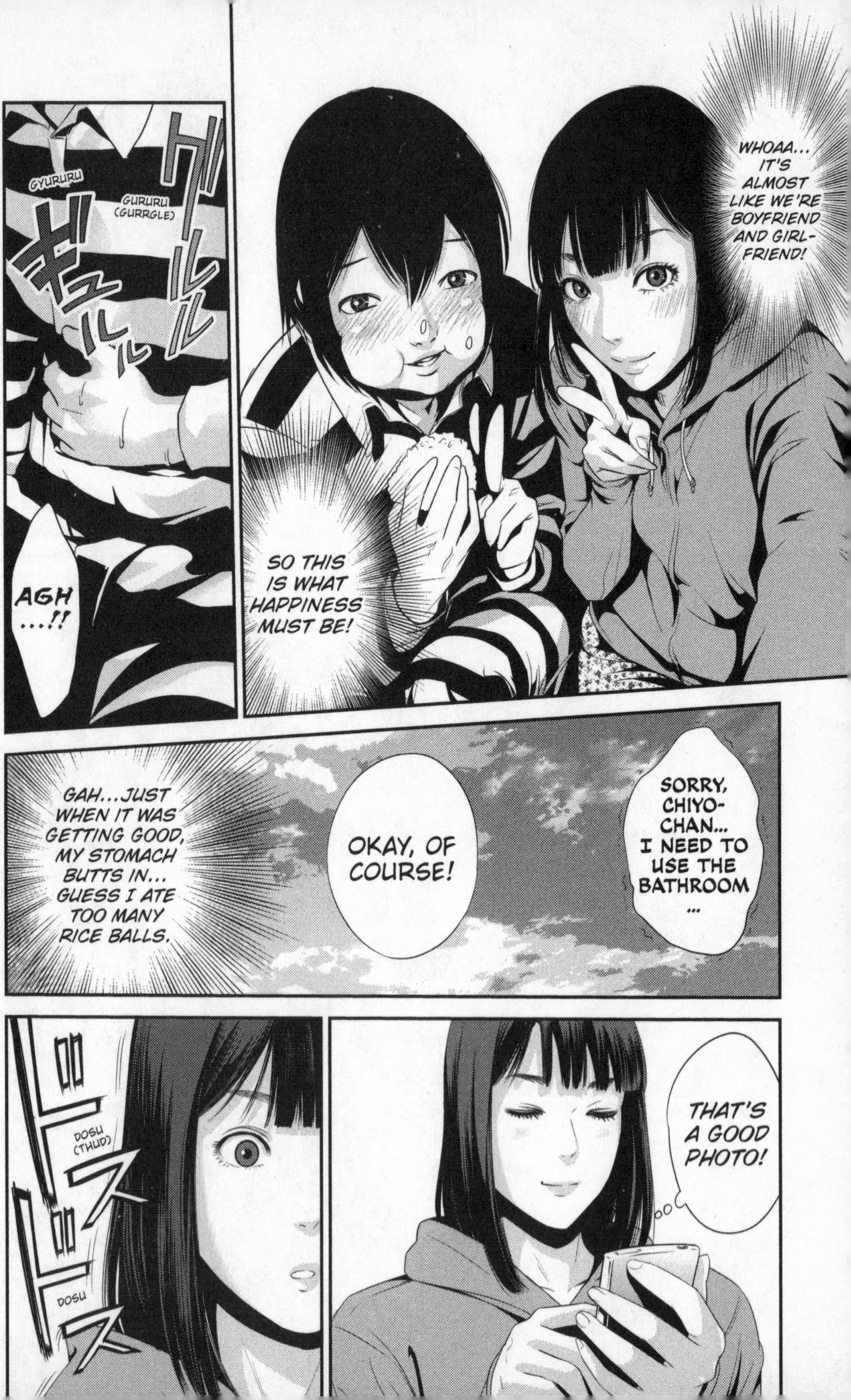
WHOAA... IT'S ALMOST LIKE WE'RE BOYFRIEND AND GIRL-FRIEND!
SO THIS IS WHAT HAPPINESS MUST BE!
GYURURU
GURURU (GURRGLE)
AGH ...!!
SORRY, CHIYO-CHAN... I NEED TO USE THE BATHROOM ...
OKAY, OF COURSE!
GAH...JUST WHEN IT WAS GETTING GOOD, MY STOMACH BUTTS IN... GUESS I ATE TOO MANY RICE BALLS.
THAT'S A GOOD PHOTO!
DOSU (THUD)
DOSU

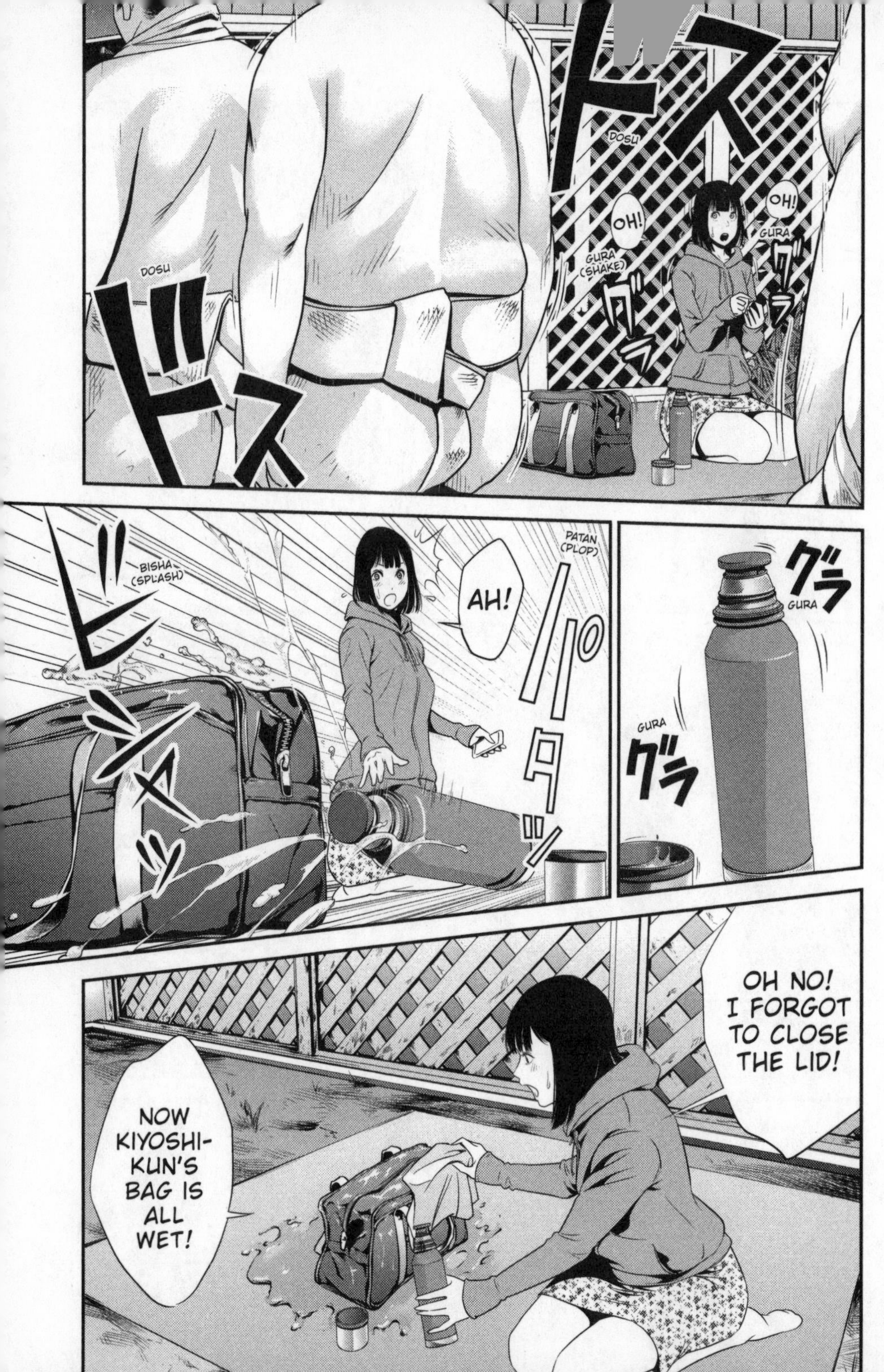
DOSU
OH!
GURA
OH!
GURA (SHAKE)
DOSU
GURA
GURA
PATAN (PLOP)
AH!
BISHA (SPLASH)
OH NO! I FORGOT TO CLOSE THE LID!
NOW KIYOSHI-KUN'S BAG IS ALL WET!

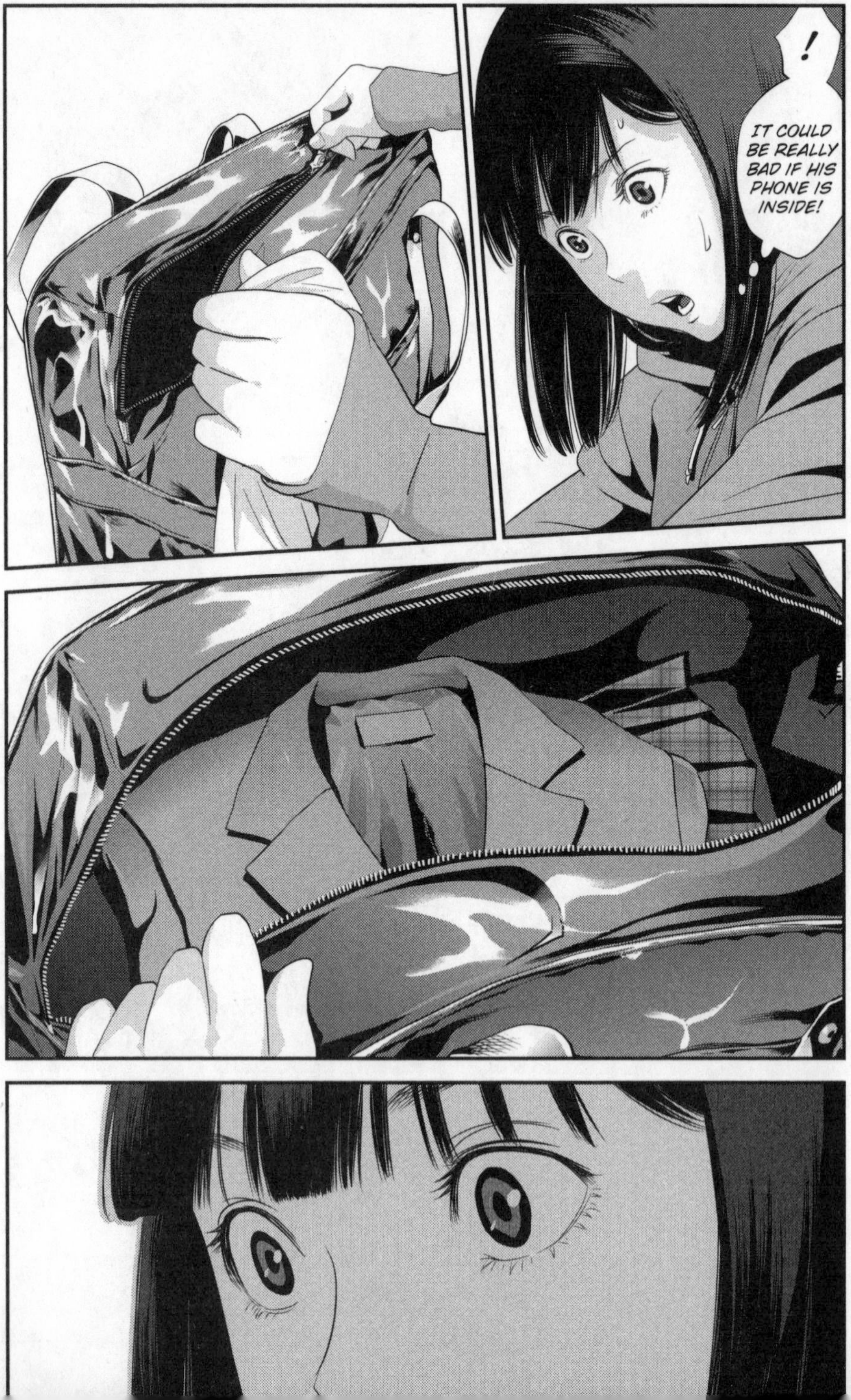
!
IT COULD BE REALLY BAD IF HIS PHONE IS INSIDE!

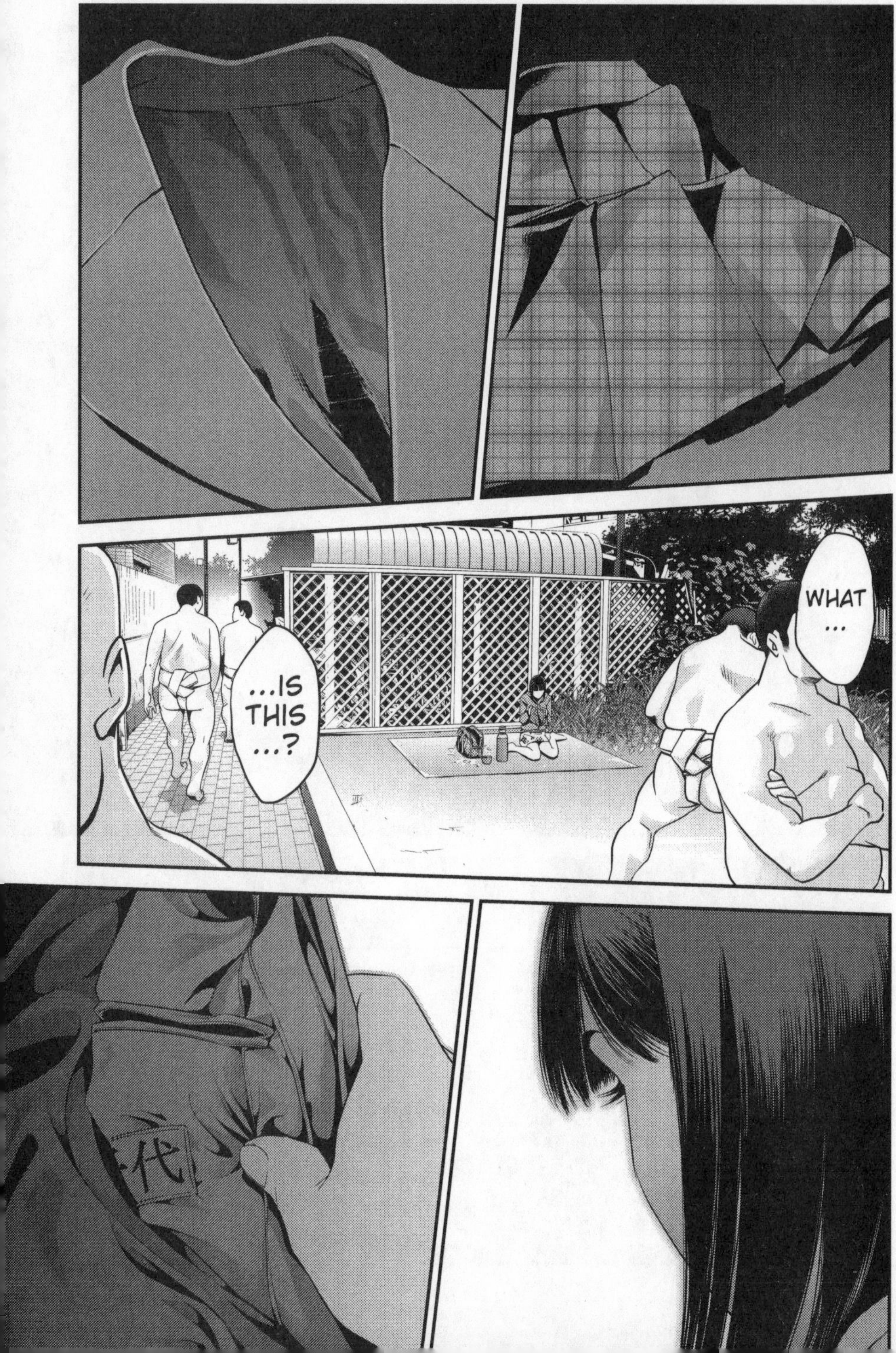
WHAT ...
...IS THIS ...?

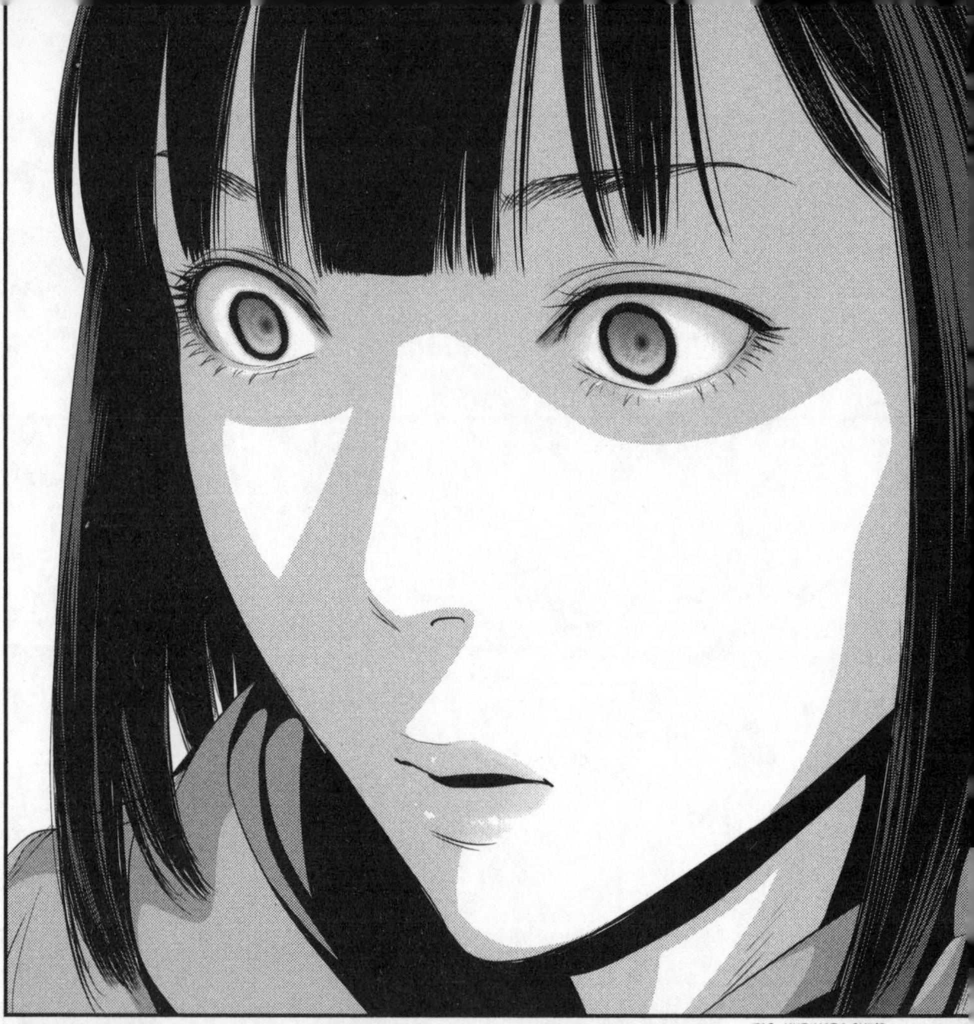

TAG: KURIHARA CHIYO

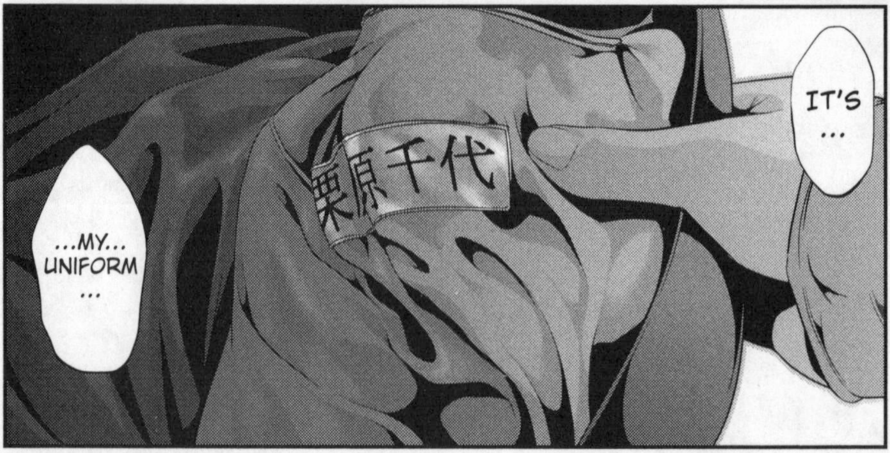
IT'S ...
栗原千代
...MY... UNIFORM ...

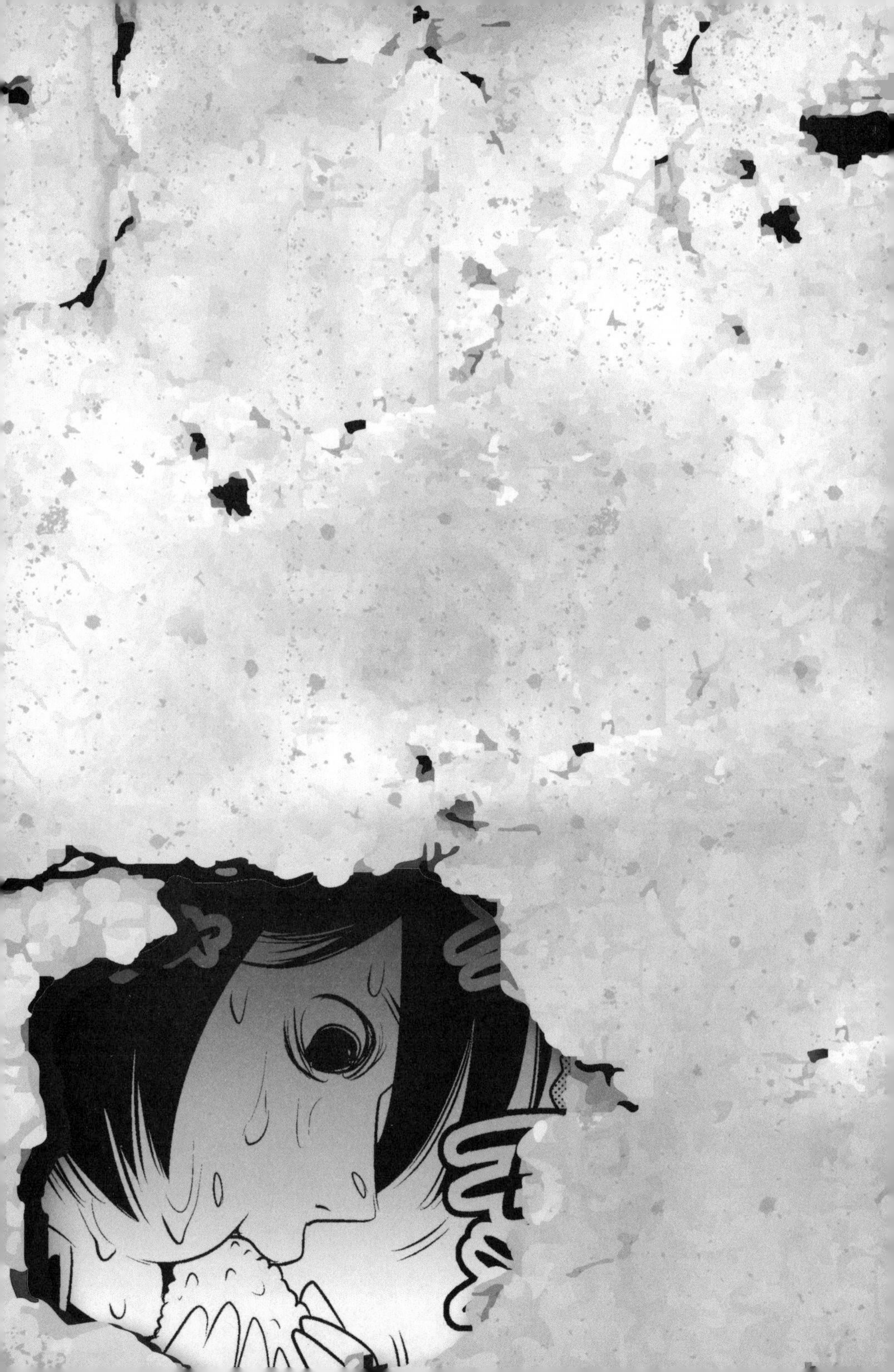

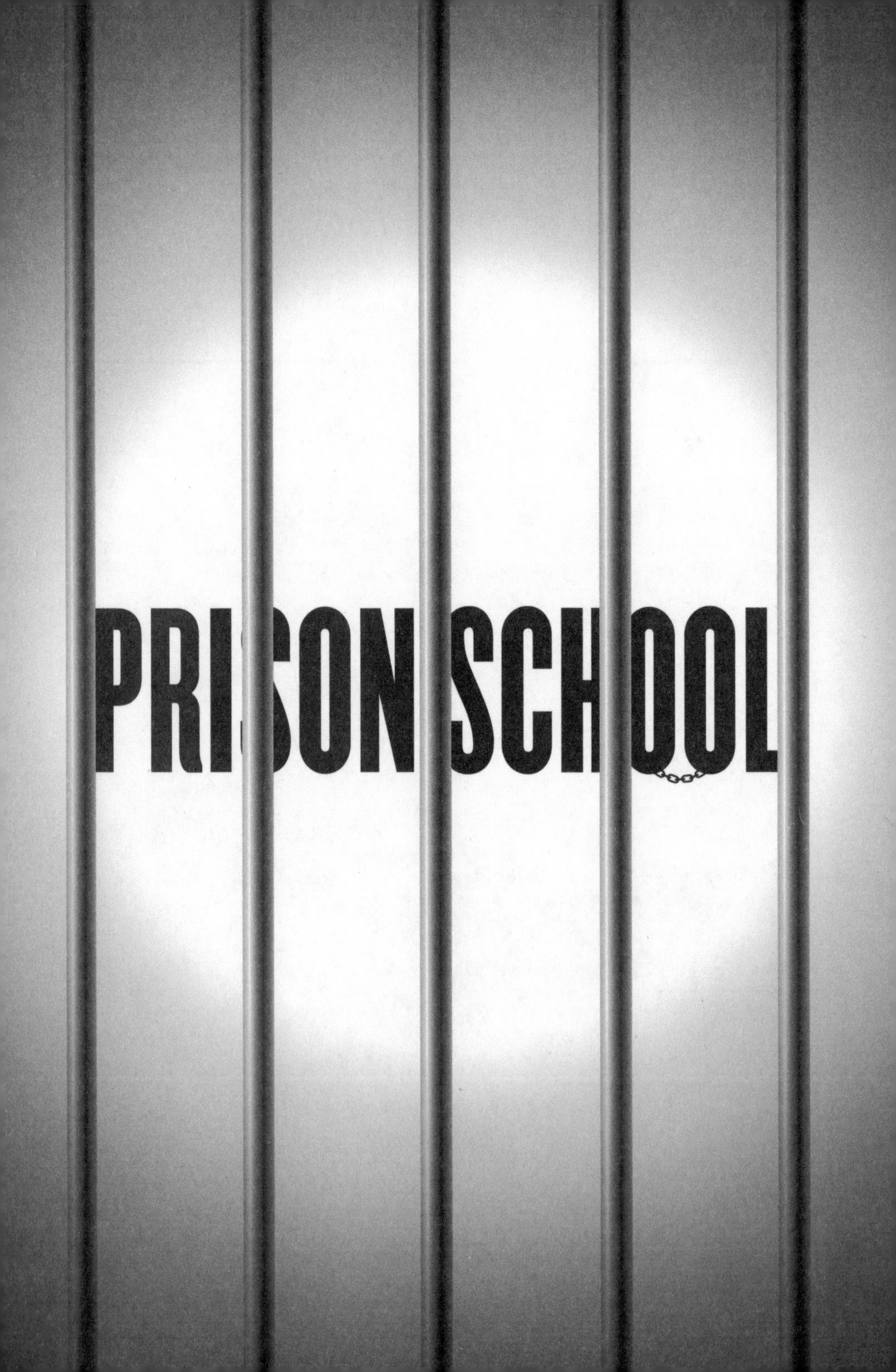
PRISON SCHOOL

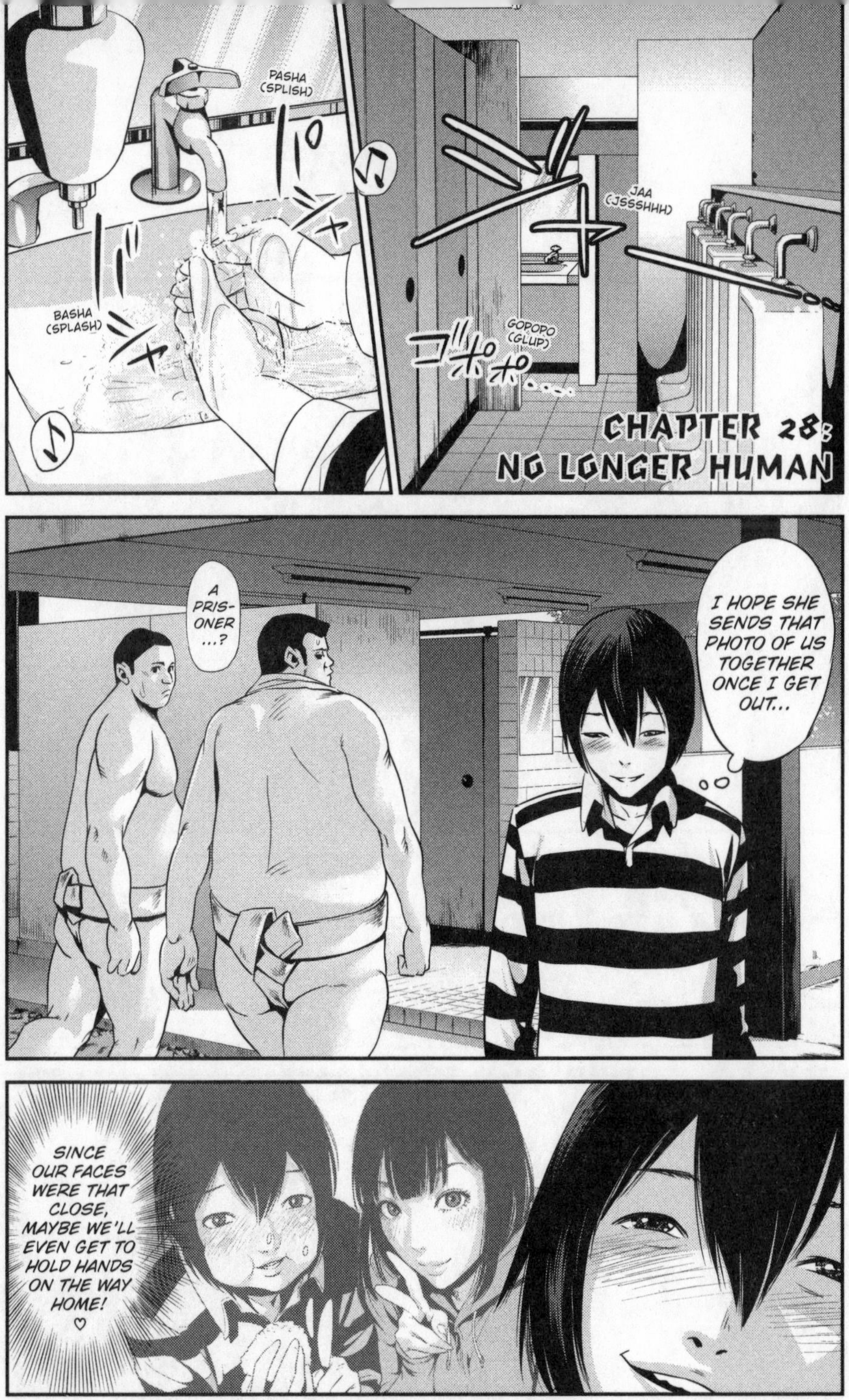
JAA
(JSSSHHH)
GOPOPO
(GLUP)
PASHA
(SPLISH)
BASHA
(SPLASH)
CHAPTER 28:
NO LONGER HUMAN
I HOPE SHE SENDS THAT PHOTO OF US TOGETHER ONCE I GET OUT...
A PRIS-ONER ...?
SINCE OUR FACES WERE THAT CLOSE, MAYBE WE'LL EVEN GET TO HOLD HANDS ON THE WAY HOME! ♡

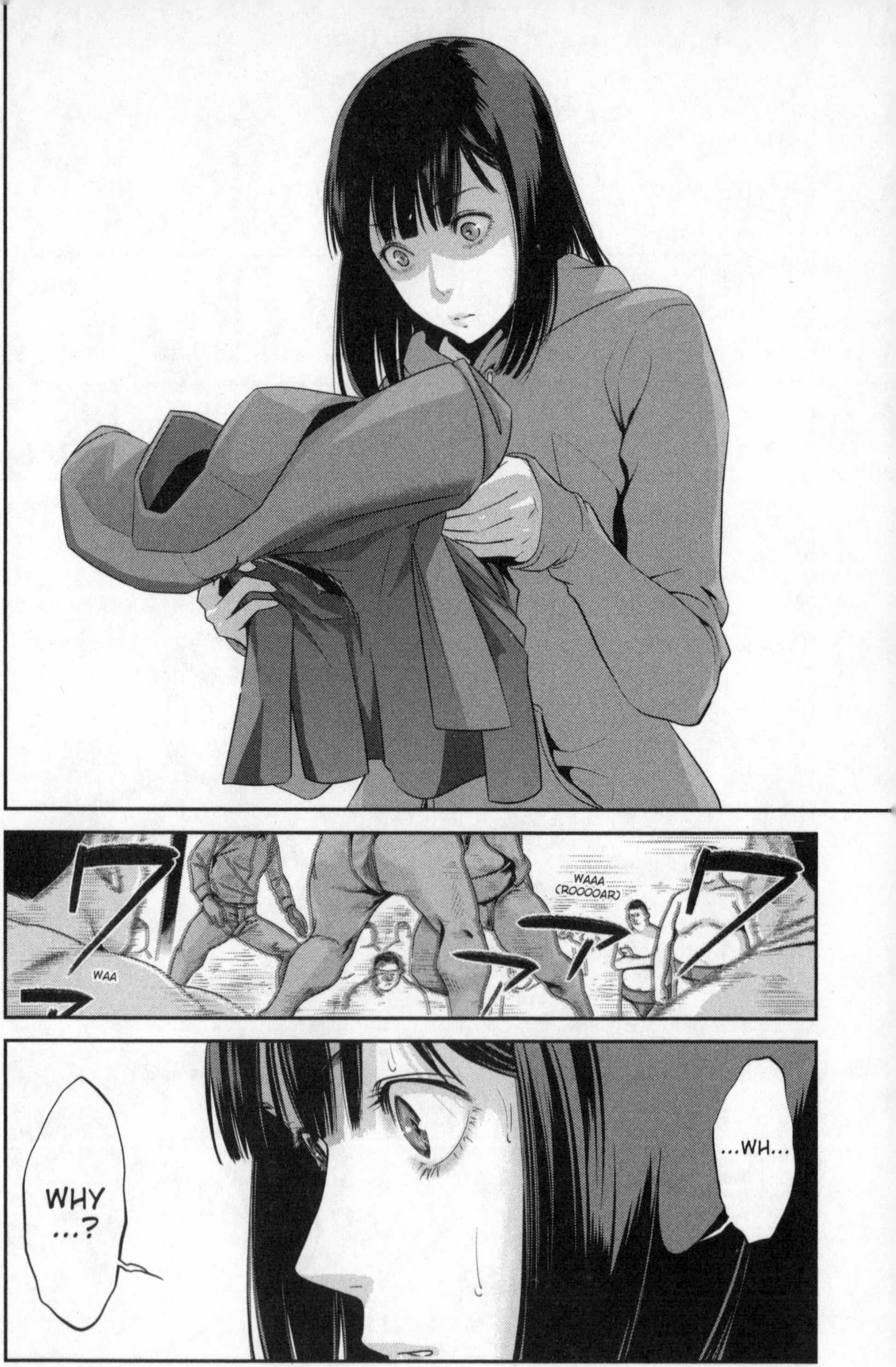
WAAA
(ROOOOAR)
WAA
...WH...
WHY
...?

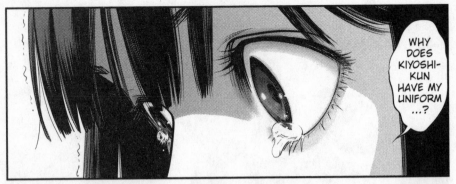

WHY DOES KIYOSHI-KUN HAVE MY UNIFORM...?

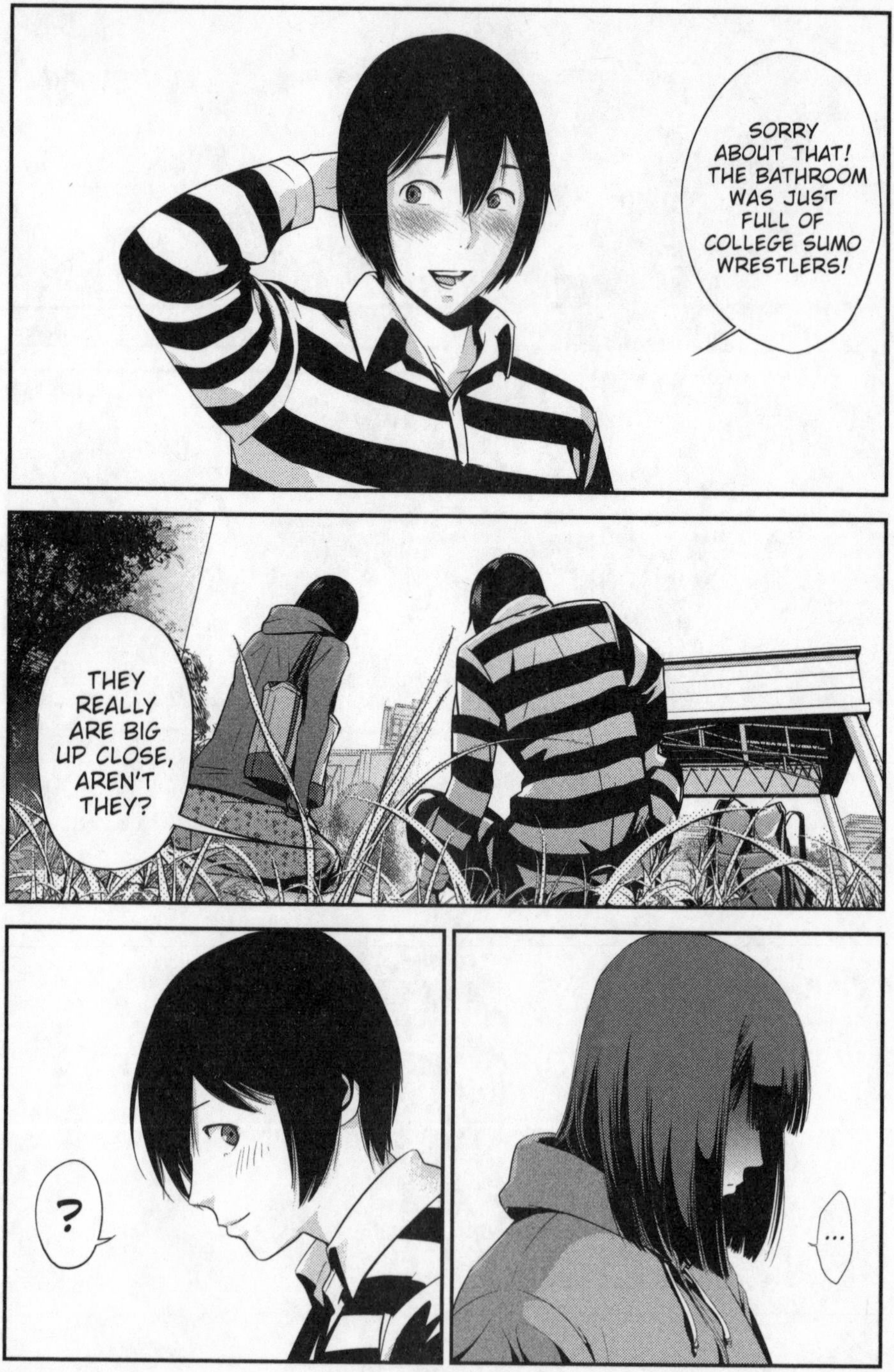
SORRY ABOUT THAT! THE BATHROOM WAS JUST FULL OF COLLEGE SUMO WRESTLERS!
THEY REALLY ARE BIG UP CLOSE, AREN'T THEY?
...
?

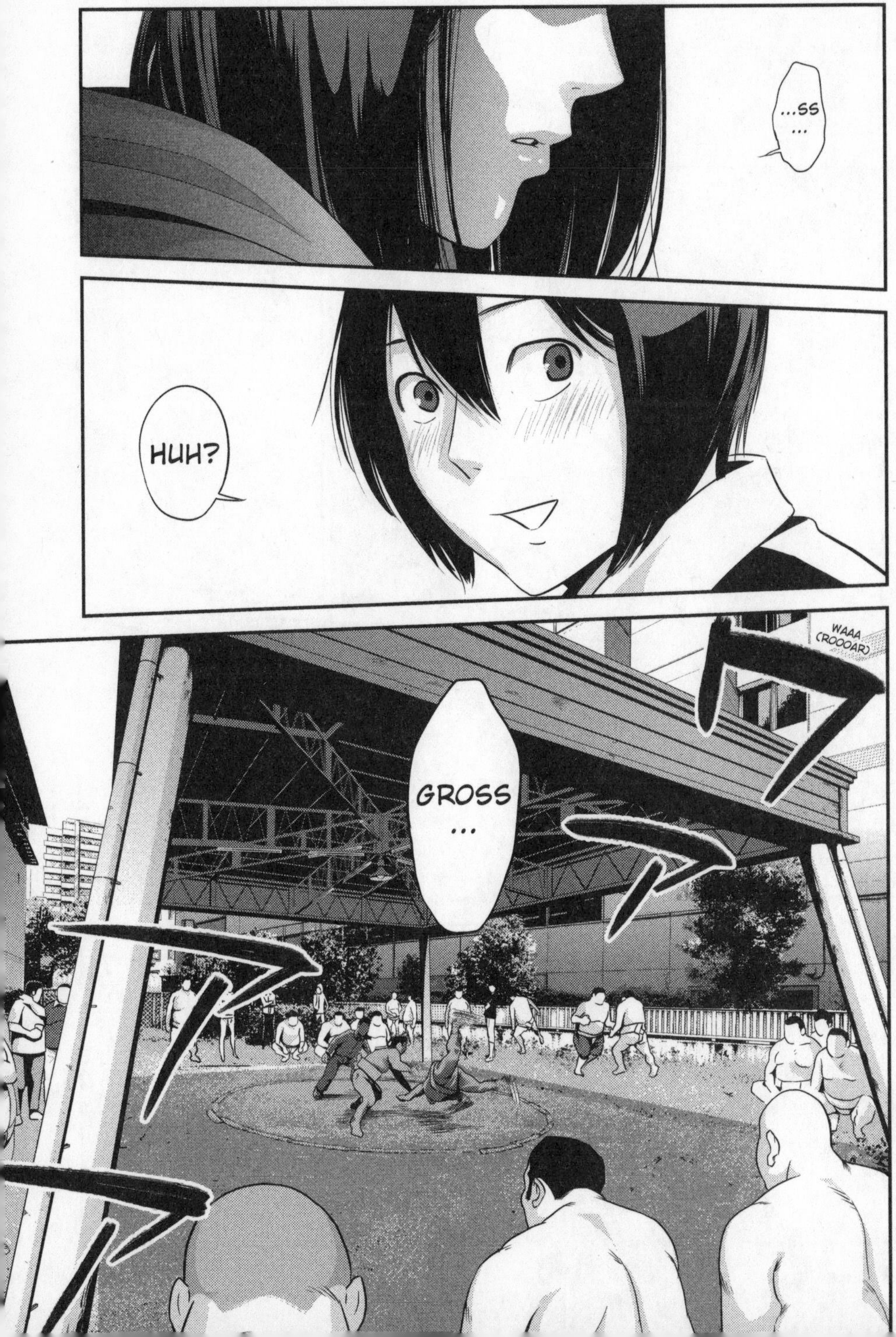
...SS
...
HUH?
WAAA
(ROOOAR)
GROSS
...

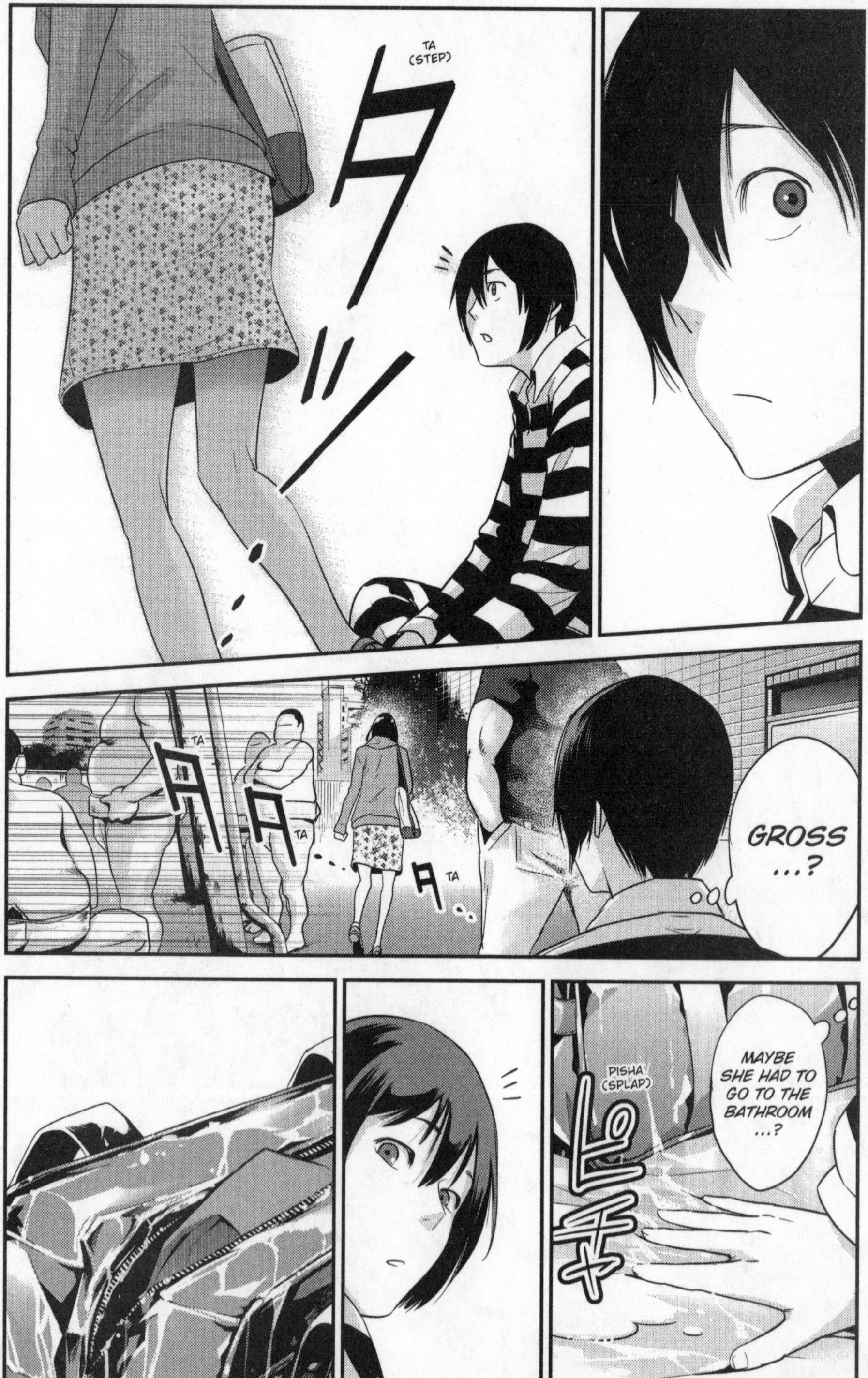
TA
(STEP)
TA
TA
TA
GROSS
...?
PISHA
(SPLAP)
MAYBE
SHE HAD TO
GO TO THE
BATHROOM
...?

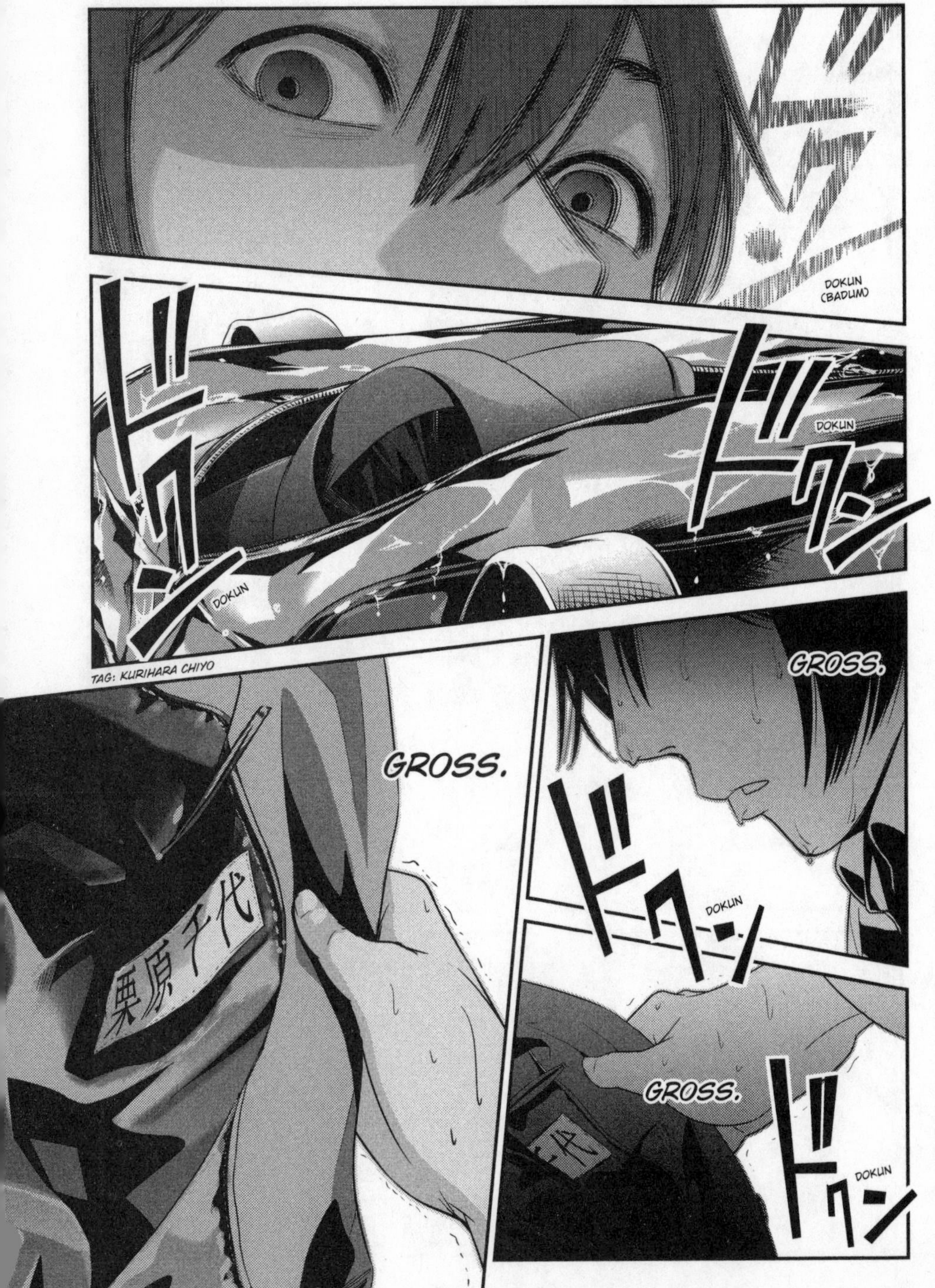
DOKUN
(BADUM)
DOKUN
DOKUN
TAG: KURIHARA CHIYO
GROSS.
DOKUN
GROSS.
栗原千代
GROSS.
DOKUN

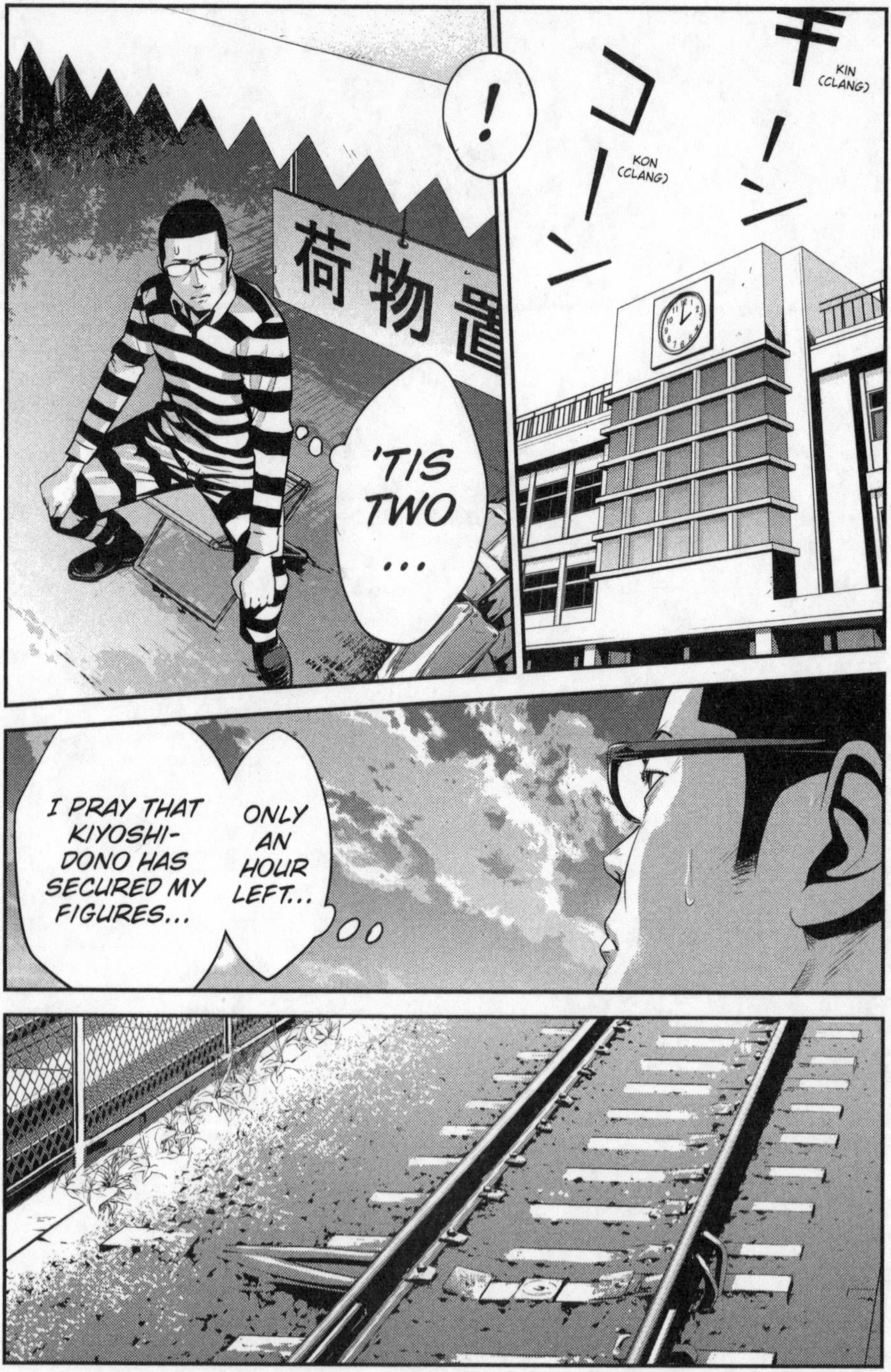

KIN (CLANG)
KON (CLANG)
!
'TIS TWO...
ONLY AN HOUR LEFT...
I PRAY THAT KIYOSHI-DONO HAS SECURED MY FIGURES...

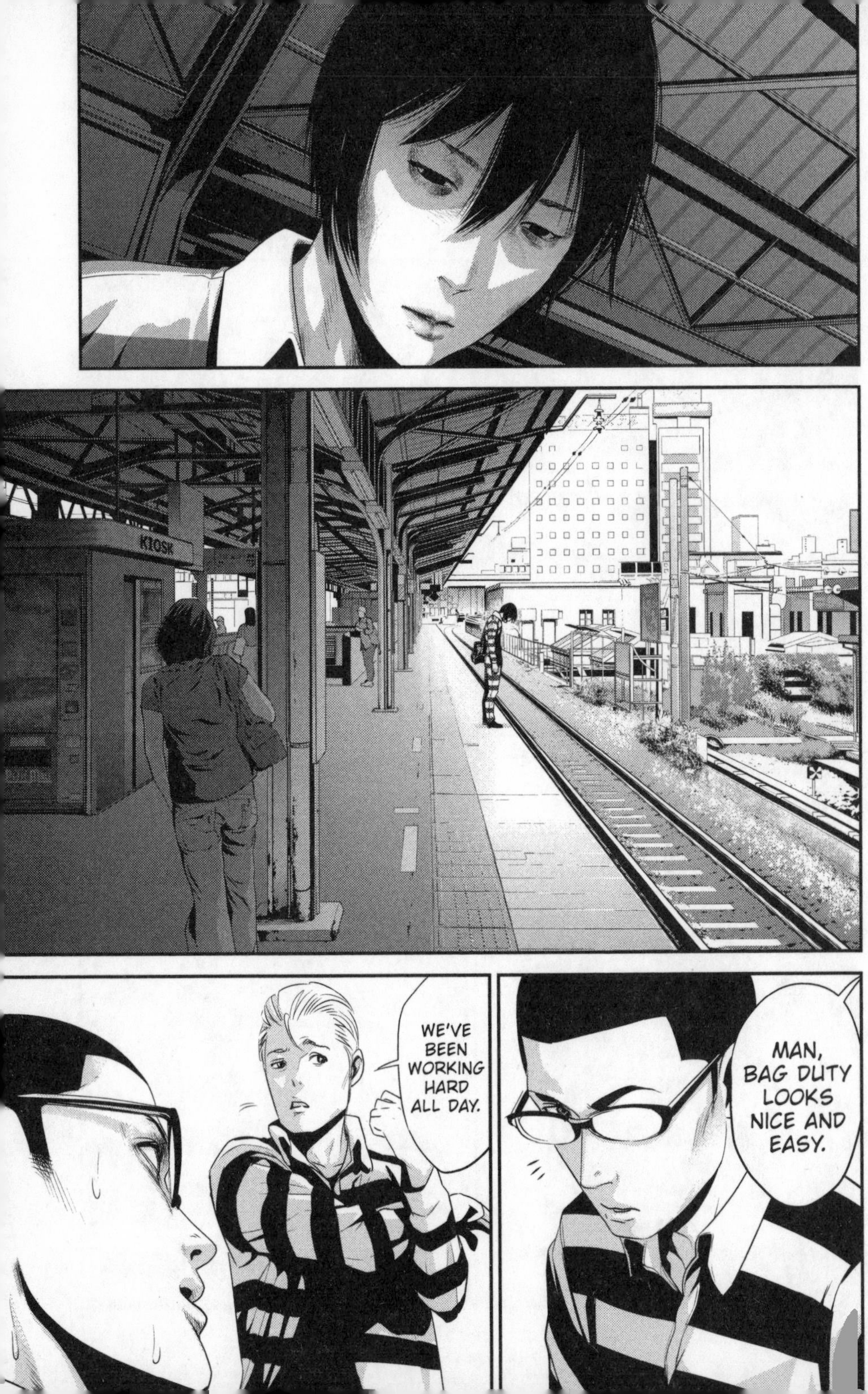
KIOSK
MAN, BAG DUTY LOOKS NICE AND EASY.
WE'VE BEEN WORKING HARD ALL DAY.

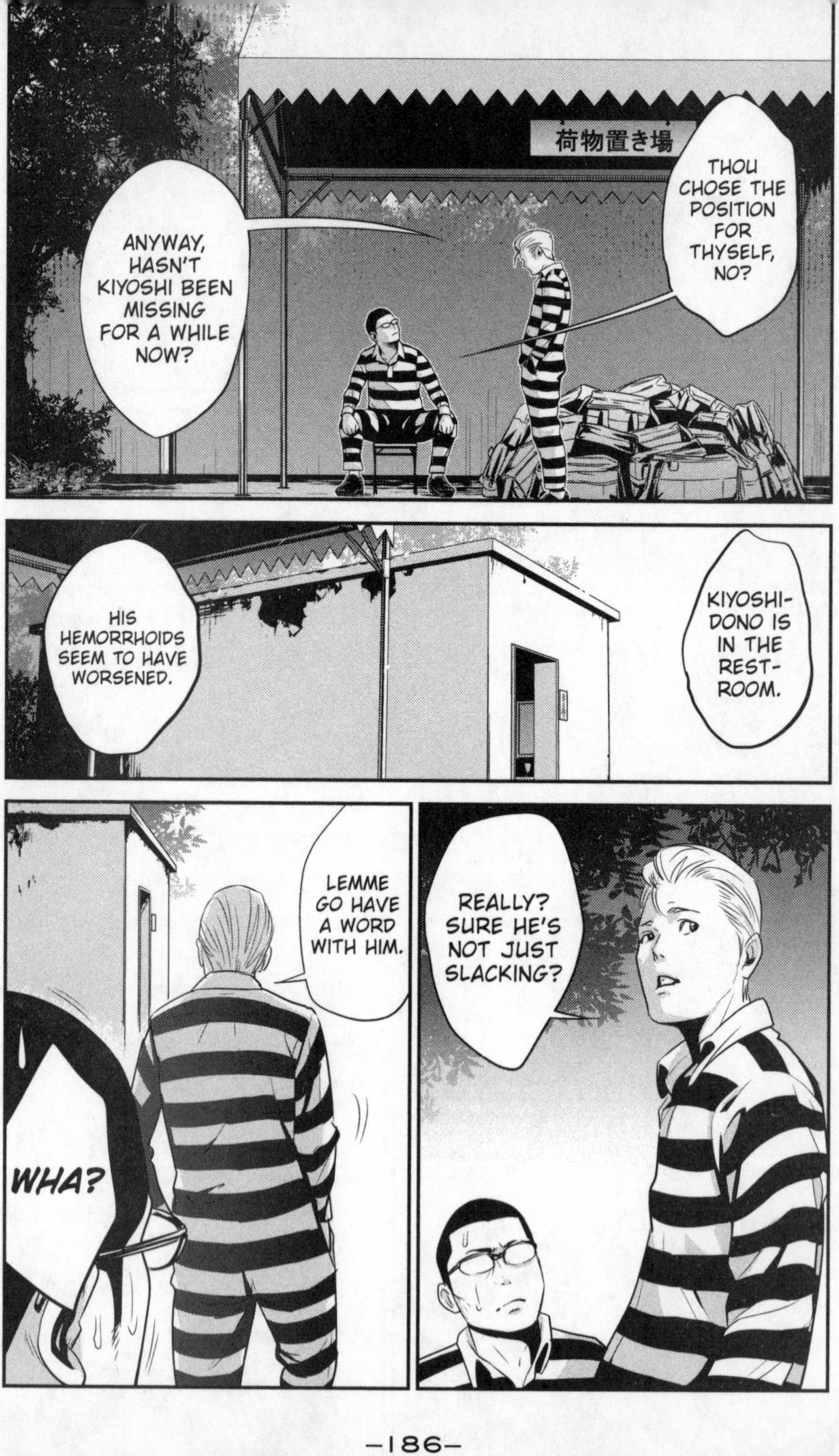
荷物置き場
THOU CHOSE THE POSITION FOR THYSELF, NO?
ANYWAY, HASN'T KIYOSHI BEEN MISSING FOR A WHILE NOW?
KIYOSHI-DONO IS IN THE REST-ROOM.
HIS HEMORRHOIDS SEEM TO HAVE WORSENED.
REALLY? SURE HE'S NOT JUST SLACKING?
LEMME GO HAVE A WORD WITH HIM.
WHA?

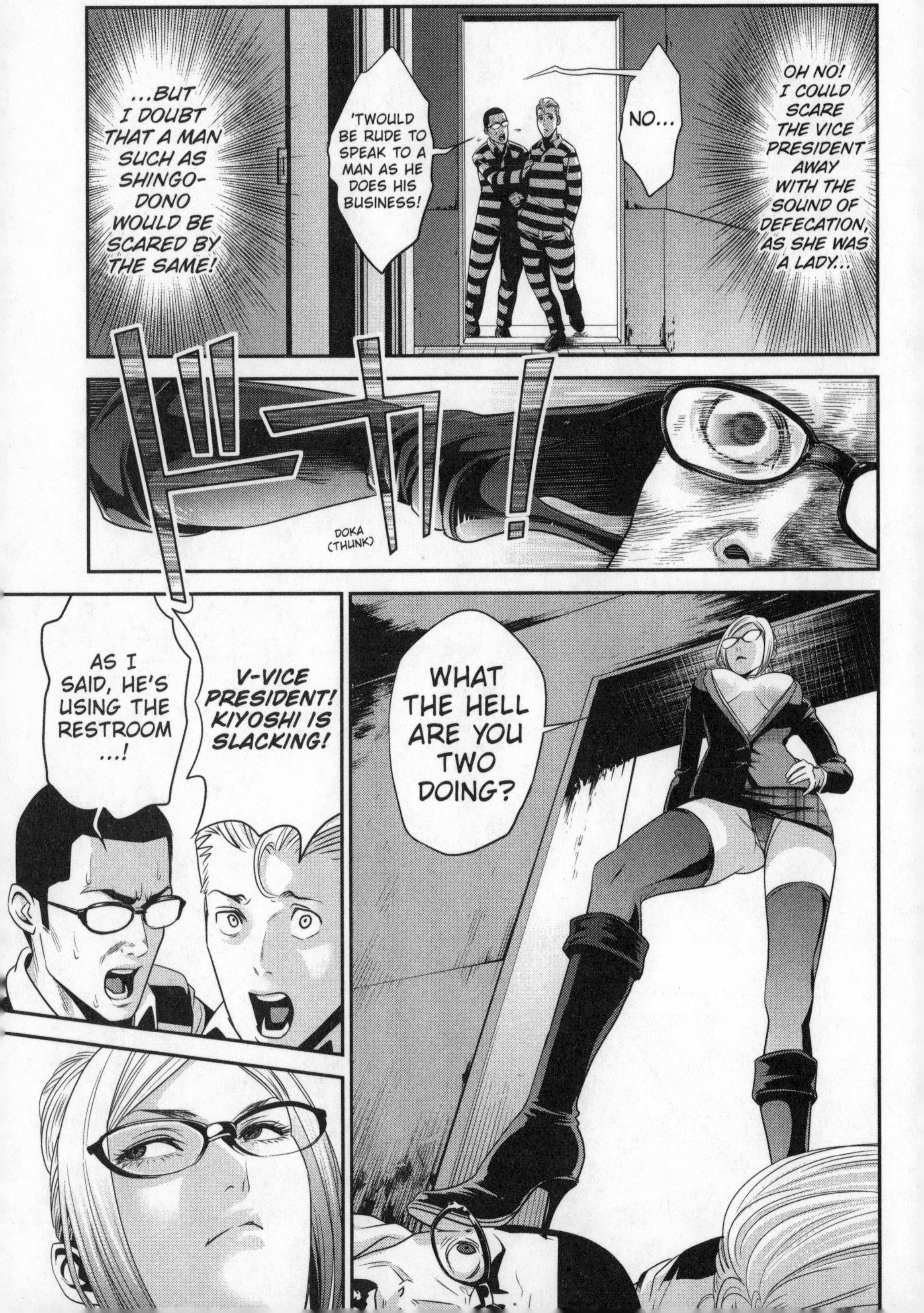
OH NO! I COULD SCARE THE VICE PRESIDENT AWAY WITH THE SOUND OF DEFECATION, AS SHE WAS A LADY...
NO...
'TWOULD BE RUDE TO SPEAK TO A MAN AS HE DOES HIS BUSINESS!
...BUT I DOUBT THAT A MAN SUCH AS SHINGO-DONO WOULD BE SCARED BY THE SAME!
ドゴッ!
DOKA (THUNK)
WHAT THE HELL ARE YOU TWO DOING?
V-VICE PRESIDENT! KIYOSHI IS SLACKING!
AS I SAID, HE'S USING THE RESTROOM ...!

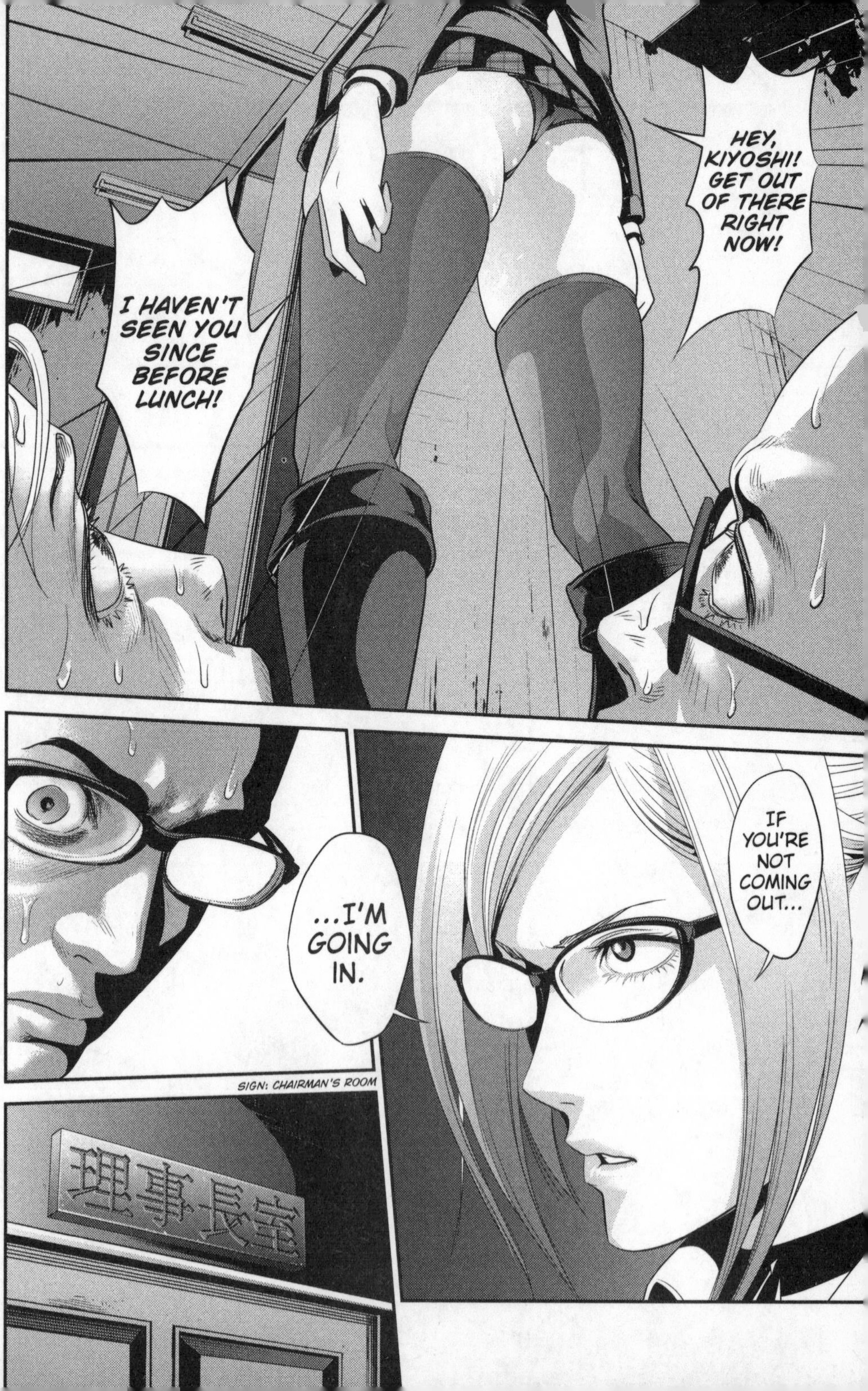
HEY, KIYOSHI! GET OUT OF THERE RIGHT NOW!
I HAVEN'T SEEN YOU SINCE BEFORE LUNCH!
IF YOU'RE NOT COMING OUT...
...I'M GOING IN.
SIGN: CHAIRMAN'S ROOM
理事長室

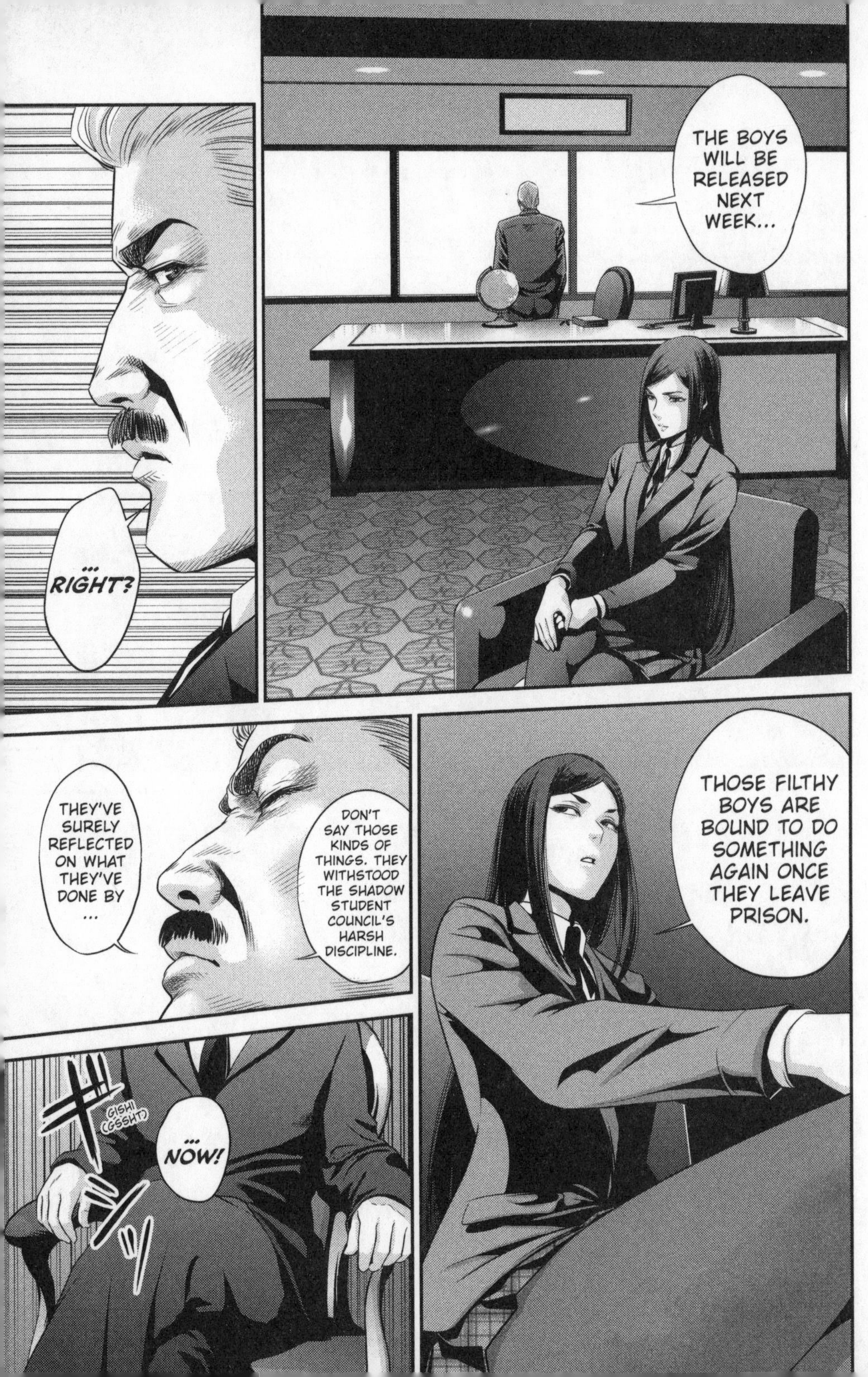

THE BOYS WILL BE RELEASED NEXT WEEK...
...RIGHT?
THOSE FILTHY BOYS ARE BOUND TO DO SOMETHING AGAIN ONCE THEY LEAVE PRISON.
DON'T SAY THOSE KINDS OF THINGS. THEY WITHSTOOD THE SHADOW STUDENT COUNCIL'S HARSH DISCIPLINE.
THEY'VE SURELY REFLECTED ON WHAT THEY'VE DONE BY ...
...NOW!
GISHI (GSSHT)

BU
(BZZZT)

BU

BU

BU BU BU

EXCUSE ME, TEXT MESSAGE...

PI

PI
(BEEP)

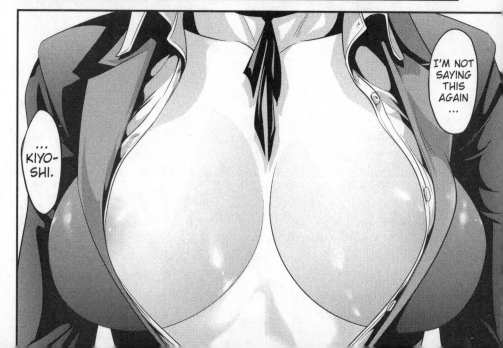

I'M NOT SAYING THIS AGAIN...

...KIYO-SHI.

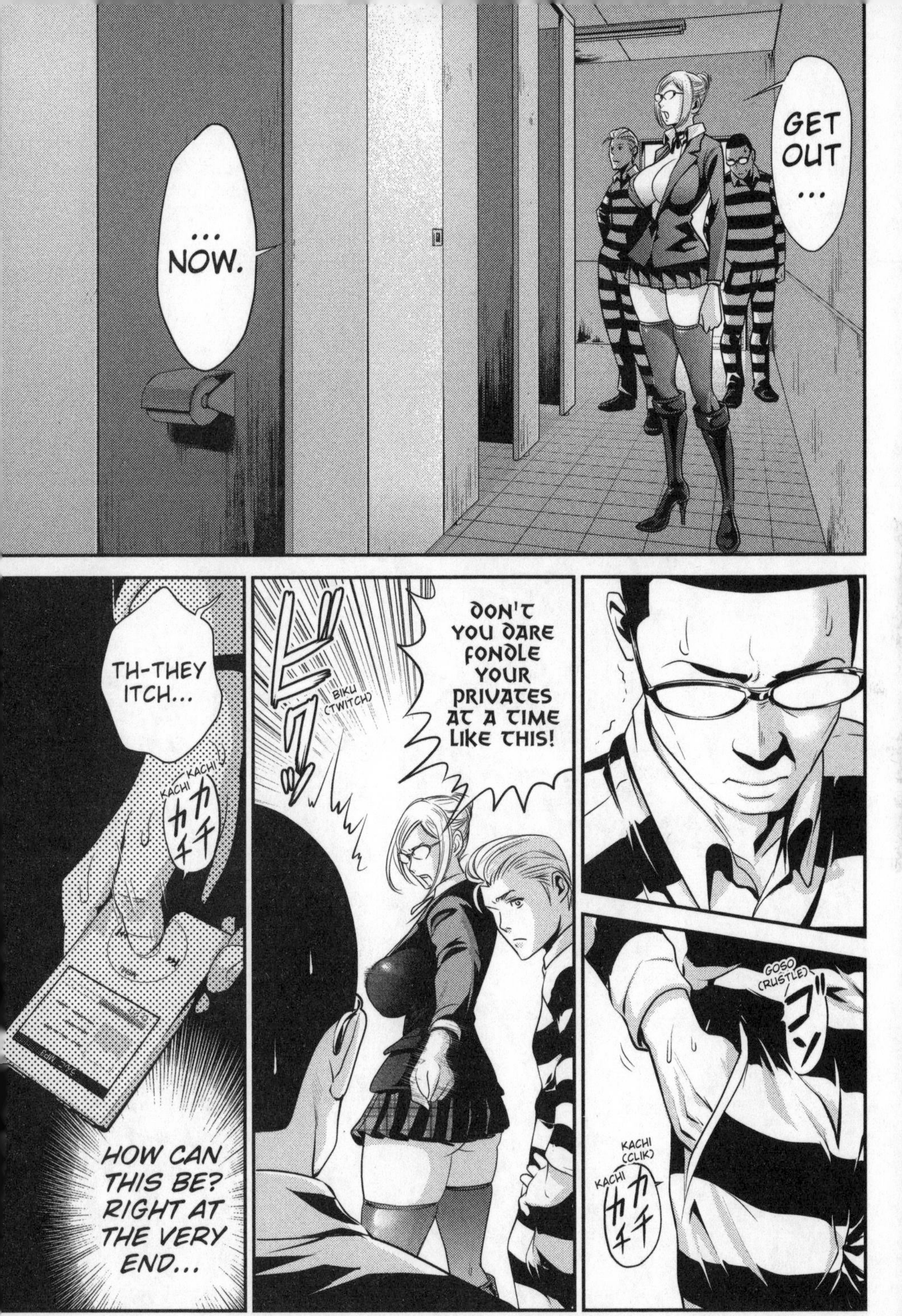
GET OUT ...
... NOW.
GOSO (RUSTLE)
ゴソ
KACHI (CLIK) KACHI
カチカチ
BIKU (TWITCH)
ビクッ
DON'T YOU DARE FONDLE YOUR PRIVATES AT A TIME LIKE THIS!
TH-THEY ITCH...
KACHI KACHI
カチカチ
HOW CAN THIS BE? RIGHT AT THE VERY END...

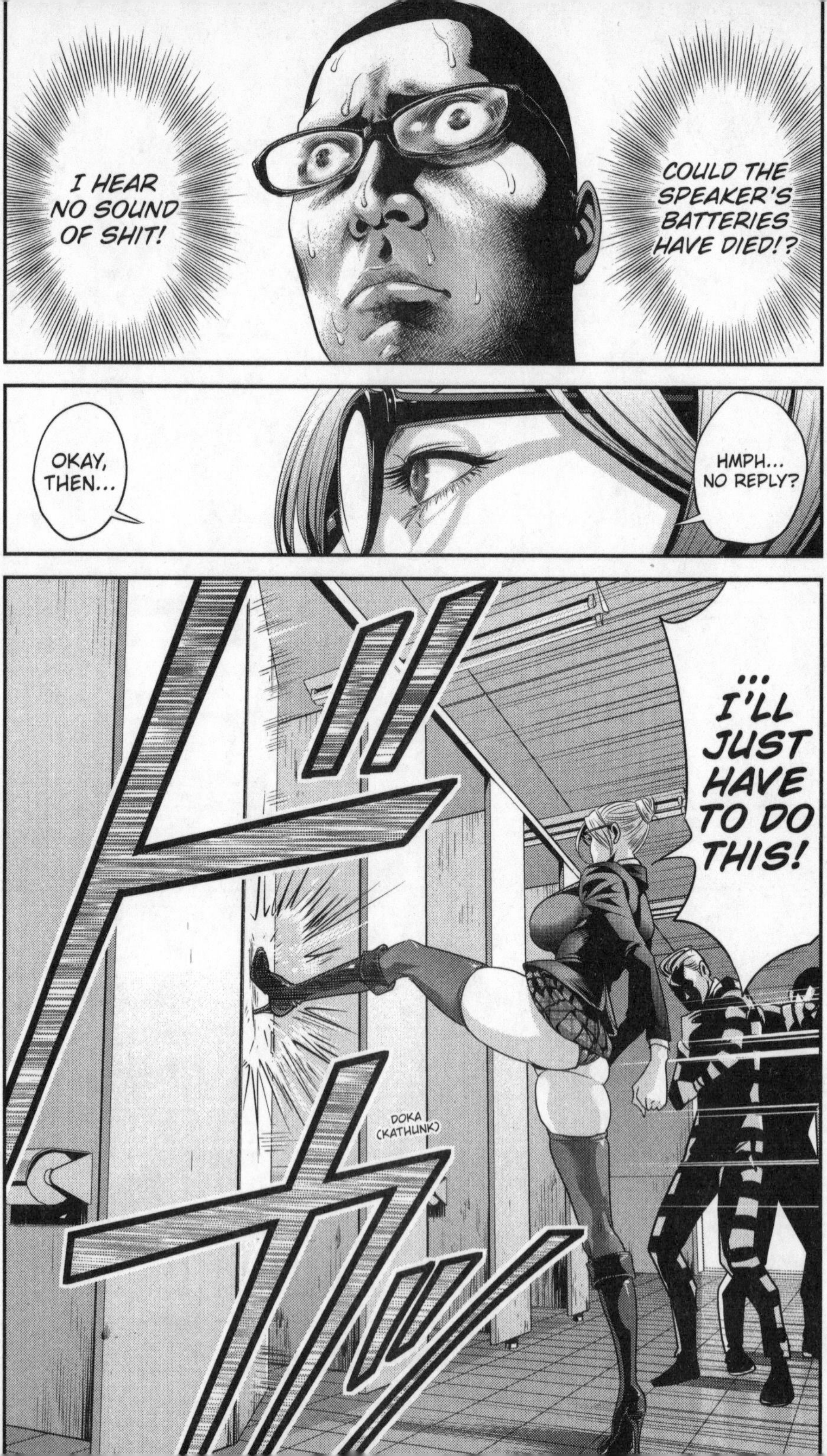
COULD THE SPEAKER'S BATTERIES HAVE DIED!?
I HEAR NO SOUND OF SHIT!
HMPH... NO REPLY?
OKAY, THEN...
... I'LL JUST HAVE TO DO THIS!
DOKA (KATHUNK)

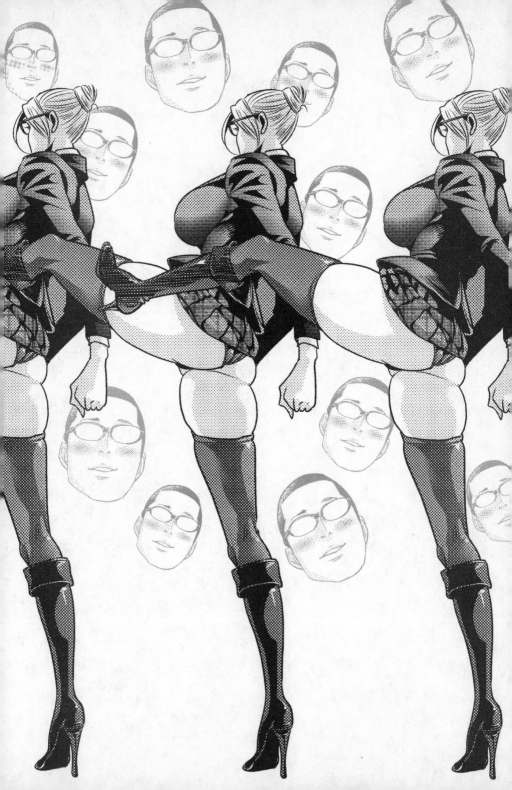

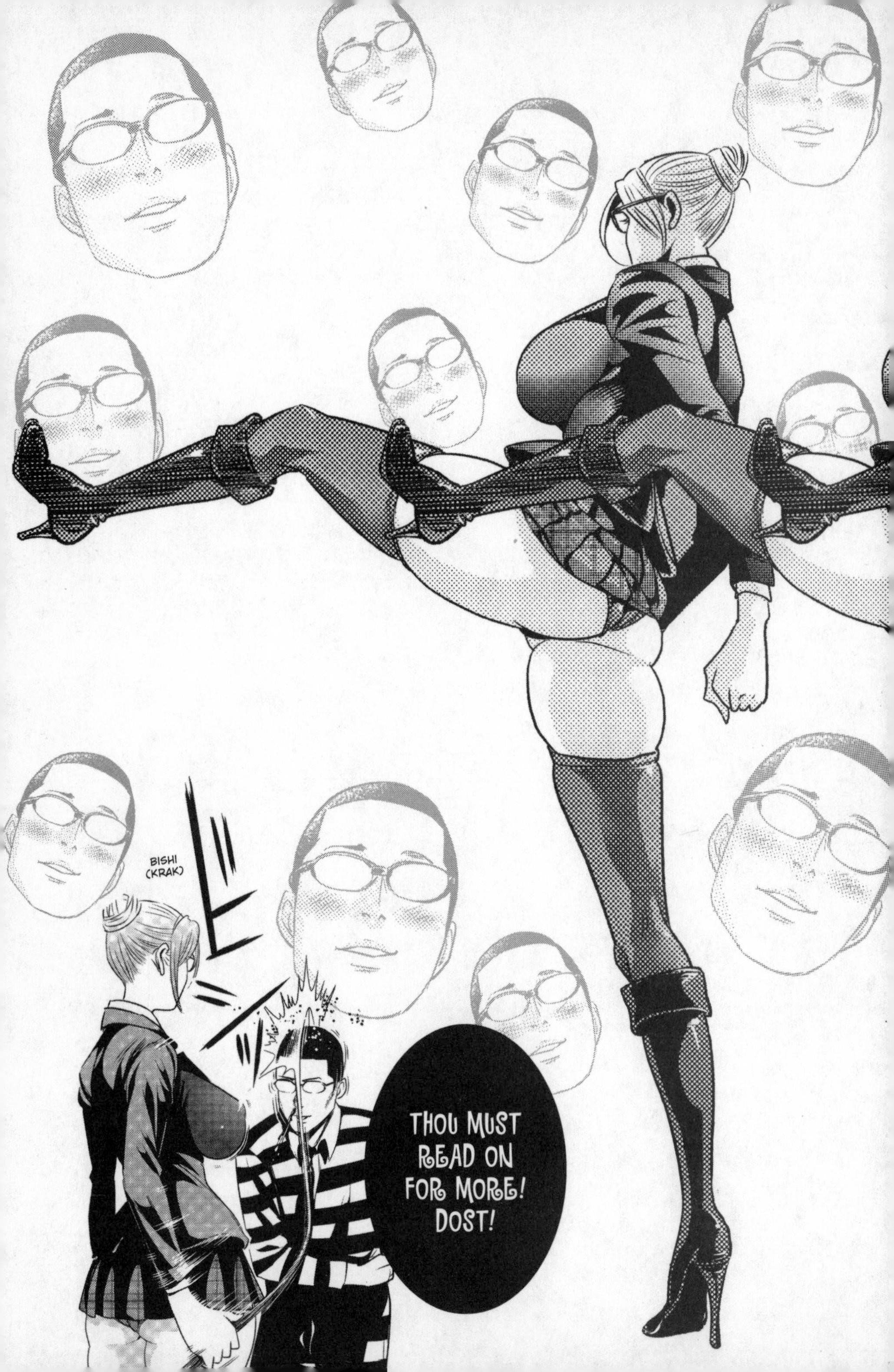
BISHI
(KRAK)
THOU MUST
READ ON
FOR MORE!
DOST!

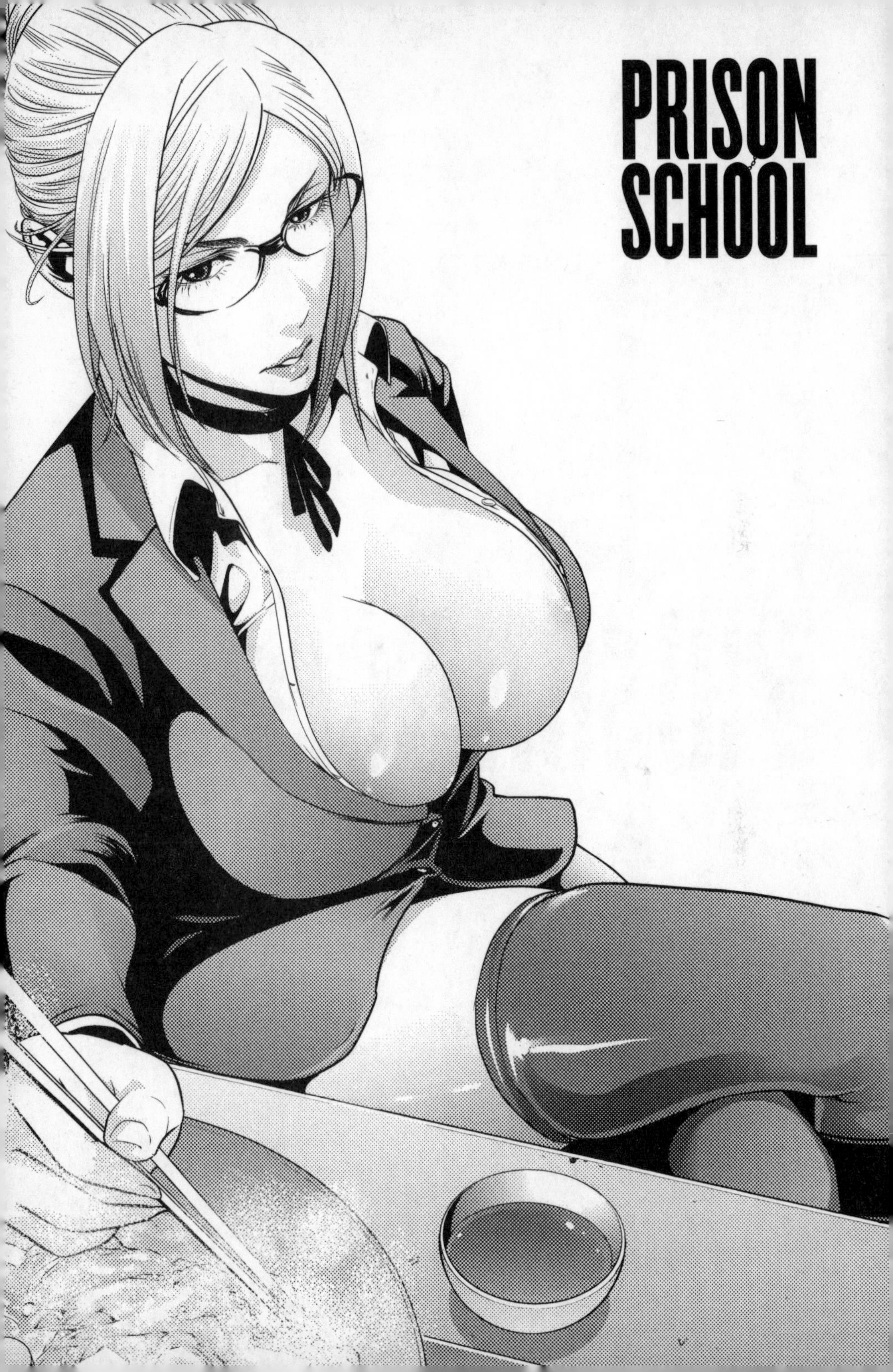
PRISON
SCHOOL

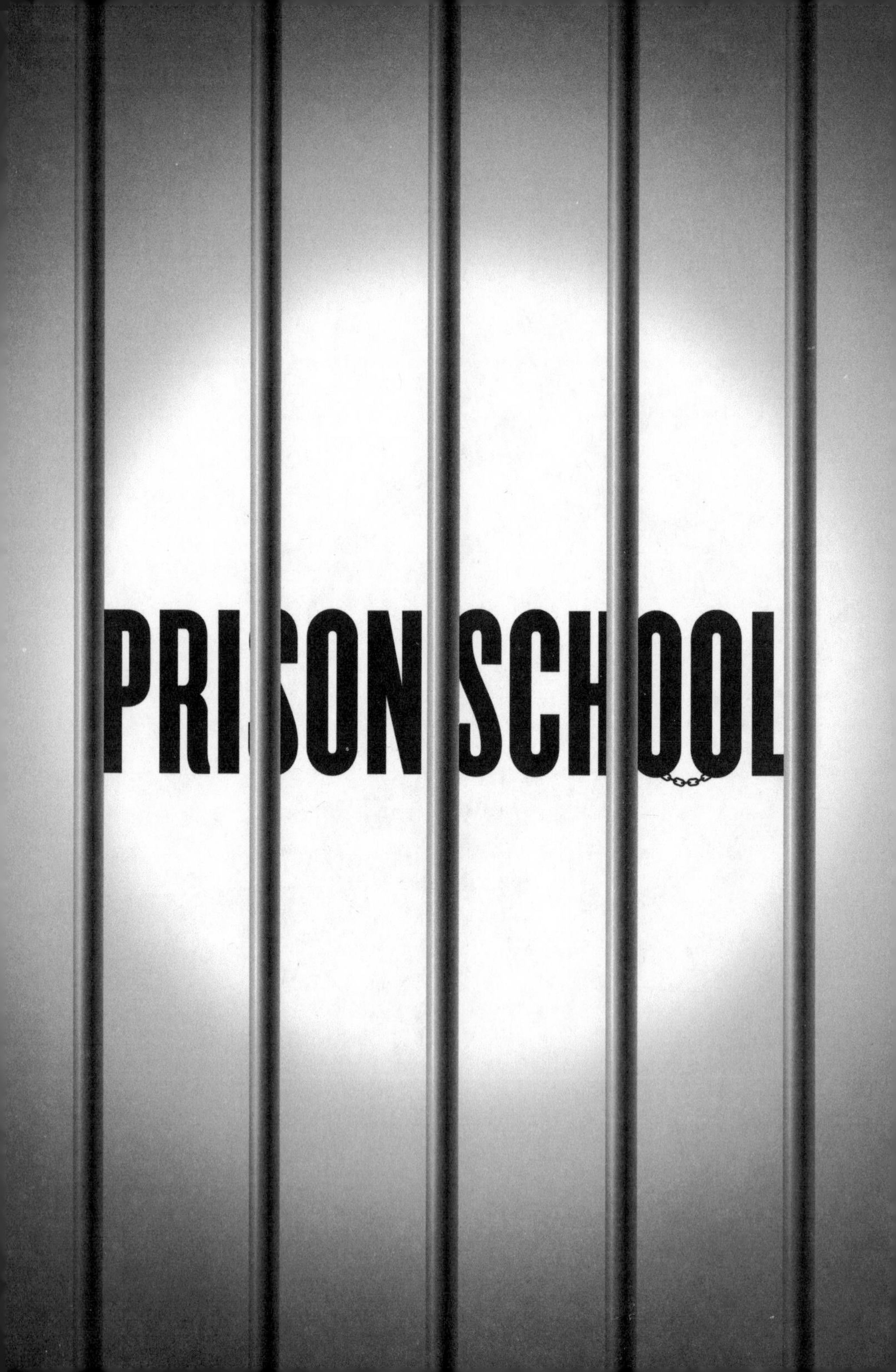
PRISON SCHOOL

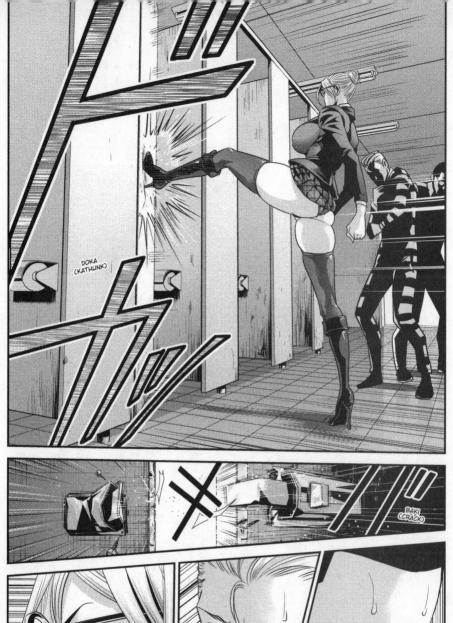

DOKA
(KATHUNK)

BAKI
(CRACK)

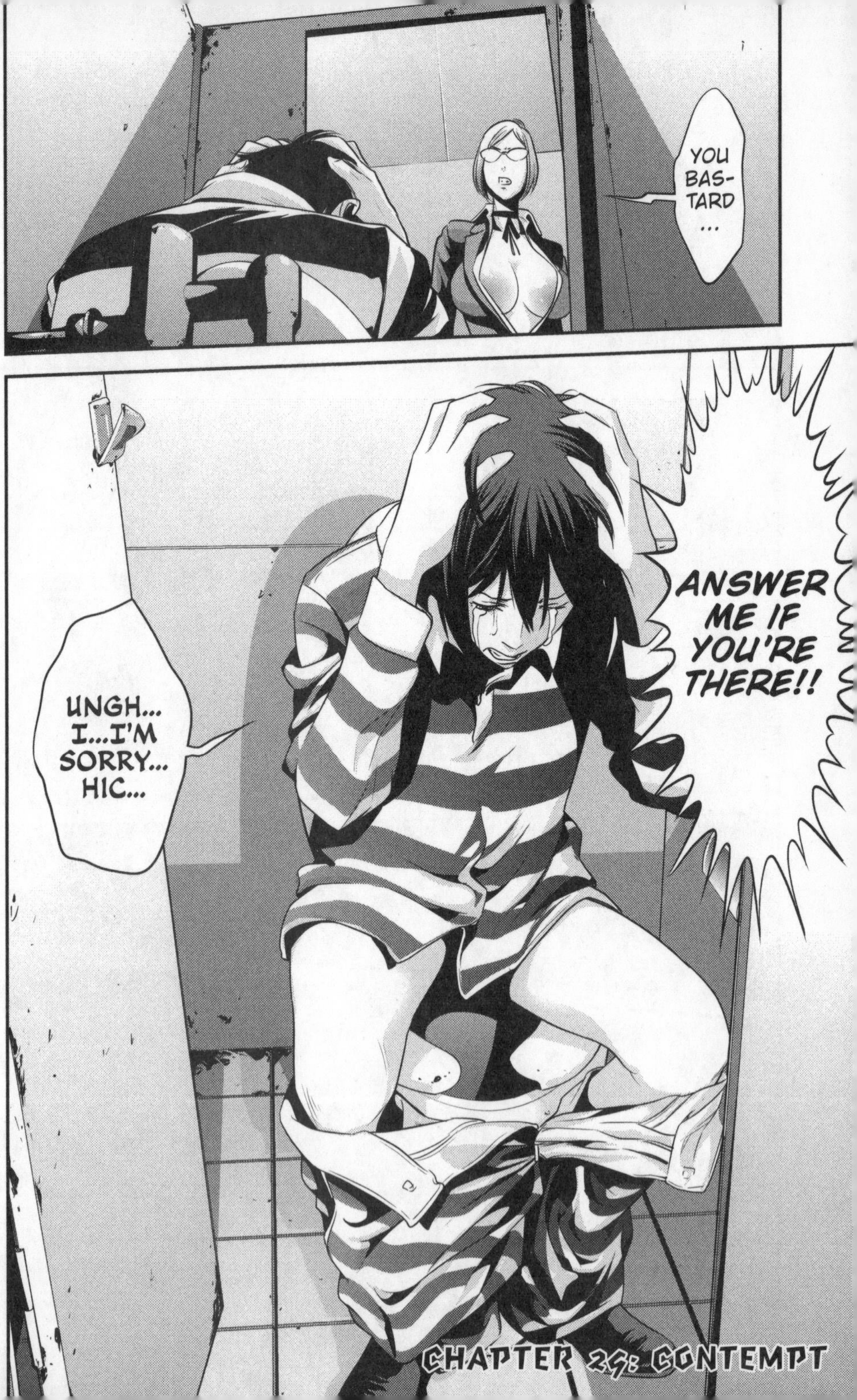
YOU BASTARD...
ANSWER ME IF YOU'RE THERE!!
UNGH... I...I'M SORRY... HIC...
CHAPTER 24: CONTEMPT

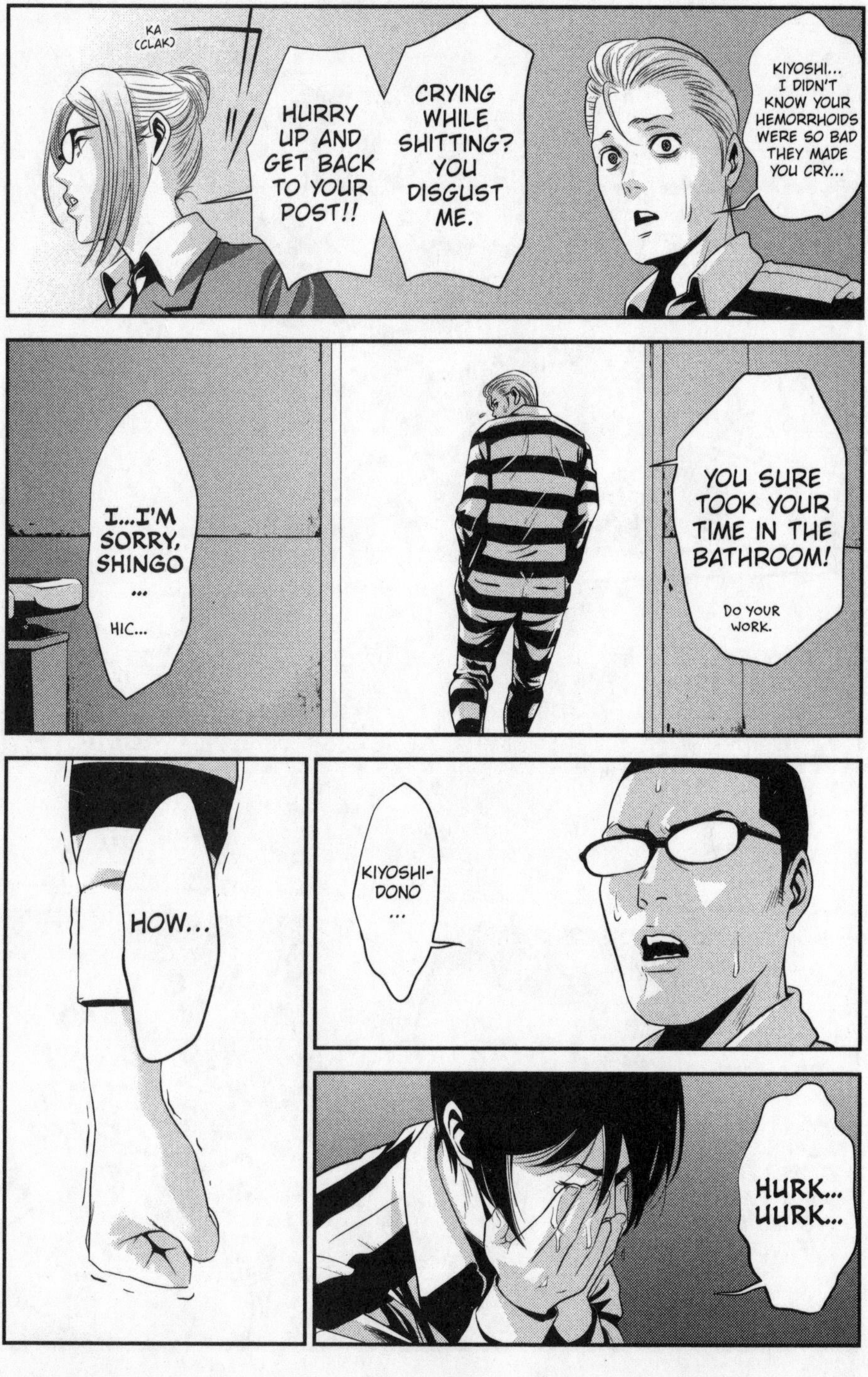
KIYOSHI... I DIDN'T KNOW YOUR HEMORRHOIDS WERE SO BAD THEY MADE YOU CRY...
CRYING WHILE SHITTING? YOU DISGUST ME.
HURRY UP AND GET BACK TO YOUR POST!!
KA (CLAK)
YOU SURE TOOK YOUR TIME IN THE BATHROOM!
DO YOUR WORK.
I...I'M SORRY, SHINGO...
HIC...
KIYOSHI-DONO...
HURK... UURK...
HOW...

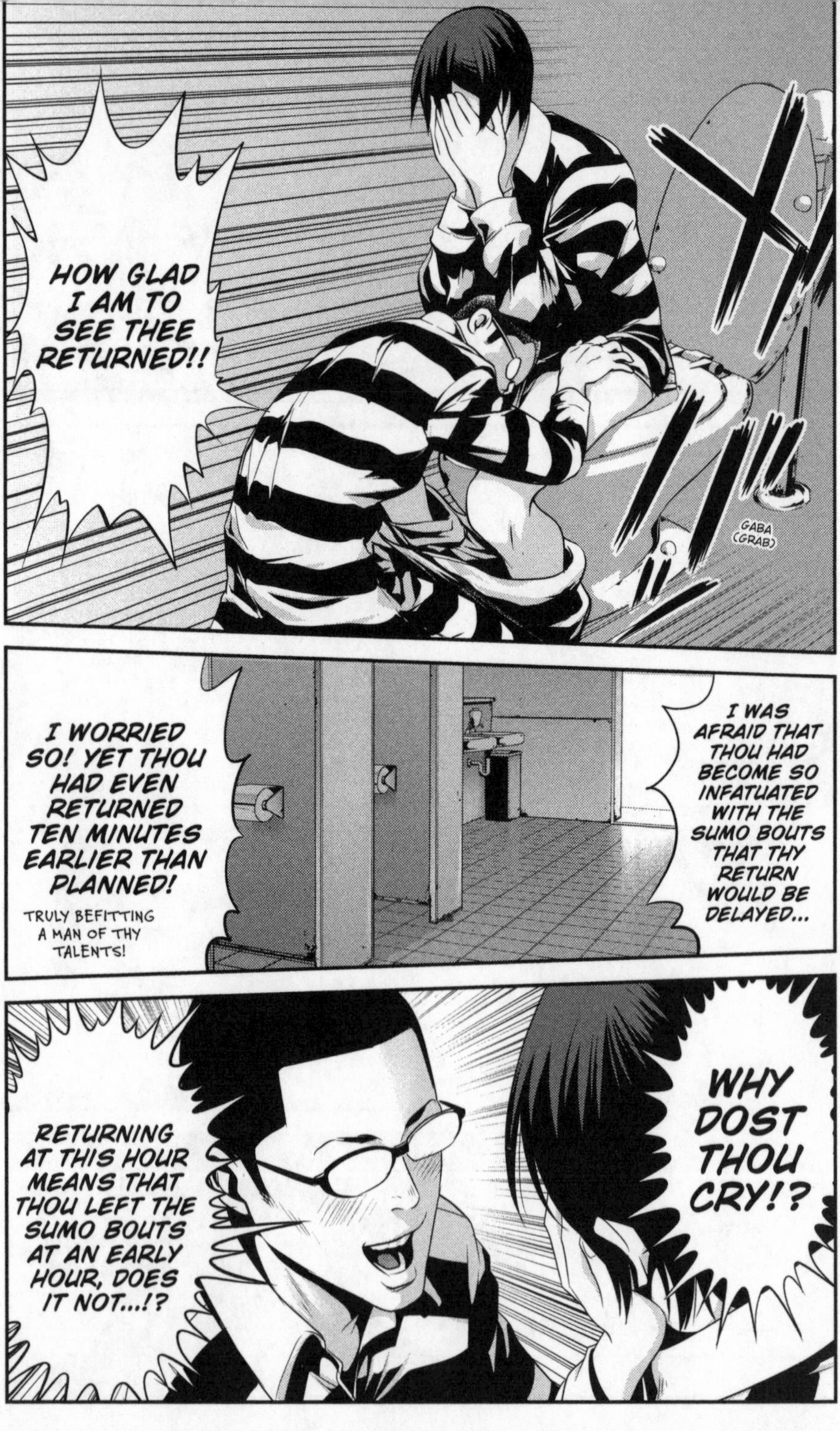
HOW GLAD I AM TO SEE THEE RETURNED!!
GABA (GRAB)
I WAS AFRAID THAT THOU HAD BECOME SO INFATUATED WITH THE SUMO BOUTS THAT THY RETURN WOULD BE DELAYED...
I WORRIED SO! YET THOU HAD EVEN RETURNED TEN MINUTES EARLIER THAN PLANNED!
TRULY BEFITTING A MAN OF THY TALENTS!
WHY DOST THOU CRY!?
RETURNING AT THIS HOUR MEANS THAT THOU LEFT THE SUMO BOUTS AT AN EARLY HOUR, DOES IT NOT...!?

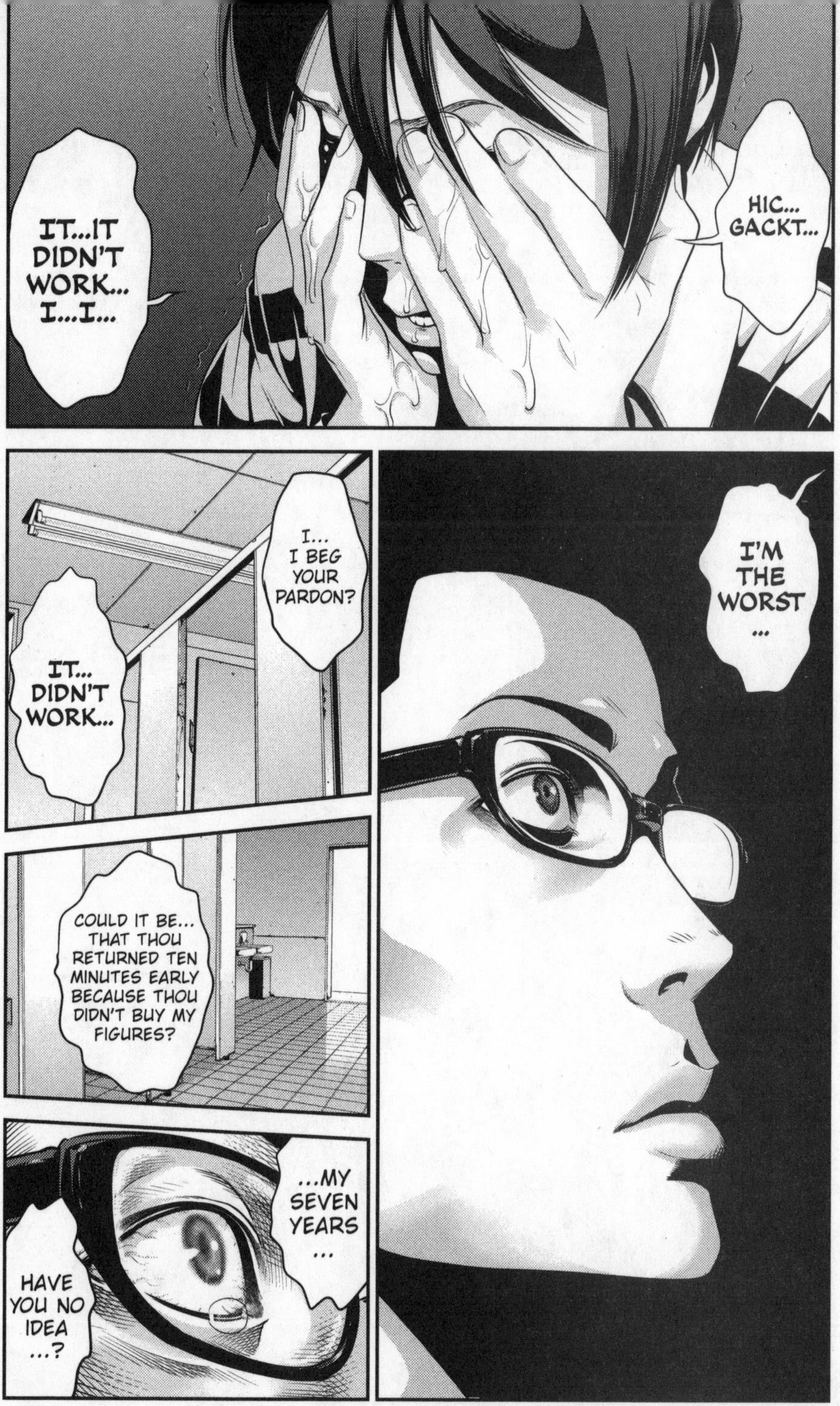
HIC... GACKT...
IT...IT DIDN'T WORK... I...I...
I'M THE WORST ...
I... I BEG YOUR PARDON?
IT... DIDN'T WORK...
COULD IT BE... THAT THOU RETURNED TEN MINUTES EARLY BECAUSE THOU DIDN'T BUY MY FIGURES?
...MY SEVEN YEARS ...
HAVE YOU NO IDEA ...?

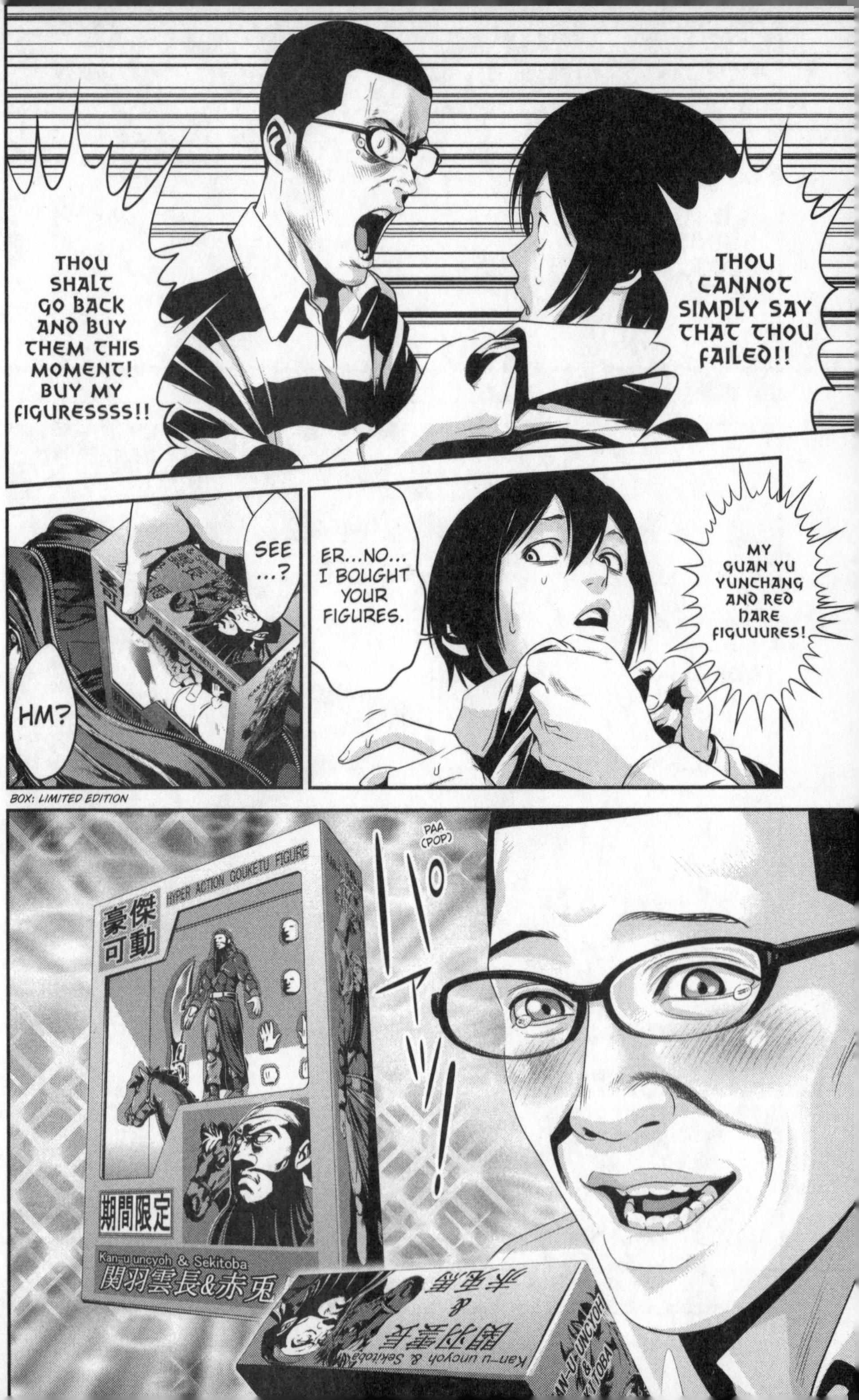
THOU CANNOT SIMPLY SAY THAT THOU FAILED!!
THOU SHALT GO BACK AND BUY THEM THIS MOMENT! BUY MY FIGURESSSS!!
MY GUAN YU YUNCHANG AND RED HARE FIGUUURES!
ER...NO... I BOUGHT YOUR FIGURES.
SEE ...?
HM?
BOX: LIMITED EDITION
PAA (POP)
豪傑可動
HYPER ACTION GOUKETU FIGURE
期間限定
Kan-u uncyoh & Sekitoba
関羽雲長&赤兎

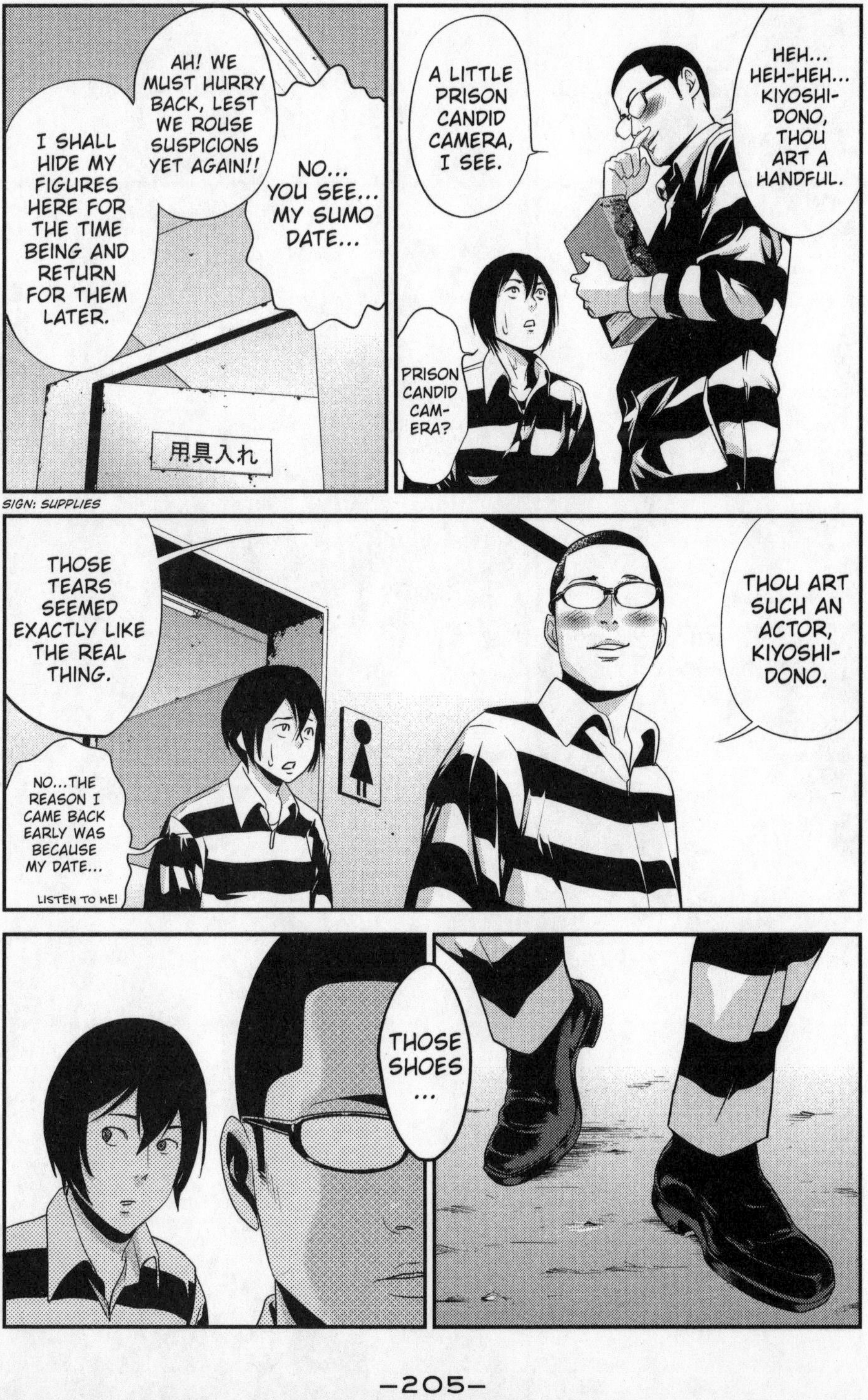
HEH... HEH-HEH... KIYOSHI-DONO, THOU ART A HANDFUL.
A LITTLE PRISON CANDID CAMERA, I SEE.
PRISON CANDID CAM-ERA?
NO... YOU SEE... MY SUMO DATE...
AH! WE MUST HURRY BACK, LEST WE ROUSE SUSPICIONS YET AGAIN!!
I SHALL HIDE MY FIGURES HERE FOR THE TIME BEING AND RETURN FOR THEM LATER.
用具入れ
THOU ART SUCH AN ACTOR, KIYOSHI-DONO.
THOSE TEARS SEEMED EXACTLY LIKE THE REAL THING.
NO...THE REASON I CAME BACK EARLY WAS BECAUSE MY DATE...
LISTEN TO ME!
THOSE SHOES ...

SIGN: SUPPLIES

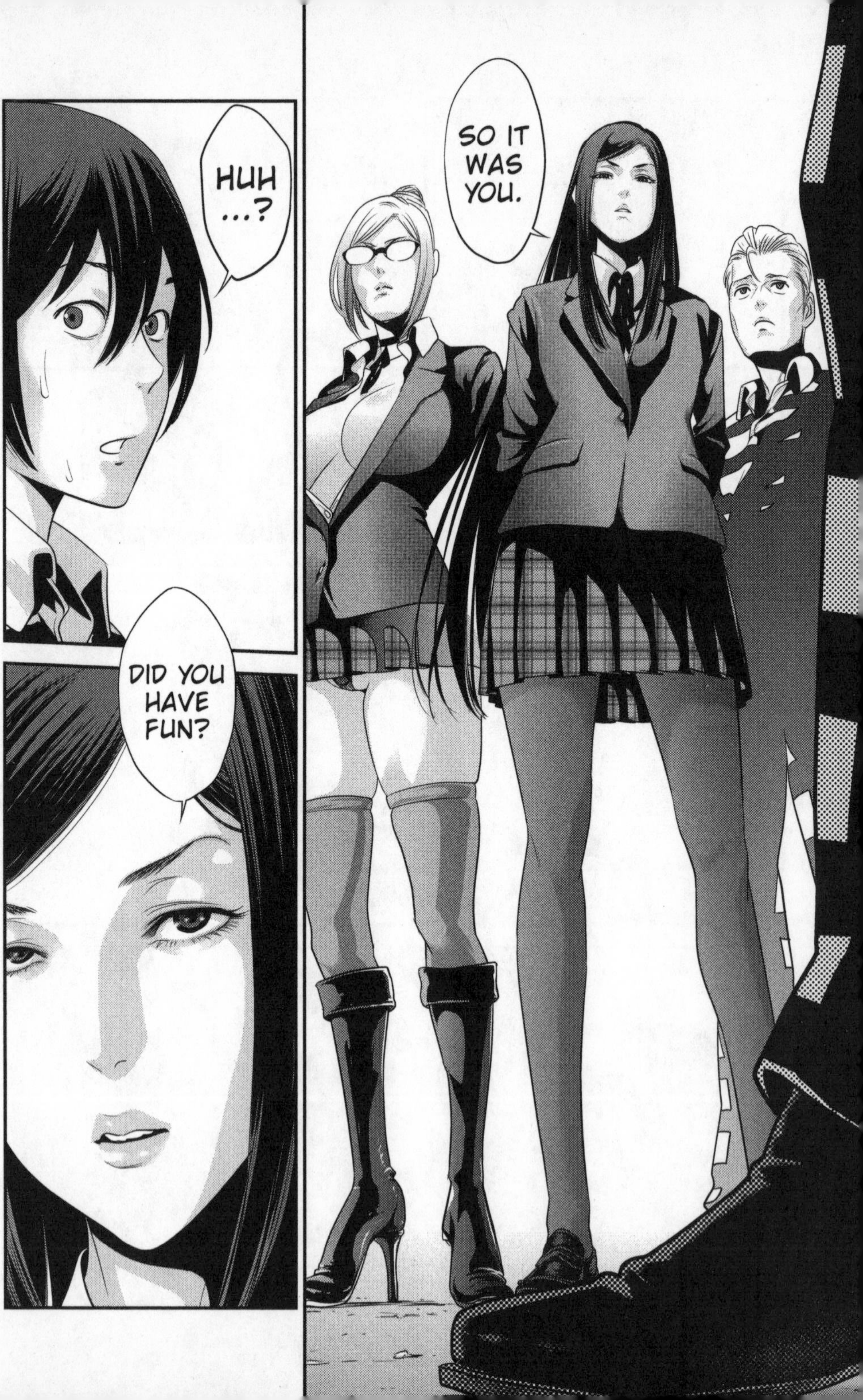
SO IT WAS YOU.
HUH ...?
DID YOU HAVE FUN?

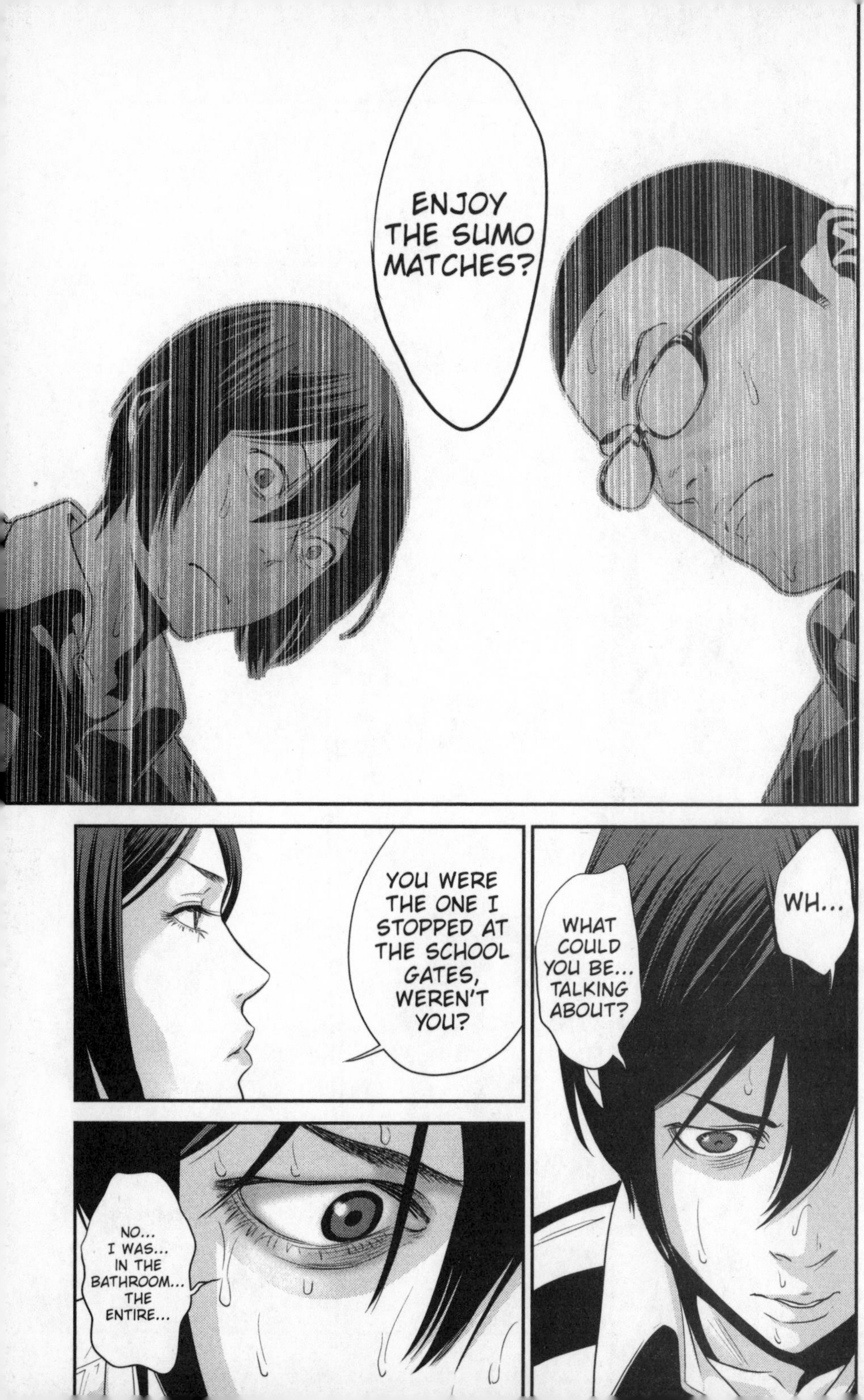
ENJOY THE SUMO MATCHES?
WH...
WHAT COULD YOU BE... TALKING ABOUT?
YOU WERE THE ONE I STOPPED AT THE SCHOOL GATES, WEREN'T YOU?
NO... I WAS... IN THE BATHROOM... THE ENTIRE...

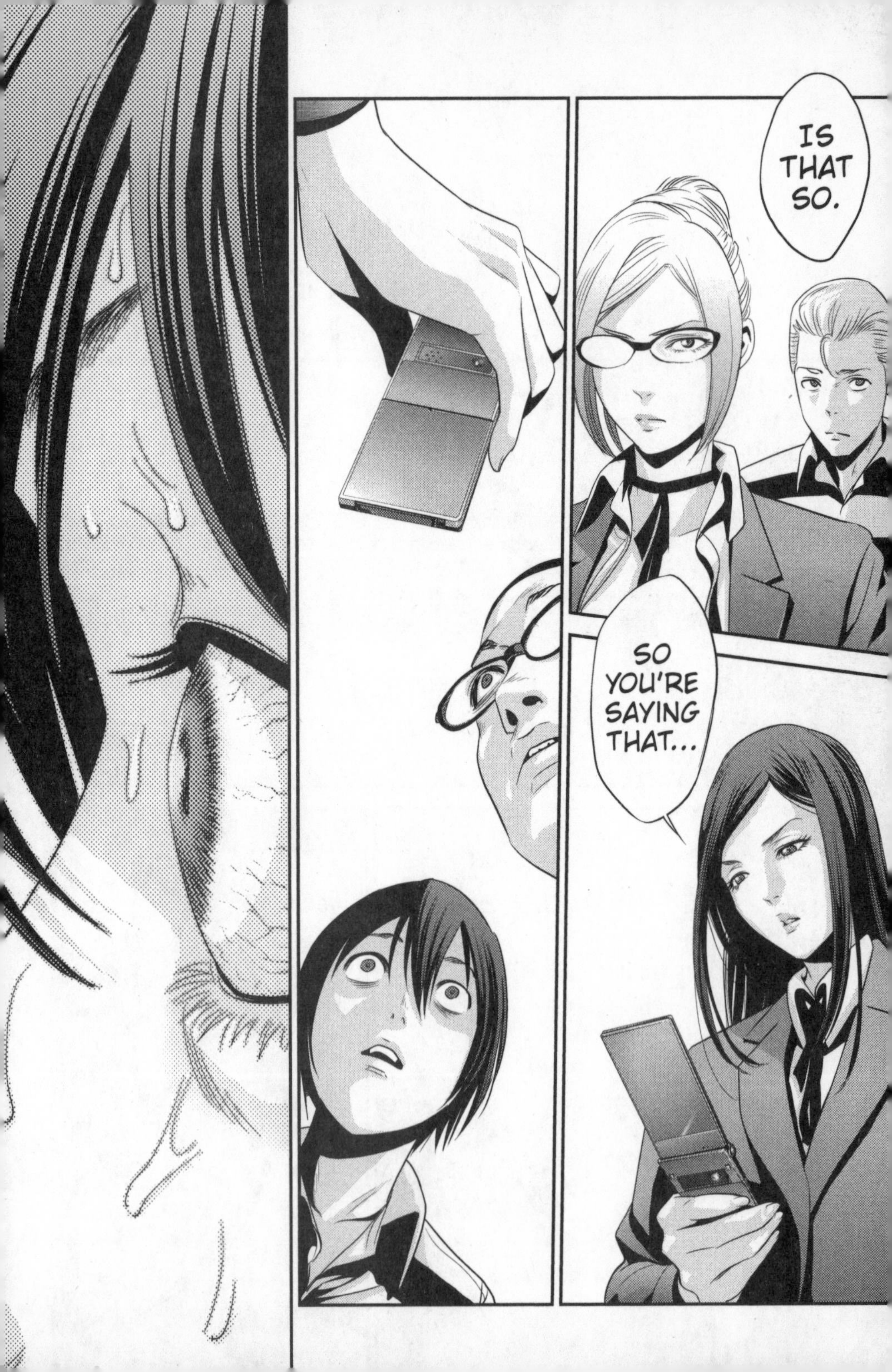
IS THAT SO.
SO YOU'RE SAYING THAT...

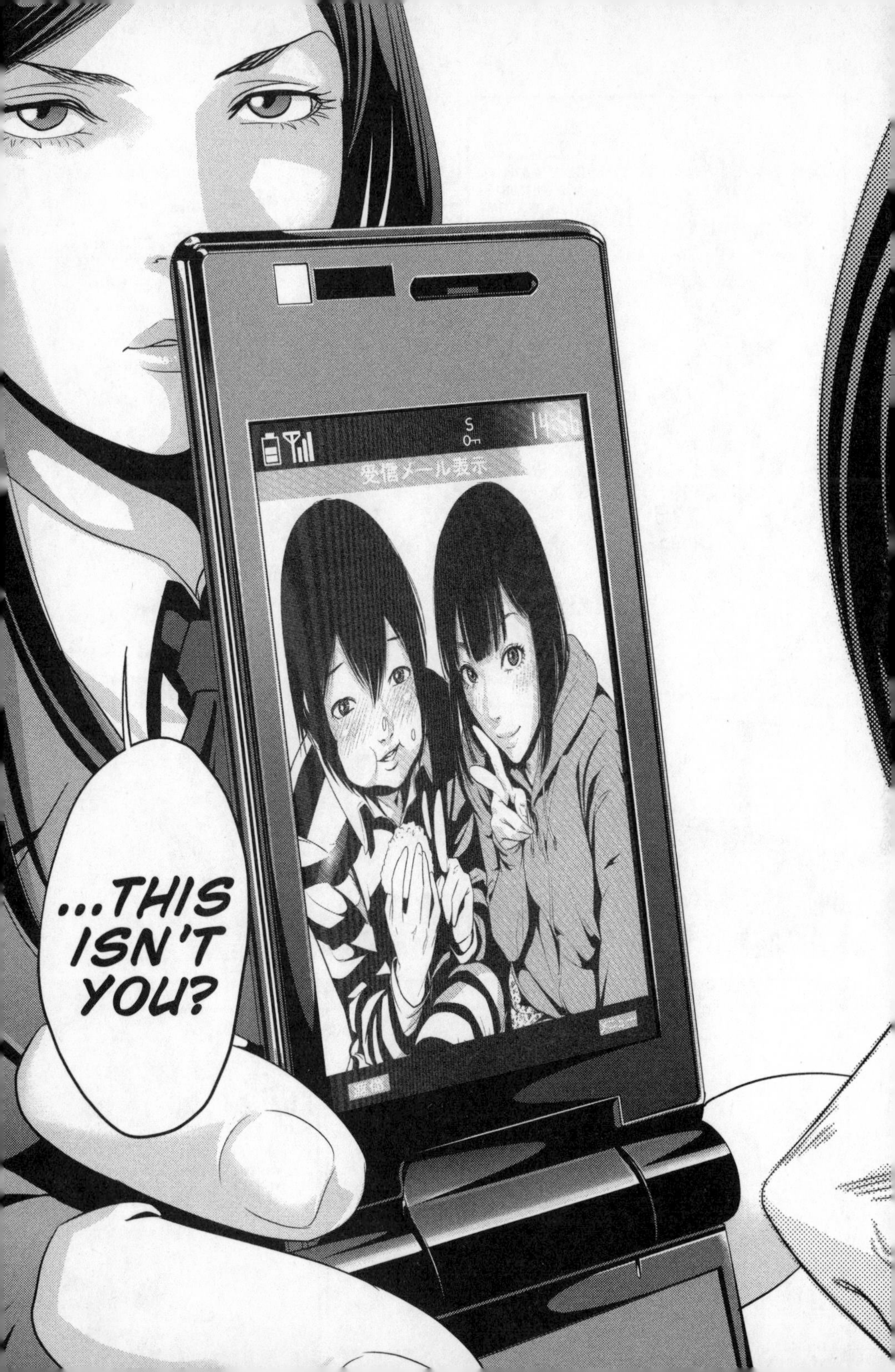
受信メール表示
...THIS ISN'T YOU?

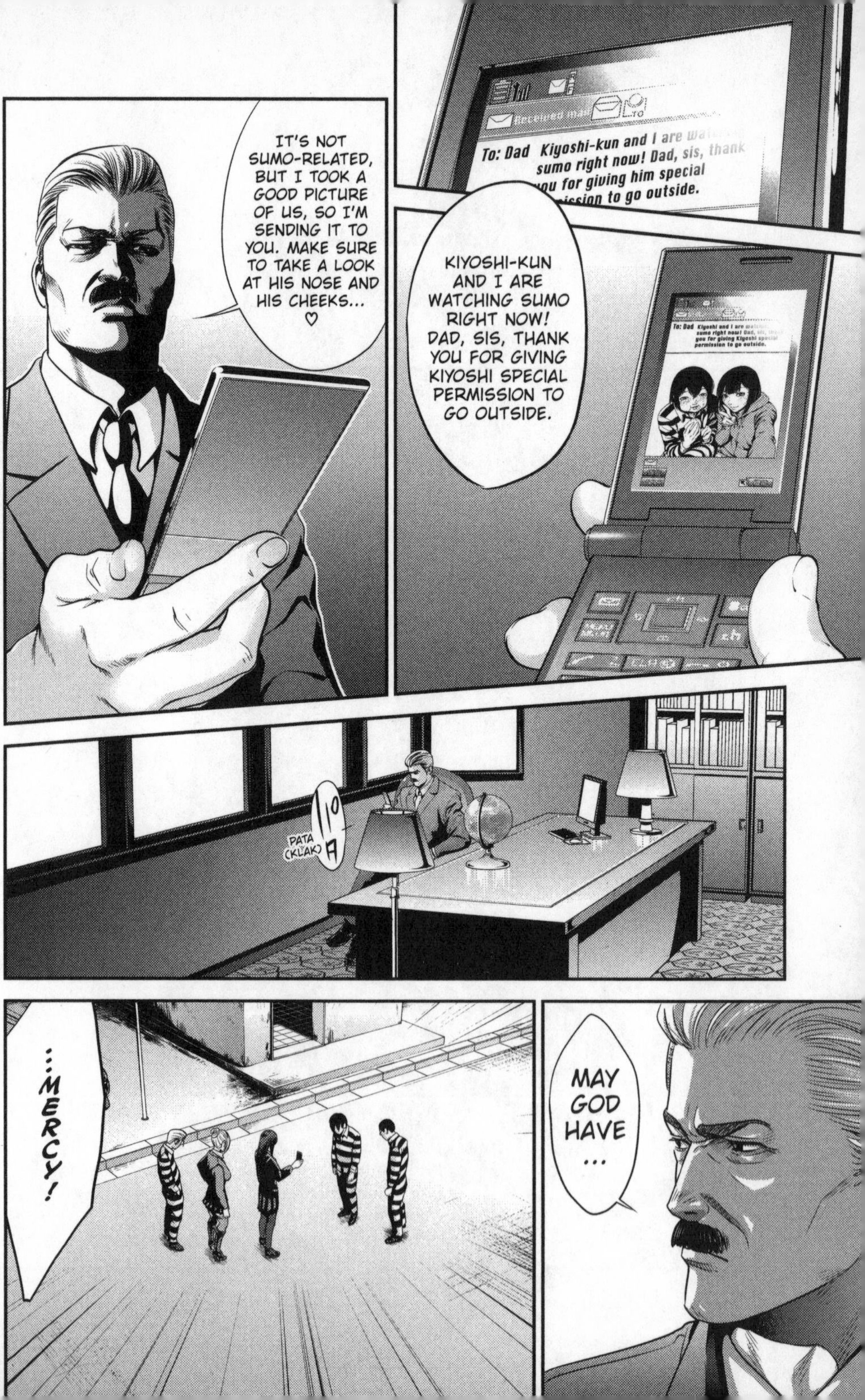

Received mail
To: Dad Kiyoshi-kun and I are watching sumo right now! Dad, sis, thank you for giving him special permission to go outside.
KIYOSHI-KUN AND I ARE WATCHING SUMO RIGHT NOW! DAD, SIS, THANK YOU FOR GIVING KIYOSHI SPECIAL PERMISSION TO GO OUTSIDE.
To: Dad Kiyoshi and I are watching sumo right now! Dad, sis, thank you for giving Kiyoshi special permission to go outside.
IT'S NOT SUMO-RELATED, BUT I TOOK A GOOD PICTURE OF US, SO I'M SENDING IT TO YOU. MAKE SURE TO TAKE A LOOK AT HIS NOSE AND HIS CHEEKS... ♡
PATA (KLAK)
MAY GOD HAVE ...
...MERCY!

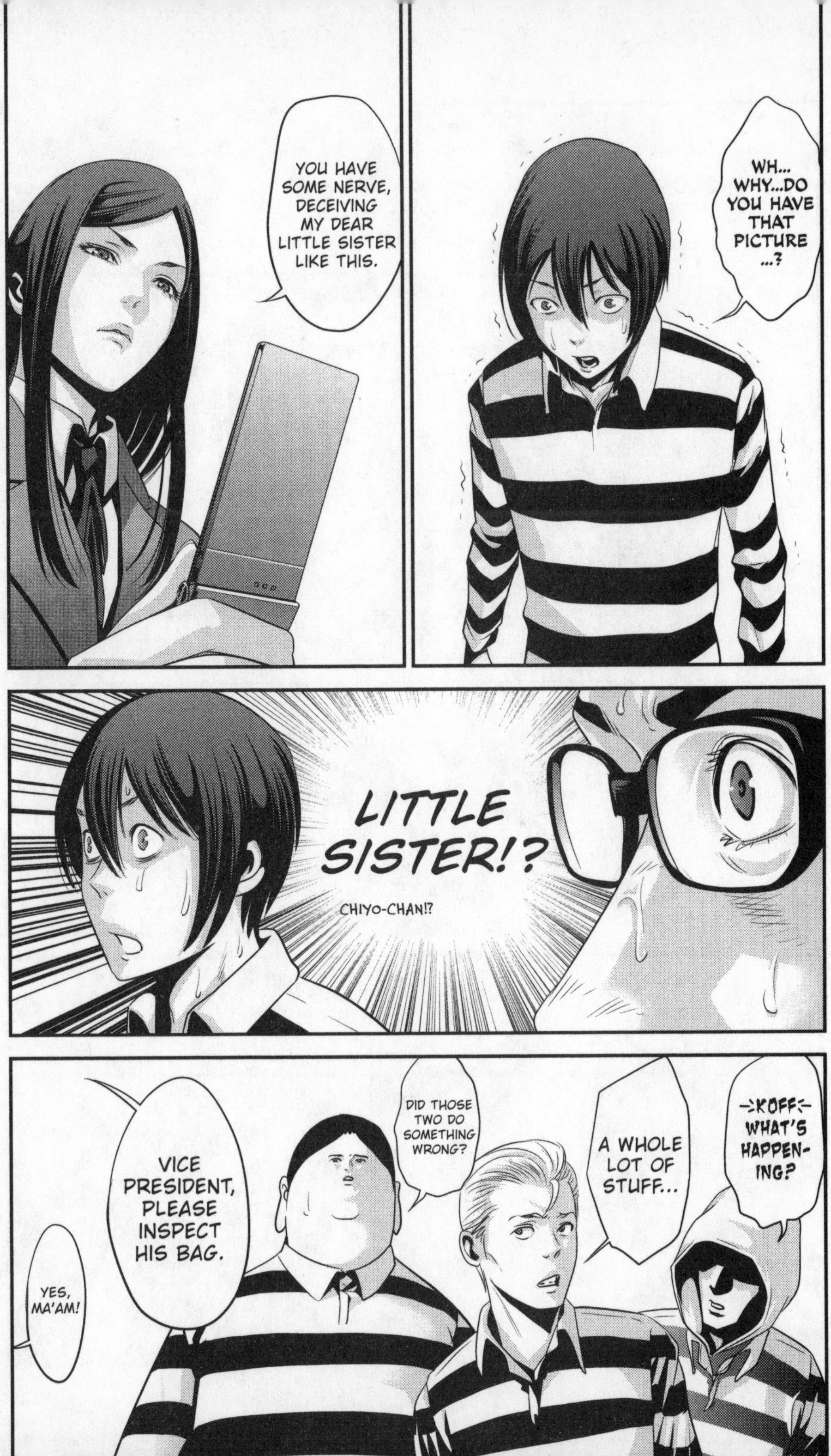
WH... WHY...DO YOU HAVE THAT PICTURE ...?
YOU HAVE SOME NERVE, DECEIVING MY DEAR LITTLE SISTER LIKE THIS.
LITTLE SISTER!?
CHIYO-CHAN!?
-KOFF- WHAT'S HAPPEN-ING?
A WHOLE LOT OF STUFF...
DID THOSE TWO DO SOMETHING WRONG?
VICE PRESIDENT, PLEASE INSPECT HIS BAG.
YES, MA'AM!

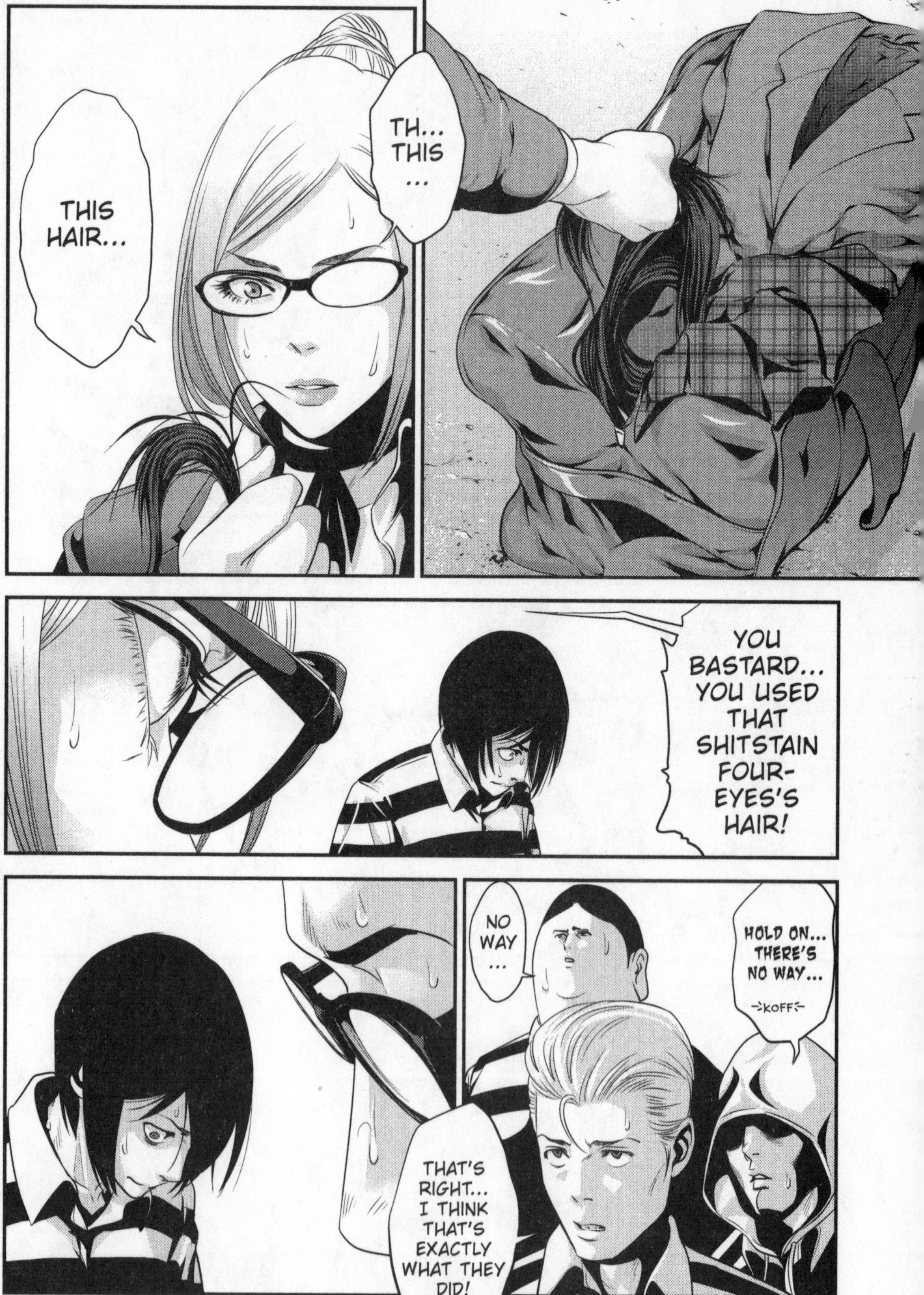
TH... THIS ...
THIS HAIR...
YOU BASTARD... YOU USED THAT SHITSTAIN FOUR-EYES'S HAIR!
HOLD ON... THERE'S NO WAY...
KOFF
NO WAY ...
THAT'S RIGHT... I THINK THAT'S EXACTLY WHAT THEY DID!

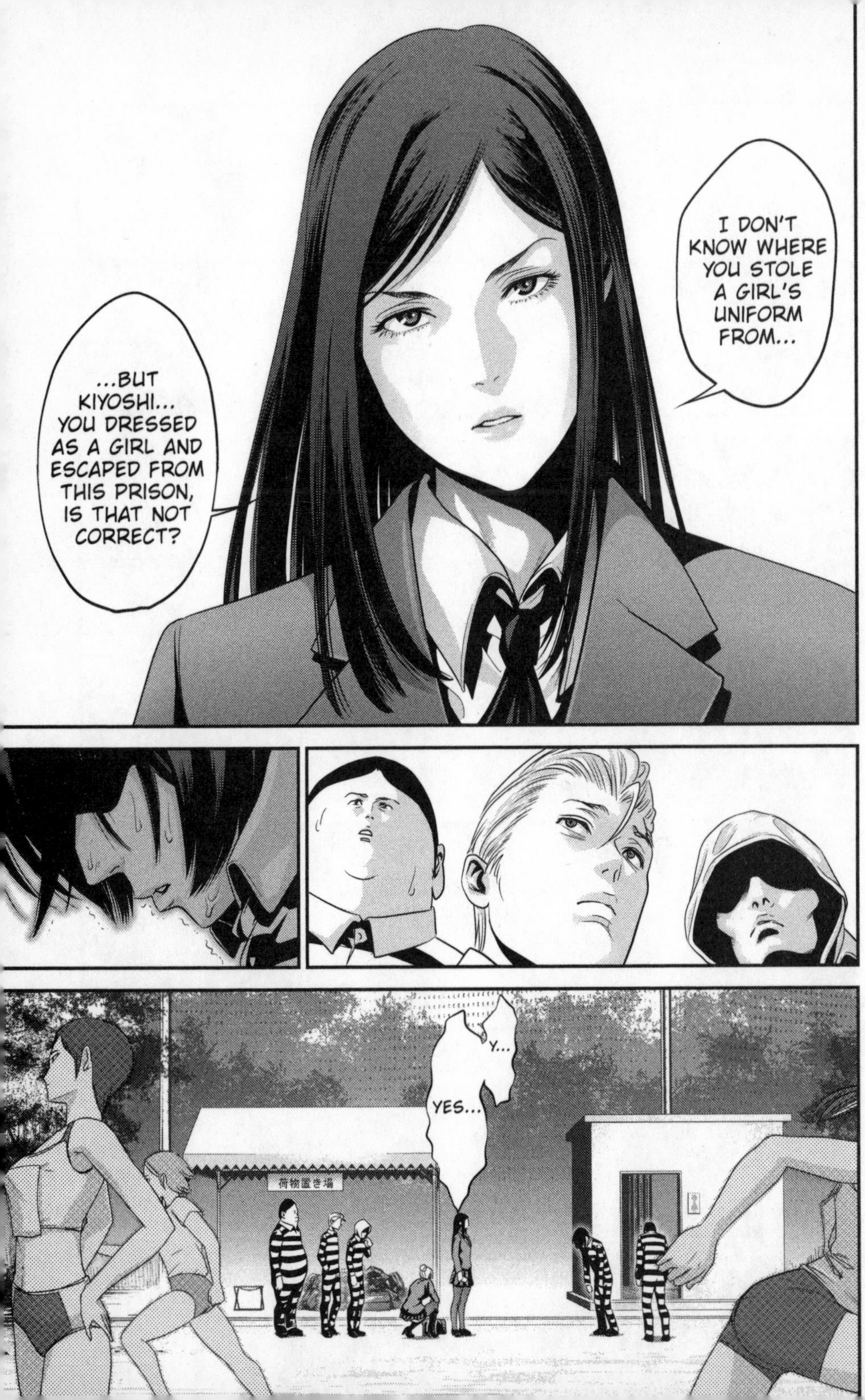
I DON'T KNOW WHERE YOU STOLE A GIRL'S UNIFORM FROM...
...BUT KIYOSHI... YOU DRESSED AS A GIRL AND ESCAPED FROM THIS PRISON, IS THAT NOT CORRECT?
Y...
YES...
荷物置き場

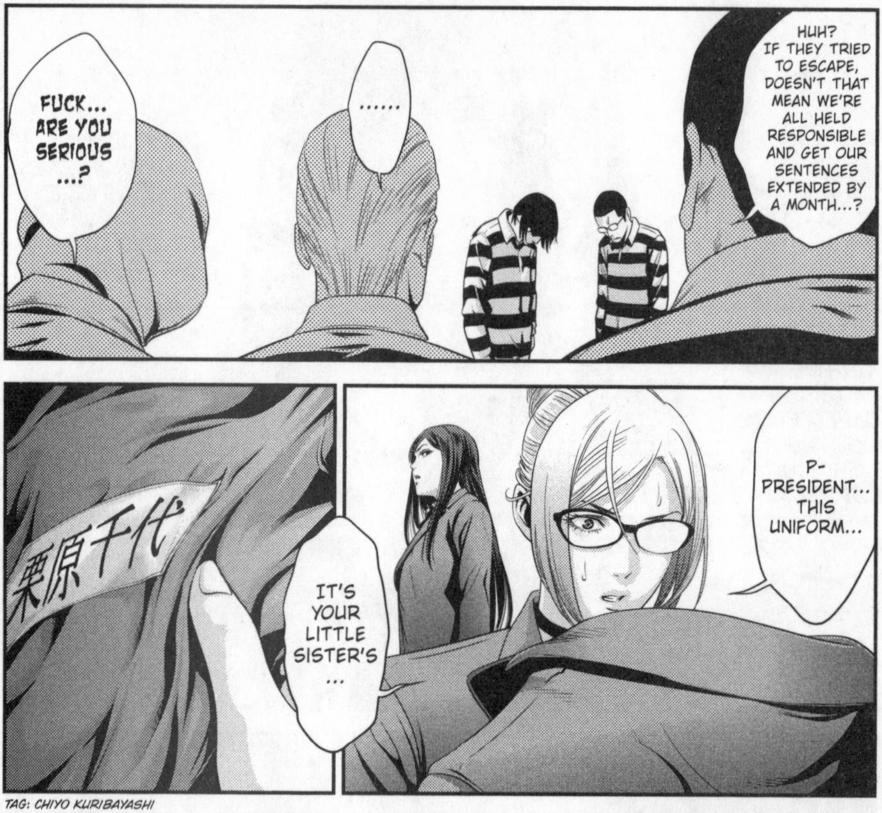
HUH? IF THEY TRIED TO ESCAPE, DOESN'T THAT MEAN WE'RE ALL HELD RESPONSIBLE AND GET OUR SENTENCES EXTENDED BY A MONTH...?
......
FUCK... ARE YOU SERIOUS ...?
P-PRESIDENT... THIS UNIFORM...
IT'S YOUR LITTLE SISTER'S ...
栗原千代

TAG: CHIYO KURIBAYASHI

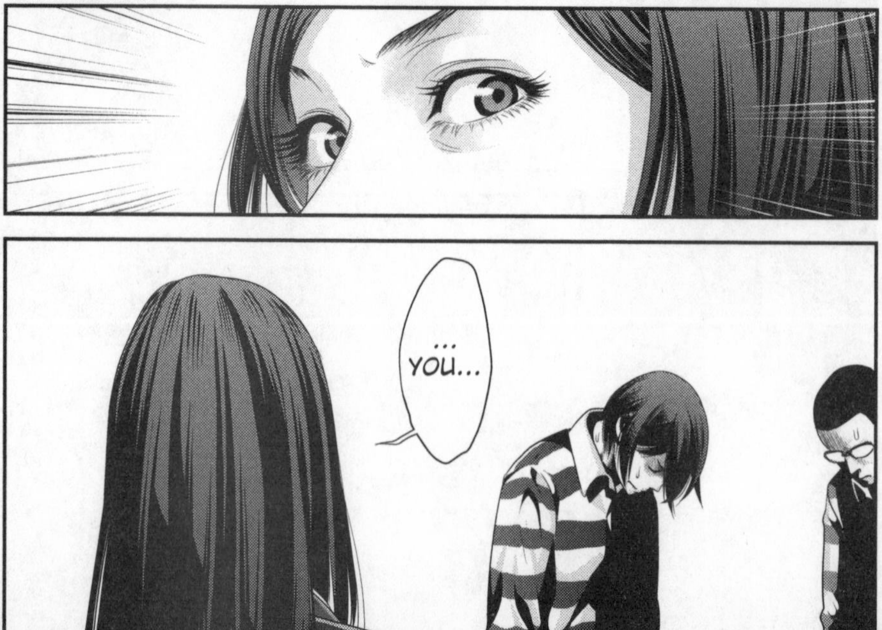
... YOU...

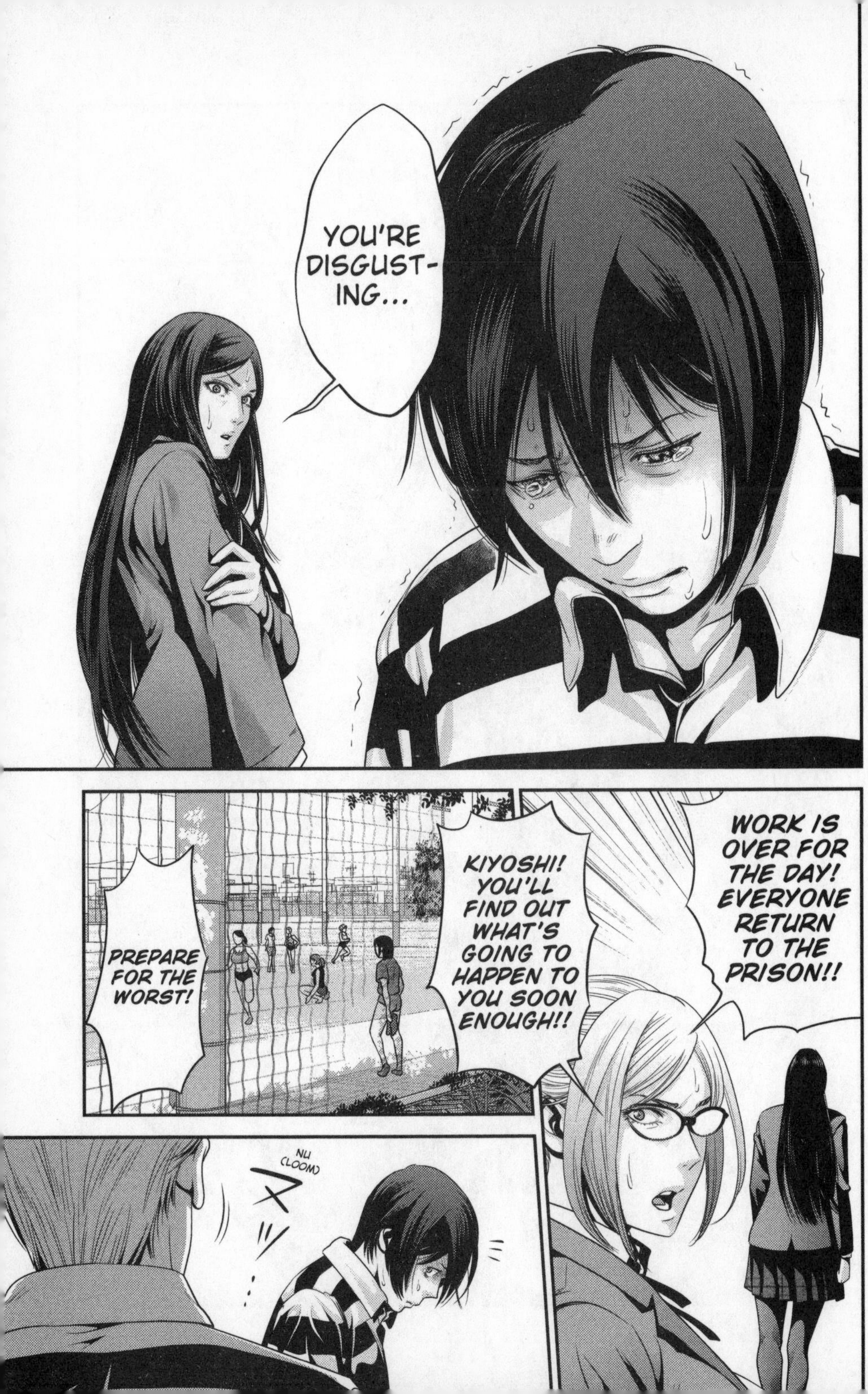
YOU'RE DISGUST-ING...
WORK IS OVER FOR THE DAY! EVERYONE RETURN TO THE PRISON!!
KIYOSHI! YOU'LL FIND OUT WHAT'S GOING TO HAPPEN TO YOU SOON ENOUGH!!
PREPARE FOR THE WORST!
NU (LOOM)

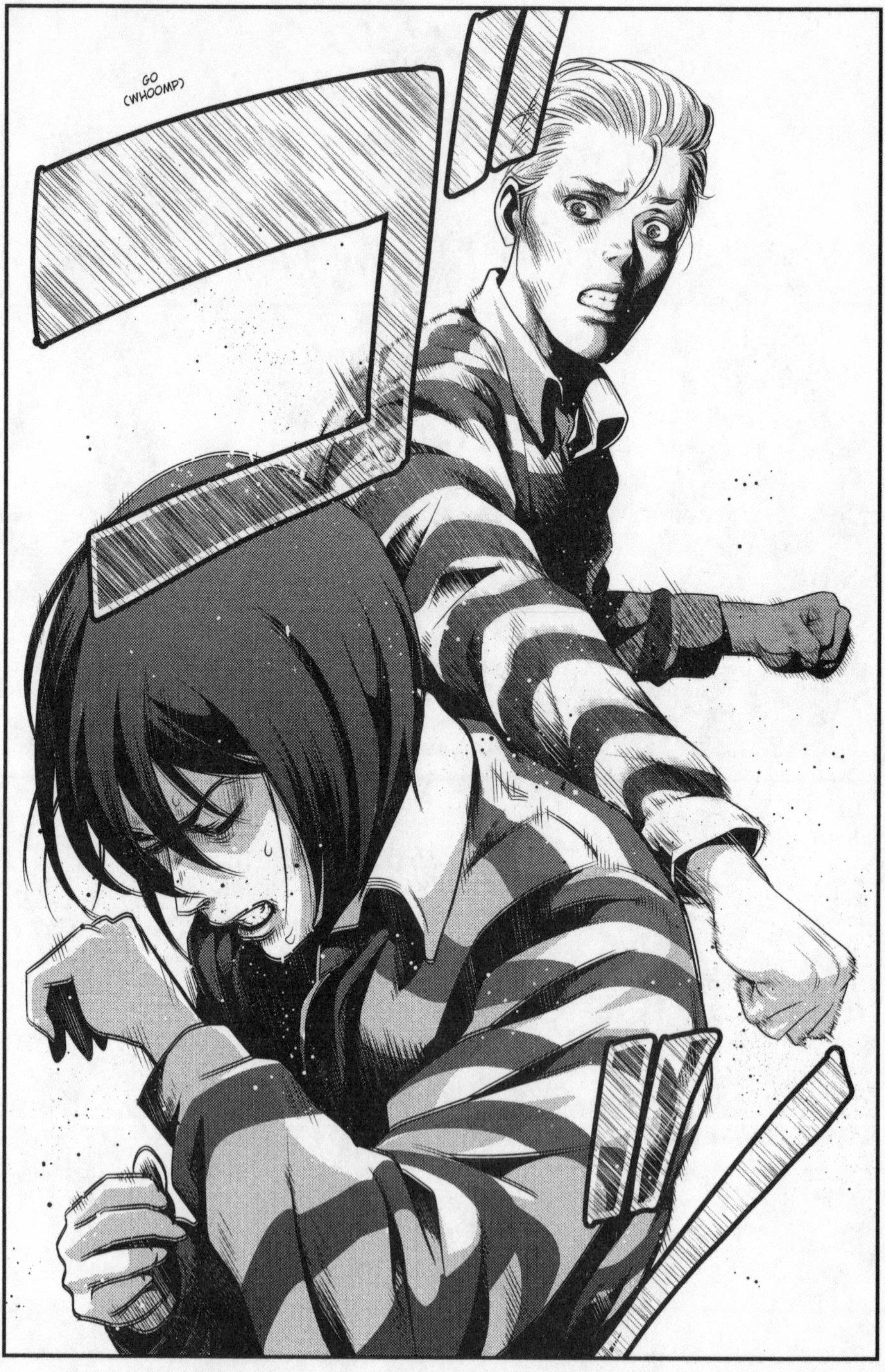
GO
(WHOOMP)

CHAPTER 30: THE VERDICT

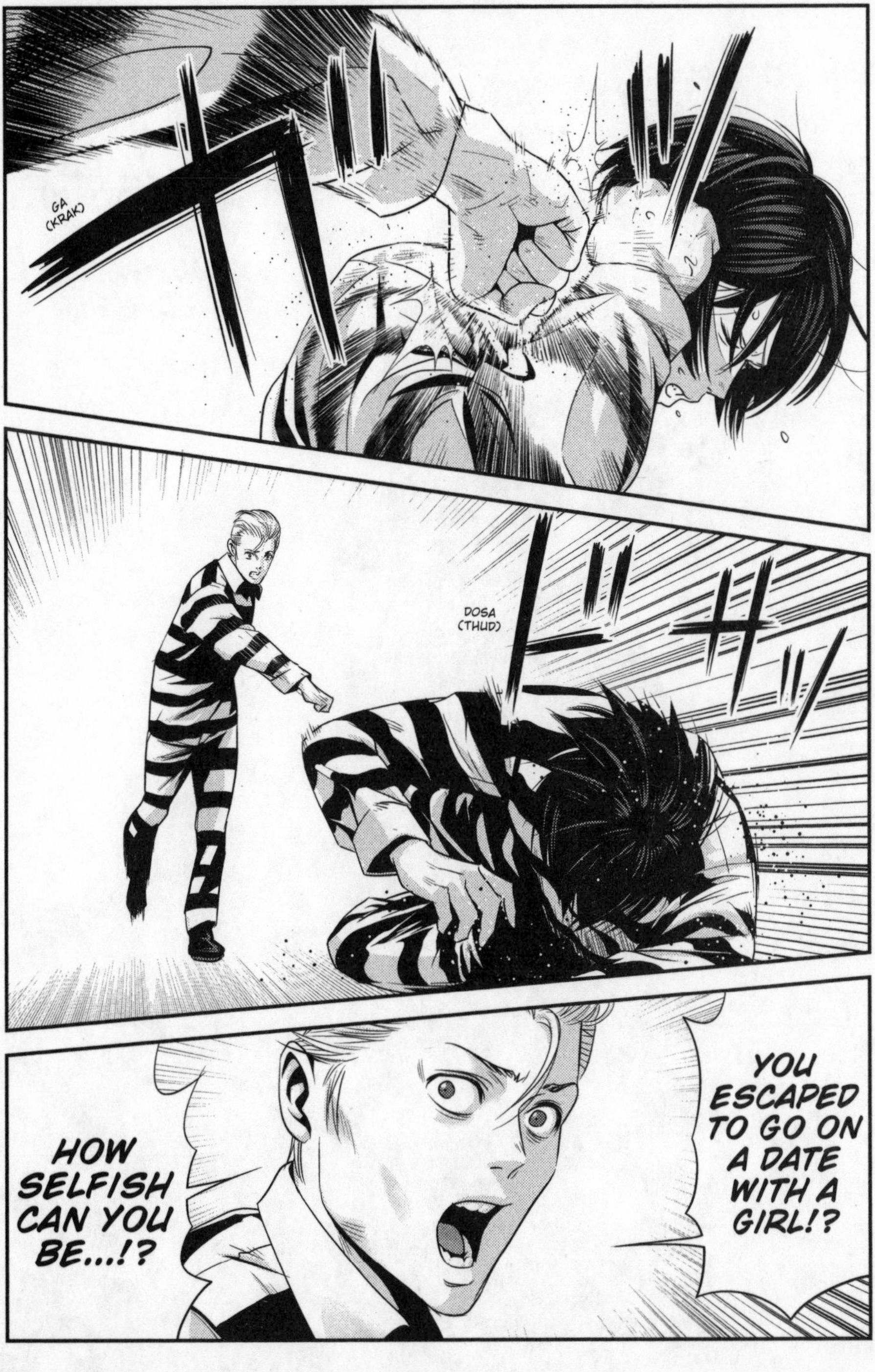
GA
(KRAK)
DOSA
(THUD)
YOU ESCAPED TO GO ON A DATE WITH A GIRL!?
HOW SELFISH CAN YOU BE...!?

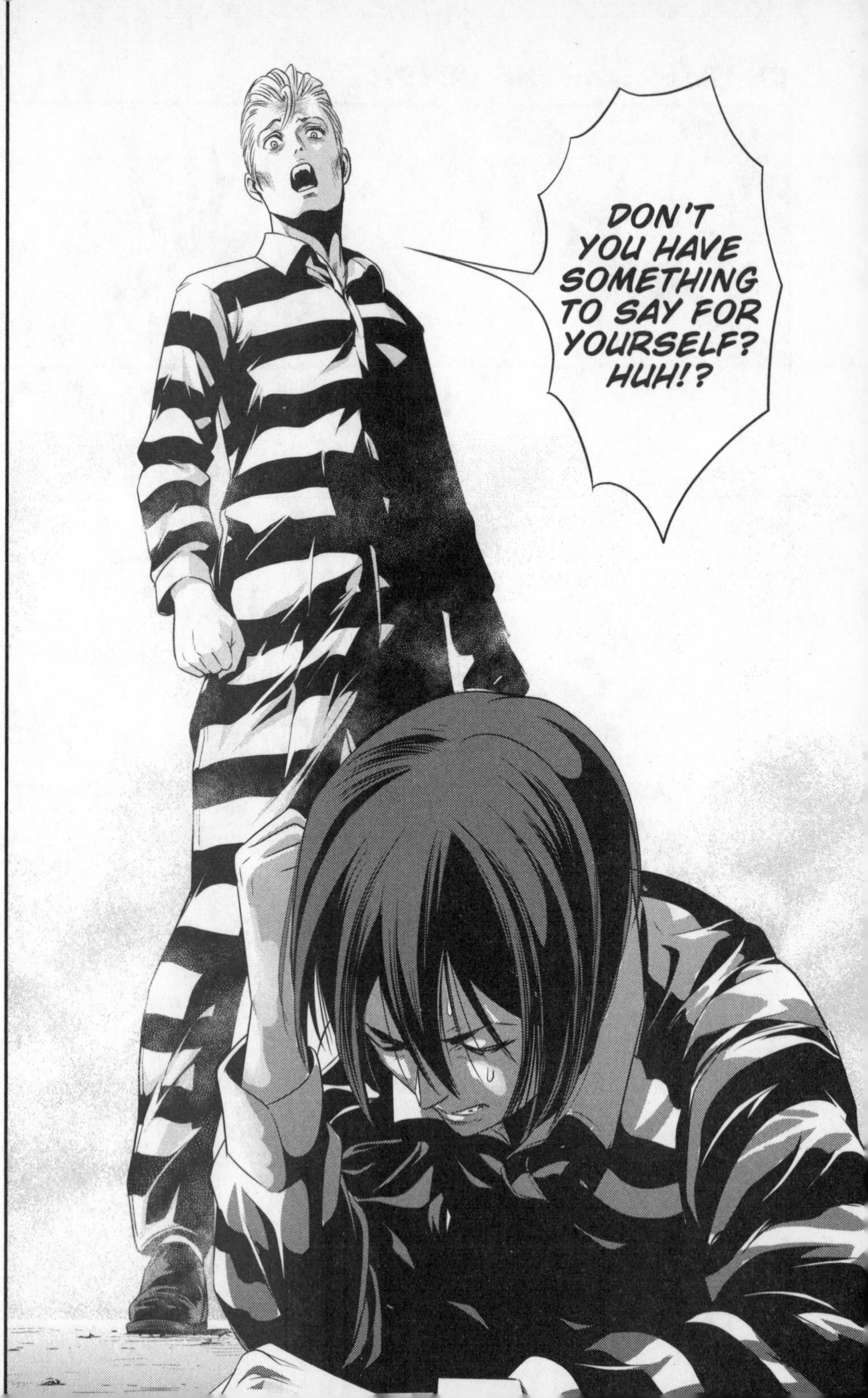
DON'T YOU HAVE SOMETHING TO SAY FOR YOURSELF? HUH!?

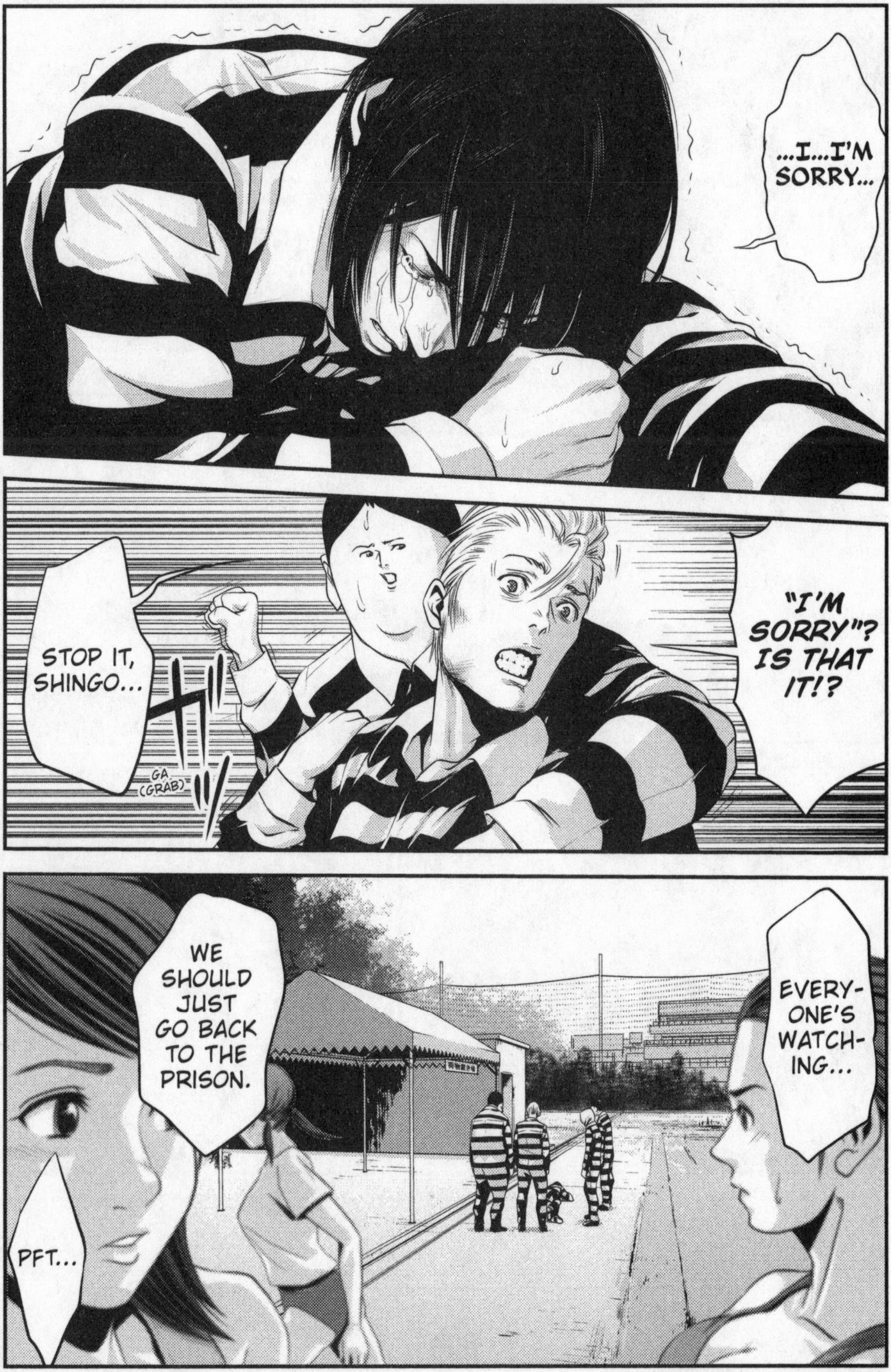
...I...I'M SORRY...
"I'M SORRY"? IS THAT IT!?
STOP IT, SHINGO...
GA (GRAB)
EVERY-ONE'S WATCH-ING...
WE SHOULD JUST GO BACK TO THE PRISON.
PFT...

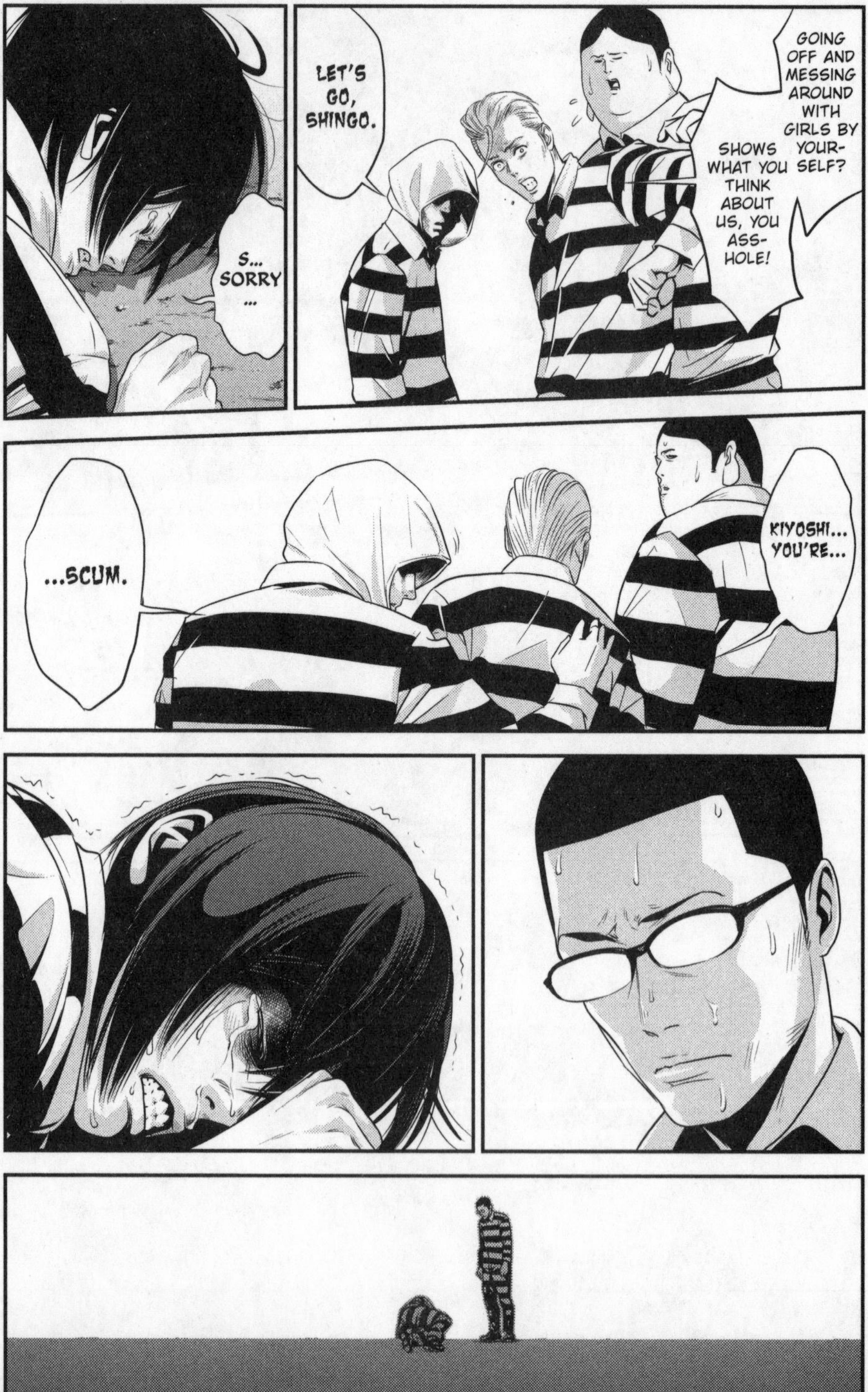
GOING OFF AND MESSING AROUND WITH GIRLS BY YOUR-SELF?
SHOWS WHAT YOU THINK ABOUT US, YOU ASS-HOLE!
LET'S GO, SHINGO.
S... SORRY ...
KIYOSHI... YOU'RE...
...SCUM.

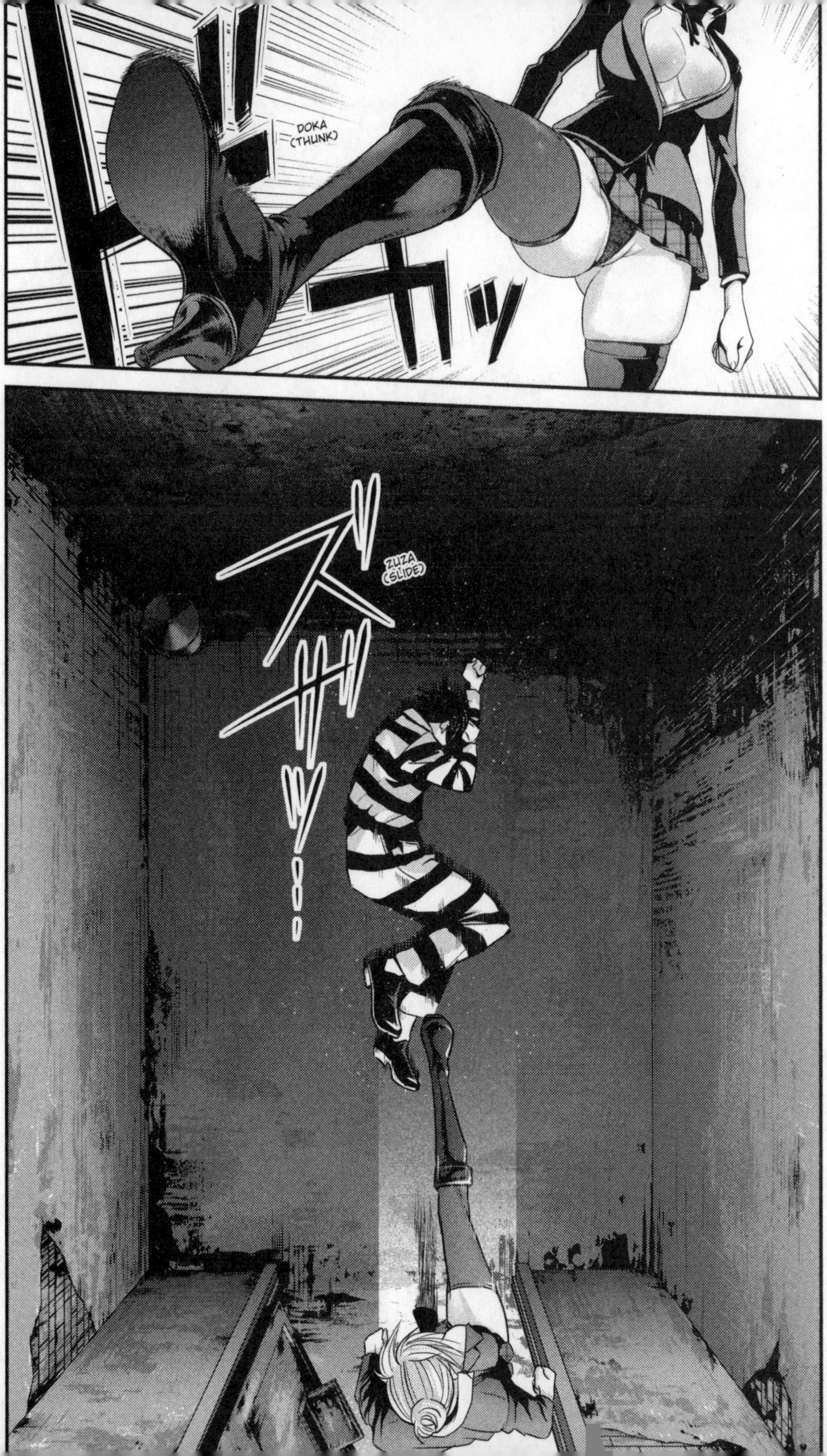
DOKA
(THUNK)
ZUZA
(SLIDE)

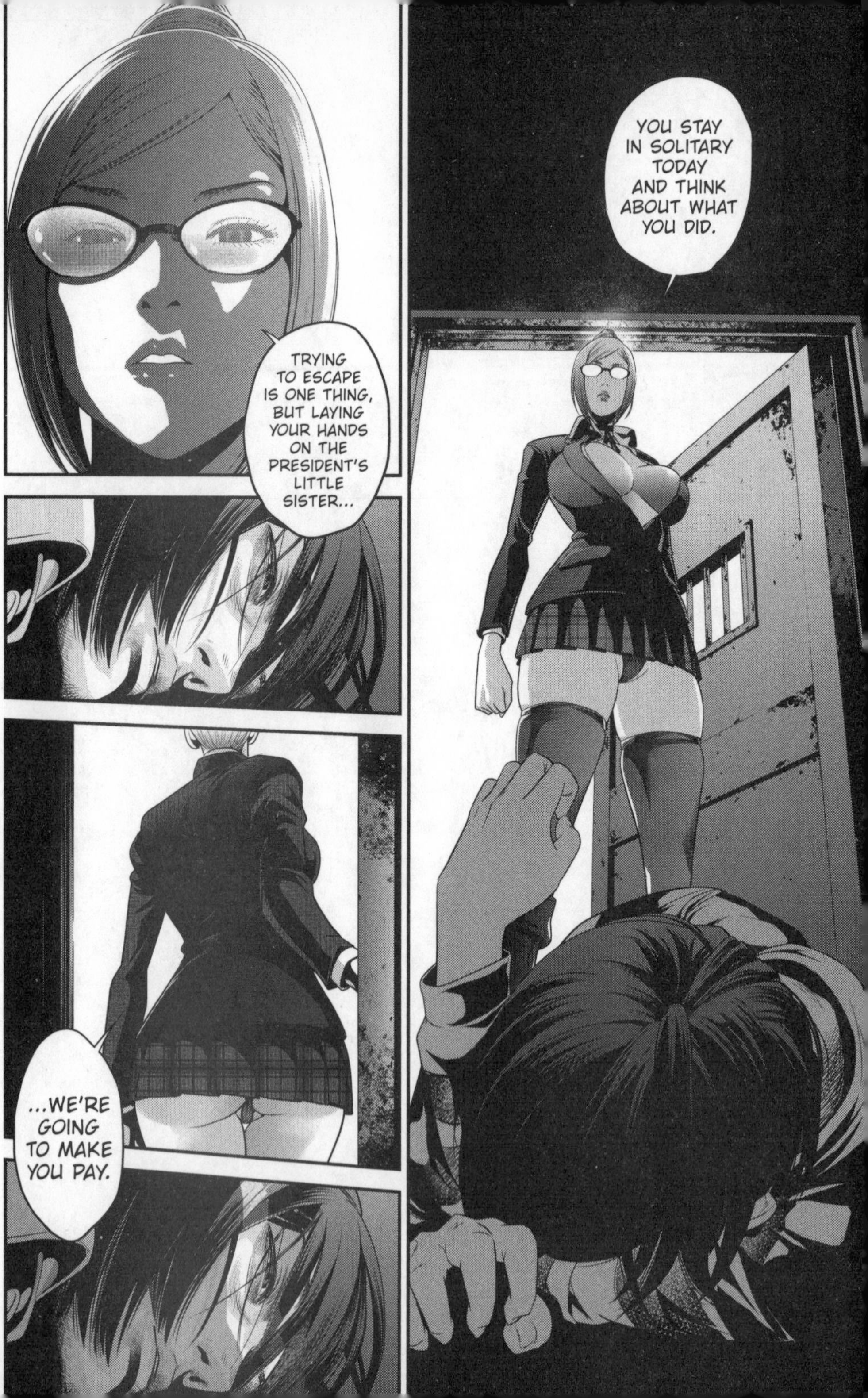
TRYING TO ESCAPE IS ONE THING, BUT LAYING YOUR HANDS ON THE PRESIDENT'S LITTLE SISTER...
...WE'RE GOING TO MAKE YOU PAY.
YOU STAY IN SOLITARY TODAY AND THINK ABOUT WHAT YOU DID.

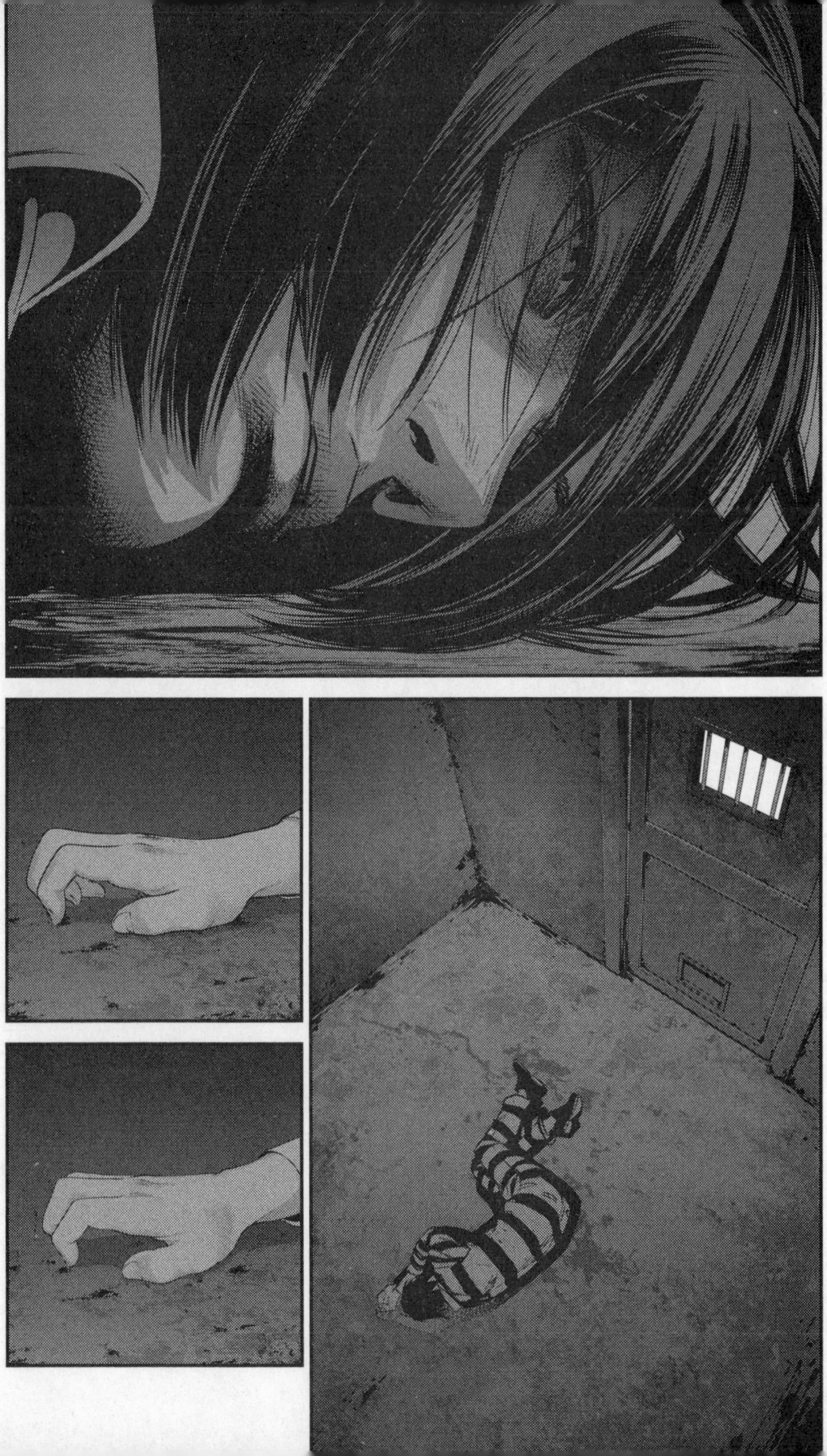

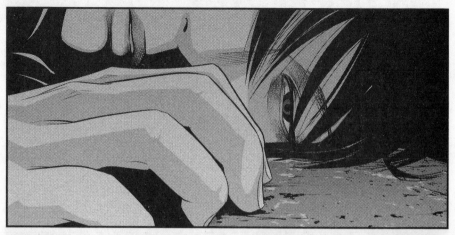

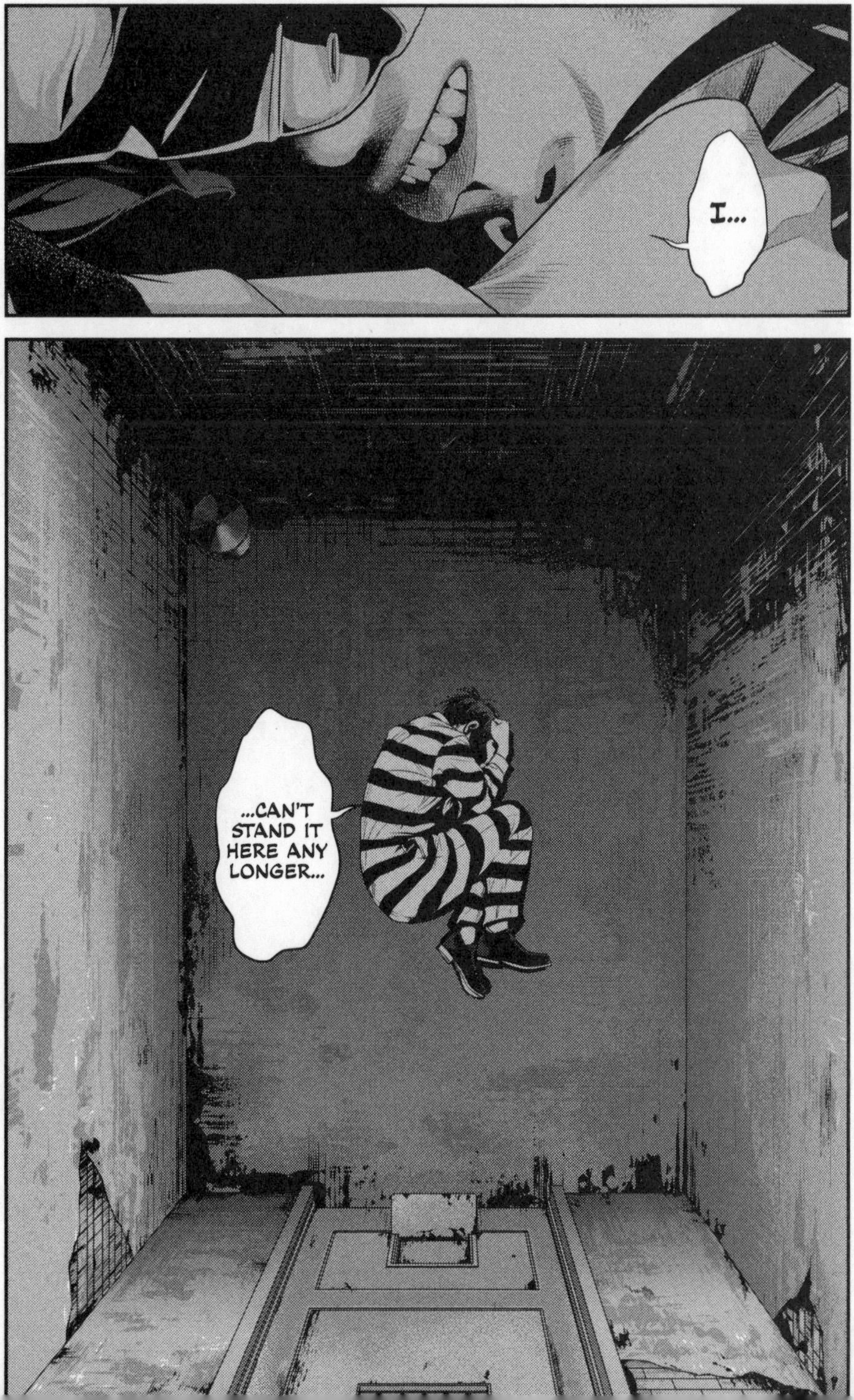
I...
...CAN'T STAND IT HERE ANY LONGER...

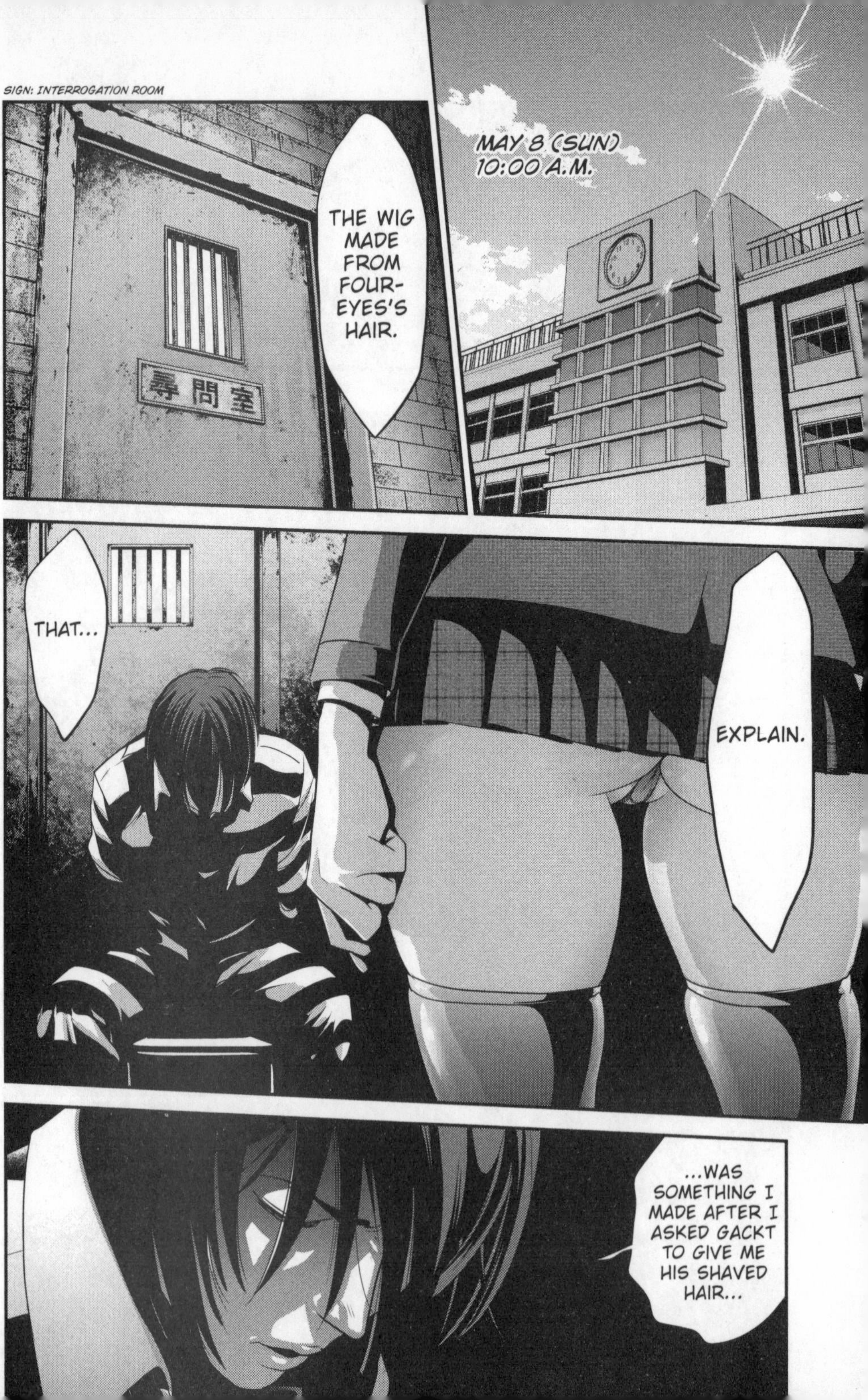
SIGN: INTERROGATION ROOM
MAY 8 (SUN) 10:00 A.M.
THE WIG MADE FROM FOUR-EYES'S HAIR.
尋問室
EXPLAIN.
THAT...
...WAS SOMETHING I MADE AFTER I ASKED GACKT TO GIVE ME HIS SHAVED HAIR...

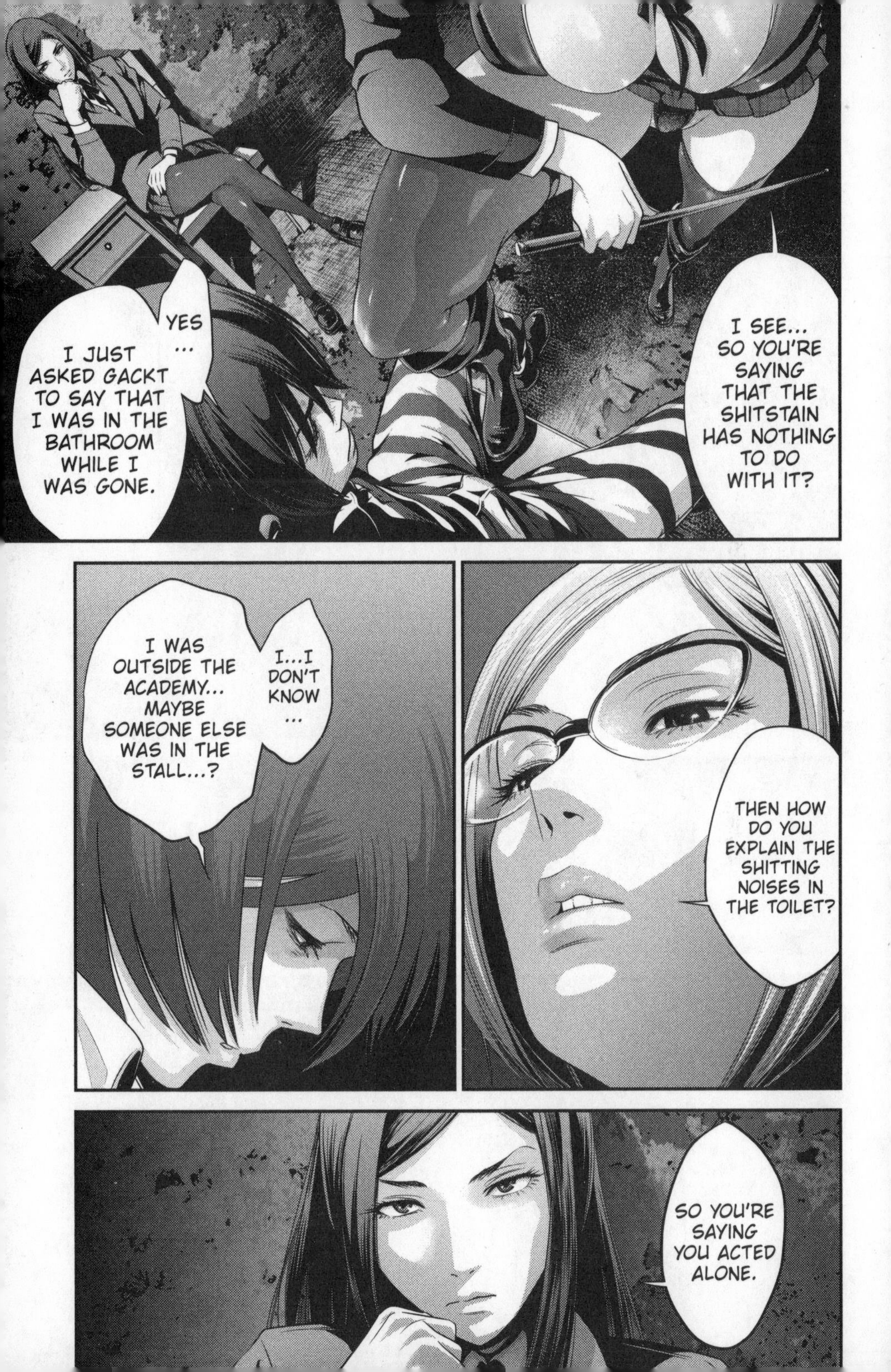
I SEE... SO YOU'RE SAYING THAT THE SHITSTAIN HAS NOTHING TO DO WITH IT?
YES ...
I JUST ASKED GACKT TO SAY THAT I WAS IN THE BATHROOM WHILE I WAS GONE.
THEN HOW DO YOU EXPLAIN THE SHITTING NOISES IN THE TOILET?
I...I DON'T KNOW ...
I WAS OUTSIDE THE ACADEMY... MAYBE SOMEONE ELSE WAS IN THE STALL...?
SO YOU'RE SAYING YOU ACTED ALONE.

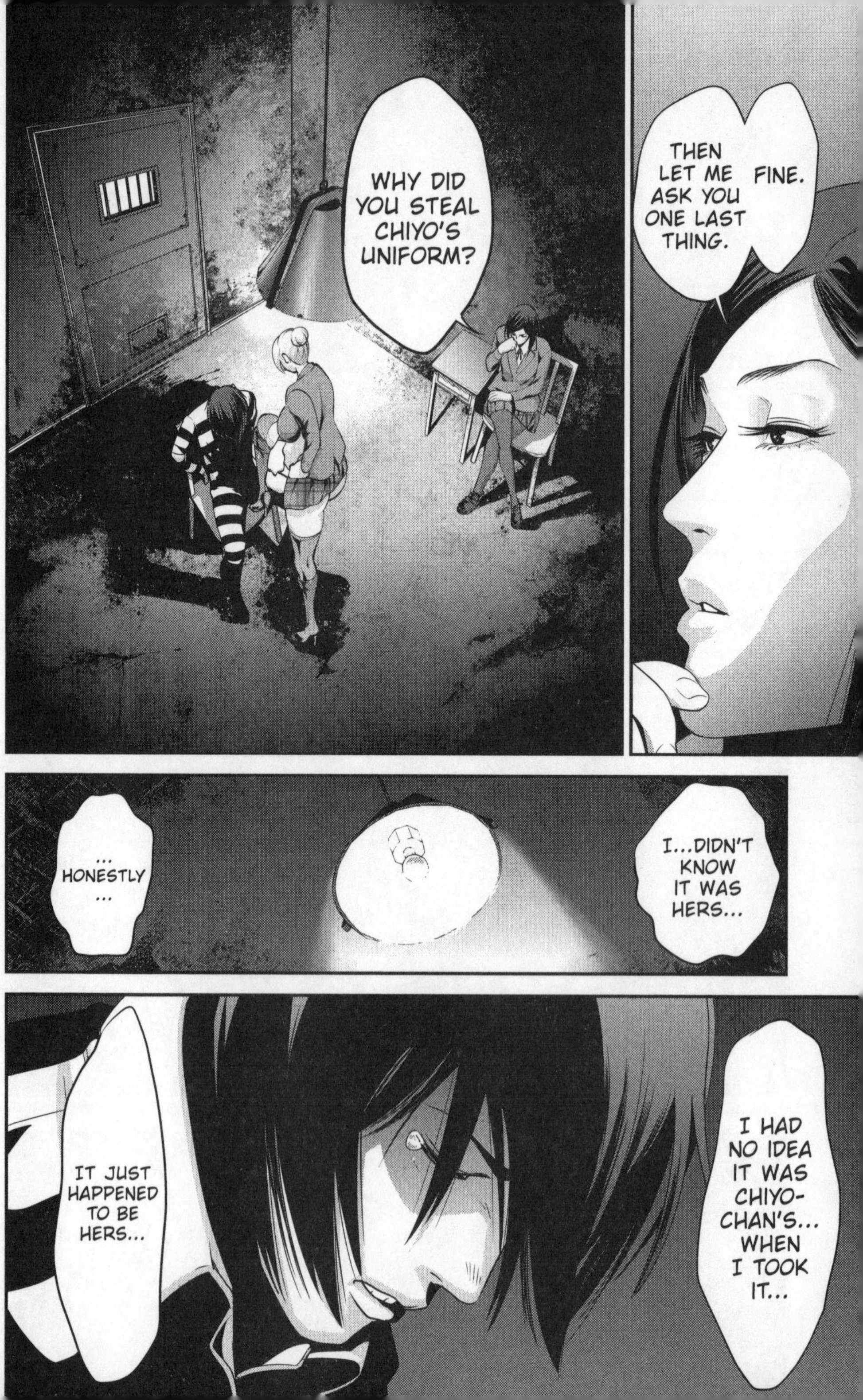
FINE.
THEN LET ME ASK YOU ONE LAST THING.
WHY DID YOU STEAL CHIYO'S UNIFORM?
I...DIDN'T KNOW IT WAS HERS...
...HONESTLY...
I HAD NO IDEA IT WAS CHIYO-CHAN'S... WHEN I TOOK IT...
IT JUST HAPPENED TO BE HERS...

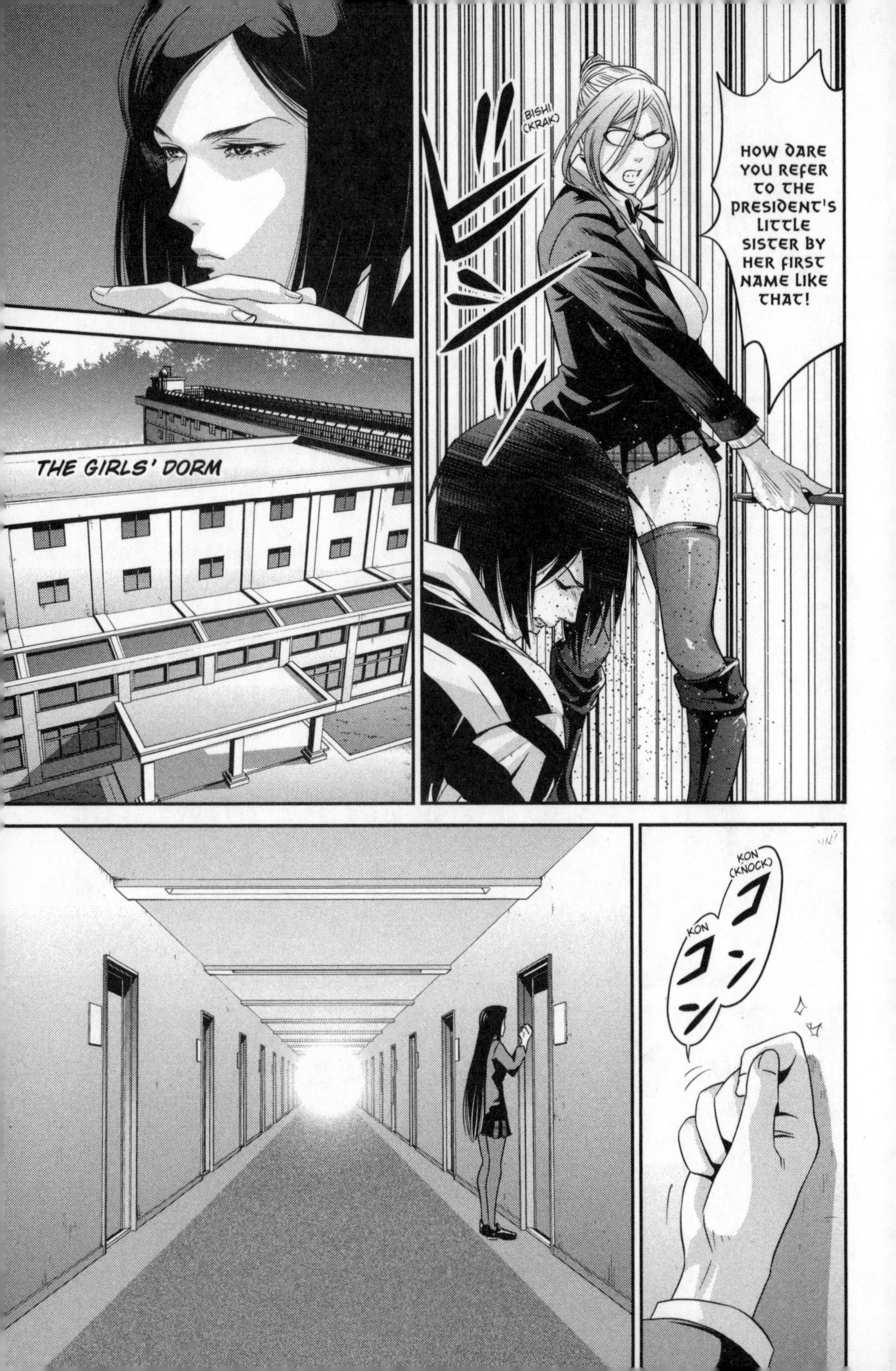

HOW DARE YOU REFER TO THE PRESIDENT'S LITTLE SISTER BY HER FIRST NAME LIKE THAT!
BISHI (KRAK)
THE GIRLS' DORM
KON (KNOCK)
KON

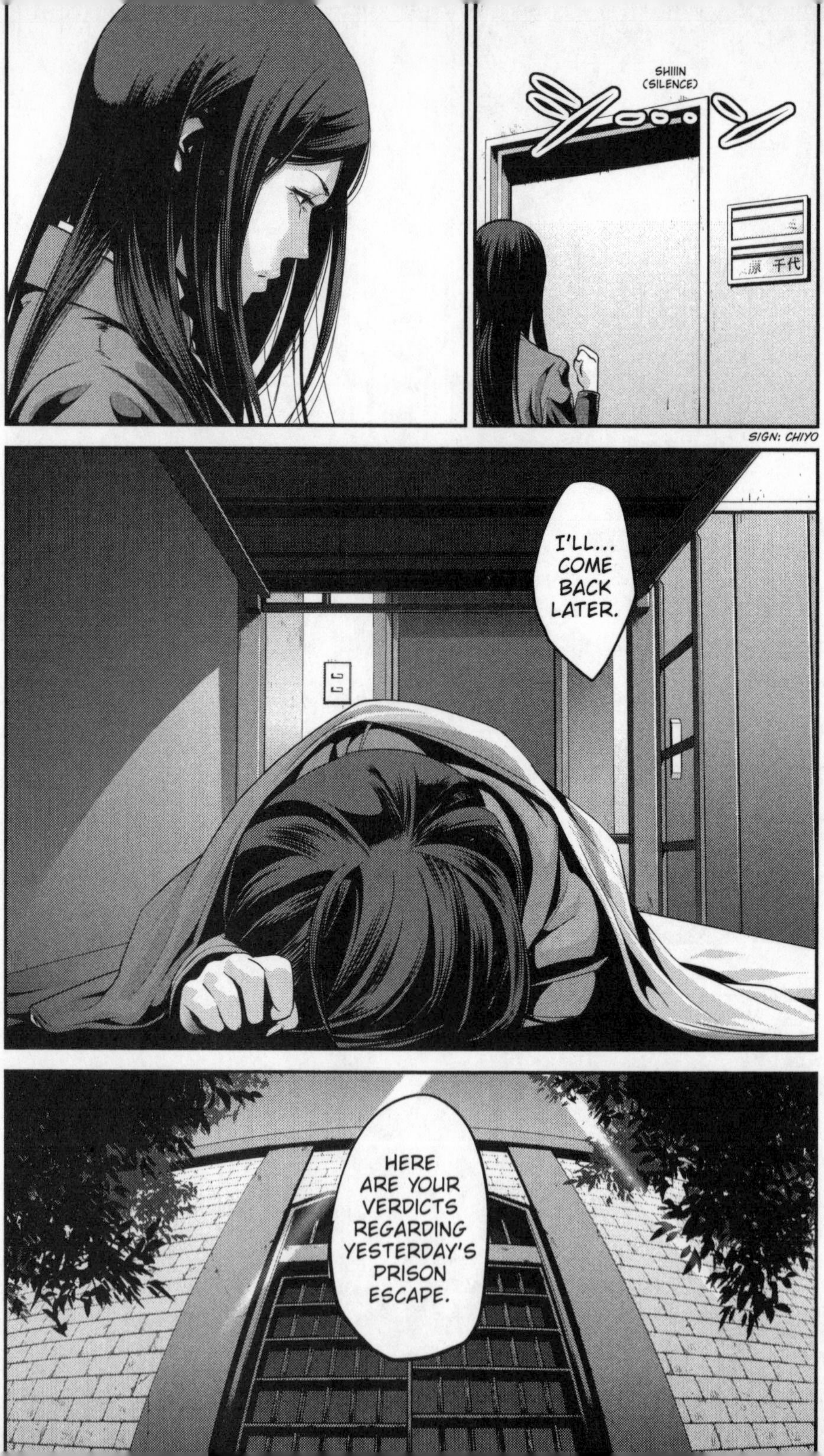
SHIIN (SILENCE)
SIGN: CHIYO
I'LL... COME BACK LATER.
HERE ARE YOUR VERDICTS REGARDING YESTERDAY'S PRISON ESCAPE.

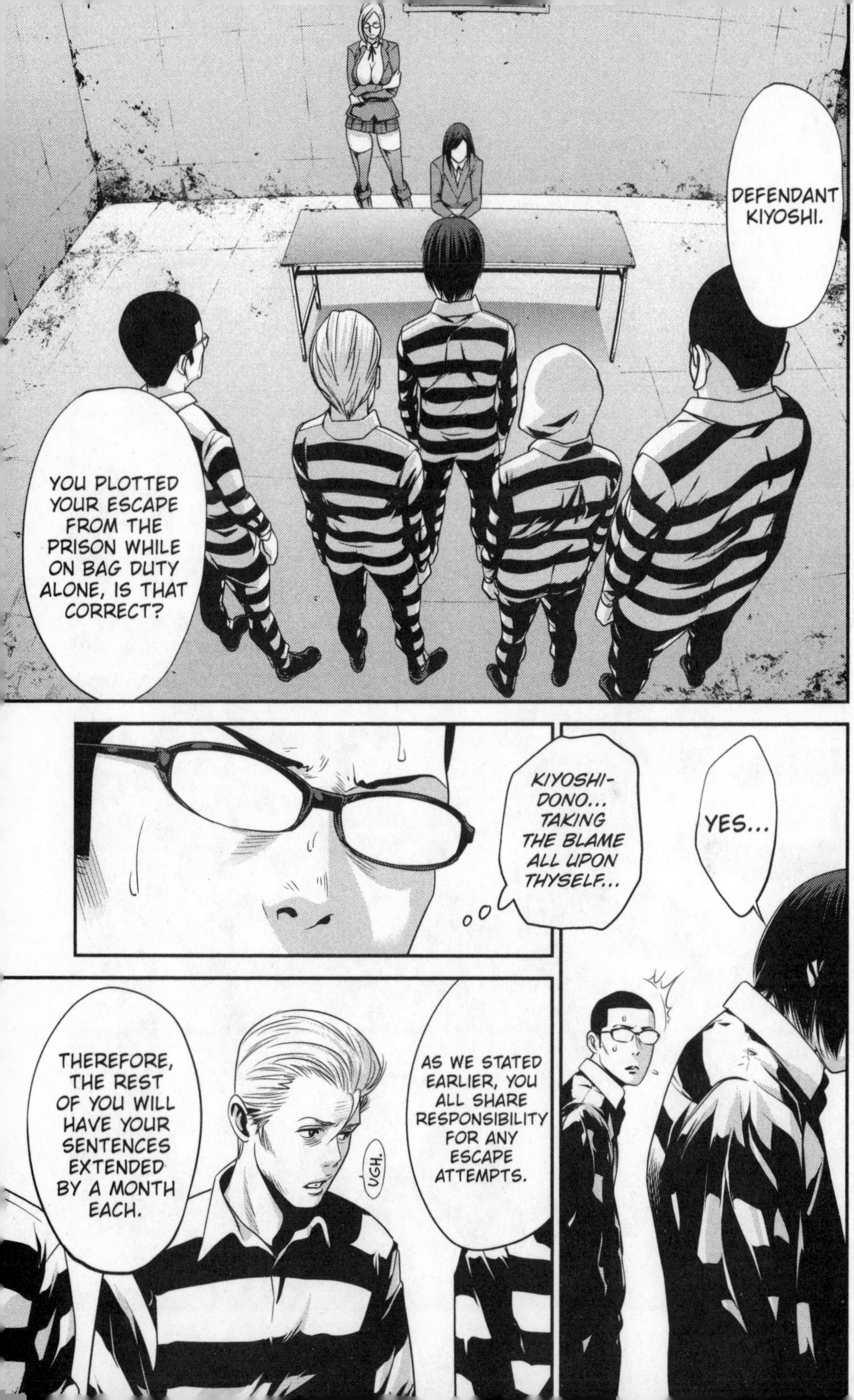
DEFENDANT KIYOSHI.
YOU PLOTTED YOUR ESCAPE FROM THE PRISON WHILE ON BAG DUTY ALONE, IS THAT CORRECT?
YES...
KIYOSHI-DONO... TAKING THE BLAME ALL UPON THYSELF...
AS WE STATED EARLIER, YOU ALL SHARE RESPONSIBILITY FOR ANY ESCAPE ATTEMPTS.
UGH.
THEREFORE, THE REST OF YOU WILL HAVE YOUR SENTENCES EXTENDED BY A MONTH EACH.

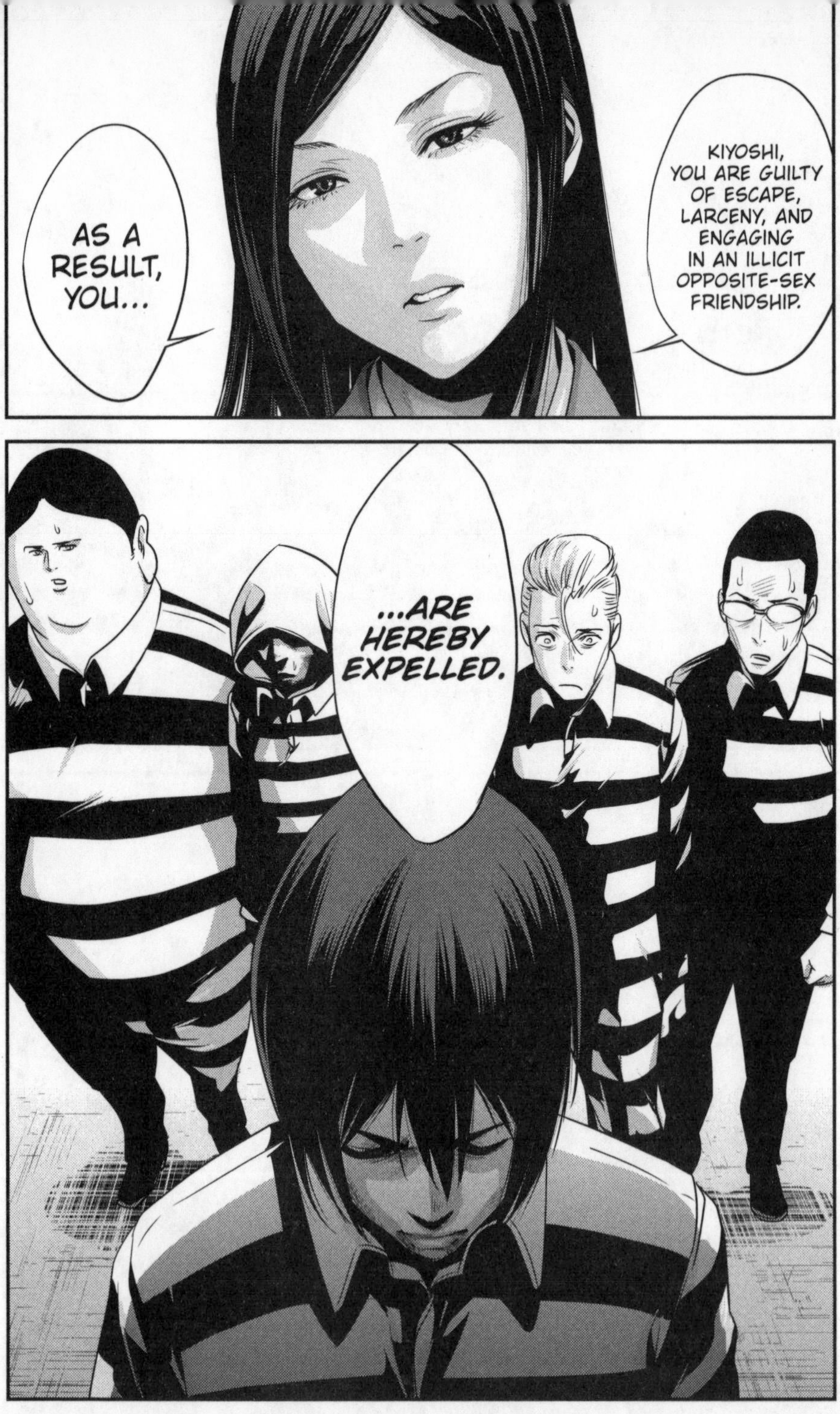
KIYOSHI, YOU ARE GUILTY OF ESCAPE, LARCENY, AND ENGAGING IN AN ILLICIT OPPOSITE-SEX FRIENDSHIP.
AS A RESULT, YOU...
...ARE HEREBY EXPELLED.

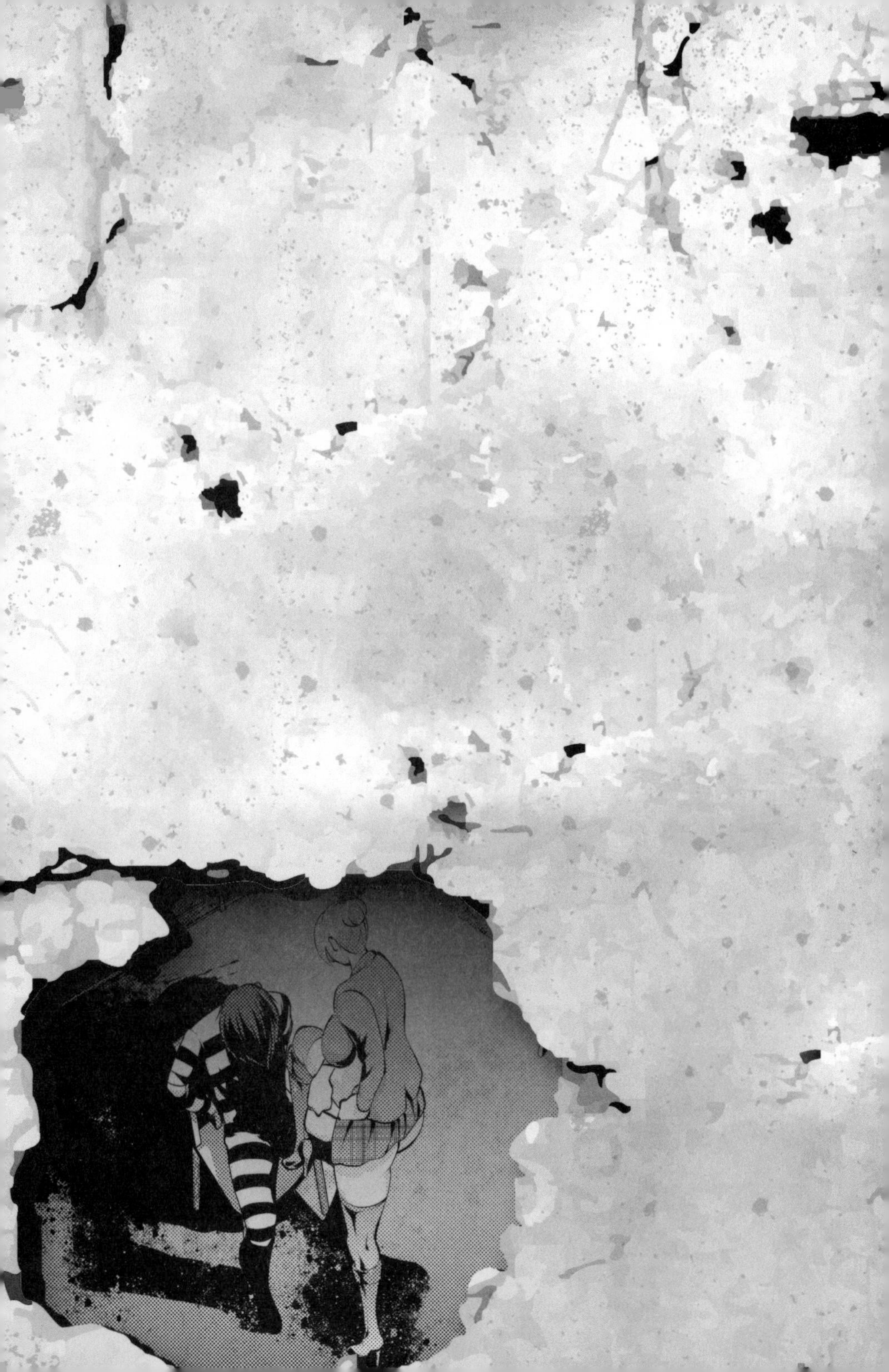

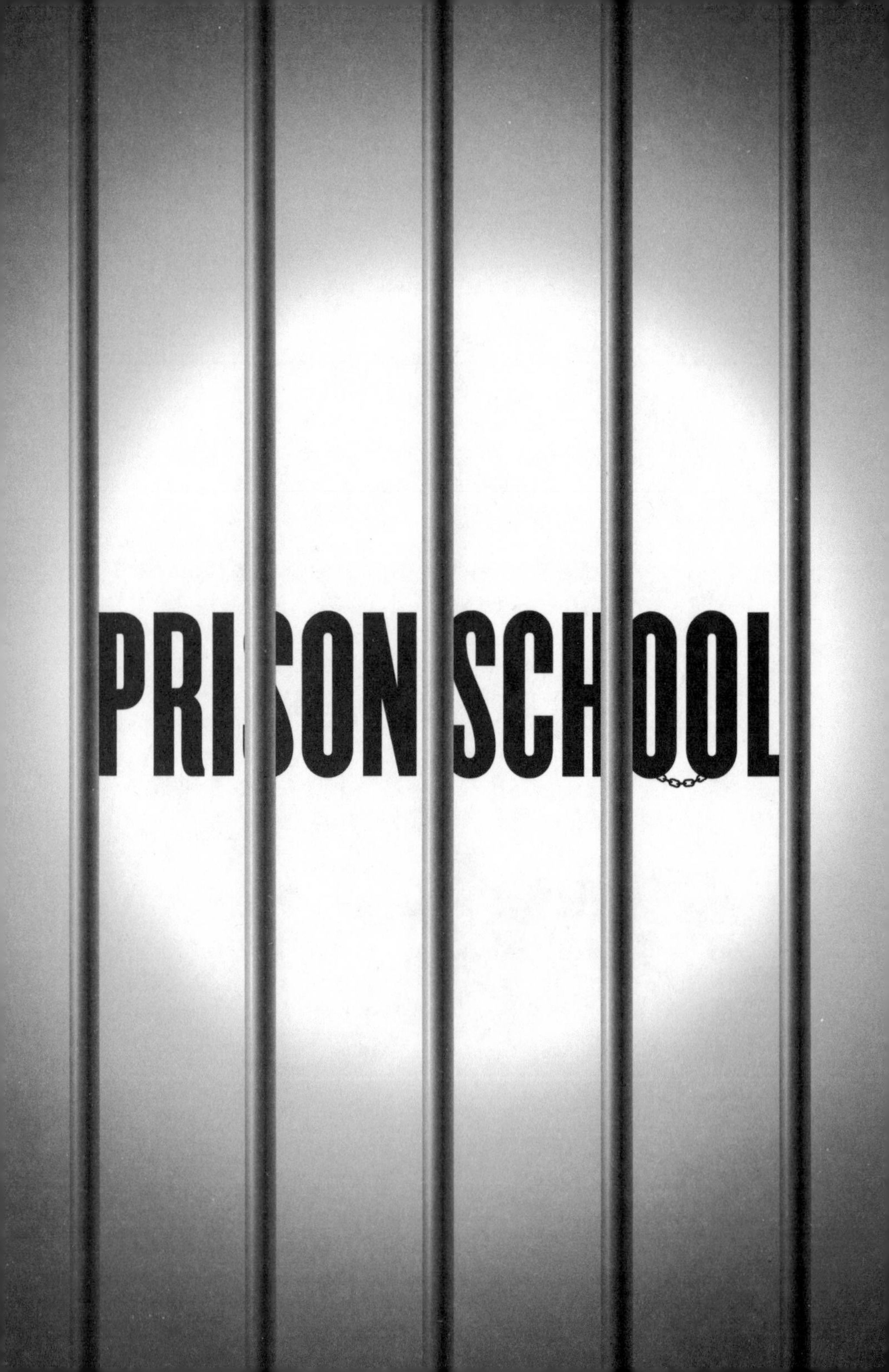
PRISON SCHOOL

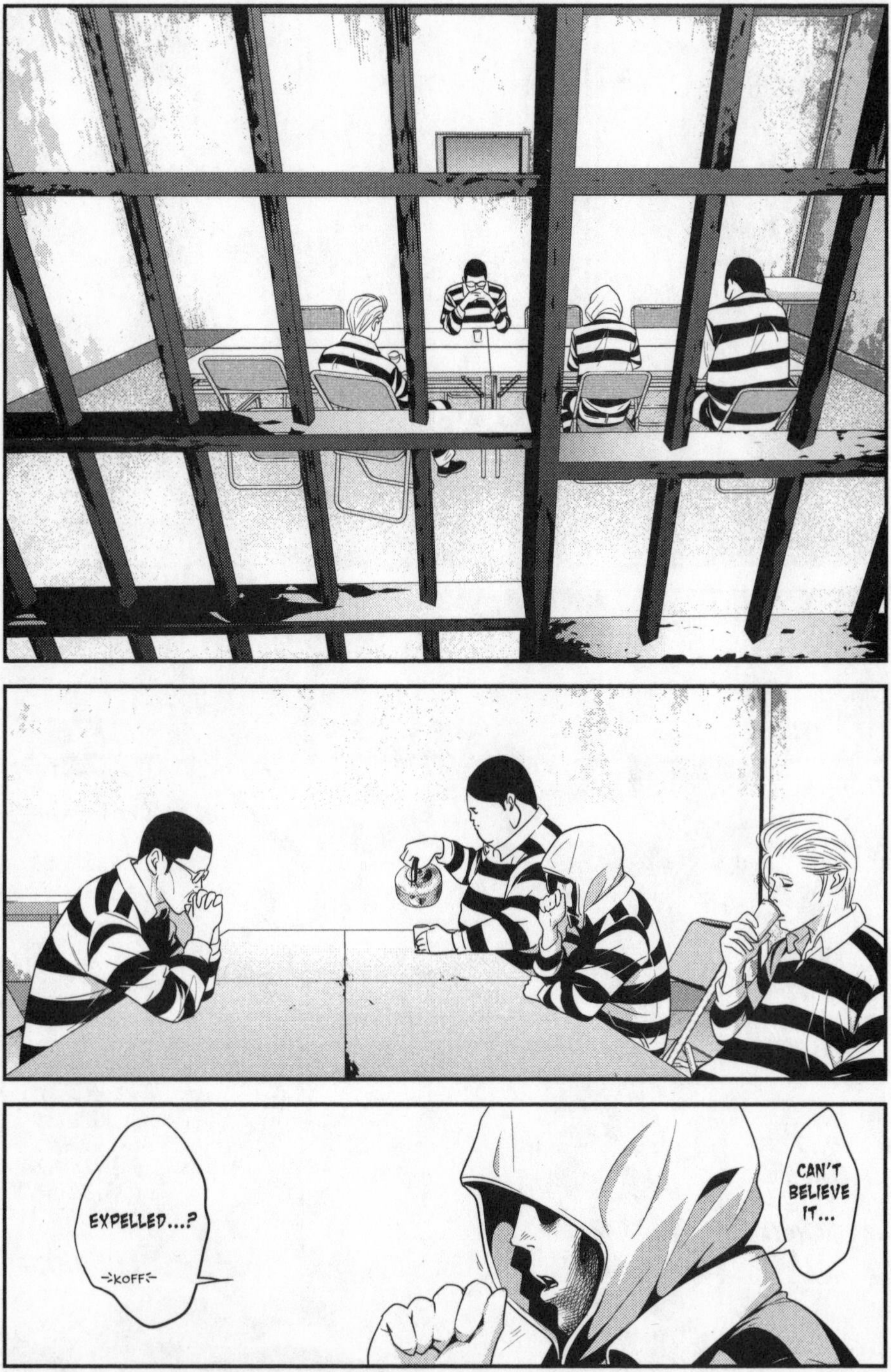
CAN'T BELIEVE IT...
EXPELLED...?
KOFF

CHAPTER 31: UNFORGIVEN

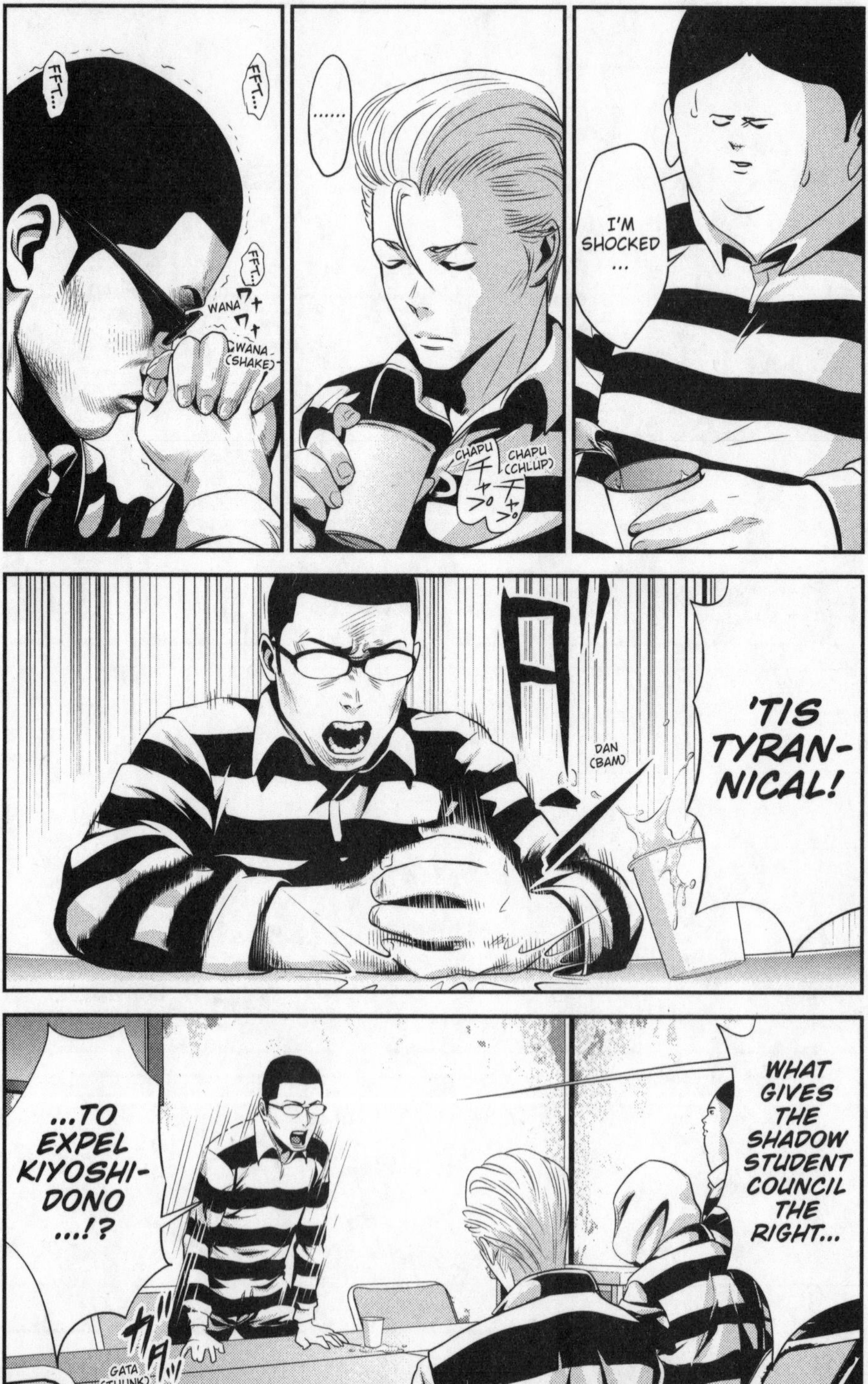
I'M SHOCKED ...
CHAPU CHAPU (CHLUP)
......
FFT...
FFT...
FFT...
WANA WANA (SHAKE)
'TIS TYRAN-NICAL!
DAN (BAM)
WHAT GIVES THE SHADOW STUDENT COUNCIL THE RIGHT...
...TO EXPEL KIYOSHI-DONO ...!?
GATA (THUNK)

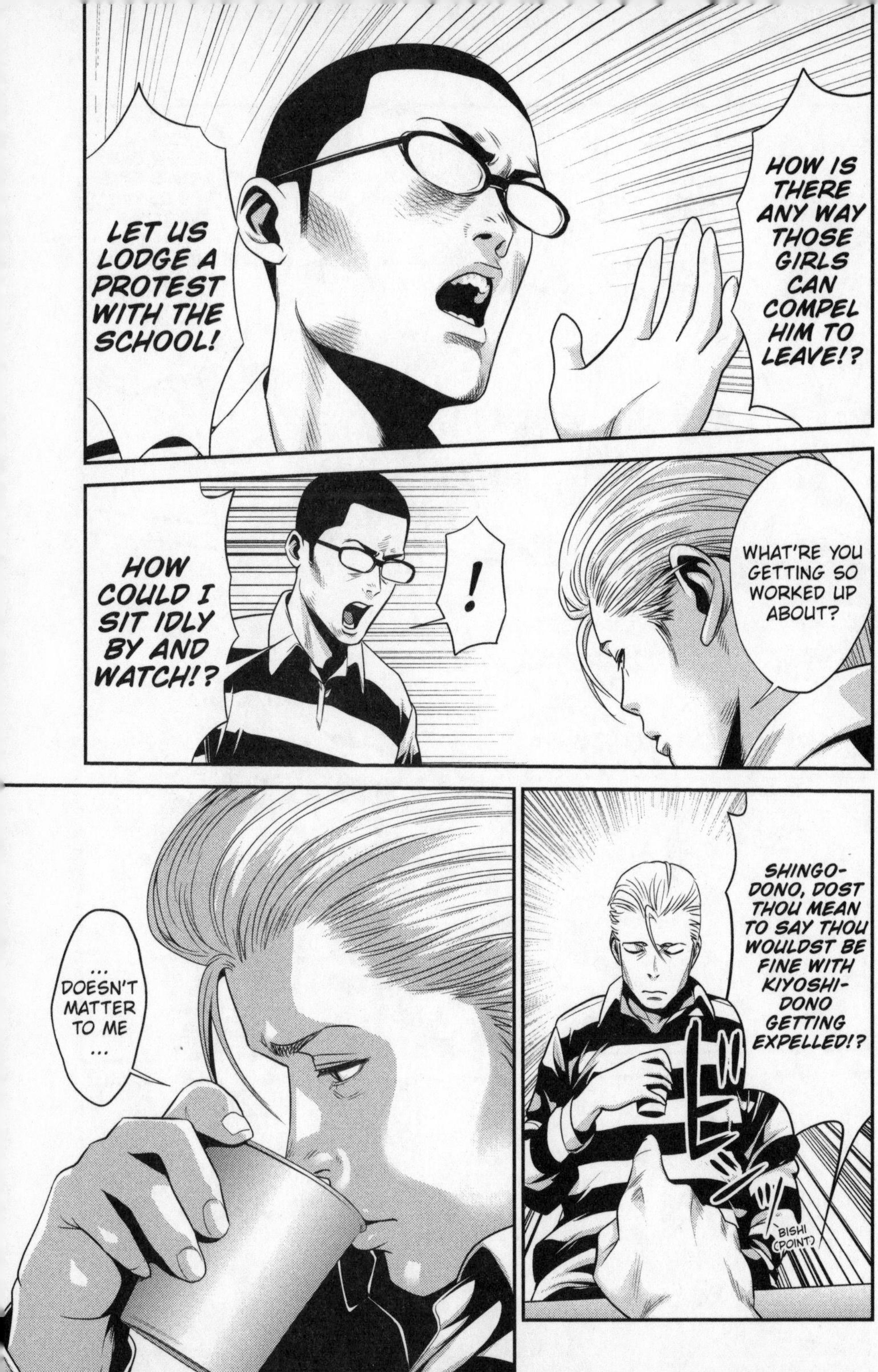
HOW IS THERE ANY WAY THOSE GIRLS CAN COMPEL HIM TO LEAVE!?
LET US LODGE A PROTEST WITH THE SCHOOL!
WHAT'RE YOU GETTING SO WORKED UP ABOUT?
!
HOW COULD I SIT IDLY BY AND WATCH!?
SHINGO-DONO, DOST THOU MEAN TO SAY THOU WOULDST BE FINE WITH KIYOSHI-DONO GETTING EXPELLED!?
BISHI (POINT)
... DOESN'T MATTER TO ME ...

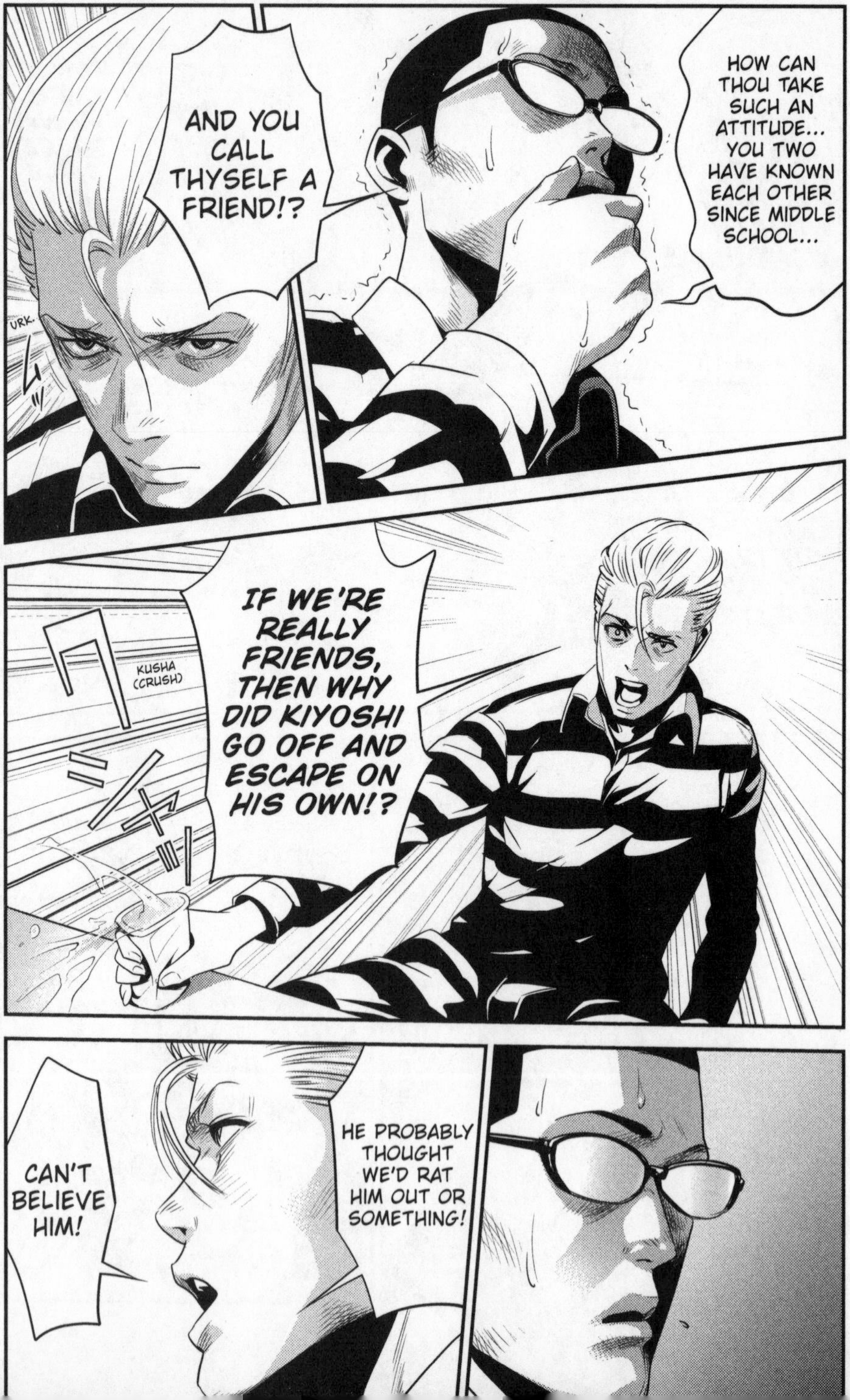
HOW CAN THOU TAKE SUCH AN ATTITUDE... YOU TWO HAVE KNOWN EACH OTHER SINCE MIDDLE SCHOOL...
AND YOU CALL THYSELF A FRIEND!?
URK.
IF WE'RE REALLY FRIENDS, THEN WHY DID KIYOSHI GO OFF AND ESCAPE ON HIS OWN!?
KUSHA (CRUSH)
HE PROBABLY THOUGHT WE'D RAT HIM OUT OR SOMETHING!
CAN'T BELIEVE HIM!

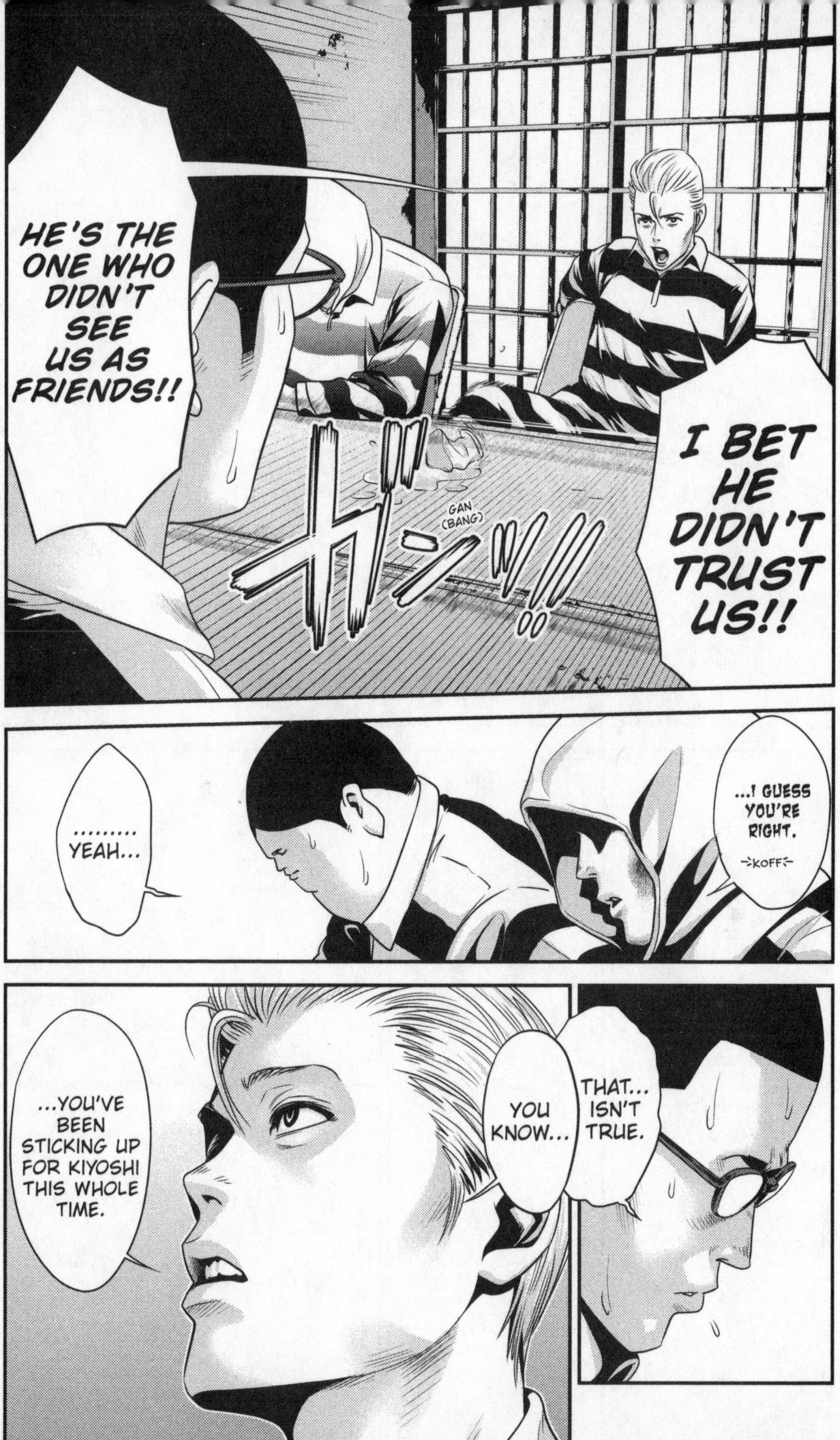
I BET HE DIDN'T TRUST US!!
GAN (BANG)
HE'S THE ONE WHO DIDN'T SEE US AS FRIENDS!!
...I GUESS YOU'RE RIGHT.
KOFF
.... YEAH...
THAT... ISN'T TRUE.
YOU KNOW...
...YOU'VE BEEN STICKING UP FOR KIYOSHI THIS WHOLE TIME.

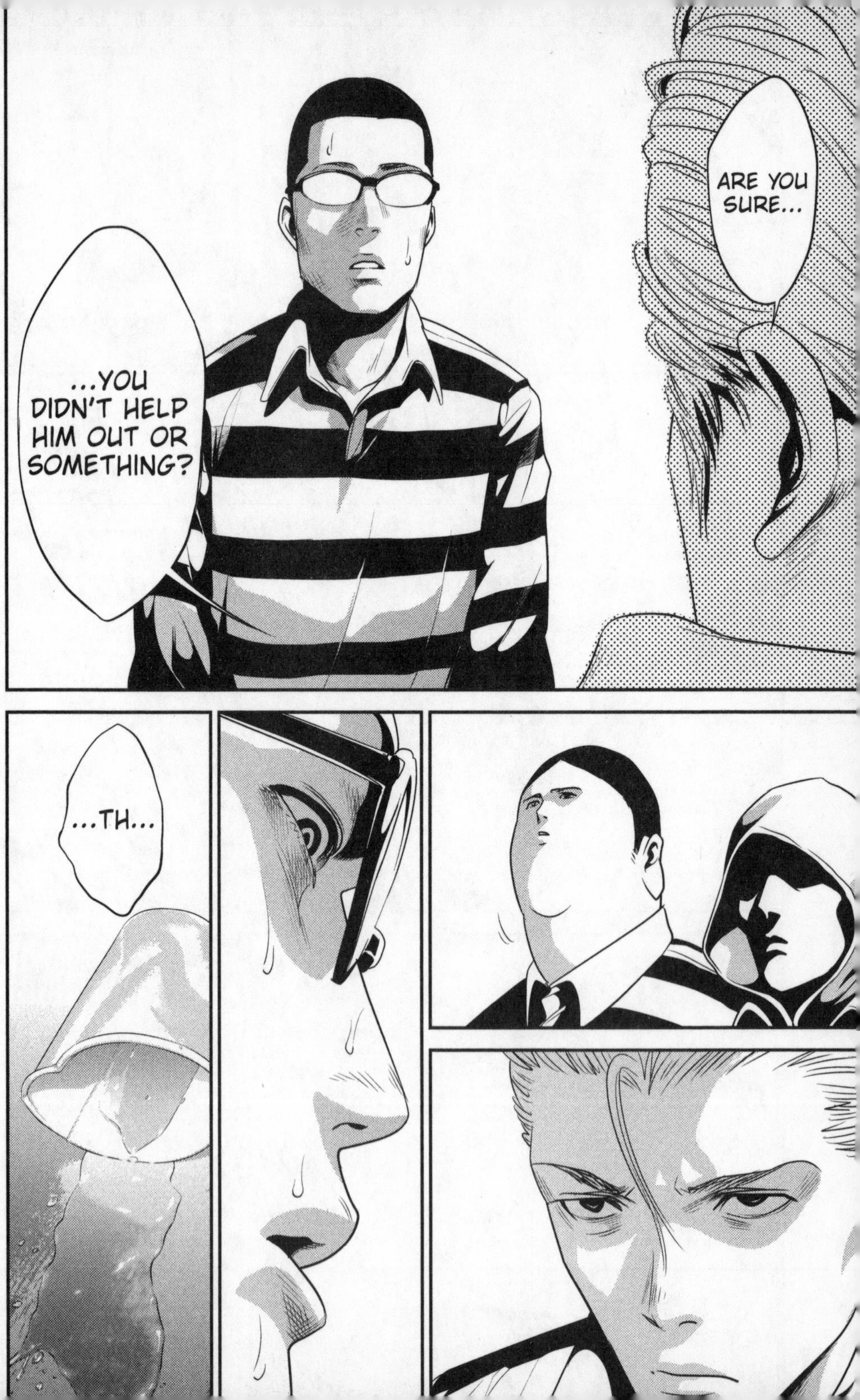
ARE YOU SURE...
...YOU DIDN'T HELP HIM OUT OR SOMETHING?
...TH...

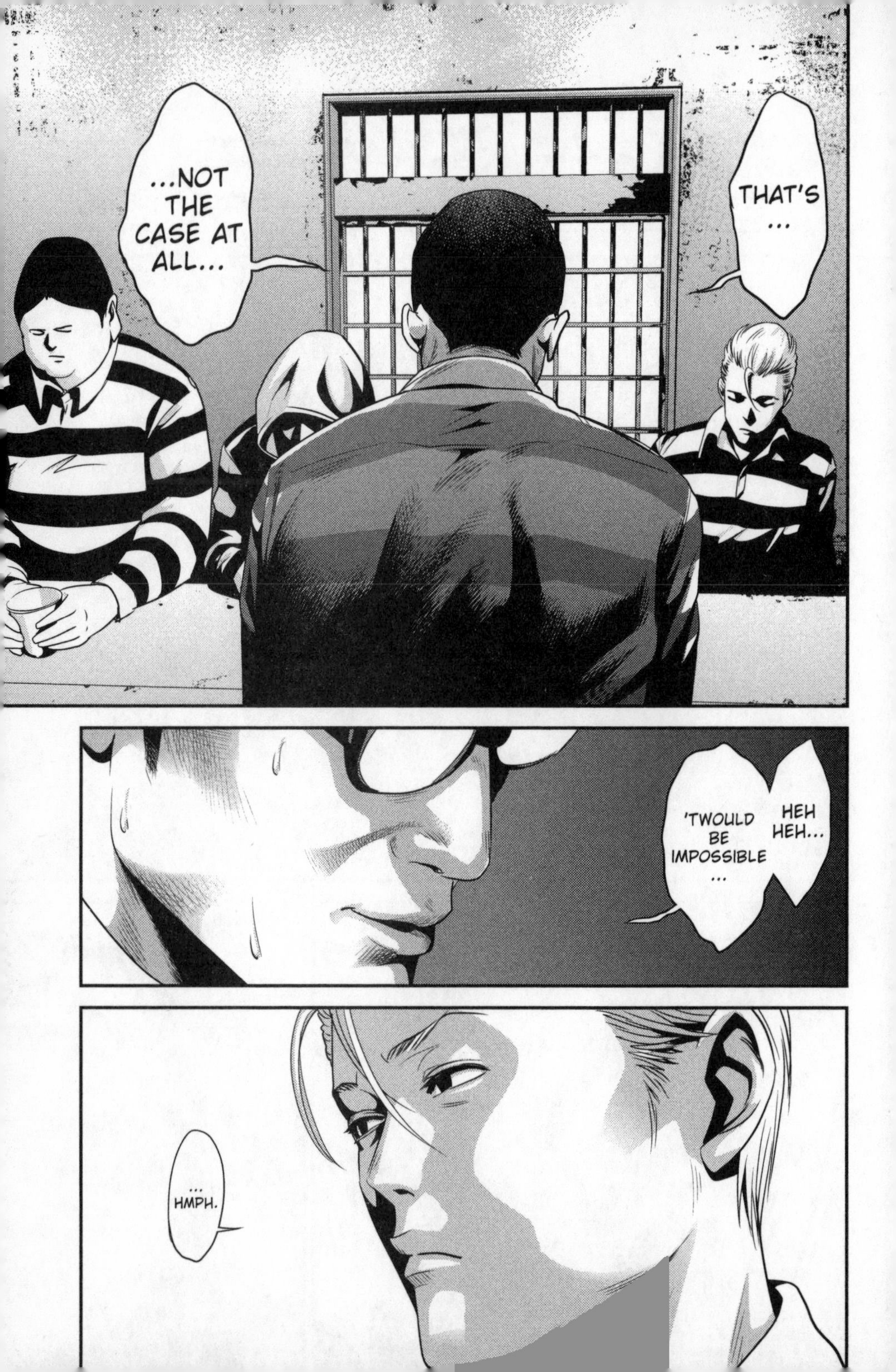
THAT'S ...
...NOT THE CASE AT ALL...
HEH HEH...
'TWOULD BE IMPOSSIBLE ...
... HMPH.

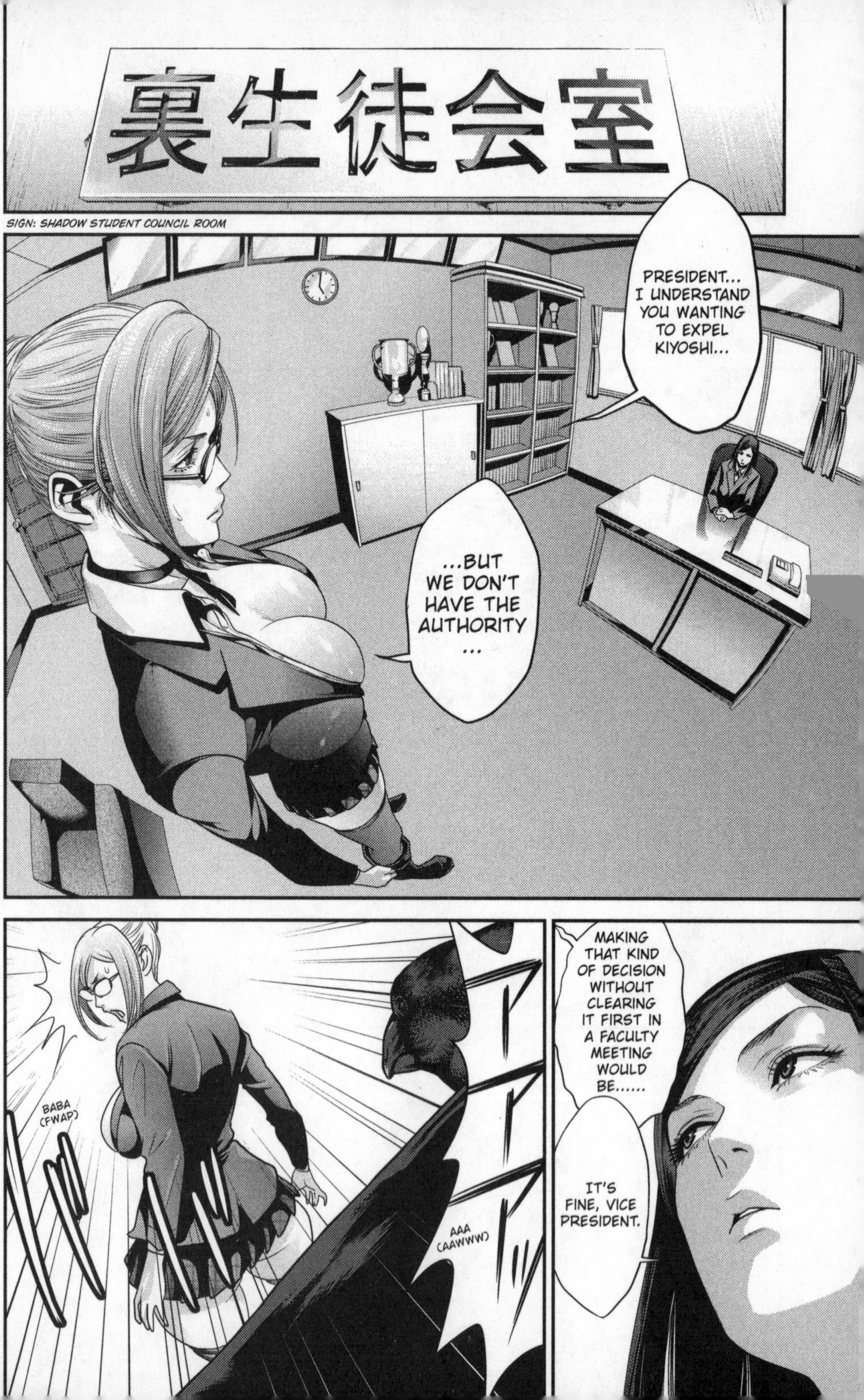
裏生徒会室
SIGN: SHADOW STUDENT COUNCIL ROOM
PRESIDENT... I UNDERSTAND YOU WANTING TO EXPEL KIYOSHI...
...BUT WE DON'T HAVE THE AUTHORITY ...
MAKING THAT KIND OF DECISION WITHOUT CLEARING IT FIRST IN A FACULTY MEETING WOULD BE......
IT'S FINE, VICE PRESIDENT.
AAA (AAWWW)
BABA (FWAP)

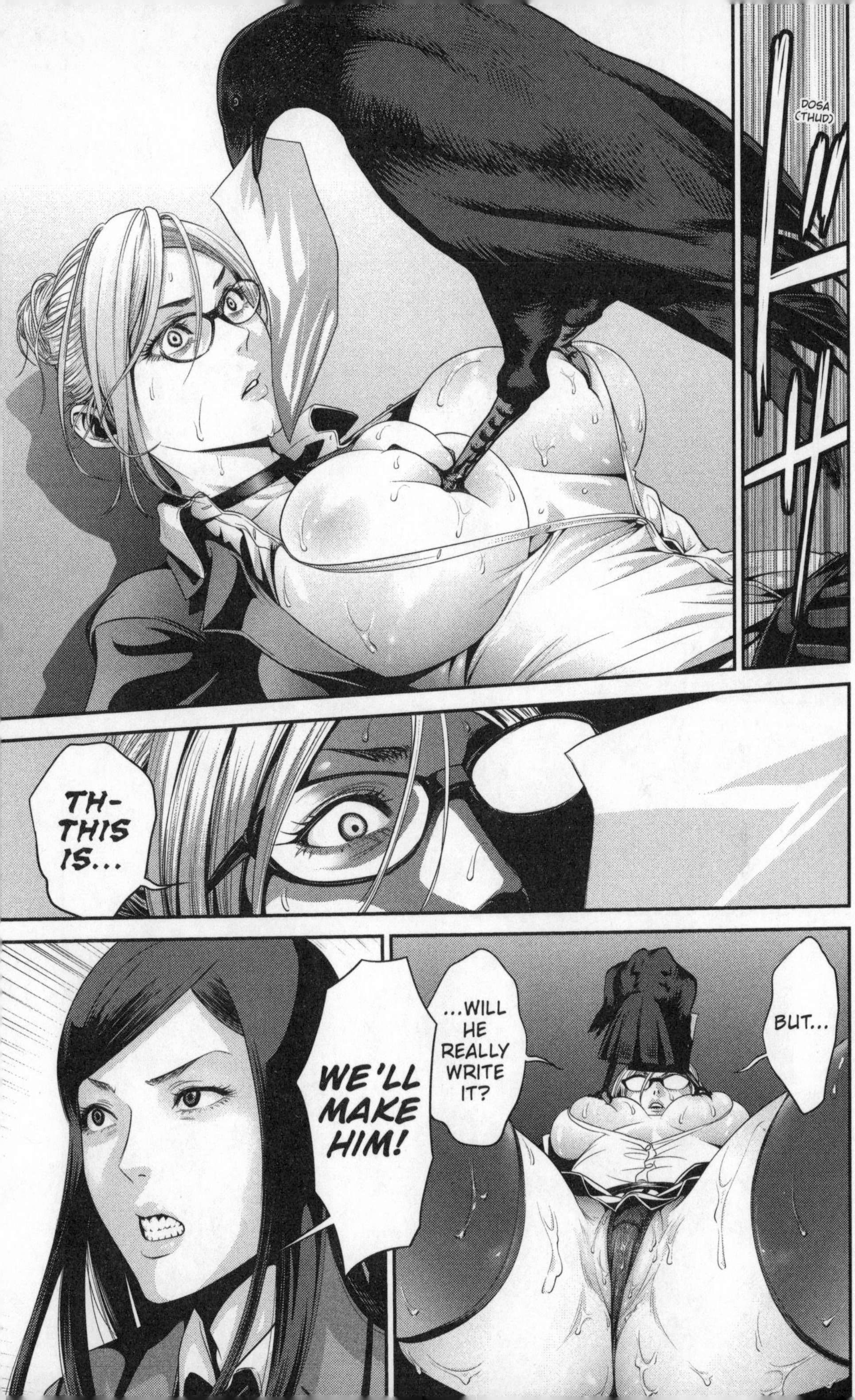
DOSA (THUD)
TH-THIS IS...
BUT...
...WILL HE REALLY WRITE IT?
WE'LL MAKE HIM!

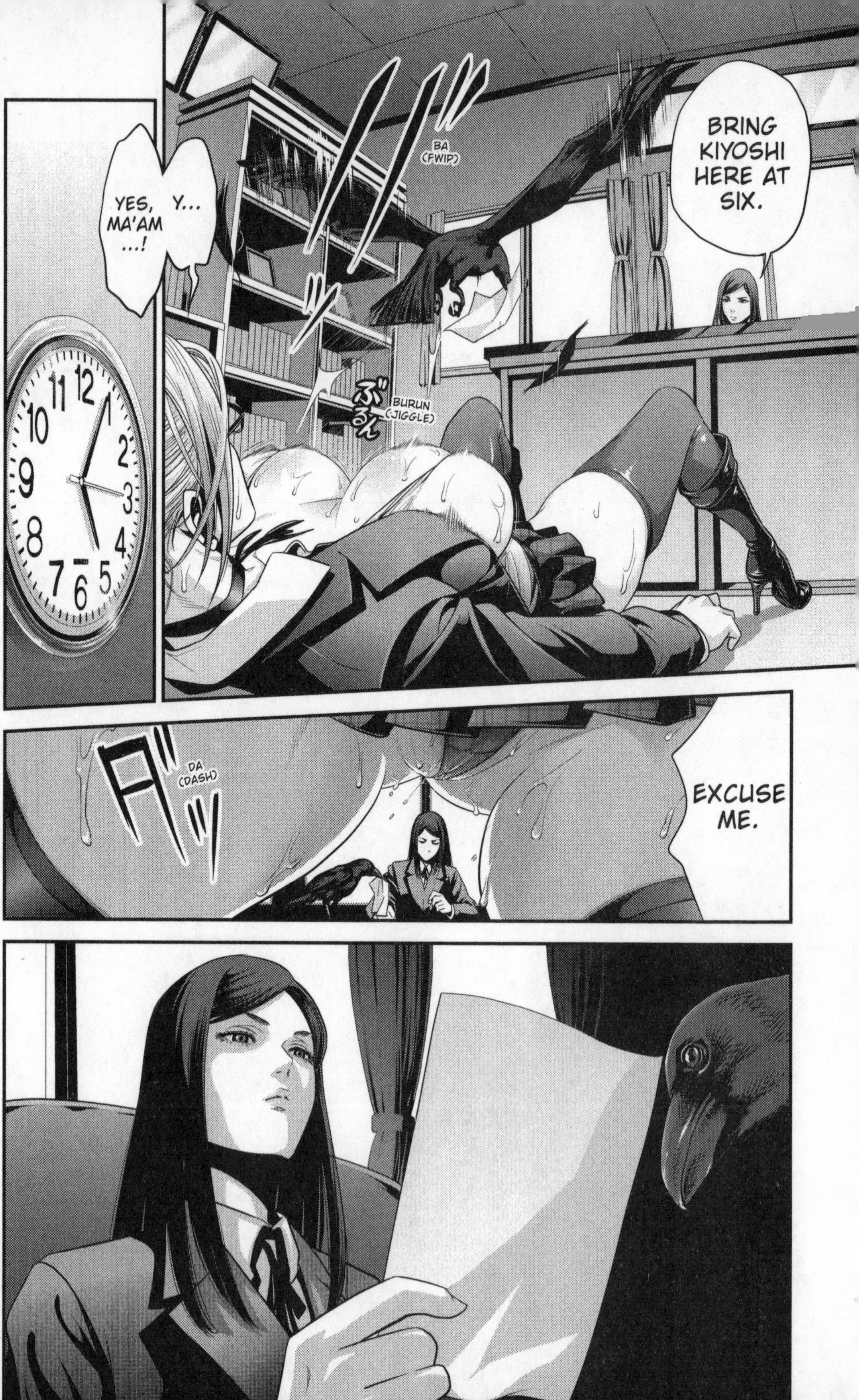
BRING KIYOSHI HERE AT SIX.
BA (FWIP)
Y...
YES, MA'AM ...!
ぶるん
BURUN (JIGGLE)
EXCUSE ME.
DA (DASH)

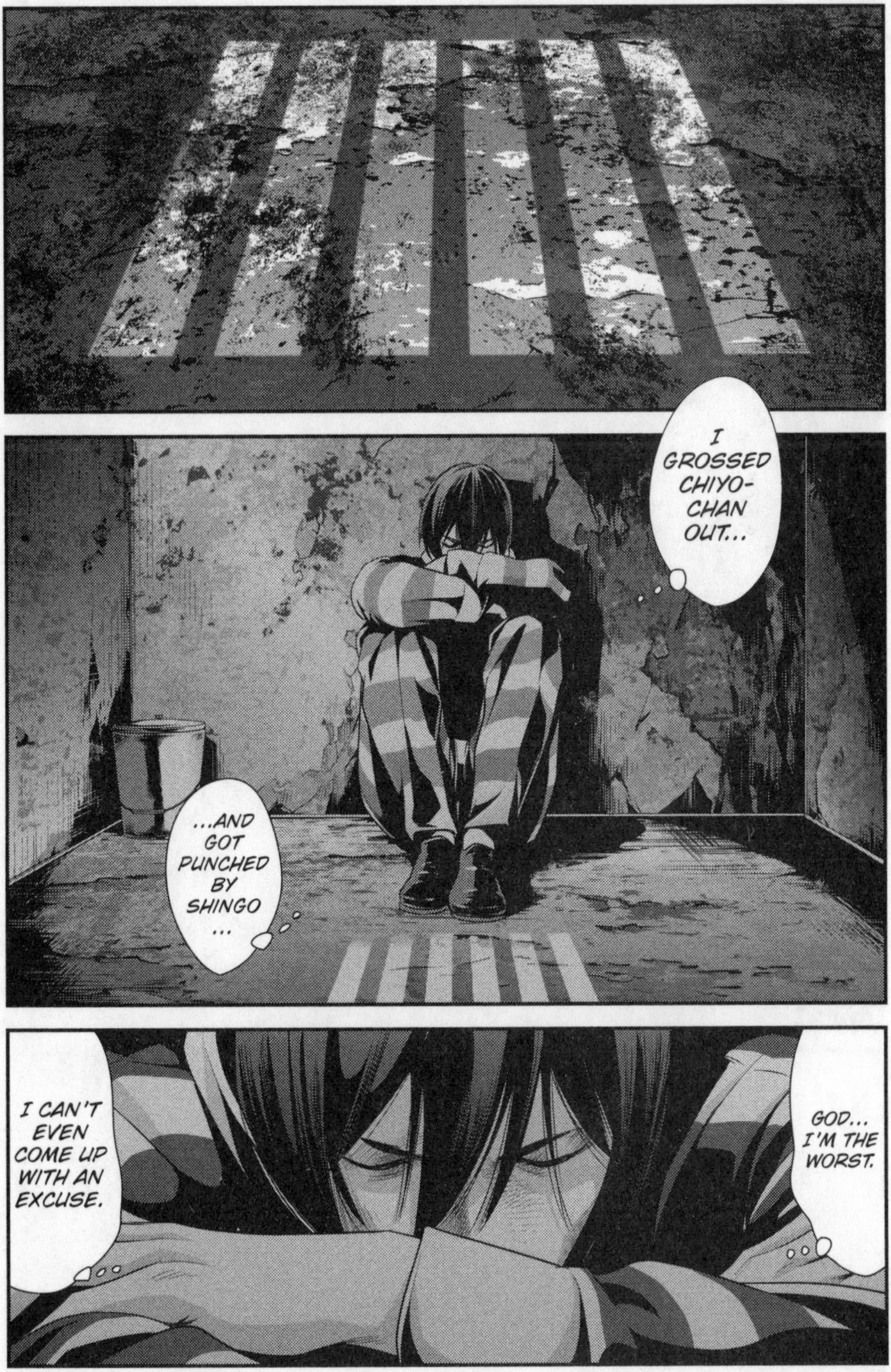
I GROSSED CHIYO-CHAN OUT...
...AND GOT PUNCHED BY SHINGO ...
GOD... I'M THE WORST.
I CAN'T EVEN COME UP WITH AN EXCUSE.

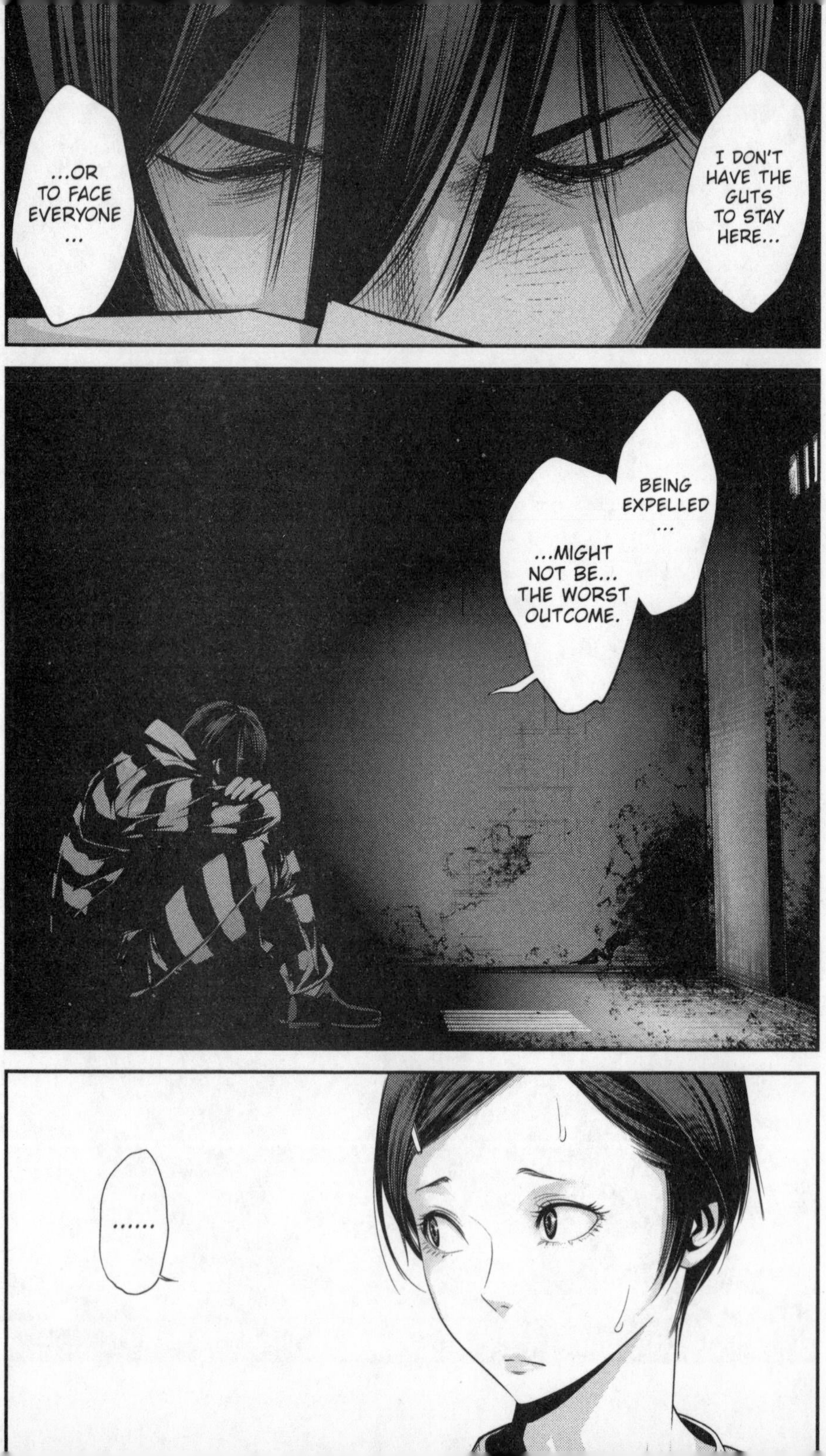
I DON'T HAVE THE GUTS TO STAY HERE...
...OR TO FACE EVERYONE ...
BEING EXPELLED ...
...MIGHT NOT BE... THE WORST OUTCOME.
......

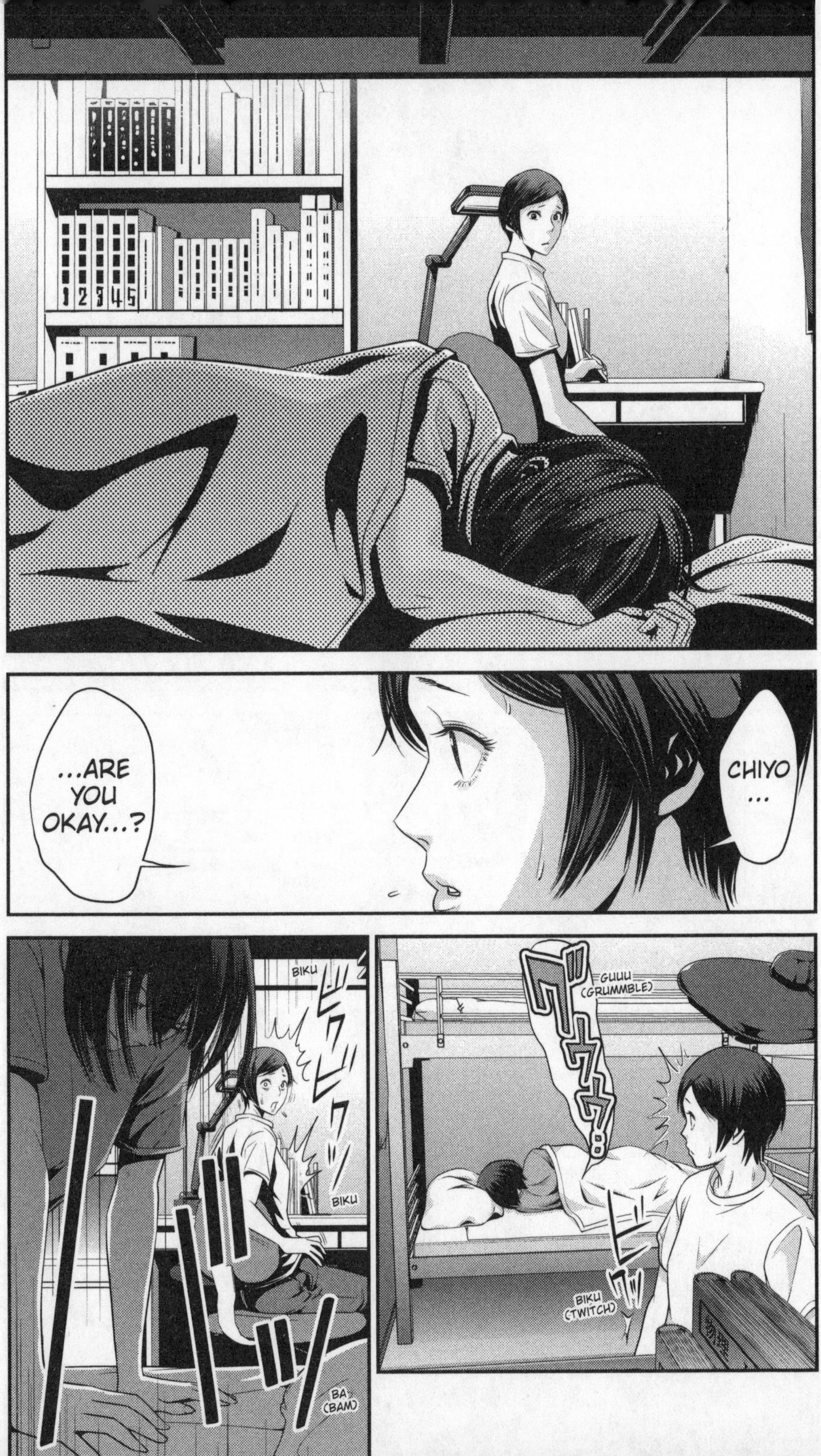
CHIYO ...
...ARE YOU OKAY...?
GUUU (GRUMMBLE)
BIKU (TWITCH)
BIKU
BIKU
BA (BAM)

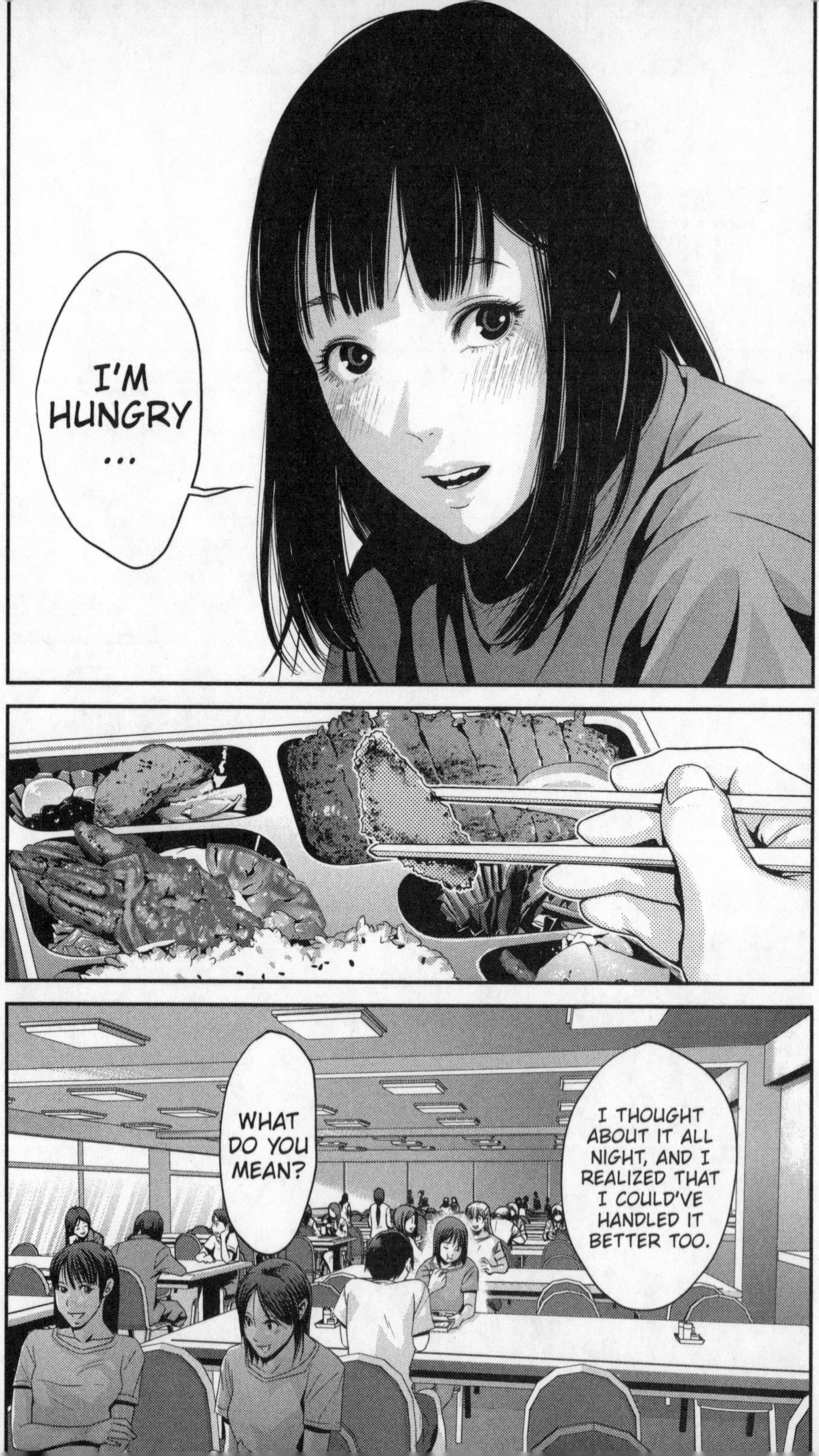
I'M HUNGRY ...
I THOUGHT ABOUT IT ALL NIGHT, AND I REALIZED THAT I COULD'VE HANDLED IT BETTER TOO.
WHAT DO YOU MEAN?

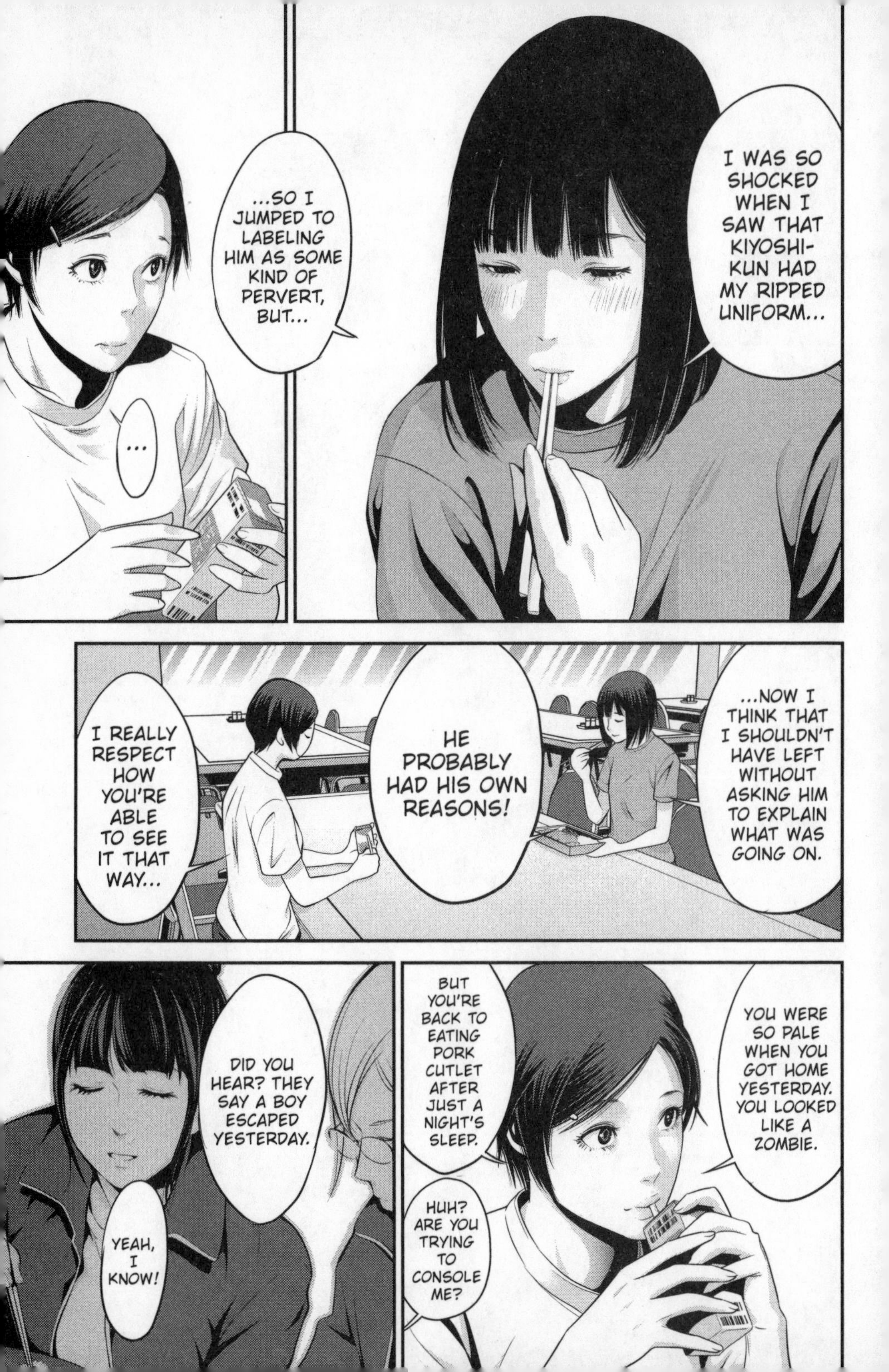
I WAS SO SHOCKED WHEN I SAW THAT KIYOSHI-KUN HAD MY RIPPED UNIFORM...
...SO I JUMPED TO LABELING HIM AS SOME KIND OF PERVERT, BUT...
...
...NOW I THINK THAT I SHOULDN'T HAVE LEFT WITHOUT ASKING HIM TO EXPLAIN WHAT WAS GOING ON.
HE PROBABLY HAD HIS OWN REASONS!
I REALLY RESPECT HOW YOU'RE ABLE TO SEE IT THAT WAY...
YOU WERE SO PALE WHEN YOU GOT HOME YESTERDAY. YOU LOOKED LIKE A ZOMBIE.
BUT YOU'RE BACK TO EATING PORK CUTLET AFTER JUST A NIGHT'S SLEEP.
HUH? ARE YOU TRYING TO CONSOLE ME?
DID YOU HEAR? THEY SAY A BOY ESCAPED YESTERDAY.
YEAH, I KNOW!

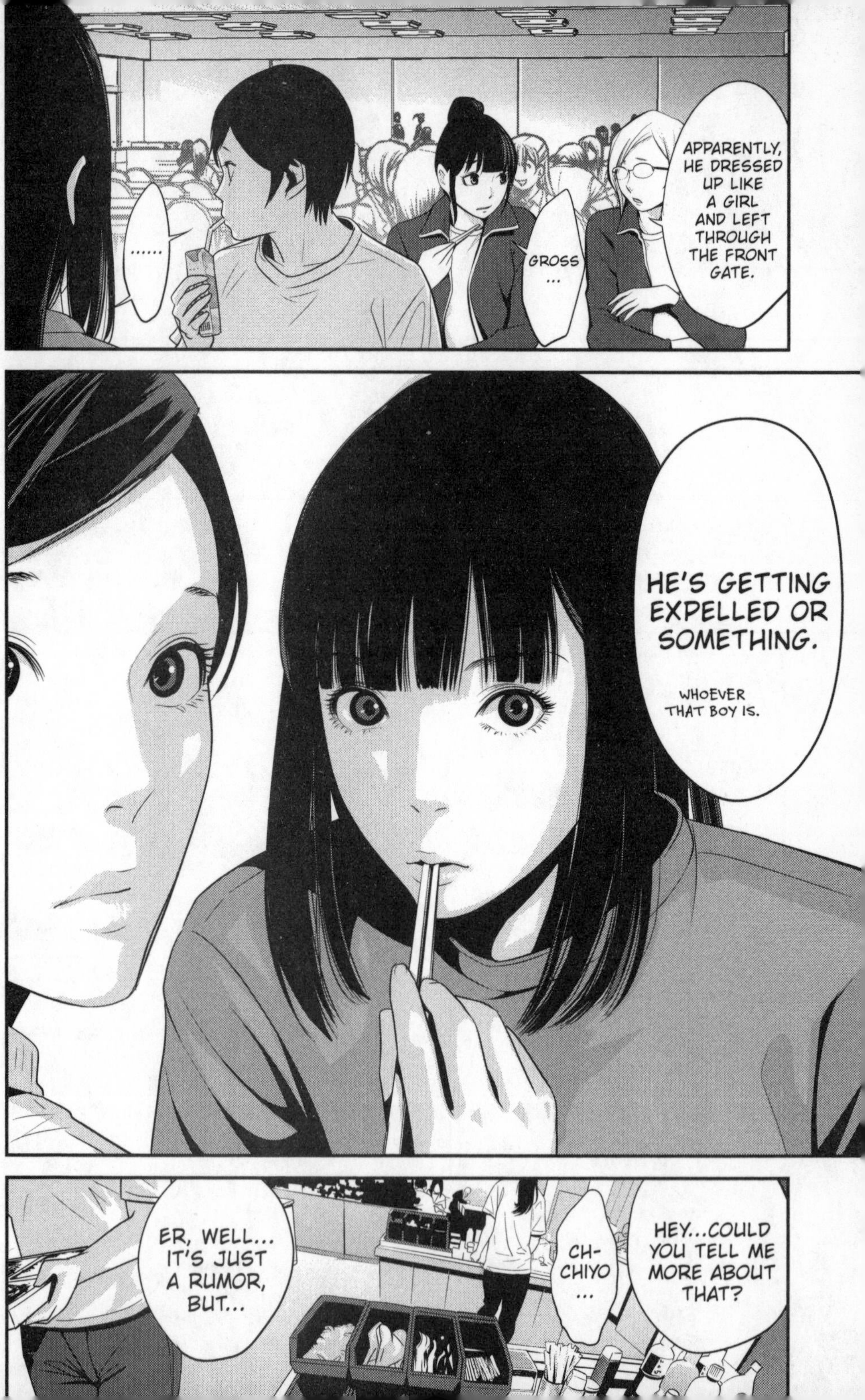
APPARENTLY, HE DRESSED UP LIKE A GIRL AND LEFT THROUGH THE FRONT GATE.
GROSS...
......
HE'S GETTING EXPELLED OR SOMETHING.
WHOEVER THAT BOY IS.
HEY...COULD YOU TELL ME MORE ABOUT THAT?
CH-CHIYO...
ER, WELL... IT'S JUST A RUMOR, BUT...

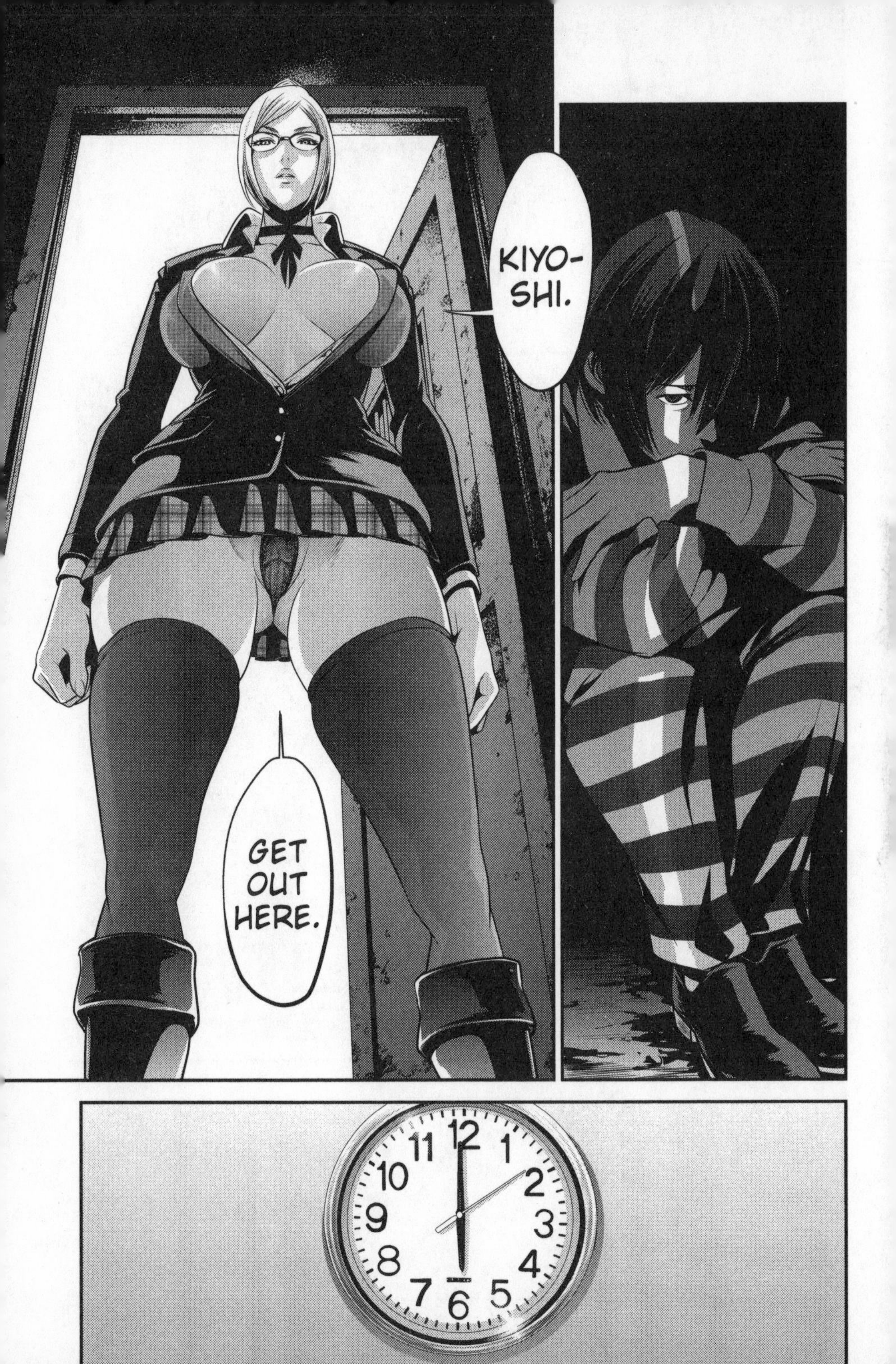
KIYO-SHI.
GET OUT HERE.

EXCUSE ME.

I'VE BROUGHT KIYOSHI.

quest to Withdraw

Year: Month: Day:

Acad··· High School Principal

Request to Withdraw

To: Hachimitsu Academy High School Pri···

Year: Month: Day:

Name

Current Address···

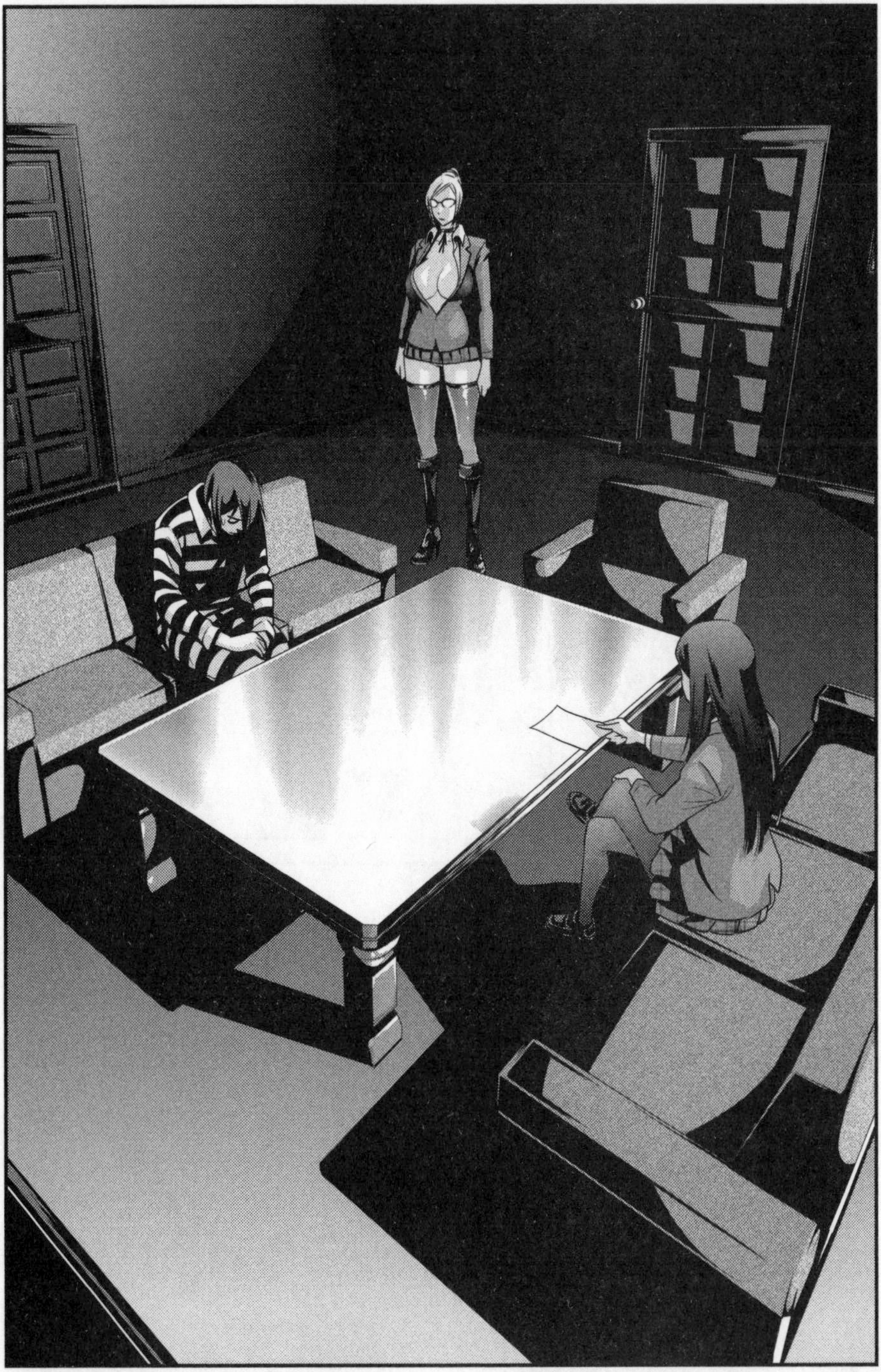

CHAPTER 32: SIGN

...TO PUT YOUR NAME ON THIS.

I WANT YOU...

Request to Withdraw

Year: Month: Day:

To: Hachimitsu Academy High School Principal

Name	
Current Address	
Telephone Number	
Student Number	

Reason for Withdrawal

I hereby requ... ...emy for the reasons listed...

THAT'S CORRECT.

A REQUEST TO WITH-DRAW...?

I THOUGHT... YOU WERE GOING TO BOOT ME OUT...

YOU WANT ME TO LEAVE THE SCHOOL VOLUNTARILY...?

THAT WOULD BE THE NATURAL THING TO DO, CONSIDERING YOUR CRIMES.

GA (GRAB)

Y-YES, MA'AM...

VICE PRESIDENT... I ASK THAT YOU STOP THREATENING HIM.

...IS FOR YOUR SAKE TOO.

THIS...

Request to Withdraw

Year: Month: Day:

To: Hachimitsu Academy High School Principal

Name	
Current Address	
Telephone Number	

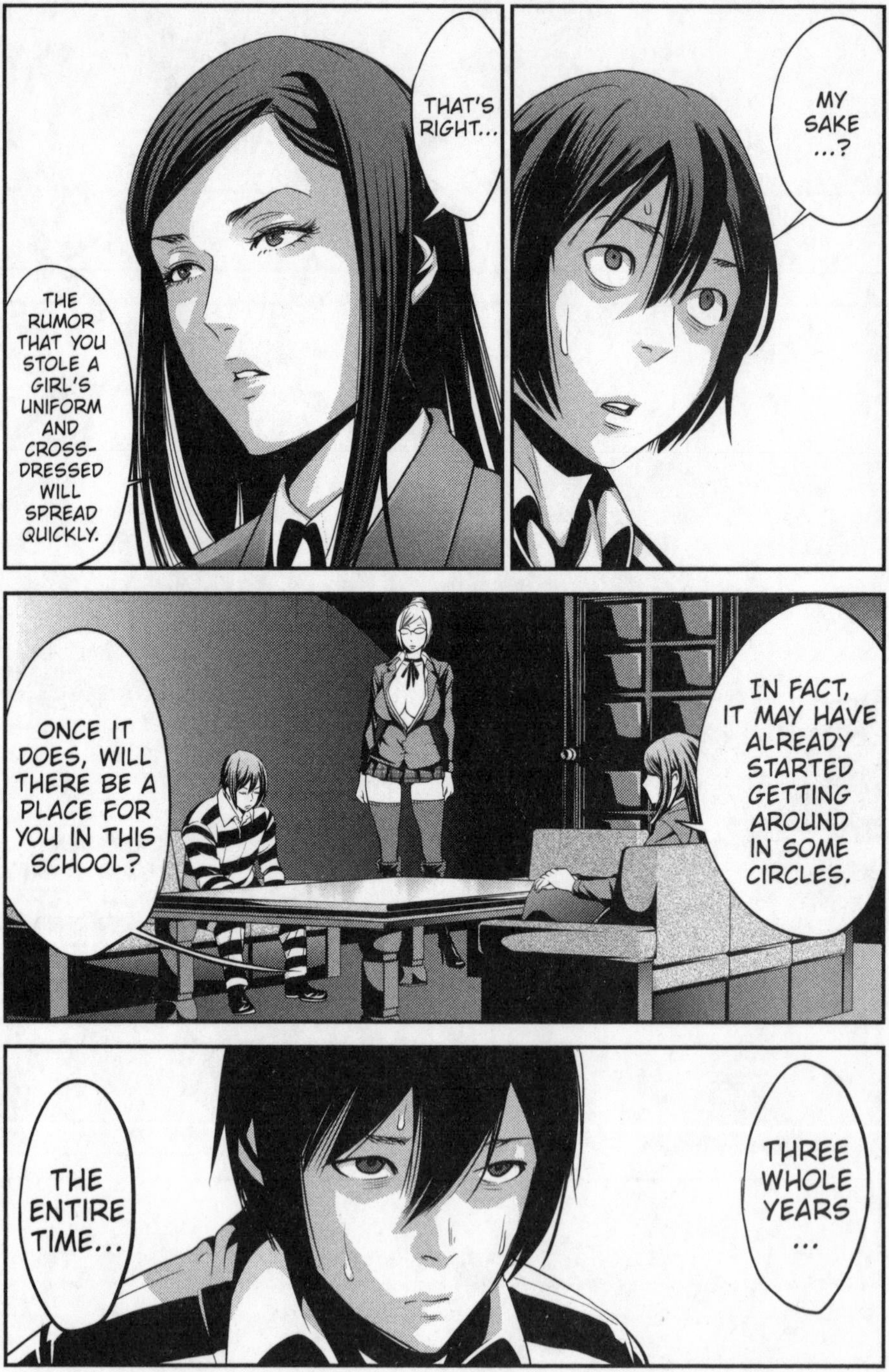
MY SAKE ...?
THAT'S RIGHT...
THE RUMOR THAT YOU STOLE A GIRL'S UNIFORM AND CROSS-DRESSED WILL SPREAD QUICKLY.
IN FACT, IT MAY HAVE ALREADY STARTED GETTING AROUND IN SOME CIRCLES.
ONCE IT DOES, WILL THERE BE A PLACE FOR YOU IN THIS SCHOOL?
THREE WHOLE YEARS ...
THE ENTIRE TIME...

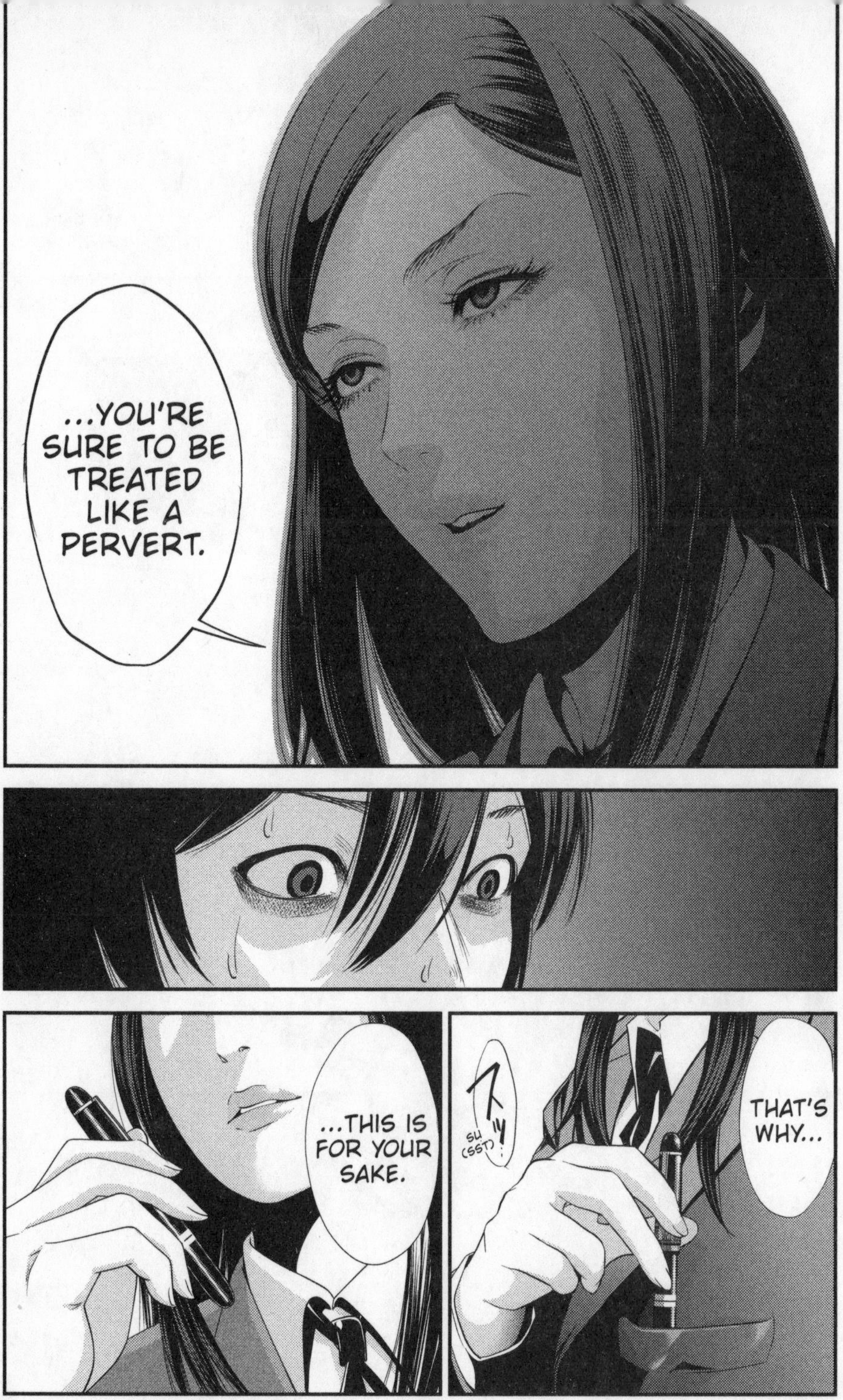
...YOU'RE SURE TO BE TREATED LIKE A PERVERT.
THAT'S WHY...
スッ
SU (SST)
...THIS IS FOR YOUR SAKE.

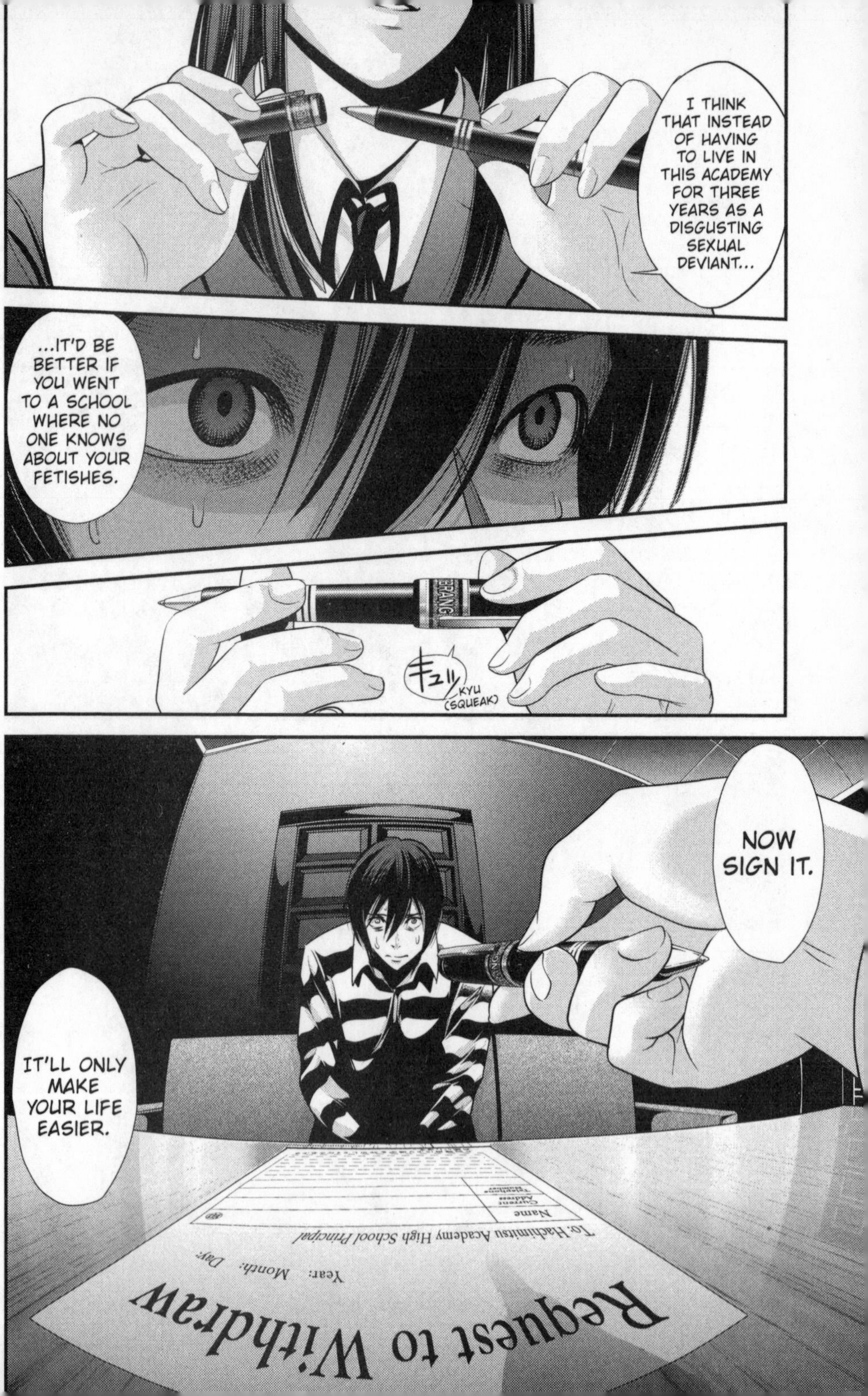
I THINK THAT INSTEAD OF HAVING TO LIVE IN THIS ACADEMY FOR THREE YEARS AS A DISGUSTING SEXUAL DEVIANT...
...IT'D BE BETTER IF YOU WENT TO A SCHOOL WHERE NO ONE KNOWS ABOUT YOUR FETISHES.
KYU (SQUEAK)
NOW SIGN IT.
IT'LL ONLY MAKE YOUR LIFE EASIER.
Request to Withdraw
Year: Month: Day:
To: Hachimitsu Academy High School Principal
Name
Current Address
Telephone Number

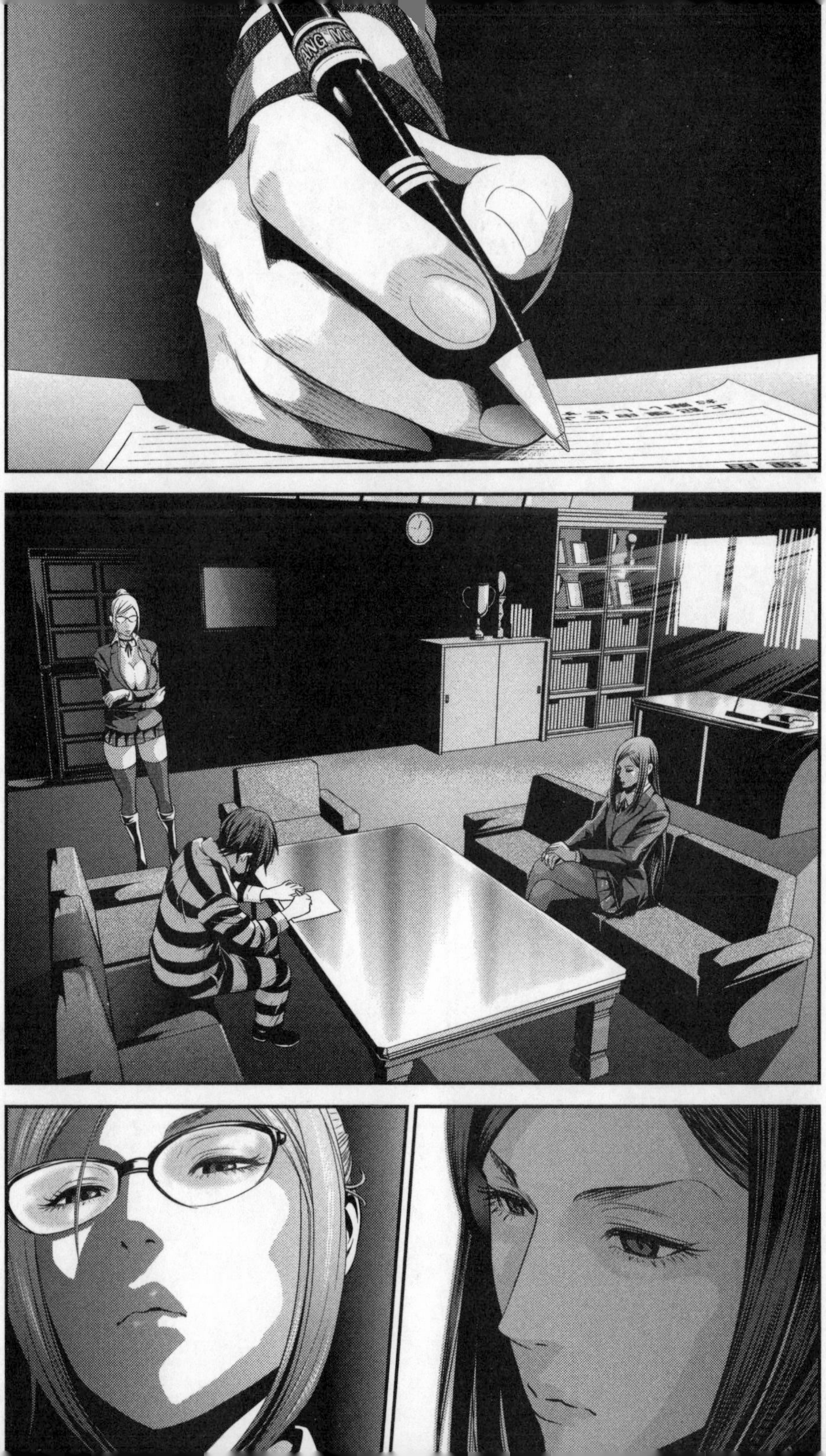

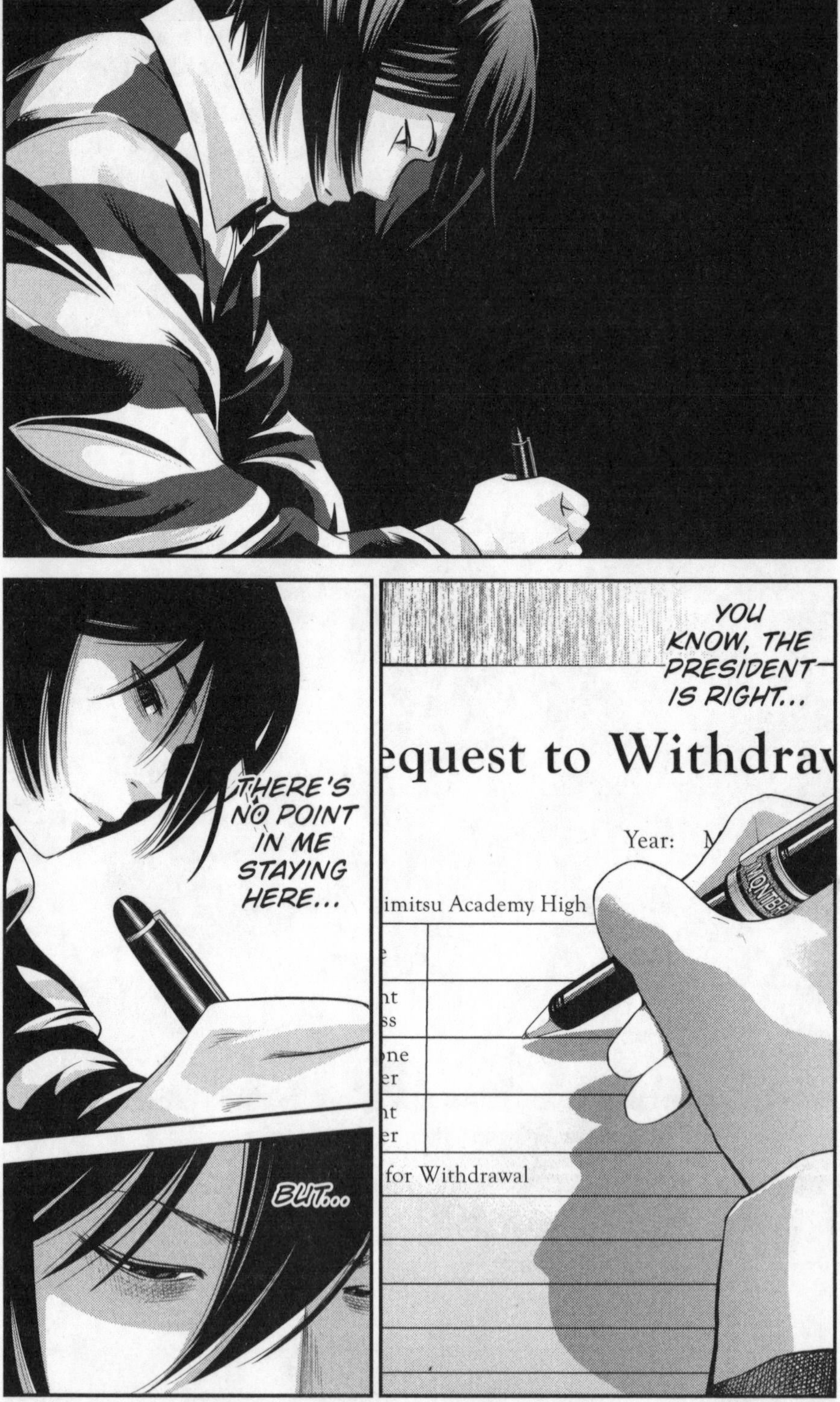
YOU KNOW, THE PRESIDENT IS RIGHT...
THERE'S NO POINT IN ME STAYING HERE...
equest to Withdraw
Year:
imitsu Academy High
for Withdrawal
BUT...

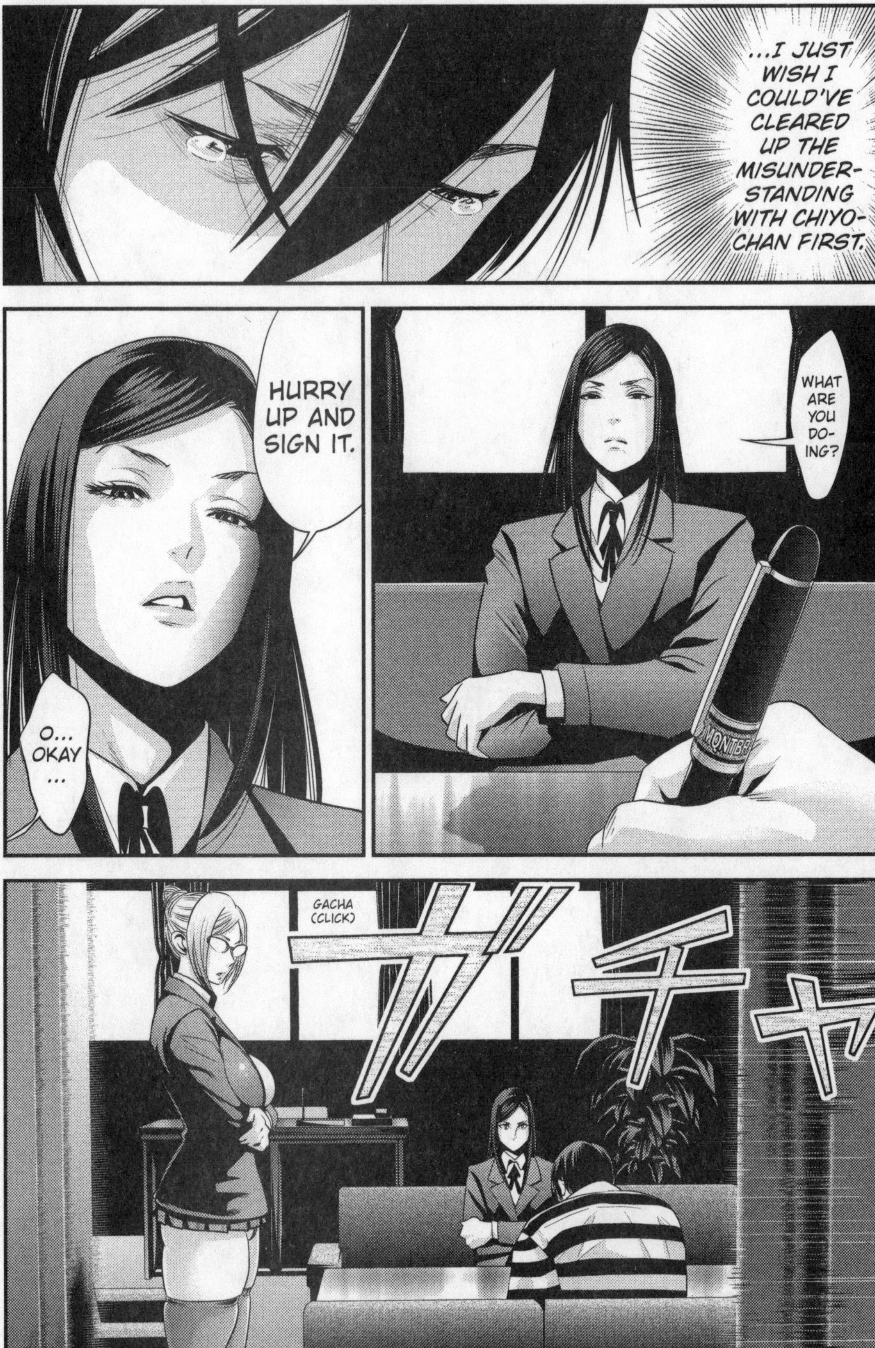
...I JUST WISH I COULD'VE CLEARED UP THE MISUNDER-STANDING WITH CHIYO-CHAN FIRST.
WHAT ARE YOU DO-ING?
HURRY UP AND SIGN IT.
O... OKAY ...
MONTBR
GACHA (CLICK)
ガチャ

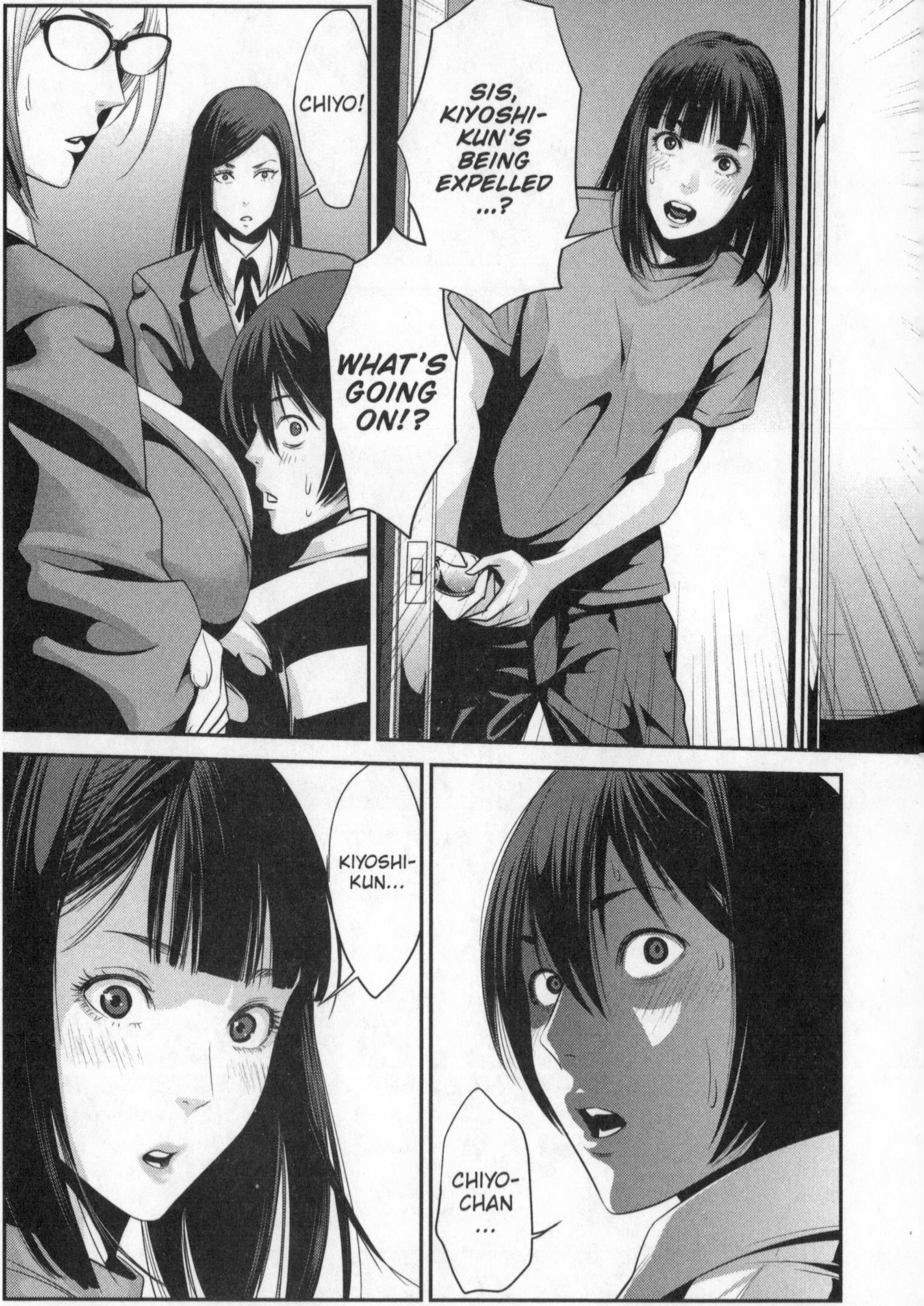
SIS, KIYOSHI-KUN'S BEING EXPELLED ...?
WHAT'S GOING ON!?
CHIYO!
CHIYO-CHAN ...
KIYOSHI-KUN...

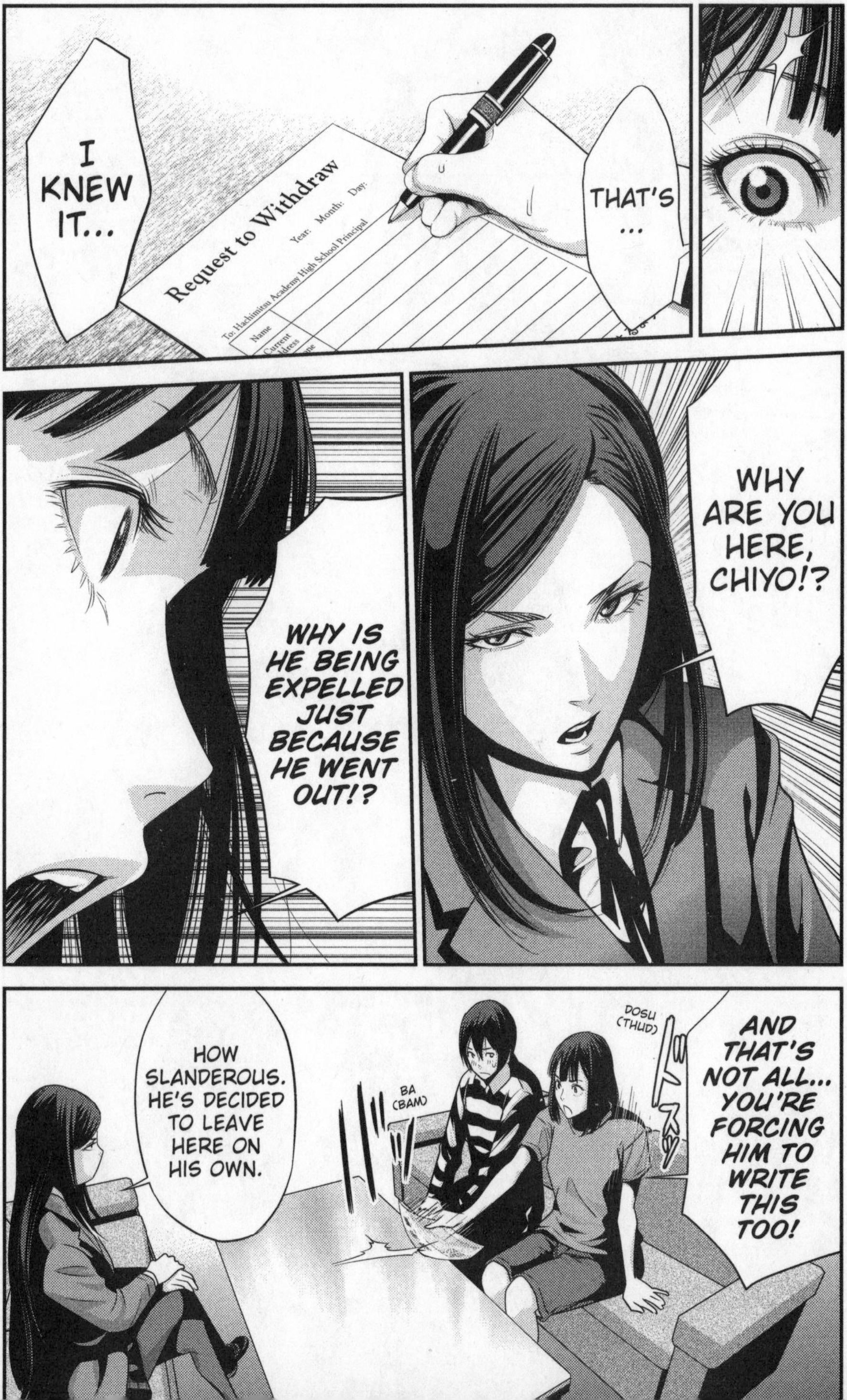

THAT'S ...
I KNEW IT...
Request to Withdraw
Year: Month: Day:
To: Hachimitsu Academy High School Principal
Name
Current Address
WHY ARE YOU HERE, CHIYO!?
WHY IS HE BEING EXPELLED JUST BECAUSE HE WENT OUT!?
AND THAT'S NOT ALL... YOU'RE FORCING HIM TO WRITE THIS TOO!
DOSU (THUD)
BA (BAM)
HOW SLANDEROUS. HE'S DECIDED TO LEAVE HERE ON HIS OWN.

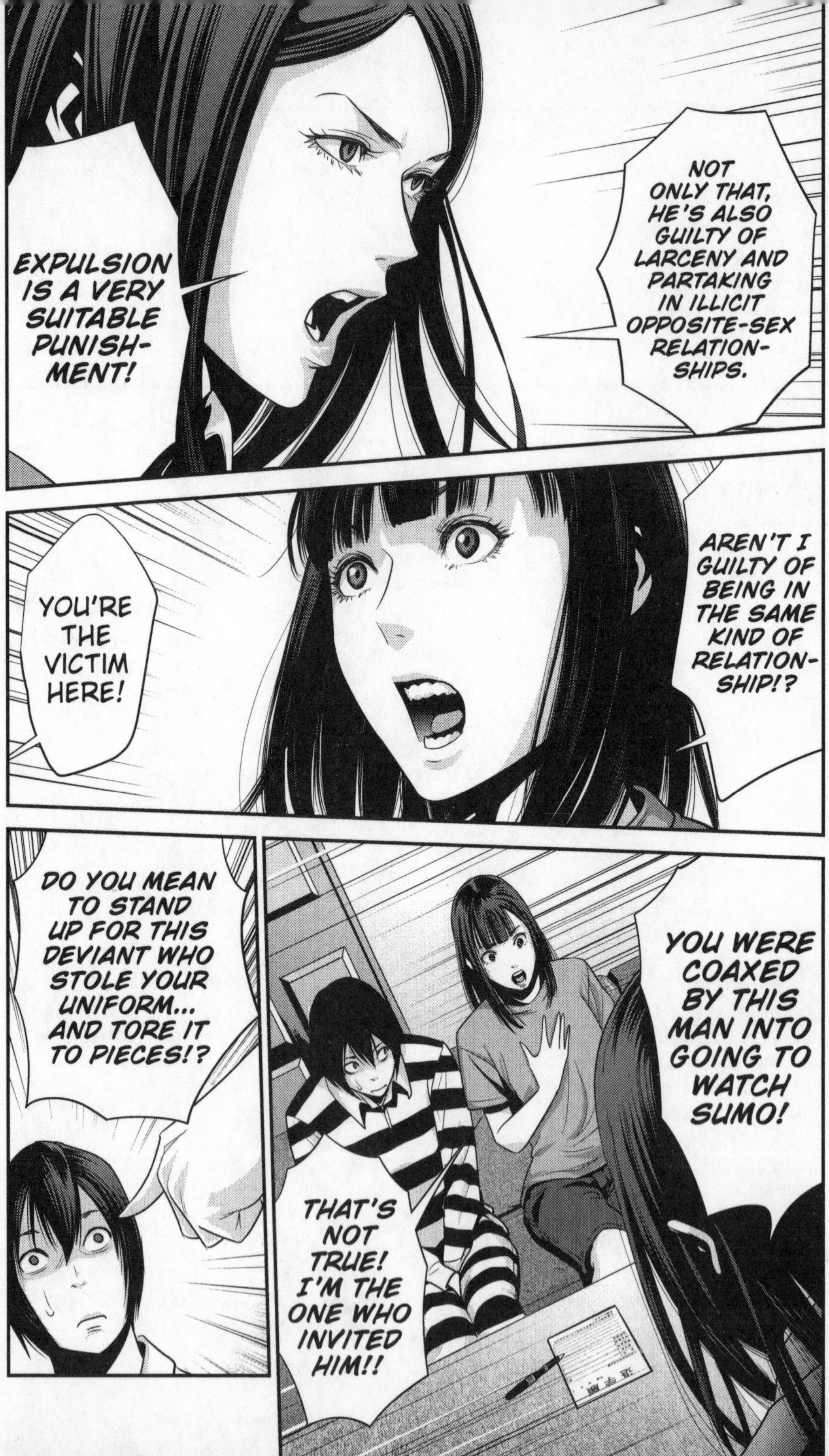
NOT ONLY THAT, HE'S ALSO GUILTY OF LARCENY AND PARTAKING IN ILLICIT OPPOSITE-SEX RELATION-SHIPS.
EXPULSION IS A VERY SUITABLE PUNISH-MENT!
AREN'T I GUILTY OF BEING IN THE SAME KIND OF RELATION-SHIP!?
YOU'RE THE VICTIM HERE!
YOU WERE COAXED BY THIS MAN INTO GOING TO WATCH SUMO!
THAT'S NOT TRUE! I'M THE ONE WHO INVITED HIM!!
DO YOU MEAN TO STAND UP FOR THIS DEVIANT WHO STOLE YOUR UNIFORM... AND TORE IT TO PIECES!?

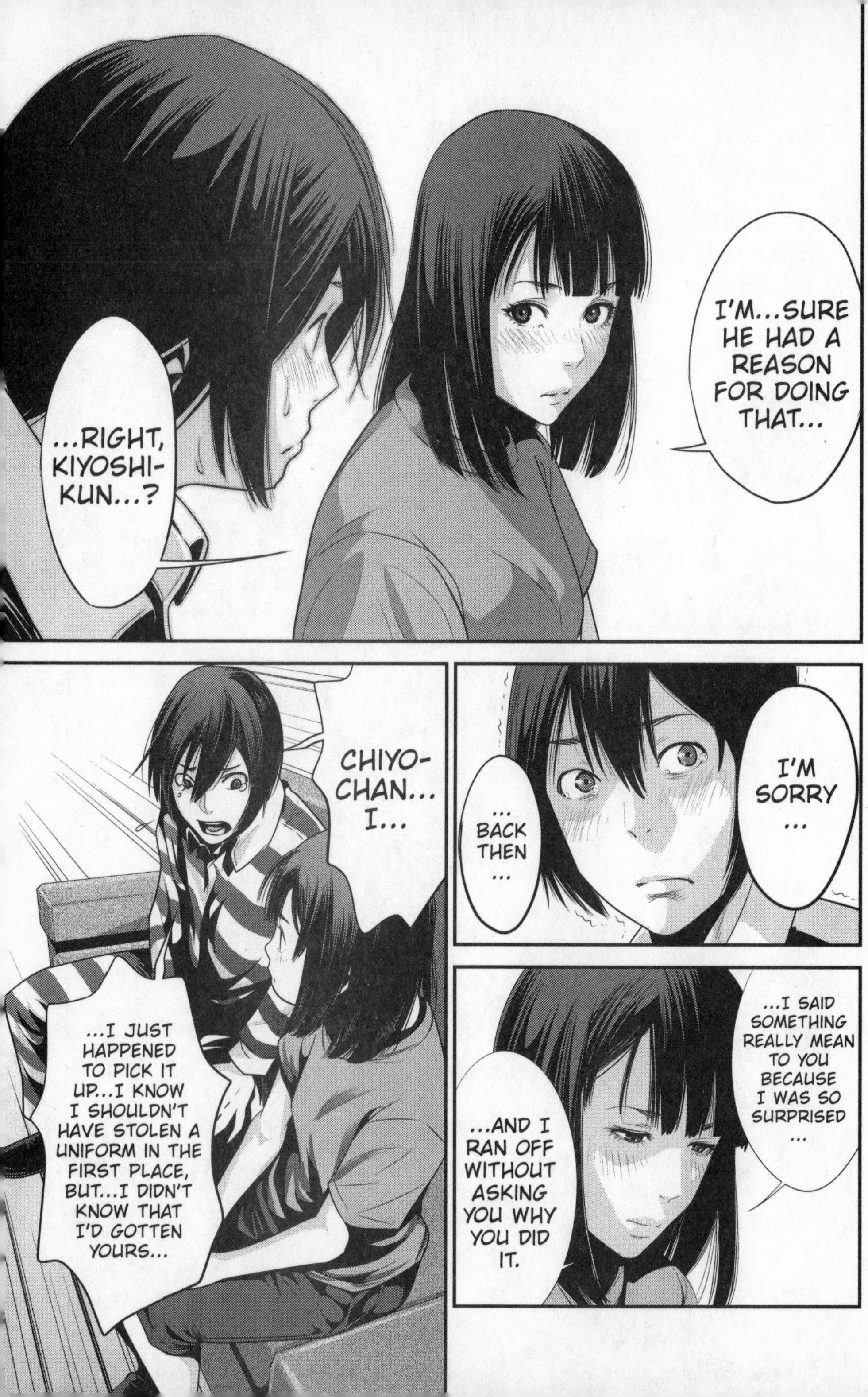

I'M...SURE HE HAD A REASON FOR DOING THAT...
...RIGHT, KIYOSHI-KUN...?
I'M SORRY ...
... BACK THEN ...
...I SAID SOMETHING REALLY MEAN TO YOU BECAUSE I WAS SO SURPRISED ...
...AND I RAN OFF WITHOUT ASKING YOU WHY YOU DID IT.
CHIYO-CHAN... I...
...I JUST HAPPENED TO PICK IT UP...I KNOW I SHOULDN'T HAVE STOLEN A UNIFORM IN THE FIRST PLACE, BUT...I DIDN'T KNOW THAT I'D GOTTEN YOURS...

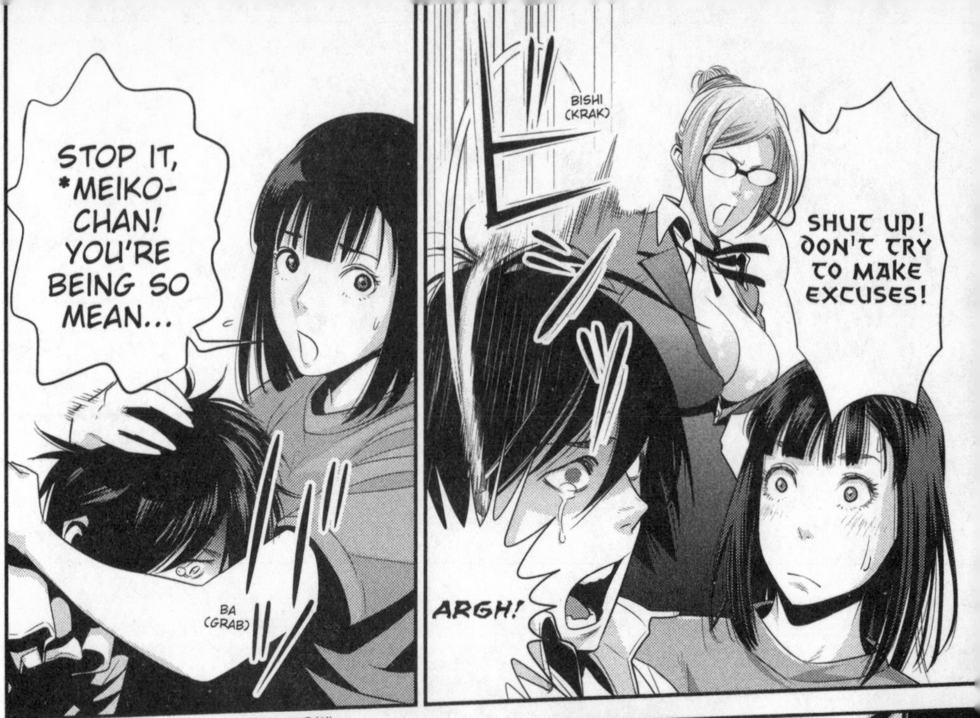
BISHI (KRAK)
SHUT UP! DON'T TRY TO MAKE EXCUSES!
ARGH!
STOP IT, *MEIKO-CHAN! YOU'RE BEING SO MEAN...
BA (GRAB)

*THE VICE PRESIDENT'S REAL NAME, MEIKO SHIRAKI

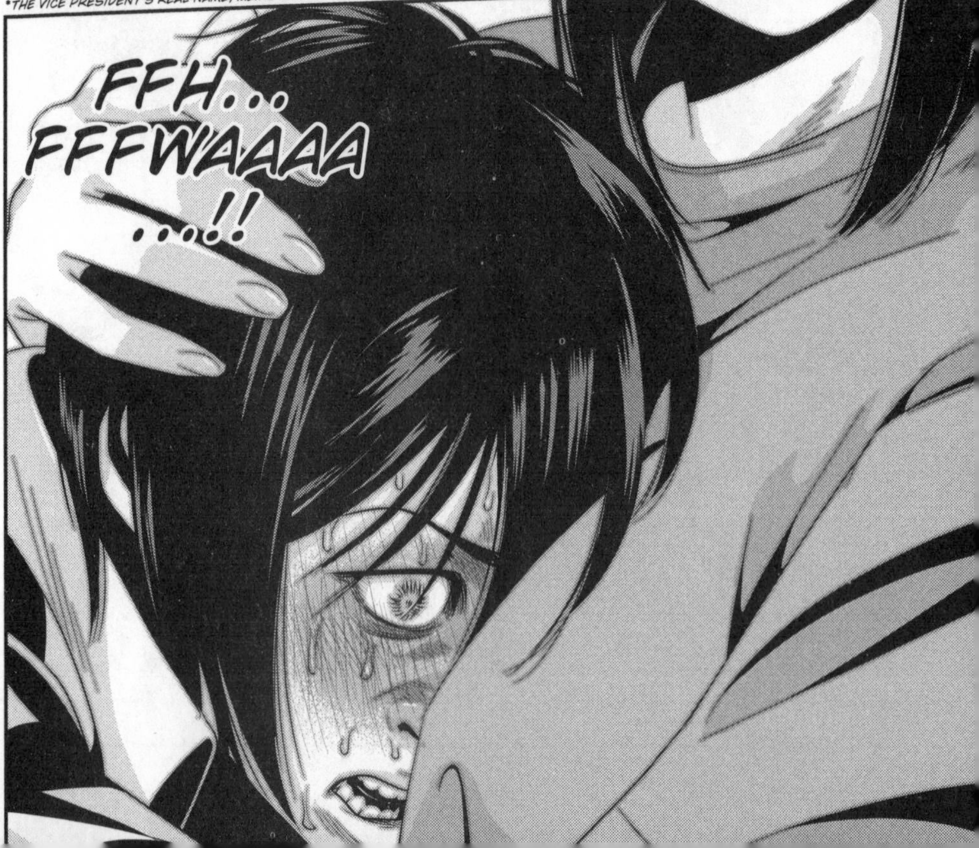
FFH... FFFWAAAA ...!!

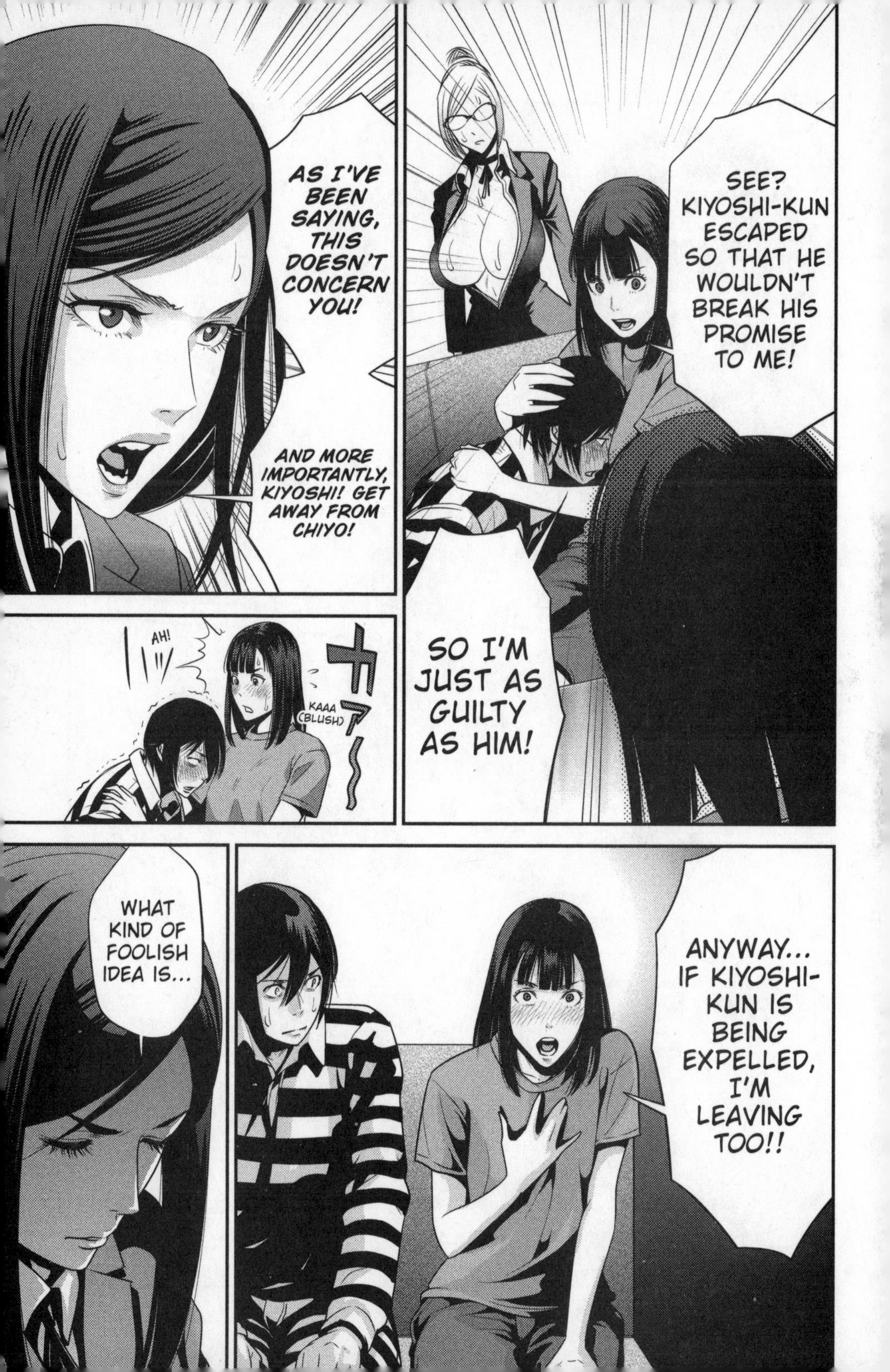
SEE? KIYOSHI-KUN ESCAPED SO THAT HE WOULDN'T BREAK HIS PROMISE TO ME!
SO I'M JUST AS GUILTY AS HIM!
AS I'VE BEEN SAYING, THIS DOESN'T CONCERN YOU!
AND MORE IMPORTANTLY, KIYOSHI! GET AWAY FROM CHIYO!
KAAA (BLUSH)
AH!
ANYWAY... IF KIYOSHI-KUN IS BEING EXPELLED, I'M LEAVING TOO!!
WHAT KIND OF FOOLISH IDEA IS...

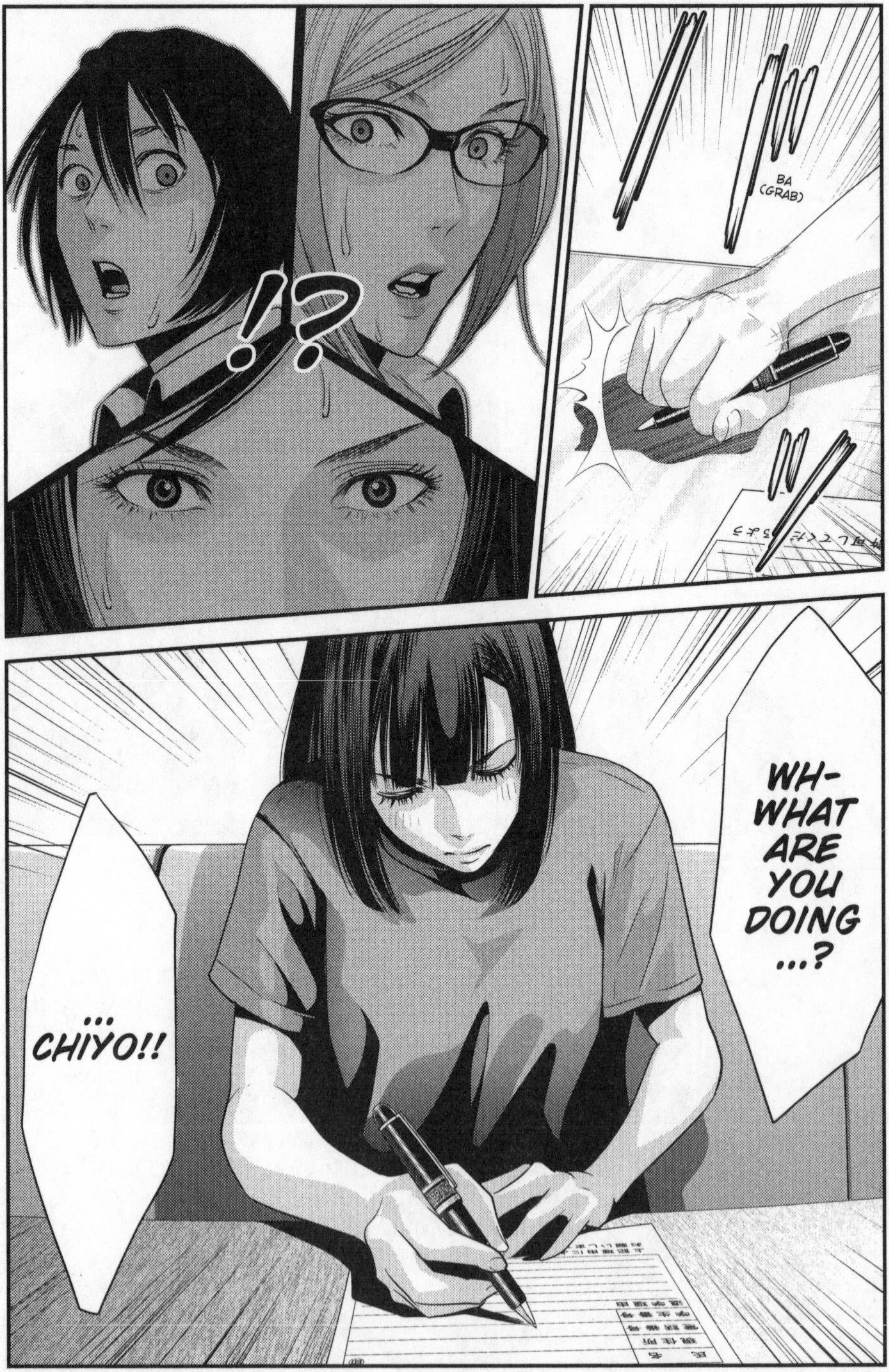
BA
(GRAB)
!?
WH-WHAT ARE YOU DOING ...?
... CHIYO!!

CHAPTER 33: REBEL WITH A CAUSE

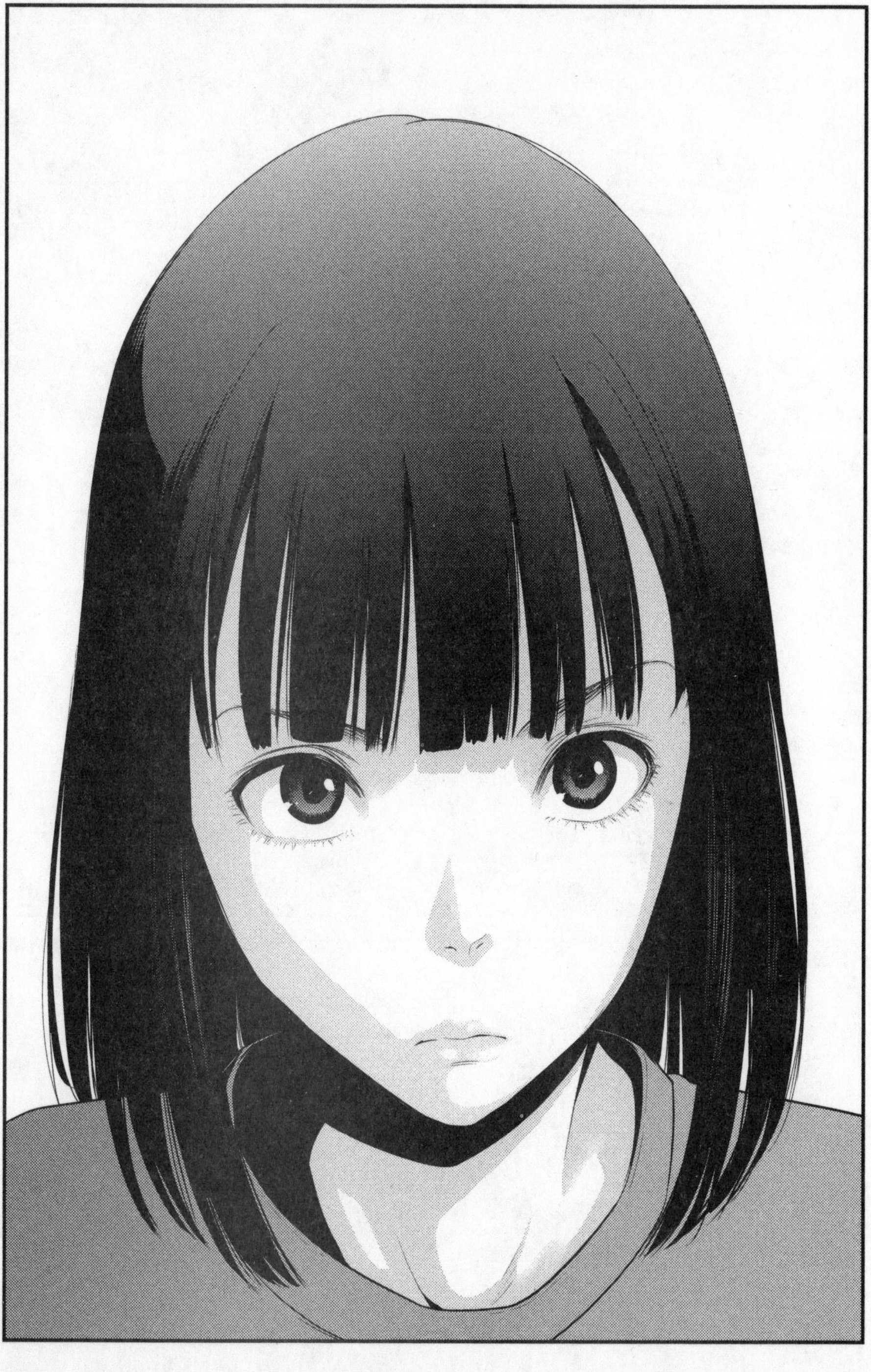

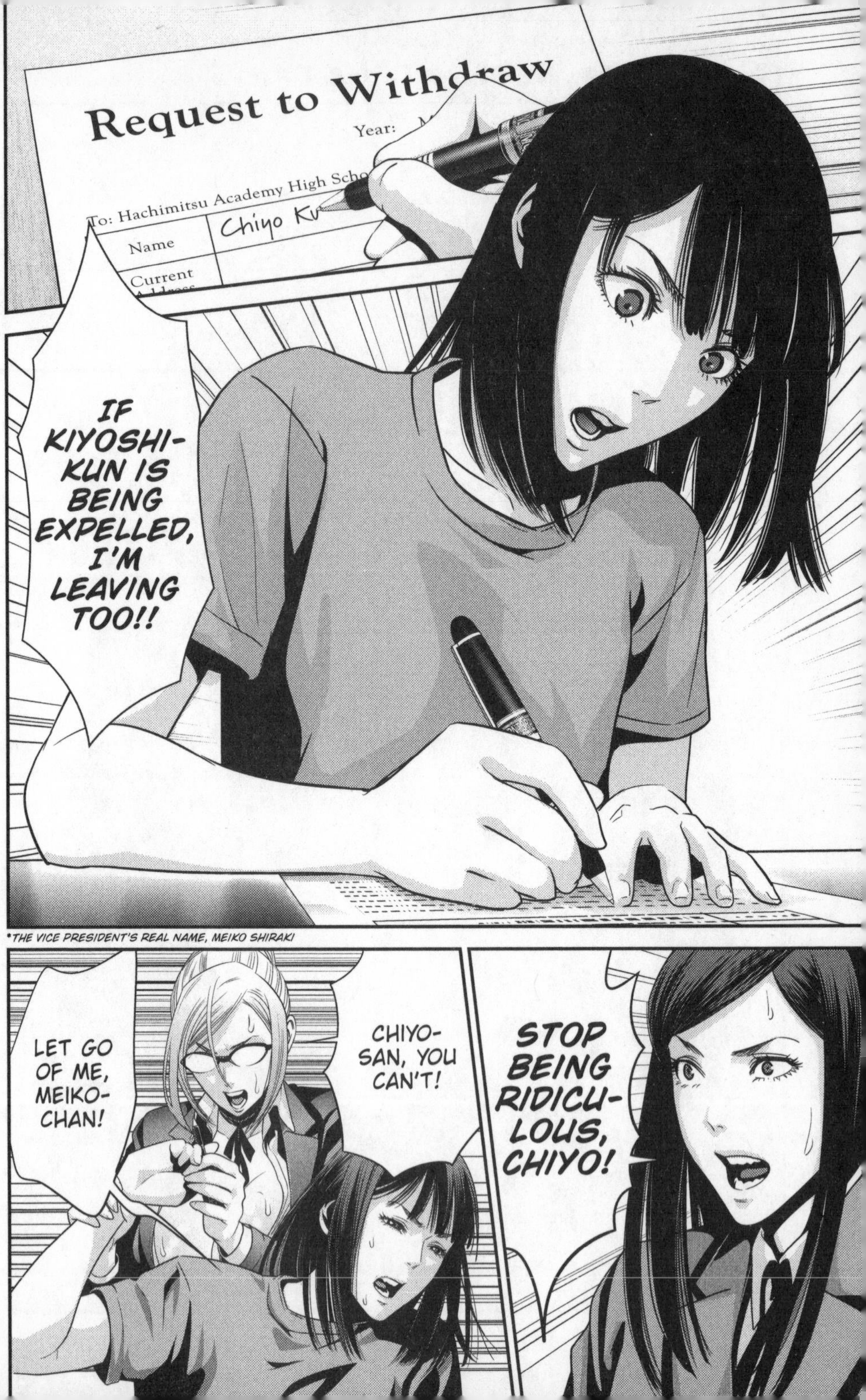
Request to Withdraw
Year:
To: Hachimitsu Academy High Scho
Name
Chiyo Ku
Current
IF KIYOSHI-KUN IS BEING EXPELLED, I'M LEAVING TOO!!
STOP BEING RIDICULOUS, CHIYO!
CHIYO-SAN, YOU CAN'T!
LET GO OF ME, MEIKO-CHAN!

*THE VICE PRESIDENT'S REAL NAME, MEIKO SHIRAKI

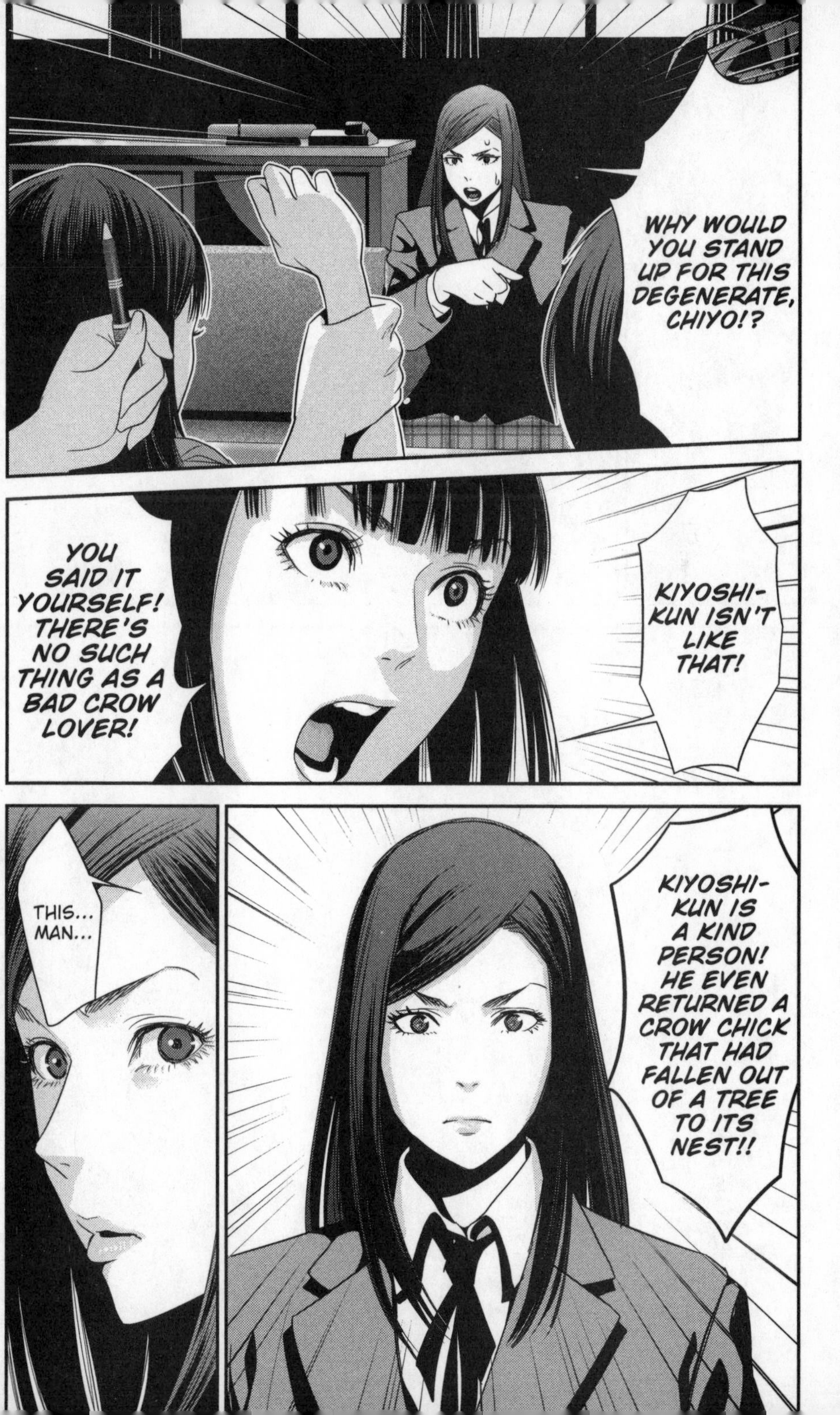

WHY WOULD YOU STAND UP FOR THIS DEGENERATE, CHIYO!?
KIYOSHI-KUN ISN'T LIKE THAT!
YOU SAID IT YOURSELF! THERE'S NO SUCH THING AS A BAD CROW LOVER!
KIYOSHI-KUN IS A KIND PERSON! HE EVEN RETURNED A CROW CHICK THAT HAD FALLEN OUT OF A TREE TO ITS NEST!!
THIS... MAN...

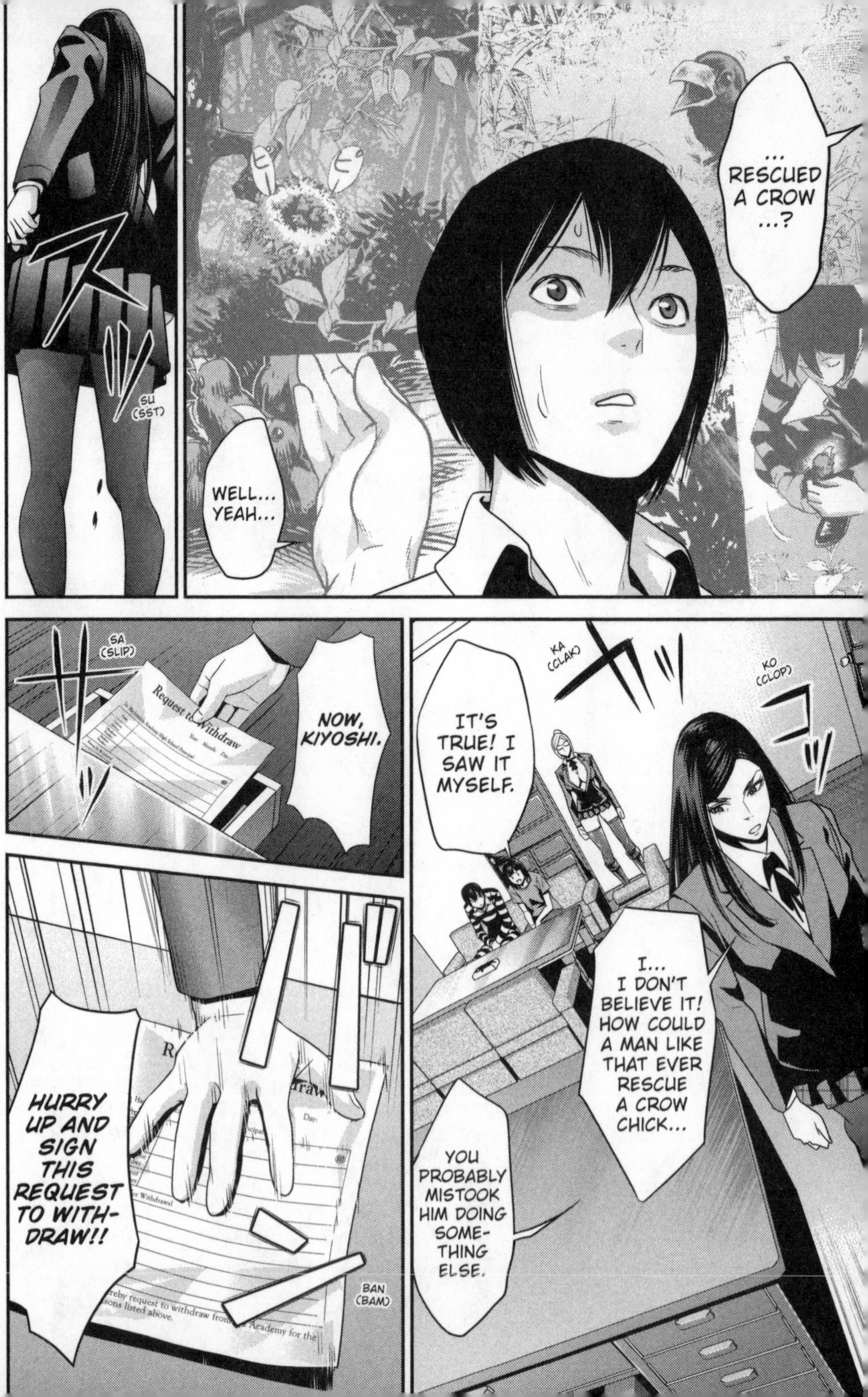
...RESCUED A CROW ...?
WELL... YEAH...
SU (SST)
KO (CLOP)
KA (CLAK)
IT'S TRUE! I SAW IT MYSELF.
I... I DON'T BELIEVE IT! HOW COULD A MAN LIKE THAT EVER RESCUE A CROW CHICK...
YOU PROBABLY MISTOOK HIM DOING SOMETHING ELSE.
NOW, KIYOSHI.
SA (SLIP)
Request to Withdraw
HURRY UP AND SIGN THIS REQUEST TO WITH-DRAW!!
BAN (BAM)

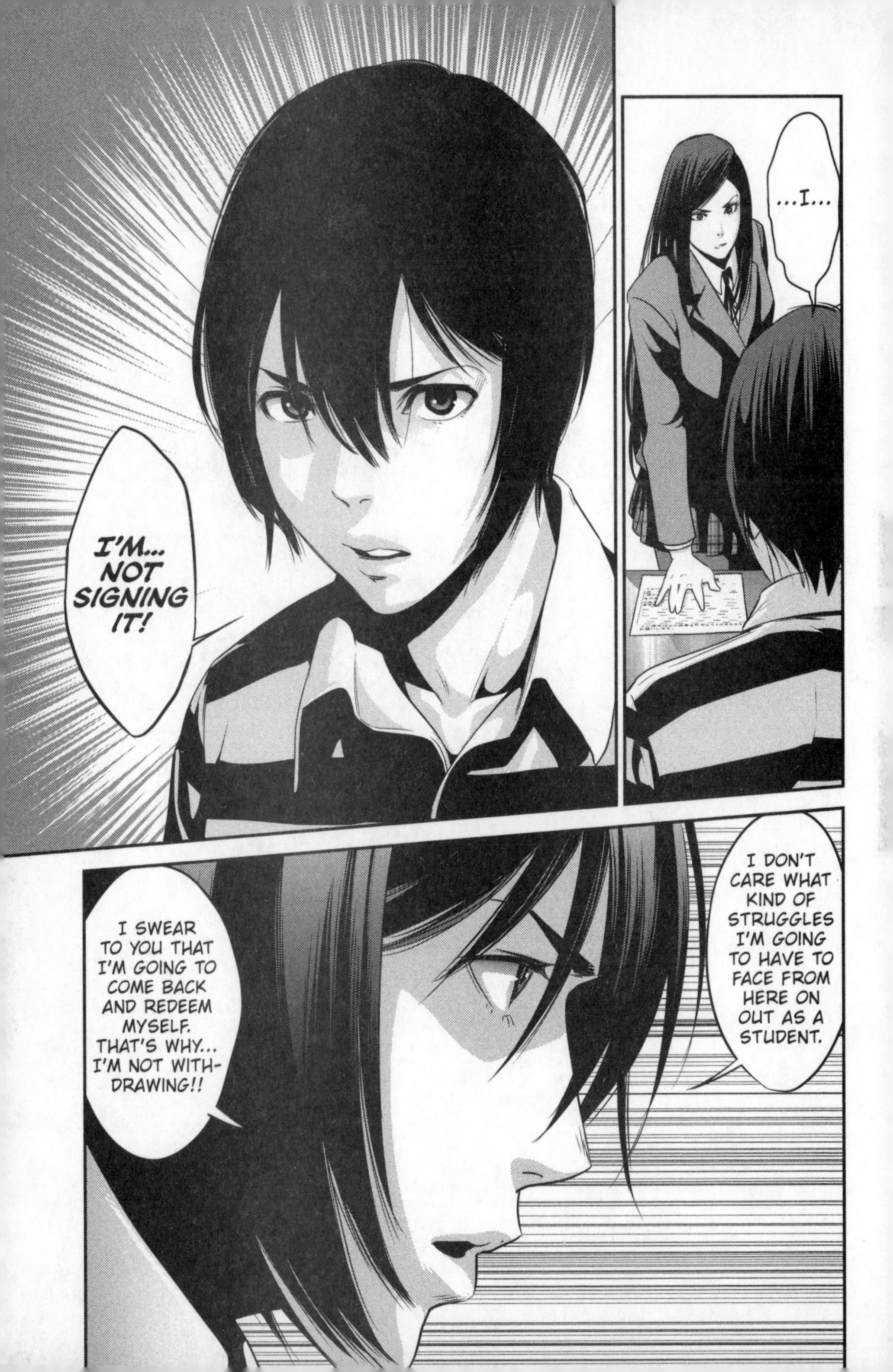
...I...
I'M... NOT SIGNING IT!
I DON'T CARE WHAT KIND OF STRUGGLES I'M GOING TO HAVE TO FACE FROM HERE ON OUT AS A STUDENT.
I SWEAR TO YOU THAT I'M GOING TO COME BACK AND REDEEM MYSELF. THAT'S WHY... I'M NOT WITH-DRAWING!!

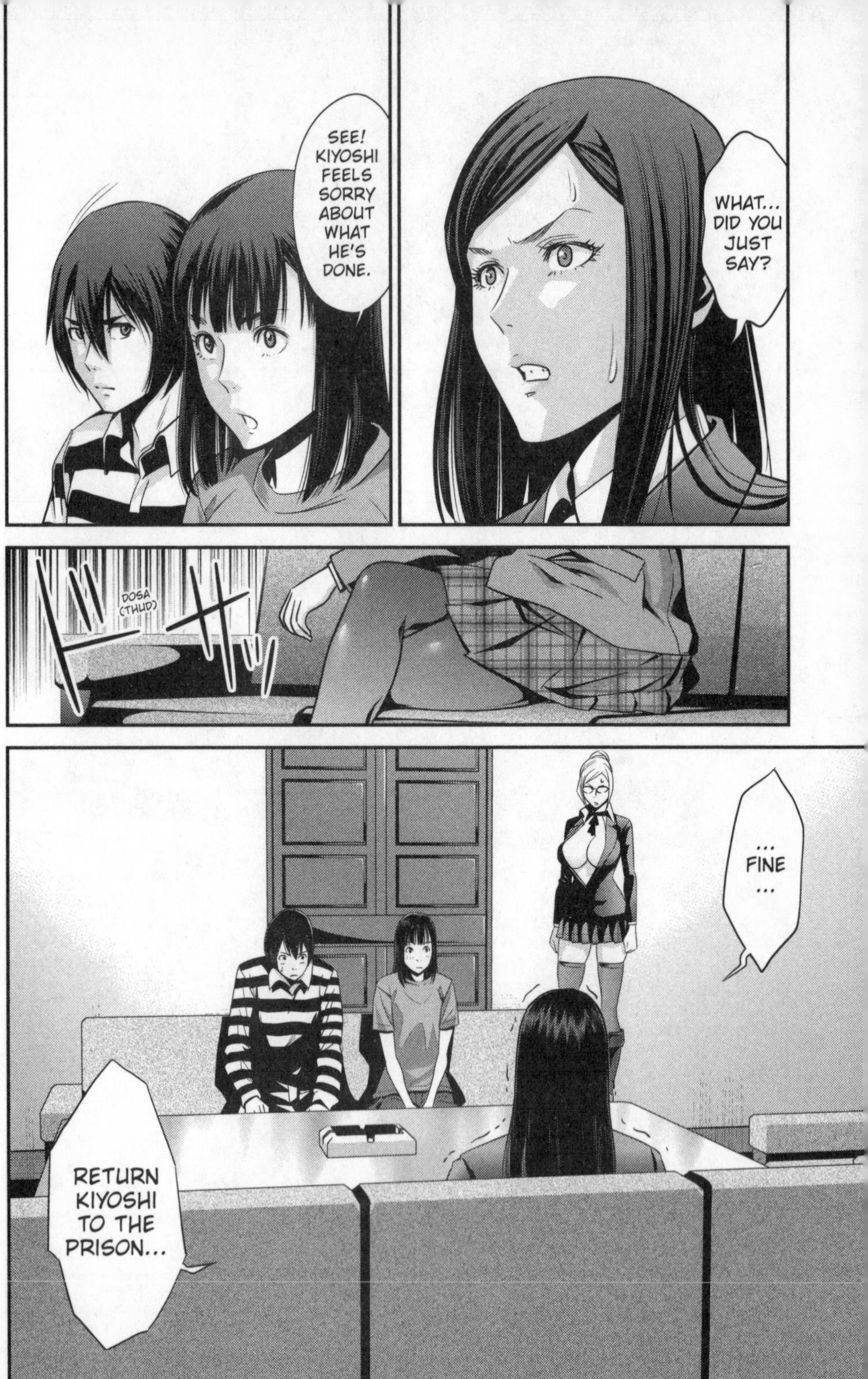
WHAT... DID YOU JUST SAY?
SEE! KIYOSHI FEELS SORRY ABOUT WHAT HE'S DONE.
DOSA (THUD)
... FINE ...
RETURN KIYOSHI TO THE PRISON...

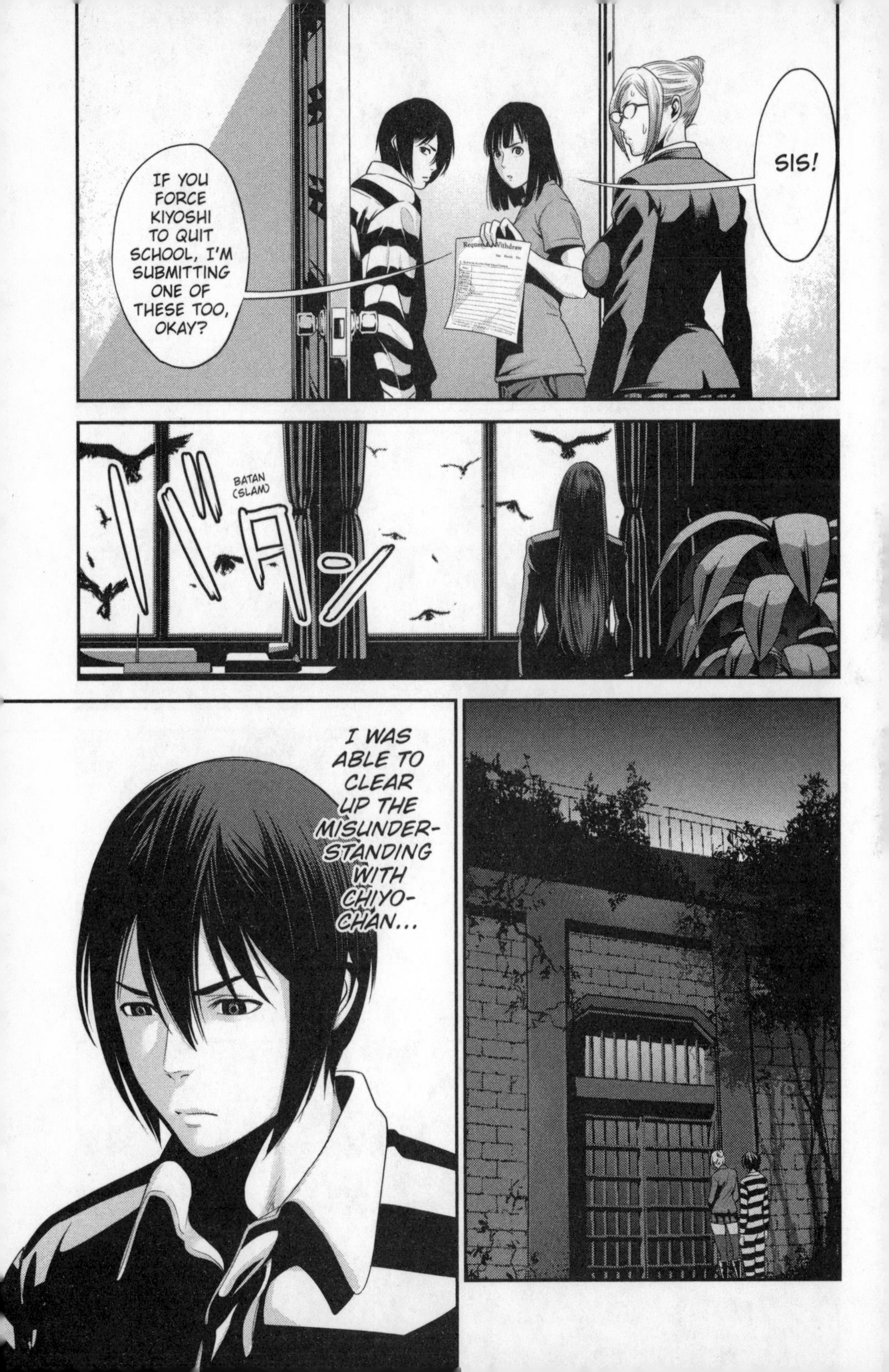
SIS!
IF YOU FORCE KIYOSHI TO QUIT SCHOOL, I'M SUBMITTING ONE OF THESE TOO, OKAY?
BATAN (SLAM)
I WAS ABLE TO CLEAR UP THE MISUNDER-STANDING WITH CHIYO-CHAN...

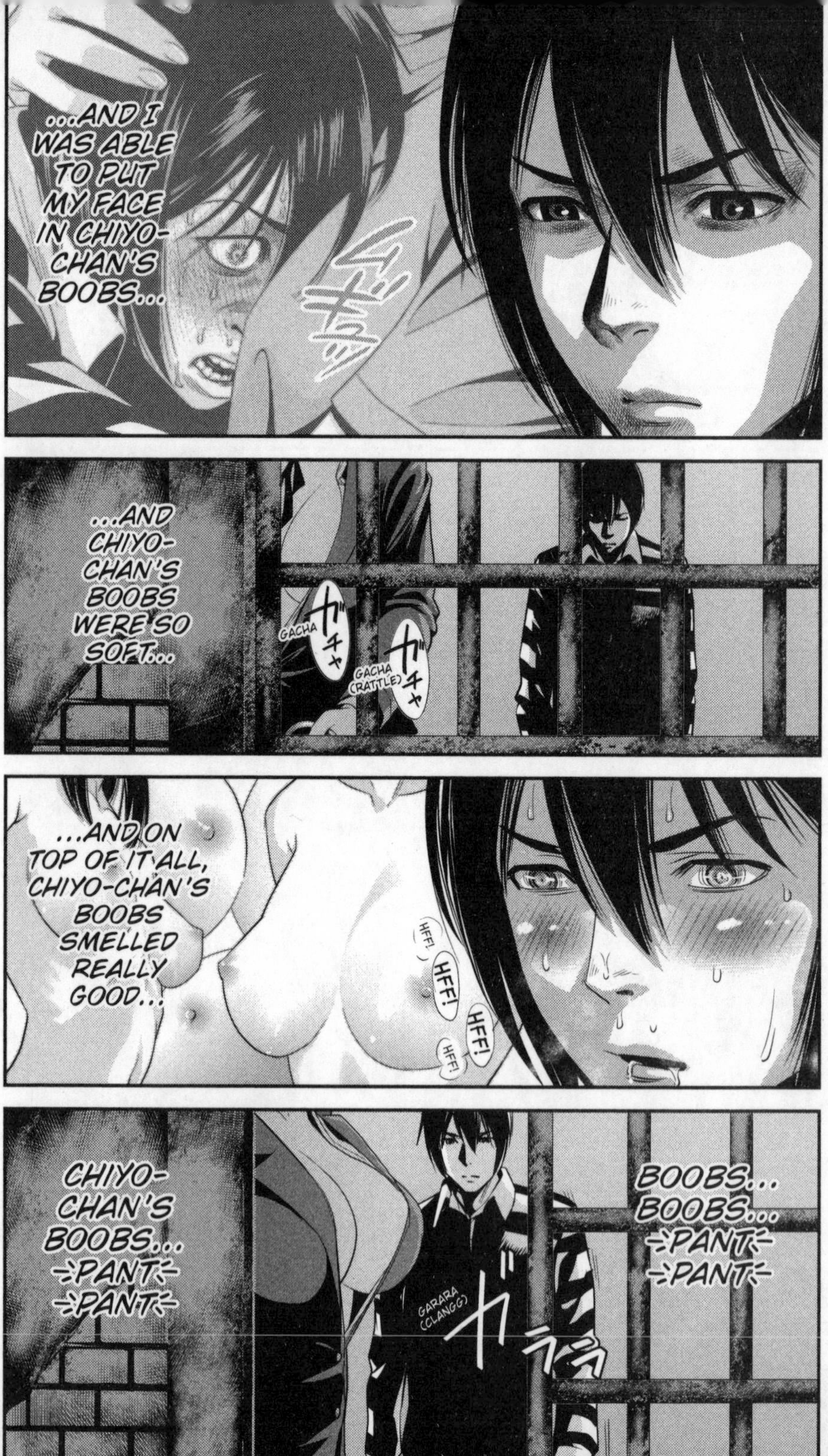
...AND I WAS ABLE TO PUT MY FACE IN CHIYO-CHAN'S BOOBS...
...AND CHIYO-CHAN'S BOOBS WERE SO SOFT...
ガチャ
GACHA
ガチャ
GACHA (RATTLE)
...AND ON TOP OF IT ALL, CHIYO-CHAN'S BOOBS SMELLED REALLY GOOD...
HFF!
HFF!
HFF!
HFF!
BOOBS... BOOBS... PANT PANT
CHIYO-CHAN'S BOOBS... PANT PANT
GARARA (CLANGG)

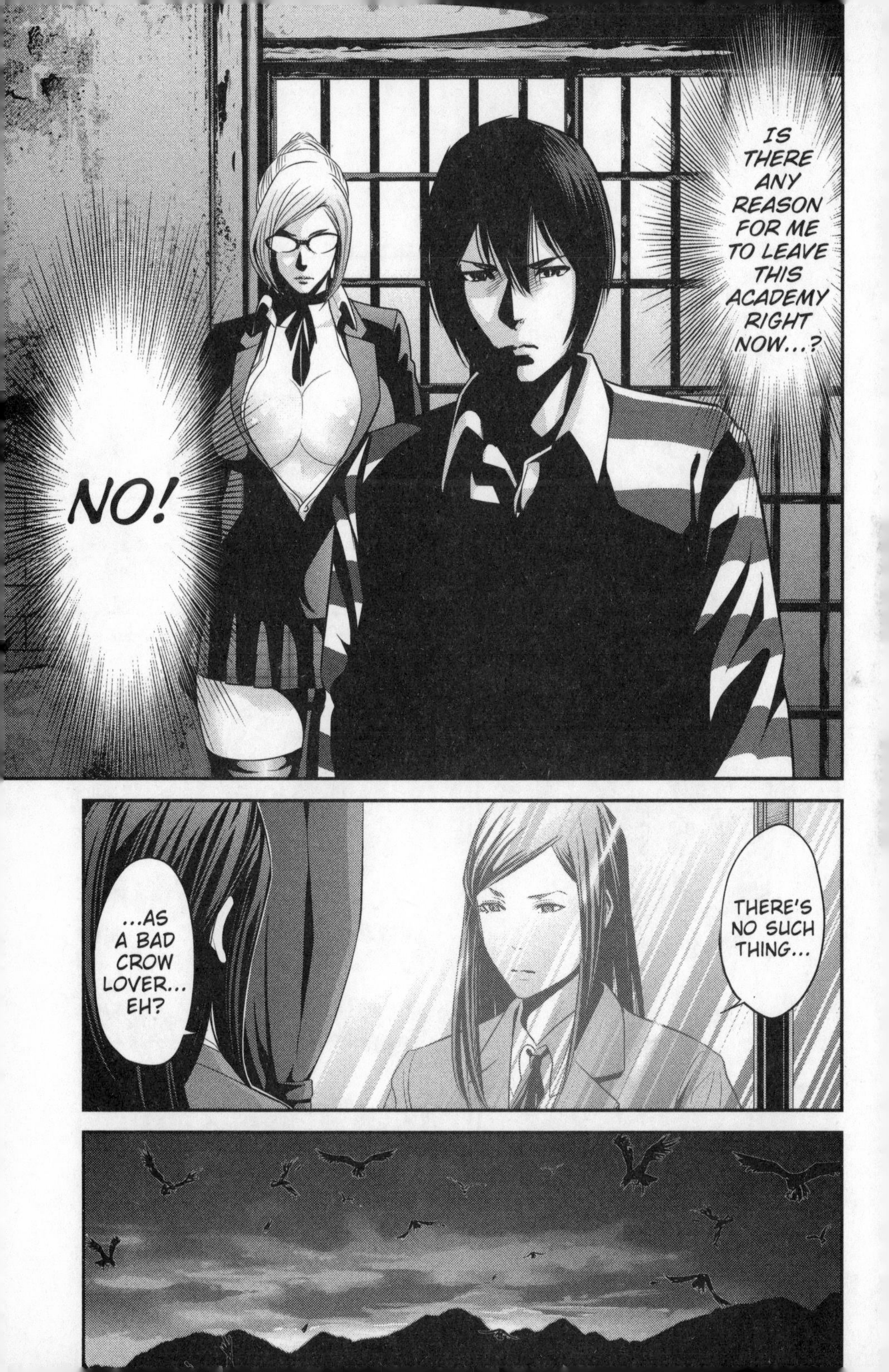
IS THERE ANY REASON FOR ME TO LEAVE THIS ACADEMY RIGHT NOW...?
NO!
THERE'S NO SUCH THING...
...AS A BAD CROW LOVER... EH?

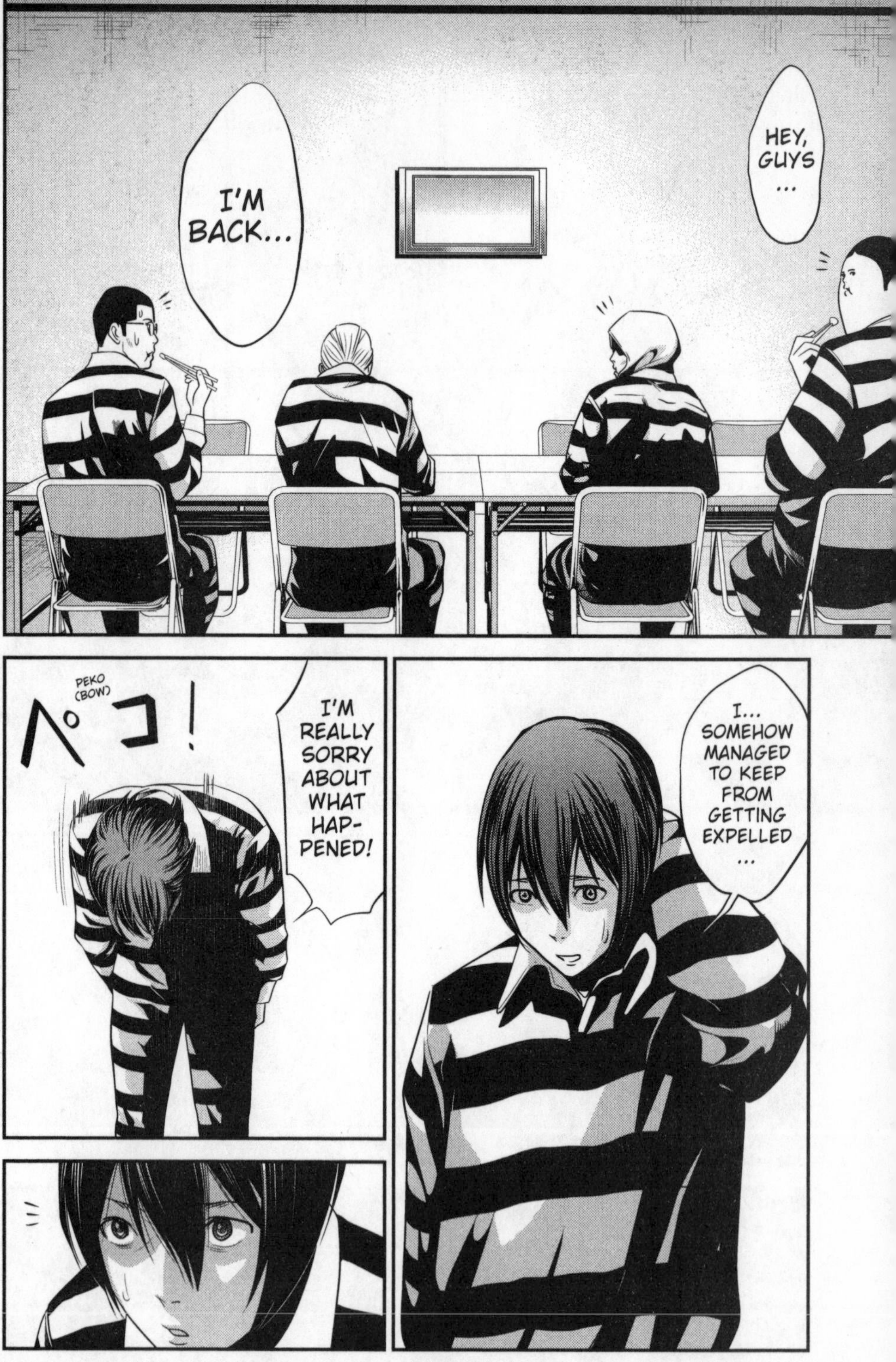
HEY, GUYS ...
I'M BACK...
I... SOMEHOW MANAGED TO KEEP FROM GETTING EXPELLED ...
I'M REALLY SORRY ABOUT WHAT HAP-PENED!
ペコ！
PEKO (BOW)

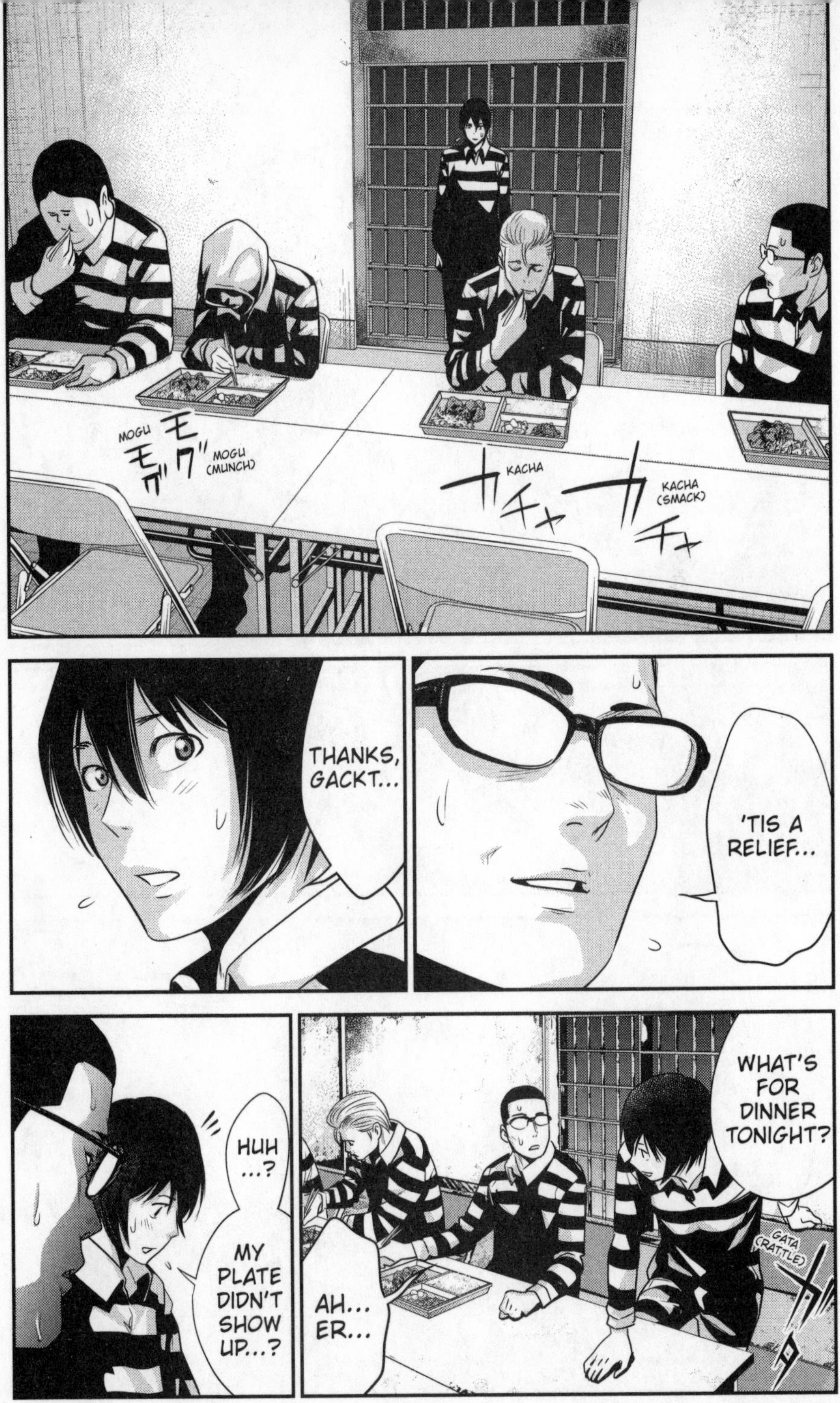
KACHA
KACHA (SMACK)
カチャカチャ
MOGU
MOGU (MUNCH)
モグモグ
'TIS A RELIEF...
THANKS, GACKT...
WHAT'S FOR DINNER TONIGHT?
GATA (RATTLE)
AH... ER...
HUH ...?
MY PLATE DIDN'T SHOW UP...?

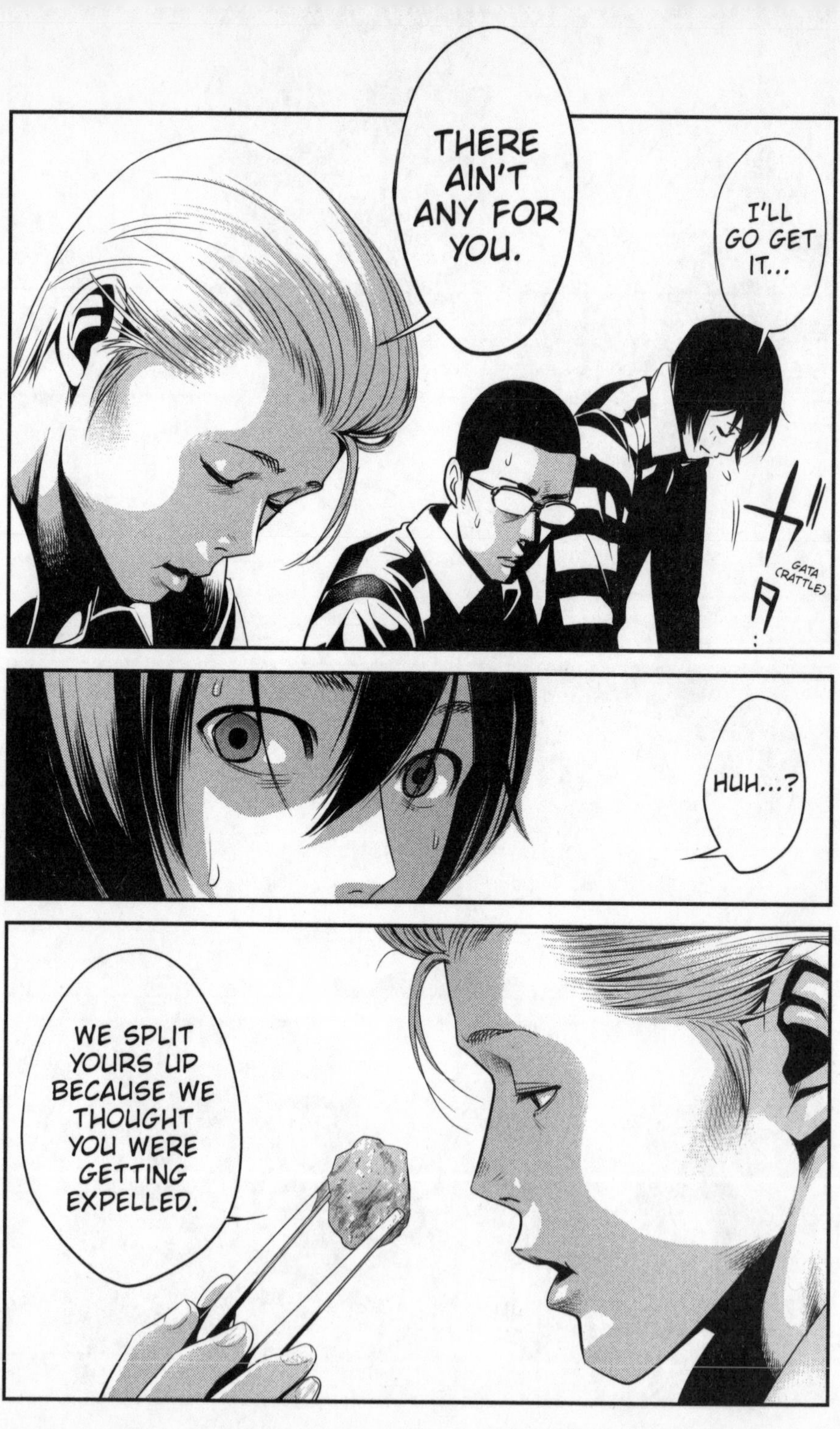
I'LL GO GET IT...
THERE AIN'T ANY FOR YOU.
GATA (RATTLE)
HUH...?
WE SPLIT YOURS UP BECAUSE WE THOUGHT YOU WERE GETTING EXPELLED.

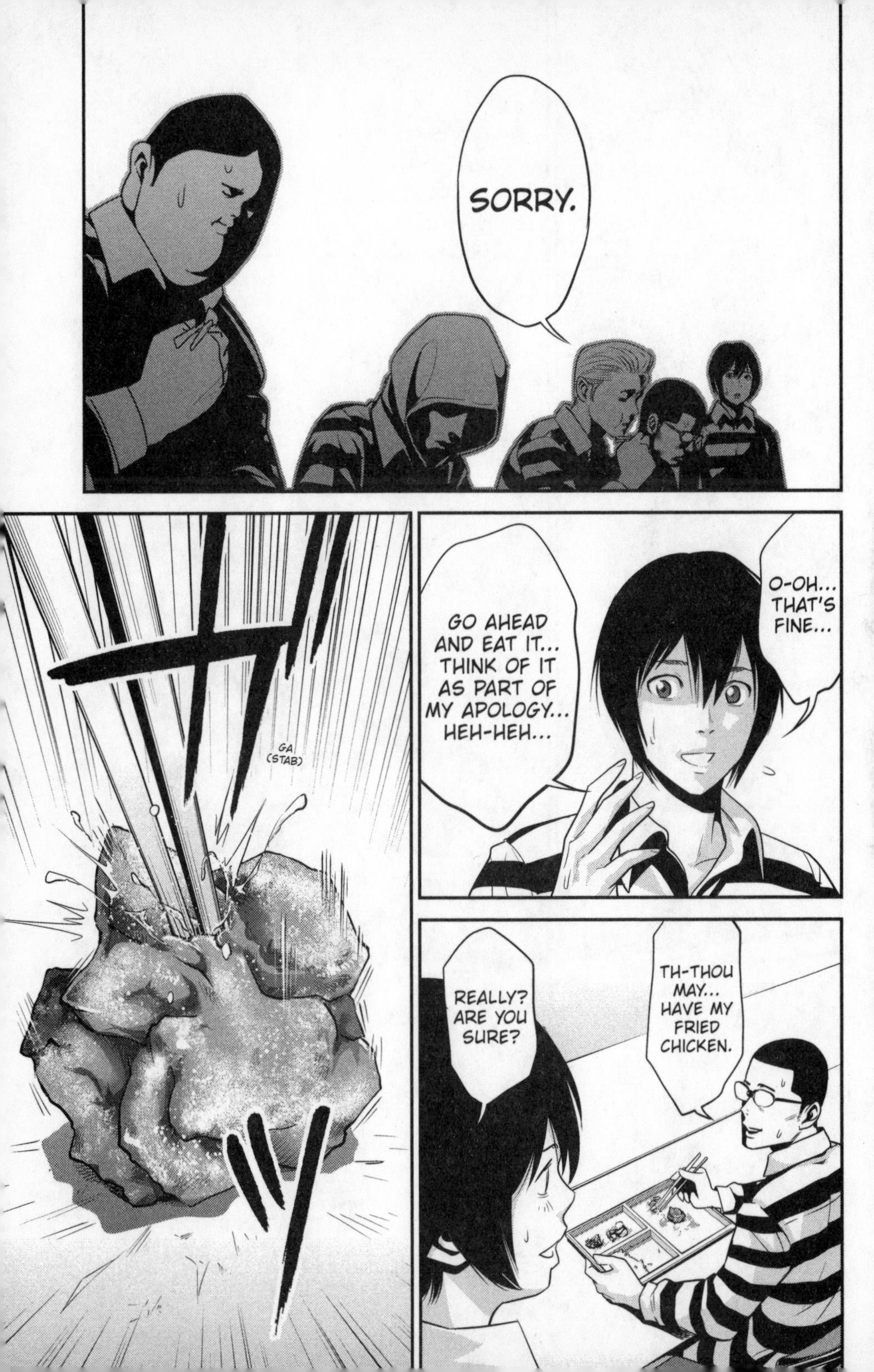
SORRY.
O-OH... THAT'S FINE...
GO AHEAD AND EAT IT... THINK OF IT AS PART OF MY APOLOGY... HEH-HEH...
TH-THOU MAY... HAVE MY FRIED CHICKEN.
REALLY? ARE YOU SURE?
GA (STAB)

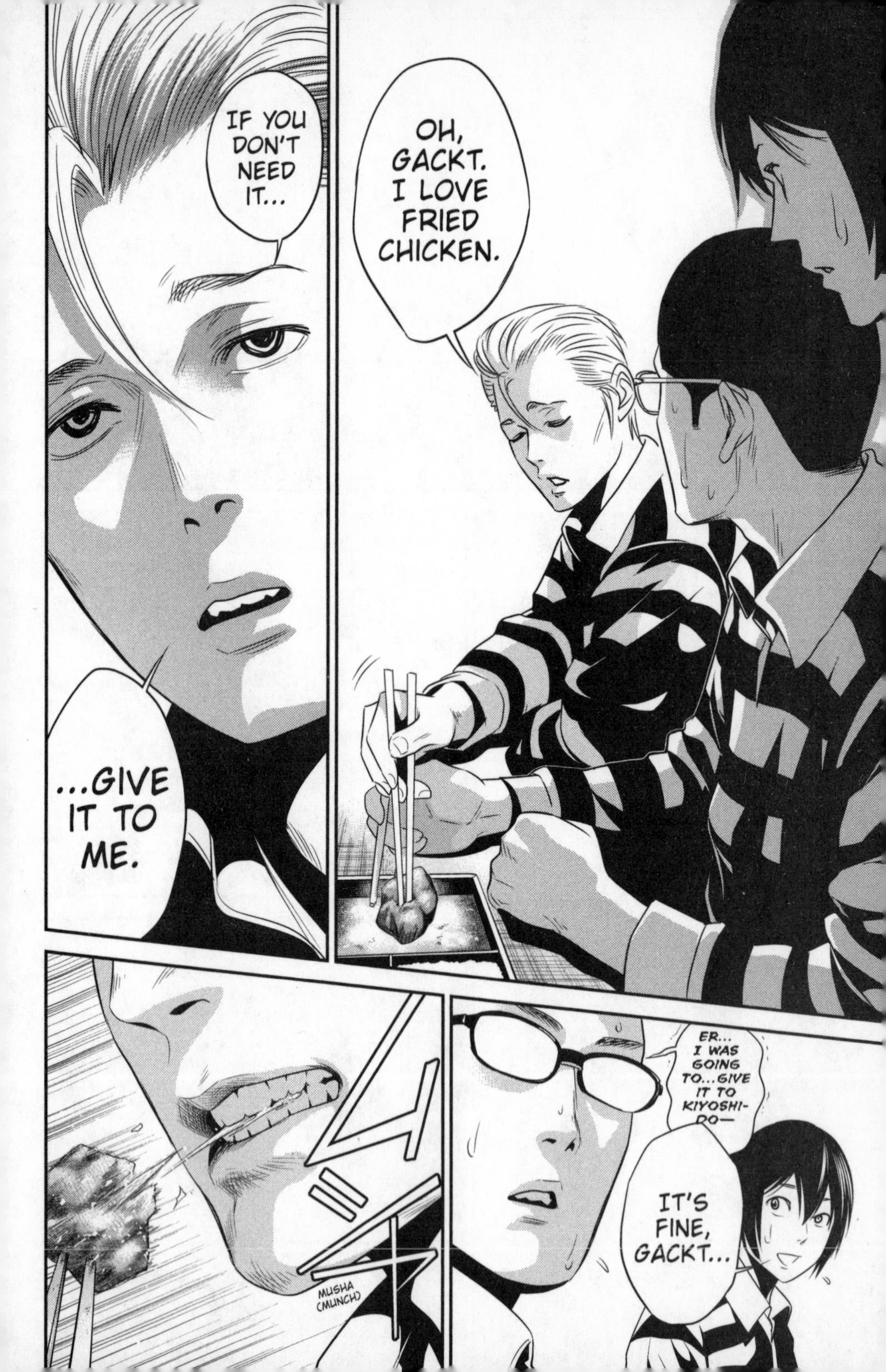

OH, GACKT. I LOVE FRIED CHICKEN.
IF YOU DON'T NEED IT...
...GIVE IT TO ME.
ER... I WAS GOING TO...GIVE IT TO KIYOSHI-DO—
IT'S FINE, GACKT...
MUSHA (MUNCH)

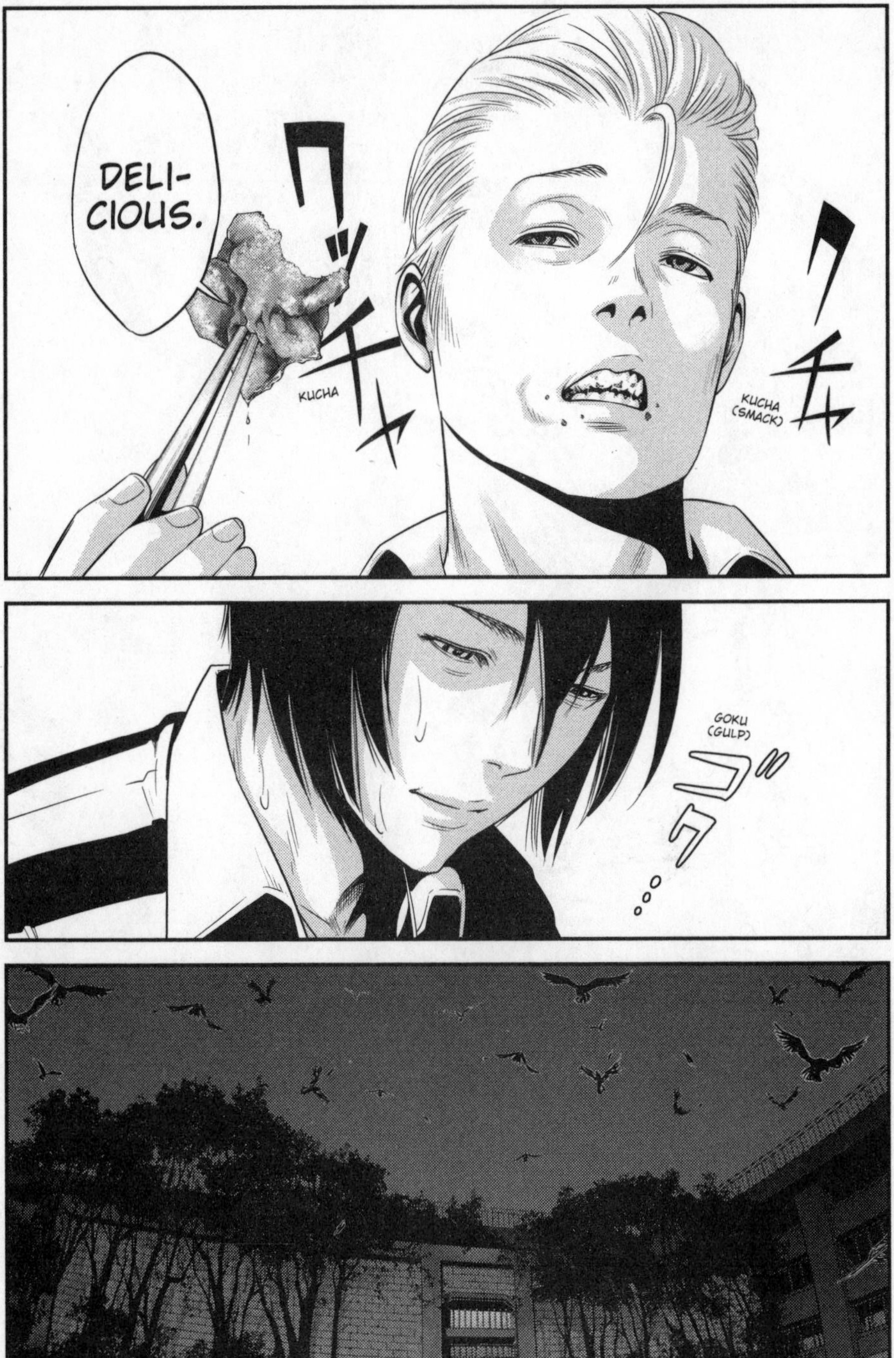
DELI-
CIOUS.
KUCHA
KUCHA
(SMACK)
GOKU
(GULP)

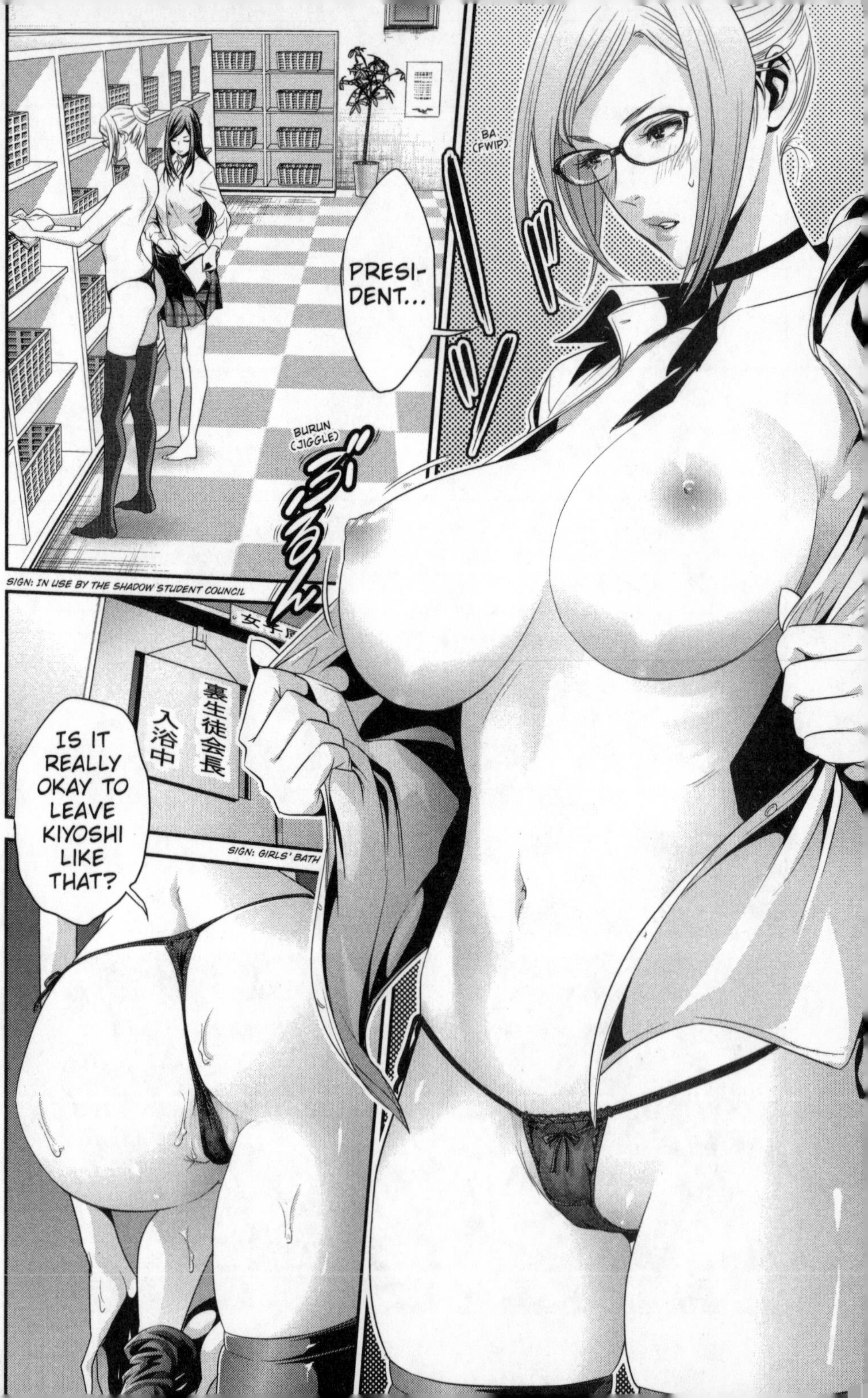
BA (FWIP)
PRESI-DENT...
BURUN (JIGGLE)
SIGN: IN USE BY THE SHADOW STUDENT COUNCIL
裏生徒会長
入浴中
IS IT REALLY OKAY TO LEAVE KIYOSHI LIKE THAT?
SIGN: GIRLS' BATH

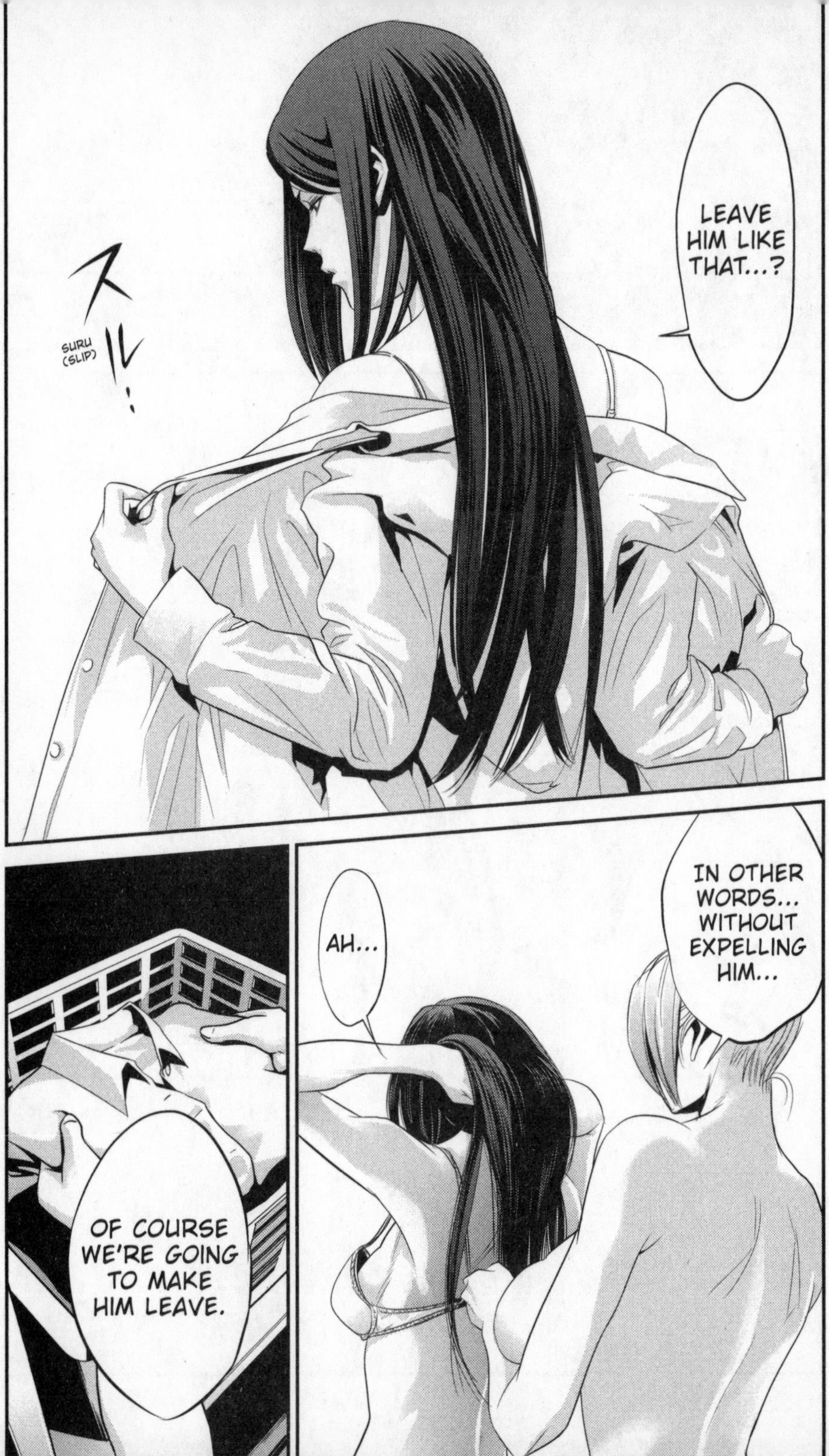

LEAVE HIM LIKE THAT...?
スル
SURU (SLIP)
IN OTHER WORDS... WITHOUT EXPELLING HIM...
AH...
OF COURSE WE'RE GOING TO MAKE HIM LEAVE.

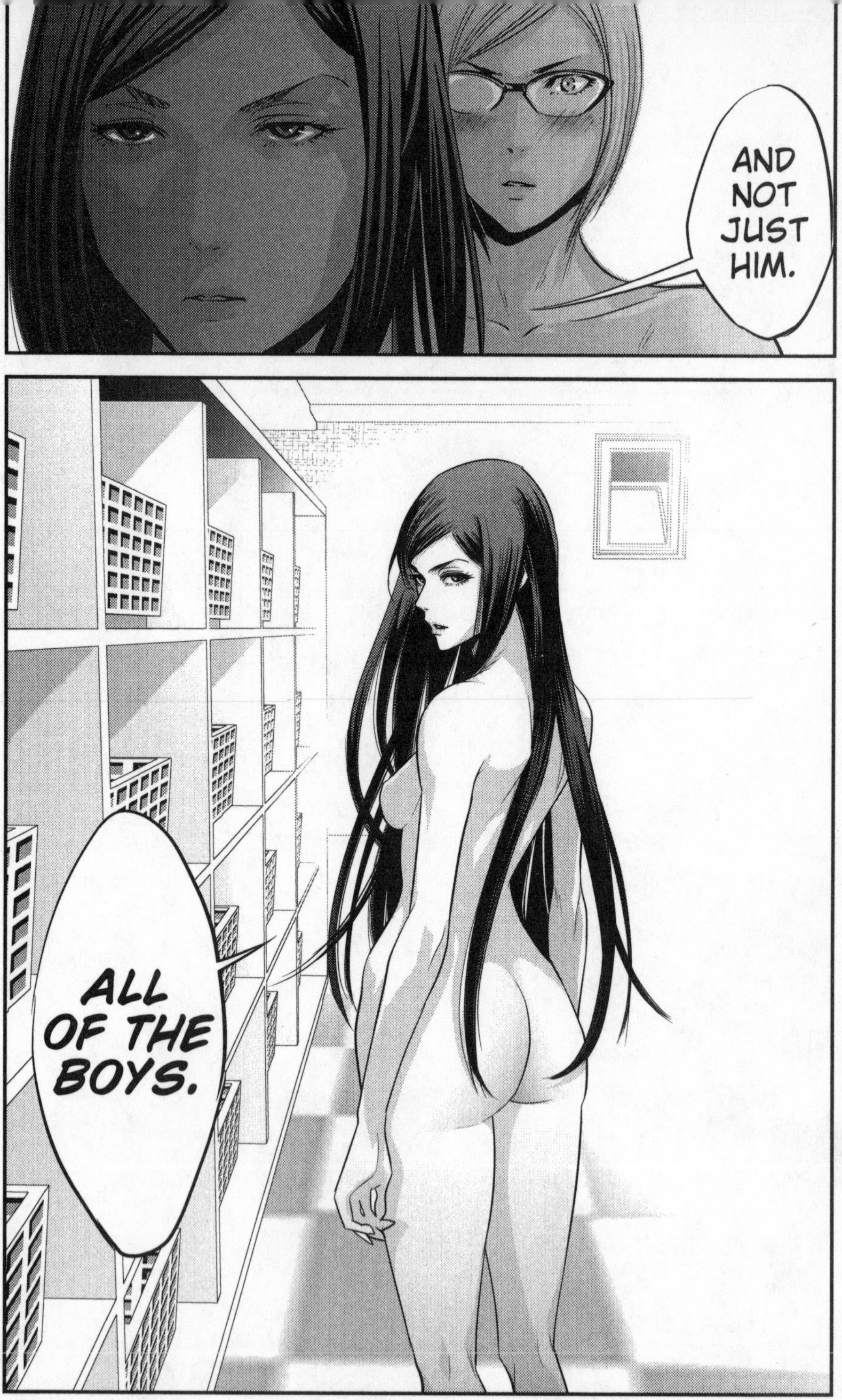
AND NOT JUST HIM.
ALL OF THE BOYS.

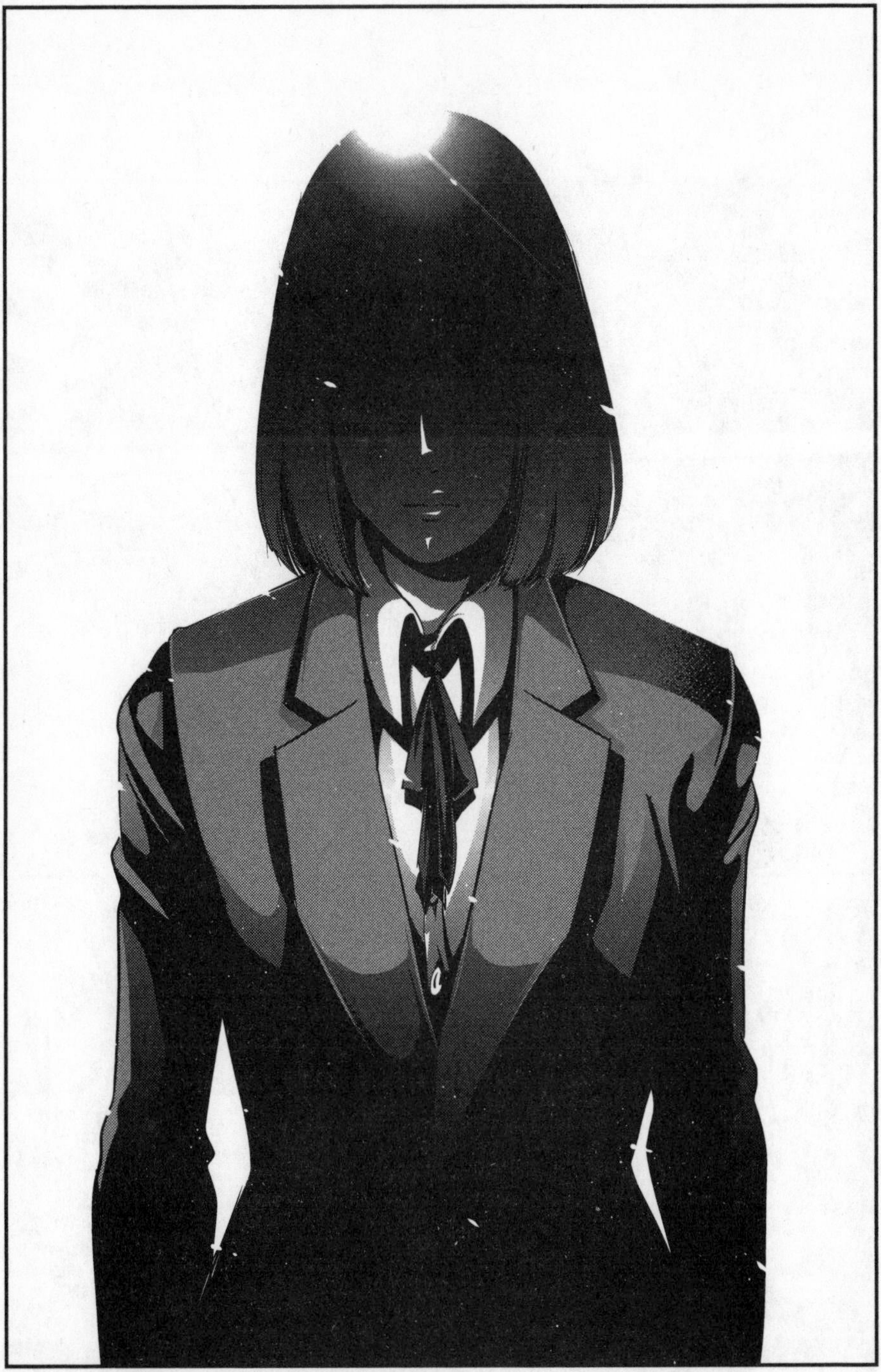

CHAPTER 34: OPERATION

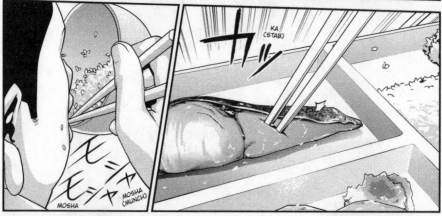

KA
(STAB)

MOSHA

MOSHA
(MUNCH)

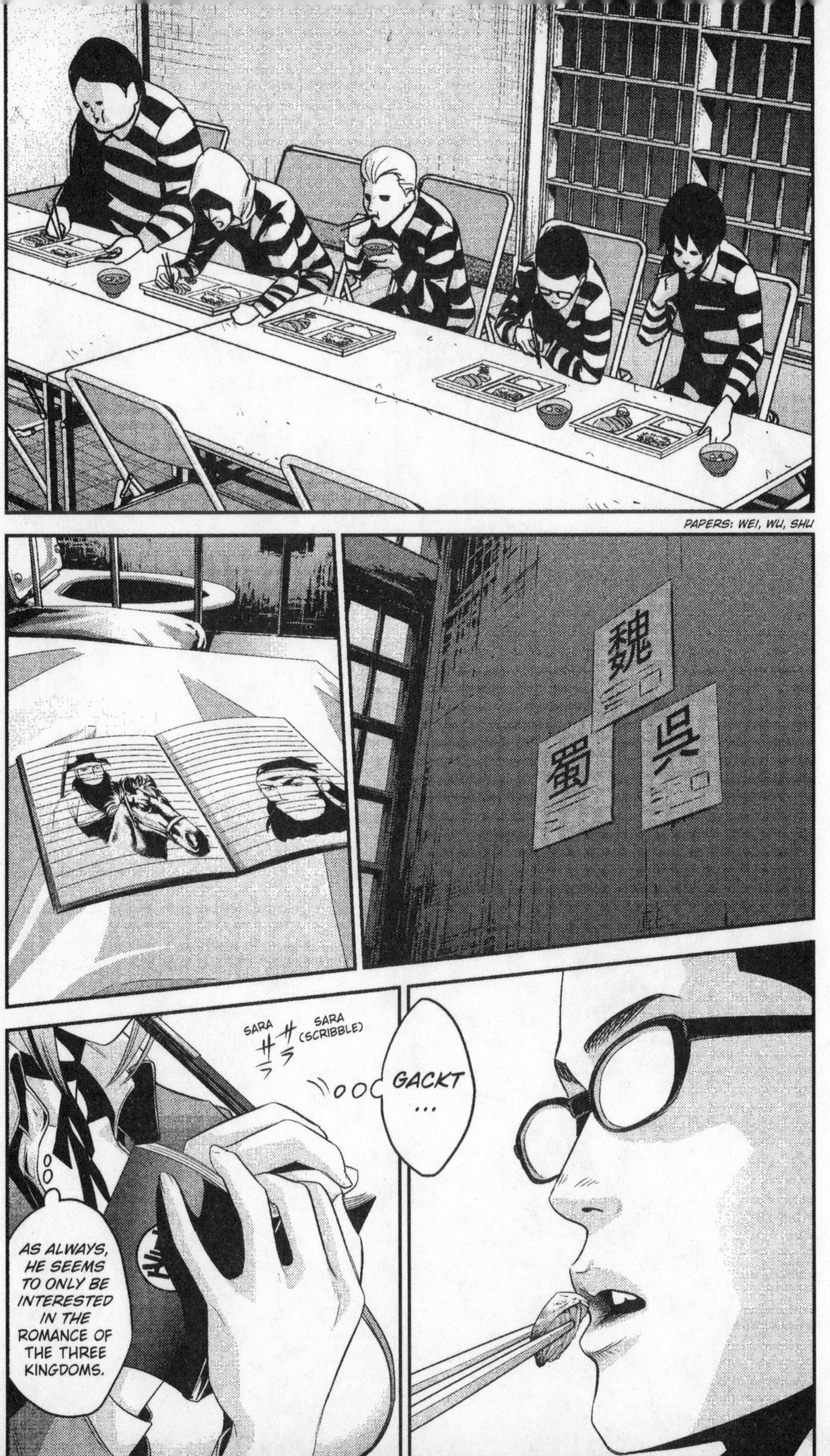
PAPERS: WEI, WU, SHU
魏
呉
蜀
GACKT ...
SARA SARA (SCRIBBLE)
AS ALWAYS, HE SEEMS TO ONLY BE INTERESTED IN THE ROMANCE OF THE THREE KINGDOMS.

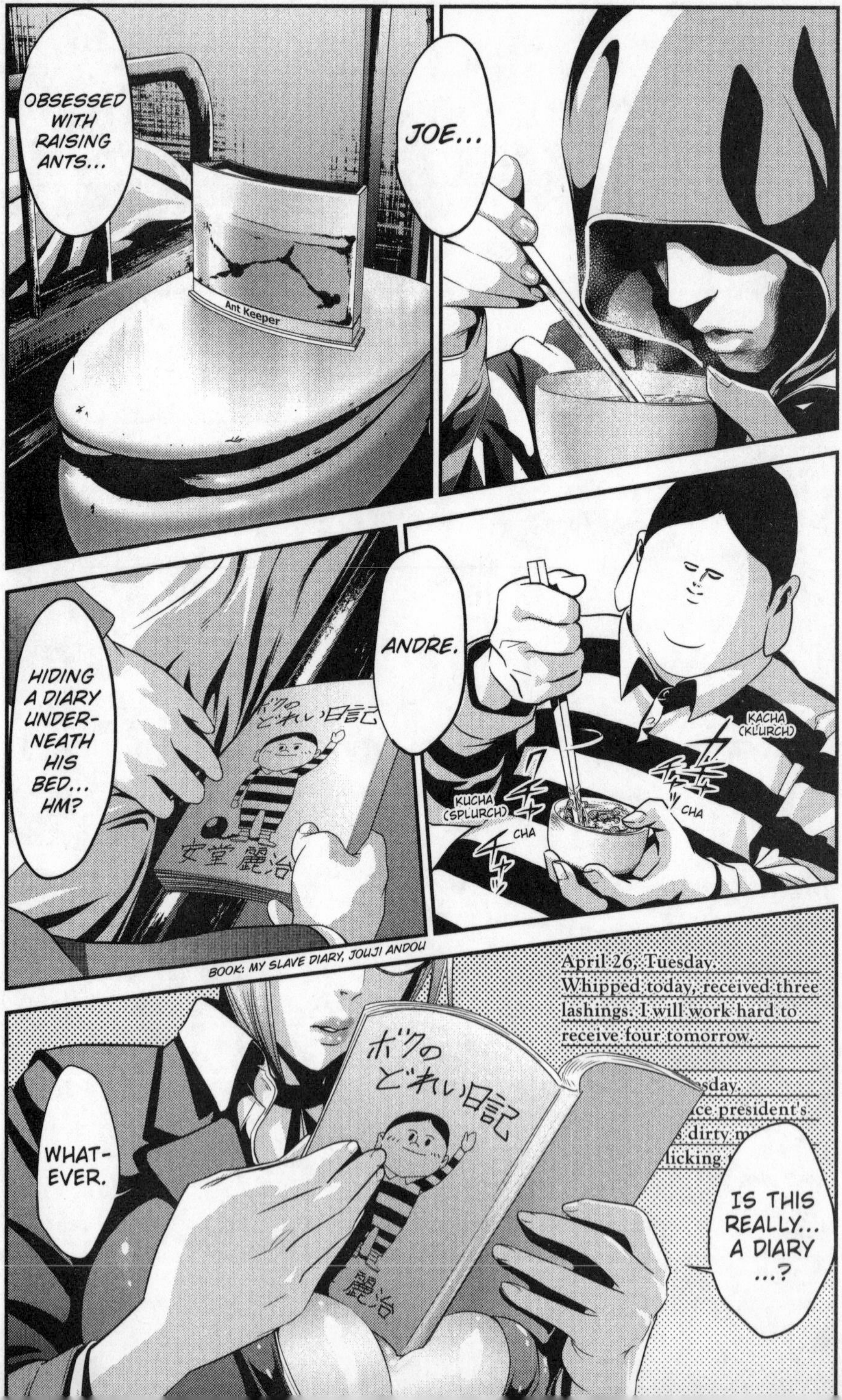
JOE...
OBSESSED WITH RAISING ANTS...
Ant Keeper
ANDRE.
KACHA (KL'URCH)
KUCHA (SPLURCH)
CHA
CHA
HIDING A DIARY UNDER-NEATH HIS BED... HM?
BOOK: MY SLAVE DIARY, JOUJI ANDOU
ボクのどれい日記
安堂麗治
April 26, Tuesday
Whipped today, received three lashings. I will work hard to receive four tomorrow.
IS THIS REALLY... A DIARY ...?
WHAT-EVER.

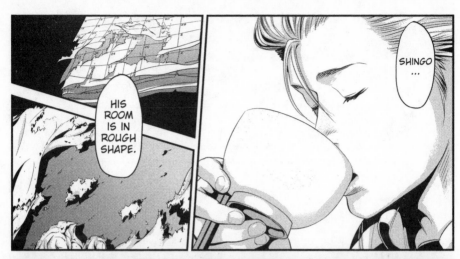

SHINGO ...
HIS ROOM IS IN ROUGH SHAPE.
HE SEEMS TO BE ANNOYED THAT HIS SENTENCE WAS EXTENDED ...
PERO (CLICK)
SARA
SARA (SCRIBBLE)

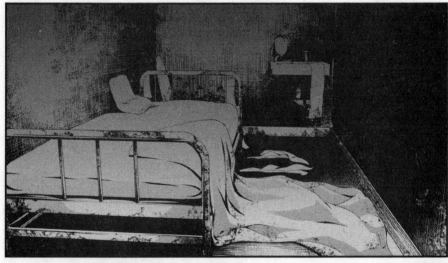

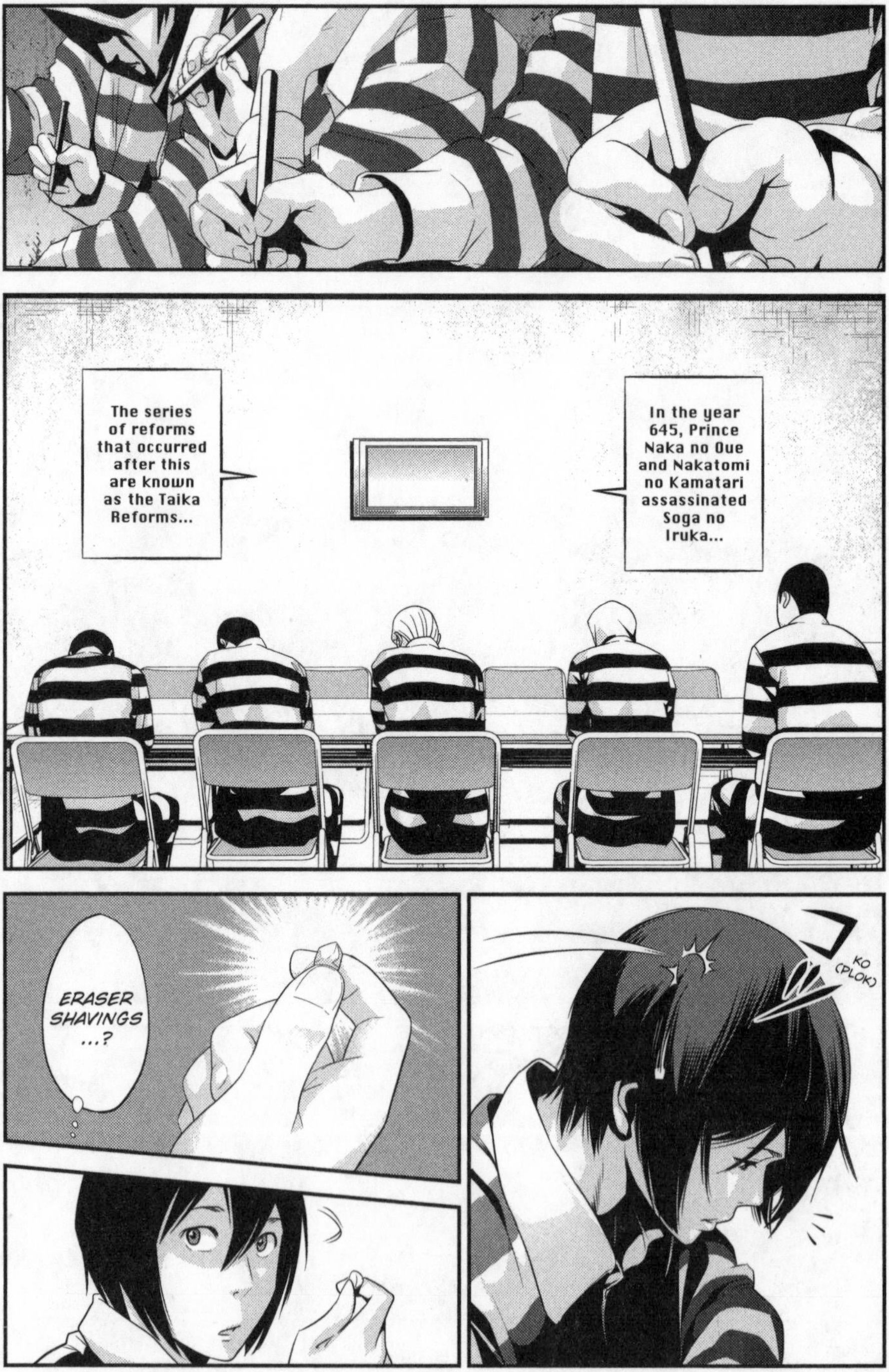
In the year 645, Prince Naka no Oue and Nakatomi no Kamatari assassinated Soga no Iruka...
The series of reforms that occurred after this are known as the Taika Reforms...
KO (PLOK)
ERASER SHAVINGS ...?

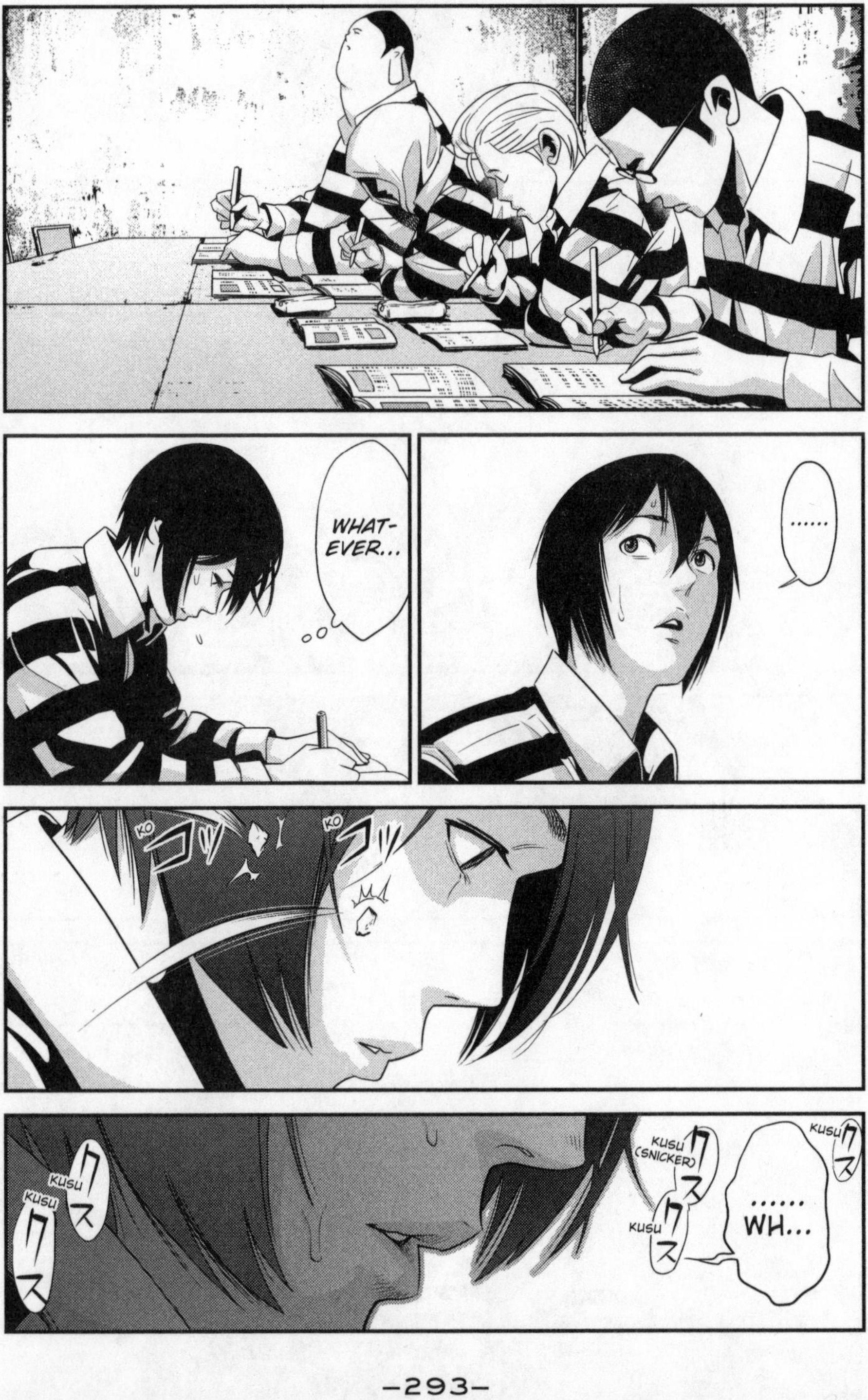
......
WHAT-
EVER...
KO コッ
KO コッ
KUSU クス
KUSU (SNICKER) クス
KUSU クス
......
WH...
KUSU クス
KUSU クス

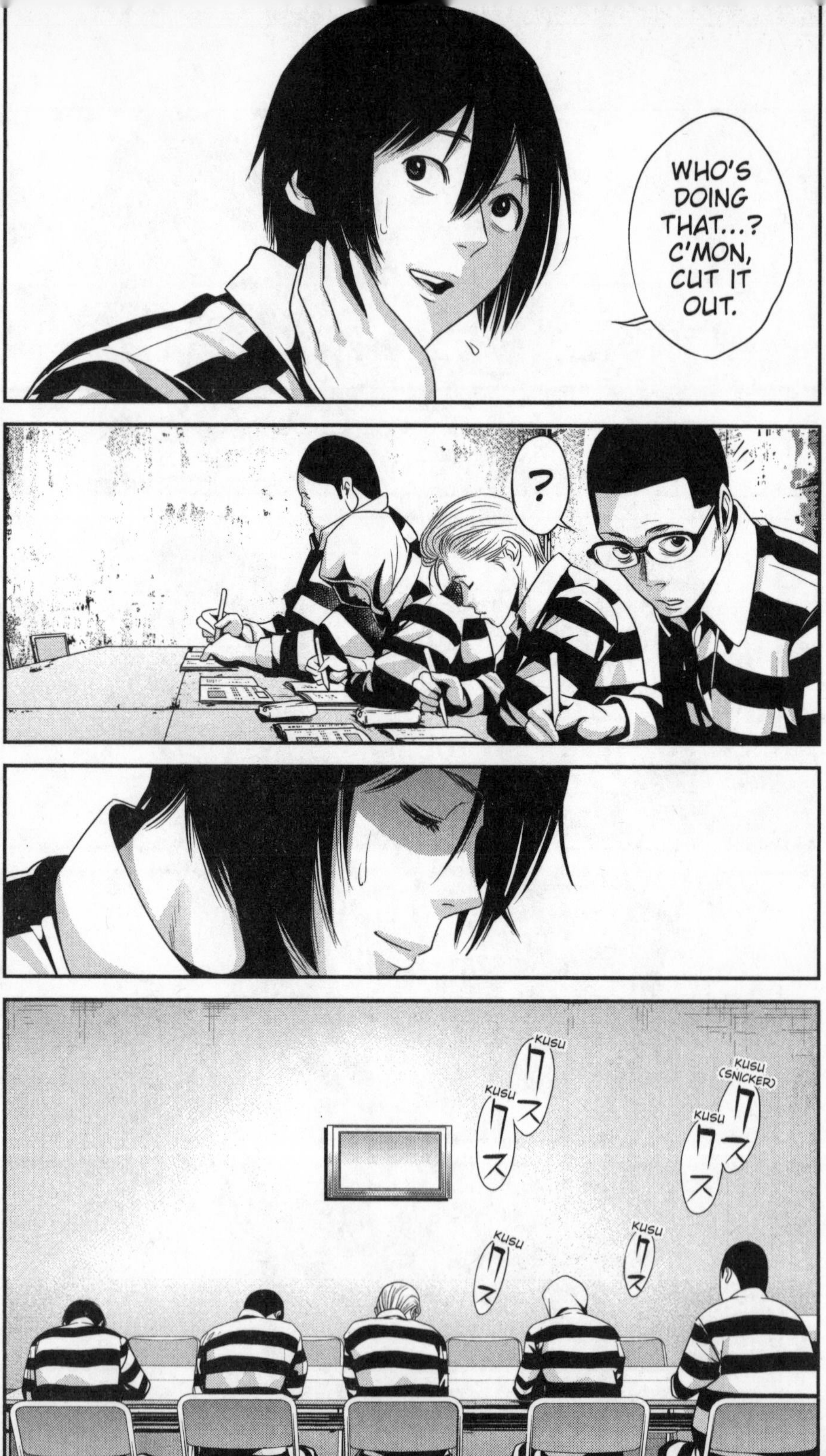
WHO'S DOING THAT...? C'MON, CUT IT OUT.
?
KUSU
クス
KUSU
クス
KUSU (SNICKER)
クス
KUSU
クス
KUSU
クス
KUSU
クス

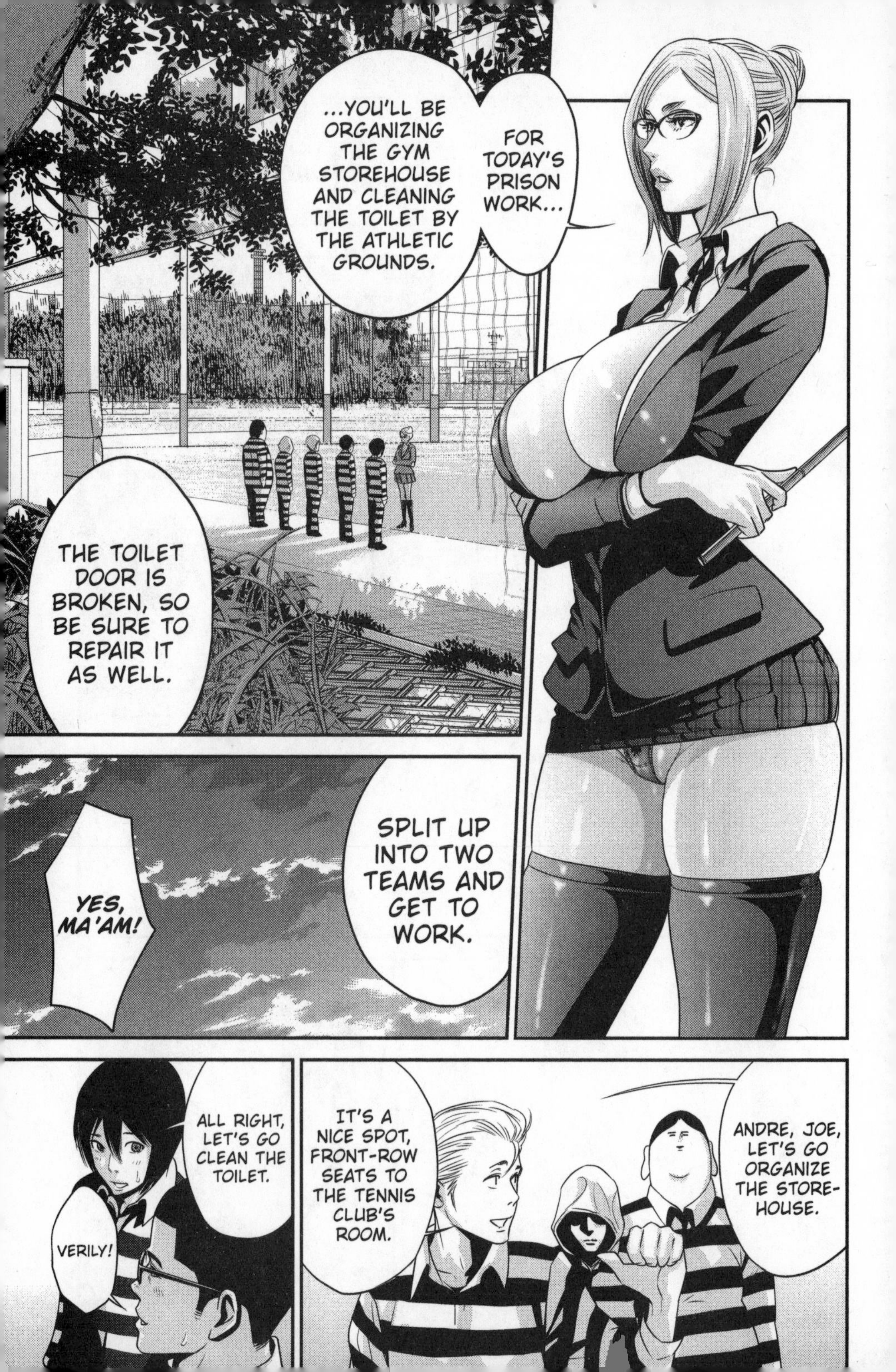
FOR TODAY'S PRISON WORK...
...YOU'LL BE ORGANIZING THE GYM STOREHOUSE AND CLEANING THE TOILET BY THE ATHLETIC GROUNDS.
THE TOILET DOOR IS BROKEN, SO BE SURE TO REPAIR IT AS WELL.
SPLIT UP INTO TWO TEAMS AND GET TO WORK.
YES, MA'AM!
ANDRE, JOE, LET'S GO ORGANIZE THE STORE-HOUSE.
IT'S A NICE SPOT, FRONT-ROW SEATS TO THE TENNIS CLUB'S ROOM.
ALL RIGHT, LET'S GO CLEAN THE TOILET.
VERILY!

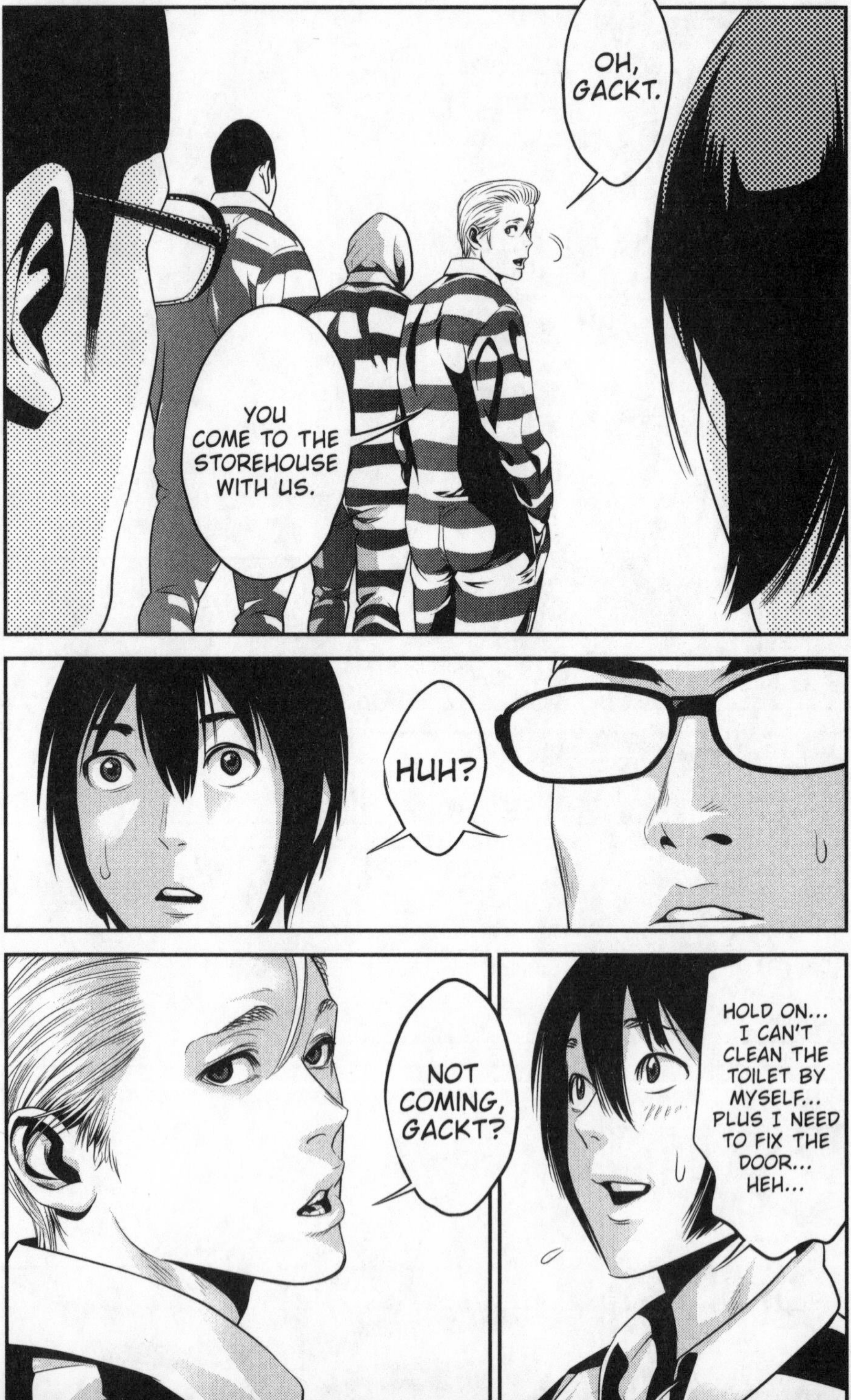
OH, GACKT.
YOU COME TO THE STOREHOUSE WITH US.
HUH?
HOLD ON... I CAN'T CLEAN THE TOILET BY MYSELF... PLUS I NEED TO FIX THE DOOR... HEH...
NOT COMING, GACKT?

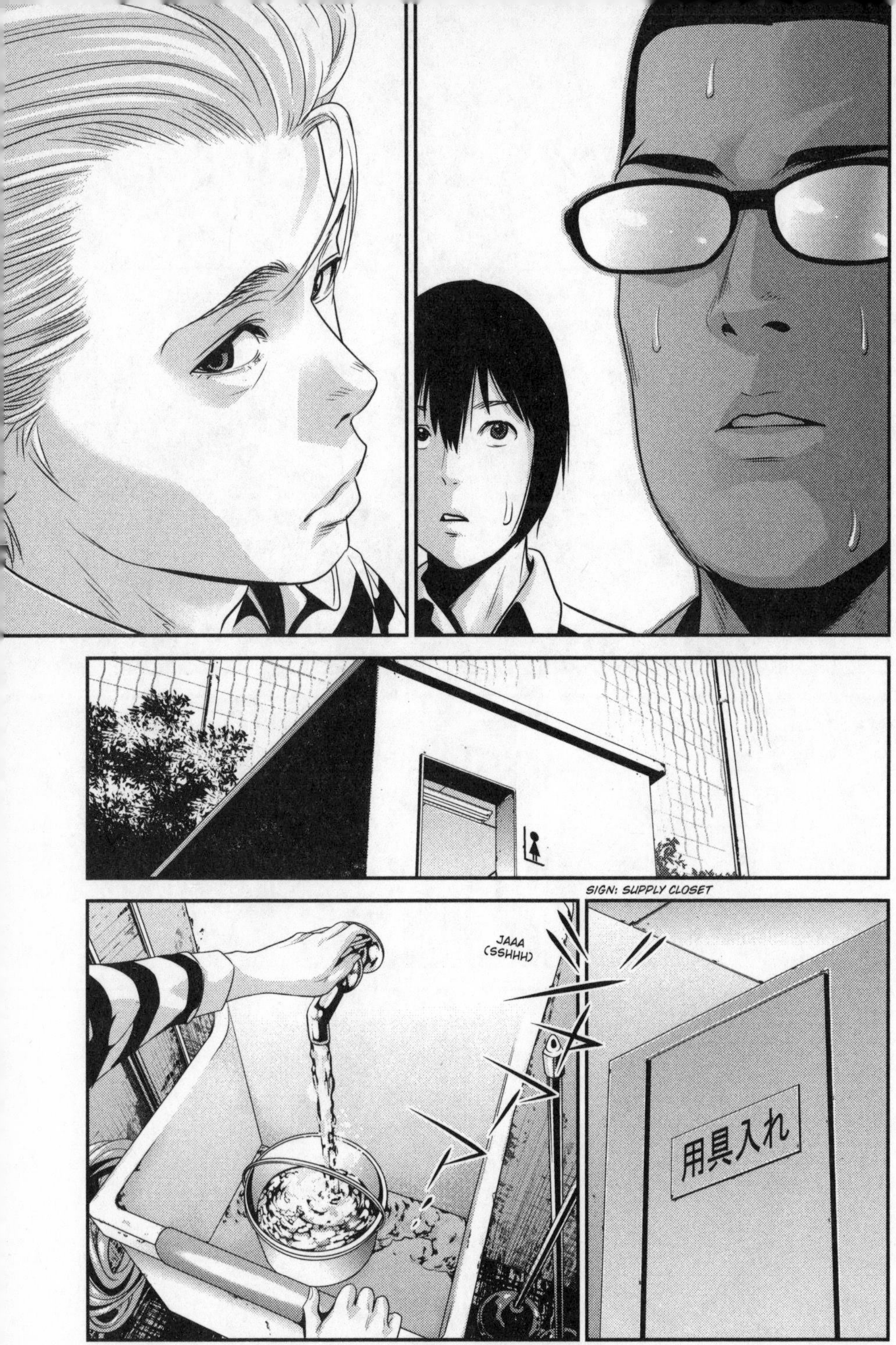
SIGN: SUPPLY CLOSET
JAAA
(SSHHH)
用具入れ

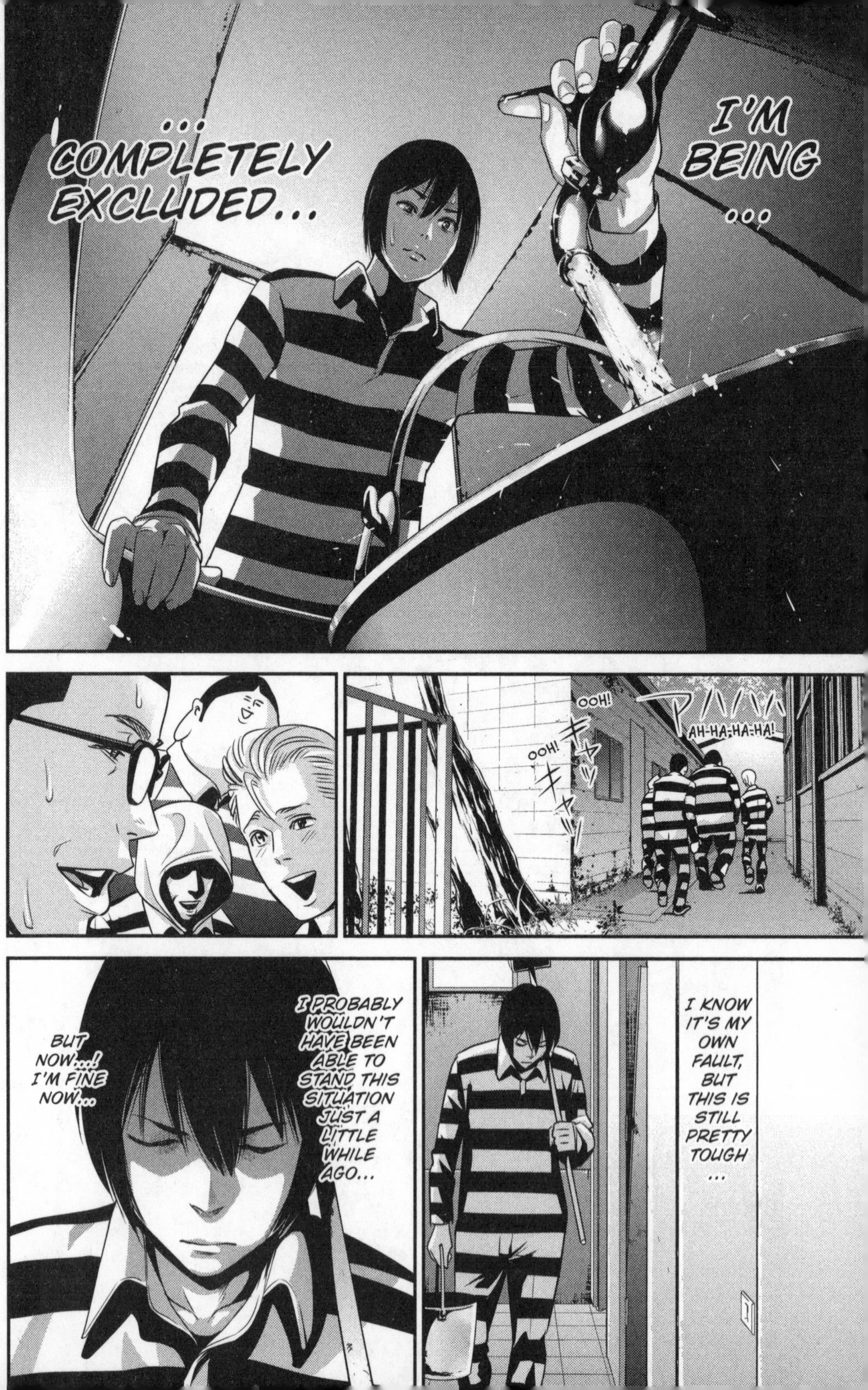
I'M BEING ...
...COMPLETELY EXCLUDED...
AH-HA-HA-HA!
OOH!
OOH!
I KNOW IT'S MY OWN FAULT, BUT THIS IS STILL PRETTY TOUGH...
I PROBABLY WOULDN'T HAVE BEEN ABLE TO STAND THIS SITUATION JUST A LITTLE WHILE AGO...
BUT NOW...! I'M FINE NOW...

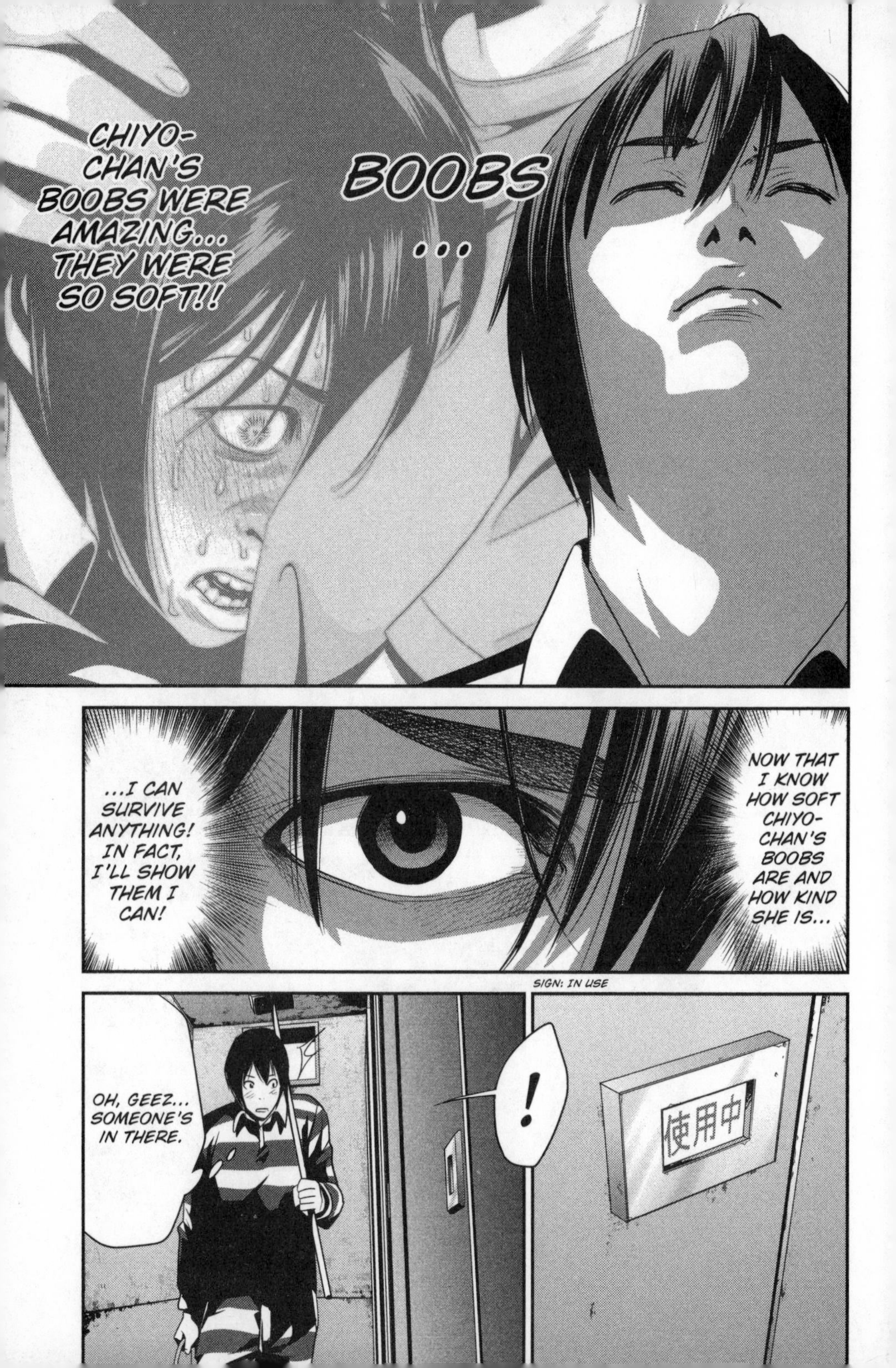
BOOBS
...
CHIYO-CHAN'S BOOBS WERE AMAZING... THEY WERE SO SOFT!!
NOW THAT I KNOW HOW SOFT CHIYO-CHAN'S BOOBS ARE AND HOW KIND SHE IS...
...I CAN SURVIVE ANYTHING! IN FACT, I'LL SHOW THEM I CAN!
SIGN: IN USE
使用中
!
OH, GEEZ... SOMEONE'S IN THERE.

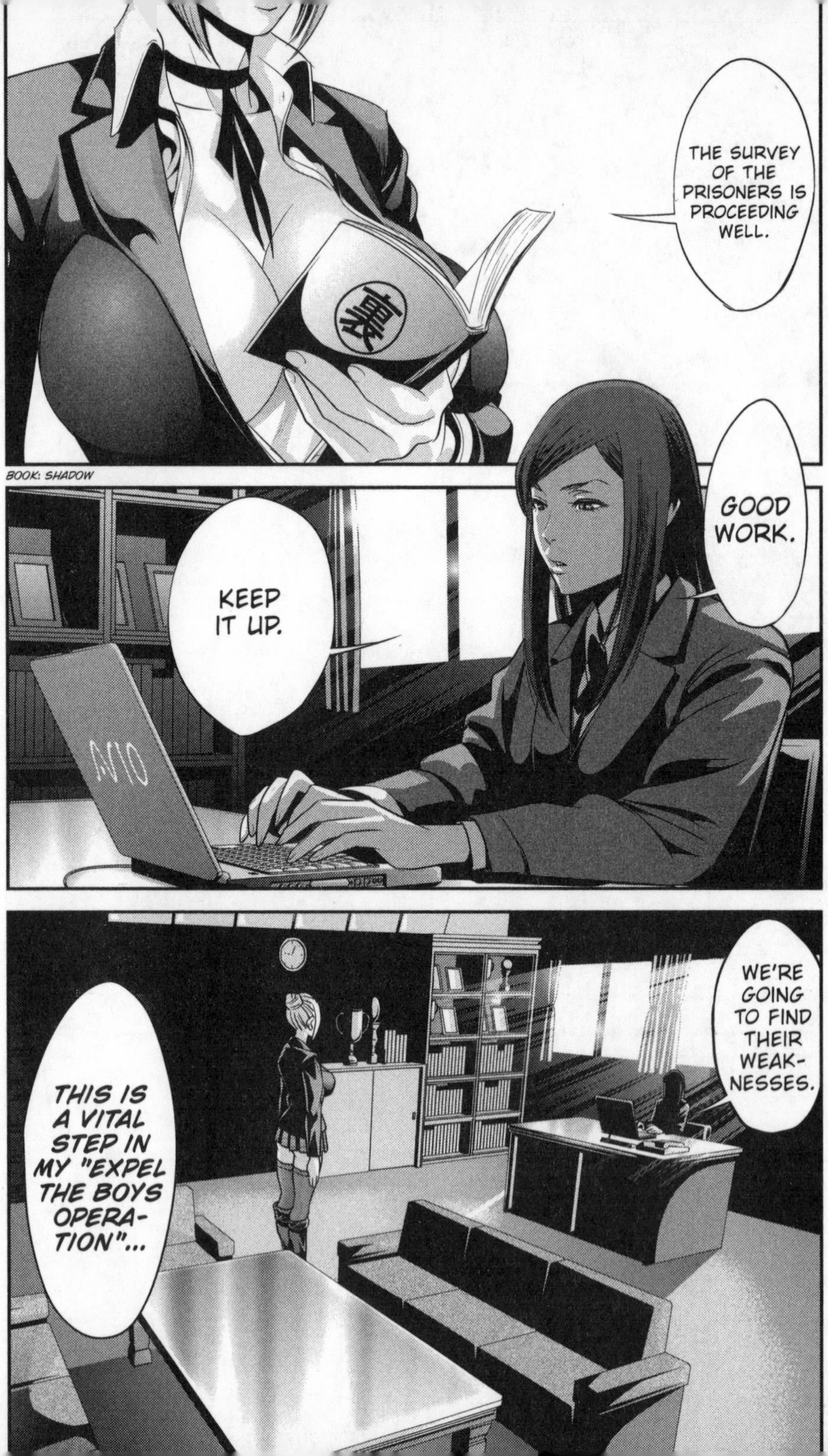
THE SURVEY OF THE PRISONERS IS PROCEEDING WELL.
裏
BOOK: SHADOW
GOOD WORK.
KEEP IT UP.
WE'RE GOING TO FIND THEIR WEAK-NESSES.
THIS IS A VITAL STEP IN MY "EXPEL THE BOYS OPERA-TION"...

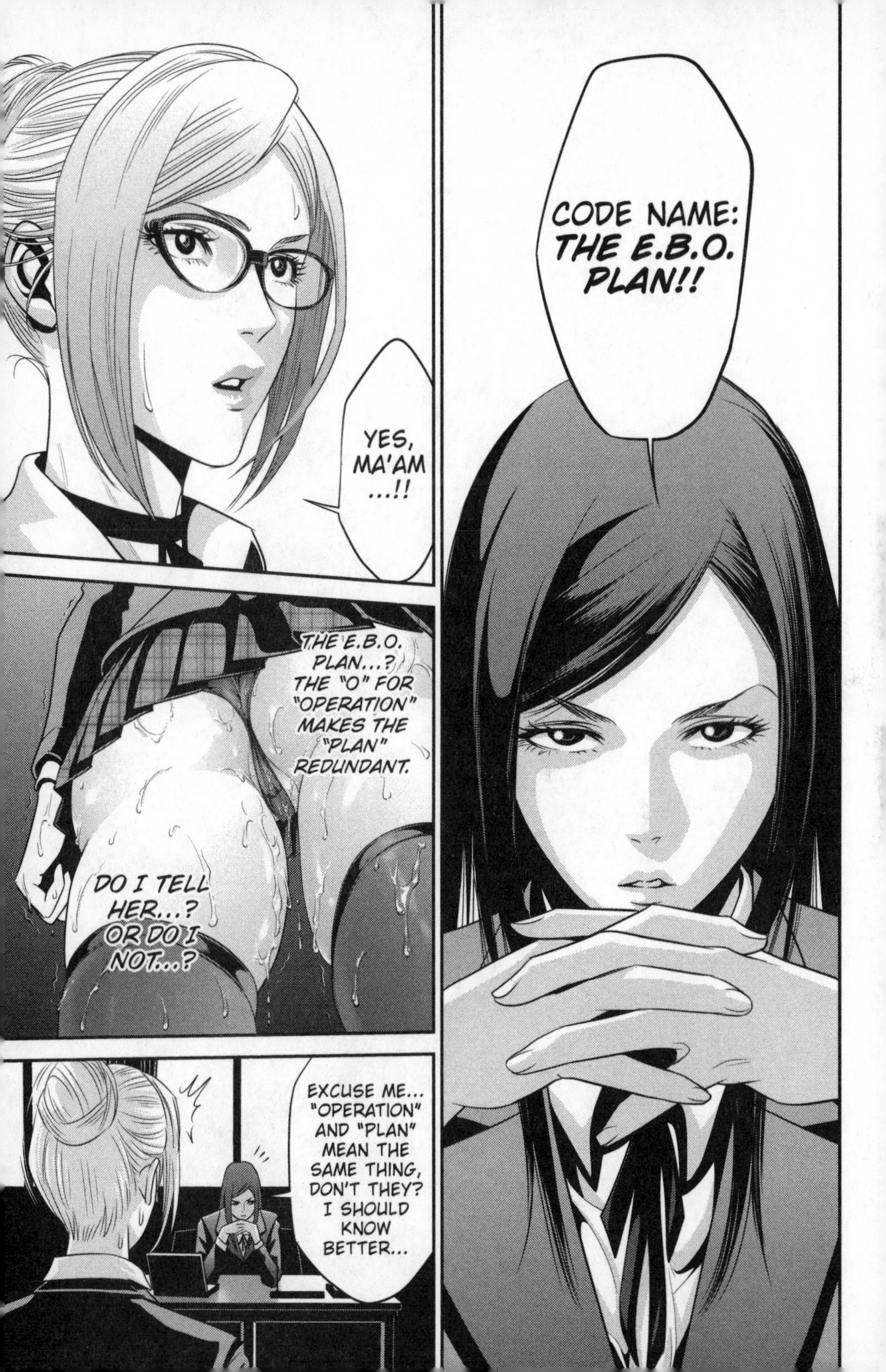
CODE NAME: THE E.B.O. PLAN!!
YES, MA'AM ...!!
THE E.B.O. PLAN...? THE "O" FOR "OPERATION" MAKES THE "PLAN" REDUNDANT.
DO I TELL HER...? OR DO I NOT...?
EXCUSE ME... "OPERATION" AND "PLAN" MEAN THE SAME THING, DON'T THEY? I SHOULD KNOW BETTER...

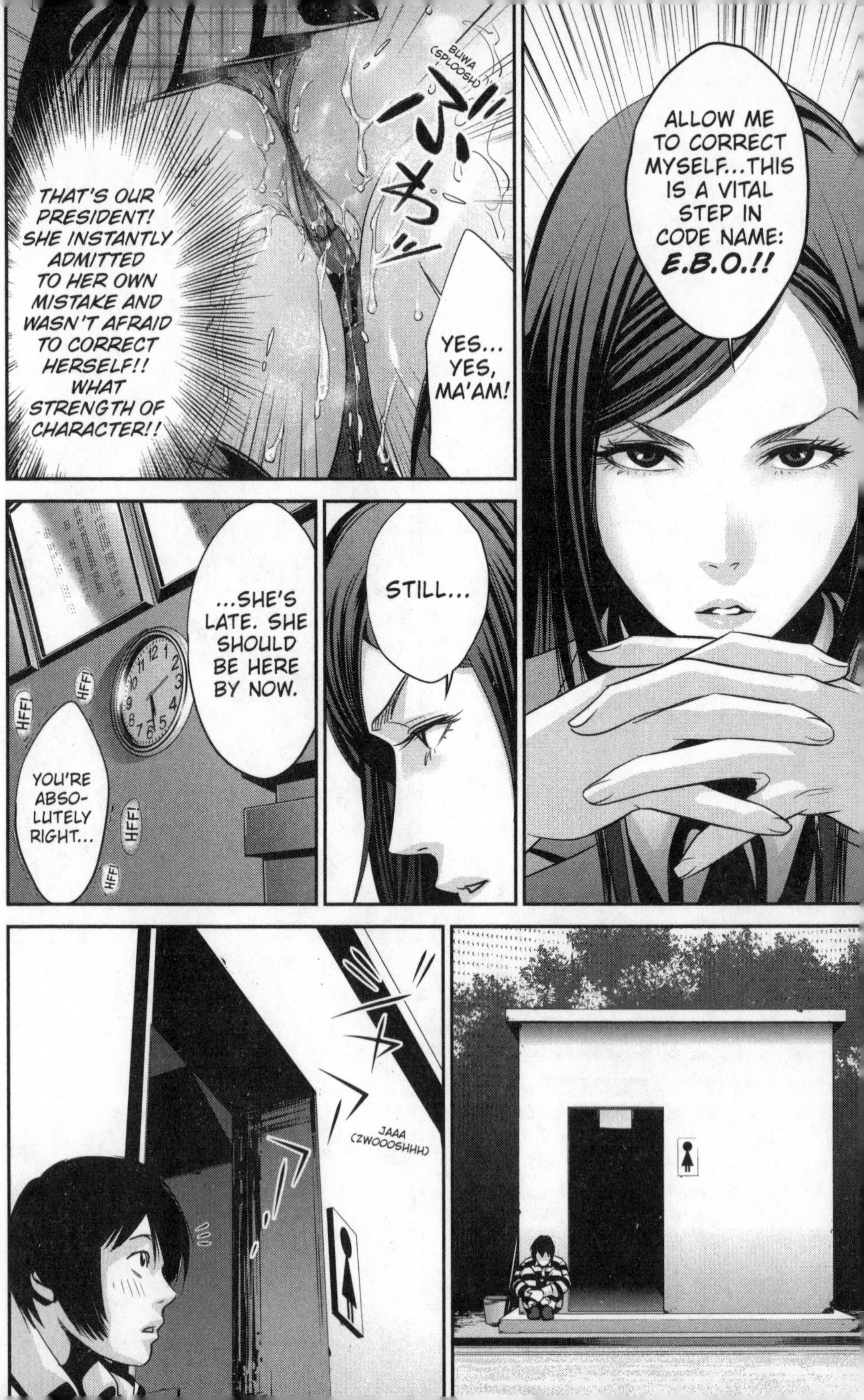
ALLOW ME TO CORRECT MYSELF...THIS IS A VITAL STEP IN CODE NAME: E.B.O.!!
YES... YES, MA'AM!
BUWA (SPLOOSH)
THAT'S OUR PRESIDENT! SHE INSTANTLY ADMITTED TO HER OWN MISTAKE AND WASN'T AFRAID TO CORRECT HERSELF!! WHAT STRENGTH OF CHARACTER!!
STILL...
...SHE'S LATE. SHE SHOULD BE HERE BY NOW.
HFF!
HFF!
YOU'RE ABSO-LUTELY RIGHT...
HFF!
HFF!
JAAA (ZWOOOSHHH)

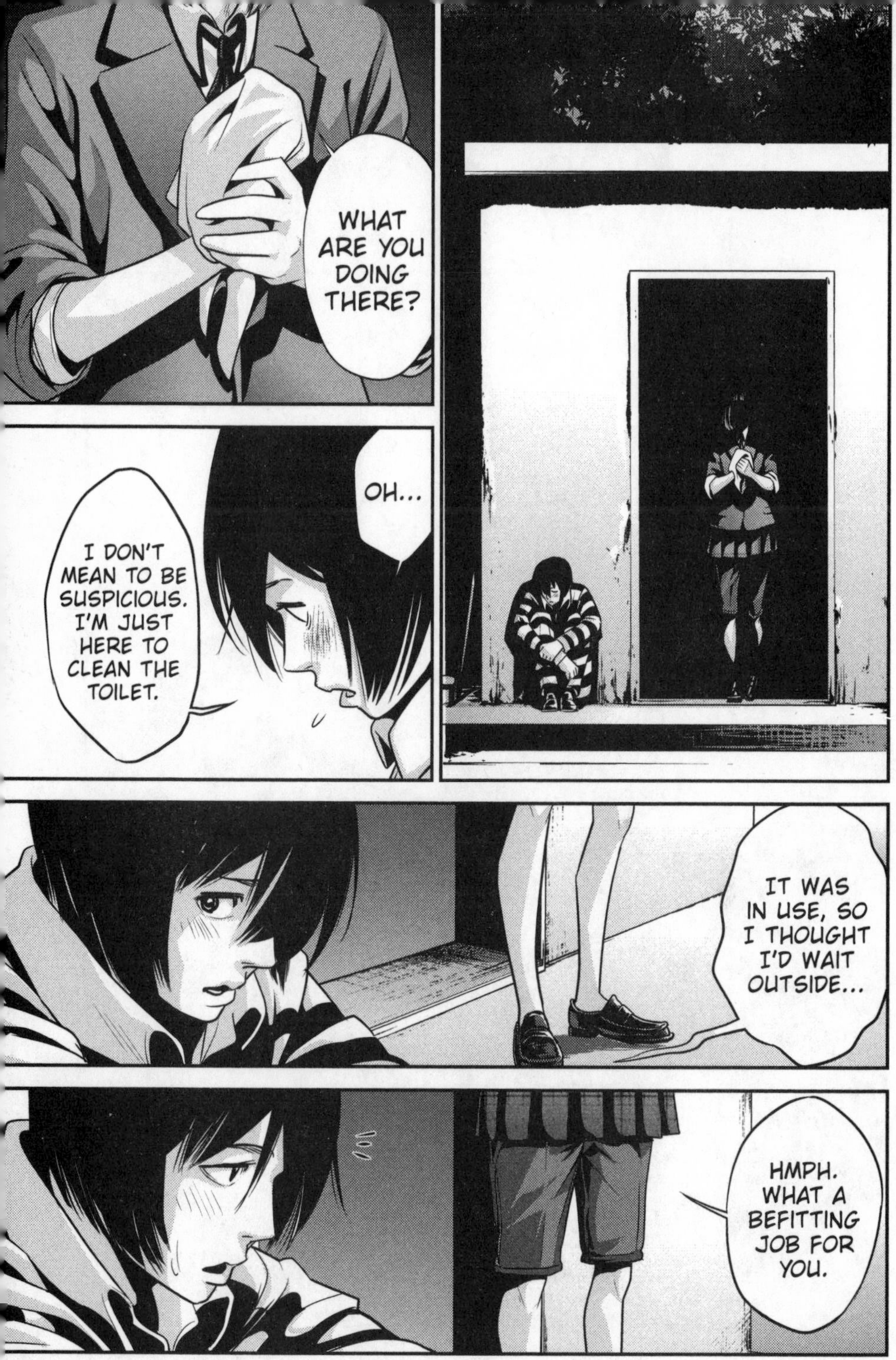
WHAT ARE YOU DOING THERE?
OH...
I DON'T MEAN TO BE SUSPICIOUS. I'M JUST HERE TO CLEAN THE TOILET.
IT WAS IN USE, SO I THOUGHT I'D WAIT OUTSIDE...
HMPH. WHAT A BEFITTING JOB FOR YOU.

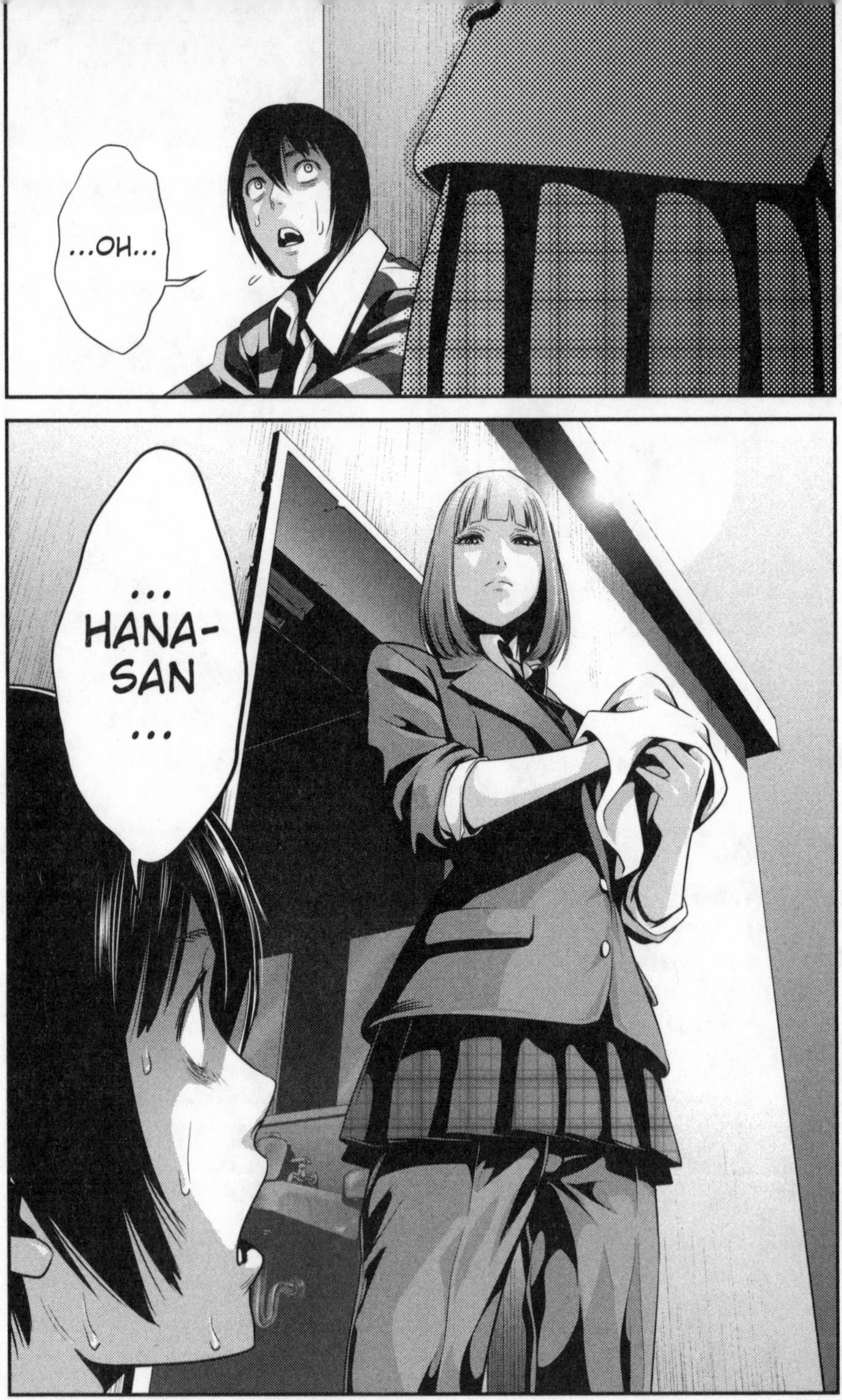
...OH...
... HANA-SAN ...

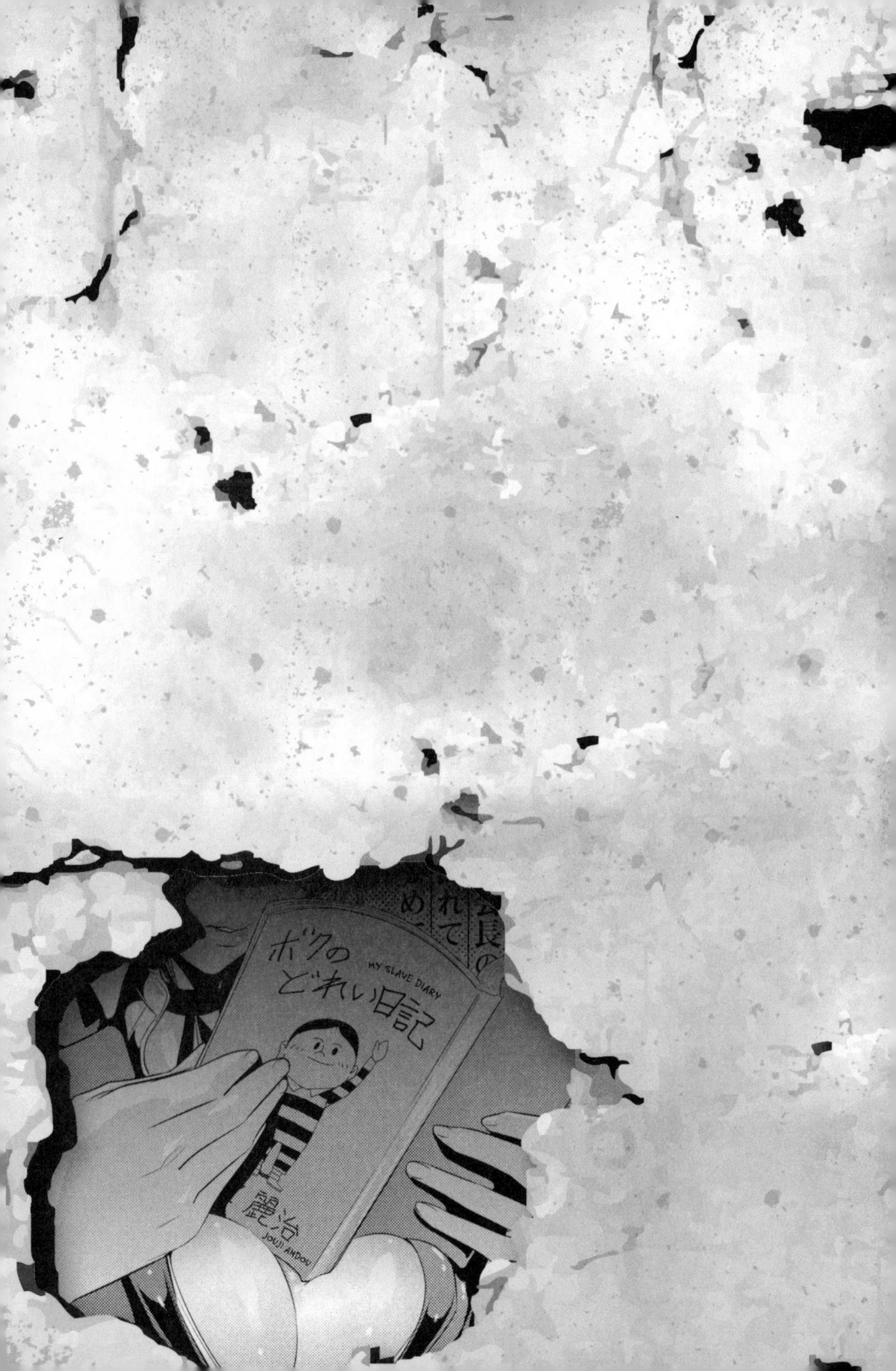
ボクのどれい日記
MY SLAVE DIARY
麗治
JOUJI ANDOU

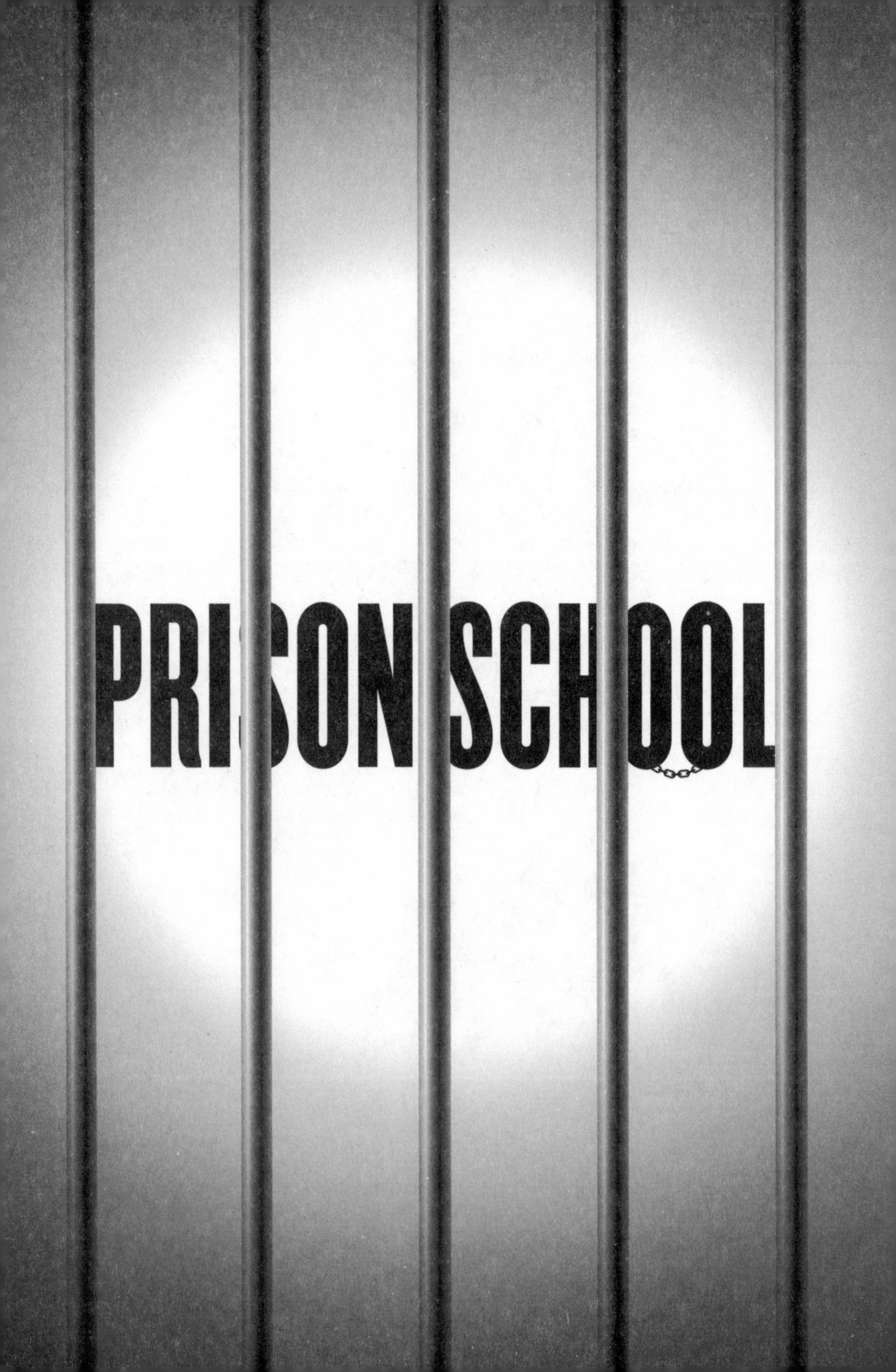
PRISON SCHOOL

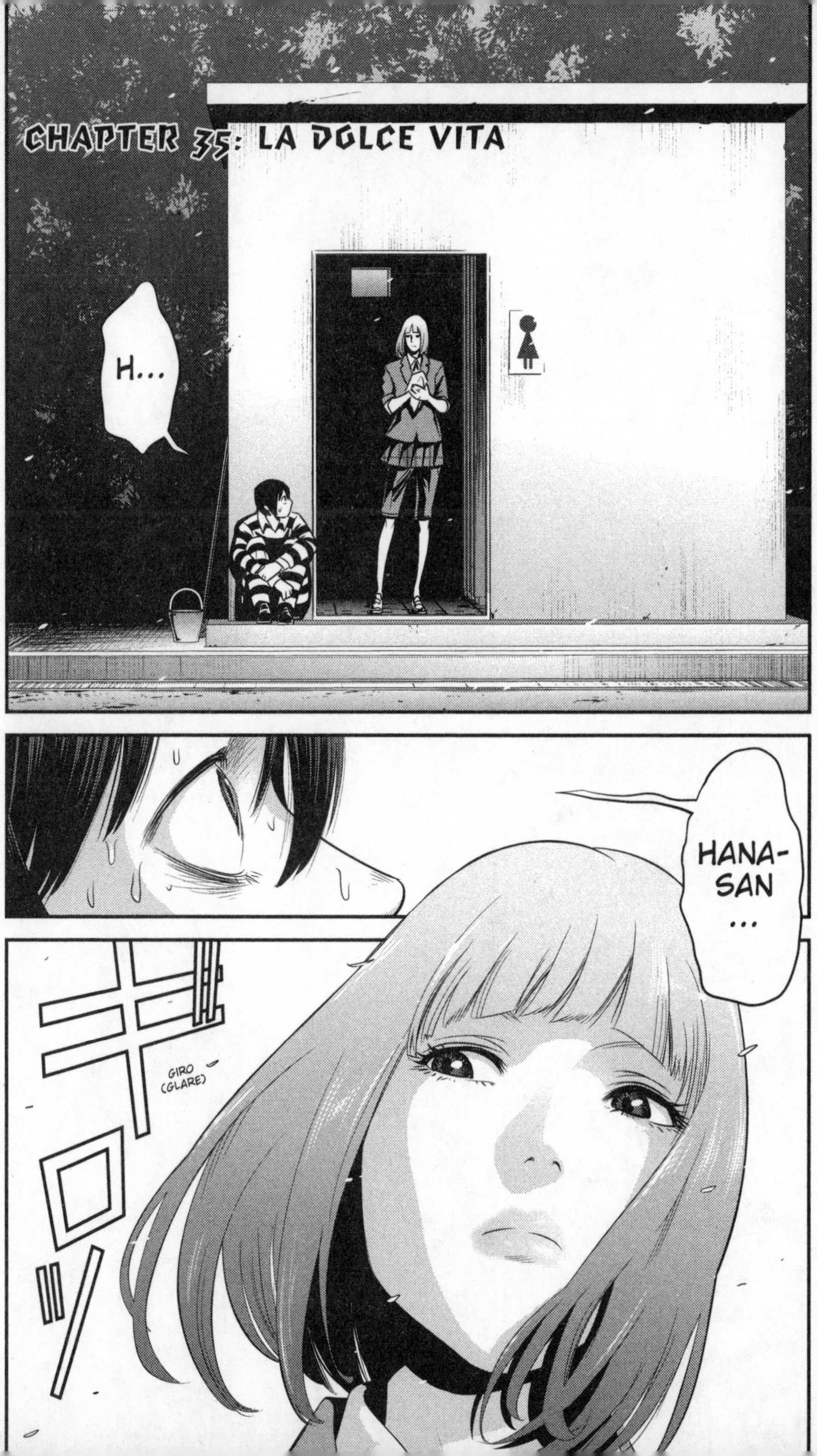
CHAPTER 35: LA DOLCE VITA
H...
HANA-SAN...
GIRO (GLARE)

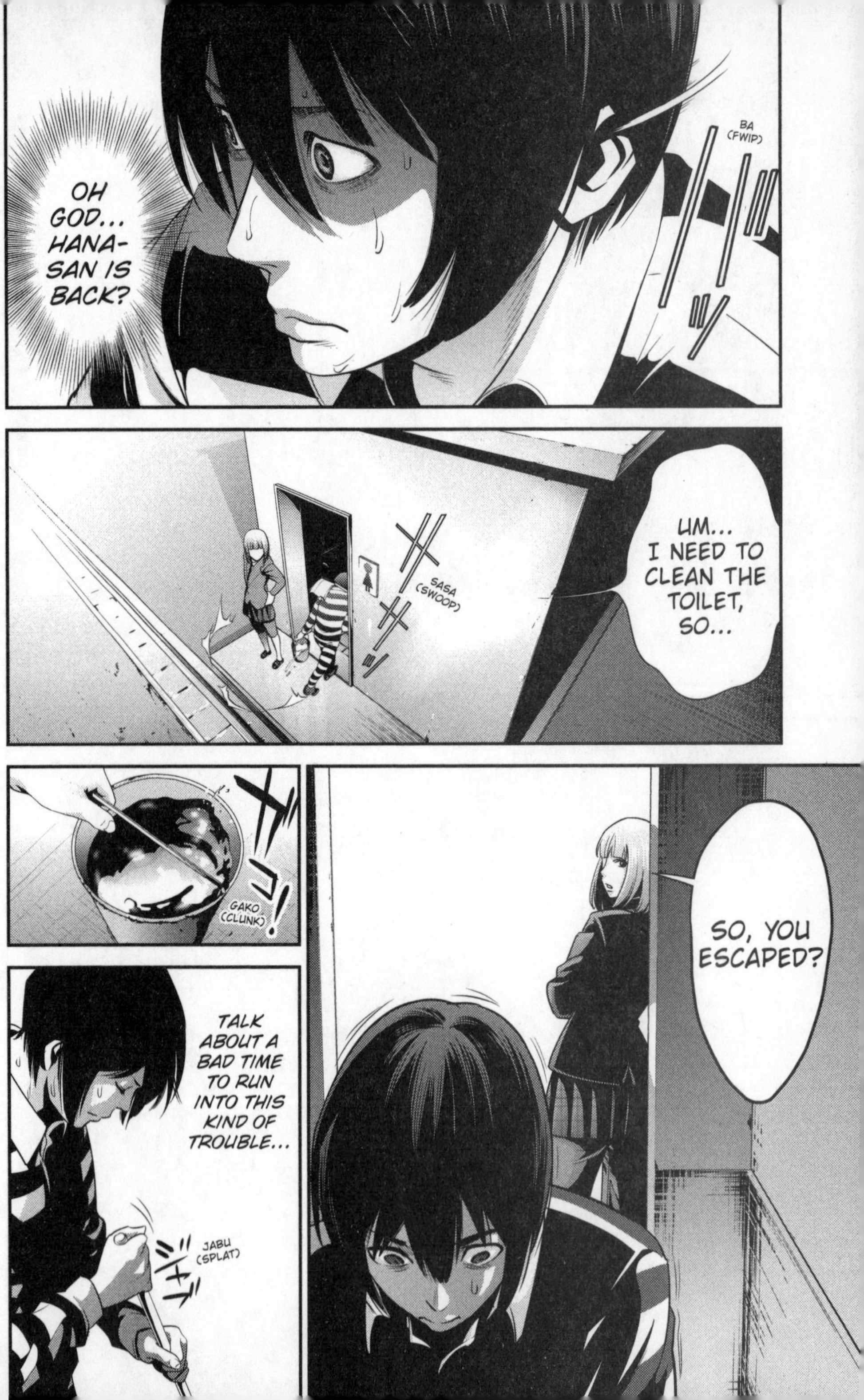
BA
(FWIP)
OH GOD... HANA-SAN IS BACK?
UM... I NEED TO CLEAN THE TOILET, SO...
SASA
(SWOOP)
SO, YOU ESCAPED?
GAKO
(CLUNK)
TALK ABOUT A BAD TIME TO RUN INTO THIS KIND OF TROUBLE...
JABU
(SPLAT)

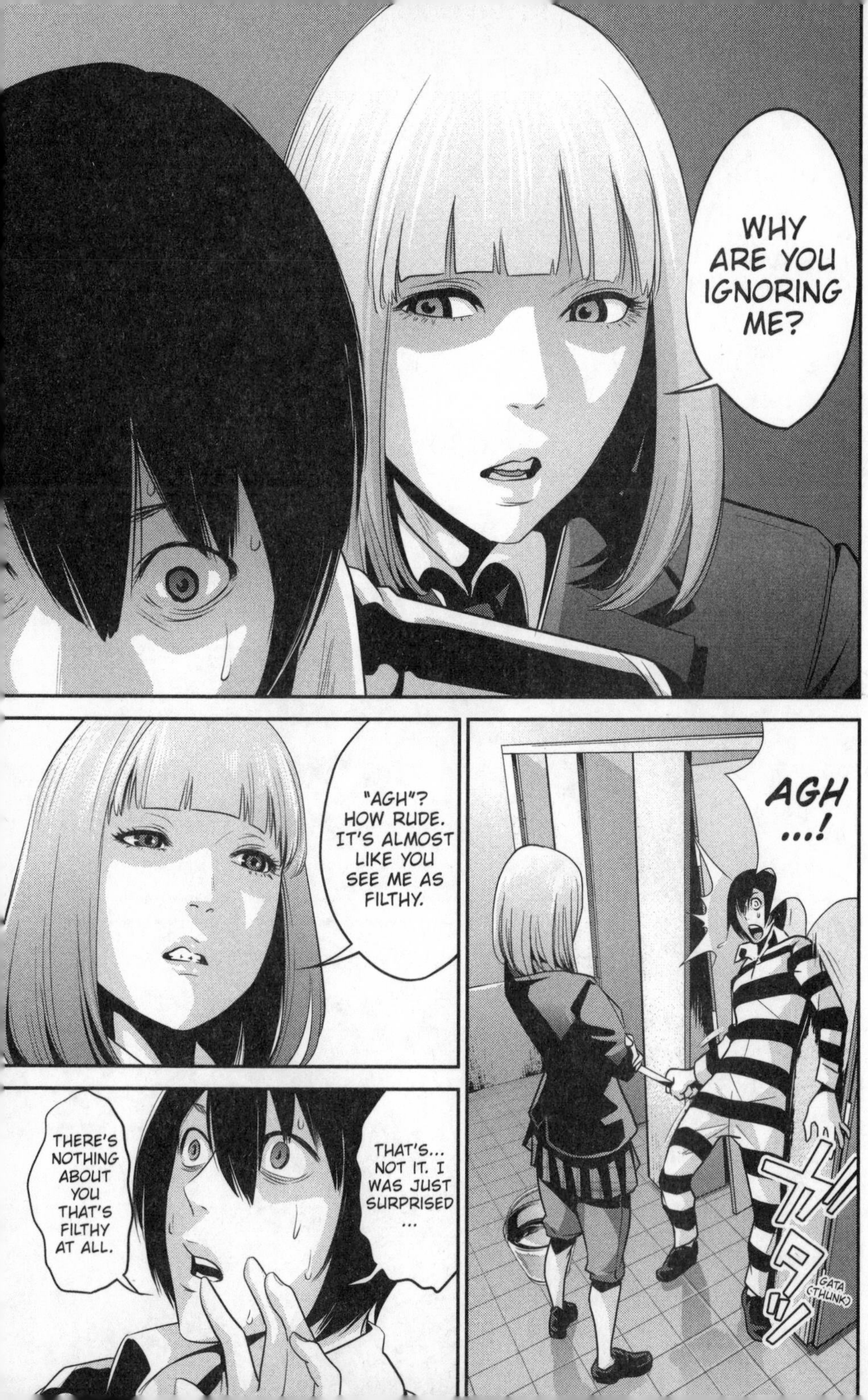
WHY ARE YOU IGNORING ME?
AGH ...!
GATA (THUNK)
"AGH"? HOW RUDE. IT'S ALMOST LIKE YOU SEE ME AS FILTHY.
THAT'S... NOT IT. I WAS JUST SURPRISED ...
THERE'S NOTHING ABOUT YOU THAT'S FILTHY AT ALL.

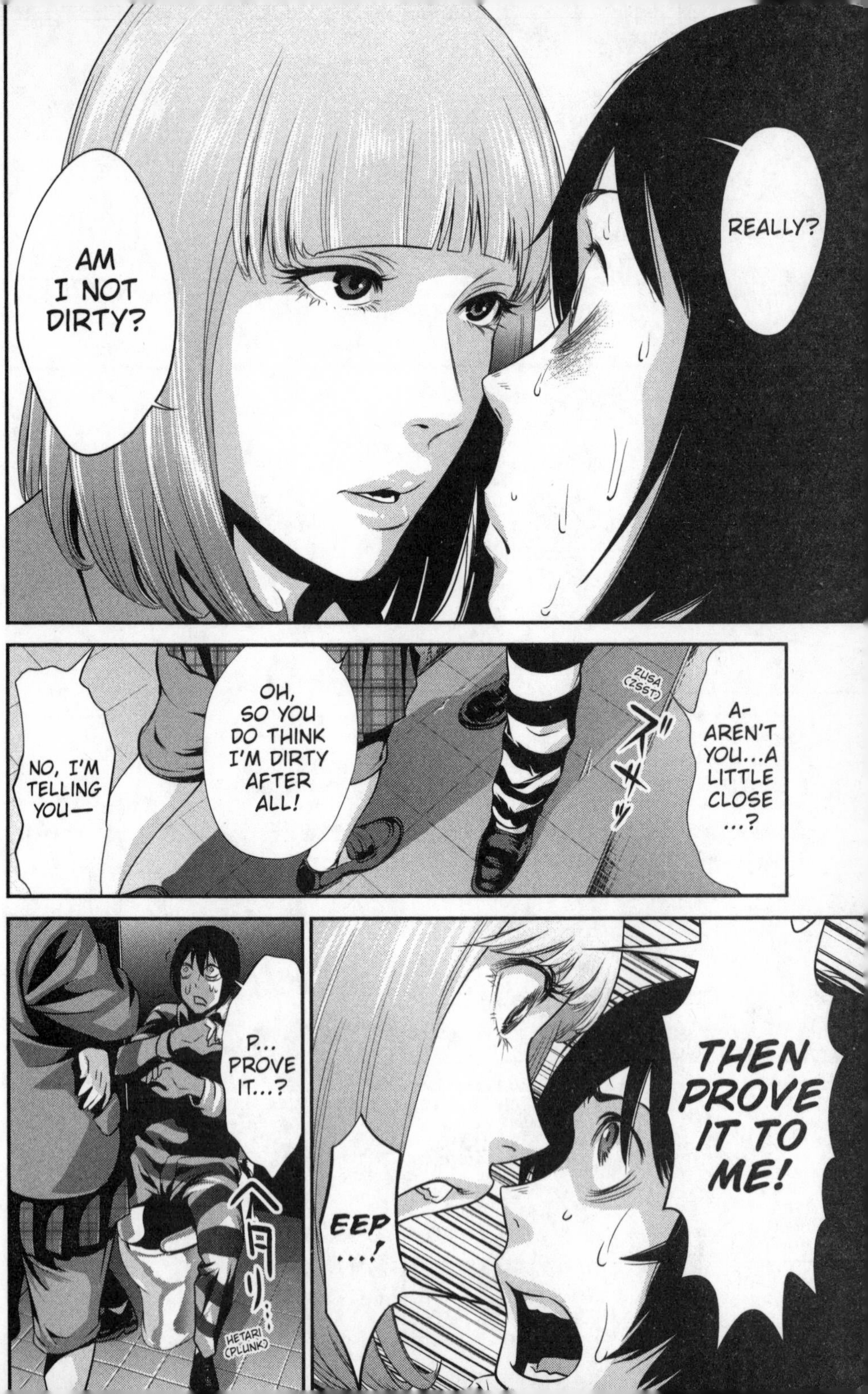
REALLY?
AM I NOT DIRTY?
A-AREN'T YOU...A LITTLE CLOSE ...?
ZUSA (ZSST)
OH, SO YOU DO THINK I'M DIRTY AFTER ALL!
NO, I'M TELLING YOU—
THEN PROVE IT TO ME!
EEP ...!
P... PROVE IT...?
HETARI (PLUNK)

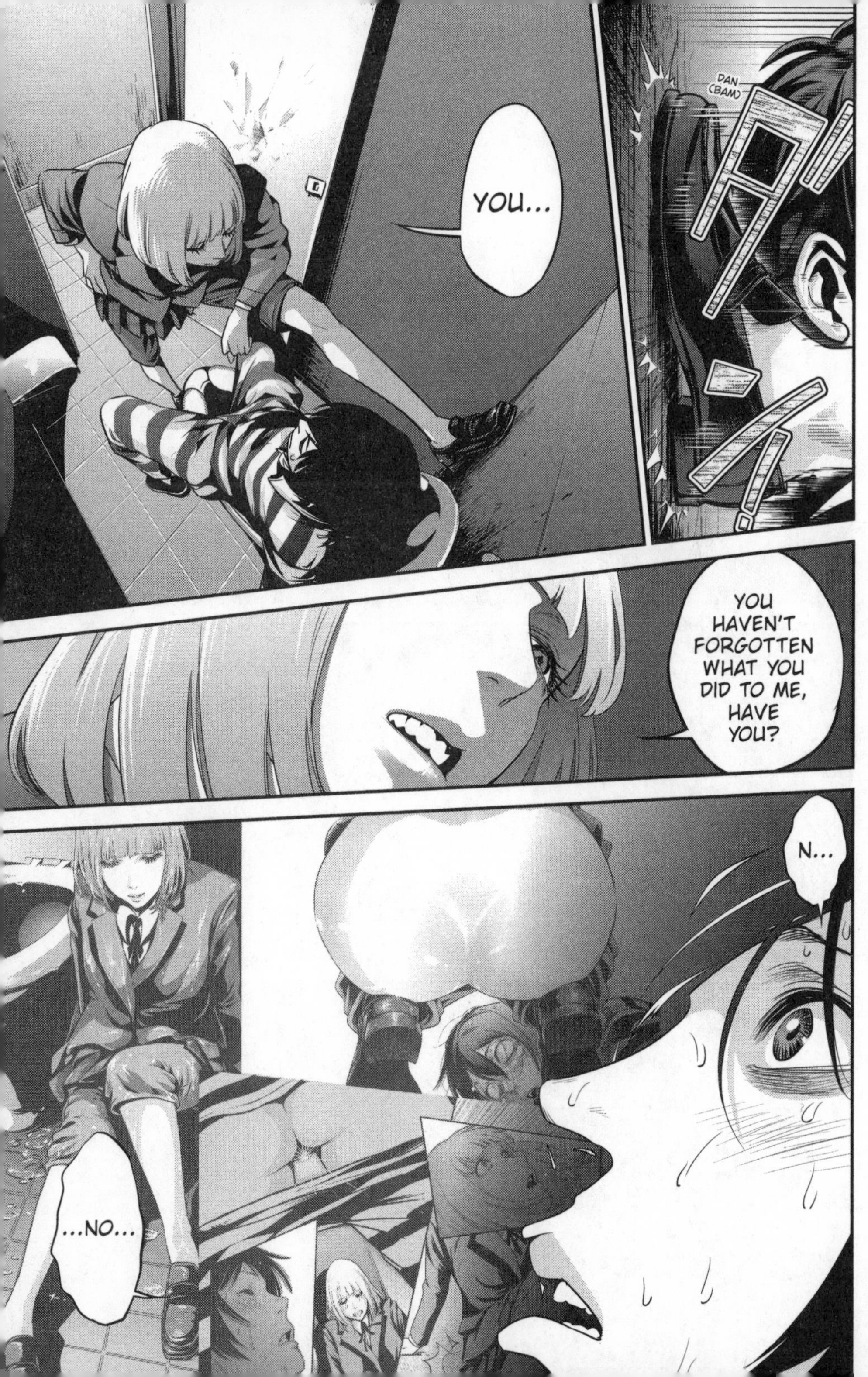
DAN (BAM)
YOU...
YOU HAVEN'T FORGOTTEN WHAT YOU DID TO ME, HAVE YOU?
N...
...NO...

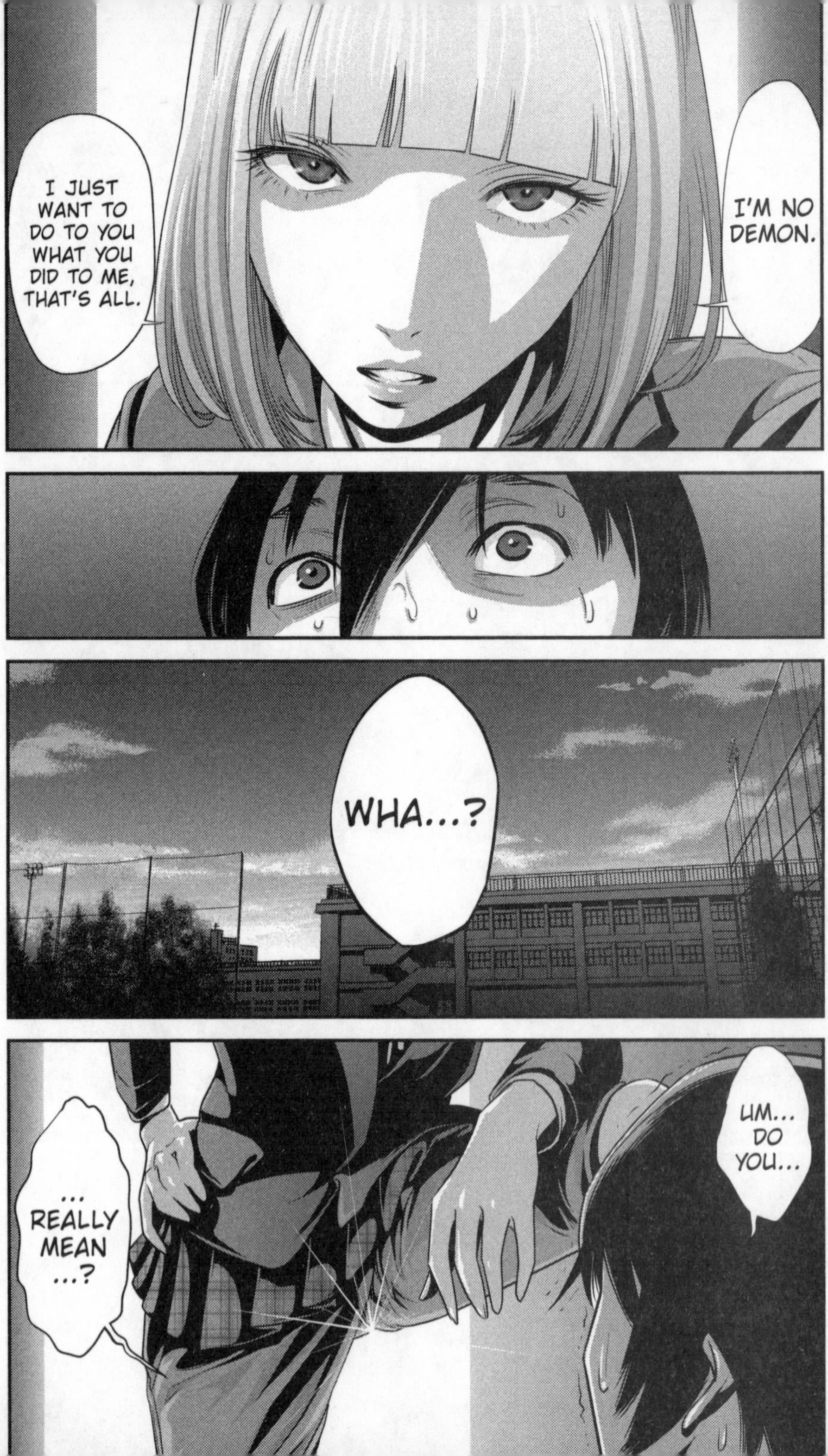
I'M NO DEMON.
I JUST WANT TO DO TO YOU WHAT YOU DID TO ME, THAT'S ALL.
WHA...?
UM... DO YOU...
... REALLY MEAN ...?

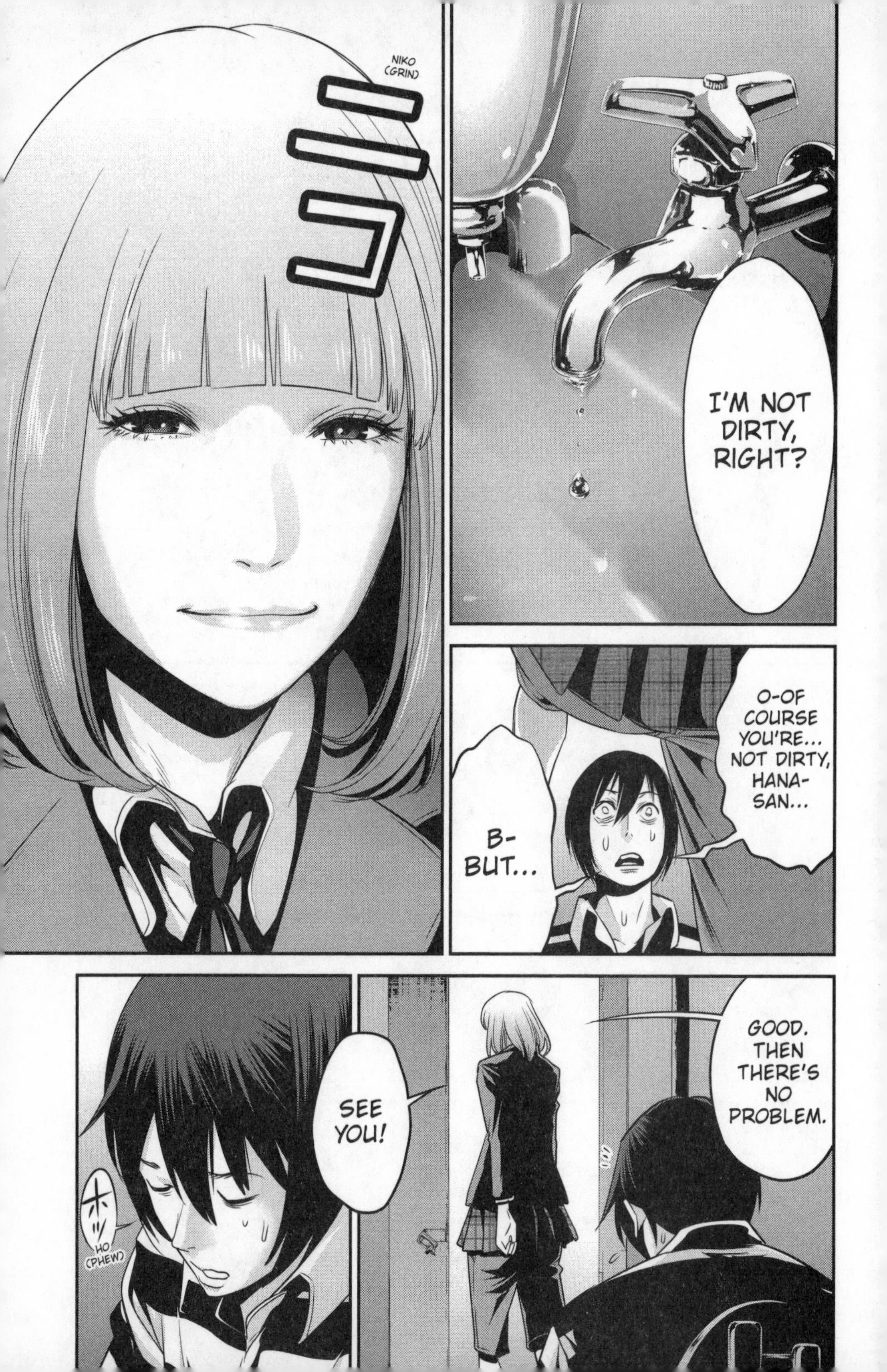
I'M NOT DIRTY, RIGHT?
O-OF COURSE YOU'RE... NOT DIRTY, HANA-SAN...
B-BUT...
NIKO (GRIN)
GOOD. THEN THERE'S NO PROBLEM.
SEE YOU!
ホッ
HO (PHEW)

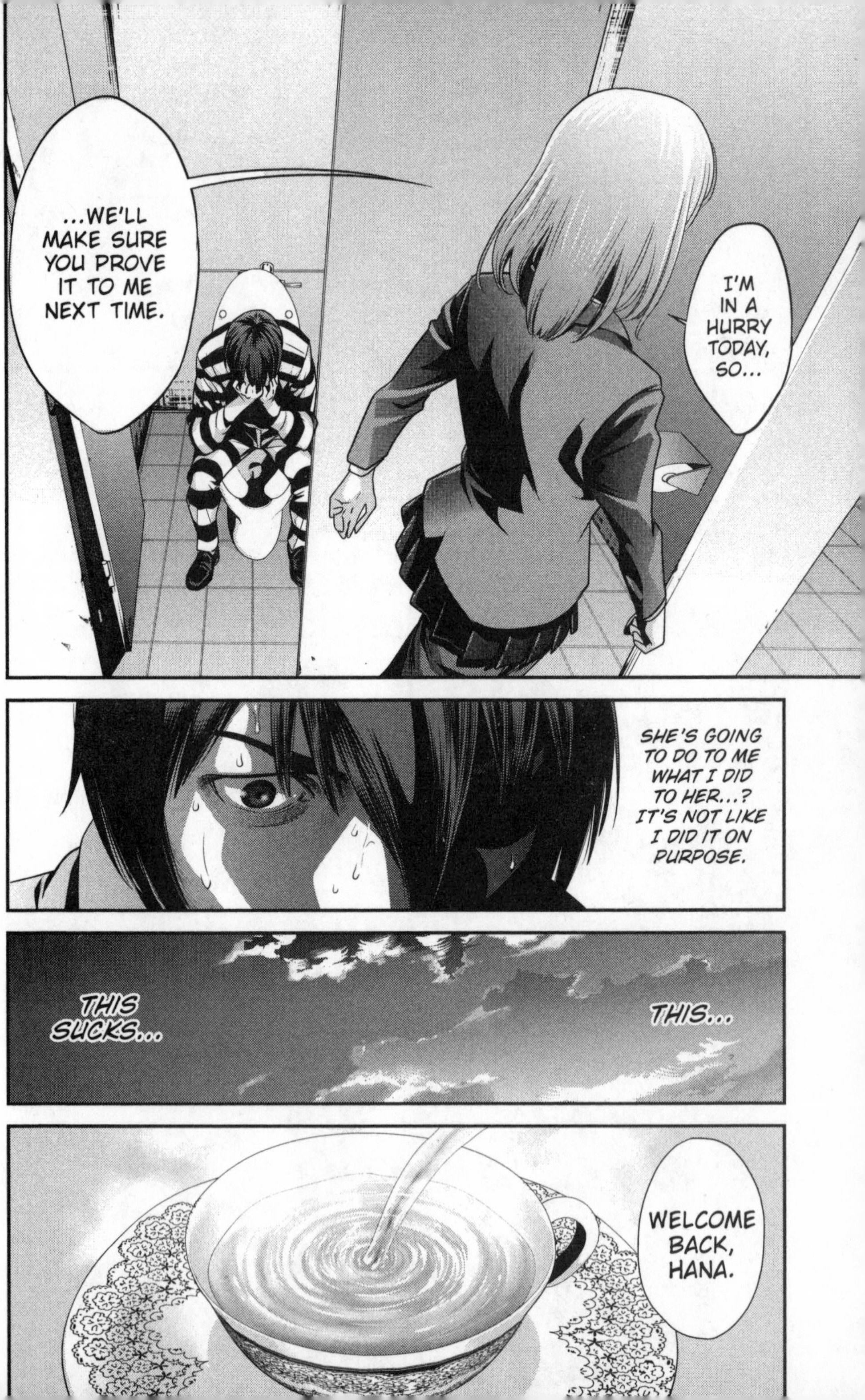
I'M IN A HURRY TODAY, SO...
...WE'LL MAKE SURE YOU PROVE IT TO ME NEXT TIME.
SHE'S GOING TO DO TO ME WHAT I DID TO HER...? IT'S NOT LIKE I DID IT ON PURPOSE.
THIS...
THIS SUCKS...
WELCOME BACK, HANA.

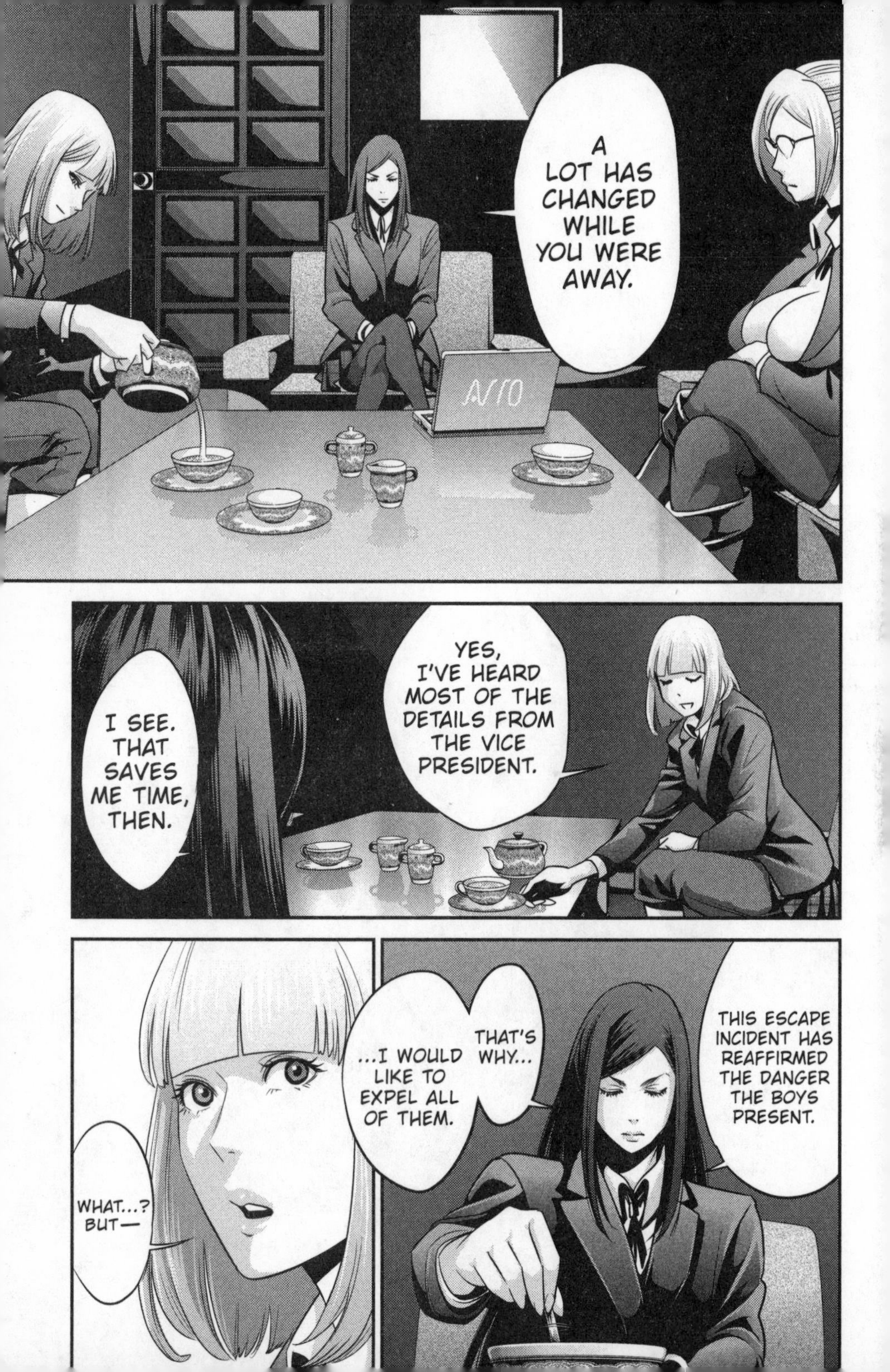
A LOT HAS CHANGED WHILE YOU WERE AWAY.
YES, I'VE HEARD MOST OF THE DETAILS FROM THE VICE PRESIDENT.
I SEE. THAT SAVES ME TIME, THEN.
THIS ESCAPE INCIDENT HAS REAFFIRMED THE DANGER THE BOYS PRESENT.
THAT'S WHY...
...I WOULD LIKE TO EXPEL ALL OF THEM.
WHAT...? BUT—

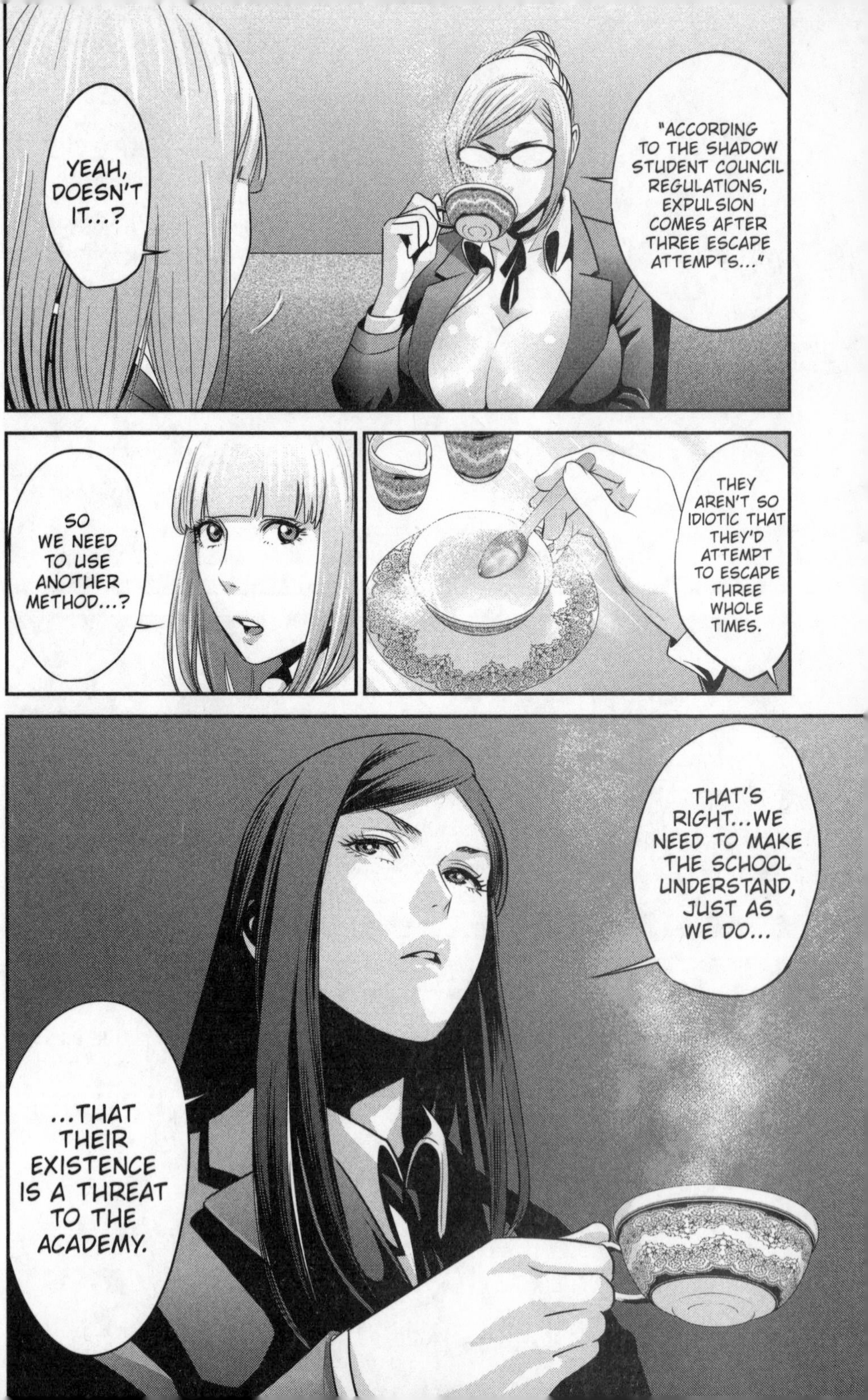
"ACCORDING TO THE SHADOW STUDENT COUNCIL REGULATIONS, EXPULSION COMES AFTER THREE ESCAPE ATTEMPTS..."
YEAH, DOESN'T IT...?
THEY AREN'T SO IDIOTIC THAT THEY'D ATTEMPT TO ESCAPE THREE WHOLE TIMES.
SO WE NEED TO USE ANOTHER METHOD...?
THAT'S RIGHT...WE NEED TO MAKE THE SCHOOL UNDERSTAND, JUST AS WE DO...
...THAT THEIR EXISTENCE IS A THREAT TO THE ACADEMY.

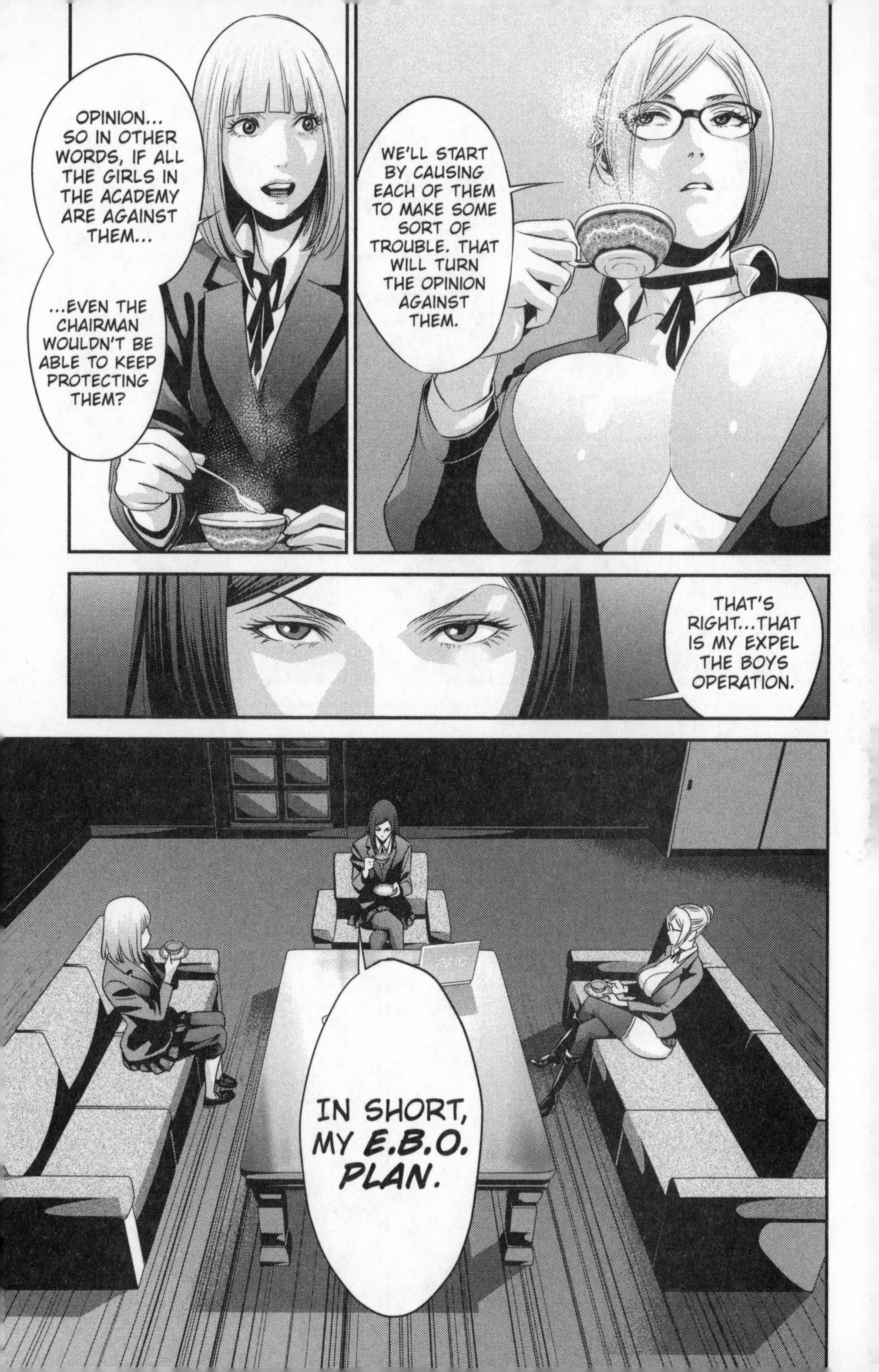
WE'LL START BY CAUSING EACH OF THEM TO MAKE SOME SORT OF TROUBLE. THAT WILL TURN THE OPINION AGAINST THEM.
OPINION... SO IN OTHER WORDS, IF ALL THE GIRLS IN THE ACADEMY ARE AGAINST THEM...
...EVEN THE CHAIRMAN WOULDN'T BE ABLE TO KEEP PROTECTING THEM?
THAT'S RIGHT...THAT IS MY EXPEL THE BOYS OPERATION.
IN SHORT, MY E.B.O. PLAN.

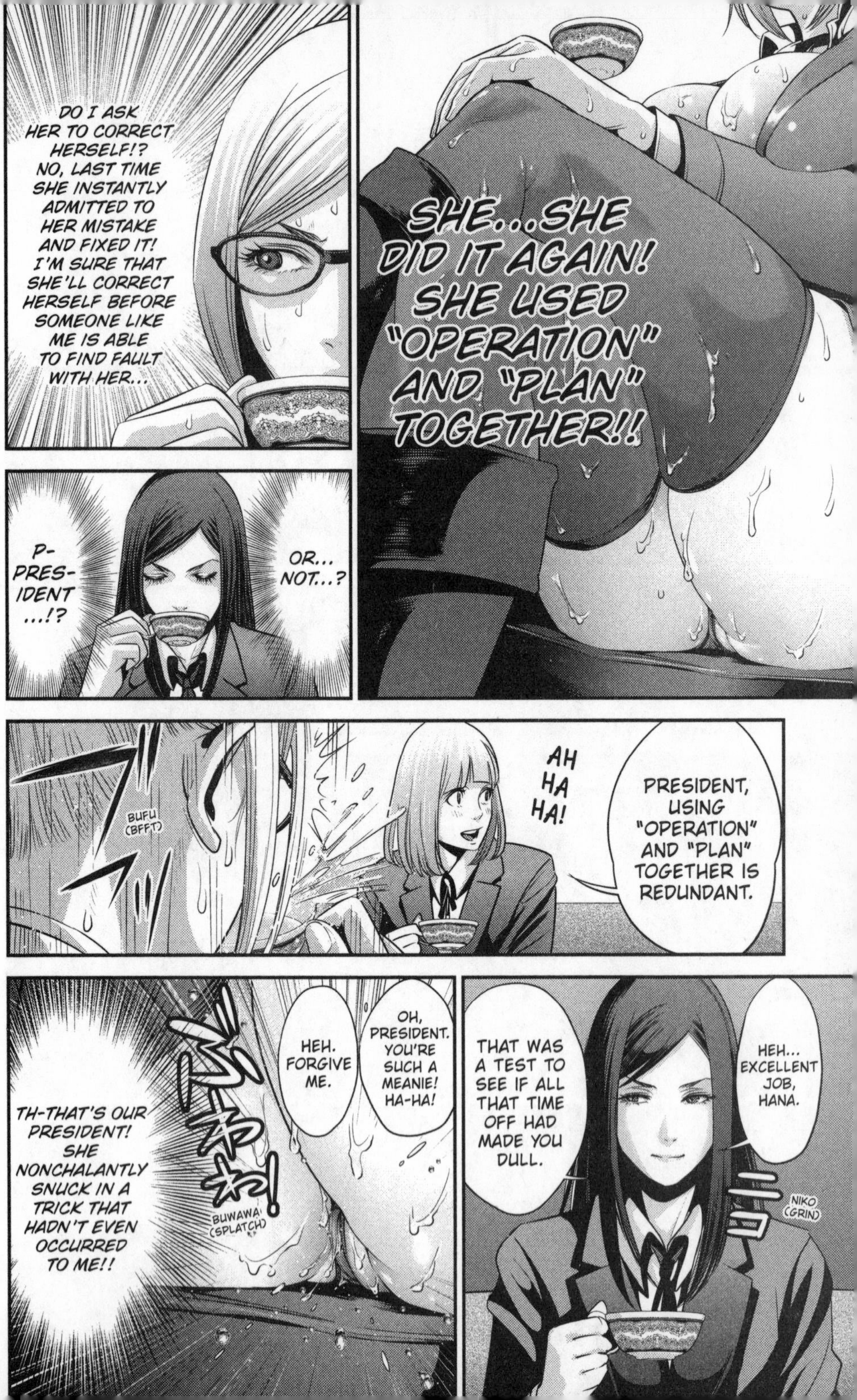

SHE...SHE DID IT AGAIN! SHE USED "OPERATION" AND "PLAN" TOGETHER!!
DO I ASK HER TO CORRECT HERSELF!? NO, LAST TIME SHE INSTANTLY ADMITTED TO HER MISTAKE AND FIXED IT! I'M SURE THAT SHE'LL CORRECT HERSELF BEFORE SOMEONE LIKE ME IS ABLE TO FIND FAULT WITH HER...
OR... NOT...?
P-PRESIDENT ...!?
PRESIDENT, USING "OPERATION" AND "PLAN" TOGETHER IS REDUNDANT.
AH HA HA!
BUFU (BFFT)
HEH... EXCELLENT JOB, HANA.
THAT WAS A TEST TO SEE IF ALL THAT TIME OFF HAD MADE YOU DULL.
NIKO (GRIN)
OH, PRESIDENT. YOU'RE SUCH A MEANIE! HA-HA!
HEH. FORGIVE ME.
TH-THAT'S OUR PRESIDENT! SHE NONCHALANTLY SNUCK IN A TRICK THAT HADN'T EVEN OCCURRED TO ME!!
BUWAWA (SPLATCH)

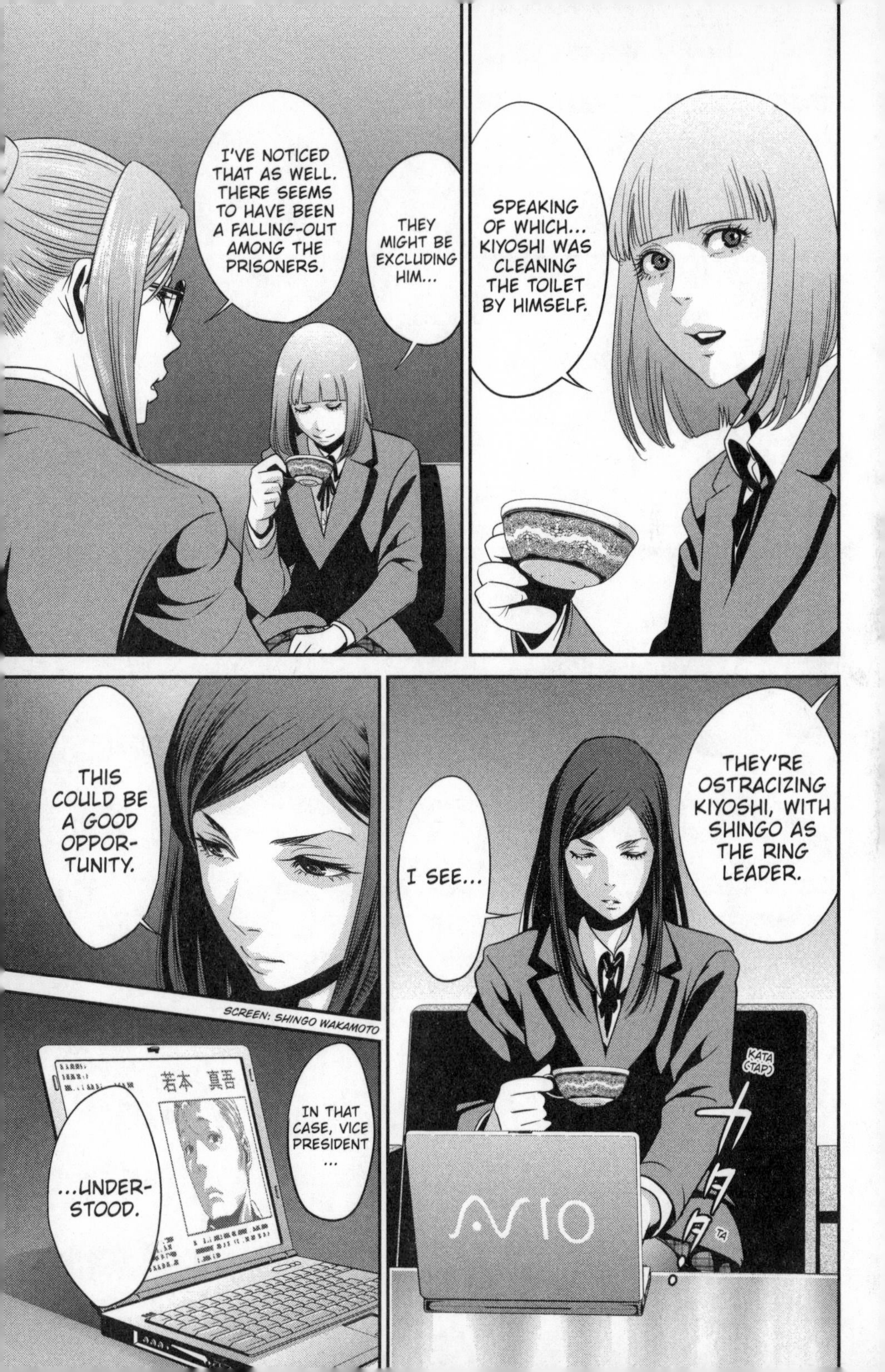
SPEAKING OF WHICH... KIYOSHI WAS CLEANING THE TOILET BY HIMSELF.
THEY MIGHT BE EXCLUDING HIM...
I'VE NOTICED THAT AS WELL. THERE SEEMS TO HAVE BEEN A FALLING-OUT AMONG THE PRISONERS.
THEY'RE OSTRACIZING KIYOSHI, WITH SHINGO AS THE RING LEADER.
I SEE...
KATA (TAP)
TA
THIS COULD BE A GOOD OPPOR-TUNITY.
SCREEN: SHINGO WAKAMOTO
若本 真吾
IN THAT CASE, VICE PRESIDENT ...
...UNDER-STOOD.

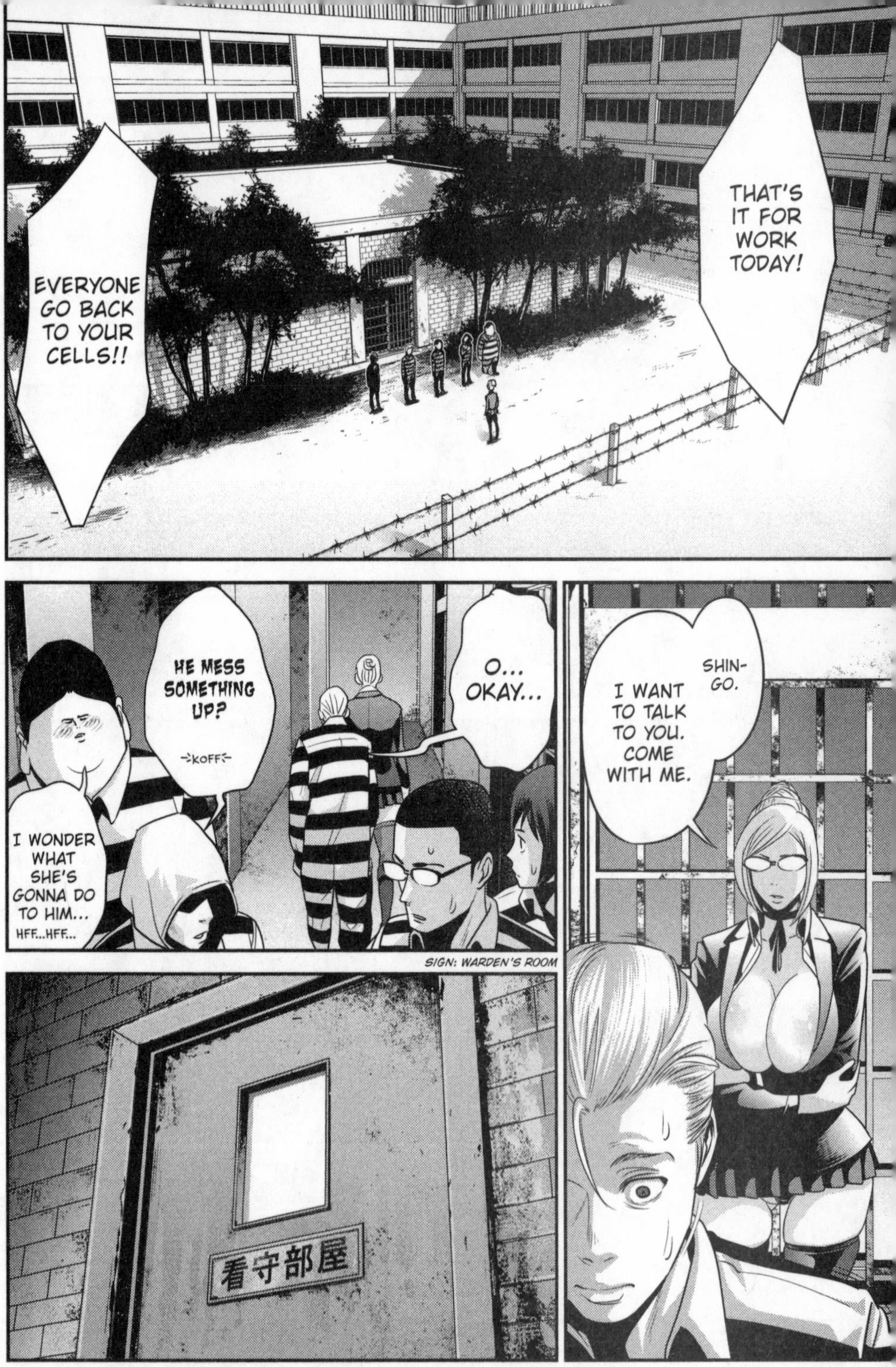
THAT'S IT FOR WORK TODAY!
EVERYONE GO BACK TO YOUR CELLS!!
SHIN-GO.
I WANT TO TALK TO YOU. COME WITH ME.
O... OKAY...
HE MESS SOMETHING UP?
KOFF
I WONDER WHAT SHE'S GONNA DO TO HIM...
HFF...HFF...
SIGN: WARDEN'S ROOM
看守部屋

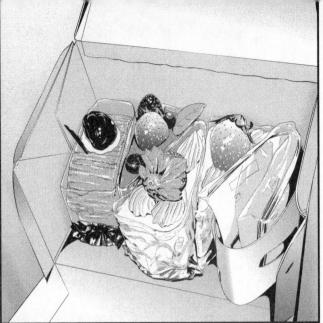

GOKURI
(GULP)

HOW'VE YOU BEEN LATELY?

HUH...? WELL...

Y-YEAH...

IT MUST BE TERRIBLE TO HAVE YOUR SENTENCE EXTENDED BECAUSE OF KIYOSHI.

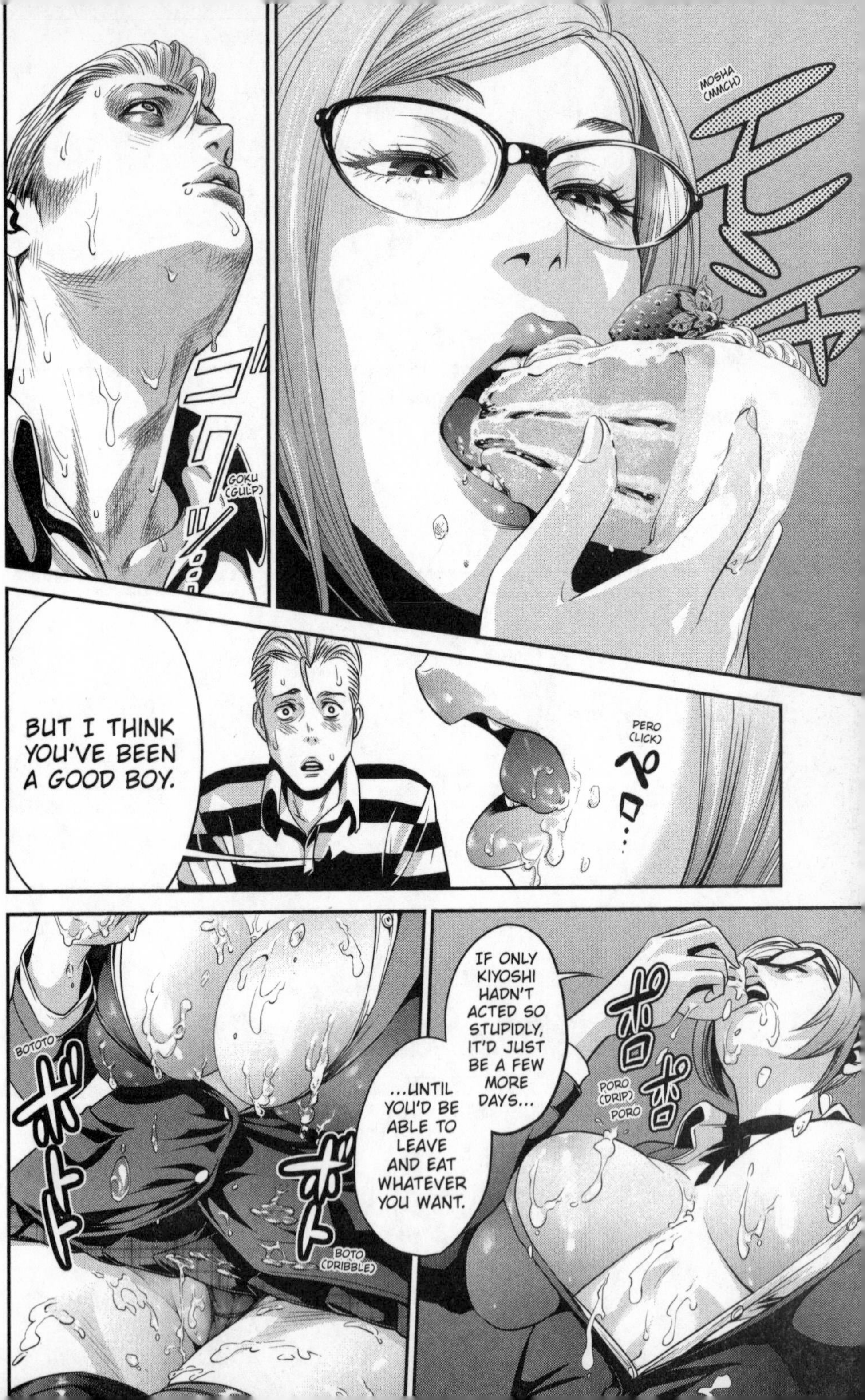
MOSHA (MMCH)
GOKU (GULP)
PERO (LICK)
BUT I THINK YOU'VE BEEN A GOOD BOY.
IF ONLY KIYOSHI HADN'T ACTED SO STUPIDLY, IT'D JUST BE A FEW MORE DAYS...
PORO (DRIP) PORO
...UNTIL YOU'D BE ABLE TO LEAVE AND EAT WHATEVER YOU WANT.
BOTO (DRIBBLE)
BOTOTO

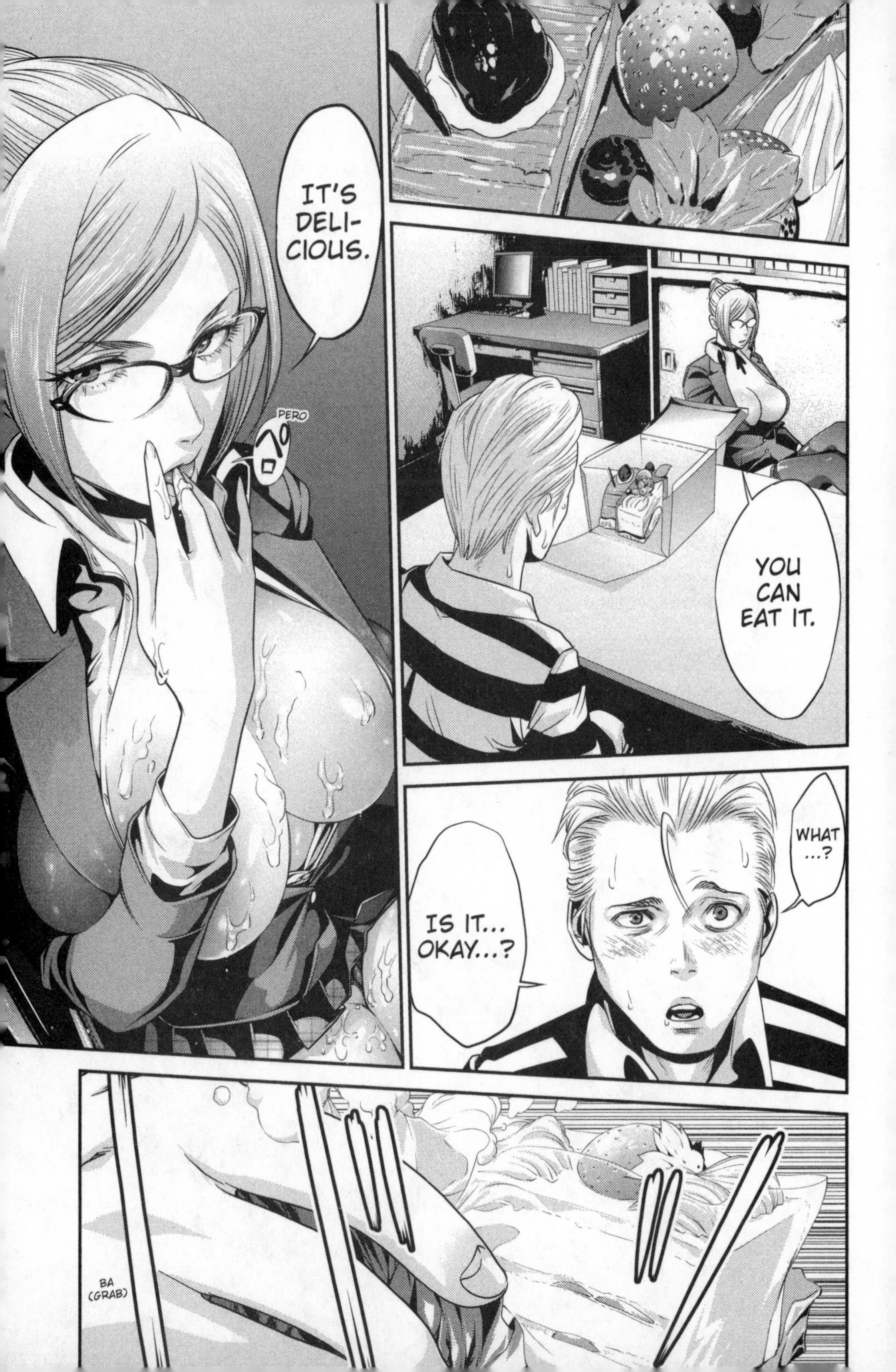
IT'S DELI-CIOUS.
PERO
YOU CAN EAT IT.
WHAT ...?
IS IT... OKAY...?
BA (GRAB)

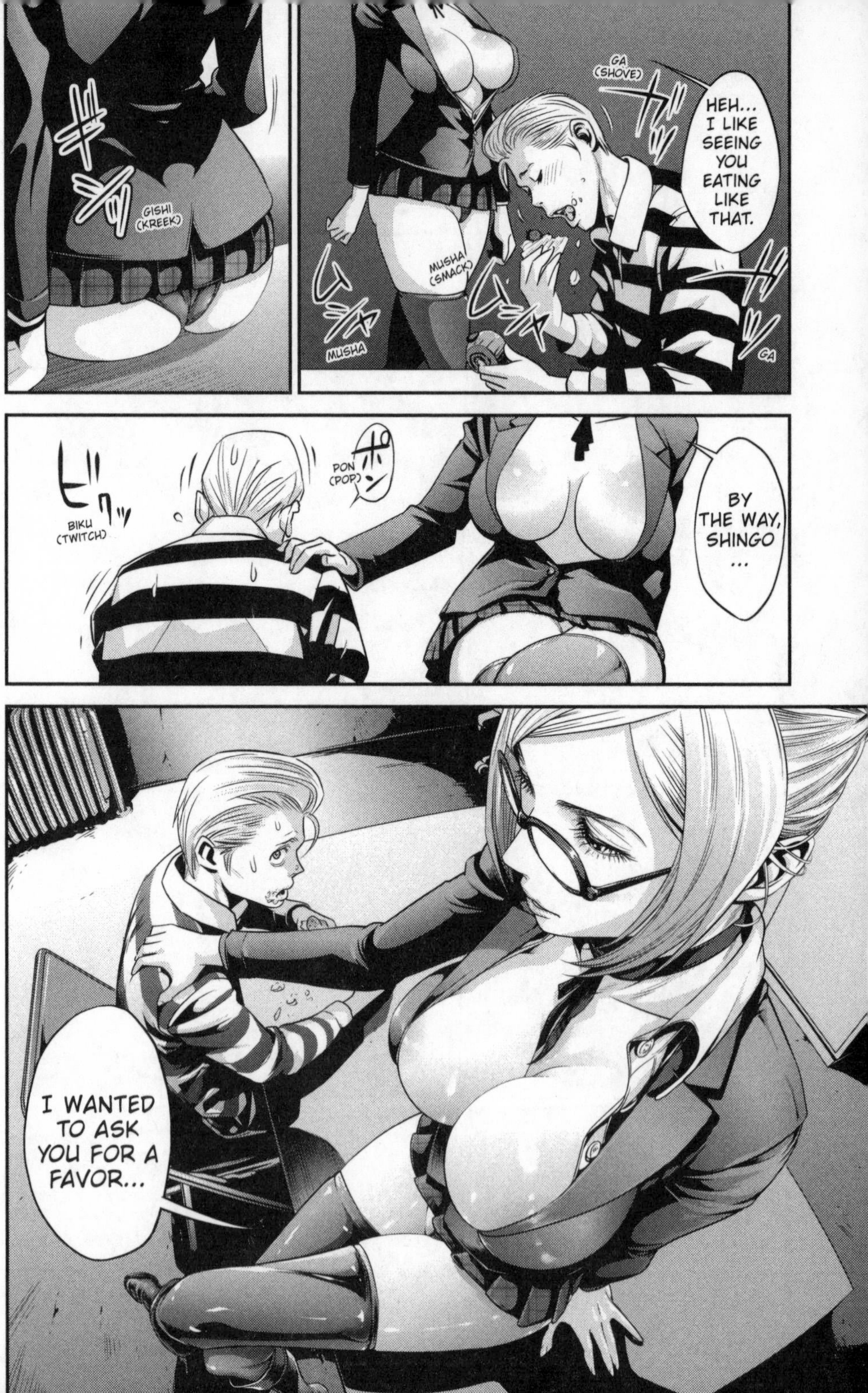
GA (SHOVE)
HEH... I LIKE SEEING YOU EATING LIKE THAT.
MUSHA (SMACK)
MUSHA
GA
GISHI (KREEK)
BY THE WAY, SHINGO ...
PON (POP)
BIKU (TWITCH)
I WANTED TO ASK YOU FOR A FAVOR...

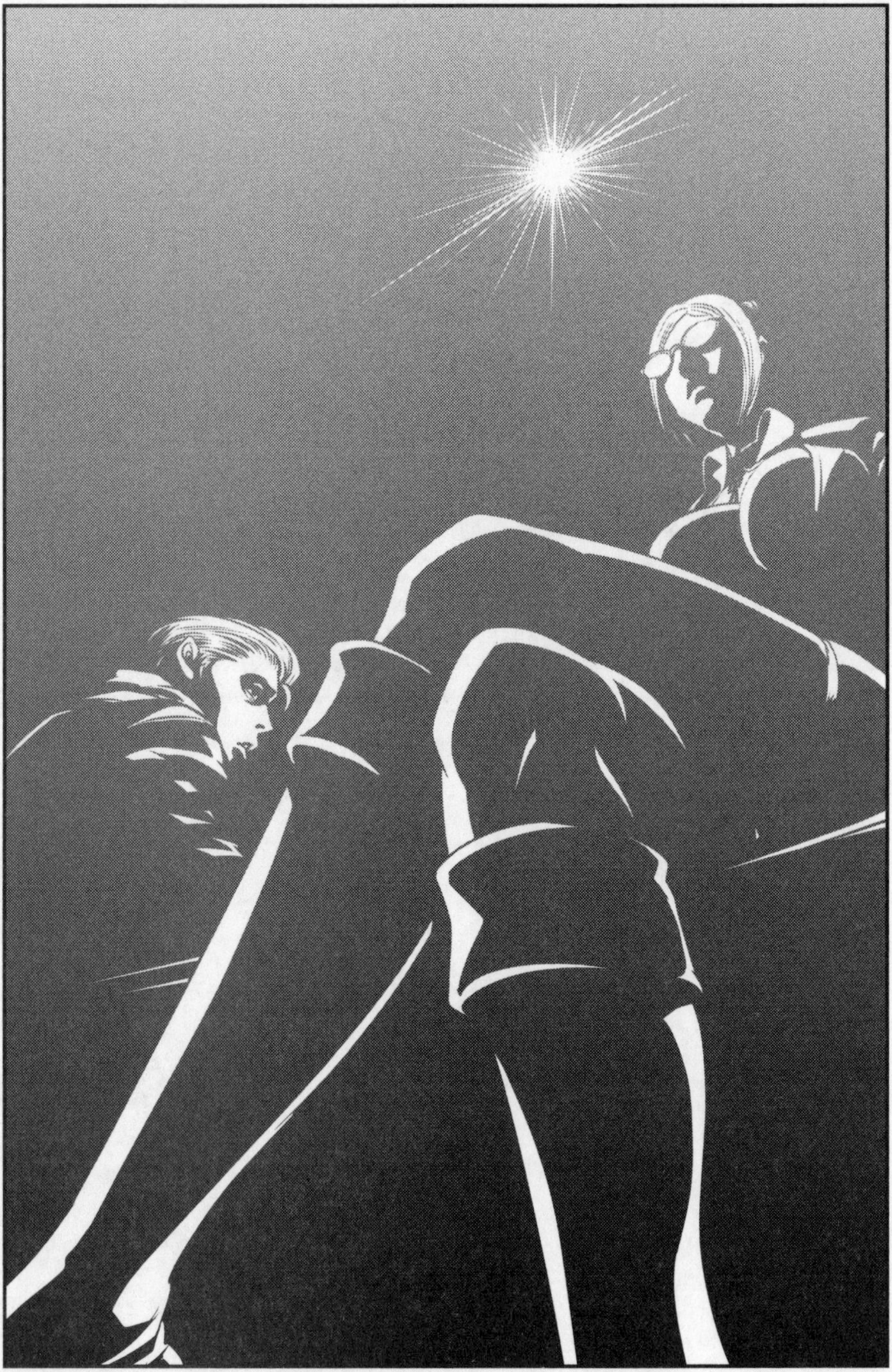

CHAPTER 36: THE SECRET

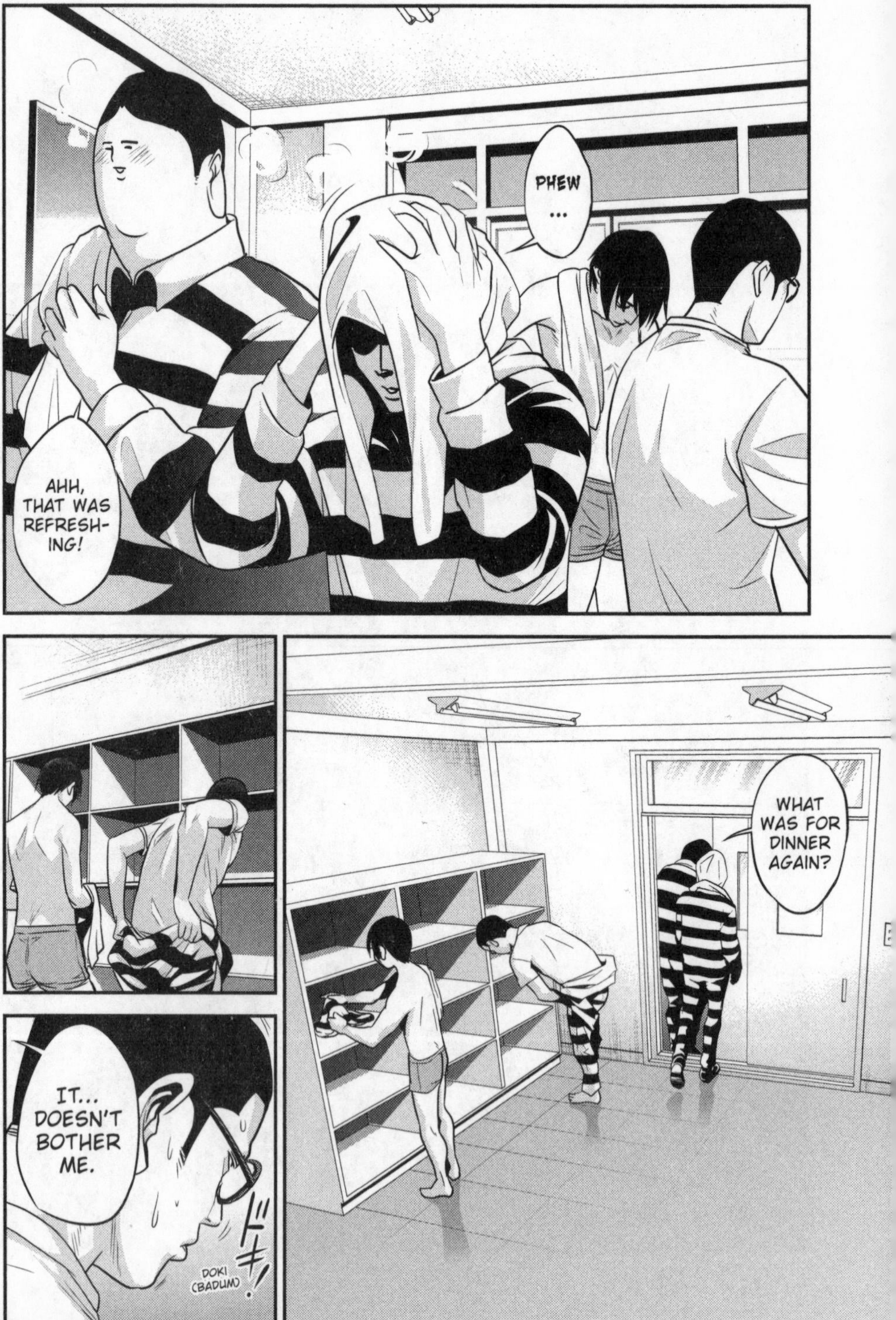
PHEW ...
AHH, THAT WAS REFRESHING!
WHAT WAS FOR DINNER AGAIN?
IT... DOESN'T BOTHER ME.
DOKI (BADUM)

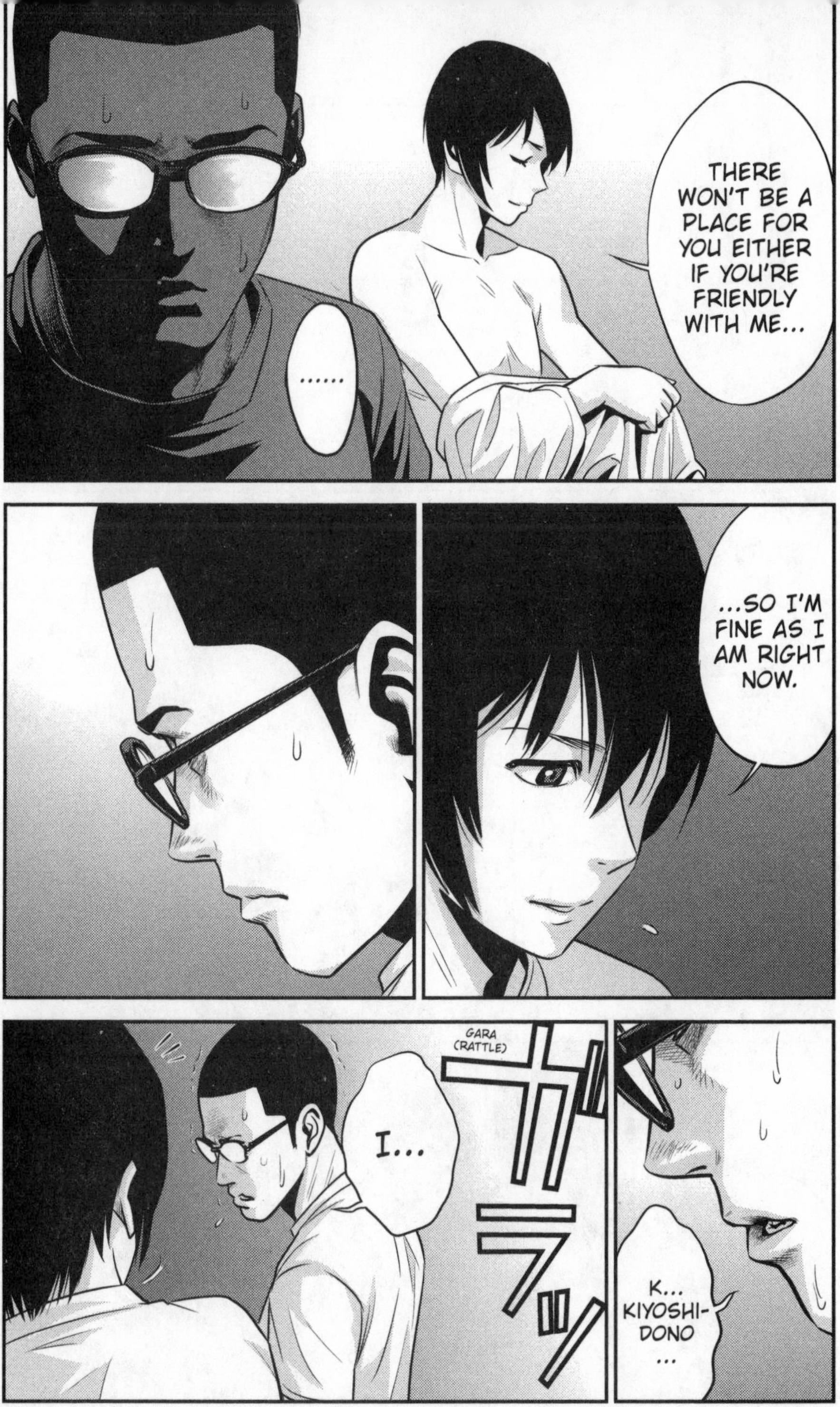
THERE WON'T BE A PLACE FOR YOU EITHER IF YOU'RE FRIENDLY WITH ME...
......
...SO I'M FINE AS I AM RIGHT NOW.
K... KIYOSHI-DONO ...
GARA (RATTLE)
I...

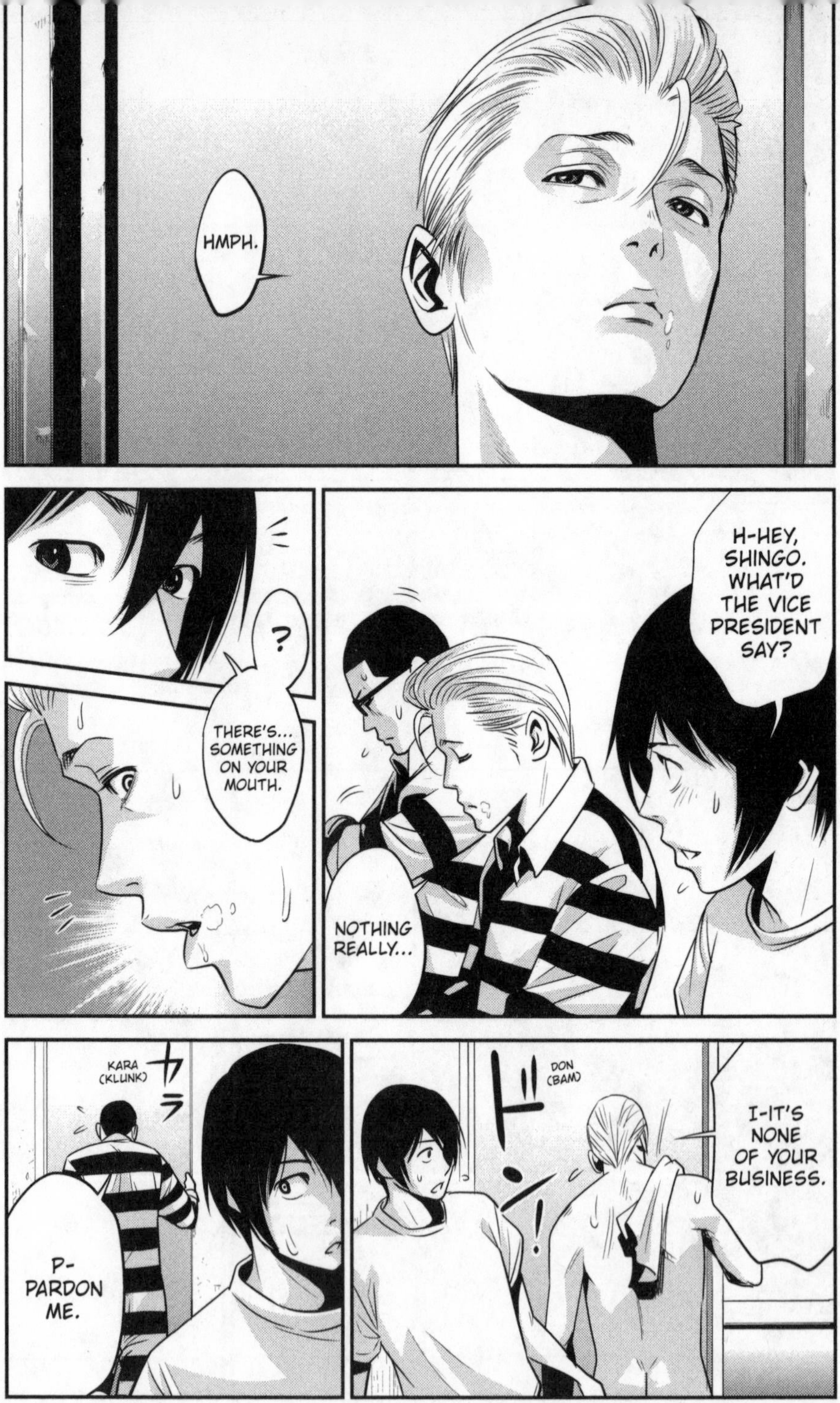
HMPH.
H-HEY, SHINGO. WHAT'D THE VICE PRESIDENT SAY?
NOTHING REALLY...
?
THERE'S... SOMETHING ON YOUR MOUTH.
I-IT'S NONE OF YOUR BUSINESS.
DON (BAM)
!
KARA (KLUNK)
P- PARDON ME.

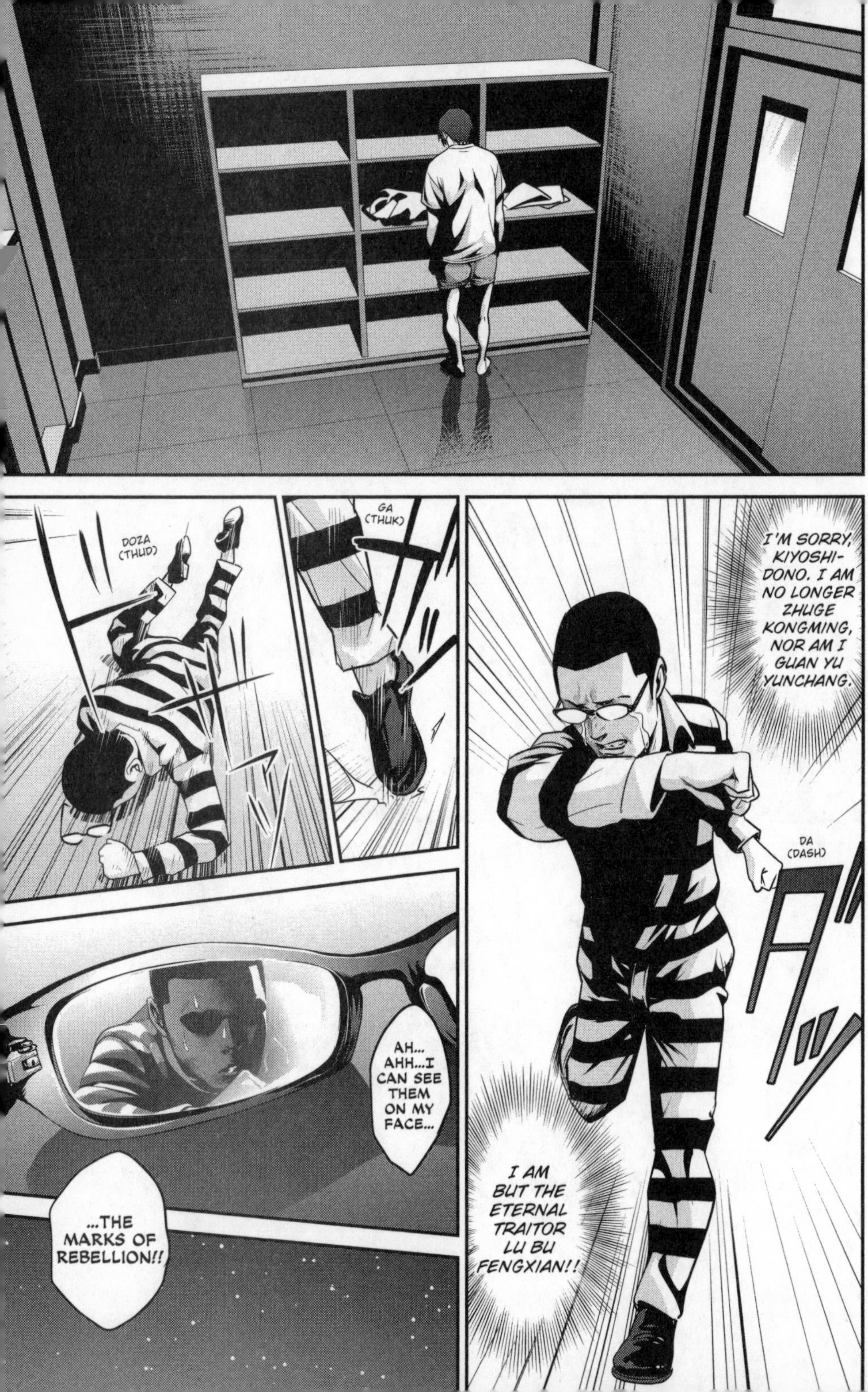
GA
(THUK)
DOZA
(THUD)
AH... AHH...I CAN SEE THEM ON MY FACE...
...THE MARKS OF REBELLION!!
I'M SORRY, KIYOSHI-DONO. I AM NO LONGER ZHUGE KONGMING, NOR AM I GUAN YU YUNCHANG.
DA
(DASH)
I AM BUT THE ETERNAL TRAITOR LU BU FENGXIAN!!

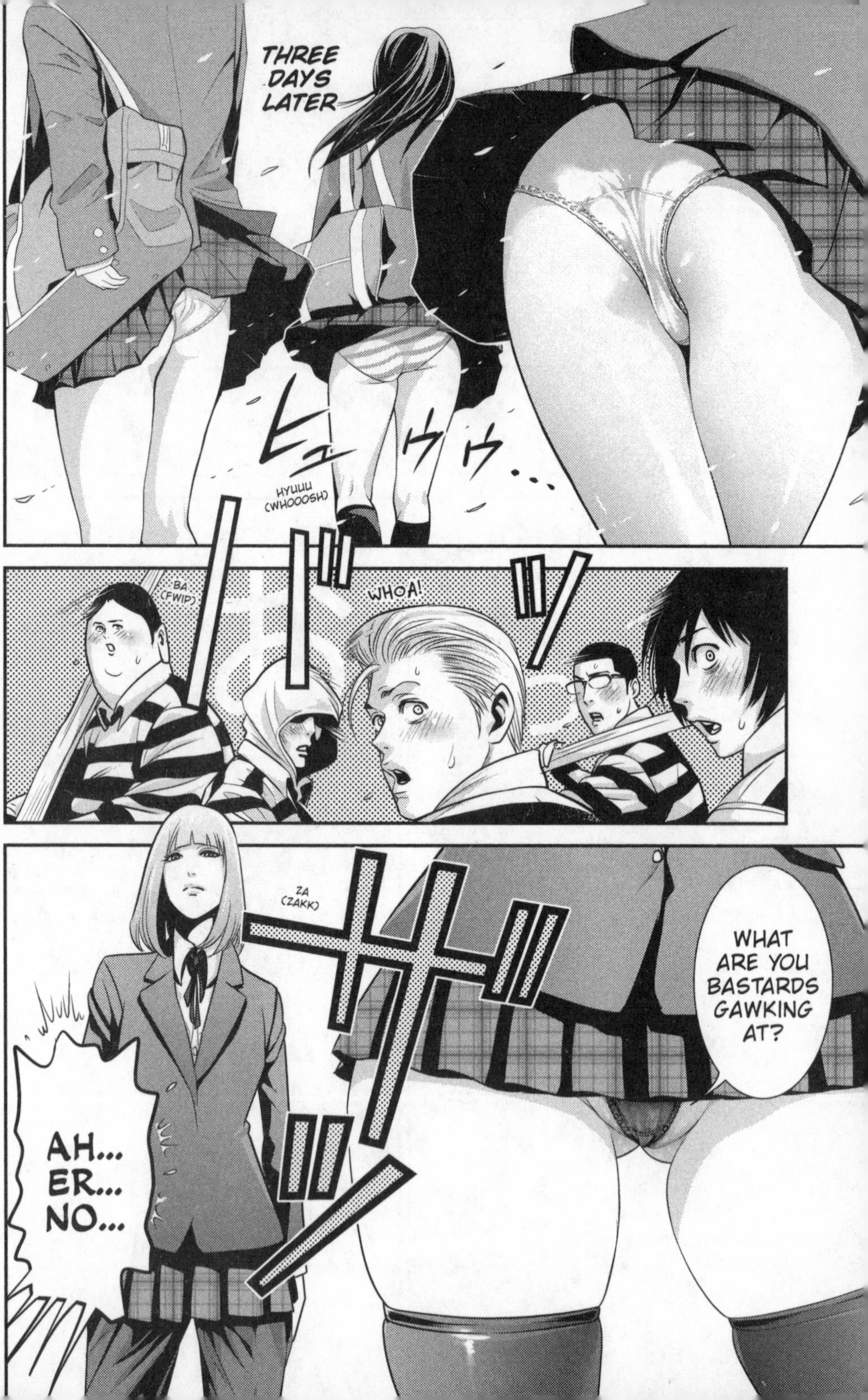
THREE DAYS LATER
ヒュウウ...
HYUUU (WHOOOSH)
バッ
BA (FWIP)
WHOA!
ザッ
ZA (ZAKK)
WHAT ARE YOU BASTARDS GAWKING AT?
AH... ER... NO...

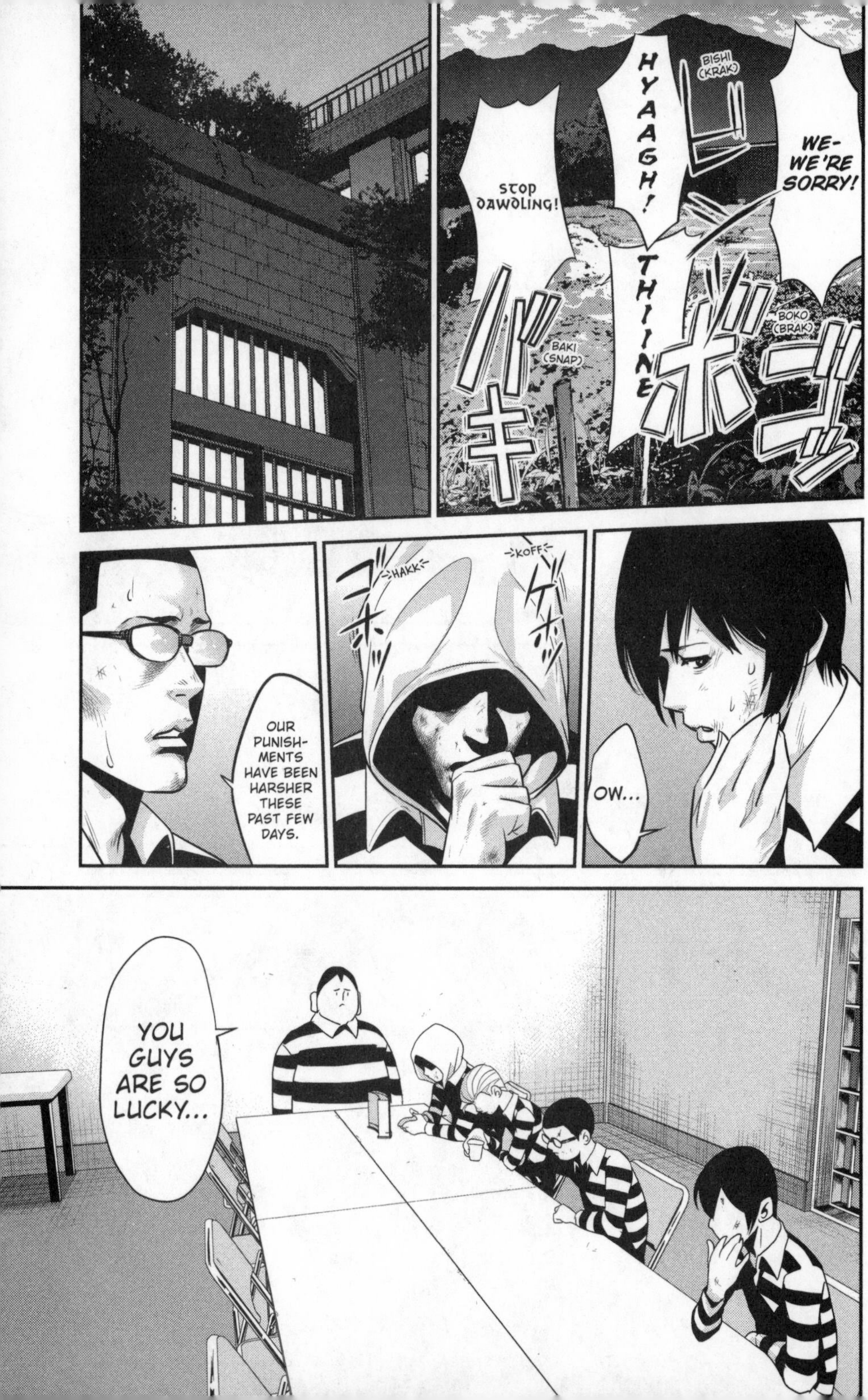
WE-WE'RE SORRY!
BISHI (KRAK)
HYAAGH!
STOP DAWDLING!
THIIINE
BOKO (BRAK)
BAKI (SNAP)
OW...
KOFF
HAKK
OUR PUNISHMENTS HAVE BEEN HARSHER THESE PAST FEW DAYS.
YOU GUYS ARE SO LUCKY...

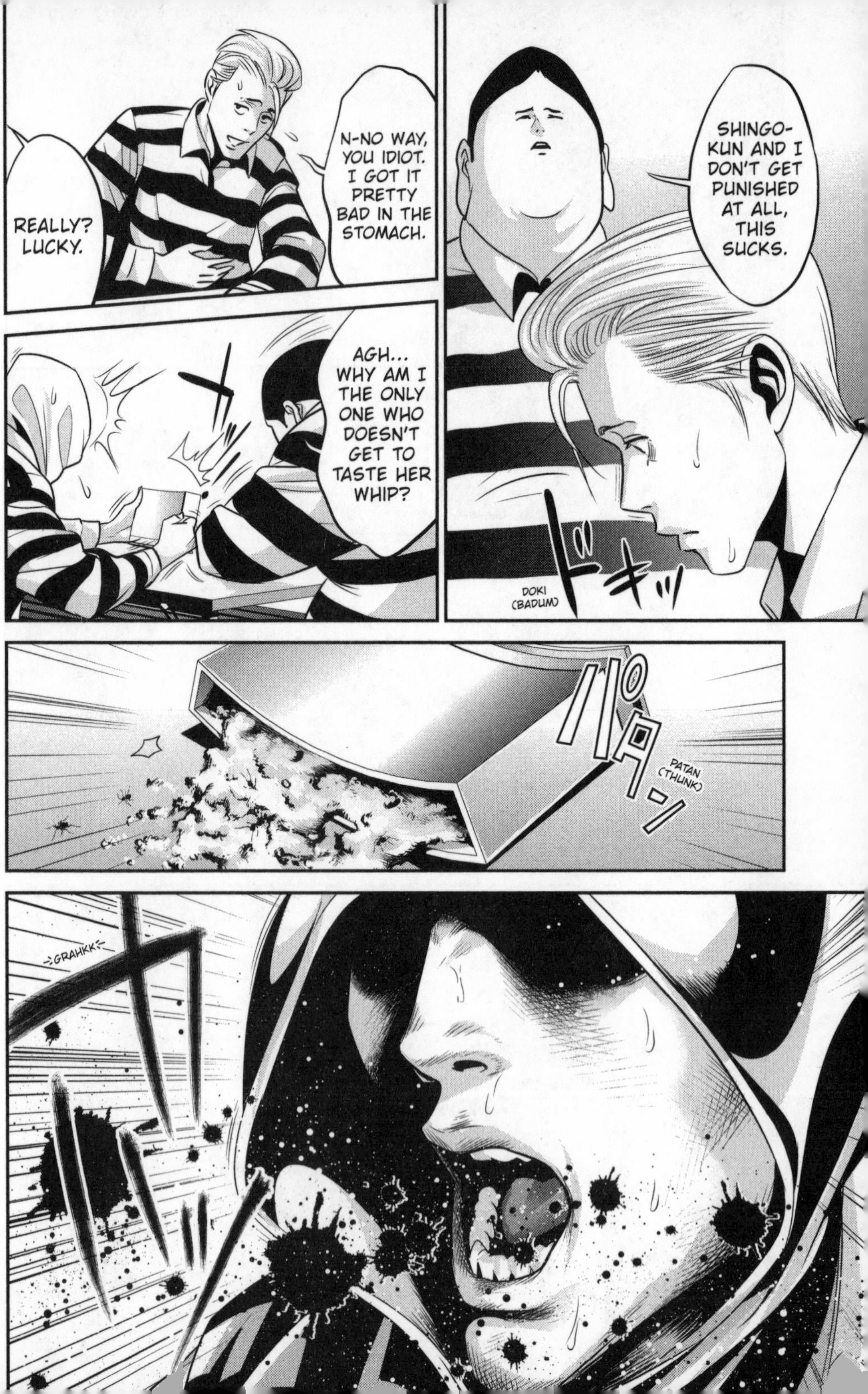
SHINGO-KUN AND I DON'T GET PUNISHED AT ALL, THIS SUCKS.
N-NO WAY, YOU IDIOT. I GOT IT PRETTY BAD IN THE STOMACH.
REALLY? LUCKY.
DOKI (BADUM)
AGH... WHY AM I THE ONLY ONE WHO DOESN'T GET TO TASTE HER WHIP?
PATAN (THUNK)
GRAHKK

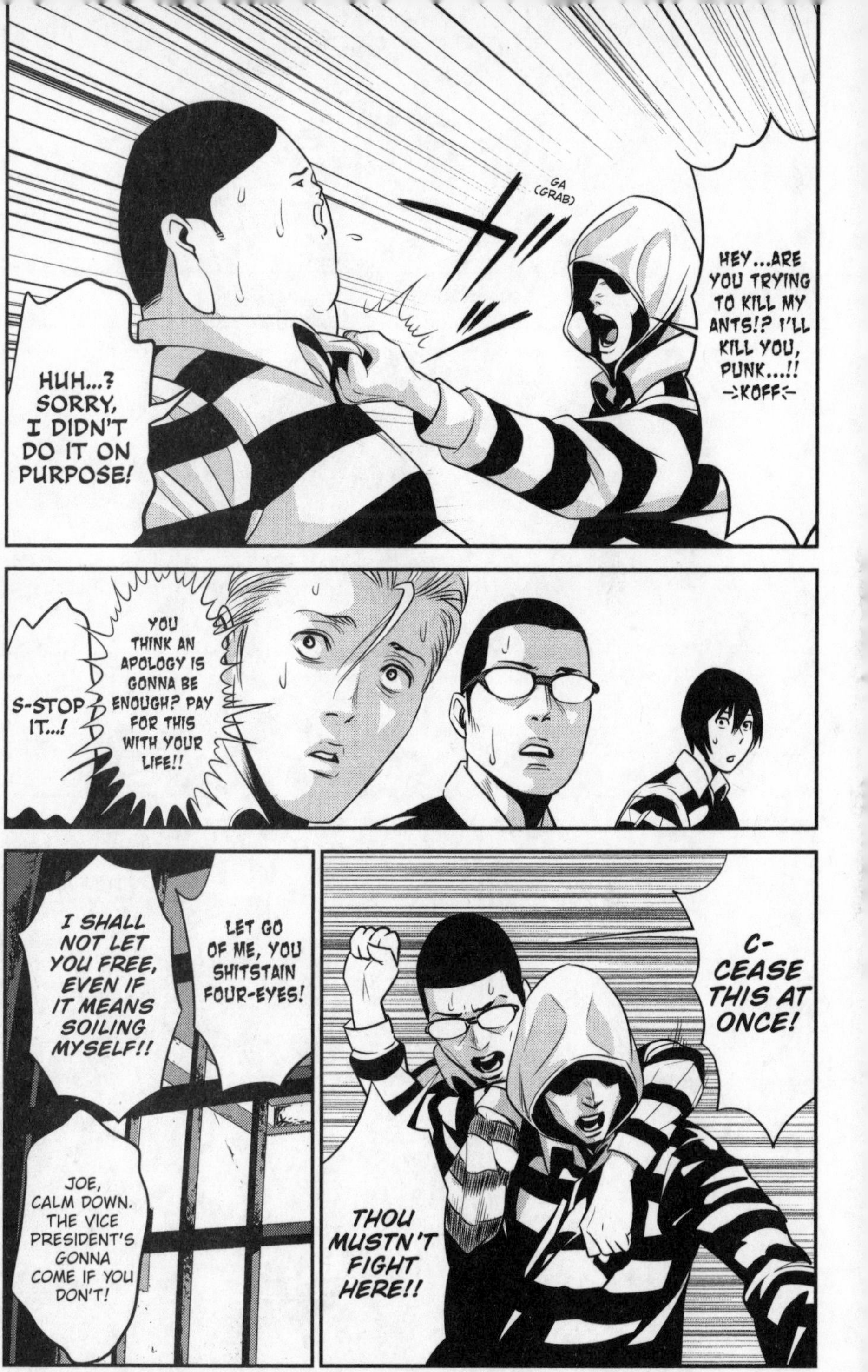

HEY...ARE YOU TRYING TO KILL MY ANTS!? I'LL KILL YOU, PUNK...!! -KOFF-
GA (GRAB)
HUH...? SORRY, I DIDN'T DO IT ON PURPOSE!
YOU THINK AN APOLOGY IS GONNA BE ENOUGH? PAY FOR THIS WITH YOUR LIFE!!
S-STOP IT...!
C-CEASE THIS AT ONCE!
THOU MUSTN'T FIGHT HERE!!
LET GO OF ME, YOU SHITSTAIN FOUR-EYES!
I SHALL NOT LET YOU FREE, EVEN IF IT MEANS SOILING MYSELF!!
JOE, CALM DOWN. THE VICE PRESIDENT'S GONNA COME IF YOU DON'T!

SIGN: WARDEN'S ROOM

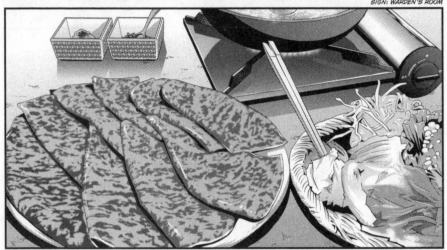

SO...?

DID YOU BRING ME THE INFORMATION LIKE I ASKED?

WELL... LET'S SEE...

I GUESS EVERYONE'S GETTING KIND OF ANNOYED?

ピタ
PITA
(STOP)

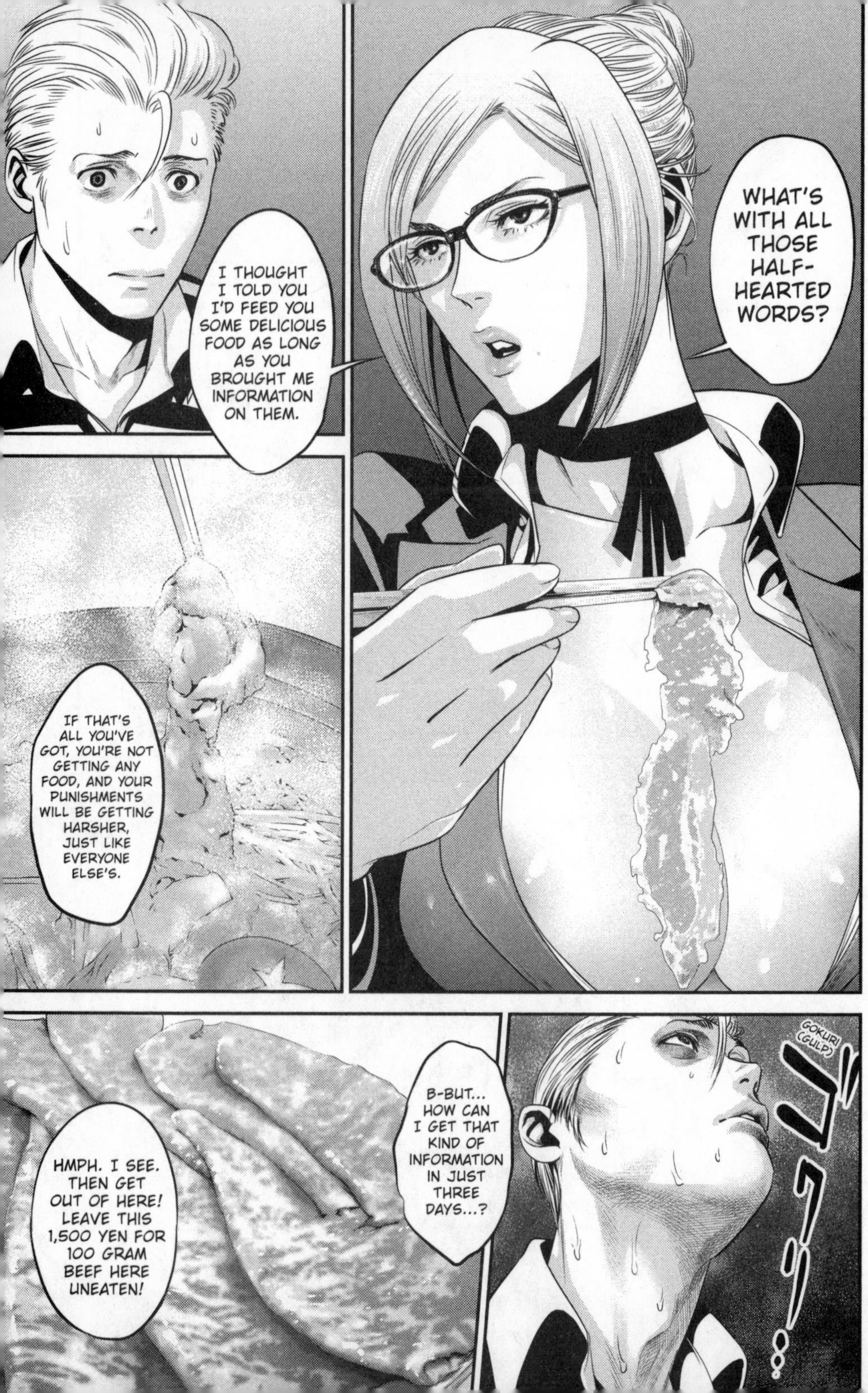

WHAT'S WITH ALL THOSE HALF-HEARTED WORDS?
I THOUGHT I TOLD YOU I'D FEED YOU SOME DELICIOUS FOOD AS LONG AS YOU BROUGHT ME INFORMATION ON THEM.
IF THAT'S ALL YOU'VE GOT, YOU'RE NOT GETTING ANY FOOD, AND YOUR PUNISHMENTS WILL BE GETTING HARSHER, JUST LIKE EVERYONE ELSE'S.
GOKURI (GULP)
B-BUT... HOW CAN I GET THAT KIND OF INFORMATION IN JUST THREE DAYS...?
HMPH. I SEE. THEN GET OUT OF HERE! LEAVE THIS 1,500 YEN FOR 100 GRAM BEEF HERE UNEATEN!

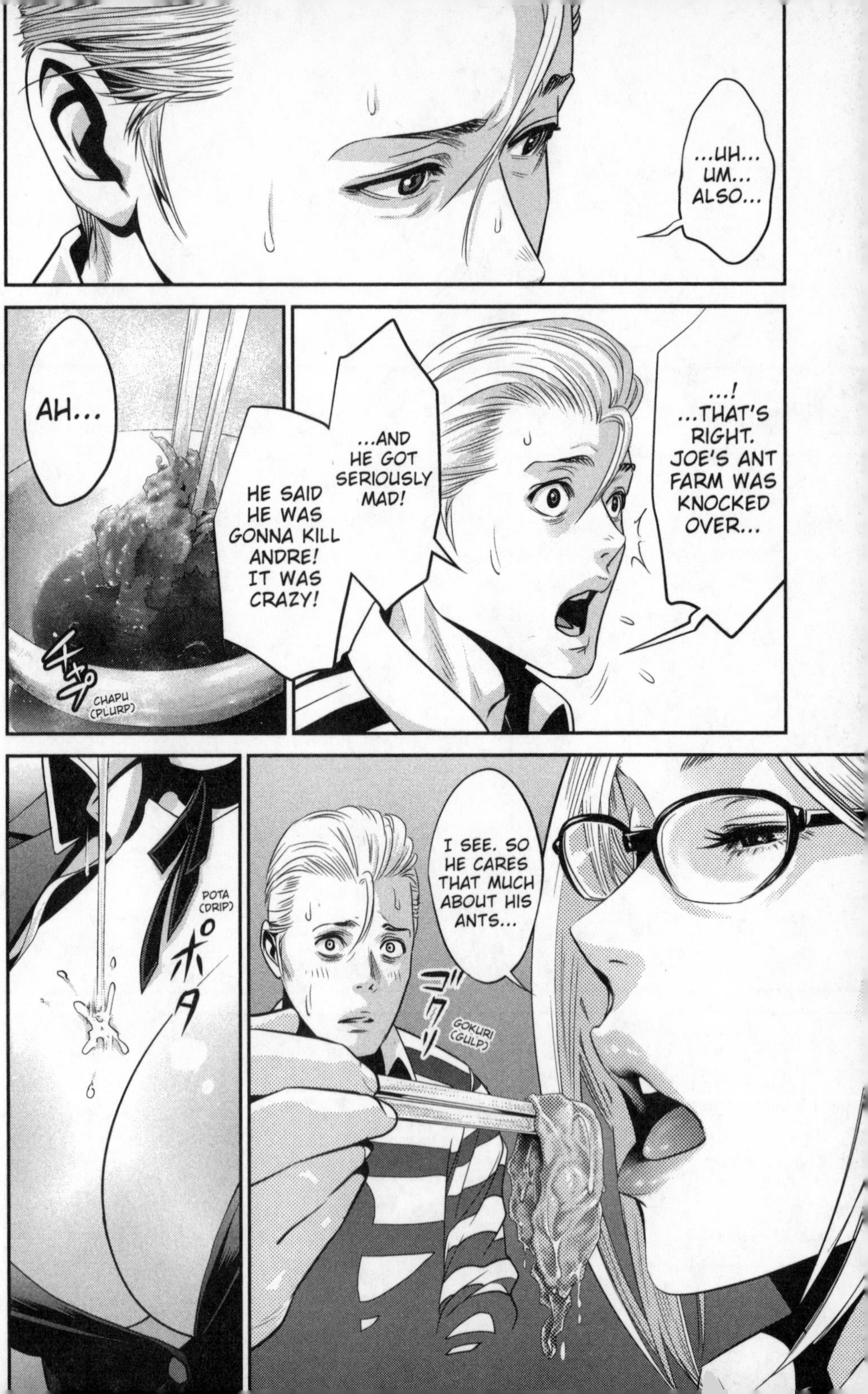
...UH... UM... ALSO...
...! ...THAT'S RIGHT. JOE'S ANT FARM WAS KNOCKED OVER...
...AND HE GOT SERIOUSLY MAD!
HE SAID HE WAS GONNA KILL ANDRE! IT WAS CRAZY!
AH...
CHAPU (PLURP)
I SEE. SO HE CARES THAT MUCH ABOUT HIS ANTS...
GOKURI (GULP)
POTA (DRIP)

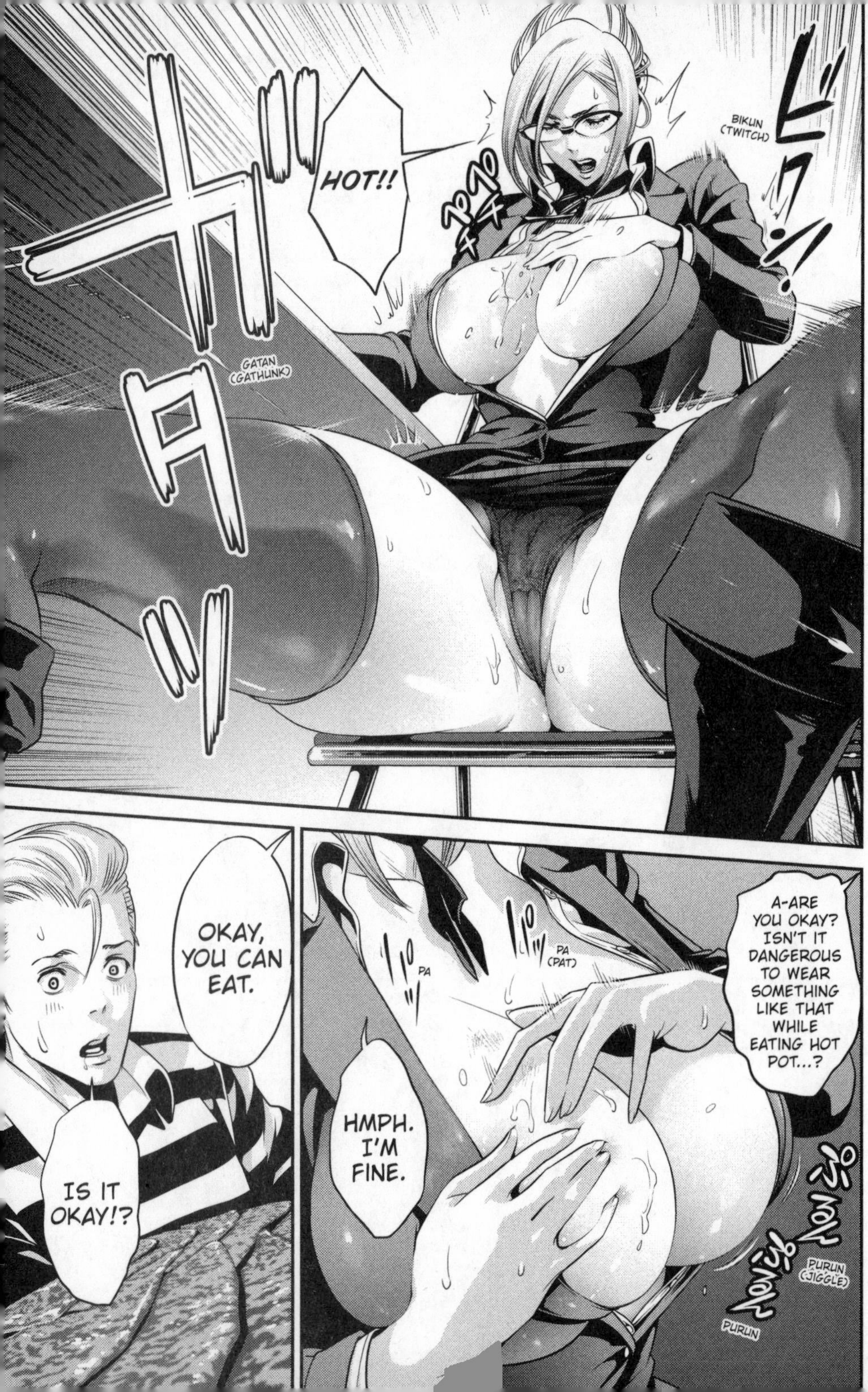
BIKUN (TWITCH)
HOT!!
GATAN (GATHUNK)
A-ARE YOU OKAY? ISN'T IT DANGEROUS TO WEAR SOMETHING LIKE THAT WHILE EATING HOT POT...?
PA (PAT)
PA
HMPH. I'M FINE.
PURUN (JIGGLE)
PURUN
OKAY, YOU CAN EAT.
IS IT OKAY!?

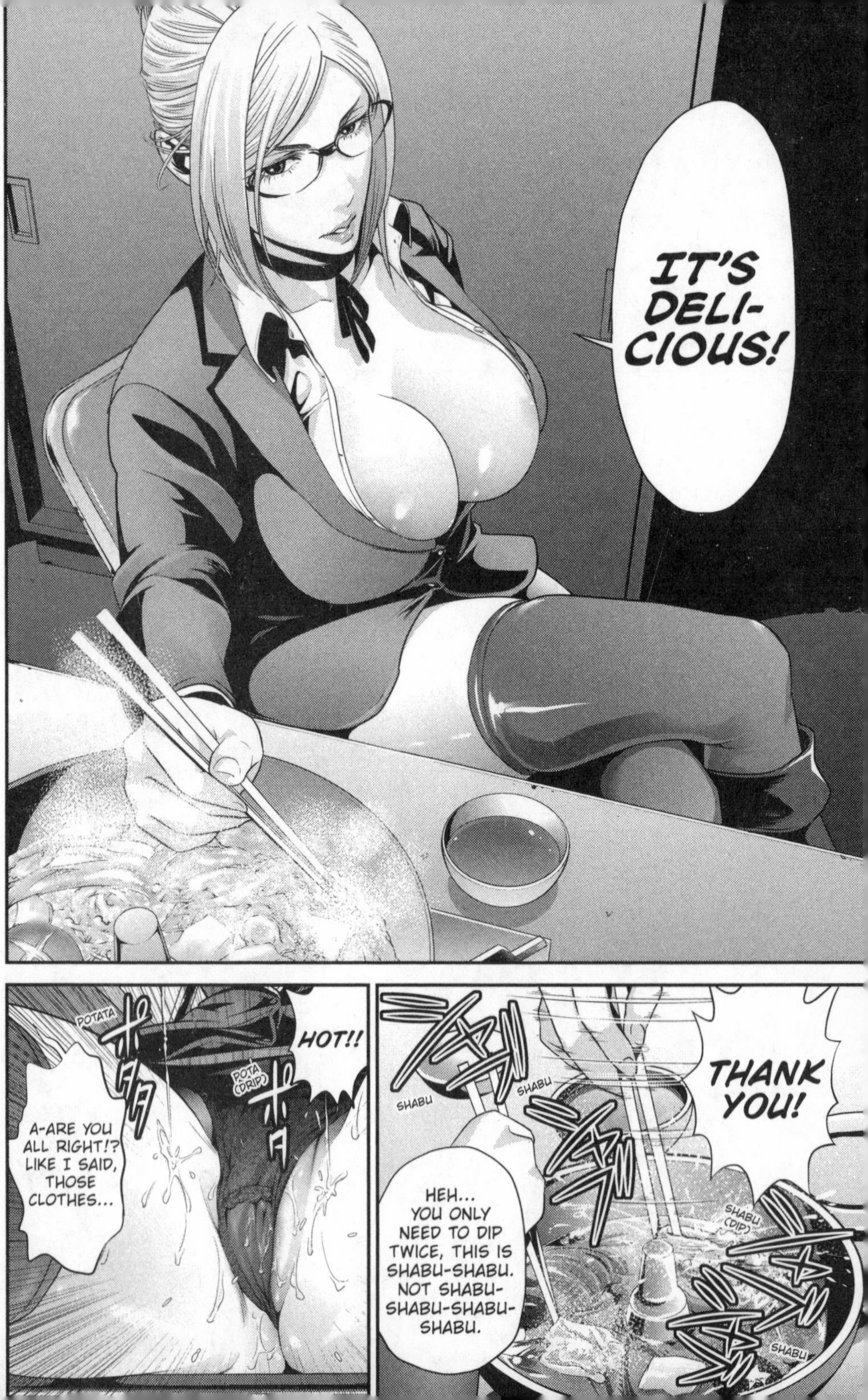
IT'S DELI-CIOUS!
THANK YOU!
SHABU
SHABU
HEH... YOU ONLY NEED TO DIP TWICE, THIS IS SHABU-SHABU. NOT SHABU-SHABU-SHABU-SHABU.
SHABU (DIP)
SHABU
HOT!!
POTATA
POTA (DRIP)
A-ARE YOU ALL RIGHT!? LIKE I SAID, THOSE CLOTHES...

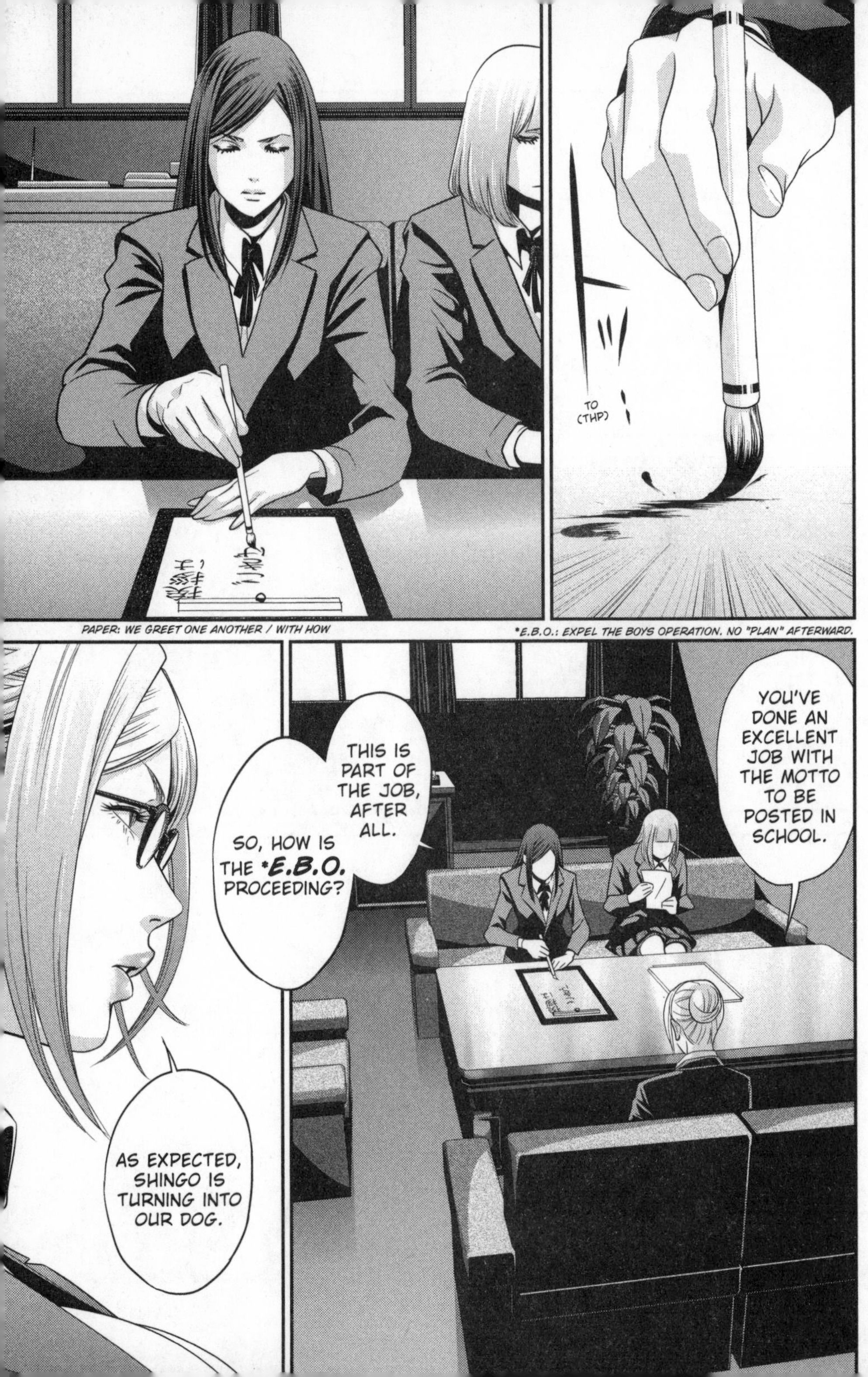
TO (THP)
YOU'VE DONE AN EXCELLENT JOB WITH THE MOTTO TO BE POSTED IN SCHOOL.
THIS IS PART OF THE JOB, AFTER ALL.
SO, HOW IS THE *E.B.O. PROCEEDING?
AS EXPECTED, SHINGO IS TURNING INTO OUR DOG.

PAPER: WE GREET ONE ANOTHER / WITH HOW

*E.B.O.: EXPEL THE BOYS OPERATION. NO "PLAN" AFTERWARD.

WITH THE HARSHER PUNISHMENTS, THEY ALL SEEM TO BE GROWING MORE STRESSED.
OF COURSE, THAT FATTY ANDRE LOOKS TO BE SUFFERING BECAUSE HE ISN'T BEING HIT!
FURTHER-MORE, JOE'S EXCESSIVE LOVE FOR HIS PET ANTS...
...SEEMS TO BE CAUSING INTERNAL TROUBLE.
PAPER: WE GREET ONE ANOTHER / WITH HOW DO YOU DO
IS THAT SO...
THE MORE STRESSED THEY ARE, THE MORE LIKELY IT IS FOR THEM CAUSE A PROBLEM.
KASA (SCURRY)
KASA
KASA
...

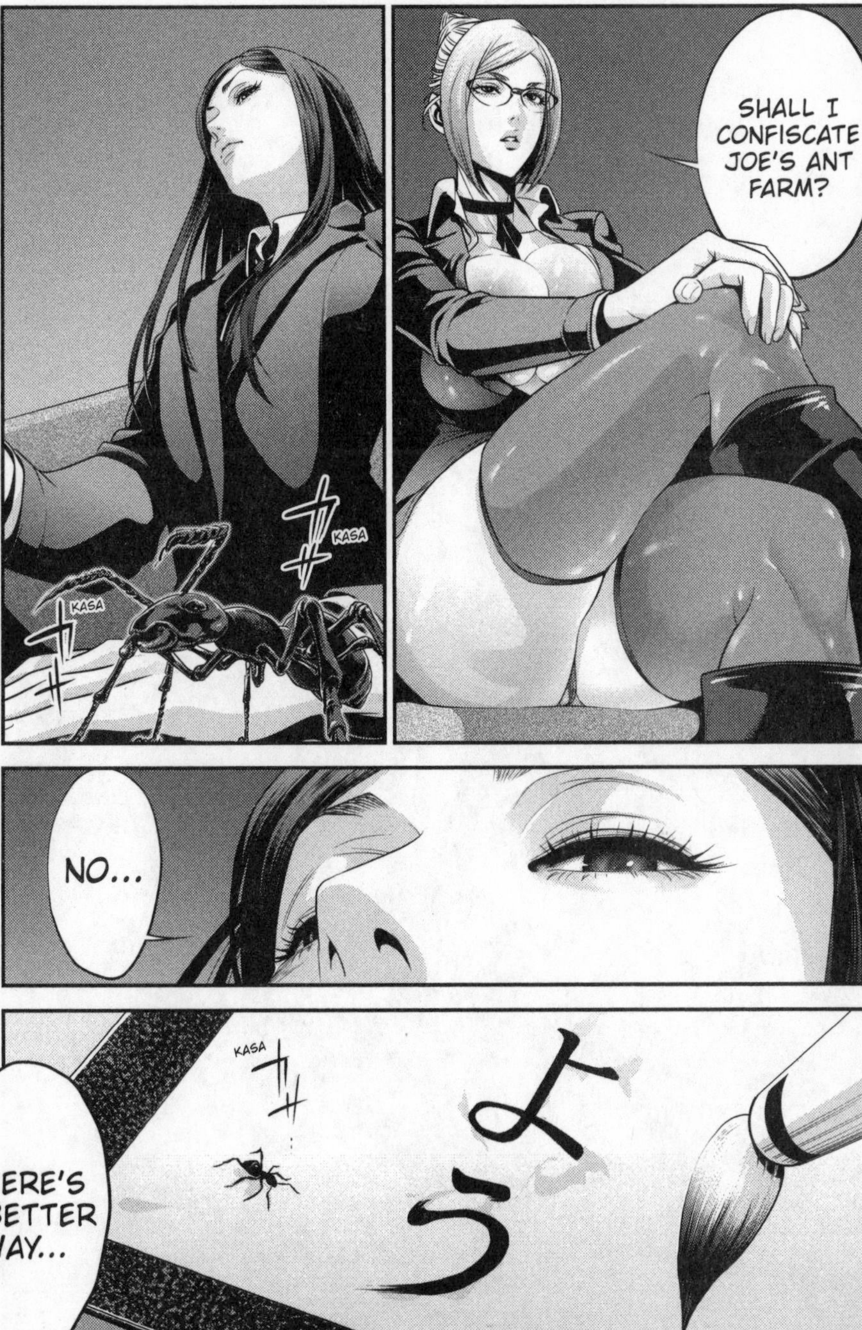
SHALL I CONFISCATE JOE'S ANT FARM?
KASA
KASA
NO...
KASA
よう
THERE'S A BETTER WAY...

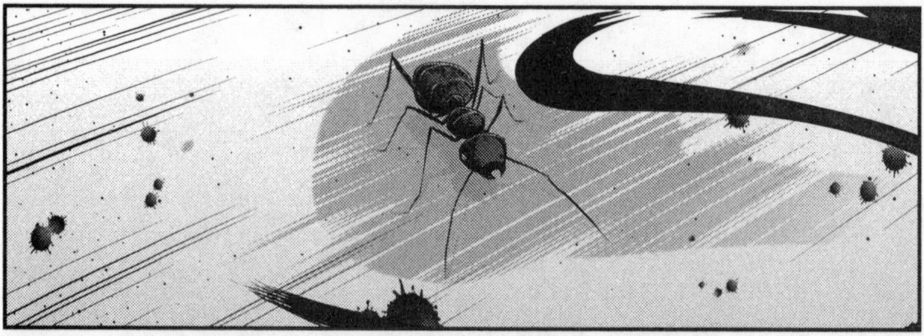

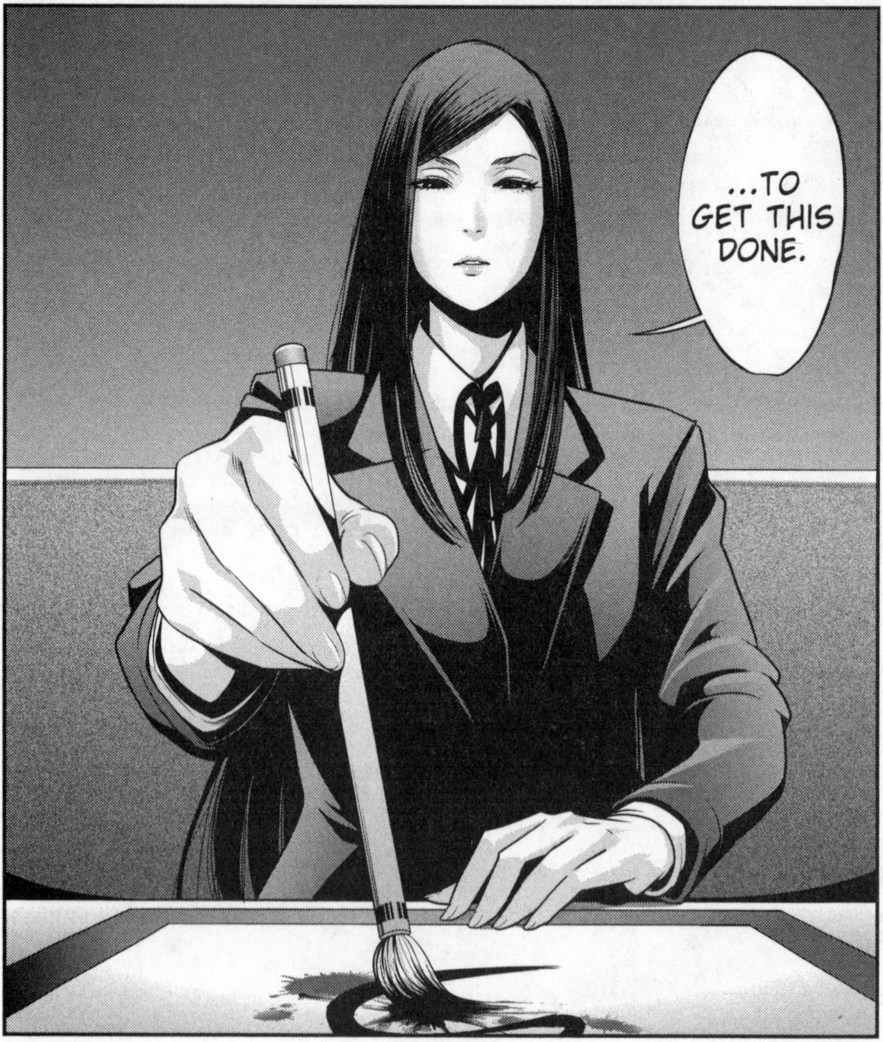
...TO
GET THIS
DONE.

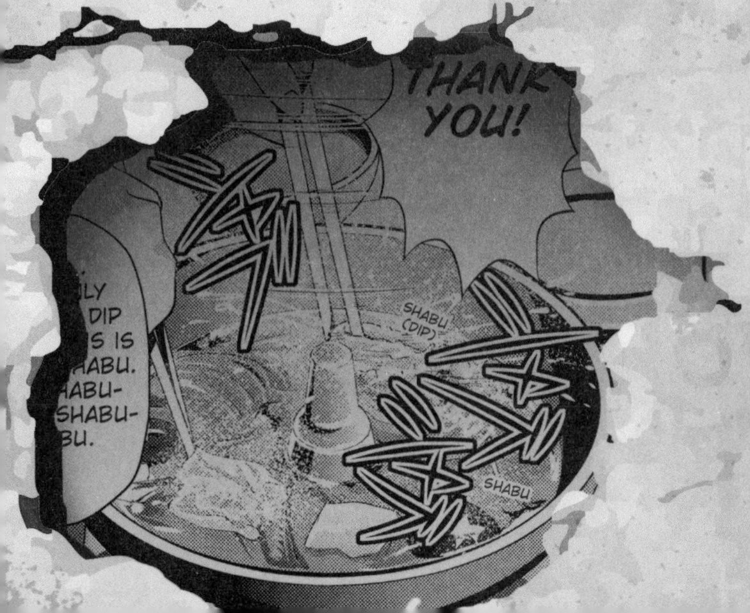
THANK YOU!
SHABU (DIP)
SHABU
LY DIP S IS HABU. HABU-SHABU-BU.

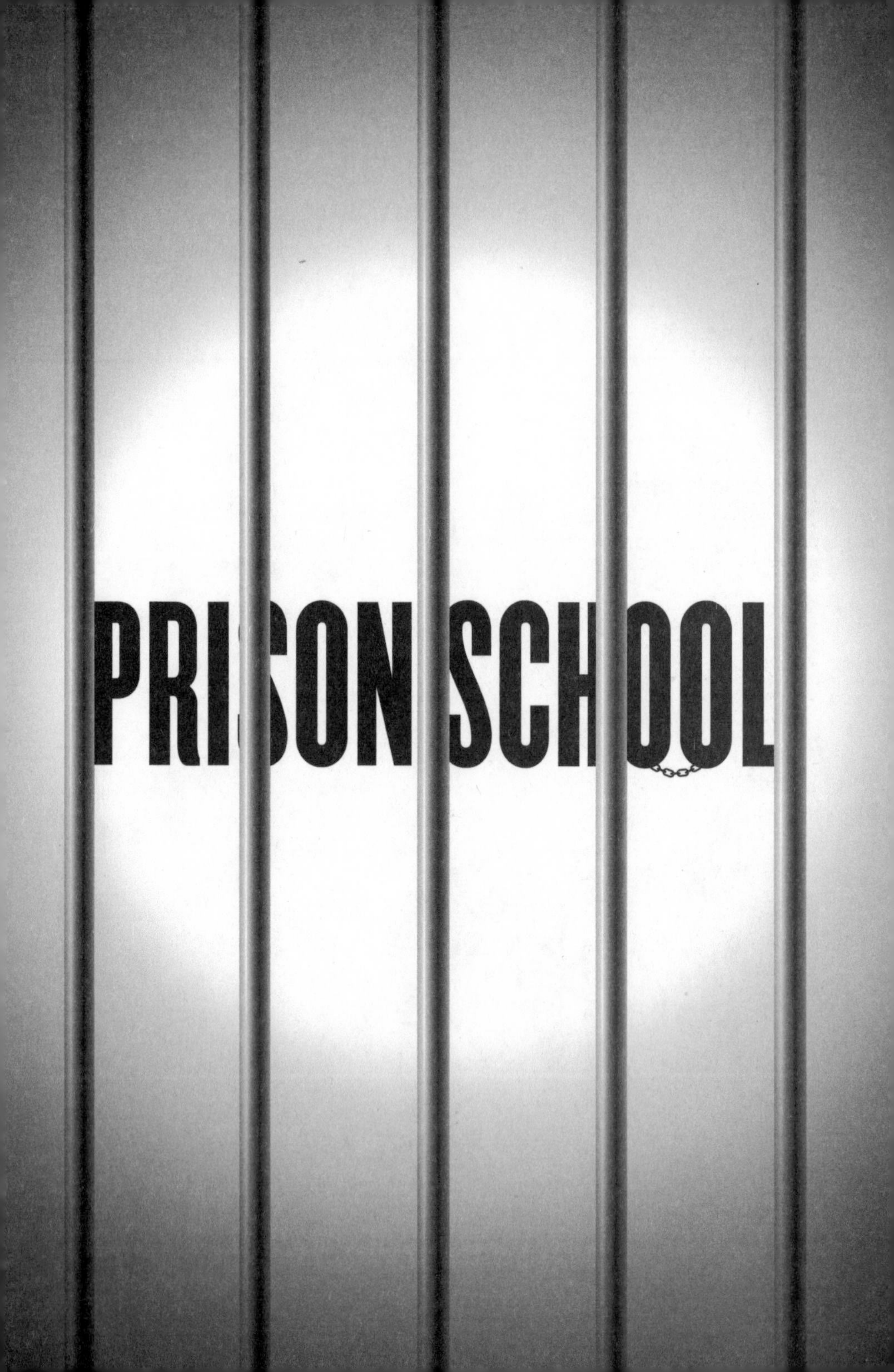
PRISON SCHOOL

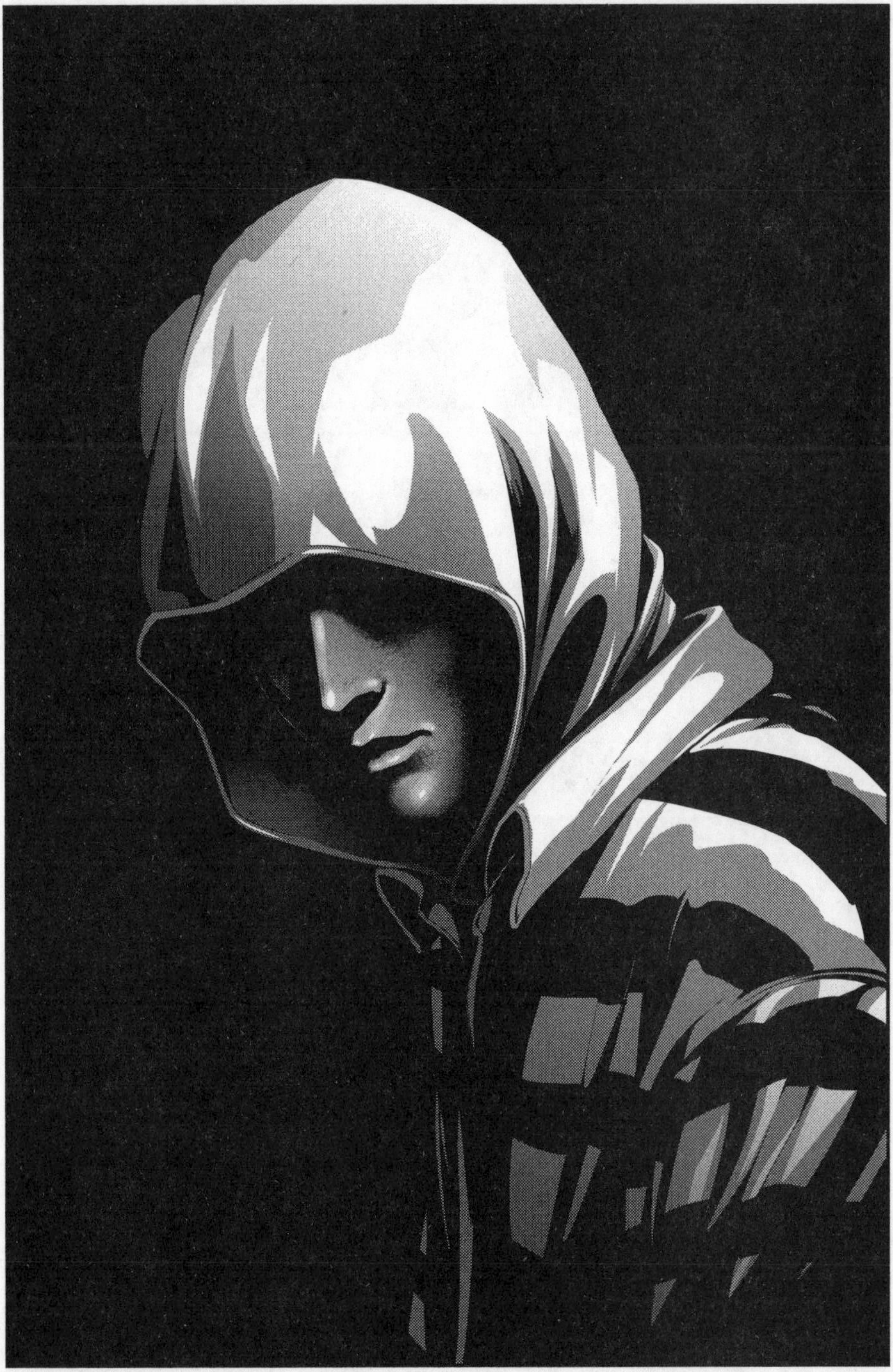

CHAPTER 37: GIANT

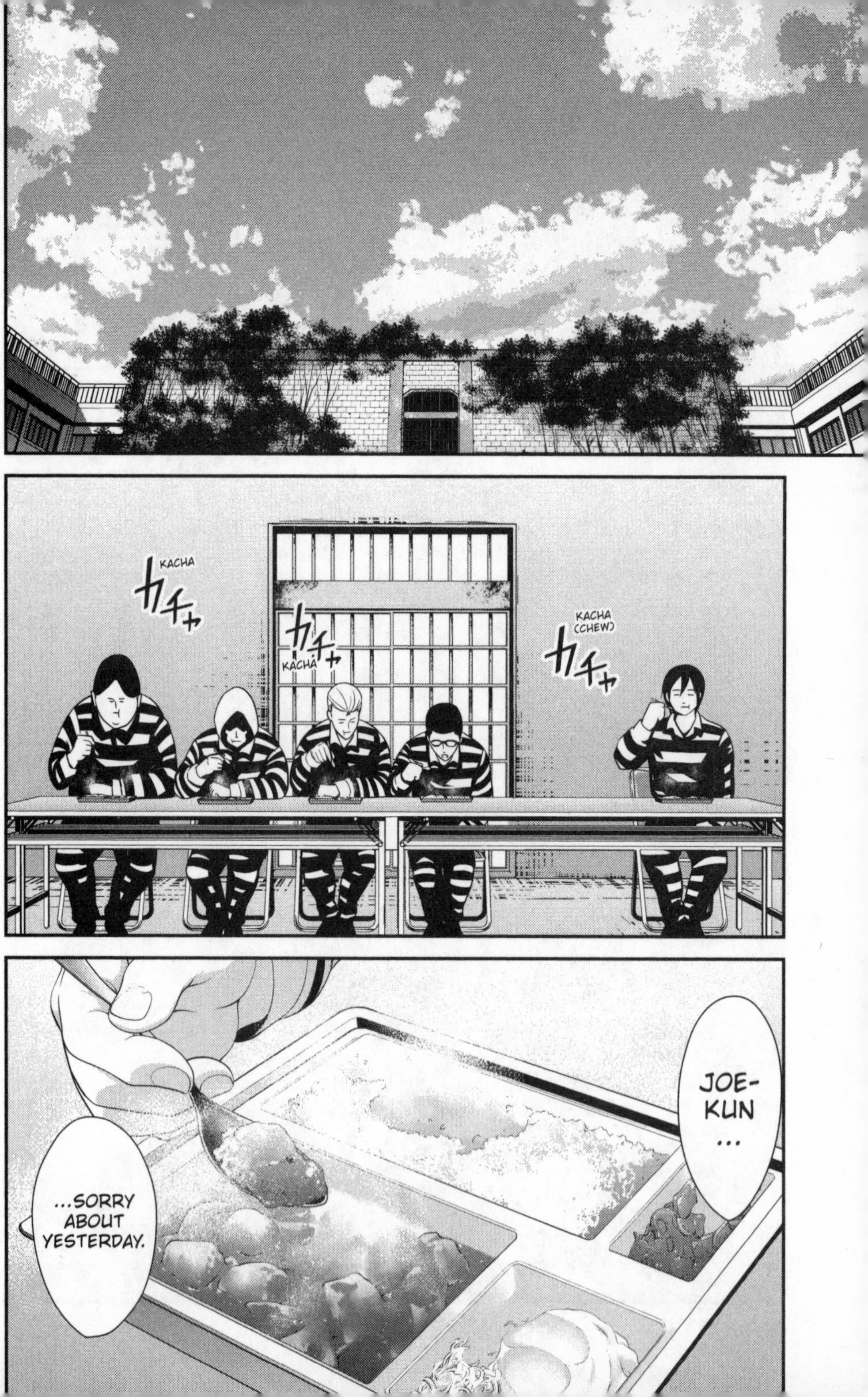

カチャ
KACHA (CHEW)
カチャ
KACHA
カチャ
KACHA
JOE-KUN ...
...SORRY ABOUT YESTERDAY.

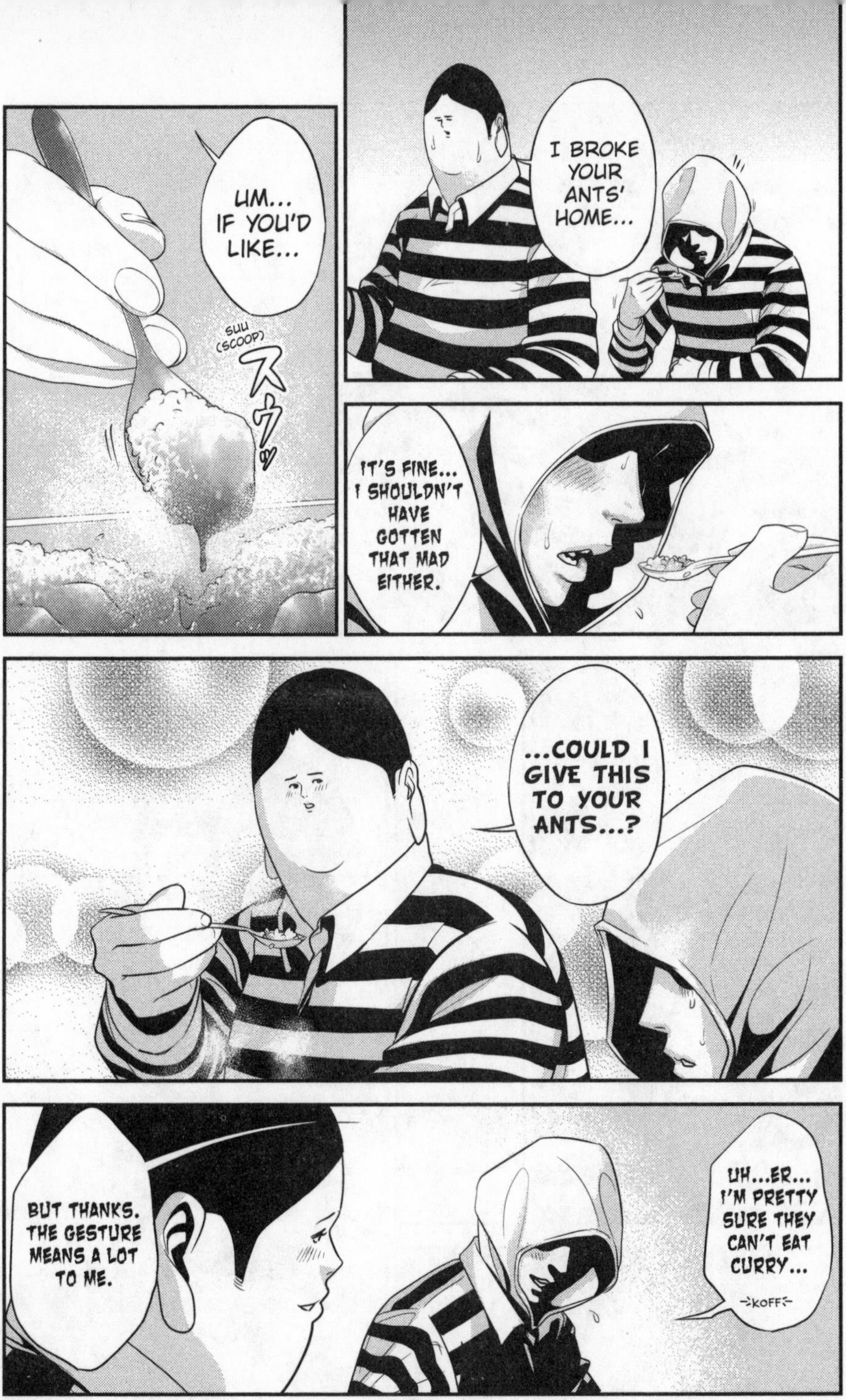
I BROKE YOUR ANTS' HOME...
IT'S FINE... I SHOULDN'T HAVE GOTTEN THAT MAD EITHER.
UM... IF YOU'D LIKE...
SUU (SCOOP)
スゥッ
...COULD I GIVE THIS TO YOUR ANTS...?
UH...ER... I'M PRETTY SURE THEY CAN'T EAT CURRY...
KOFF
BUT THANKS. THE GESTURE MEANS A LOT TO ME.

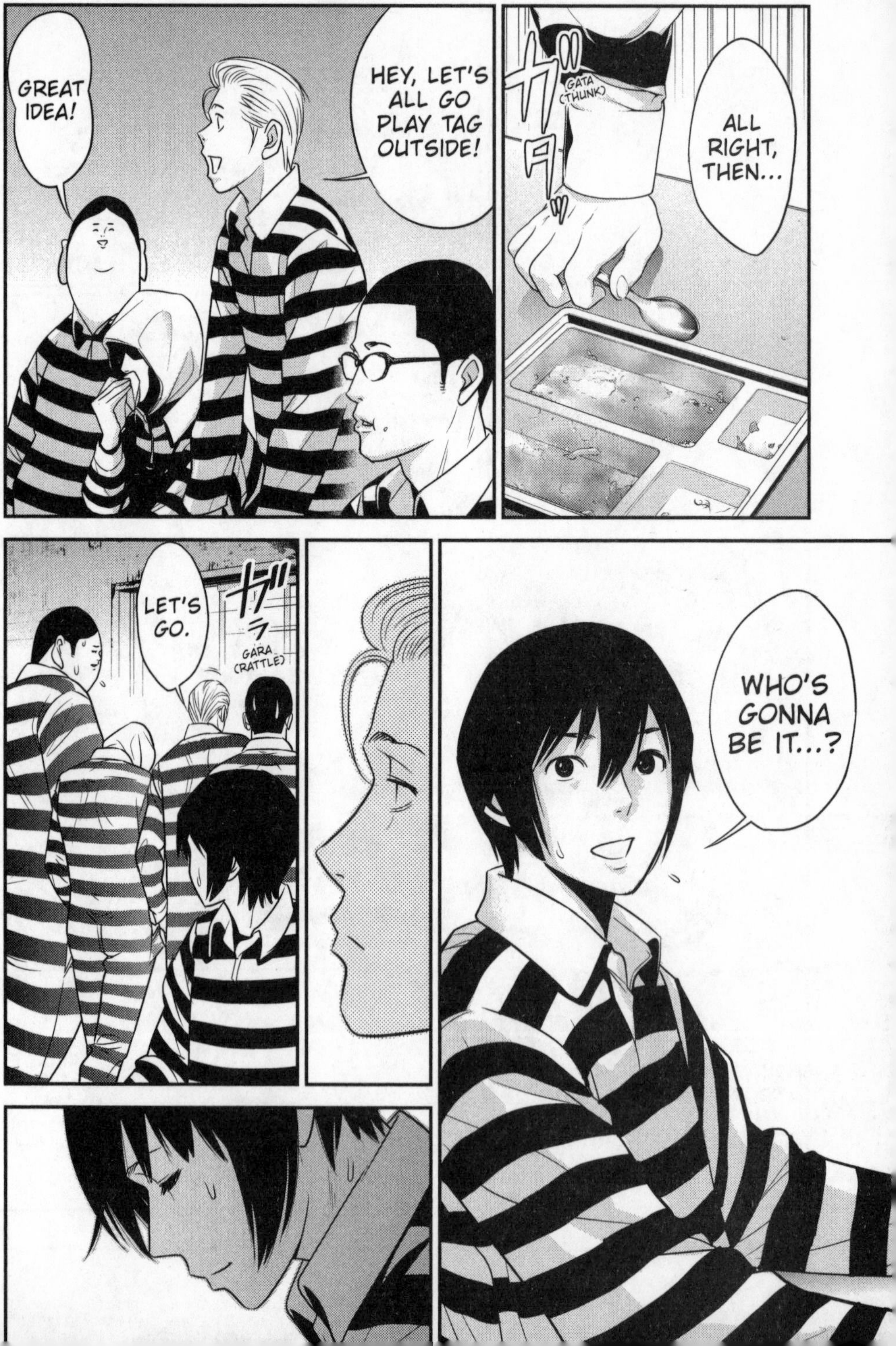
GATA (THUNK)
ALL RIGHT, THEN...
HEY, LET'S ALL GO PLAY TAG OUTSIDE!
GREAT IDEA!
WHO'S GONNA BE IT...?
GARA (RATTLE)
LET'S GO.

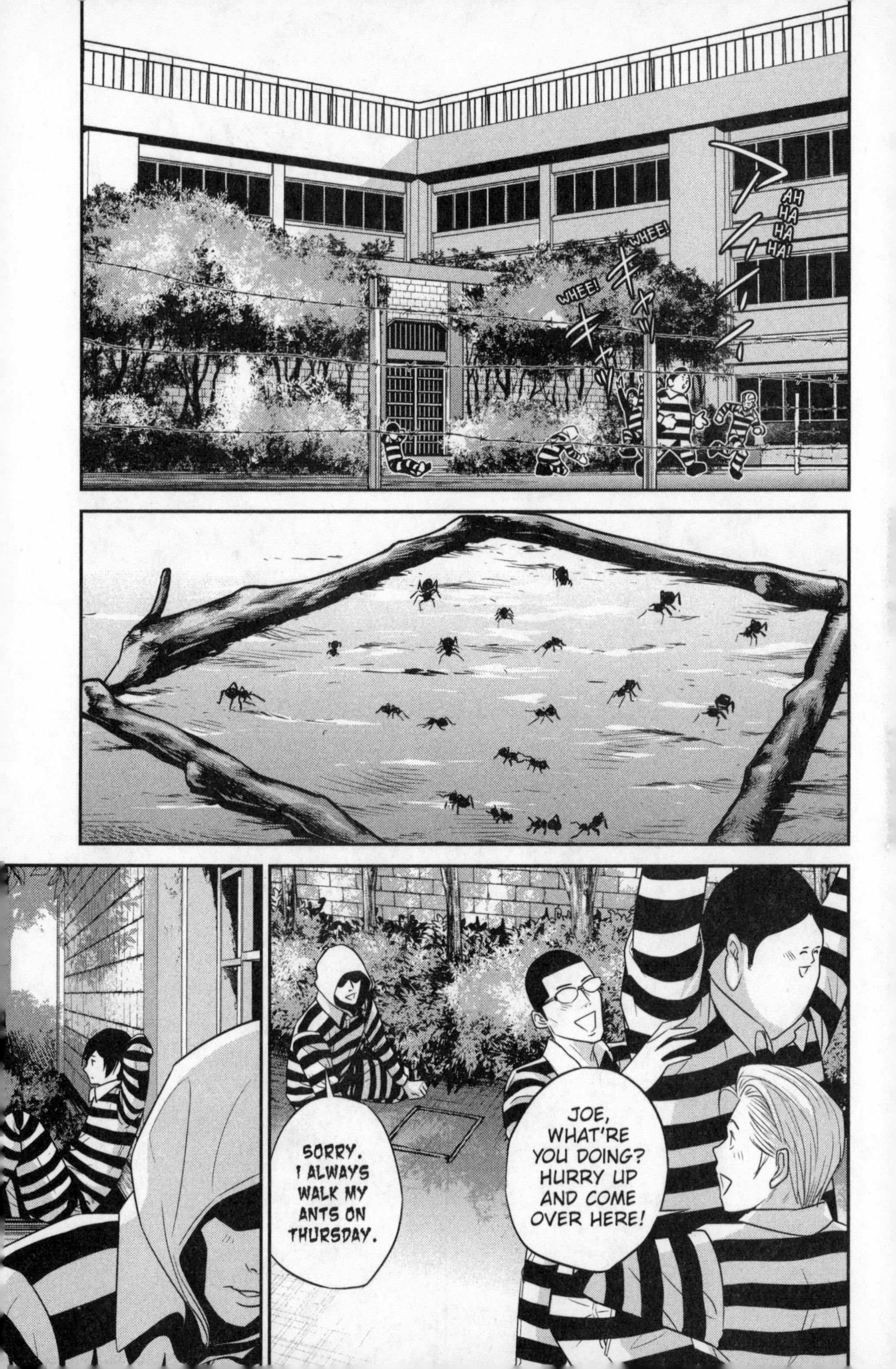
AH HA HA HA!
WHEE!
WHEE!
JOE, WHAT'RE YOU DOING? HURRY UP AND COME OVER HERE!
SORRY. I ALWAYS WALK MY ANTS ON THURSDAY.

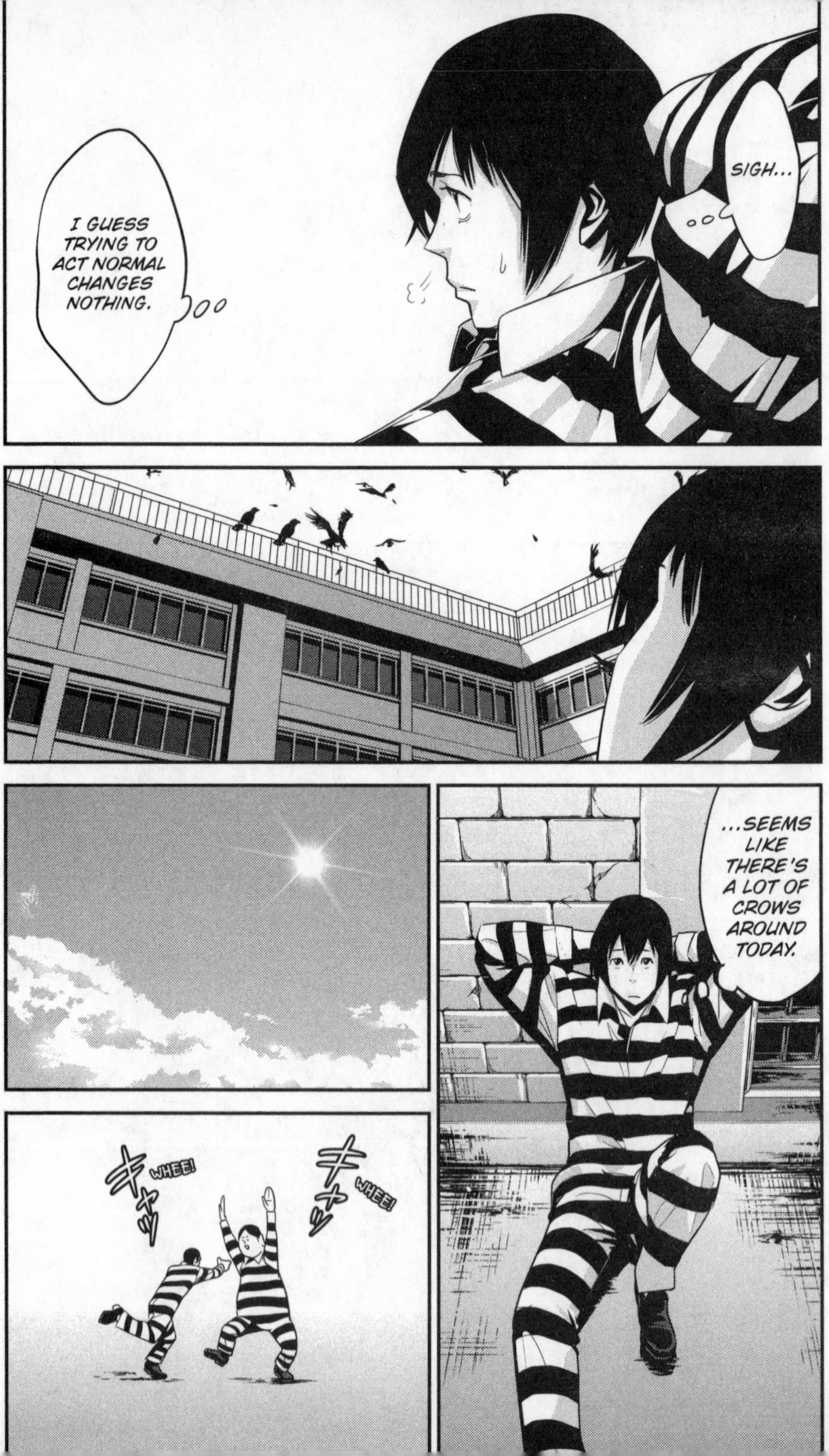
SIGH...
I GUESS TRYING TO ACT NORMAL CHANGES NOTHING.
...SEEMS LIKE THERE'S A LOT OF CROWS AROUND TODAY.
キャッ
WHEE!
キャッ
WHEE!

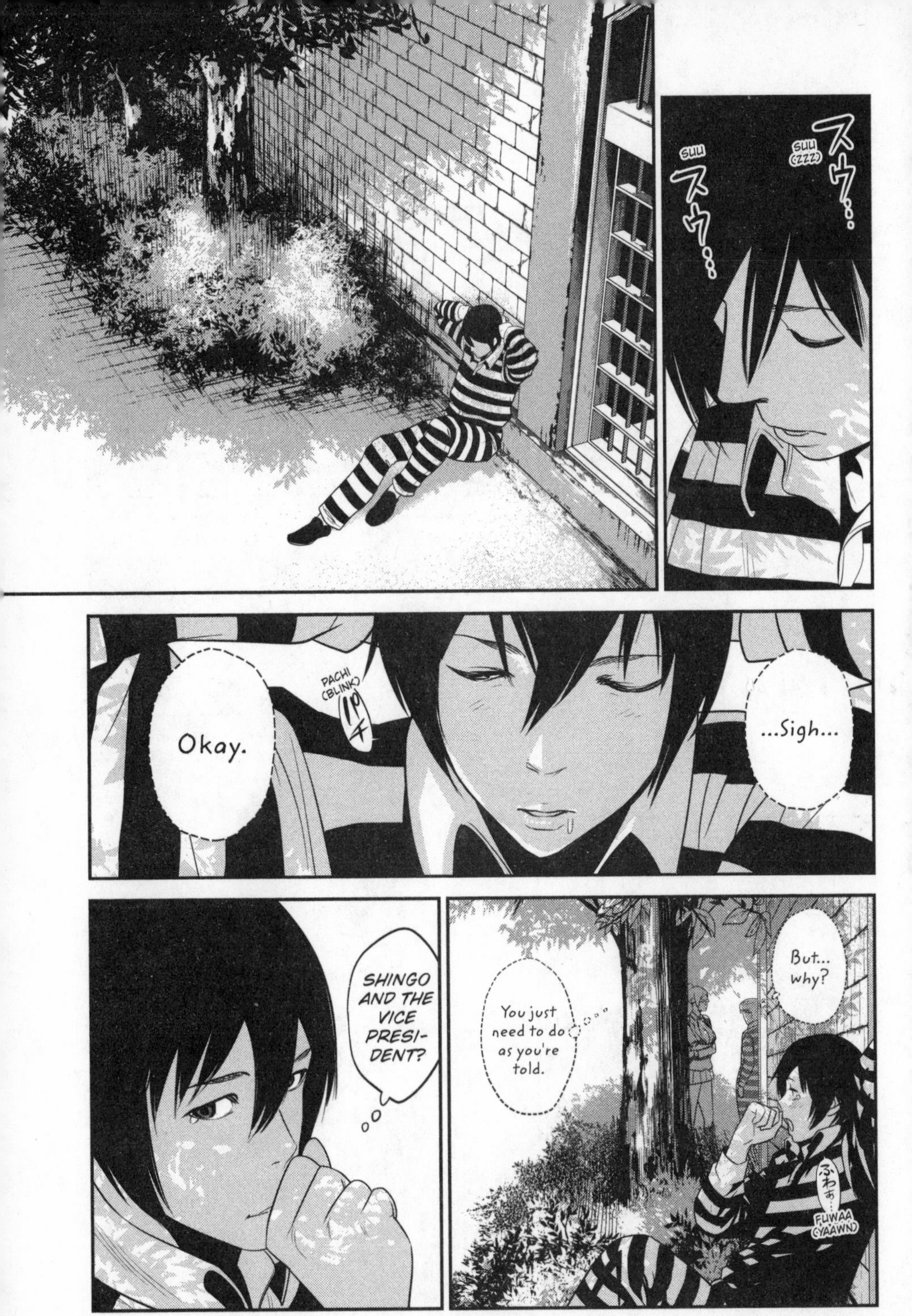
スウ…
SUU (ZZZ)
スウ…
SUU
…Sigh…
ハチ
PACHI (BLINK)
Okay.
But… why?
You just need to do as you're told.
ふわぁ…
FUWAA (YAAWN)
SHINGO AND THE VICE PRESI-DENT?

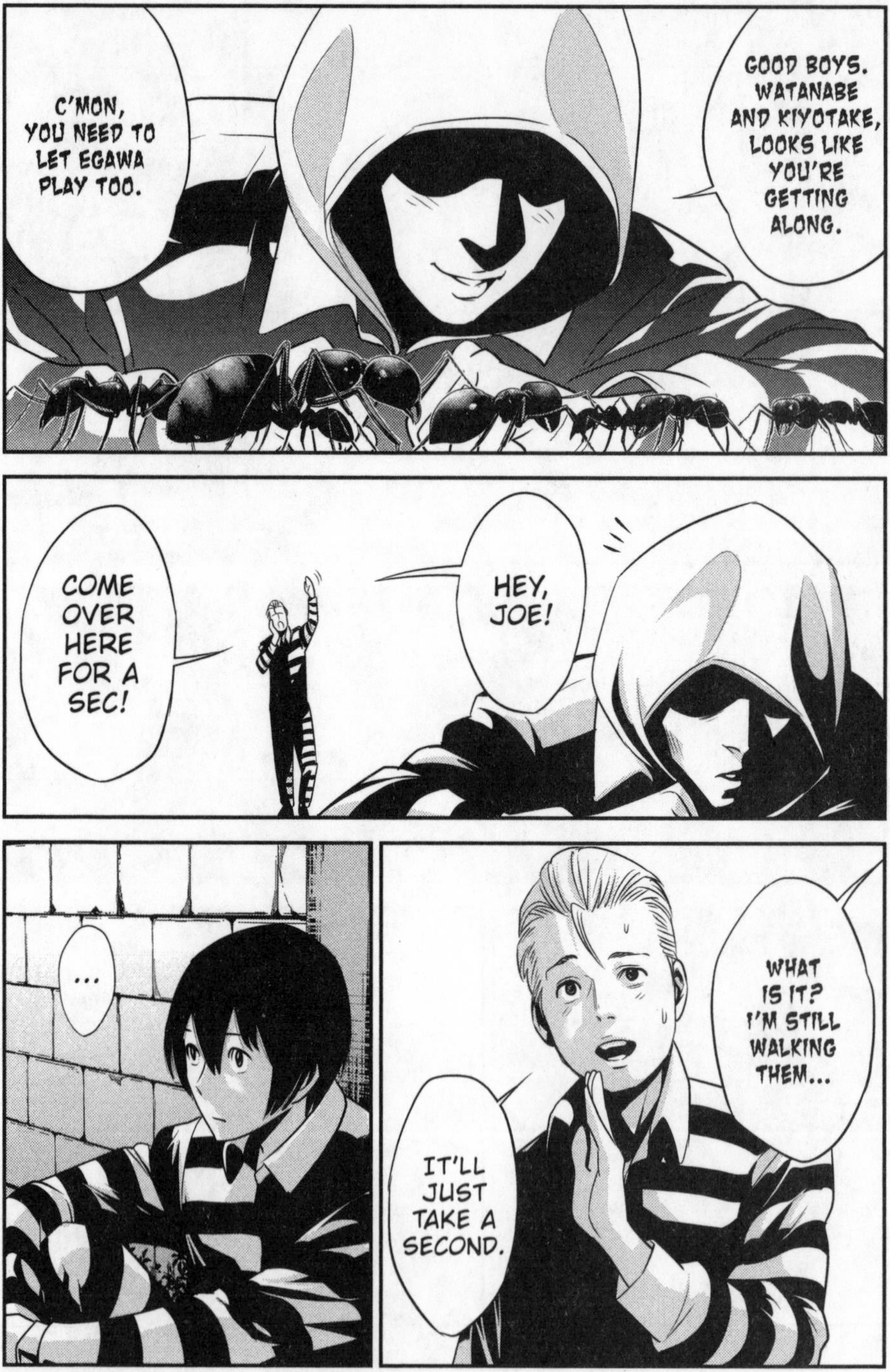
GOOD BOYS. WATANABE AND KIYOTAKE, LOOKS LIKE YOU'RE GETTING ALONG.
C'MON, YOU NEED TO LET EGAWA PLAY TOO.
HEY, JOE!
COME OVER HERE FOR A SEC!
WHAT IS IT? I'M STILL WALKING THEM...
IT'LL JUST TAKE A SECOND.
...

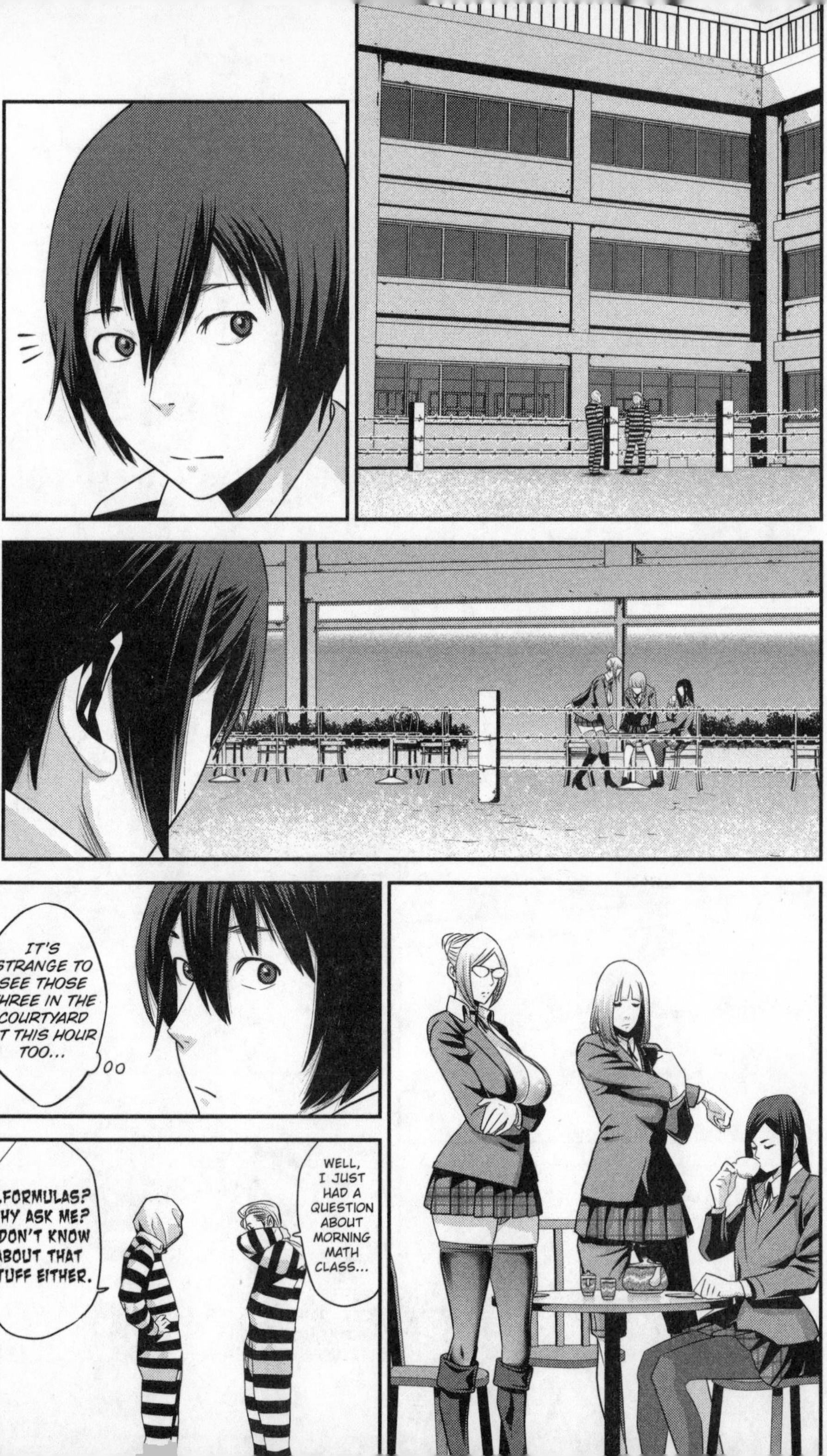
IT'S STRANGE TO SEE THOSE THREE IN THE COURTYARD AT THIS HOUR TOO...
WELL, I JUST HAD A QUESTION ABOUT MORNING MATH CLASS...
...FORMULAS? WHY ASK ME? I DON'T KNOW ABOUT THAT STUFF EITHER.

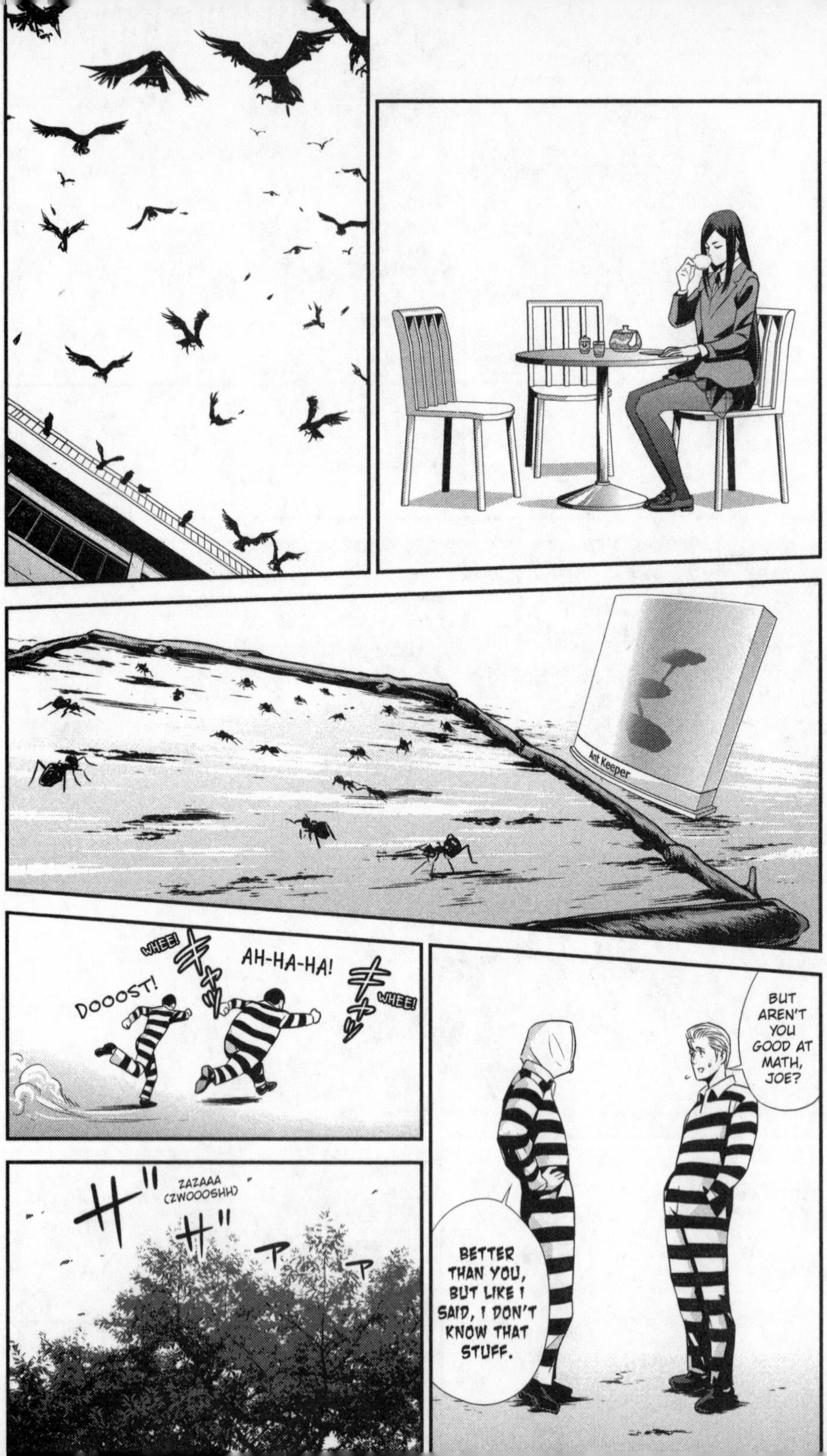
Ant Keeper
BUT AREN'T YOU GOOD AT MATH, JOE?
BETTER THAN YOU, BUT LIKE I SAID, I DON'T KNOW THAT STUFF.
WHEE!
AH-HA-HA!
DOOOST!
WHEE!
ZAZAAA (ZWOOOSH)

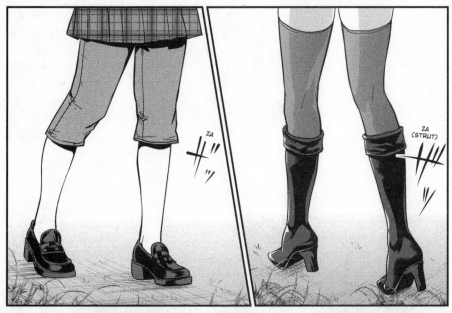

ZA

ZA
(STRUT)

......

KACHA
(CLINK)

YOUR ANTS...

JOE-KUN!

~GHKLAAK~

AA (CAAW)

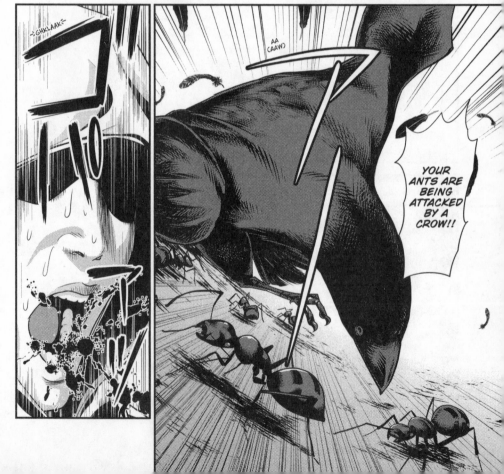

YOUR ANTS ARE BEING ATTACKED BY A CROW!!

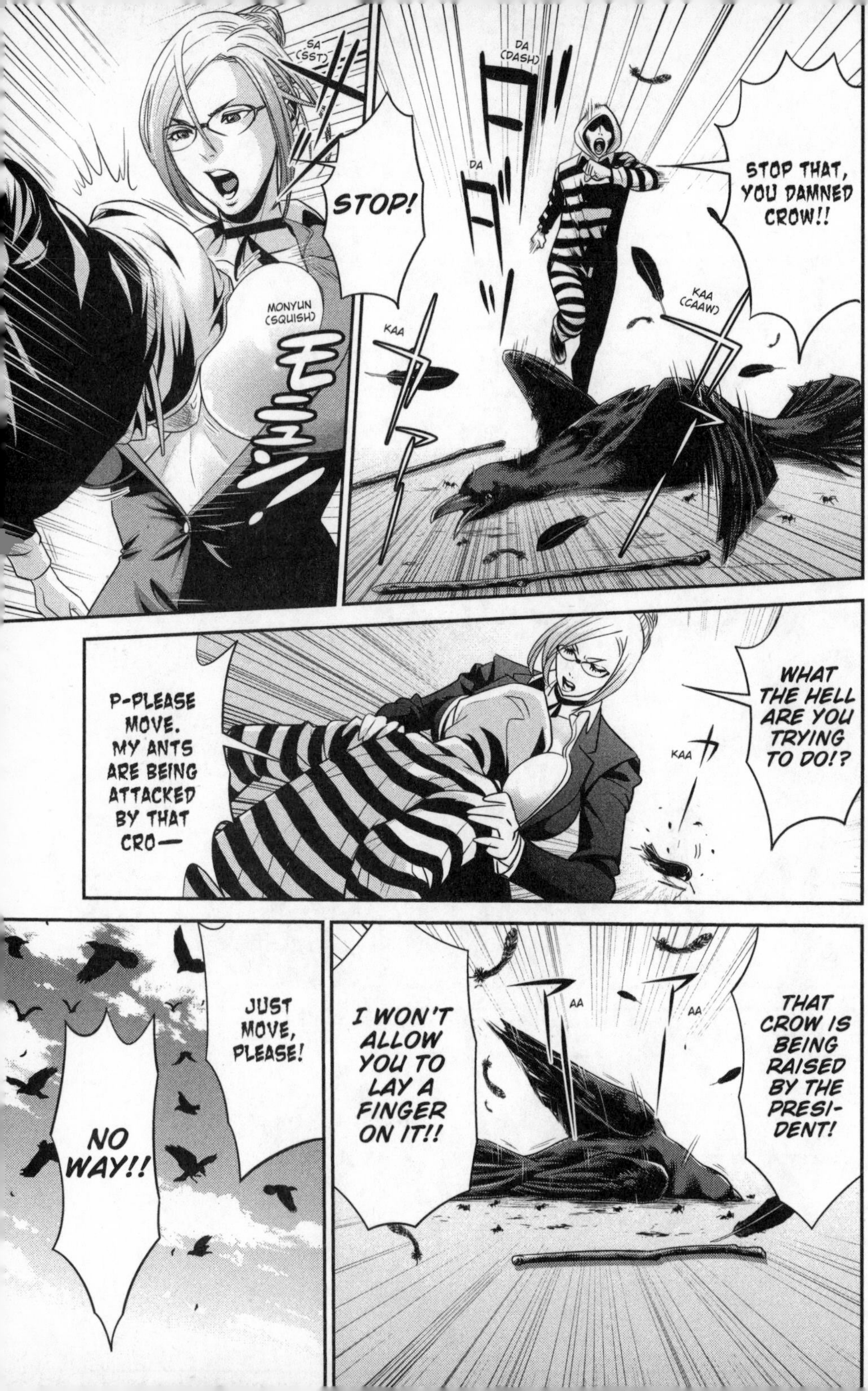
DA
(DASH)
DA
STOP THAT, YOU DAMNED CROW!!
KAA
(CAAW)
KAA
SA
(SST)
STOP!
MONYUN
(SQUISH)
WHAT THE HELL ARE YOU TRYING TO DO!?
KAA
P-PLEASE MOVE. MY ANTS ARE BEING ATTACKED BY THAT CRO—
THAT CROW IS BEING RAISED BY THE PRESI-DENT!
AA
AA
I WON'T ALLOW YOU TO LAY A FINGER ON IT!!
JUST MOVE, PLEASE!
NO WAY!!

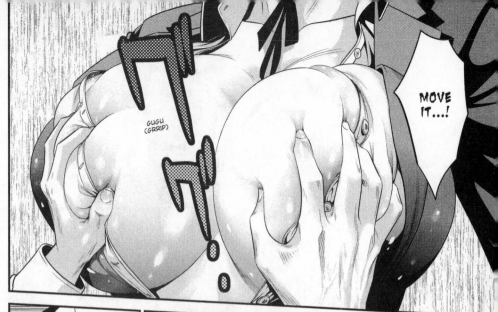

MOVE IT...!

GUGU (GRRIP)

MY ANTS...

DON (BOOM)

BURUN (THUD)

SUPAN (PAKRAK)

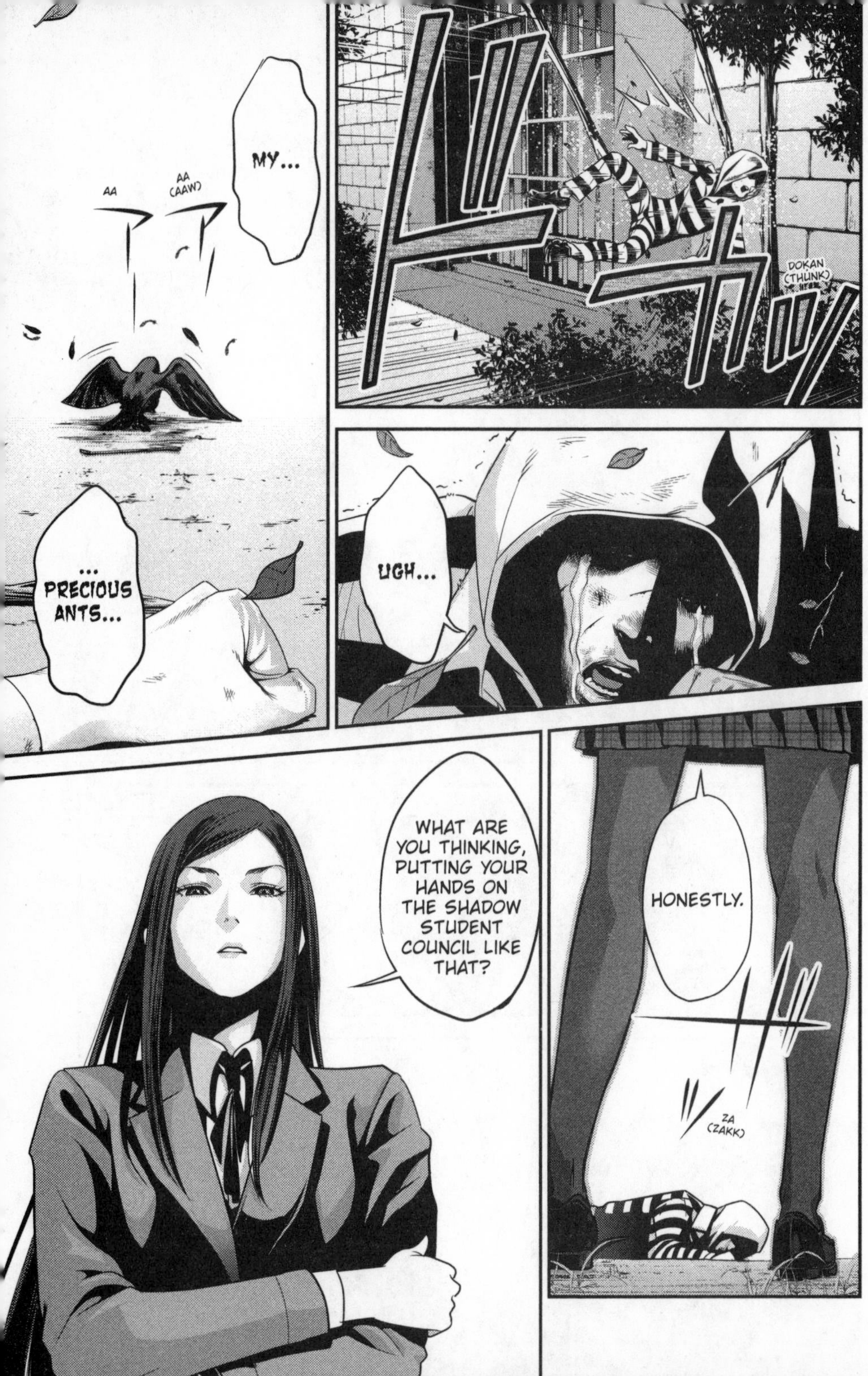
DOKAN
(THUNK)
UGH...
MY...
AA
(AAW)
AA
... PRECIOUS ANTS...
HONESTLY.
ZA
(ZAKK)
WHAT ARE YOU THINKING, PUTTING YOUR HANDS ON THE SHADOW STUDENT COUNCIL LIKE THAT?

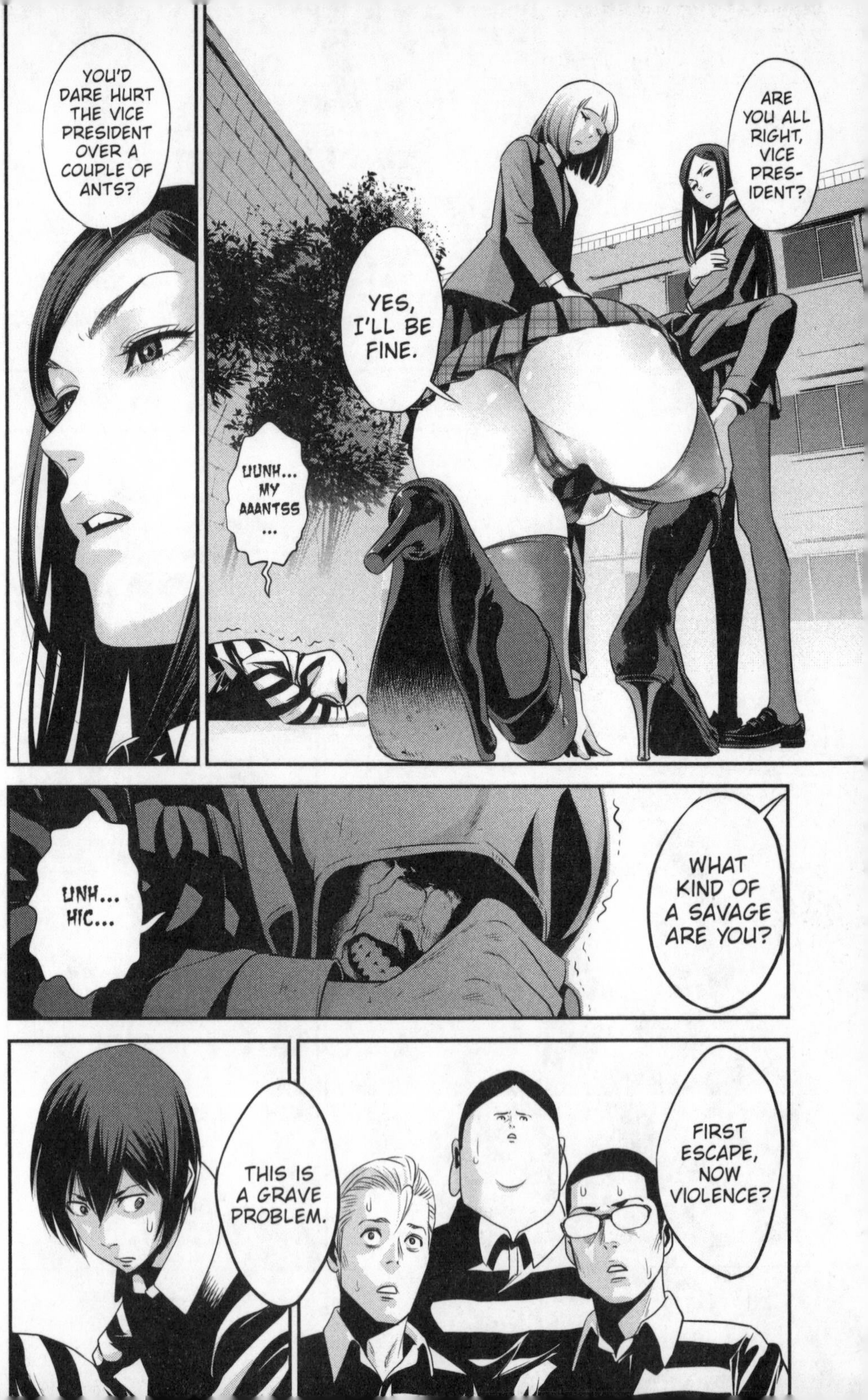
ARE YOU ALL RIGHT, VICE PRES-IDENT?
YES, I'LL BE FINE.
UUNH... MY AAANTSS ...
YOU'D DARE HURT THE VICE PRESIDENT OVER A COUPLE OF ANTS?
WHAT KIND OF A SAVAGE ARE YOU?
UNH... HIC...
FIRST ESCAPE, NOW VIOLENCE?
THIS IS A GRAVE PROBLEM.

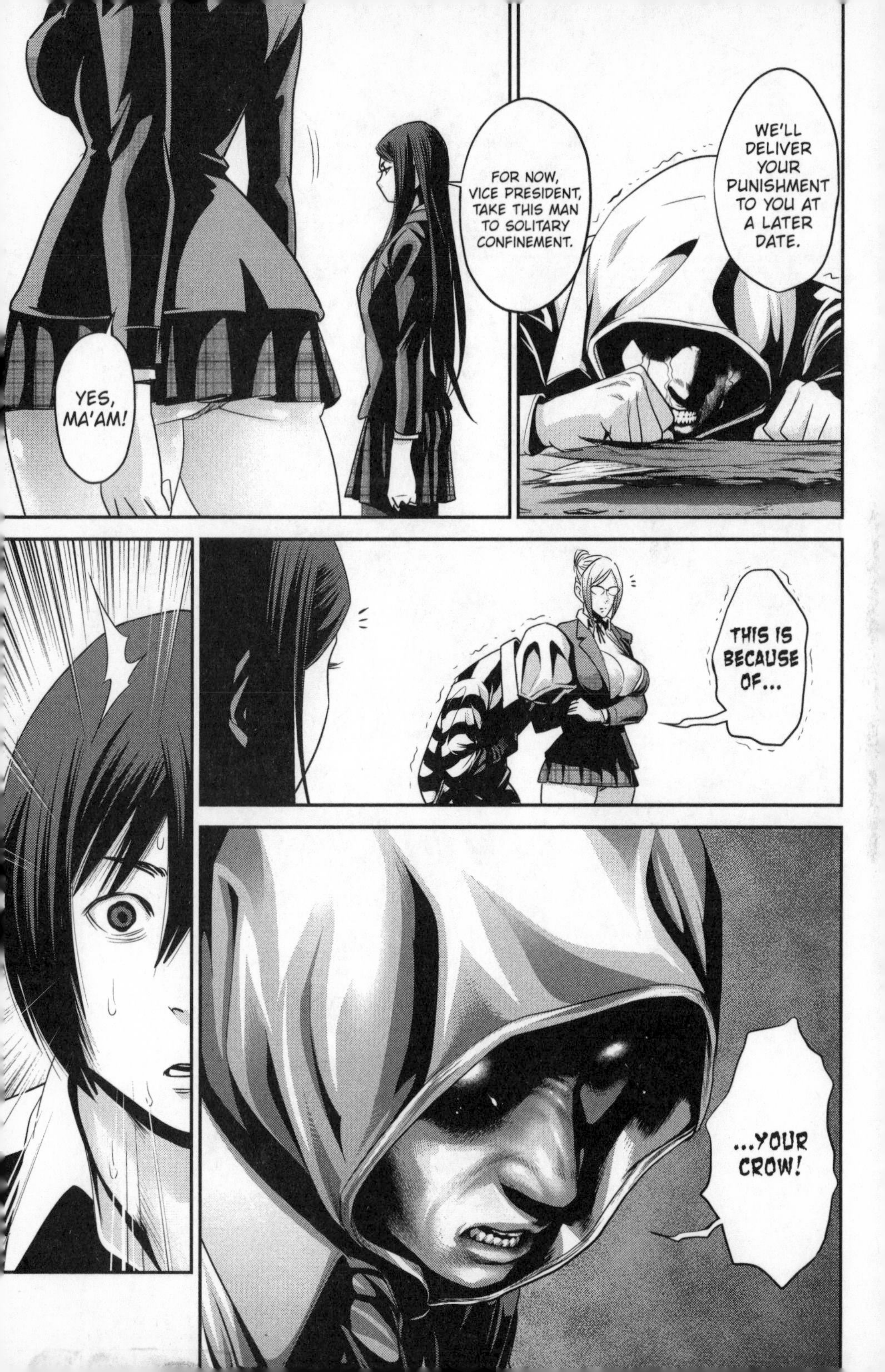
WE'LL DELIVER YOUR PUNISHMENT TO YOU AT A LATER DATE.
FOR NOW, VICE PRESIDENT, TAKE THIS MAN TO SOLITARY CONFINEMENT.
YES, MA'AM!
THIS IS BECAUSE OF...
...YOUR CROW!

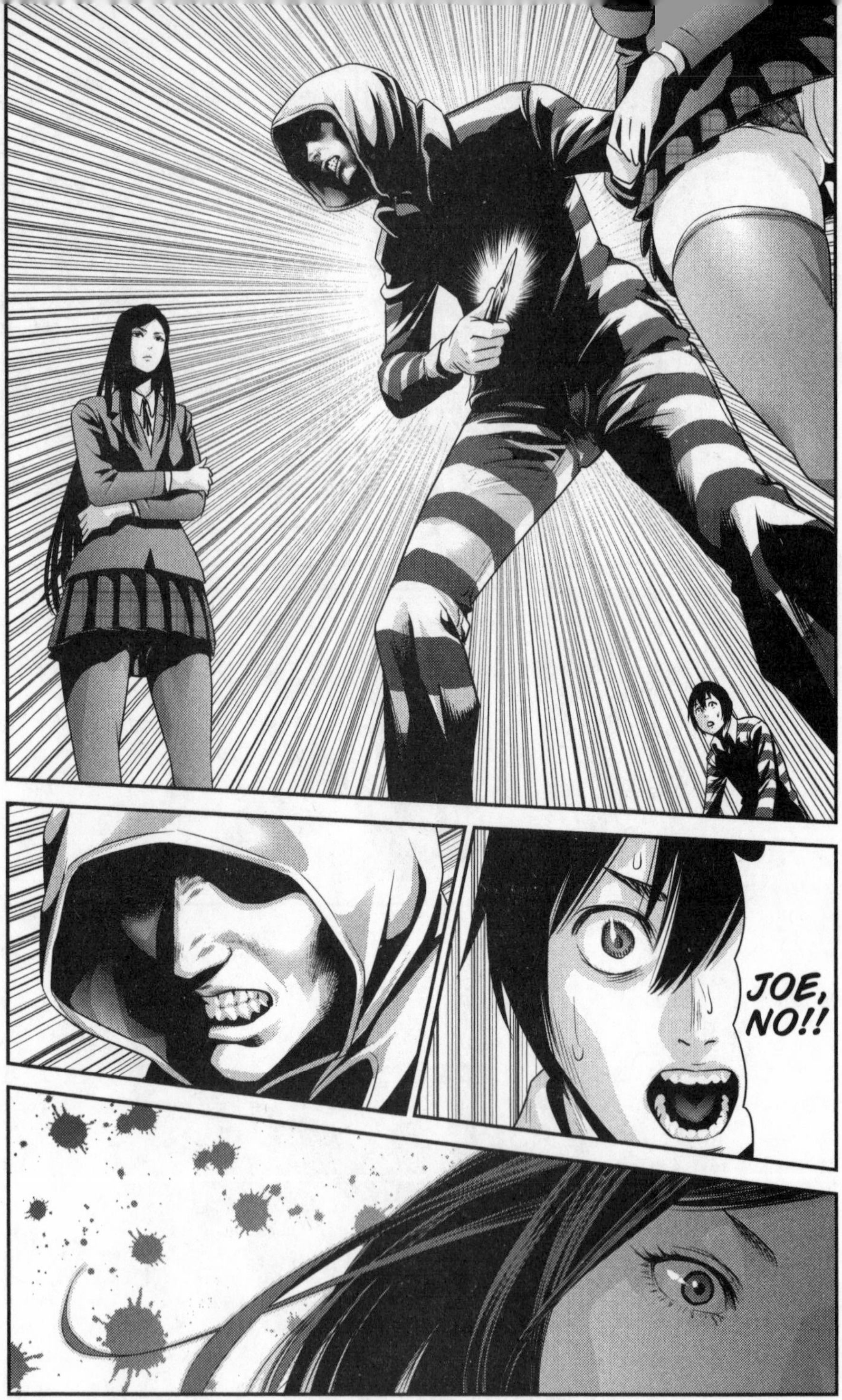
JOE, NO!!

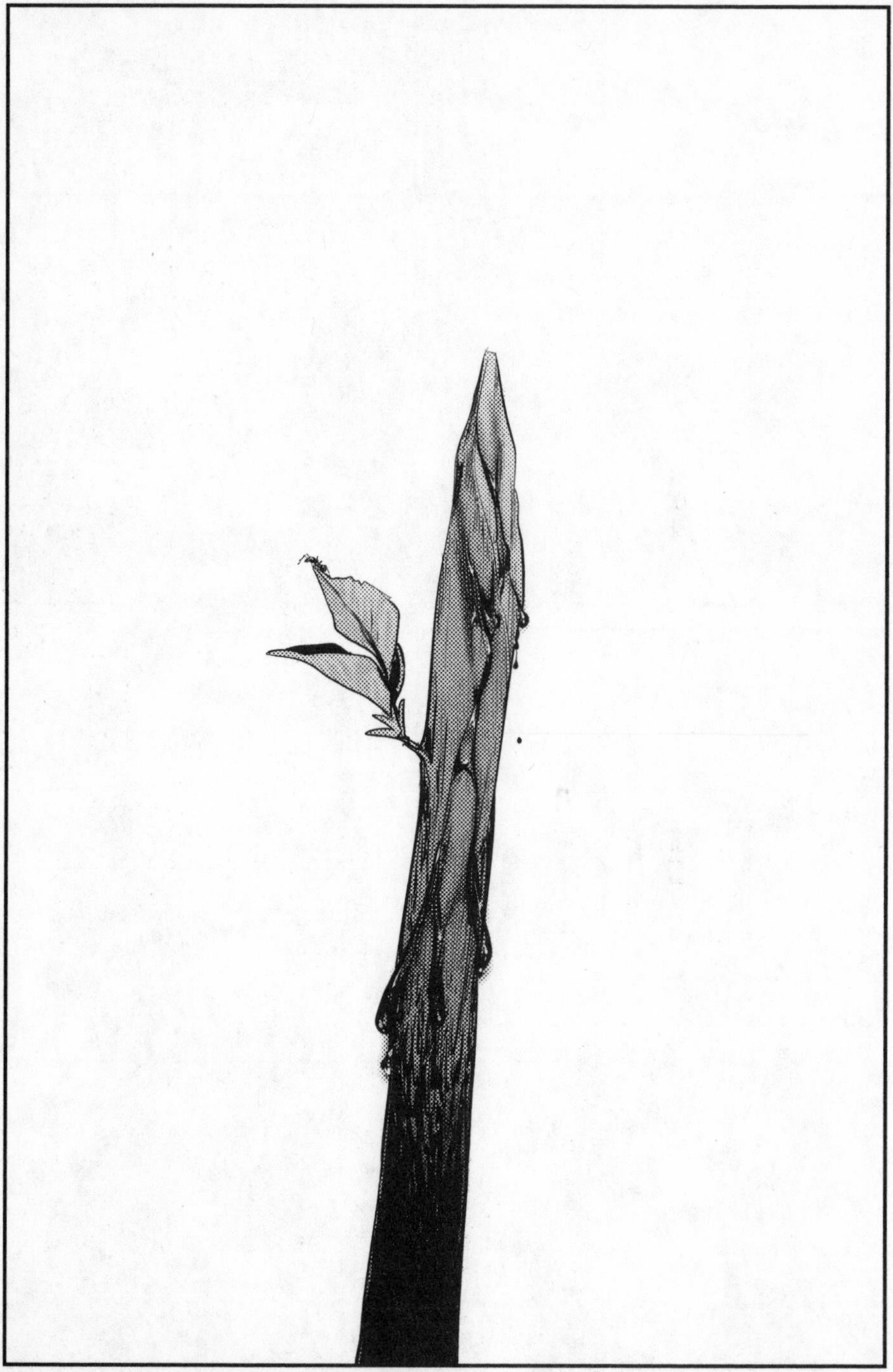

CHAPTER 38: ALI

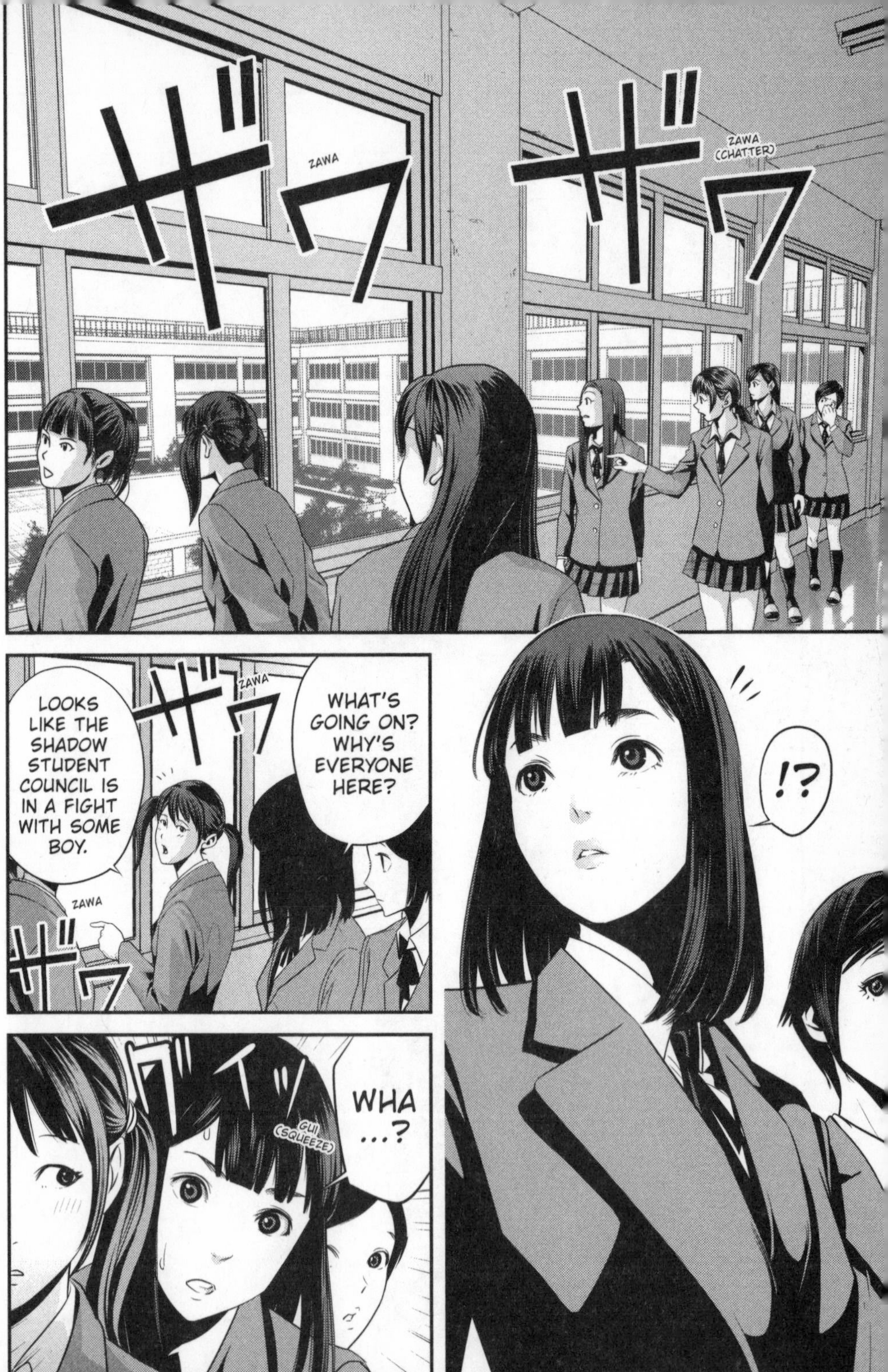
ZAWA (CHATTER)
ZAWA
!?
WHAT'S GOING ON? WHY'S EVERYONE HERE?
ZAWA
LOOKS LIKE THE SHADOW STUDENT COUNCIL IS IN A FIGHT WITH SOME BOY.
ZAWA
WHA ...?
GUI (SQUEEZE)

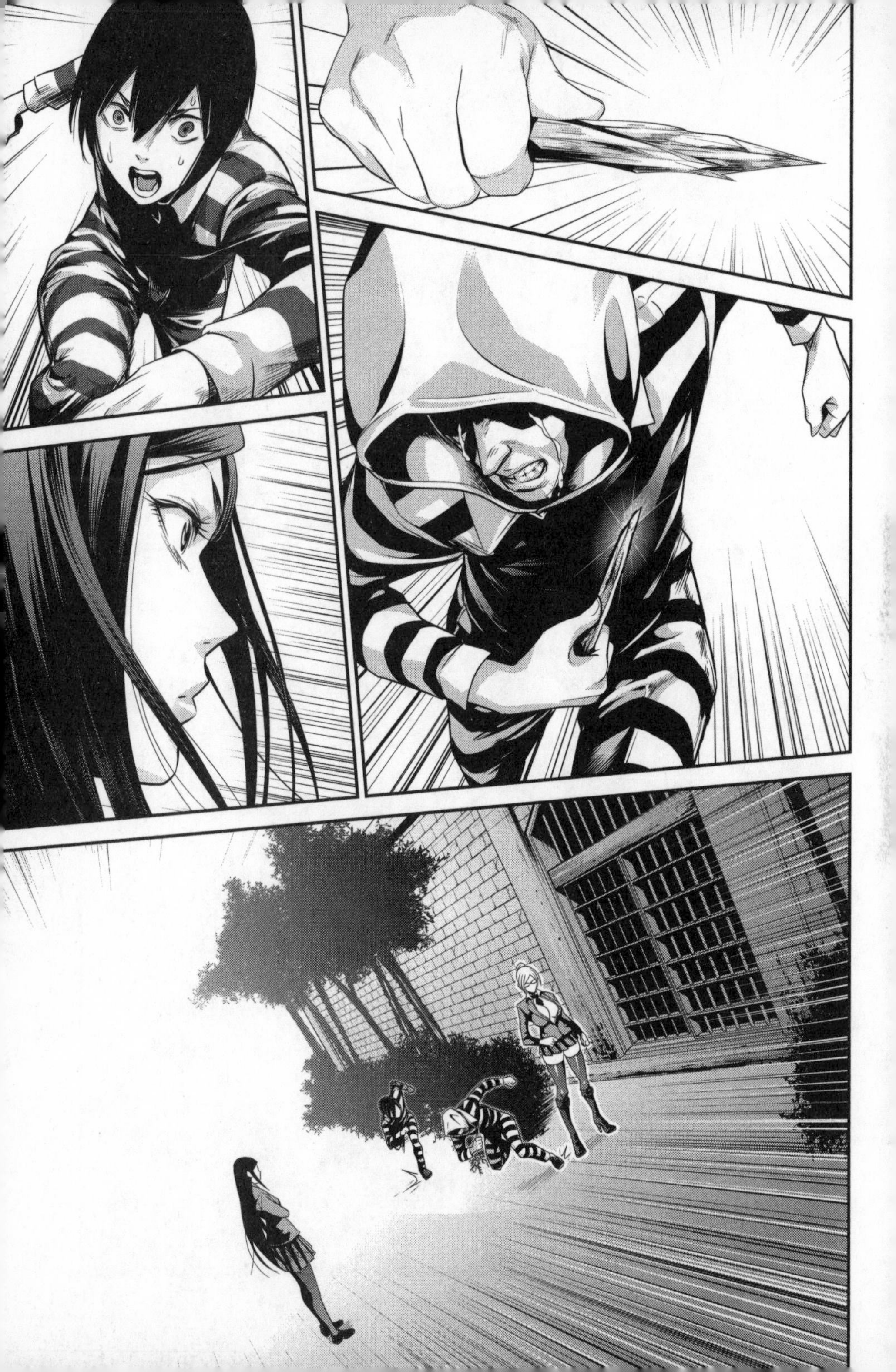

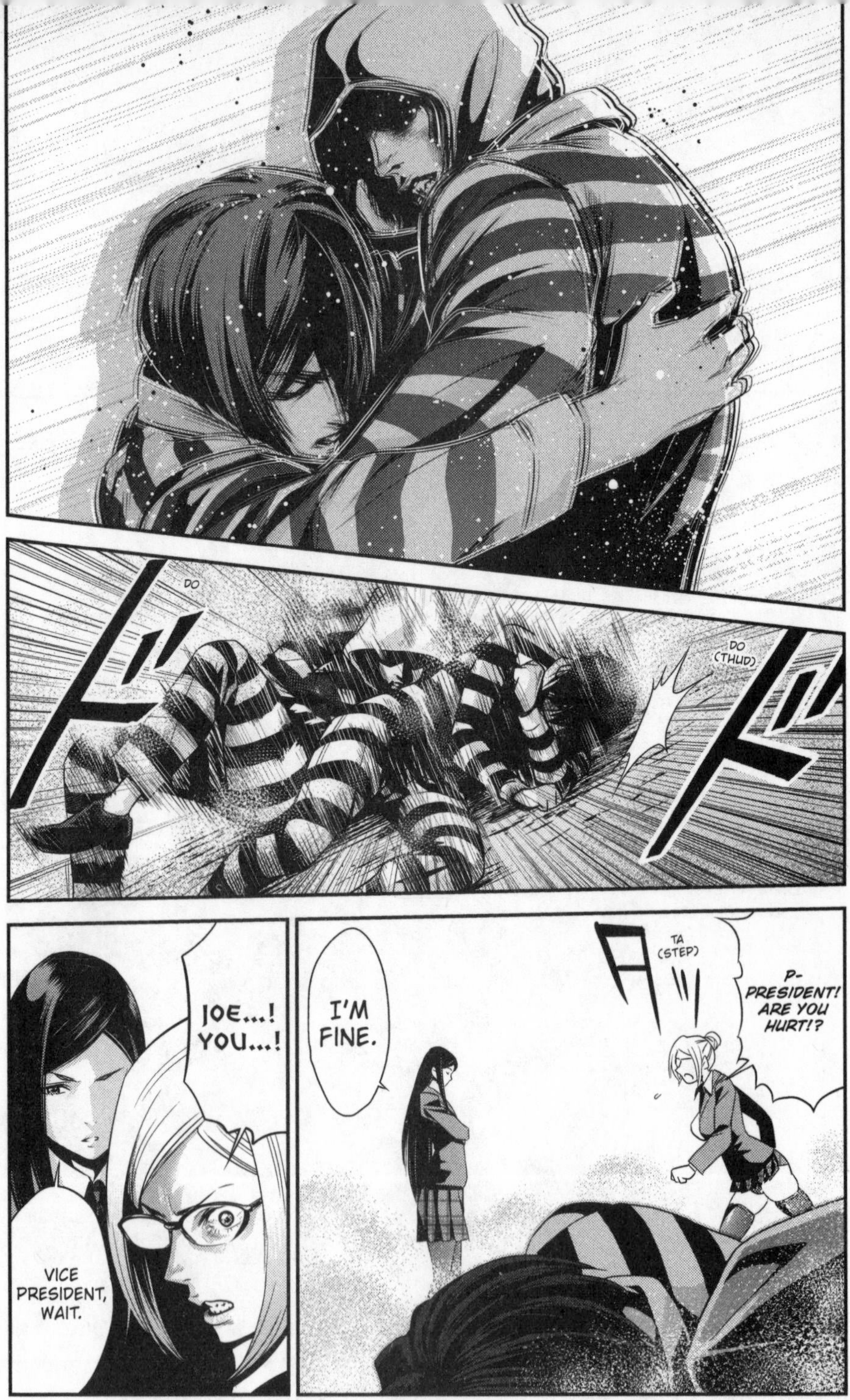
DO (THUD)
DO
TA (STEP)
P-PRESIDENT! ARE YOU HURT!?
I'M FINE.
JOE...! YOU...!
VICE PRESIDENT, WAIT.

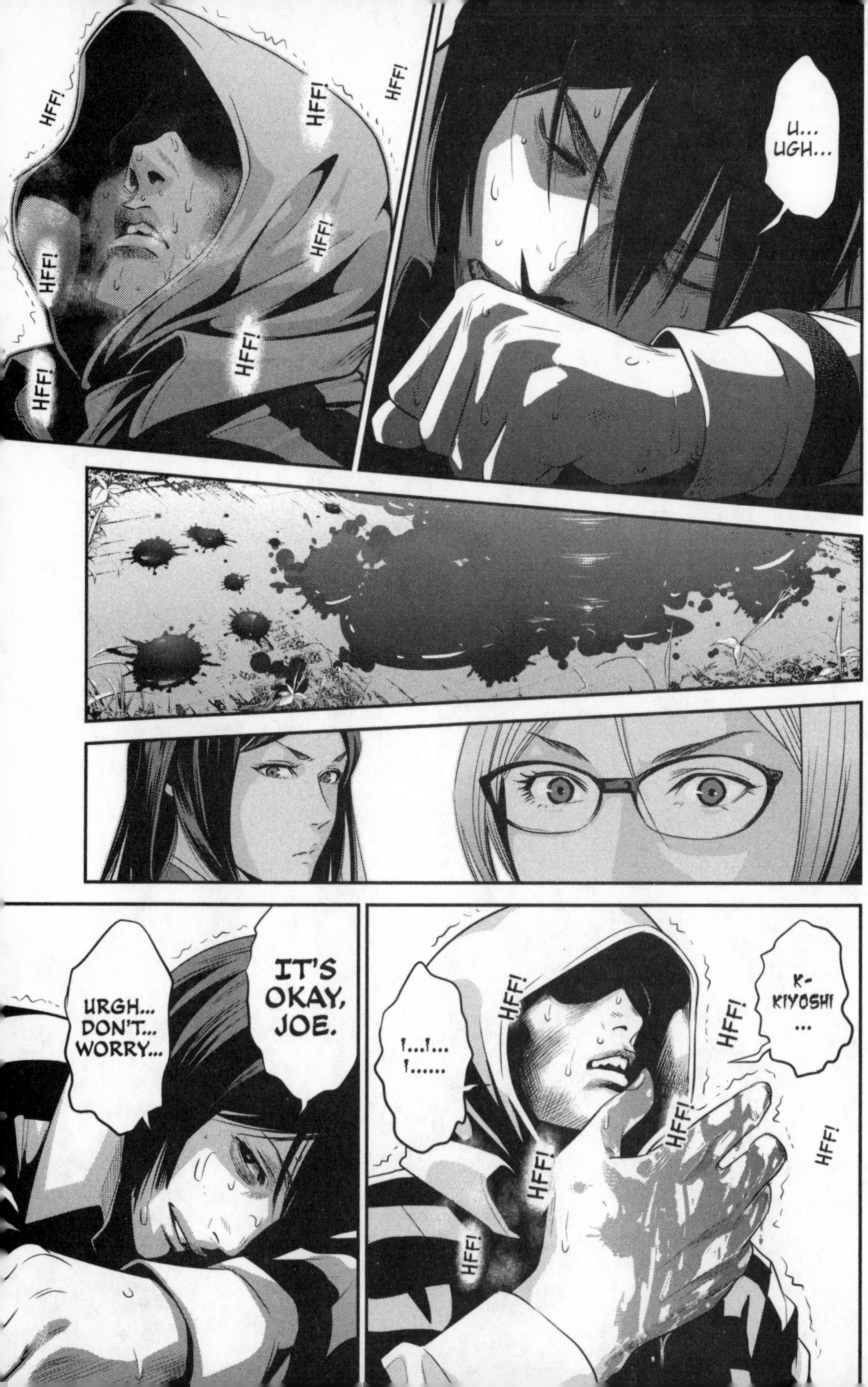

U... UGH...
HFF!
HFF!
HFF!
HFF!
HFF!
HFF!
HFF!
K-KIYOSHI ...
!...!... !......
HFF!
HFF!
HFF!
HFF!
HFF!
HFF!
IT'S OKAY, JOE.
URGH... DON'T... WORRY...

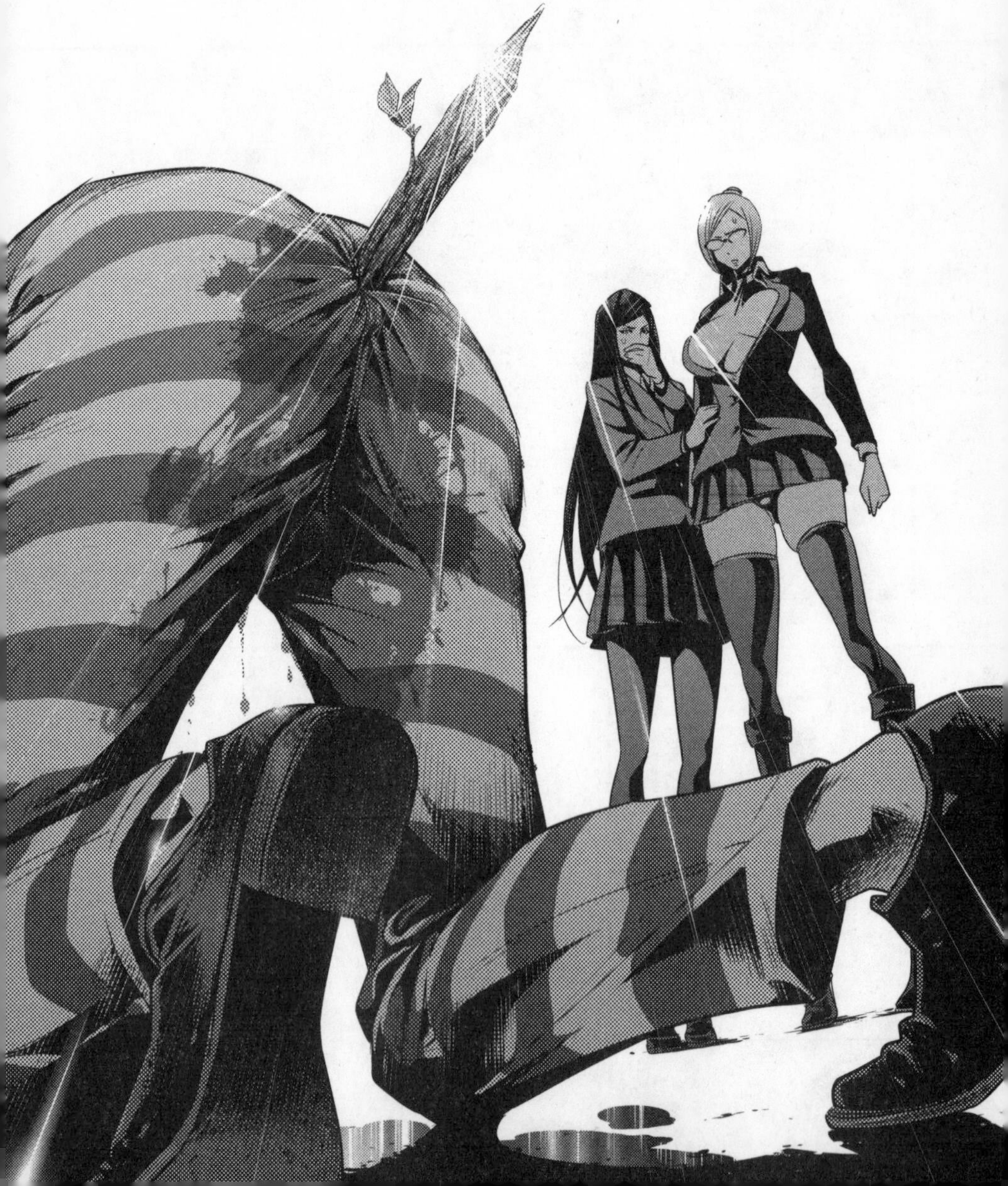

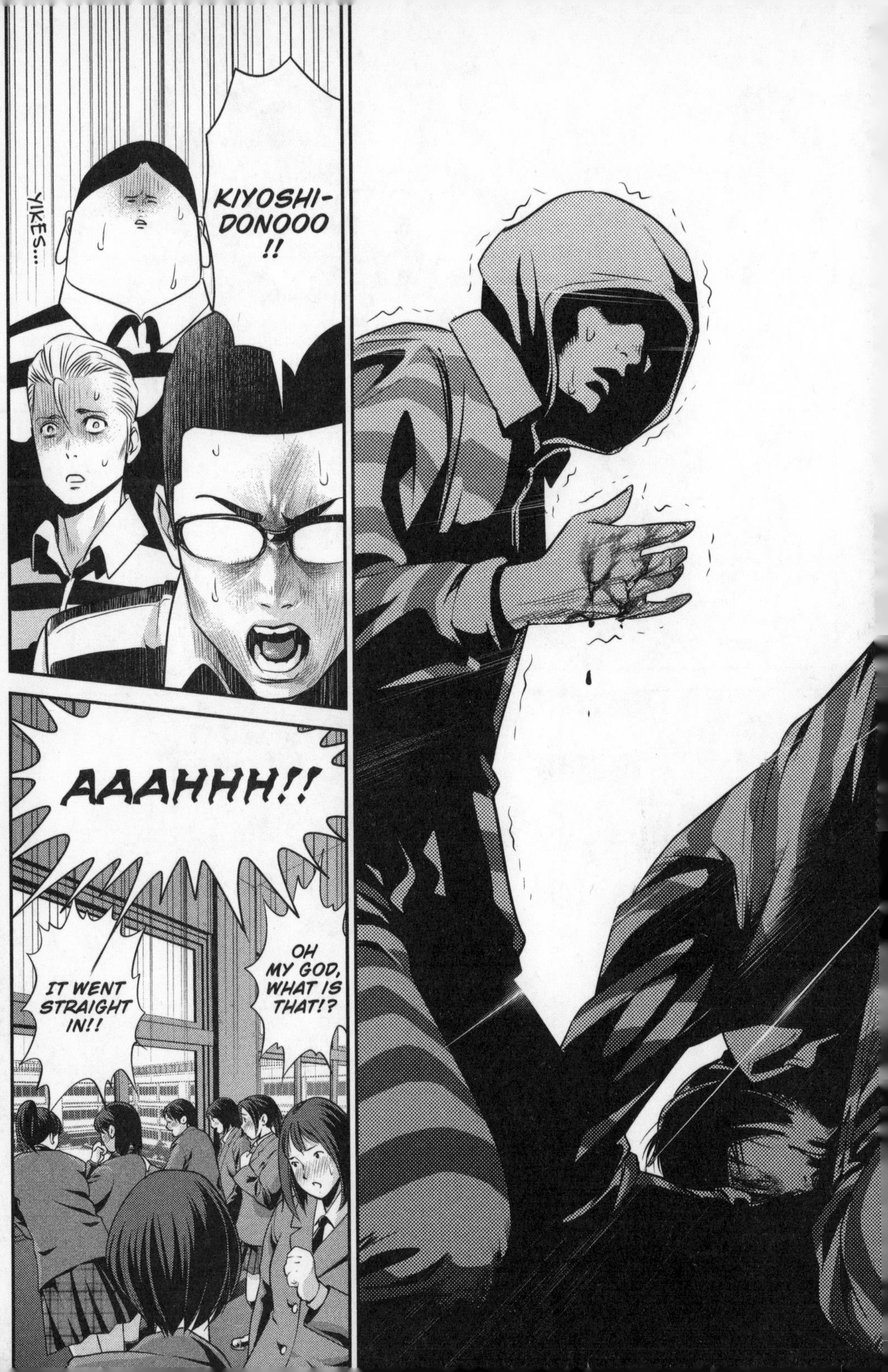

KIYOSHI-DONOOO!!
YIKES...
AAAHHH!!
OH MY GOD, WHAT IS THAT!?
IT WENT STRAIGHT IN!!

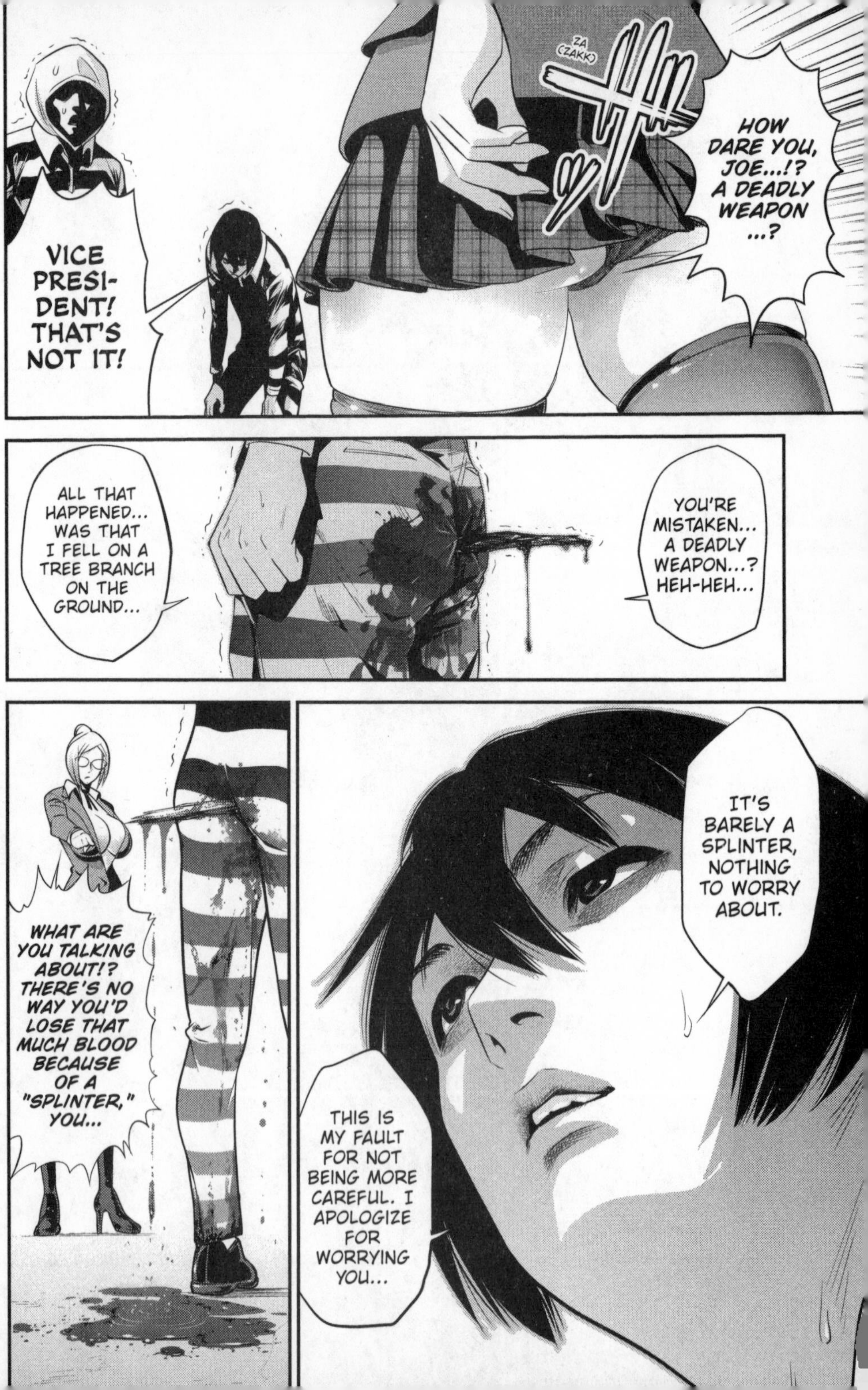
ZA (ZAKK)
HOW DARE YOU, JOE...!? A DEADLY WEAPON ...?
VICE PRESIDENT! THAT'S NOT IT!
YOU'RE MISTAKEN... A DEADLY WEAPON...? HEH-HEH...
ALL THAT HAPPENED... WAS THAT I FELL ON A TREE BRANCH ON THE GROUND...
IT'S BARELY A SPLINTER, NOTHING TO WORRY ABOUT.
THIS IS MY FAULT FOR NOT BEING MORE CAREFUL. I APOLOGIZE FOR WORRYING YOU...
WHAT ARE YOU TALKING ABOUT!? THERE'S NO WAY YOU'D LOSE THAT MUCH BLOOD BECAUSE OF A "SPLINTER," YOU...

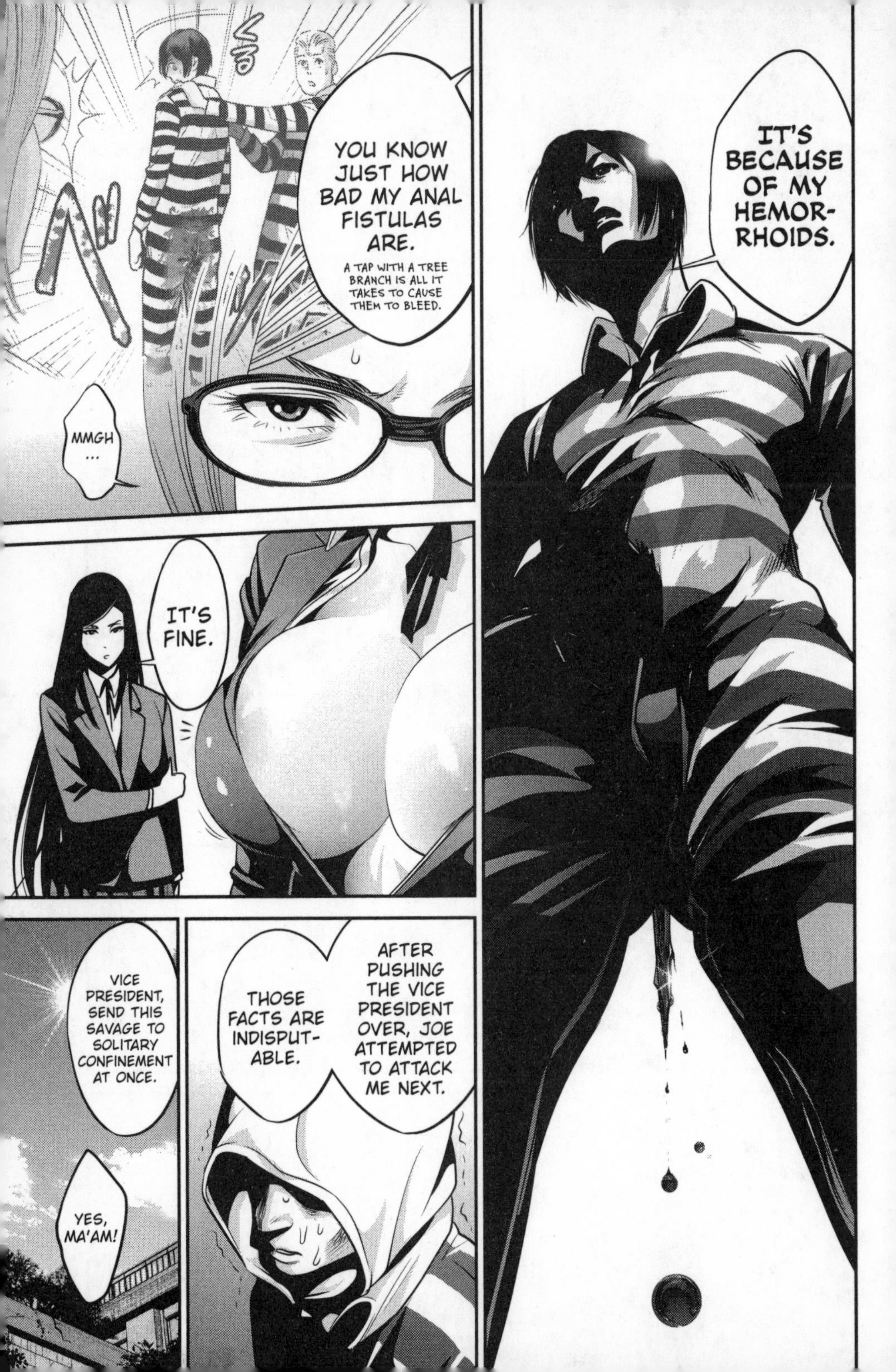
IT'S BECAUSE OF MY HEMOR-RHOIDS.
くる
YOU KNOW JUST HOW BAD MY ANAL FISTULAS ARE.
A TAP WITH A TREE BRANCH IS ALL IT TAKES TO CAUSE THEM TO BLEED.
MMGH ...
IT'S FINE.
AFTER PUSHING THE VICE PRESIDENT OVER, JOE ATTEMPTED TO ATTACK ME NEXT.
THOSE FACTS ARE INDISPUT-ABLE.
VICE PRESIDENT, SEND THIS SAVAGE TO SOLITARY CONFINEMENT AT ONCE.
YES, MA'AM!

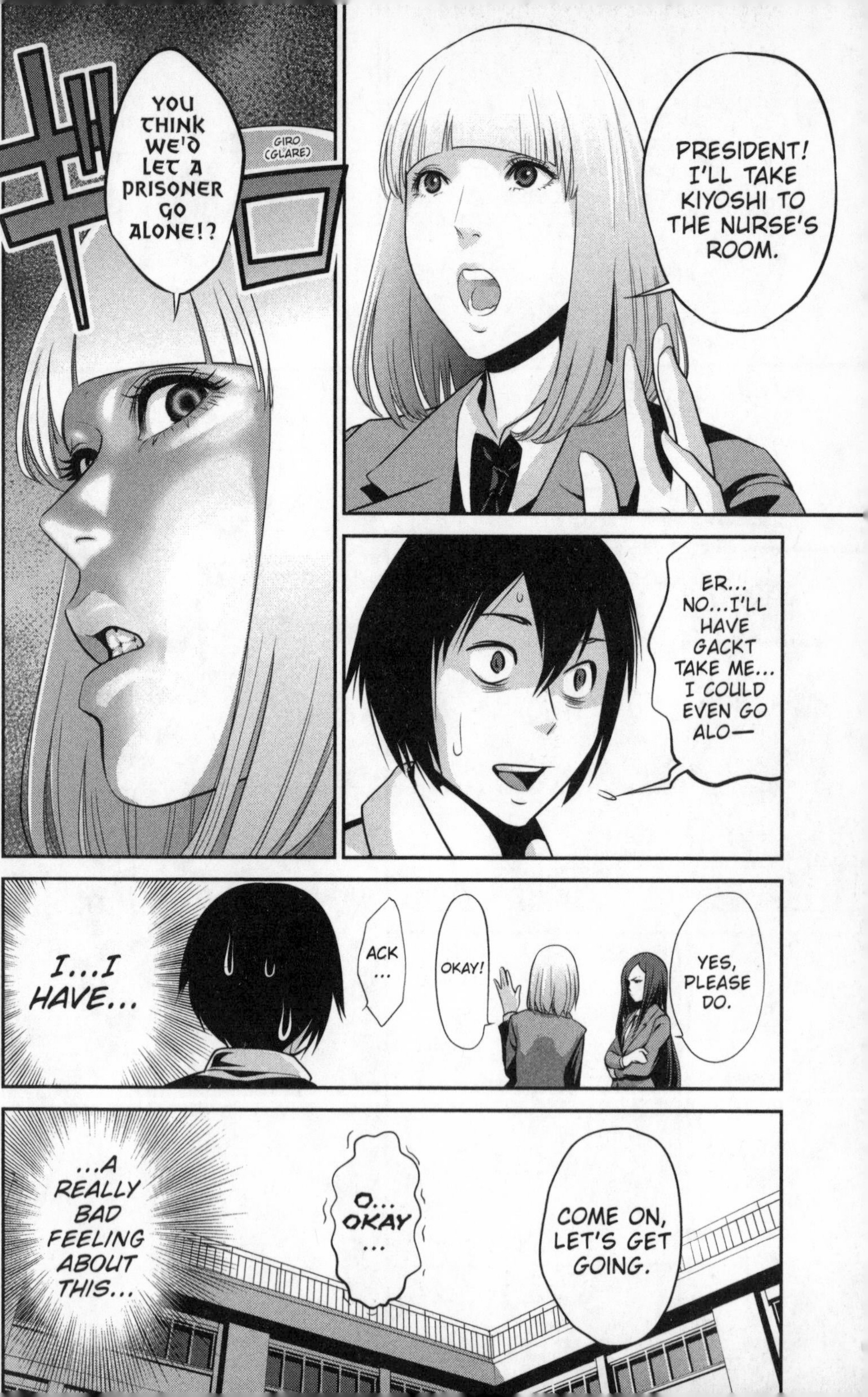
PRESIDENT! I'LL TAKE KIYOSHI TO THE NURSE'S ROOM.
GIRO (GLARE)
YOU THINK WE'D LET A PRISONER GO ALONE!?
ER... NO...I'LL HAVE GACKT TAKE ME... I COULD EVEN GO ALO—
YES, PLEASE DO.
OKAY!
ACK...
I...I HAVE...
COME ON, LET'S GET GOING.
O... OKAY...
...A REALLY BAD FEELING ABOUT THIS...

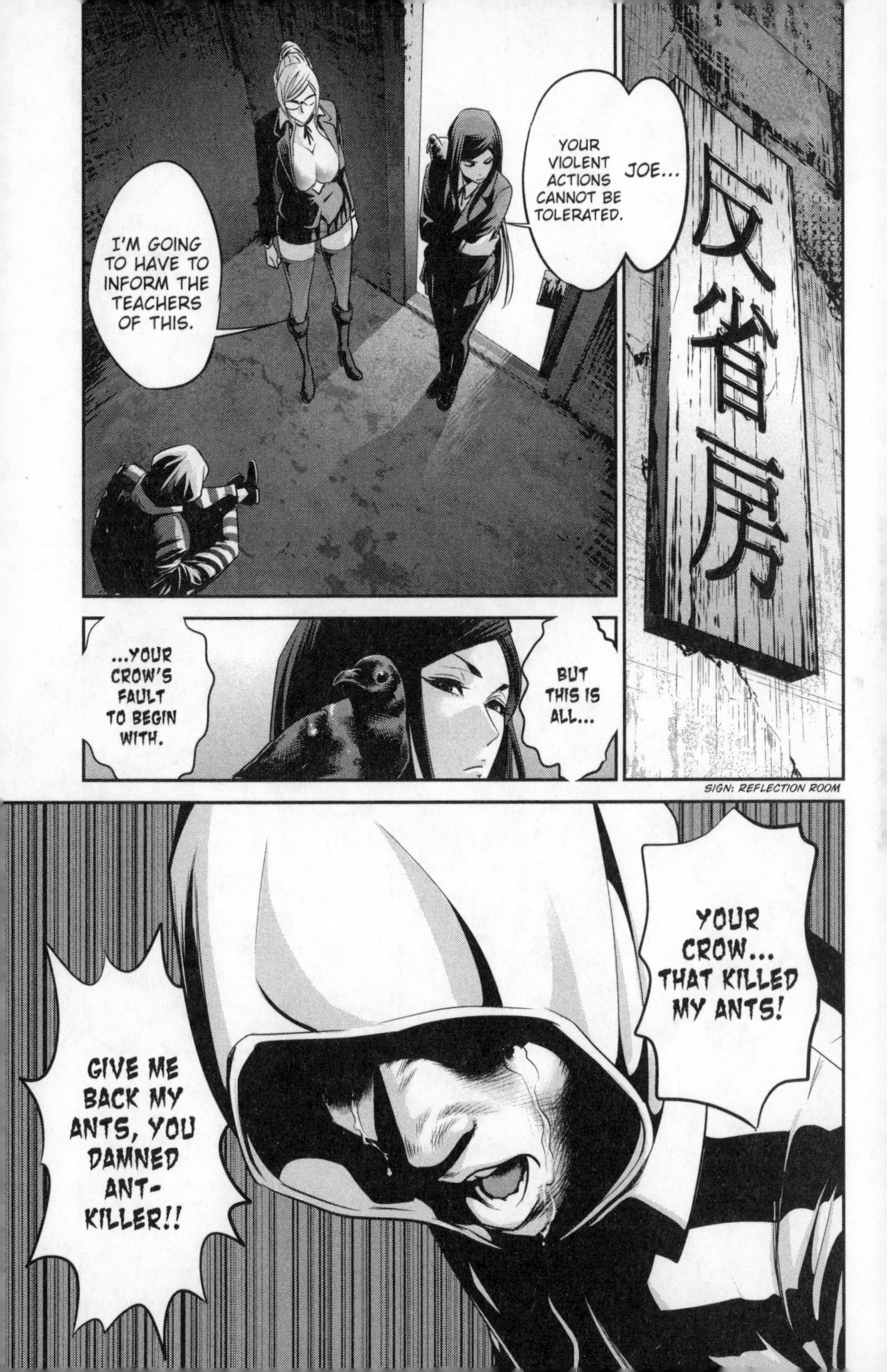
JOE...
YOUR VIOLENT ACTIONS CANNOT BE TOLERATED.
I'M GOING TO HAVE TO INFORM THE TEACHERS OF THIS.
反省房
BUT THIS IS ALL...
...YOUR CROW'S FAULT TO BEGIN WITH.
YOUR CROW... THAT KILLED MY ANTS!
GIVE ME BACK MY ANTS, YOU DAMNED ANT-KILLER!!

SIGN: REFLECTION ROOM

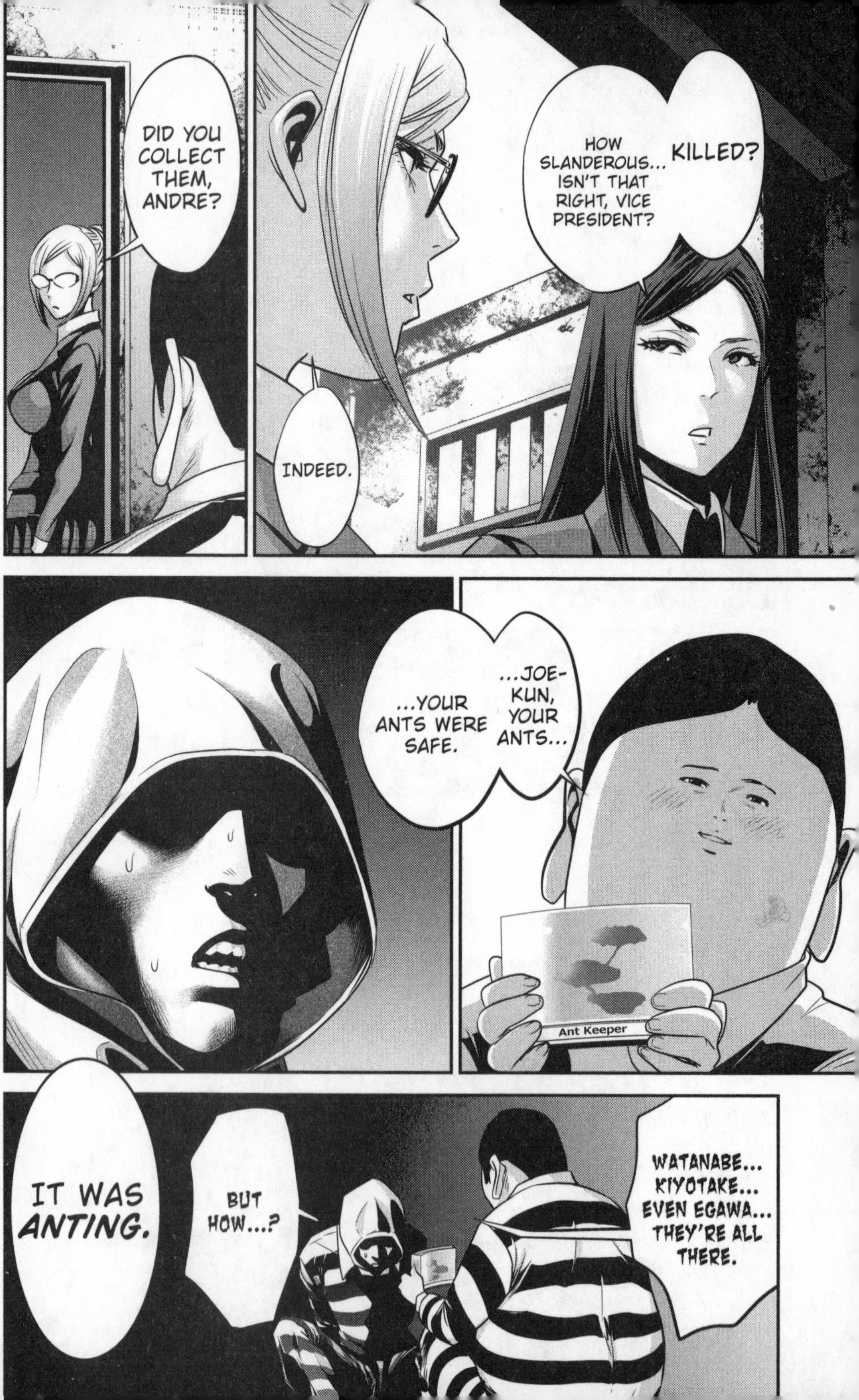
KILLED?
HOW SLANDEROUS... ISN'T THAT RIGHT, VICE PRESIDENT?
INDEED.
DID YOU COLLECT THEM, ANDRE?
...JOE-KUN, YOUR ANTS...
...YOUR ANTS WERE SAFE.
Ant Keeper
WATANABE... KIYOTAKE... EVEN EGAWA... THEY'RE ALL THERE.
BUT HOW...?
IT WAS *ANTING.*

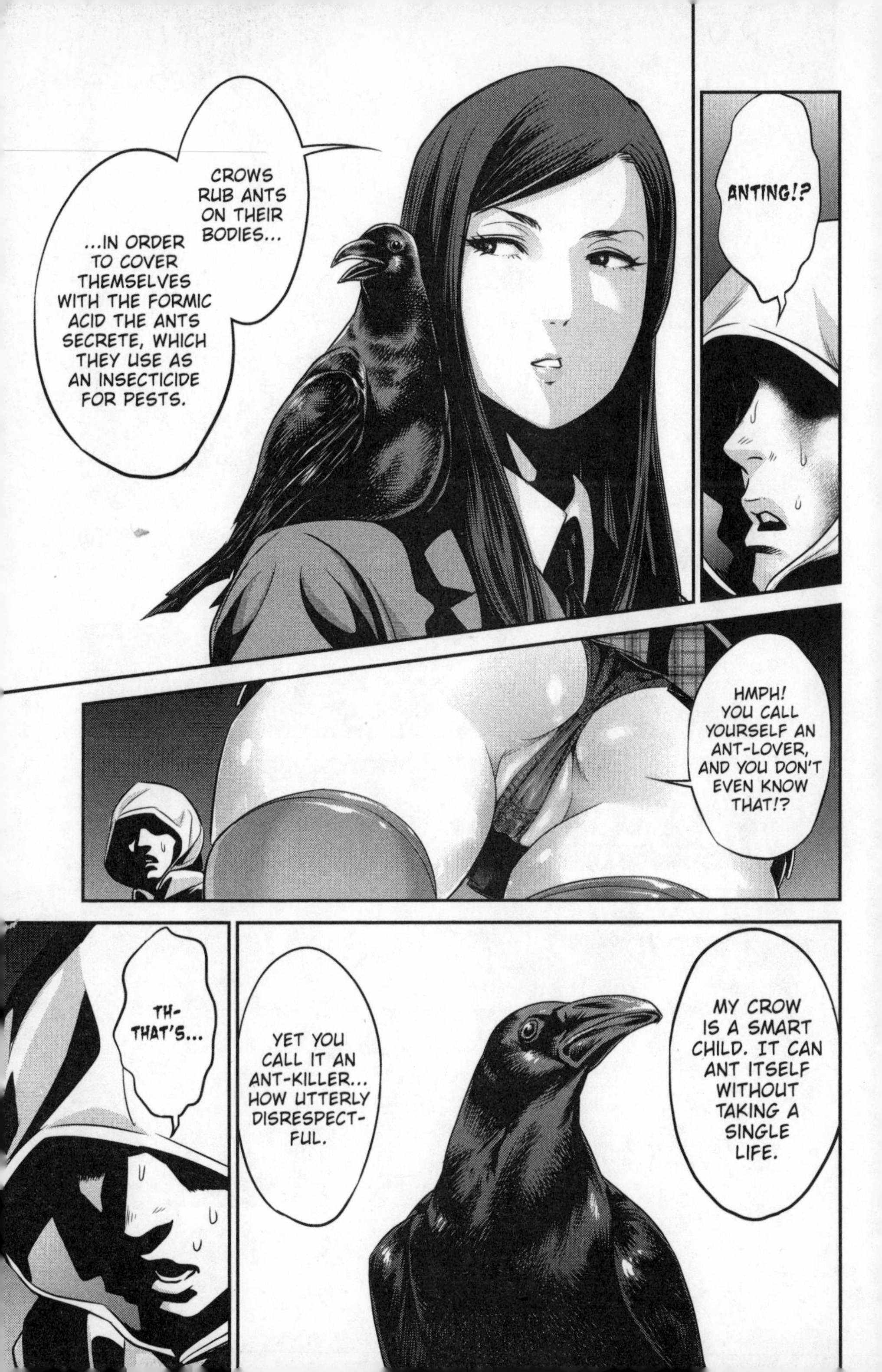

ANTING!?
CROWS RUB ANTS ON THEIR BODIES...
...IN ORDER TO COVER THEMSELVES WITH THE FORMIC ACID THE ANTS SECRETE, WHICH THEY USE AS AN INSECTICIDE FOR PESTS.
HMPH! YOU CALL YOURSELF AN ANT-LOVER, AND YOU DON'T EVEN KNOW THAT!?
MY CROW IS A SMART CHILD. IT CAN ANT ITSELF WITHOUT TAKING A SINGLE LIFE.
YET YOU CALL IT AN ANT-KILLER... HOW UTTERLY DISRESPECT-FUL.
TH-THAT'S...

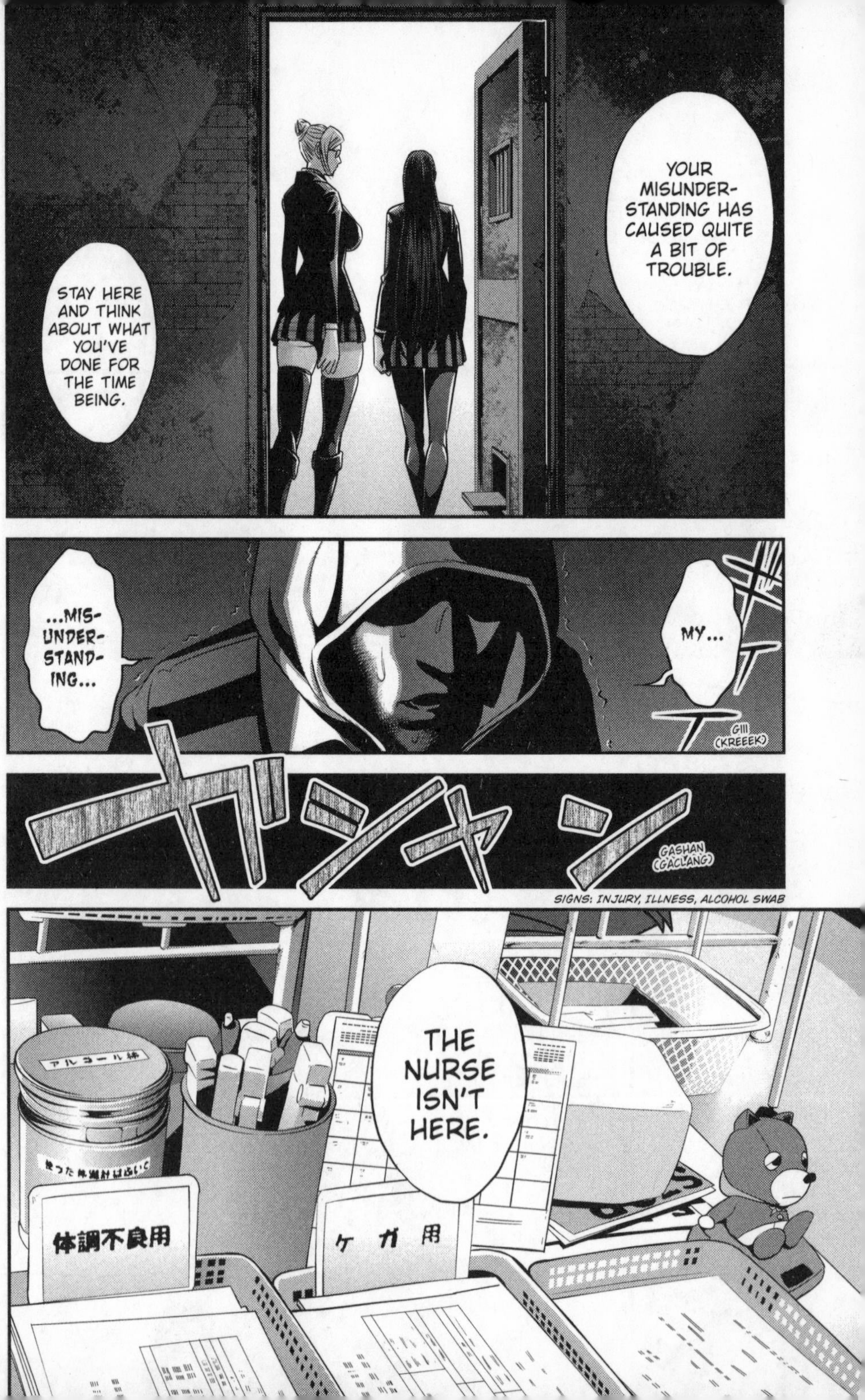
YOUR MISUNDERSTANDING HAS CAUSED QUITE A BIT OF TROUBLE.
STAY HERE AND THINK ABOUT WHAT YOU'VE DONE FOR THE TIME BEING.
MY...
...MISUNDERSTANDING...
GIII (KREEEK)
GASHAN (GACLANG)
SIGNS: INJURY, ILLNESS, ALCOHOL SWAB
アルコール綿
体調不良用
ケガ用
THE NURSE ISN'T HERE.

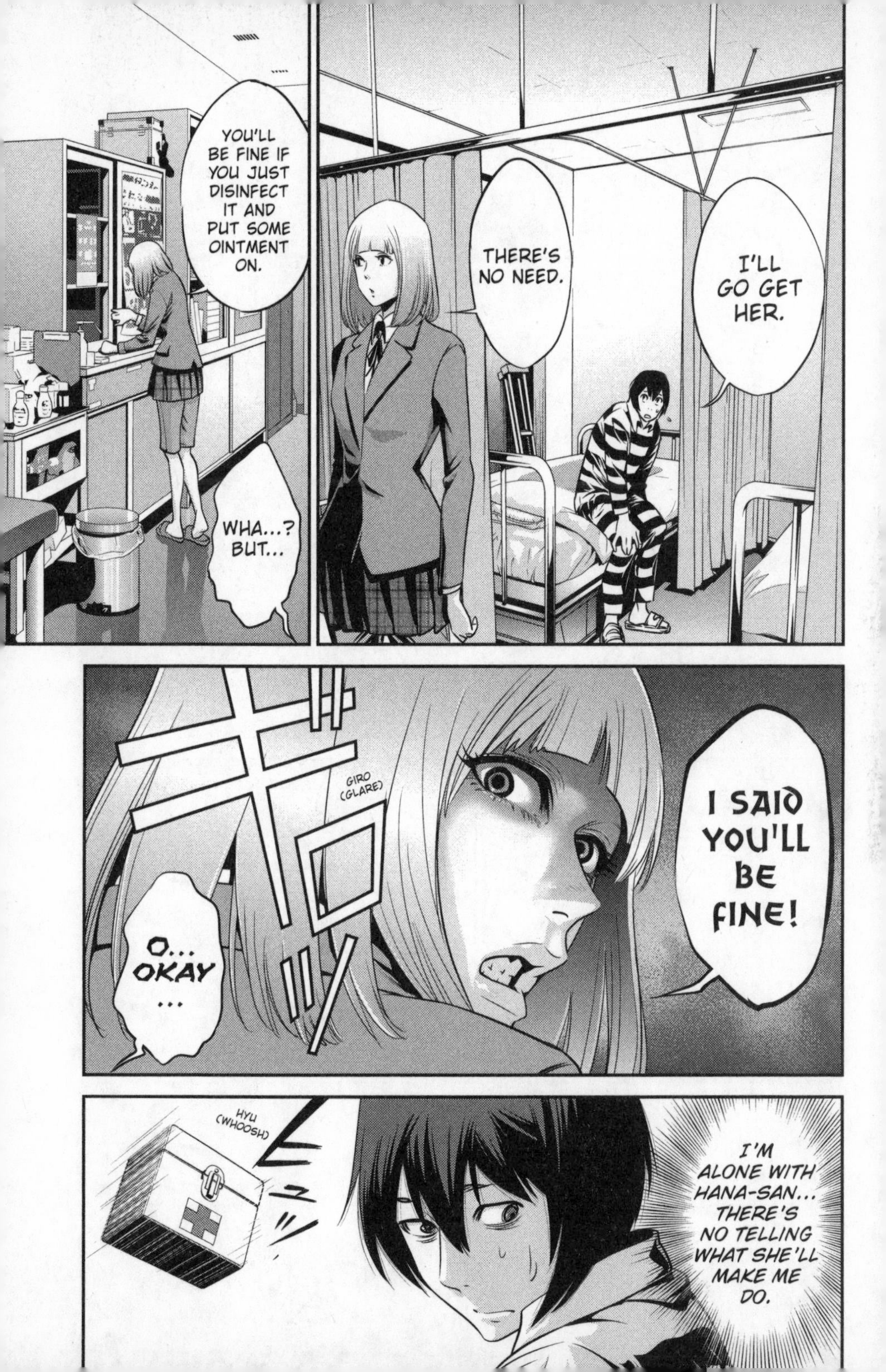
I'LL GO GET HER.
THERE'S NO NEED.
YOU'LL BE FINE IF YOU JUST DISINFECT IT AND PUT SOME OINTMENT ON.
WHA...? BUT...
I SAID YOU'LL BE FINE!
GIRO (GLARE)
O... OKAY ...
I'M ALONE WITH HANA-SAN... THERE'S NO TELLING WHAT SHE'LL MAKE ME DO.
HYU (WHOOSH)

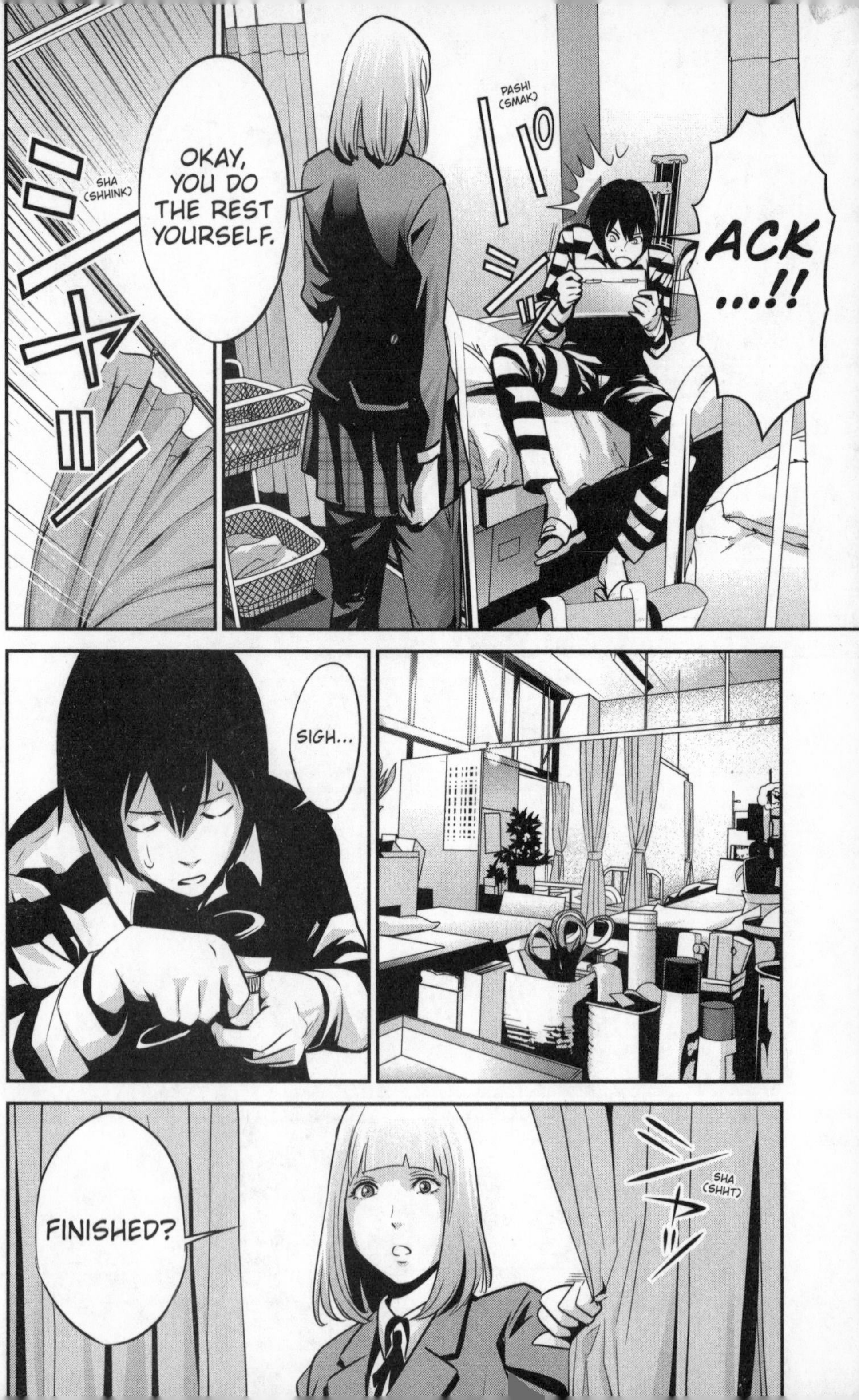
ACK ...!!
PASHI (SMAK)
OKAY, YOU DO THE REST YOURSELF.
SHA (SHHINK)
SIGH...
SHA (SHHT)
FINISHED?

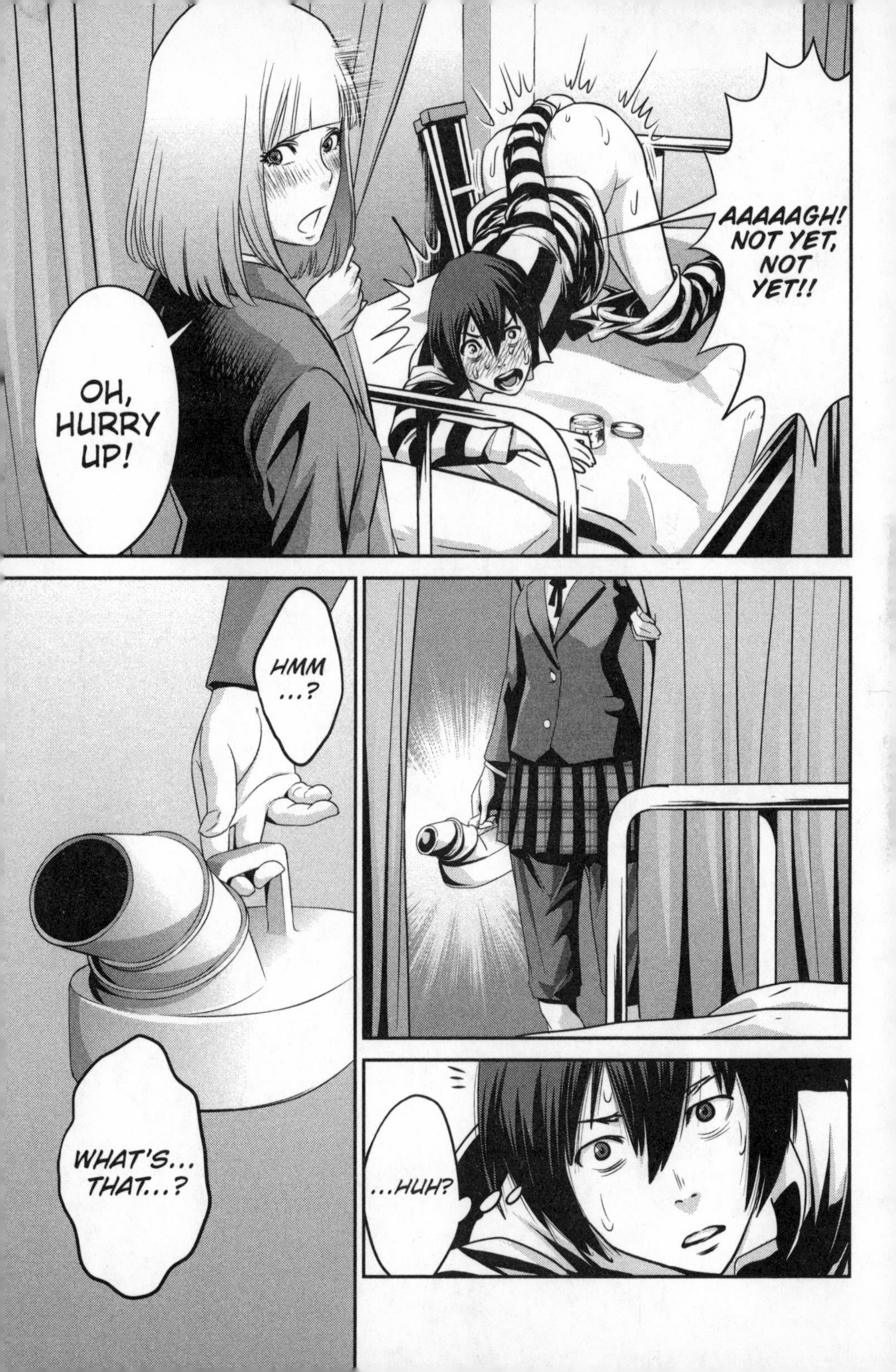
AAAAAGH! NOT YET, NOT YET!!
OH, HURRY UP!
HMM ...?
...HUH?
WHAT'S... THAT...?

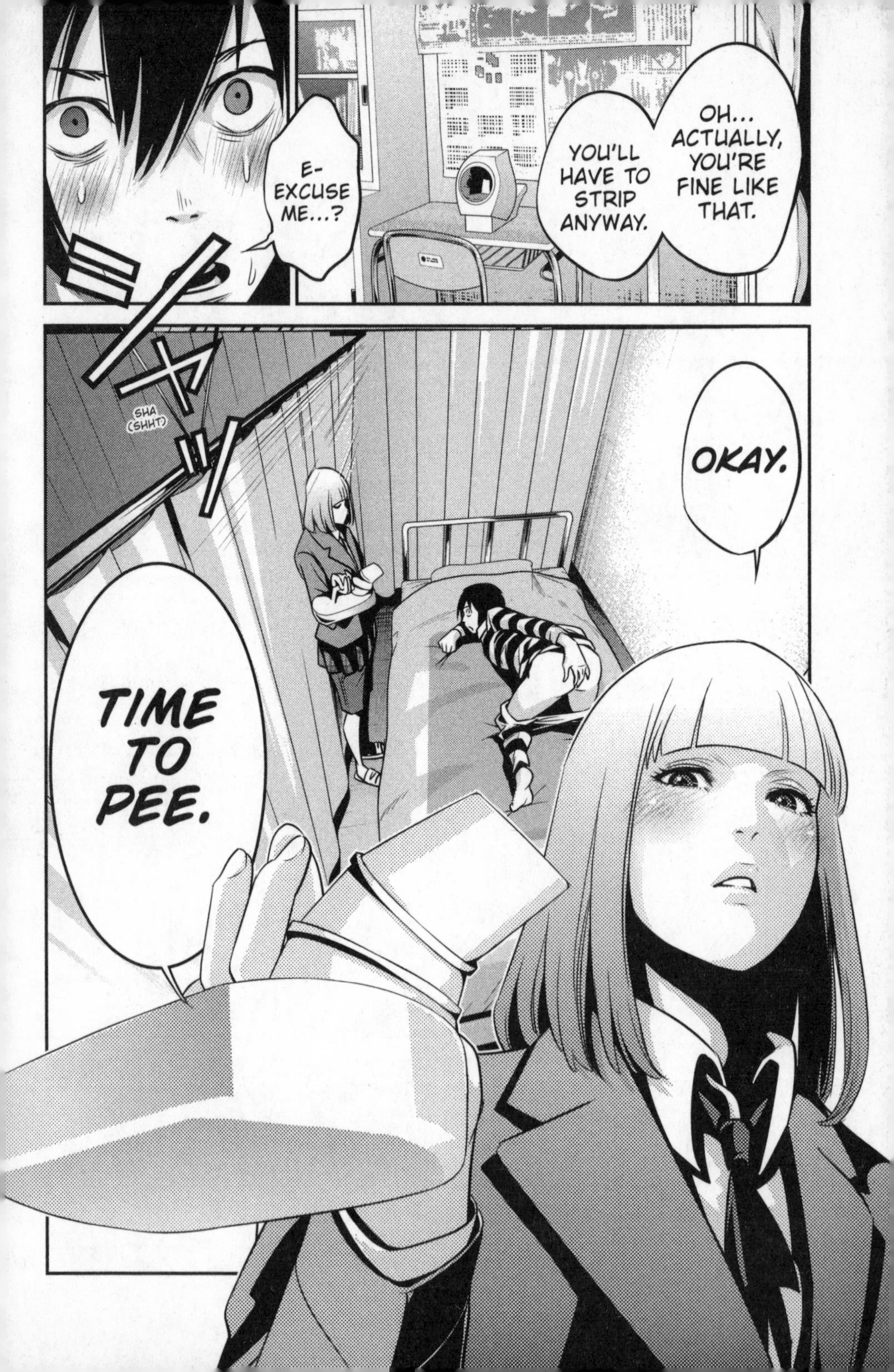
OH... ACTUALLY, YOU'RE FINE LIKE THAT.
YOU'LL HAVE TO STRIP ANYWAY.
E-EXCUSE ME...?
SHA (SHHT)
OKAY.
TIME TO PEE.

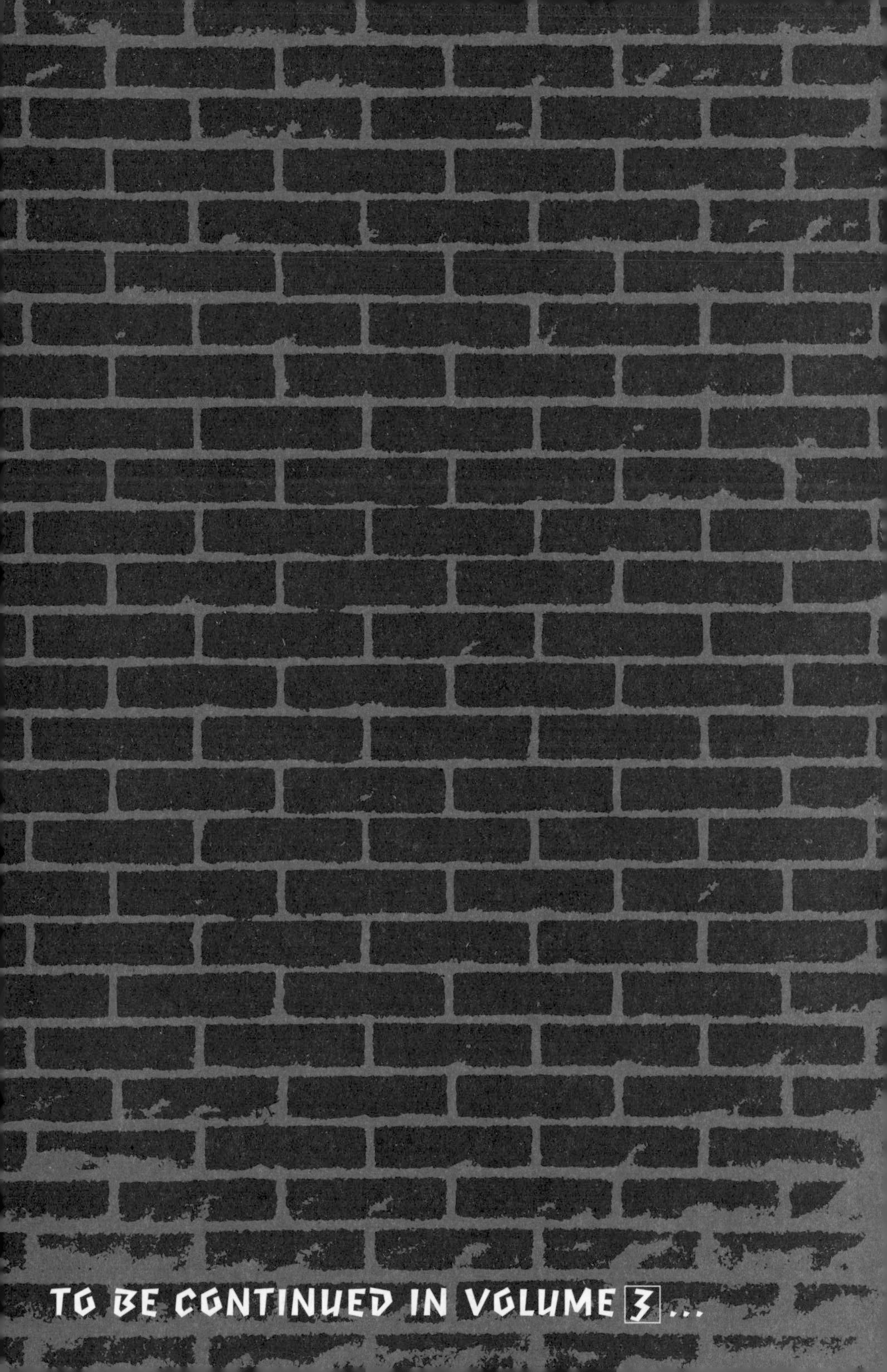
TO BE CONTINUED IN VOLUME 3 ...

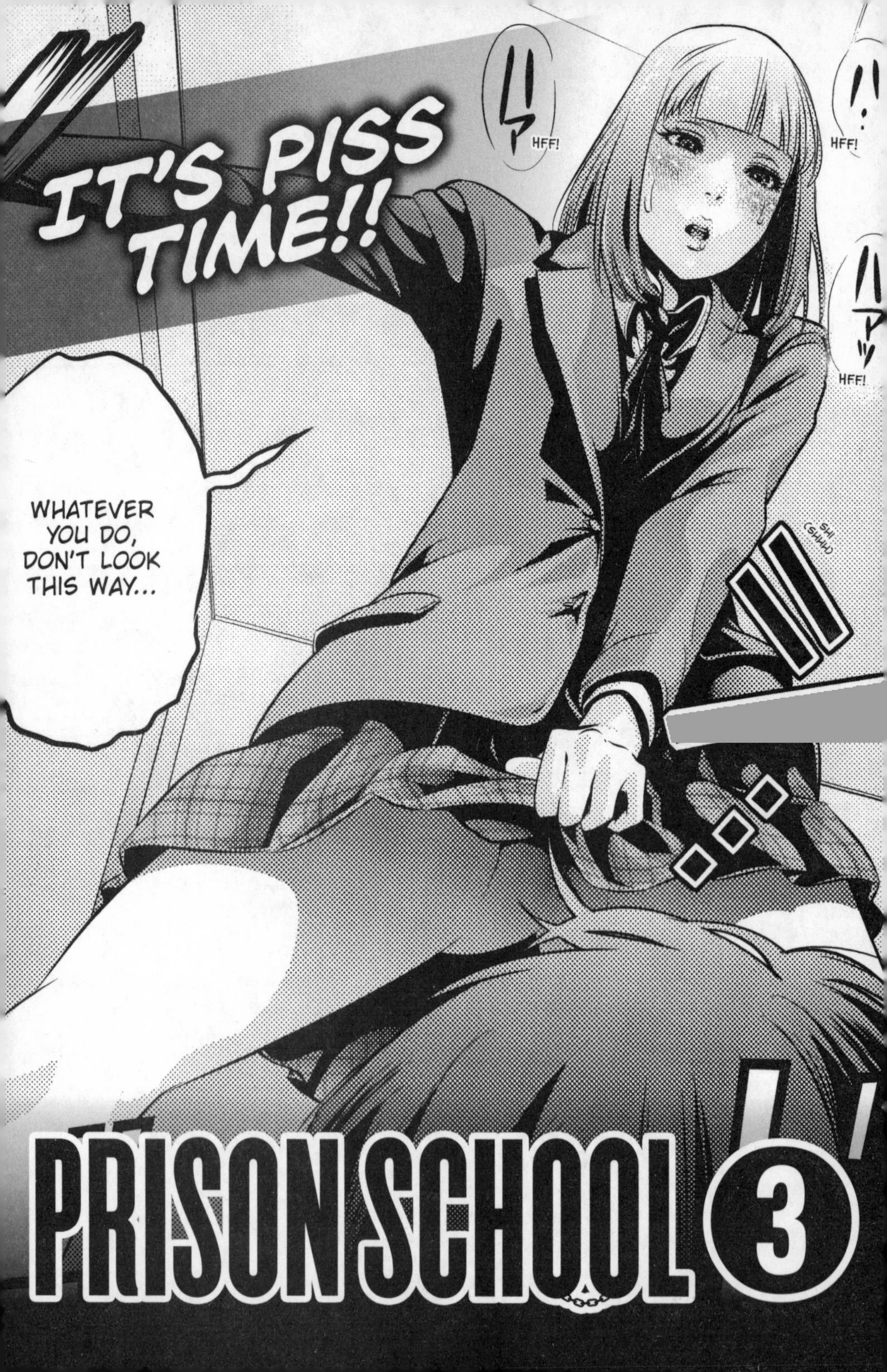
HFF!
HFF!
HFF!
IT'S PISS TIME!!
SHI (SHHH)
WHATEVER YOU DO, DON'T LOOK THIS WAY...
PRISON SCHOOL 3

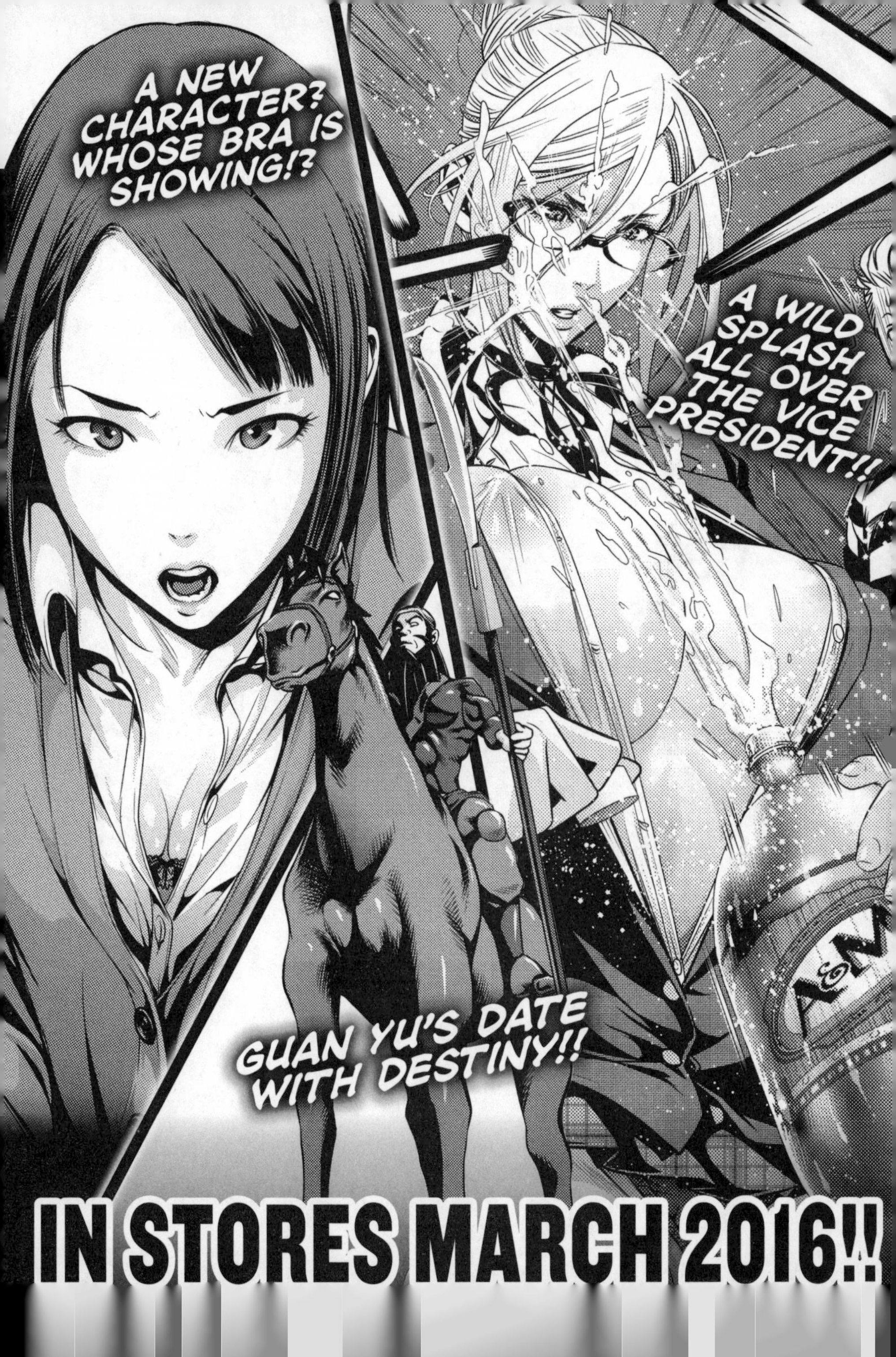
A NEW CHARACTER? WHOSE BRA IS SHOWING!?
A WILD SPLASH ALL OVER THE VICE PRESIDENT!!
GUAN YU'S DATE WITH DESTINY!!
IN STORES MARCH 2016!!

TRANSLATION NOTES

Common Honorifics

no honorific: Indicates familiarity or closeness; if used without permission or reason, addressing someone in this manner would constitute an insult.

-san: The Japanese equivalent of Mr./Mrs./Miss. If a situation calls for politeness, this is the fail-safe honorific.

-dono: Conveys an indication of respect for the addressee.

-kun: Used most often when referring to boys, this indicates affection or familiarity. Occasionally used by older men among their peers, but it may also be used by anyone referring to a person of lower standing.

-chan: An affectionate honorific indicating familiarity used mostly in reference to girls; also used in reference to cute persons or animals of either gender.

-senpai: A suffix used to address upperclassmen or more experienced coworkers.

Yen conversion: While exchange rates fluctuate daily, a convenient conversion estimation is about ¥100 to 1 USD.

PAGE 52
One hundred grams is approximately 3.5 ounces.

PAGE 132
Yokozuna is the highest rank in Sumo that can be achieved in Japan.

Hiroshi Wajima is the 54th *yokozuna* of sumo.

PAGE 155
Gottsuan desu is a slang term used in sumo to say "thank you."

PAGE 289
Wei, Wu, and Shu are the three major states during China's Three Kingdoms period.

PRISON SCHOOL

PRISON SCHOOL ❷

AKIRA HIRAMOTO

Translation: Ko Ransom

Lettering: Alexis Eckerman

This book is a work of fiction. Names, characters, places, and incidents are the product of the author's imagination or are used fictitiously. Any resemblance to actual events, locales, or persons, living or dead, is coincidental.

Yen Press
150 West 30th Street, 19th Floor
New York, NY 10001

Visit us at yenpress.com
facebook.com/yenpress
twitter.com/yenpress
yenpress.tumblr.com
instagram.com/yenpress

First Yen Press Edition: November 2015

Yen Press is an imprint of Yen Press, LLC.
The Yen Press name and logo are trademarks of Yen Press, LLC.

The publisher is not responsible for websites (or their content) that are not owned by the publisher.

Library of Congress Control Number: 2015373915

ISBN: 978-0-316-34612-2

10 9 8 7

WOR

Printed in the United States of America